Banking in Oklahoma
1907–2000

Banking in Oklahoma
1907–2000

Michael J. Hightower
Foreword by Frank Keating

University of Oklahoma Press : Norman

Also by Michael J. Hightower
Inventing Tradition: Cowboy Sports in a Postmodern Age
   (Saarbrücken, Germany, 2008)
Frontier Families: The Records and Johnstons in American History
   (Oklahoma City, 2010)
The Pattersons: A Novel (Charlottesville, Va., 2012)
Banking in Oklahoma Before Statehood (Norman, Okla., 2013)

An earlier version of chapter 7 was published as "Penn Square: The Shopping Center Bank That Shook the World, Part 1—Boom," *Chronicles of Oklahoma* 90, no. 1 (Spring 2012): 68–99. An earlier version of chapter 8 appeared as "Penn Square: The Shopping Center Bank That Shook the World, Part 2—Bust," *Chronicles of Oklahoma* 90, no. 2 (Summer 2012): 204–36.

Library of Congress Cataloging-in-Publication Data

Hightower, Michael J.
   Banking in Oklahoma, 1907–2000 / Michael J. Hightower ; foreword by Frank Keating.
       pages cm
   Includes bibliographical references and index.
   ISBN 978-0-8061-4495-5 (cloth)
   ISBN 978-0-8061-6323-9 (paper)
   1. Banks and banking—Oklahoma—History—20th century. 2. Oklahoma—History—20th century. I. Title.
   HG2611.O5H538 2014
   332.109766'0904—dc23

                                                                                2014010472

The paper in this book meets the guidelines for permanence and durability of the Committee on Production Guidelines for Book Longevity of the Council on Library Resources, Inc. ∞

Copyright © 2014 by the University of Oklahoma Press, Norman, Publishing Division of the University. Paperback published 2019. Manufactured in the U.S.A.

All rights reserved. No part of this publication may be reproduced, stored in a retrieval system, or transmitted, in any form or by any means, electronic, mechanical, photocopying, recording, or otherwise—except as permitted under Section 107 or 108 of the United States Copyright Act—without the prior written permission of the University of Oklahoma Press. To request permission to reproduce selections from this book, write to Permissions, University of Oklahoma Press, 2800 Venture Drive, Norman OK 73069, or email rights.oupress@ou.edu.

I dedicate this book to C. C. Hightower, Frank P. Johnson, Hugh M. Johnson, and Wilbur E. "Billy" Hightower—bankers and community builders who shared an extraordinary commitment to Oklahoma's economic development. Their portraits and photographs watched my every move when I was growing up in the house built by my great-grandparents, Frank and Aida Johnson, at the corner of Northwest Fifteenth Street and Walker in Oklahoma City, and I was never sure what to make of them. Nowadays, I think I know what was on their minds. I just hope I got their stories straight.

Contents

List of Illustrations ix
Foreword, by Frank Keating xi
Preface xiii

Part I. Frontier to Region
1. A Brand-New State 3
2. The War Years 37
3. The Roaring Twenties 65
4. The Dawn of Conservative Banking 94

Part II. Depression, Surge, Boom, and Bust
5. The Home Front 129
6. Postwar Oklahoma 156
7. Boom 191
8. And Bust 217

Part III. Road to Recovery
9. The Rest of the Story 257
10. The Change 288
11. Great Expectations 319
12. Toward the New Millennium 357

Epilogue: Crossroads of Communities 389

Notes 407
Bibliography 453
Index 461

Illustrations

Exchange National Bank of Tulsa under construction, ca. 1910	22
American National Bank, Oklahoma City, 1909	24
Socialist camp meeting near Antlers, September 1910	46
El Reno Interurban Line	51
Carney, Oklahoma, unit of the Lincoln County Vigilance Committee, 1925	77
Oklahoma City branch of the Federal Reserve Bank of Kansas City	87
Oil gusher near Cushing	96
First National Bank Building and Ramsey Tower under construction	100
Abandoned farm in Cimarron County, 1939	111
Bank in Arcadia, 1937	134
International Petroleum Exposition, Tulsa, May 1936	137
Party in the First National Bank lobby, Oklahoma City, 1941	142
NAACP's Freedom Now march, Oklahoma City, April 3, 1965	170
Teller's deposit receipt machine, July 1947	176
Bank lobby, June 1948	177
Advertisements for Penn Square Bank, 1981	222–24
Penn Square Bank at its closing on July 5, 1982	239
Oil rig in the Anadarko Basin	276
BancFirst Corporation in the former Tradesmen's National Bank Building, Oklahoma City	337

Foreword

By Frank Keating

As the Oklahoma Historical Society's bank and commerce historian and a descendant of pioneer bankers, Michael J. Hightower is uniquely positioned to tell the story of Oklahoma banks and their dynamic role in the birth, adolescence, and adulthood of America's forty-sixth state. In this lively and entertaining story, he vividly describes the furious gales that whipped through the state in its early years, its experimental young adulthood, and its maturity as a First World urban and rural economy.

Under the leadership of the irascible Charles N. Haskell, the brand-new state of Oklahoma created the nation's first state-chartered deposit guarantee system, funded by a stout 1 percent assessment on bank assets. Oklahoma remained true to its frontier roots by religiously advocating local control of currency and credit and resisting the infection of big-city bankers and their plump and greedy urban allies. It was an Oklahoma regulator who prohibited banks from honoring bounced checks as a stain on good morals and good judgment.

Banks nourished the muscle and sinew of the state's economy. It was early Oklahoma bankers who pursued improvements to agriculture, encouraged better crop yields, and helped promote a successful rural economy. Those same bankers pressed for modern roads and small-business lending. Bankers knew that small businesses created jobs and wealth, and they shaped their business models accordingly.

Hightower lights a prairie fire in his depiction of early-day Oklahoma as a Socialist hothouse and a crucible of wild-eyed speculation. While bandits such as Pretty Boy Floyd were ransacking banks across the state, Governor "Alfalfa Bill" Murray sent the National Guard to force the temporary closing of the First National Bank of Enid, whose president, H. H. Champlin, resisted the governor's order for a bank holiday during the early days of the Great Depression.

The rise and fall of Penn Square Bank, and the role that bank played in the dizzy frenzy of combustion and speculation in the oil patch, merit two chapters. The contagion brought down two national titans, Continental Illinois and Seattle First National Bank. In the ensuing depression and flurry of bank failures, Oklahoma bankers were among the last in the nation to acknowledge the futility of unit banking and embrace branching and multibank holding companies.

This book reminds us that a great industry needs leaders of vision and integrity. They are here in scores: Chuck Vose, Gene and David Rainbolt, George Records, George Kaiser, and many others throughout the state whose interviews with Hightower constitute a major component of his research. As Hightower amply demonstrates, many of today's community banks remain operated by a third or fourth generation of family owners. Those owners have transitioned from a time of frontier regulation, light-touched and populist, to a modern regulated banking system with the latest technologies, every product offering, and the ability to serve the needs of Oklahomans in both national and international business arenas.

Queried about managing his bank's assets, Bristow's Tracy Kelly summoned his pioneer father's homespun wisdom: "Leave the woodpile higher than you found it." The story of banks and bankers in Oklahoma is a woodpile-building story.

Banking in Oklahoma, 1907–2000 is a necessary read for everyone who is fascinated by the state's special story.

Preface

Like my previous book, *Banking in Oklahoma Before Statehood,* this story of Oklahoma banking rests on the twin pillars of narrative and social history. Many historians, including this one, consider narratives to be the purest form of historical analysis, and these accounts are preserved in memoirs, oral histories, correspondence, and various forms of journalism. To capture narratives requires immersion in social history, sometimes described as history "from the bottom up." Social history drops us into the messy swirl of everyday life, and its lessons are often missing in books that rely on opinion leaders who, by virtue of their wealth or position or notoriety or, most likely, all of the above, command a disproportionate share of the spotlight. Although this history of Oklahoma banking in the twentieth century certainly relies on perspectives from the corner office, it aims to balance those perspectives with voices that are harder to hear, and with stories that failed to capture the headlines.

The story begins with a marriage ceremony in Guthrie, Oklahoma, on November 16, 1907, when Mr. Oklahoma and Miss Indian Territory exchanged vows to become the forty-sixth state in the union. Those who read my previous book will, I hope, find a seamless transition to Oklahoma banking after statehood. If you skipped that book, you can certainly read this one as a stand-alone volume, but with a caveat: you are missing out on a raucous adventure, unique in American history, and exceptional by any standard. As wellsprings of community development and stewards of other people's money, bankers hastened the Oklahoma and Indian Territories' acceptance of sound business principles and did yeoman's work in paving the bumpy road to statehood. The more we know about their role in frontier settlement, the more we realize that pioneer bankers earned, as much as any cowboy or Indian or gunslinger ever did, a place in the West of our imagination.

Part I, "Frontier to Region," takes us from the aforementioned nuptials between Mr. Oklahoma and Miss Indian Territory to the creation of the Federal Deposit Insurance Corporation (FDIC) in 1934. If these events seem worlds apart, that is because they are. Between 1907 and 1934, Oklahoma shed its frontier persona and wove itself ever more tightly into national networks of banking and commerce. Along the way, the brand-new state legislature set the standard for Progressive legislation with a guarantee that depositors in state-chartered banks would never lose a penny; land and oil investors and the bankers who fueled their dreams raised get-rich-quick (and often get-poor-quick) schemes to an art form; Oklahoma City stole the state capital from Guthrie; the Federal Reserve Bank set up shop in Oklahoma City; Oklahomans showed the nation how to finance a war by purchasing war bonds in record numbers; Governor Jack Walton captured the national spotlight for hosting the world's biggest-ever barbecue; the state legislature gave up on bank deposit guaranty (see above) and put it out of its misery; the Oklahoma Bankers Association (OBA) sent armed vigilantes into the countryside with a mandate to convince bank robbers to reconsider their career options or face the consequences; and the economy went belly-up.

Federal programs and regulations aimed at rescuing a nation in distress in the 1930s sparked heated debates about the proper role of government in the economy. As far as most Oklahoma bankers were concerned, legislators in faraway Washington, D.C., were overstepping their bounds in saddling the banking industry with endless regulations. Others recognized that the so-called mixed economy in which the federal government serves the dual role of referee and business partner was here to stay and might even prove to be a satisfactory arrangement. Either way, the die was cast, and future generations of bankers and businesspeople were left to sort out the details.

Part II, "Depression, Surge, Boom, and Bust," spans the Depression and World War II era to the demise of Penn Square Bank in July 1982, an event that was both cause and effect of the most severe economic downturn in the oil patch since the 1930s. Milestones that preceded the 1980s depression include Tulsa's rise to prominence as "the Oil Capital of the World"; bankers' participation in luring military facilities to Oklahoma; the postwar boom; the evolution of a mixed economy that blended private, state, and federal funding, and whose potential was realized in the McClellan-Kerr navigation system; the Leo Winters banking scandal; and various episodes in the federal government's stubborn insistence on regulating banks. The Penn Square Bank story, a woeful tale that unfolds with the force of Greek drama, warrants two chapters—one on the rise and one on the fall. Even in a state renowned for its creativity in commerce, Penn Square Bank was in a league of its own. For once, the lessons of history are crystal clear, and we ignore them at our peril.

Part III, "Road to Recovery," brings the story of Oklahoma banking from its nadir in the 1980s to the dawn of the new millennium. The state's slow road to recovery was threatened at every turn by bank failures that made the FDIC one of the state's few growth industries. Challenges in the closing decades of the twentieth century fall under the rubric of "the change," and they stemmed from a combination of globalization, technological advances, and Reagan-era deregulation that opened the door to free marketeering not seen since the Gilded Age. Highlights include the fallout from Penn Square Bank's demise, most notably the federal government's rescue of Continental Illinois National Bank and the subsequent firestorm over the "too-big-to-fail" argument; the crisis on the farm in the 1980s and subsequent resurgence of agriculture in the 1990s; the proliferation of nonbank banks, which gave banks, quite literally, a run for their money; and legislation that put an end to unit banking and ushered in a brave new world of branch banking and multibank holding companies. American finance hit rock bottom during the savings and loan crisis—a catastrophe stewed in the toxic juices of greed and unwise legislation, and remembered (if it is remembered at all) as an all-time low in the American government's guardianship of the financial-services industry.[1] The book closes on an upbeat note as banks returned to profitability. In the epilogue, I give Oklahoma bankers a bully pulpit to describe the opportunities and challenges they face in the second decade of the twenty-first century and to explain what community banking is all about.

For better and worse, bankers' stories remind us that Oklahoma is closer in time to its frontier roots than any other state. At the time of this writing in 2014, many bankers were operating banks founded by their ancestors and were only three or four generations removed from the land runs and lotteries and migrations that dropped the curtain on the frontier. They were also wrestling with the same conflict between democracy and capitalism that roared to life in the early national period when Thomas Jefferson and Alexander Hamilton nearly came to blows over centralized banking. Then and now, banking lies at the heart of America's most persistent dilemma: how to preserve America's promise as a land of opportunity for all in a capitalist system that consistently—and, it seems, inevitably—favors the few against the many.

So, where does Oklahoma stand in the tug-of-war between democracy and capitalism? Well, I think we have to accept the fact that the jury is still out. The tugging and warring continue, with no end in sight. For generations, people have been lured to Oklahoma by the promise of opportunity or, in the case of many Native Americans, prodded to the area at the point of a bayonet. Some have succeeded, while others have been chewed up and spit out by a capitalist system that rewarded someone else's opportunity and then slammed the door shut, often aided by a push from a politician with his or (less likely but certainly possible) her hand in the till. And so it goes. It is hardly original to suggest that capitalism and democracy, however compatible they are supposed to be, often act like the couple that can live neither with nor without the other.[2]

I would like to spread some credit to the people who made this book possible: Dr. Bob Blackburn, executive director of the Oklahoma Historical Society (OHS), for bringing me in as principal researcher for the Oklahoma Bank and Commerce History Project; George J. Records, chairman of MidFirst Bank, for his ongoing support; the Oklahoma Bankers Association and Community Bankers Association of Oklahoma (CBAO) boards of directors and staffs for their practical assistance and moral support; bankers and businesspeople who shared their stories in taped interviews; OHS members who caught wind of what I was doing and told stories that I never would have discovered otherwise; archivists at the Oklahoma Historical Society in Oklahoma City and the Western History Collections in Norman for prowling their collections to locate documents and photographs; Frank Keating for writing the foreword; and Judy Walston Hightower, a Virginian who probably knows more about Oklahoma history than anyone else in her native state, for her emotional support and technical expertise—a rare combination that helped move this book to completion. Finally, thanks go to Kelly Parker for her editorial acumen and my friends at the University of Oklahoma Press for their professionalism at every stage of the publishing process.

And now, to quote the Sooners and Boomers whose vision gave us the forty-sixth state: *On to Oklahoma!*

MJH
Oklahoma City and Charlottesville
Fall 2014

PART I

Frontier to Region

CHAPTER ONE

A Brand-New State

> Down east here they sneer at everything that comes from Oklahoma. It is a joke. It is "reub [sic]," has hayseed in its hair, and is wild of eye and altogether peculiar. But the people of the West are not so cynical. Oklahoma is young and progressive and enterprising. Perhaps Oklahoma has gone too fast, possibly has made mistakes. But it is American; it is a part of us, of our own people, and is entitled to be judged on merits, on performance.
>
> "Deposits Guaranty Wins West,"
> *Guthrie Daily Leader*, August 29, 1908

Between 1889 and 1906, no fewer than thirty-one bills were introduced in Congress for the admission of the Oklahoma and Indian Territories to the Union as either one or two states. Few bills made it to the floor, and most languished in committee until Congress adjourned. Prior to 1900, legislators dismissed statehood on the grounds that the Twin Territories were too small and undeveloped to warrant admission. The census of 1900, however, showed Congress that their populations and resources were more than adequate for statehood.[1]

Confronted with irrefutable evidence that statehood was warranted, debates in Congress turned from statistics to politics. In 1902, northern and eastern senators denied statehood because they did not want to upset the sectional balance between parties. By 1904, plans for admission were being derailed by rancorous debates over the admission of Arizona and New Mexico. When President Roosevelt weighed in on the issue in

December 1905, he recommended that the Oklahoma and Indian Territories be admitted as one state, and Arizona and New Mexico as another. "There is no justification for further delay," railed the Rough Rider in his annual message to lawmakers, "and the advisability of making the four Territories into two States has been clearly established."[2]

It was not until January 22, 1906, that Representative Hamilton, cochairman of the two committees on territories in Congress, pointed the way out of the impasse with House Bill 12707. His bill called for admitting two states out of the four territories. Spirited debate in the ensuing months, including passionate appeals for single statehood from Oklahoma bankers and the territorial delegate, Bird McGuire, untangled the Twin Territories from their neighbors to the west. Further negotiations revolved around the sale of intoxicating liquors. Prior to 1889, the federal government banned liquor from the Indian Territory, but no such prohibition had been extended to the Oklahoma Territory when it was created by the Organic Act of 1890. Ultimately, Congress decided to extend prohibition over the entire state.

On June 16, 1906, President Roosevelt signed the Enabling Act, which called for joining the Twin Territories into a single state. Proponents of single statehood were vindicated when the census of 1910 showed population figures that warranted eight representatives from the new state for the next ten years. Oklahoma thus became the first state since the original thirteen to be admitted into the Union with as many as five representatives.[3]

Machinations in Washington, D.C., were paralleled by events in the Oklahoma Territory. With the support of the Oklahoma City Commercial Club and major newspapers throughout the Twin Territories that banded together in the Single Statehood Press Association, single statehood gained momentum.[4] In 1902, single statehood made its way into the Democratic Party's platform: "We here and now declare our firm conviction that we are entitled to the rights, privileges and responsibilities of American statehood. Nor are we unmindful of our brethren of the Indian Territory. Appreciating their splendid capacity and wonderful resources and achievements, we desire union with them in order that jointly we may build up the greatest of Western states. We, therefore, favor admission into the Federal Union, of Oklahoma and the Indian Territory as a single state."[5]

Governor Frank Frantz and members of the Oklahoma constitutional convention set September 17, 1907, as the date for popular ratification of the constitution. As delegates rolled up their sleeves and went to work in Guthrie, prescient observers sensed that something new was in the wind. "It was not merely the birth of a new state; it was the birth of a new kind of state," wrote Frederick Upham Adams in the *Saturday Evening Post*. "Its founders claim that it is the first real democracy, the pioneer in the experiment of a true form of republican government. Its detractors assert that the visionaries and radicals from all other states poured into Oklahoma, and that the more rabid of them met and consolidated their theories into a hodge-podge which is certain to result in ever-lasting ruin; but I am of the opinion that it will take more than a freak constitution to hold Oklahoma back."[6] When the appointed day of ratification arrived, voters approved the constitution by a vote of 180,333 to 73,059.[7] At 95 pages and 45,000 words, Oklahoma's constitution was one of the longest such documents ever written.[8]

In their first gubernatorial election, Oklahomans rejected territorial governor Frank Frantz and elected Charles N. Haskell of Muskogee, Indian Territory. In keeping with his Populist roots, Governor-elect Haskell, dubbed "Boss" Haskell in Guthrie's Republican-leaning *Oklahoma State Capital*, promised a barbecue at his inaugural as a way of thanking the farmers and laborers who had supported his candidacy.[9] Meanwhile, the entire slate of Democratic candidates for executive positions glided into office on Haskell's coattails. The legislature, whose initial session was slated for December 2, 1907, consisted of ninety-three Democrats and sixteen Republicans in the lower house and thirty-nine Democrats and five Republicans in the Senate.[10]

Politics aside, the first order of business was a party, and what a party it was! The festivities at the temporary state capital of Guthrie began at 10:00 A.M., November 16, 1907, in front of the Carnegie Library, where Oklahoma Territory secretary Charles H. Filson, joined on stage by the governor-elect, read President Roosevelt's proclamation declaring Oklahoma a state. Next, to represent the union of the Twin Territories, the Reverend W. H. Dodson of the First Baptist Church of Guthrie performed nuptials between Mr. Oklahoma—personified by Gristmill Jones—and Miss Indian Territory—played by a young woman from Muscogee, described by veteran journalist Irvin Hurst as "a beauty of

Cherokee descent."[11] (The details of the highly symbolic and fascinating wedding are found in the epilogue of *Banking in Oklahoma before Statehood*.)

The marriage of east and west that brought Oklahoma into being was greeted with typical frontier boosterism across the length and breadth of the brand-new state. Speeches, parades, feasting, and surely a bit of drinking on the sly signaled that a new day was dawning—that the banking and commercial interests of the Oklahoma Territory and the natural resources of the Indian Territory would become an unbeatable combination. But flowing beneath the euphoria like an underground aquifer was awareness of a union of even deeper significance. Thanks to the marvels of communication and transportation, commercial practices spawned by the exigencies of the frontier were conforming to modern ways of doing business. Regulations were putting an end to fly-by-night banks and fostering ever more conservative banking practices. And for the first time in their careers, bankers were reacting to events rather than initiating them.[12]

Oklahoma's statehood celebration coincided with the Panic of 1907. Even though financial downturns were a staple of the nineteenth-century economy, few saw this one coming, and for good reason: during the decade following the 1896 recession, agricultural prices rose to the point that farmers were able to shed debt to an extent unknown since the beginning of settlement in the Mississippi valley. Harvests of staple crops in 1907 were down a bit, but high prices made up for the shortfall. Railroads were in good shape too; if anything, they were suffering from growing pains as traffic increased and infrastructure had to be expanded. With the exception of coffee, commodities were flowing through the marketplace, from warehouses to retailers to consumers, in an orderly fashion, unhampered by inventory bottlenecks or price resistance.[13]

Such was the pace of economic activity that the nation's annual growth rate between the mid-1890s and the end of 1906 was an astonishing 7.3 percent. The absolute size of all industrial production had thus doubled in only ten years.[14] Capital markets in the United States and abroad were showing some strains, but not enough to signal an immediate crisis. According to one scholar of the time, "It would be difficult to find an equally long period of business activity at the close of which the relative development of different industries would seem to have been similarly satisfactory."[15]

Yet trouble was coming, and it announced its arrival on April 18, 1906, when San Francisco was rocked by a catastrophic earthquake. Fueled by wood-frame buildings, massive fires consumed four square miles of the city—about half of the urban area. Five hundred people perished, and a half million people were made homeless.[16] The natural disaster was followed by a financial one as stocks plummeted and enormous amounts of cash and gold were shipped to the stricken city. Outflows of gold from England raised fears of a liquidity crisis and fanned rumors in New York that British financial houses were in trouble. The Bank of England responded to the depletion of gold supplies by raising interest rates. Central banks throughout Europe followed suit. By the winter of 1906–1907, a credit crunch was in the making.

In the ensuing months, markets and the confidence they depended on were buffeted by declining stock prices and tightening credit. Clearly, the tempest was rising, but even the most prescient observers missed the warning signs. A key player in the escalating drama was Fritz Augustus Heinze, a swashbuckling adventurer who spent his twenties and most of his thirties in the copper-mining camps of Montana. Mergers after 1898 left three dominant companies in the nonferrous metals industry: Heinze's United Copper Company, Amalgamated Copper, and the American Smelting and Refining Company.[17] By the time Heinze returned to his native New York, he had amassed enough money to purchase the Mercantile National Bank. In February 1907, he became the bank's president, and positions as director of other financial institutions were soon to follow.

Now that he was on a roll, Heinze bought a seat on the New York Stock Exchange for his brothers, Otto and Arthur, and established a brokerage house under the name Otto C. Heinze & Company. Relying on his experience and contacts in the copper business, he and his brothers used their brokerage house to unleash a scheme in October 1907 to corner the stock of United Copper Company.[18] A contemporary economist, O. M. W. Sprague, characterized the target of their ambitions as "a copper company of secondary importance."[19]

The plan promptly went down in flames. Rumors spread like wildfire as the usual constellation of factors—impending bank failures, revelations of swindles, and precipitous drops in the prices of securities and commodities—coalesced into a perfect storm.[20] Frantic depositors lined up to empty their accounts, and the panic was on. Brokerage houses and banks that had participated in the plan tumbled like dominoes, including the third-largest trust company in New York—the Knickerbocker Trust Company, with deposits totaling $62 million.[21] As the magnitude of the crisis sank in, spooked depositors throughout the country hoarded cash to the tune of $296 million, according to the United States Treasury.[22]

Total disaster in October 1907 was averted when J. P. Morgan, the colossus of turn-of-the-century finance, summoned the presidents of major New York banks to his Italian Renaissance–style palace on Madison Avenue, locked the bronze doors to his fabled library, and kept them there until they agreed to pony up a collective $25 million. Acting like a one-man Federal Reserve System, the cigar-chomping titan decided which firms would succeed and which ones would fail. By engineering what amounted to a financial bailout of New York City, Morgan added his considerable heft to the too-big-to-fail argument.[23] Predictably, the panic fanned out to all parts of the country, including the Twin Territories—just three weeks shy of statehood, primed for a big-time celebration, and hardly in the mood for a financial meltdown.

Early on, the Oklahoma Territory's business community was unfazed by the hubbub back east. Journalist Fred L. Wenner described Saturday, October 26, 1907, as the end of a week of fine weather and record harvests.[24] "Oklahoma City has nothing to fear," declared Frank P. Johnson a year after his rise to presidency of the American National Bank. Declaring that the Knickerbocker Trust Company's failure was the result of stock speculation and "the efforts of the copper crowd to corner the Heinze interests," the Oklahoma City banker touted the territory's resilience. "Local banks carry so little money on deposit in New York banks that any failure would hardly hit any of us. Our bank carries only a small account for checking purposes when a customer wants eastern exchange. There is plenty of money here to carry on our business independent of the New York financial dealings."[25]

The *Daily Oklahoman,* Democratic to the core and, like its readers, wary of goings-on in New York, touted the Oklahoma Territory's independence from Wall Street as the best defense against the looming crisis.[26] Declaring that "there never was a time in the history of the west when there was less excuse for a panic," the *Blackwell Times-Record* assured its readers that the flurry would soon pass and that "the banks of this city and county never were in better condition, and are unquestionably solvent."[27] The news from Shawnee on October 29 was equally upbeat: "Reports from the Trust Companies all over the city late today state that normal conditions obtained and that incipient runs on several minor companies had failed to develope [sic]."[28]

But as the contagion spread across the land, complacency turned to conviction that something had to be done about mounting withdrawals from banks and dwindling supplies of cash. The cancellation of currency shipments from Kansas City and Saint Louis left banks without a source of the cash required for marketing grain and cotton and moving livestock. In desperation, bankers from Guthrie, Oklahoma City, Tulsa, Ardmore, Muskogee, and Enid gathered in the acting governor's office on Sunday evening, October 27, to request a banking moratorium.[29] For political leaders, the situation was awkward in the extreme. The Twin Territories had just ratified a constitution and curbed Republican control in Guthrie by electing a heavily Democratic slate of legislators. The last thing they needed on the eve of statehood was a full-blown bank panic.

Having lost his bid for the governor's office to Charles N. Haskell, territorial governor Frank Frantz was in Washington, D.C., to await Roosevelt's statehood proclamation. In his absence, acting governor Charles H. Filson, pressured by bankers and supported by Herbert H. Smock—who served as the last territorial banking commissioner and who would soon be appointed to that office in the new state—proclaimed a bank holiday beginning on Monday, October 28.[30] Filson's proclamation, issued at four o'clock that morning, was both a plea for cooperation and a paean to the can-do spirit of his fellow Oklahomans, and it left no doubt about the gravity of the crisis:

> Invoking the patience and indulgence of the citizens of Oklahoma, I entreat them to show that high forbearance and consideration and confidence in themselves and in their financial institutions and neighbors that has given Oklahoma such high place in the business and banking world and to refrain from making such comments or remarks as may be calculated to destroy confidence in Oklahoma institutions, firmly believing that conditions will soon become normal; and that necessity

exists for the issuing of this proclamation and for the protection and maintenance of our financial institutions which, without warning, are confronted with a situation without parallel in the history of the world.[31]

News of a different sort arrived in Guthrie via telegram from Washington, D.C., at noon. In a message to the people of the Oklahoma and Indian Territories, President Roosevelt announced that he would approve Oklahoma's famously verbose constitution and grant statehood to the two territories on November 16, 1907. That was certainly good news, but it did little to dispel the gathering gloom. By the terms of Filson's proclamation, banks in the Oklahoma Territory were to remain closed until Saturday, November 2; their counterparts in the Indian Territory had to be handled separately because they were under federal authority. In virtually every town except Tulsa and Muskogee, depositors were limited to cash withdrawals of $5.00 a day or $20.00 a week from deposits made prior to the banking holiday. Limits in Tulsa and Muskogee were $10.00 and $40.00, respectively.[32] Compliance with acting governor Filson's orders was far from uniform and depended on local economies. Some bankers refused to close their doors at all. Others came up with their own restrictions on withdrawals, and some circulated their own certificates and currencies. Merchants cooperated as best they could by accepting payment in whatever medium of exchange passed through their hands or by expanding credit sales.[33]

In the meantime, clearinghouses in Oklahoma City, Tulsa, and other cities issued scrip in lieu of disappearing currency.[34] Two kinds of currency substitutes were issued: clearinghouse loan certificates in large denominations for the settlement of bank balances; and clearinghouse certificates in small denominations for general circulation. The total amount issued in the Oklahoma Territory, beginning on November 1 and retired on January 1, 1908, was $200,000.[35]

Bankers thus found themselves stuck between the proverbial rock and a hard place. Even as they agreed that a bank holiday was the proper response to a panic that had gone global, they insisted that their institutions were sound. "No one locally has been unfair enough to even intimate that our banks are not all right," asserted the *Blackwell Times-Record* with a not-so-subtle message that pessimists should keep their own counsel, "and a majority of our farmers, business men and laboring men who have deposits with the local banks, realize that they have done the wise thing in closing, and will patiently wait until matters become adjusted."[36] Frank Johnson, who was also head of the Oklahoma City Clearing House, assured the public that the city's nine banks had reserves three times the legal minimum of 15 percent. Smock put the average reserve ratio at 40 percent for state-chartered banks. But there was no escaping the reality that, large as they were, the reserves were largely inaccessible because they resided as deposits in reserve banks where payments were restricted.[37]

Strictly speaking, clearinghouse certificates were illegal, but nobody thought about prosecuting. Much of the issue was subject to a 10 percent tax, but nobody gave much thought to collecting. Most certificates bore the words "payable only through the clearing house" to remind people that they could not demand cash. "In plain language," wrote A. Piatt Andrew, assistant secretary of the treasury in the Taft administration, a year after the debacle, "it was an inconvertible paper money issued without the sanction of law, an anachronism of our time, yet necessitated by conditions for which our banking laws did not provide."[38]

The worst of the money crunch was over within two weeks, and Oklahoma's statehood festivities on November 16 proceeded on schedule even though currency was still scarce and clearinghouse certificates were still in circulation as legal tender.[39] The bank holiday "was taken in stride" and "met by prompt effectiveness," asserted a headline in the *Daily Oklahoman*'s fiftieth-anniversary edition on April 23, 1939. "Oklahoma and Indian territory banks remained closed for about a week, then gradually resumed normal operations."[40]

Writing in 1909, Alexander D. Noyes, a bespectacled and professorial market watcher and longtime financial editor of the *New York Times,* cautioned against underestimating the shock whose worst effects were mitigated by J. P. Morgan's quick thinking and deep pockets: "The Panic of 1907 was a panic of the first magnitude, and will be so classed in future economic history, along with such financial episodes as the crises of 1893, 1873, 1857, and 1837." It bore all five characteristics of a classic panic: (1) hoarding by banks and the suspension of credit; (2) hoarding by individuals, which depleted bank reserves and put a premium on currency; (3) financial helplessness and substantial borrowing, and purchasing, of gold from foreign sources; (4) manufacturing shutdowns occasioned by loss of credit and slackening demand; and (5) a dearth of demand nationwide.[41] Banks in the South and West were particularly anxious to hang onto their cash. As Andrew wrote in 1908, "A large number of bankers, especially in the West and South, appear to have become panic-stricken along with the general public, and to have adopted the fatal policy of *sauve qui peut*."[42] By all accounts, bank hoarding made the panic worse by adding to the premium placed on currency, exacerbating the general collapse of credit, and contributing to the issuance of illegal money substitutes.

The Panic of 1907 was the most severe breakdown in the nation's credit mechanism since the national banking system was established in the 1860s.[43] On the eve of another banking crisis in 1931, Frank Johnson's memories of the week from hell remained vivid. "That's a long time ago, but I remember it well," he said in an interview for the *Daily Oklahoman*. "I lost my voice during that period, talking at meetings after meetings to explain that all was well but it would take a little time." Leaning back in his chair and chuckling, the veteran banker and, at the time of his interview in 1931, president of the First National Bank and Trust Company of Oklahoma City, reminisced about what it was like to be at the vortex of an old-fashioned bank panic: "The people were white of face and shaky of hand, and the bankers were about as scared as the rest of them." Working at Frank Johnson's side at American National Bank in 1907 was cashier D. W. Hogan, who went on to become president of City National Bank in Oklahoma City. What Hogan recalled most clearly about the Panic of 1907 was the inelasticity of currency: "At that time we had an inelastic currency which would neither expand in the crop moving seasons of the year nor contract when they were over. As the business of the United States expanded and when business was more active at the crop moving season, all of the currency available was brought into active use. It did not grow as the country grew and in 1906 there was barely enough to go around at the crop moving season."[44]

The economic contraction from May 1907 to June 1908 might have happened in any case, but it was probably intensified by the banking crisis. From the second quarter of 1907 to the first quarter of 1908, the stock of money fell 6.8 percent. Estimates of the decline in real gross national product (GNP) from 1907 to 1908 range from 4.3 to 5.6 percent.[45] When the dust settled and life returned to normal, even the most ardent opponents of centralization recognized the urgency of banking reform. State legislatures enacted banking laws throughout the late 1800s, but it was not until the Panic of 1893 that regulations began to converge. The regulatory impulse crested after the Panic 1907.[46] As the economist Sprague noted once the storm had passed, "Somewhere in the banking system of a country there should be a reserve of lending power, and it should be found in its central money market."[47] Senator Nelson Aldrich was blunter: "Something has got to be done. We may not always have Pierpont Morgan with us to meet a banking crisis."[48]

Economists back east scrambled to pinpoint the causes of the breakdown. Some blamed President Roosevelt's assault on monopolies. Others claimed that defects in the nation's currency system had finally come home to roost. Mindful of the Heinze brothers' attempt to corner the copper market, Noyes cited reckless banking in New York City as a primary culprit. He further suggested looking further afield for answers—not only to the San Francisco earthquake and its counterpart in Valparaiso, Chile, in August 1906, which added their miseries to financial turbulence, but also to countries as far-flung as Egypt and Japan whose markets were experiencing severe growing pains.[49]

The blame game was accompanied by post-panic assurances that it would never happen again. An extraordinary vision coalesced in the so-called sunshine movement, which was embodied in the Prosperity League. The movement's happy-go-lucky supporters summoned collective action to persuade communities that, if they believed themselves to be prosperous, then by golly, they would be prosperous! Nowhere was the Prosperity League's buoyancy better expressed than in the public advice of one of the organization's branch presidents. Poised at the brink of a new banking paradigm in the second decade of the twenty-first century, we would do well to ponder the purposeful amnesia that he preached to victims of the Panic of 1907: "Let the people resume business the way they were doing twelve months ago, start everything with a hurrah, and we will forget all about the panic in a day or two."[50]

Our final postmortem for the Panic of 1907 comes from Federal Reserve Board chairman Ben Bernanke. Speaking at a conference on November 8, 2013, Bernanke drew parallels between the subprime mortgage debacle of 2008, which he helped to tame, and the Panic of 1907. "The recent crisis echoed many aspects of the 1907 panic," said Bernanke. Topping his list of similarities were reckless speculation and a dearth of regulations pertaining to financial institutions. In both instances, restoring public confidence in the nation's finances depended on temporary public and private guarantees, measures to strengthen financial institutions' balance sheets, and public disclosure of the conditions of financial firms. "The challenge for policymakers," said the Fed chairman in conclusion, "is to identify and isolate the common factors of crises, thereby allowing us to prevent crises when possible and to respond effectively when not."[51]

While academics and businessmen searched for causes of the panic and solutions to the nation's banking woes, legislators in Guthrie, Oklahoma, set their sights on more provincial concerns: how to protect depositors in their state from ruin when their banks failed. The legislature met for the first time on December 2, 1907—a couple of weeks after the formal declaration of statehood on November 16, and a month after the bank holiday occasioned by the Panic of 1907. Article XIV of the Oklahoma Constitution contained an enabling clause calling for the legislature to create a banking department under a commissioner to be appointed for a four-year term by the governor, with the consent of the state senate. The clause granted the commissioner "sufficient" power to regulate all banks and trust and guaranty companies in Oklahoma, and maximum interest rates were established.[52]

All this was pretty typical legislation, but the circumstances were anything but typical. Credit was tight, banks were struggling to maintain their cash reserves, depositors were spooked, clearinghouse certificates were still in circulation—these and other signs of financial distress created a charged atmosphere in Guthrie. In a legislature weaned on prairie populism and infused with William Jennings Bryan's calls for reform, nobody doubted that something big was in the wind.

In his first message to the legislature on December 2, Governor Haskell, "admired by his many friends, feared and hated by his enemies," upped the ante with his insistence on legislation that would guarantee the safety of bank deposits. Such was the governor's enthusiasm for guaranteed deposits that he had tried to write it into Oklahoma's constitution but had failed by one vote.[53] But in a state and nation still reeling from a bank panic, vindication was at hand. The press, bankers, and key political figures in the new state agreed that Oklahomans deserved assurance that their money was safe.[54]

The legislature moved with dispatch. Its first piece of legislation in December 1907, offered by Senator Clint Graham of Marietta and Representative C. A. Skeen of Wapanucka, declared that railroad companies should provide separate coaches and depot waiting rooms for people of African descent.[55] Having disposed of this vexing issue, the legislature turned its attention to the guarantee of bank deposits. On December 5, Representative J. Roy Williams of Lawton introduced House Bill 11A. Although Senator Reuben M. Roddie of Ada was credited as its author, the bill bore the unmistakable imprint of Governor Haskell's brand of Populism in its promise that depositors would never lose a penny. "This is perhaps as important a measure as will likely come up during the session and has attracted much attention over the entire country," intoned the *Guthrie Daily Leader*. "It provides for the establishment of a guaranty fund for the protection of depositors, and for regulating banks and banking. This is the first attempt at legislation of this kind. Oklahoma is taking the lead in this matter and her experiment will be watched with interest throughout the nation."[56] Ominously, the bill afforded no way for national banks to avail themselves of the new law in a way that would satisfy the comptroller of the currency. Convinced that national banks would never be permitted to tap their capital and surplus to finance a state insurance fund, the executive committee of the Oklahoma Bankers Association met with Governor Haskell, U.S. senators Robert L. Owen and Thomas P. Gore, and members of the state legislature to find a way out of the impasse. The bill was promptly sent back to the committee on banks and banking.[57]

Subsequent debate, as brief as it was inconclusive, failed to allay national bankers' concerns that a state guarantee fund would put them at a disadvantage vis-à-vis state banks. The Roddie-Williams bill passed the lower house on December 17 and was promptly approved by an enthusiastic governor whose political capital was invested in deposit guarantee.[58] "Governor Haskell has made history," gushed the *Guthrie Daily Leader*. "He rose to the occasion when the people needed action. Without hesitancy, knowing full well that failure meant political ruin, he bridged the awful chasm between prosperity and calamity, tearing loose from all ancient and useless customs. Oklahoma, thanks to a militant chief executive, steps to the fore in the banking world, and says not only to her own but all other people that she will pledge her great, boundless and widely diversified resources to the protection and safety of their savings."[59] National banks were left in limbo insofar as they were welcomed to participate in the program, but only in a way that would satisfy the state banking board, the state banking commissioner, and the comptroller of the currency. Senator Owen pledged to advocate for a law that would enable national banks to offer their depositors the same protection that Oklahoma now offered to depositors in state banks.[60] As state bankers relished the prospect of a barrage of deposits from national banks and Comptroller of the Currency William Barret Ridgely awaited an opinion from the Department of Justice before rendering a final decision, Oklahoma was charging hell-for-leather into history not only as the newest state but also as the first state to guarantee deposits in state-chartered banks.[61]

The key provision of this landmark law was the creation of a bank guarantee fund, to be raised by a levy of 1 percent of the average daily deposits in all state-chartered banks. Additional assessments were authorized in case of emergency. The state banking commissioner, under the supervision of a board consisting of the governor, lieutenant governor, president of the board of agriculture, state treasurer, and state auditor, was charged with administering the program.[62] In cases of bank failures or closings, all assets of the bank were to be liquidated, and whatever additional funds were needed to meet depositors' claims were to be drawn from the guarantee fund. The two outstanding characteristics of the law were that it was compulsory and that depositors were to be paid at once. As Thomas Bruce Robb, then associate professor of Economics at the University of Missouri, wrote in his exhaustive treatment of the deposit guaranty movement of the 1920s: "The law was to take effect in sixty days. During its swift and harmonious passage through the legislature, little patience was manifested in either house with attempts to amend the bill. The only record of any debate on the bill is where the press reports state that the House is agreeing to a Senate amendment debated for an hour the proposition of substituting the word 'active' for 'acting' in a certain clause."[63]

Writing in 1913, President Taft's assistant secretary of the treasury, A. Piatt Andrew, expressed nothing short of dismay with passage of "a law without any precedent in any other country, and with only one dimly remembered, unsuccessful precedent in the United States—a law which nevertheless presented what was probably the most far-reaching and drastic experiment in banking legislation that had been made anywhere in the world for at least two generations."[64] Andrew's "dimly remembered, unsuccessful precedent" was the safety fund system in New York State that limped along from 1829 to 1842 before it was discarded in the wake of the Panic of 1837. Oklahoma's bank guaranty law faced the additional challenge of regulating banks from neighboring, yet vastly different regions: western Oklahoma, with a reasonably coherent set of banking codes; and eastern Oklahoma, where territorial banks had not even been required to incorporate. The fledgling legislature seemed to be promising people that they could deposit money and achieve high dividends and, in case of failure, look forward to bailouts courtesy of conservative, low-dividend investors.

As we so often do, we rely on the French language for its brevity of expression: *plus ça change*.[65]

Enthusiasm for the bank guarantee law surged when, on December 21, 1907, the Great Commoner from Nebraska, William Jennings Bryan, was an honored guest at a joint session of the Oklahoma legislature in Guthrie's Brooks Theatre. Even the House chaplain was filled with the spirit of the occasion. After a lengthy prayer on Bryan's behalf, he spiraled toward his crescendo: "Lord . . . if it is according to Thy will, let him be the next president of the United States." After a unanimous "Amen" from rapturous Democrats, Speaker William H. Murray of Tishomingo, lambasted in the *Oklahoma State Capital* as "Cocklebur" Murray long before he earned the nickname "Alfalfa Bill," intoned, "All in favor of that make it known by saying 'Aye!'" Shouts of "aye!" gushed forth, followed by thunderous applause.[66]

Stressing the need to protect the little man, the yeoman farmer, and the town laborer, Bryan heaped praise on the state's progressive constitution for acknowledging the people as the locus of all sovereignty.[67] Bryan was praised for his good work, and the heavily Democratic legislature pledged its support for his 1908 presidential campaign.[68] Meanwhile, back in Nebraska, cooler heads were questioning the wisdom of Oklahoma's effort to quell financial panics by legislative fiat. "The Oklahoma law was a mistake," asserted a statesman from Nebraska in January 1909.

> The people down there realize it and are trying to get away from it. . . . Deposits from all parts of the country are flowing to

Oklahoma, attracted by the apparent security obtained. At the first breath of suspicion that the law is not safe and sound, these deposits will disappear, as if by magic. Meantime, the banks will have loaned a large part of the money and things will be in sad shape. Nebraska is not going to put herself in any such position. Her citizens are conservative.[69]

Apparently, they were not conservative enough. On March 25, 1909, Nebraska became the second state to promise worry-free deposits with passage of the Nebraska Deposit Guaranty Law. Kansas followed suit in 1909, followed by Texas (1910), Mississippi (1914), South Dakota (1915), North Dakota (1917), and Washington (1917).[70] It comes as no surprise to find that unit banking was encoded in the DNA in the eight states that adopted some form of deposit insurance between 1908 and 1917. Wary of outside influence, America's pioneers in deposit insurance failed to recognize a more viable route to safety and stability that was, even then, gaining traction in other states: branch banking. Then as now, the benefits of intrastate branching included diversification of risk, coordination of responses to economic crises, and an efficient allocation of capital across regions, all of which minimize costs to banks and help depositors sleep better at night. From an economic standpoint, it seems clear that the commitment to unit banking in Oklahoma and its ideological peers stemmed not from clearly articulated economic policies but, rather, from Populist distrust of big-city bankers and their nefarious ways.[71]

With typical frontier temerity, Oklahoma legislators and their Populist brethren across America's heartland gave little thought to the weaknesses inherent in deposit insurance. The problem was twofold: first, insurance has a tendency to relax vigilance; and second, it raises the danger of concentration of risk, especially in agricultural regions where poor crops mean shrinking bank assets that would likely strain deposit guaranty funds. Such concerns made it to the floor of the Oklahoma legislature, but they were not enough to stem a revolution in the making.

As Robb noted, "The very fact that people are on the frontier shows that they were restive under the restraints and conventions of older civilizations; and Oklahoma was the last frontier."[72] One observer from back east saw something charming in Oklahoma's prairie chutzpah and went so far as to suggest that cynical easterners might even learn something from the new state's experiment in deposit guarantee.

If the tradesman, the farmer or the salaried man wants an object lesson of the value of deposit guarantee or insurance, he finds it in the Oklahoma system. Down east here they sneer at everything that comes from Oklahoma. It is a joke. It is "reub [sic]," has hayseed in its hair, and is wild of eye and altogether peculiar. But the people of the West are not so cynical. Oklahoma is young and progressive and enterprising. Perhaps Oklahoma has gone too fast, possibly has made mistakes. But it is American; it is a part of us, of our own people, and is entitled to be judged on merits, on performance.[73]

Predictably, the guarantee of bank deposits was a big hit among bankers and beleaguered depositors. Many banks still reeling from the Panic of 1907 renounced their national charters in favor of state charters so they could participate in the program. From February 1908 to January 1911, the number of state banks increased from 470 to 695, and their deposits skyrocketed from $18 million to $55 million. During that same period, the number of national banks decreased from 312 to 219.[74] As Robb wrote with an economist's flair for understatement, "Deposit guaranty proved so popular with the masses that this movement continued until the great avalanche of bank failures in 1910 and 1911 put an end to it."[75]

Failure of his pet project was far in the future when Governor Haskell, flush from victory in the legislature, cobbled together an examination of state banks prior to the deposit guarantee law's effective date of February 14, 1908. Working the phones, Governor Haskell appointed thirty-one special examiners to shine their analytical lights on balance sheets and loan portfolios. They were probably good bankers, but they were not necessarily trained examiners. As noted in the *First Annual Report of the Bank Commissioner* in 1908, "While a large number of banks were technically not in harmony with every provision of the banking laws, their general condition was such that the department did not feel justified in closing them and upon their promise to correct the objectionable features of their business they were allowed to continue in operation."[76]

One bank that was allegedly on the ropes was the International Bank of Coalgate in southeastern Oklahoma. On May 21, 1908, Commissioner Smock called Governor Haskell from Coalgate to report "gross irregularities" in the bank's conduct. The governor wasted no time in ordering Smock to shut it down. He then summoned a meeting of the banking board. Forty-two minutes later, Smock received detailed orders to pay off depositors in accordance with the bank guaranty law. Most depositors were paid within three days, and the incident was dismissed as a tempest in a teapot. When one farmer learned by telephone that the brouhaha was over and that he could come to town to get his money, he is said to have responded, "Well, I'm in no hurry. I'll be in next week." But bank officials had a different take on the closing, including bank president Dr. L. A. Conner, who insisted that the bank was closed for no other reason than to enhance Governor Haskell's status at the Democratic National Convention slated to open in Denver in early July.[77]

Even as examiners of questionable competence fanned across the state to do their governor's bidding, Governor Haskell was encouraged by good news from the courts. Wary of the state's interference in the banking business, the Noble State Bank took its concerns to district court, charging that the legislature did not have the authority, either under state or federal statutes, to pass regulations pertaining to the protection of bank depositors. Judge Huston's ruling was unequivocal: "My conclusion is that the provision of this law for raising a safety fund to protect all depositors of state banks, is a legitimate exercise of the police power of the state, and that the law does not infringe upon any of the provisions of the constitution of Oklahoma nor of the constitution of the United States."[78]

Case closed. Chalk up a win for Governor Haskell and deposit guarantee. But there was a catch. Such was the resistance to mandatory assessments that State Treasurer James A. "Sunny Jim" Menefee was compelled to issue a warning that state deposits would be withdrawn after June 1, 1908, from banks that had not complied with the new law.[79]

Meanwhile, the extension of deposit guarantee to national banks was going down in flames. In a letter that was published in the state press from T. P. Cane in the Department of the Treasury to Guthrie National Bank of Commerce president J. W. McNeal, national bankers received a preview of what to expect from the attorney general. "This question is of sufficient magnitude and importance to the banks of Oklahoma to obtain an official opinion from the Department of Justice, if it can be obtained," wrote Cane. "And until this office advises you in regard to the matter, you would not be justified in expending any money under the law of Oklahoma. In my opinion national banks have no right to avail themselves of the terms of the Oklahoma law relative to insuring deposits and until the Attorney General or the courts decide otherwise I shall so hold."[80]

As it turned out, Cane's assessment of the situation was right on target. Three months after Cane's letter was published, Charles J. Bonaparte—the grandson of Napoleon Bonaparte's brother, Jerome; onetime investigator of fraud in Indian land sales; and now U.S. attorney general—weighed in on Governor Haskell's effort to force national banks into compliance with the state guarantee law. In a letter to the secretary of the treasury dated July 28, 1908, Bonaparte refused to sanction assessments on national banks as a means of strengthening the guaranty fund: "I find no provision of the national banking law authorizing any such action on their part, and, in my opinion, a business of this nature would be essentially foreign to the legitimate functions of a national bank as an instrument of the government."[81]

Stymied but undeterred, Governor Haskell had an uphill battle on his hands to extend deposit guarantee beyond state-chartered banks. In response to a telegram from the *New York World* about the attorney general's ruling, Haskell went on the offensive. "Bonaparte's decision does not interest us," wired the defiant governor to the big-city newspaper. "If it did we would seriously question its correctness." Declaring that banking was a semipublic business and that depositors' rights needed to be protected as well as those of stockholders, Haskell gave a preview of what was to come in Oklahoma's battle of the banks: "The present antiquated and inefficient national banking law inspires no confidence in our people, and the smaller national banks fully realize that the national banking law operates to the benefit of the large banks only."[82]

While deposit guarantee was capturing the headlines, trouble was brewing in the oil fields of eastern Oklahoma. Even though agriculture dwarfed other interests in banks' loan portfolios, oil was quickly becoming the preferred route to riches. Ground zero for the looming disaster was the Columbia Bank and Trust Company of Oklahoma City, whose principals included its president, W. L. Norton, a well-known oil speculator; Vice President Herbert Smock, the former banking commissioner with connections all over eastern Oklahoma; and State Treasurer James A. Menefee, who was not bashful about encouraging the deposit of public funds in his bank.

Exchange National Bank of Tulsa under construction, ca. 1910. Tulsa's banks became engines of economic development in the early 1900s when vast oil deposits were discovered in northeastern Oklahoma. Within a few short years, Tulsa was known worldwide as the "Oil Capital of the World." Courtesy Oklahoma Historical Society.

Hastily organized in 1905, the bank's deposits grew by an astonishing 700 percent—from $365,686.01 to $2,806,008.61—during the twelve months ending September 1, 1909.[83] Using strategies that ran the gamut from the legitimate to the ridiculous, Columbia Bank's principals touted the safety of deposits under Oklahoma's state bank guaranty law to entice deposits from oil speculators and country bankers eager to hop in bed with their big-city colleagues. They also circumvented state laws by paying interest rates on time deposits of 6 percent, far more than the legal maximum rate of 4 percent. In some instances, they sweetened the pot with commissions.[84] As Columbia Bank's day of reckoning neared, about half of its assets represented deposits from smaller, local banks—119, to be exact.[85] Robb summed up the prelude to disaster: "Now all these and other reckless methods were employed to get business, but at all times the guaranty law was worked for all it was worth, and one cannot avoid the conclusion that this was directly responsible for most of the mushroom growth."[86]

What happened next was a shocking reminder of capitalism's susceptibility to financial bubbles. The comptroller of the currency, long suspicious of oil paper accumulating in Oklahoma banks, sent special examiners to eastern Oklahoma with instructions to charge off suspicious paper whether it was due or not. They complied, and paper began to gather like the leaves of autumn in the woodlands of eastern Oklahoma. In September 1909, Columbia Bank suspended operations; liquidation of assets and an inquiry ensued.[87] Reporting to an increasingly indignant public, journalist Frederick S. Barde claimed that the bank's $200,000 in capital stock was "heavily impaired by heavy loans upon doubtful securities." Moreover, two months before it was closed, the bank was examined by the state and found to be in good condition. Whatever mischief ensued must have occurred during the thirty days preceding its failure.[88]

Failure of the state-chartered Columbia Bank and Trust Company gave bankers with national charters a golden opportunity to assail the bank guaranty law for its tendency to foster wildcat banking. Apparently deciding that the best form of defense was attack, Governor Haskell donned his Populist mantle and issued a signed statement denying that any national banks had offered assistance to the floundering institution.[89] The governor's message was clear: national banks were tethered to big money and cared little about the fate of their Oklahoma brethren, while state bankers demonstrated their compassion for depositors every day through the bank guaranty law. Thus resurrected, the ghosts of Hamilton and Jefferson resumed their vendetta in the brand-new state of Oklahoma, where campaigns to tether banks to eastern capital were stymied by Populist insistence on maintaining local control of currency and credit.

As the rhetoric turned ugly, American National Bank president Frank Johnson found himself in the familiar role of mediator. His membership in the Oklahoma City Clearing House Association gave him the clout he needed to set the record straight. In a statement to a reporter for the *Oklahoma City Times,* he explained in laborious detail that the Clearing House Association had voted to provide State Banking Commissioner A. M. Young with $250,000 "if they could be sure that this money would save the Columbia and if the loan was properly secured by good assets of the distressed bank."[90] Young declined the proposal, but the point was made. "There is absolutely no dissension between the state and national

American National Bank Building in Oklahoma City, 1909. Courtesy Oklahoma Historical Society.

banks of Oklahoma City, as they are all standing shoulder to shoulder for the common good," declared Johnson. But he was not done yet. "It is a matter of record that the committee appointed to save the Columbia, if possible, was appointed on a motion of a national banker."[91]

Subsequent goings-on are sketchy. Robb tells us that "practically all the records of the bank were destroyed or stolen, and when large depositors came for their money they were permitted to go through the note-case and select such paper as they wished to offset their account. No records exist of the details of these transactions."[92] Not surprisingly, the fiasco had dire implications for the guaranty fund that had proven to be such a lure for W. L. Norton and his associates. The *Daily Oklahoman* reported simply that, when the Columbia Bank and Trust Company in Oklahoma City failed in 1909, it "broke the depositors' guaranty fund."[93]

Well, not quite. At the time of the failure, the guaranty fund contained $380,000, $50,000 of which was in the defunct bank.[94] Like a commander massing his troops for battle, Governor Haskell seized control of the situation. He and the state banking board imposed an emergency levy of three-fourths of 1 percent on member banks to fatten the guaranty fund to $693,000, and special shipments of currency were ordered from Kansas City. Meanwhile, individual depositors were invited to claim their funds, which they did with surprisingly little drama.[95] As a result of these measures, the guaranty fund was rescued from oblivion, destined to vex lawmakers for another fourteen years.

It came as no surprise to find Governor Haskell and State Banking Commissioner Young in the hot seat, accused of complicity in the shenanigans that brought down the Columbia Bank. An editorial on October 19, 1909, riddled with capital letters for readers who were slow to get the point, turned the heat on full blast:

> Governor Haskell, and Commissioner Young:
> The facts—the REAL facts—of the Columbia failure will come to the surface, and you KNOW IT!
> Why don't you talk facts, instead of talking innuendoes, and set yourselves right with the public, instead of bellowing "politics."
> The TRUTH won't injure either of you, only you think that you have to play politics all the time.
> Tell the TRUTH![96]

Meanwhile, the dominoes were tumbling in eastern Oklahoma. One of them was the Farmers National Bank of Tulsa whose president, E. F. Blaise, pinned the blame squarely on W. L. Norton, who maintained a heavy debt load at Farmers National Bank. "I will force Mr. Norton into bankruptcy," ranted the irate bank president. "He is worth a half million dollars and must pay these obligations. The depositors at Farmers National will be paid in full."[97]

In February 1911, a federal grand jury in Muskogee returned indictments against both bankers. Norton was charged with making false entries in the books of the American National Bank of Bartlesville, making a false report to the comptroller of the currency, and misappropriating funds. Blaise was on the hook for making a false report on the Farmers National Bank of Tulsa's condition to the comptroller of the currency and for misapplication of funds. Norton and Blaise, uneasy bedfellows at best, were on the same page in their insistence that government accountants had nothing to show but some technical errors after a year and five months of working the case. Both men looked forward to the opportunity to "make things look considerably different" when their case came to trial in federal court.[98]

The collapse of Columbia Bank and Trust Company did little to dampen the spirits of speculators who were converging on Oklahoma City's outskirts to cash in not on oil, but real estate. The most infamous member of this cadre of frontier boosters was I. M. Putnam, a rather unstructured businessman who had been dabbling in real estate since 1905.[99] Putnam saw his star rising when bids went out to relocate the state capital. In 1910, the companies that he controlled owned more than eight thousand acres with an average value of $1,000.00 per acre. The highest valuation was placed on 133 acres on the west interurban some nine miles from Oklahoma City that comprised the townsite of Putnam City, which Putnam claimed to be worth $2,400 per acre.[100]

Suspecting that Oklahoma City would be the likely winner of the capital sweepstakes, Putnam and an increasingly enthusiastic group of bankers and developers mounted a campaign blitz to lure the capital to their swaths of windswept prairie.[101] One of his closest associates was Abner Davis, a businessman who would soon earn a reputation in the oil fields as an "unprincipled promoter."[102] Davis was president of the Night and Day Bank, a position that he achieved in 1910 without the expenditure of any of his own funds, but rather by manipulating stock in Putnam's varied land companies.[103] Putnam was fortunate to count on Governor Haskell's support for his real estate venture. Reflecting Edenic imagery that would have passed muster with David L. Payne and his true believers in the Boomer movement, the townsite that might one day blossom into a state capitol complex carried the lyrical moniker "Oklacadian."[104] Once again, we rely on the economist Robb for a frank assessment of frontier boosterism on steroids: "These outrageous values placed upon barren open-country land nine miles from Oklahoma City were accepted as safe by the parties from whom Putnam obtained his money. These wild estimates were the product of the febrile mind of the promoter and any foundation they might have was contingent upon the location of the capitol building at Putnam City."[105]

While speculators were drawing up plans for their prairie mansions, events were conspiring against them. To sort out conflicting versions of those events, we turn to two individuals whose accounts seem most plausible and tend to corroborate one another: Fred L. Wenner, an early-day journalist who went on to serve as secretary of the Guthrie Chamber of Commerce and the Guthrie Capital Campaign Committee; and Mrs. A. S. Heaney, formerly Alice Beitman, who founded the Young Ladies' Seminary in Oklahoma City in the fall of 1889 and left her mark as one the Oklahoma Territory's most illustrious educators, and whose husband was a well-known real estate developer.[106]

Our story begins in Guthrie, designated in the Enabling Act of 1906 as the state capital until 1913, and the place where Governor Haskell seethed with indignation over the *Oklahoma State Capital*'s rough treatment of him and his family. On or about June 1, 1910, he summoned into his office three men whom he accused of controlling the newspaper through their banking interests and demanded that they do something about it. His listeners insisted that they had no control over the paper's editorial content, but to no avail. The governor threatened that, unless they exercised their influence to produce editorials more to his liking, he would move the capital to Oklahoma City. As the trio left, Haskell walked into his private office and dictated a proclamation calling for an election to determine, once and for all, the location of the state capital. The contenders were Guthrie, Oklahoma City, and Shawnee.

During the election on Saturday, June 11, Governor Haskell was in Tulsa campaigning against William Murray's run for the governor's office. At nine o'clock that night, before a single county had completed its canvas of the election, the governor declared that Oklahoma City had defeated its rivals by an overwhelming majority. The governor then boarded a special train for Oklahoma City. Shortly after his arrival, he opened his office at the Lee Huckins Hotel.

The plot thickened the night of Sunday, June 12, when Governor Haskell's secretary, W. B. Anthony, slipped past deputy sheriffs in the courthouse capitol building in Guthrie, stuffed the official state seal and special records in a suitcase, jumped out a back window, and ran down a back alley where a getaway car was waiting.[107] The ensuing late-night dash across the prairie, seared into Oklahomans' collective memory as a particularly brazen display of political chicanery, ended at the Lee Huckins Hotel, serving as the de facto capitol of Oklahoma until more permanent digs could be provided. For safekeeping, the state seal was wrapped in soiled clothing and stashed under a bed pillow in a top-floor apartment occupied by Mr. and Mrs. Heaney, who were, by now, two of Oklahoma City's most prominent citizens.[108] A handwritten sign bearing the simple inscription "Governor's Office" was placed over the clerk's desk. With characteristic confidence bordering on hubris, Governor Haskell responded to critics by asserting that he had simply done his duty under the law.[109] For many years after the heist and last-ditch efforts to undo the governor's sleight of hand, no party for politicos and public officials at the Heaney apartment in the Lee Huckins Hotel was complete without a retelling of how the Heaneys' bed had been, however briefly, the capital of Oklahoma.[110]

Guthrie citizens had their own take on the incident. Headlines in the *Oklahoma State Capital* blared with fury on Tuesday, June 14, after allegedly phony election results came in and the capital heist came to light. Less concerned with grammar than cold, hard rage, front-page editorials accused Governor Haskell and his fellow "brigands from the south" of conspiring to move the capital through trickery, lying, and a criminal misallocation of the people's money. "Boss" Haskell, rebranded "Czar Charles" and "Charles I" for his parody of Old World despots, had relinquished his right to serve the good people of Oklahoma: "Delegating to himself the power of a Russian Czar, trampling under foot all civil law and defying the process of a high court of this state, Gov. Charles N. Haskell (Charles I) from temporary 'executive offices' in Lee-Huckins hotel here at an early hour Monday morning issued his imperial ukase declaring Oklahoma City—'legally and ethically' the capital of the state of Oklahoma."[111]

Over the years, the removal of the state capital from Guthrie to Oklahoma City has served as a reminder that history is a messy business, and that memory is never free of bias and collective consciousness as well as old-fashioned self-interest. Citing, among other things, an interview with Governor Haskell some twenty-two years after the incident, *Daily Oklahoman* reporter Irvin Hurst dismissed W. B. Anthony's stealthy getaway as more myth than fact. His evidence further suggests that the governor was not quite the villain depicted in the Guthrie press and that folks in Oklahoma City, allegedly a den of liars and thieves and cutthroats, were as surprised as their neighbors to the north by the sudden turn of events.[112]

Further inquiry into what might be Oklahoma's most famous imbroglio, interesting and entertaining though it might be, would send us on a major detour from our mission: to weave a narrative of Oklahoma banking and commerce in the twentieth century. For present purposes, suffice it to say that the capital removal marked a decisive shift in Oklahoma history. Less than three years after statehood, the former capital and beehive of business activity morphed into just another small town whose charm and architectural jewels had to make do as compensation for the losses it had suffered. Oklahoma City newspaperman, civic leader, and educator Angelo C. Scott offered a eulogy for Guthrie's lost status as a capital city: "Guthrie was a grand fighting town. I always admired the grit of her fighting men who cherished so long the dream of the capital and struggled so long for their dream. But the final loss of the capital broke her spirit. Many (not all, by any means) of her leading citizens went to Oklahoma City or Tulsa, and nearly all attained conspicuous success, for Guthrie was justly famed for able men and women."[113]

For better or worse, all roads now led to Oklahoma City.

Recognizing the urgency of determining a capitol site, a group of business leaders gathered at the Lee Huckins Hotel—headquarters of the American National Bank before fire had leveled the hotel in August 1908—to review the options. Headed by Henry Overholser, the site location committee began meeting soon after Oklahoma City stole the capital from Guthrie in June 1910 and included Governor Haskell, Sidney L. Brock, W. L. Alexander, American National Bank president

Frank P. Johnson, and onetime cowboy, then lawman, and now real estate mogul Charles F. Colcord.[114] Having served as treasurer of the capital relocation committee, Johnson was an obvious choice to help figure out where, exactly, the capitol was to be built. Johnson had much to ponder as he sorted through the options on the very spot where his bank had been nearly destroyed less than two years earlier.

The capitol location committee's decision supported a consensus that was building in the state legislature, and it was not good news for I. M. Putnam. Nor was it good news for banks carrying loans that he and other speculators had taken out to support their scheme, including the Night and Day Bank and the Planters and Mechanics Bank. Such was the magnitude of real estate loans in the portfolios of these and other banks that they were dubbed "Putnam paper."[115]

A bubble was in the making, and it burst when Putnam City was rejected as the site for the state capitol in favor of land to the northeast that was donated by J. J. Culbertson and W. F. Harn.[116] History does not reveal what Putnam paper was called after the site selection committee's bombshell hit the streets. Nor do we know if the high-flying developer was on hand on July 20, 1914, when Governor Lee Cruce, a former cashier and president of the Ardmore National Bank, whose financial acumen complemented his prowess on the links, swung a pick rather than a golf club to break ground for the state capitol building, many miles east of the stillborn mecca of Oklacadian.[117]

What we do know is that real estate prices plummeted in 1910 after the site relocation committee made its decision. Land that had been advertised at inflated values of $250.00 to $1,000.00 per acre dropped to $50.00 to $75.00 per acre. The ripple effect was dramatic: stock in Putnam's companies crashed, and banks holding real estate paper quickly closed their doors, including the Night and Day Bank and the Planters and Mechanics Bank. Bank failures triggered a flow of funds from an already depleted bank guaranty fund and, for the first time, necessitated the use of emergency warrants to pay depositors.[118]

Bank failures were not the only things with an offensive smell. As it turned out, Mother Nature had the last word in thwarting Putnam's plans and those of his following of wannabe real estate moguls. According to Irvin Hurst, "Everything was going lovely to build the capitol out there at Putnam City, but in the meantime, the packing plants were in operation, and in those days, we didn't have air conditioning, and that south breeze brought that odor up there, and people were—" Hurst paused to ponder the malodorous stockyards. "You remember how it used to be in Putnam City and Bethany," he continued. "For years and years, they were stultified in their growth because of it."[119]

The failures of the Columbia Bank and Trust Company, the Night and Day Bank, the Planters and Mechanics Bank, and others caught up in the maelstrom severely weakened the bank guaranty fund. But Putnam was not the only one with imperial ambitions. What he was doing northwest of Oklahoma City was duplicated on a smaller scale elsewhere. In June 1911, the *St. Louis Post-Dispatch* cautioned its readers to beware of swindlers who were doing their best to maintain Oklahoma's reputation for outlawry.

> When real estate values began advancing in Oklahoma about ten years ago, and new country and new towns were being opened up by new lines of railroads, the real estate grafter cast his eye over the landscape. Townsite companies were platted and tracts of land worthless for any purpose were cut up into town lots. There was no substantial ground for believing or even hoping that the townsite would ever be valuable enough to support a crossroads post office, yet it was advertised—in newspapers outside Oklahoma—as the nucleus of a great industrial center, where men could buy a home for a song and live in a community where there would be a constant demand for both skilled and unskilled labor at high wages, where churches would lift their steeples to the sky and schools be found upon every hand. Thousands of persons were fleeced.[120]

Making do with total appropriations for his department of $86,800 over two years, State Banking Commissioner J. D. Lankford (1911–19) did his best to protect his fellow Oklahomans from the money grabbers.[121] Early in his term he threw down the gauntlet, warning grafters that a new sheriff was in town.[122] Under the no-nonsense headline "Proclamation that Announced Fight," Lankford announced the creation of a department in the state banking commissioner's office "for the purpose of giving information as to the financial standing of companies whose stock is offered for sale to the people of our State."[123] He also insisted that bankers obtain certificates of title or title insurance policies before making real estate loans. The crusading banking commissioner was still going strong in the summer of 1915 when he warned officers and directors of state banks, in no uncertain terms, that old-fashioned customs would no longer be tolerated: "For the reason that the practice of paying checks which overdraw accounts is both illegal and out of harmony with sound business principles, you are hereby advised that in the future this practice must be discontinued and you will so inform your customers." Lankford closed his letter of July 1, 1915, with instructions that the letter be read at semiannual meetings of banks' boards of directors and that "a suitable resolution in conformity with this ruling" be passed and "be spread upon your minutes as a permanent record."[124]

Yet speculators were not about to let sound business principles get in the way of quick profits. Banks routinely invested in development schemes far out on the prairie; when schemes collapsed, their real estate paper became worthless. Safe havens were hard to come by. As Robb noted, "One class of bankers was in collusion with the speculator; the other was the speculator's victim—together they dealt a blow that staggered the infant guaranty system."[125]

Another outbreak of bank failures (eight in all) rocked the state's finances in 1911. Only three small banks failed in 1912, but sixteen succumbed to an epidemic of statewide failures in 1913—the most in any year since statehood. Another five toppled in the first half of 1914, a year that Charles F. Colcord recalled as one of the roughest ever for Oklahoma City businessmen. "Crops throughout the state were bad and the city was depressed," wrote Colcord. "Men were so hard pressed trying to save their businesses that practically nothing of a constructive nature could be accomplished." To pay $53,000 in rent for offices occupied by state officials while the capitol was under construction, Oklahoma City mayor Whit Grant declared a holiday so that business leaders could canvas the city for money. "It was hard work," wrote Colcord, "but we got all the money needed and thereby kept the word of the city."[126]

Financial troubles came as no surprise to state banking board member J. C. McClelland, who shared Lankford's concerns about the sorry state of banking in general and loose lending requirements in particular. Yet he reserved special opprobrium for the bank guaranty law: "The condition of the banks in the State of Oklahoma at the time the guaranty law went into effect was most deplorable, and there were a number of banks which were allowed to come under the wing of protection of the guaranty fund that should never have been admitted. A great many of these banks have changed hands, and there are still some of these same banks that cause the department more or less anxiety, and are a source of constant care and vigilance."[127]

Just three years after its inception, the State Bank Guaranty Law was under assault by state bankers who balked at mandatory assessments and demanded up-to-date financial reporting. When told that an examiner would soon be knocking on his door to close his bank unless he coughed up his assessment, one banker threatened insurrection. "When he comes," growled the enraged banker in April 1911, "send the militia with him, for he will have to close my bank over my dead body. Mine is a solvent institution, prepared to pay every cent due its depositors, and I'll be damned if I'll pay any more assessments until I know where the money has gone."[128]

Governor Haskell's pet project, a milestone of progressive banking legislation unmatched in its audacity since the age of Jackson, hung on by a thread before it was put out of its misery by legislative fiat on March 31, 1923.[129] Although insurance premiums were eventually discontinued, the state banking board continued to issue warrants to depositors of failed banks. When the law was repealed in 1923, the state scraped up enough money to pay about 7 percent on the outstanding warrants.[130] Emergency measures and strong-arm tactics from the governor's office enabled Haskell to proudly declare that, from its inception in the first state legislature in 1907 to 1920, no depositor in an Oklahoma state-chartered bank lost a penny.[131]

Governor Haskell's nemesis in Guthrie, the *Oklahoma State Capital,* was downright giddy on Haskell's final day in office. "'The King Is Dead'—Welcome Gov. Lee Cruce," blared the headline on June 10, 1911.[132] As fate would have it, the paper folded a year to the day after Haskell's proclamation calling for an election to determine the location of the state capital.[133] In his final message to the legislature on January 7, Haskell heaped praise on the cornerstone of his Populist policies, the Bank Guaranty Law of 1908, which had weathered three years of "the most vicious assaults and untruthful criticism."

> Never have the services of a policeman been required to aid in the conduct of the state banking business in Oklahoma. We have had our bank failures, and doubtless always will have so long as

human nature remains unchanged. And it is for the purpose of protecting the public against loss and disaster that Oklahoma has a law to successfully manage and liquidate insolvent banks; and where the answer to the anxious depositor, in a failed bank operating under other laws, when he may get his money invariably is, "God only knows," under Oklahoma state banking law, the answer to such inquiry is, "you can get it now."[134]

Oklahoma's economic expansion in the immediate post-statehood period was hamstrung by a lack of good roads. Even though automobiles were replacing horses, many of the thoroughfares they traveled on remained as primitive as they were in territorial days. Caddo County oilman George Gorton knew all about the appalling state of Oklahoma roads, but he knew what to do. "I'd hate to recount how many times I was stuck in mud or sand those days," he recalled, "and for real bad road conditions it was hard to beat a model T Ford, with four good husky men inside, an axe, a shovel and coil of strong manila rope."[135] To persuade the state legislature to fund the development of a transportation infrastructure commensurate with the needs of the new century, community groups formed good roads associations whose ultimate goal was to establish a highway department as a division of state government. Their efforts paid off in 1909 when the legislature empowered counties to create road improvement districts.[136]

None were more persuasive in promoting good roads than Chandler banker and businessman Hugh M. Johnson, the brother of Oklahoma City banker Frank P. Johnson. In an October 1909 address to farmers and businessmen in Logan County, Hugh Johnson made an appeal to build roads as the first step in linking farmers and ranchers with commercial centers. Lincoln County voters had recently voted to spend $1 million to reclaim swamps, build thirty miles of hard-surfaced roads, and eradicate Texas cattle tick fever, and folks in Logan County wanted to know the secret of their success.[137] Johnson boiled it down to simple arithmetic. "There is more money wasted by farmers on bad roads than on the greatest commercial enterprises combined," explained the Chandler banker to what was surely a rapt audience. "The waste is staggering. Get the facts from sources that cannot be disputed and the farmers will believe them. We tried it in Lincoln County and got 80 per cent of all the votes cast. . . . Get right down to business and be frank with the farmers. Give them facts and figures and you can build a good road anywhere."[138]

While Hugh Johnson and his ilk were lobbying for good roads to replace the tangle of trails and rutted byways that had compromised economic development in the Twin Territories, Oklahoma City businessmen were adjusting to the rhythms of the new state's boom-bust cycle. The economist Robb borrowed figures from the city auditor's report of June 1, 1916, and *Harlow's Weekly,* the city's leading business newspaper, to illustrate the combined effects of population growth, railway expansion, economic development, downtown and residential construction, and a nascent oil industry that was poised for takeoff. Those same figures tell a story of precipitous decline when frenzied growth reaped the whirlwind.

	BUILDING PERMITS	BANK CLEARINGS
1907	$1,853,629	—
1908	1,734,938	$46,182,000
1909	5,903,270	83,650,000
1910	5,493,203	122,821,000
1911	2,828,256	104,853,000
1912	885,246	85,415,000
1913	174,727	91,800,000

"But this was a diseased growth," wrote Robb. "We now know that it was the result of that 'hectic orgy of speculation' that swept so many towns off their feet in the granger states a generation ago."[139] Drawing on his literary repertoire, Angelo Scott borrowed from Marc Antony to suggest that men had lost their reason and had reached a stage of "boom psychology"—"the stage of impossible additions, impossible expectations, impossible prices, impossible dreams of wealth. It was a huge phantasmagoria. This continued for a few years longer, possibly three or four. And then, suddenly, came the great cessation, the years of taking up the slack. This was absolutely typical; every great boom has suffered this identical experience."[140] Not for the first time and certainly not the last, Oklahoma's speculators and the bankers who fueled their dreams had flown too high. Their descent was all but foreordained.

It is easy to see runaway growth in the brand-new state as a cautionary tale of capitalism run amuck. Caught in the crossfire were bankers who were responsible for financing economic development and, at the same time, building their institutions. Sometimes, everybody came out winners. But all too often, bankers and their customers wound up in the same sorry mess.

In its transition from frontier scarcity to consumer abundance, Oklahoma was the latest venue for the tug-of-war between capitalism and democracy. The former championed the benefits of an unfettered marketplace, while the latter held the promise of opportunities open to everyone. In their first few years of statehood, Oklahomans showed just how precarious that balance could be.

CHAPTER TWO

The War Years

> You cannot build a great commonwealth with a wail of pessimism, but you can make great progress every day in the year by placing yourself on an optimistic platform where you can see many wise laws, many conscientious public officials and unprecedented development in every part of Oklahoma.
> — Sydney J. Roy, secretary, Shawnee Chamber of Commerce, vice president, State Federation of Commercial Clubs

Congress's response to the Panic of 1907 was the Aldrich-Vreeland Act of May 30, 1908.[1] In addition to legalizing and regulating what had happened spontaneously during the panic, the act created a National Monetary Commission to investigate the monetary system and propose reforms.[2] The commission's twenty-four-volume report, published on January 11, 1911, identified the national banking system as the cause of panics and inelastic currency.[3] No precise policy prescriptions were offered, but there was a clear consensus that the United States, the only major industrial power without a central bank, needed a lender of last resort.

The National Monetary Commission's report was hailed as a landmark of progressivism. Years later, reformers were chagrined to learn that recommendations came not from deliberations in the halls of Congress, but from a secret meeting—the dreaded cabal!—of government officials and Wall Street insiders that convened in November 1910 at Jekyll Island, Georgia. Attendees arrived at the onetime hunting retreat for wealthy northerners under a veil of secrecy that would have impressed the cloak-and-dagger set in our own time. The gathering of financial heavyweights included Henry Davison, the conclave's organizer and senior partner in the House of Morgan; Senator Nelson W. Aldrich, chair of the National Monetary Commission; Frank A. Vanderlip, president of National City Bank, the nation's largest bank; Paul Warburg of the illustrious Hamburg banking family, a partner at Kuhn Loeb and an expert on central banking; A. Piatt Andrew, assistant secretary of the treasury and a former Harvard professor; and Benjamin Strong, president of the Bankers Trust Company, who was destined to become the first governor of the Federal Reserve Bank of New York. Served by a skeleton staff during their ten-day visit to the deserted island and laboring under an oath of confidentiality, these masters of finance wined and dined like royalty and deliberated late into the night to craft a system of centralized banking for a nation whose antipathy toward centralization in any guise was in for a rude awakening.[4]

Under the authorship of Vanderlip and Strong, what came to be known as the Aldrich Plan proposed the creation of a Reserve Association of America or National Reserve Bank, a central bank in everything but name whose nationwide branches would be authorized to issue currency and make loans to commercial banks. Although the federal government was to be represented on the association's board of directors, the association would be owned and controlled by banks to constitute a sort of bankers' cooperative.[5] The Aldrich Plan made its way into the National Monetary Commission's report and influenced subsequent legislation, but its debt to financiers who gathered at Jekyll Island did not become public knowledge until four years later when a magazine published the details. Twenty years would pass before the Aldrich Plan architects would publicly acknowledge their undercover operation. It was not without a dose of irony that the institution known to subsequent generations simply as "the Fed" was a child of the "money trust" that struck fear into the hearts of progressives who thought they had cornered the market on enlightened monetary policy.

For the next three years, the ghosts of Jefferson and Hamilton grappled for control of the nation's banking system. The stakes ramped higher when a committee led by Congressman Arsène P. Pujo of Louisiana issued a scathing report on the money trust that was channeling investment capital into the hands of a few oligarchs bent on controlling the country.⁶ Upon his election to the presidency in November 1912, Woodrow Wilson asked the chairman of the House Committee on Banking and Currency, Carter Glass of Virginia, to take up the National Monetary Commission's report and spearhead legislation in accordance with its recommendations.

Congressman Glass's coalition included two Democrats from Oklahoma: Robert L. Owen, chair of the Senate Committee on Banking and Currency, a native Virginian of Cherokee ancestry who practiced law on behalf of the Five Tribes in the Indian Territory before launching his political career and who based his successful campaign for the U.S. Senate in 1907 on opposition to monopolies and trusts and a promise to push for removal of restrictions on the sale of Indian lands;⁷ and Claude Weaver, a native Texan who was elected to the House of Representatives from Oklahoma's Fifth District in 1907 and quickly earned membership on the Committee on Banking and Currency.⁸ Such was the extent of Senator Owen's influence that the legislation passed into law on December 23, 1913, as the Owen-Glass Federal Reserve Act. Praise from such august organizations as the American Bankers Association (ABA) notwithstanding, skeptics were on hand to criticize the boldest banking regulation in generations. Alleging that the Federal Reserve Act was pure politics, Representative George McLean of Connecticut sneered, "There is not one man in ten thousand who cares anything about the subject . . . and his ignorance in this regard is as natural and excusable as his ignorance of the Chinese language."⁹

But we can be sure that Oklahoma's beleaguered bankers cared about it. A Federal Reserve Board was appointed by the president; the first governor of the Federal Reserve Bank of New York was Benjamin Strong. Reserve banks were established in twelve cities: Boston, New York, Philadelphia, Cleveland, Richmond, Atlanta, Chicago, Saint Louis, Minneapolis, Kansas City, Dallas, and San Francisco. High-powered money in the form of gold, national banknotes, subsidiary silver and minor coin, together with a hodgepodge of relics from earlier episodes of monetary reform—greenbacks, silver dollars, silver certificates, and Treasury notes of 1890—yielded to the Federal Reserve note as a means to solve the problem of inelasticity.¹⁰ The notes were to be backed by commercial credit and reserves of gold representing at least 40 percent of the amount of the notes issued.¹¹ All national banks were forced to join the system by depositing from one-half to two-thirds of their legal reserves in a common account. The Federal Reserve banks provided pools of money to banks nationwide, and they were restricted to dealing only with the Treasury Department and member banks. The greatest power bestowed on the new Federal Reserve System was establishment of the *discount rate*—the rate of interest charged by the banks when lending to member institutions. Raising the discount rate was supposed to slow the economy; lowering it was supposed to stimulate economic activity.

The Owen-Glass Federal Reserve Act of 1913 was a milestone in banking reform whose architects looked forward to less turbulence and more elasticity in the nation's finances. Prior to its passage, Vanderlip had expressed the sentiments of many in the banking community in a speech before the Commercial Club of Chicago. "The whole world is united in agreement that we have about the worst system of banking that there is anywhere in existence," declared the fed-up bank president. "It makes of us . . . an international nuisance."[12] For bankers who agreed with Vanderlip's bleak assessment of their industry, the Federal Reserve System illuminated the path to an efficient and prosperous future. Back in Oklahoma, editors at the *Daily Oklahoman* had their doubts, particularly when Senator Aldrich insisted that he was beholden not to "the interests" but rather to the exigencies of statesmanship and the public welfare. "The public is as well prepared to believe this," declared the newspaper, "as it would a declaration that the moon consists of green fromage."[13]

Prescient observers recognized an Achilles' heel that continues to thwart the Fed's efforts to regulate the nation's finances. Simply put, the Federal Reserve System began operations with no effective legislative criteria for determining the total stock of money. With the stroke of a pen, the quasi-automatic discipline of the gold standard yielded to the discretionary judgment of Federal Reserve governors—hardly a recipe for the smooth flow of currency and credit that Hamilton's ideological heirs were after. As the years passed, the benefits of centralized banking were often eclipsed by erratic dips and swings in the money supply, causing many to wonder if, in slaying one beast, they had simply spawned another.[14]

Nevertheless, the creation of the Federal Reserve System was a game changer insofar as it wrested control of the nation's money supply from capitalists of J. P. Morgan's ilk and bestowed it upon the presidentially appointed and senatorially approved Federal Reserve Board. Arguably, no single reform has ever shifted the balance between capitalism and democracy more decisively than the Federal Reserve Act of 1913. Granted, the linkage was loose. Once appointed, the Federal Reserve governors were beyond recall and effectively insulated from political pressure. Yet as stewards of what was, in effect, a central bank, they answered not to shareholders of the Federal Reserve System's member banks, but to the people of the United States.[15]

The Federal Reserve Act of 1913 was a few months in the future when Ethlyn Johnson, the daughter of American National Bank of Oklahoma City president Frank Johnson and his wife, Aida, made her debut in showbiz. Touted as the "leading lady," Ethlyn participated with five other young women in a moving picture, filmed in August 1913, aimed at showcasing Oklahoma City. Chosen by a secret committee, Ethlyn and her costars joined Colin Campbell—a member of the exclusive Pickwick Club, one of the city's most eligible bachelors, and a man whose family lived two blocks west of the Johnsons—to put their thespian talents into the service of public relations.

The opening scene of *Seeing Oklahoma City* was filmed at the Frisco station, where the six women, billed as "pilgrims," arrived as out-of-town visitors. They disembarked, climbed into Campbell's car, and were whisked away for a grand tour of the city. Their first stop was a tea party at the Johnson home at 439 Northwest Fifteenth Street. "Miss Johnson and her mother poured tea and entertained their guests while the camera man ground merrily on," ran a feature article in the *Daily Oklahoman*.[16] Refreshed, the entourage proceeded to other elegant homes. In four days of filming, the pilgrims visited hotels, department stores, office buildings, packing plants, and industrial sites. In all likelihood, the pilgrims dropped by the American National Bank to showcase the city's prominence in state finances. In a foretaste of media's ability to shape perception, residents were asked to heighten the buzz by gathering in large numbers at the starlets' venues.

Heralded as "the hit of the season," the feature consisted of four reels. The first was a rollicking glimpse of Oklahoma City "in the days of '89," complete with the land run and the staking of lots, and brought to life with a full complement of gun-toting horsemen, Indians, cowboys, and soldiers. The tempo settled a bit in the second and third reels to feature Oklahoma City's businesses, residential sections, parks, boulevards, and schools—more alluring, perhaps, to potential newcomers than fast horses and gunplay. Reel number four, a comedy stretching to a thousand feet, was an added attraction, but it had to be cut due to the length of the first three reels. Admission was a modest twenty cents for adults and ten cents for children, and viewers were promised thirty electric fans and ice-cooled air to mitigate the misery of a blazing Oklahoma summer. Readers of the *Oklahoma City Times* were probably won over by the time they scanned one advertisement's final seduction: "Don't Miss This Show—IT'S THE BEST EVER."[17]

According to breathless accounts in the Oklahoma City press, motion picture fans were not disappointed: "'Have you seen the picture?' is a question asked on every hand—no need to ask which picture—there is but one talked of now." The Overholser Theater "was taxed to capacity" with young and old alike and included a sprinkling of Boomers and probably Sooners. One early settler was heard to say that the first reel depicting the Run of '89 "was so true as to detail and assemblage that it seemed to have been taken on the ground when the original run took place." Much praise was heard for the artistry that went into selecting young ladies to play the part of the pilgrims. Special acclaim was reserved for the belle of the community: "Miss Ethlyn Johnson in the leading role is a real 'movie' star and each of the young ladies carries her part like a professional."[18]

A private screening was held at the Overholser before the public unveiling. Guests included Frank and Aida Johnson, their daughter—not only the belle of the community but now the "Queen of the Movies"—three other pilgrims, the dashing Colin Campbell, and various other insiders and newspaper reporters. Edith C. Johnson (no relationship to the banking family), the *Daily Oklahoman*'s society editor, reported that the suspense was terrible as guests waited in the lobby. Tensions rose as the "picture machine" sputtered to life. "Finally," Johnson reported, "the white screen was dropped on the stage, the lights went off and Manager Lamb called for a little slow music." More sprightly airs soon emanated from the orchestra pit. When "Seeing Oklahoma City" flashed on the screen, one of the pilgrims cried out, "O, mamma, I'm so scared."

"But she need not have been," continued the society maven, "for six prettier, cheerier, livelier pilgrims could not be imagined. Vivacity and grace were in every movement. With unflagging interest and energy they climbed in and out of the big auto time after time in the sightseeing tour of the city. They smiled at everything and everybody and took in the sights indefatigably." Colin Campbell rose to the occasion as well—gallant to a fault, and treating his precious cargo with the grace and deference they deserved as Oklahoma City's original pop stars.[19]

Newspaper accounts do not tell us if Frank Johnson was home to enjoy the pilgrims' tea party on the first day of filming. Nor do we know if Frank's brother and Chandler banker Hugh Johnson and his wife, Mary, were there to see what all the hoopla was about.[20] If so, the brother bankers might have observed the festivities from behind a Doric column on the front porch of the Johnsons' imposing home, where they were beyond the gaze of the cameraman and free to discuss the goings-on in business and banking.

Sweltering under an August sun, the Johnson brothers would have had much to talk about: the harrowing Panic of 1907 that felled banks across the land; a bank guaranty law that seemed to promise depositors more than it could deliver; manic speculation in land and oil that led some to riches, others to ruin, and many to both; the prospects of returning to centralized banking, realized later that year with the creation of the Federal Reserve System; and bank failures that were the inevitable consequence of unwise business decisions. Did Frank and Hugh congratulate one another on surviving the perils of their modernizing age? Did they share strategies to cope with banking challenges yet to come?

There is no way to know. Maybe they were content to sip their tea and enjoy the scene unfolding before them on the lawn, where a cameraman was capturing a Victorian tea party with technology symbolizing the triumph of modernity. Stretching to the horizon, a hastily built city, fueled by a capitalist juggernaut that leveled everything in its path, was lurching into the twentieth century with all the grace of a bull in a china shop, exploiting resources for all they were worth, and apparently blind to the consequences of unfettered growth.

And behind them was the frontier—tamed, perhaps, but far from vanquished.

Ethlyn Johnson's debut on the silver screen and the Owen-Glass Federal Reserve Act of 1913 were a few years in the future when, in the spring of 1907, an unassuming German from the tiny Bavarian village of Achstetten showed up in Oklahoma City. Upon his arrival, he made straight for Main Street to locate the office of Otto Branstetter, a onetime homesteader in the Cherokee Strip and trade unionist in Kansas City who had been appointed secretary of the Socialist Party of Oklahoma in 1906. The newcomer needed to get the lowdown on Oklahoma farmers and the likelihood of enticing them into the Socialist fold. Branstetter knew better than most the fractious history of Oklahoma radicals, and he had no illusions about imposing centralized party authority on their movement. As his visitor wrote many years later in his memoir, *If You Don't Weaken,* "The secretary confessed there wasn't much of a proletariat in Oklahoma to build a proletarian revolution on, and with."[21]

The visitor was Oscar Ameringer, and to follow his trail through Oklahoma is to glimpse the vast underbelly of the American Dream. Known to posterity as "the Mark Twain of American Socialism," Ameringer was born to the cadence of cannon fire during the Franco-Prussian War, and he spent his youth steeped in a culture of rural poverty and rigid class structure. He also spent enough time reading radical writings to become a staunch defender of the disadvantaged. Once in America, he synthesized the democratic principles of Jefferson with the individualism of the frontier and sprinkled them with a tolerant, nonsectarian brand of Marxism to formulate what he called "industrial democracy": industry of the people, by the people, and for the people. Raising storytelling to an art form, Ameringer depicted in both his writing and his speeches the plight of dispossessed Oklahomans, but not without a folksy wit that earned him a niche in the tradition of southwestern humor.[22]

The marriage of Mr. Oklahoma Territory and Miss Indian Territory notwithstanding, Ameringer and his fellow organizers proselytized in a state that was deeply divided between east and west. Thanks to the relative ease of communication and transportation, the flatlands to the west were fertile ground for entrepreneurship. Cities attracted entrepreneurs who not only were competitive but who also understood the role of currency and credit in fostering sound business practices.[23] The Homestead Act of 1862 did not apply to the Indian Territory, but it certainly lured to the nation's midsection farmers who were likewise attuned to the rhythms of commerce.

As predatory businesses spread their tentacles across the plains, some farmers sought refuge in the Farmers' Alliance, an organization founded in Texas in the 1870s as a vehicle for collective action against monopolies. One of the alliance's main goals was to form cooperatives as a means of strengthening producers' influence in buying their supplies and marketing their products.[24] Hamstrung by lack of capital, poor management, and insufficient patron support, cooperative enterprises fell by the wayside, and farmers whose grievances remained unmet flocked to the banner of Populism.[25] With the demise of the Populist movement in the late 1890s, disgruntled farmers had a choice: they could either cast their lot with a Democratic Party that was losing touch with farmers and working-class constituents; or they could heed the siren call of socialism, stewed in the juices of European social theory and homegrown frustrations.

In the three campaigns after Oklahoma statehood, election results told the story of unhappy farmers willing to launch yet another bold experiment. From a base of fewer than 10,000 votes in 1907, the Socialists' following grew to more than 21,000 in 1908, nearly 25,000 in 1910, and more than 41,000 in 1912.[26] In 1910, the party's dues-paying, "red-card" membership was not only the largest in the Southwest; it was the largest in the nation. With 5,482 official members, Oklahoma's Socialist Party had precisely 800 more than the state with the second highest membership, New York, and paid more dues to the national office ($3,800) than any other state, thus supplying the Oklahoma party with an impressive war chest with which to finance its candidates.[27] Such was the extent of Socialist strength in Oklahoma that Oscar Ameringer garnered 23 percent of the vote in a three-way race for mayor of Oklahoma City in 1911. More than a hundred Socialists were elected to local office, including six to the state legislature.[28] In the presidential race of 1912, Socialist candidate Eugene Debs captured 6 percent of the national vote; in Oklahoma, that percentage ballooned to 16 percent.[29] What is more, the Sooner State led the nation in subscriptions—22,276 at their peak—to socialism's leading journal, *Appeal to Reason*. In 1908, its publishers in Crawford County, Kansas, rewarded the banner state with a special Oklahoma City edition.[30] Served by fifty-five weekly Socialist Party newspapers in Oklahoma, Texas, Louisiana, and Arkansas, the party faithful had plenty to talk about at summer encampments that drew people by the thousands throughout the Southwest.[31]

Unforgiving though they were, the economic challenges of northern and western Oklahoma paled in comparison to problems in the old Indian Territory, where life was never easy. The federal Homestead Act did not apply to the Indian Territory, and forty years of erosion and single-crop agriculture had left the soil depleted and its tillers impoverished.[32] In the absence of a commercial culture that facilitated entrepreneurship among their neighbors to the west, farmers in the east were easily pushed into

Socialist camp meeting near Antlers, September 1910. Courtesy Oklahoma Historical Society.

tenancy. Their problems were exacerbated when the Panic of 1907 led to an increase in absentee landlordism. As urban creditors foreclosed on farms and prosperous planters moved to town, absentee landlords joined businessmen and politicians who were well schooled in the arts of making false promises to honest workers.[33]

In 1910, tenants operated 54.8 percent of farms in the state; by 1925, the percentage had risen to 58.6. Some counties groaned under the weight of 75 to 80 percent tenancy.[34] *Harlow's Weekly* was unambiguous in identifying tenant farmers "whose family are ill clothed, inadequately fed and squalidly housed, and whose children are growing up uneducated" as a major drag on the state's economy. "What we need to recognize," ran a story in Oklahoma City's premier business newspaper, "is that we have with us a type of incompetent, present in large numbers; the economically incompetent, just as truly incompetent as the intellectually or morally incompetent. And the state owes them some kind of responsibility."[35]

The number of tenant farms in the Southwest was increasing at twice the national rate,[36] and they were served in eastern Oklahoma by financial institutions that, according to a 1914 study, "should not even be called banks." The author of the study and editor of the *Farmer-Stockman* in Oklahoma City, Carl Williams, calculated that the typical bank had only $10,000 in capital and thus faced the impossible goal of loaning $45,000 annually while keeping interest at the mandated rate of 10 percent. As if high overhead, ignorance of sound banking practices, a shortage of currency and capital, and the risky nature of frontier banking were not enough to stymie eastern Oklahoma's growth, usury was systemic. Even in prosperous counties, interest rates ranged from 12 to 60 percent, and the average was 25 percent.[37]

Bankers throughout eastern Oklahoma struggled to strike a balance between profits and public service in an environment that was positively hostile to sound banking practices. Meanwhile, their nemeses in the Socialist movement had plenty of readers for their journals and attendees for their encampments. The Socialist blueprint for a just society ranged from reform to revolution, and it included various forms of agricultural collectivism, an enlarged role for the state, and tighter regulations on the hours, conditions, and wages of workers in nonfarm industries. Oscar Ameringer spoke for many in the movement when he linked farmers with laborers in their struggles against exploitation. In his estimation, city wage workers were exploited because they did not own their own tools, much as farmers were exploited because they did not own the land they tilled. In the countryside and to some extent in the city, the movement aimed to remove parasitic bankers, landlords, and other artificial forces from productive processes so that people could exert their natural energies upon nature's bounty. Unlike their ideological kin in Europe who toiled under the banner of scientific Marxism, Oklahoma reds never strayed too far from their Bibles. Like modern-day marketers who know their customers, local Socialists built their base in Oklahoma on old-time religion, proven morality, and a sense of righteous conviction.[38]

Clearly intimidated by the rising tide of rural radicalism, bankers responded with pleas for thrift on the part of impoverished tenants. In Marshall County, where tenancy rates were among the highest in the region and Socialists obtained their largest percentages of the vote between 1910 and 1916, the Madill National Bank advertised its services with a not-so-subtle hint of class envy: "Some people are always POOR," ran the heading with bold caps to drive home the bank's message, "because they never save any proportion of what they earn. It just melts away from day to day, with nothing in the end to show for it. A savings account at this bank will put you in the OTHER class."[39]

Socialism was a toxic brew for a young state struggling to outgrow its hardscrabble roots, and it posed a threat to bankers and businessmen who wanted nothing more than inclusion in the national polity. Experimental legislation, lax regulation, wild-eyed speculation, bank robberies, and systemic usury among rural banks were enough to tarnish the young state's image. Toss in a homegrown version of Marxism, and you have a perfect storm capable of keeping even the most sanguine of businessmen up at night.

The specter of revolution reared its ugly head in the tragicomic Green Corn Rebellion of August 1917. The catalyst for violence came on August 2 when a sheriff's posse on the lookout for draft dodgers was ambushed near Lone Dove in Seminole County. The rebels' resentment toward bankers and landlords had erupted in hostilities on numerous occasions; now, it was the government's turn to reap the whirlwind for enlisting workingmen as cannon fodder in a rich man's war. Following the ambush, a thousand rebels scattered across the Canadian River valley were poised to march all the way to Washington, D.C., and survive on ripened corn along the way. Their plan was to subject the "Big Slick" (a.k.a. President Woodrow Wilson) to citizens' arrest, to end the war, and to "restore to the working class the full product of its labor."[40]

Within three days, the jig was up. Green Corn rebels were hunted down and prosecuted like common criminals while the war in Europe raged on. Authorities promised to leave no stone unturned in their effort, as the *Ada Star-Democrat* put it, to "corral every objector and agitator and place them behind the bars where they will not be able to incite further resistance to the government."[41] Aside from acres of uneaten corn, the most important consequence of the stillborn uprising was that socialism became associated with treason. Socialist leaders did their best to distance themselves from the fracas, but to no avail. In a prelude to the Red Scare following the Bolshevik Revolution of October 1917, Socialist newspapers were denied mailing privileges, agitators were silenced, and armed vigilantes escorted rabble-rousing scalawags to the state borders. Waxing apocalyptic, the editor of the *Ada Star-Democrat* concluded that if law-abiding citizens continued to tolerate "this revolutionary and anarchistical [sic] movement," they would be as foolish as the citizens of France who had "wallowed in luxury" while the vagabond Rousseau penned "the bloodiest page in all history."[42]

The movement to remake Oklahoma in the workingman's image entered its twilight, and Oklahomans were left to ponder yet another distinction: theirs was the only state where socialism posed a genuine threat not only to the adoption of conservative banking principles but also to the governing party.[43]

As far as bankers and businessmen were concerned, the demise of socialism left one less obstacle in Oklahoma's tortuous path to inclusion in national networks of banking and commerce.

Even in the wake of bank failures occasioned by real estate and oil speculation, on the eve of World War I banks were showing evidence of renewed prosperity. On October 12, 1912, *Harlow's Weekly* reported total deposits in state banks of $80 million. A total of 914 banks—293 national banks and 621 state banks—reported capital stock of $22,782,250. Loans were on the rise, and the average reserve statewide was 43.8 percent. Following the failure of the Columbia Bank and Trust Company and others caught in the subsequent depression, many state banks had taken out national charters. As prosperity returned, this tendency slowed, "and the prospects are again brightening materially for the increase of our state banking system."[44] On October 31, 1912, the Clearing House Association of Oklahoma City showed a $2 million increase in bank deposits over the previous year. The increase was "wholly occasioned" by an increase in farm and manufactured products in the Oklahoma City trade area. Most was attributed to the marketing of increased crop production—all in all, a "splendid evidence of returned prosperity and revived business."[45]

In April 1913, the *Daily Oklahoman* reported that deposits in fifteen Oklahoma City banks had reached the highest point in five years, and "that in no time in the history of Oklahoma City have the local financial institutions been in such good shape as the present." Topping the list was the American National Bank with capital of $500,000, surplus and profits of $73,300, and deposits of $2,429,400. In a clear effort to drive a stake through the heart of past bank practices, the article's author, Allen J. Cash, attributed the good times to banking on a "conservative footing": "Banks in Oklahoma City today are not loaning money on prospective increases in real estate valuations. For every dollar loaned, 100 cents in gilt edge securities is exacted. When banks settle down to doing business on this basis, and only then, can they be considered in a healthy condition as to securities."[46]

Regulations and sound business principles were clearly having an effect on Oklahoma banking, but symbols of safety were far from passé. Cash cited two banks of which Oklahomans were particularly proud: the State National Bank, which towered to a height of twelve stories; and the eight-story American National Bank—both situated on corners of Main Street and Robinson Avenue in Oklahoma City, and destined to merge in 1927 to become the First National Bank and Trust Company of Oklahoma City. "The former cost in the neighborhood of $400,000," wrote Cash, "is fireproof in construction throughout, and the material used in the outer walls is white stone. It is one of the most attractive buildings in the city, besides being one of the most substantial.... The American National bank building, erected at a cost in the neighborhood of $275,000, is built of white agonite [sic] stone and is one the buildings to which citizens of Oklahoma City point with pride."[47]

The reporter lavished praise on American National Bank president Frank P. Johnson. Yet his paean to the pioneer banker could just as easily have been written about bankers throughout the state whose conservative principles enabled them to weather the downturns and promote economic development. "F. P. Johnson of the American National, Oklahoma City, is one of the most successful financiers in the Southwest," ran a news brief in the *Oklahoma Banker* in September 1911. "With some years to go yet before he is forty Mr. Johnson has accumulated a large fortune and built up a splendid bank. He has made practically all he has in Oklahoma City and is one of the pillars of the metropolis."[48]

Successes notwithstanding, Oklahomans continued to worry about their image as a Populist state with an attitude toward business. Some claimed that such concerns were much ado about nothing. Citing the galloping pace of economic development as evidence of Oklahoma's progress, Sydney J. Roy, secretary of the Shawnee Chamber of Commerce and vice president of the State Federation of Commercial Clubs, blamed political demagogues for misrepresenting the state in the court of public opinion. "We are making great progress and investments are absolutely safe," asserted the chamber executive. "You cannot build a great commonwealth with a wail of pessimism, but you can make great progress every day in the year by placing yourself on an optimistic platform where you can see many wise laws, many conscientious public officials and unprecedented development in every part of Oklahoma."[49]

Roy's tribute to Oklahoma business might have flown at a chamber luncheon. But as far as the national press and its readers were concerned, Oklahoma was still a rough-and-tumble frontier where Populist laws confounded sound business principles at every turn. Upon returning from a trip back east in the spring of 1908 to promote investment in

The El Reno Interurban Line, officially opened on December 3, 1911, was a boost to economic development in Canadian County. Modern transportation was vital in transforming rural communities into vibrant centers of business and banking. Courtesy Ronald J. Norick Downtown Library, Oklahoma City.

Oklahoma, members of the Tulsa Commercial Club were so vexed by businessmen's impressions of the new state that they summoned commercial clubs statewide to a conference in Guthrie to mitigate the damage done "by freak laws and unsound public officials."[50] The Tulsa Commercial Club's resolutions, drawn up while the delegation was en route from Chicago to Kansas City (they could not even wait to get home!) and made public upon its return to Tulsa, called on every right-minded citizen to "insure to capital a cordial welcome and fair treatment, thereby stimulating the growth of all our cities, the building of industrial enterprises, the creation of a better market for our farm and factory products, the employment of labor, and the happiness and prosperity of all our people."[51] Delegates convened in Guthrie in August 1908 and promptly established a three-part action plan that included the creation of public relations offices in Oklahoma City, the appointment of a representative to facilitate a statewide PR campaign, and the formation of a committee, headquartered in Guthrie, whose purpose would be to publicize important bills and kill "freak legislation" at birth.[52]

While big-city bankers were situating themselves in webs of regulation and responsibility and amassing their fortunes and businessmen were burnishing their state's image, country bankers were busy fending off frontier lawlessness. In January 1911, two masked men stepped out of the shadows, drew their revolvers, and opened fire on Brigam Young, a policeman who was making his rounds near the Bank of Ochelata. Slightly wounded, Young dropped to the ground and emptied his chambers before running for reinforcements. When he and a dozen armed citizens returned to the scene, the brigands were long gone. The word on the street was that one had suffered a serious wound.[53] The next month, bandits blew open the safe at the First State Bank of Mead, a tiny hamlet ten miles west of Durant, and made away with its entire store of cash amounting to $14,500. Just before the robbery, the men had cut all wires leading into town. One suspect was apprehended, but others were on the loose. A reward of $500 was offered for information leading to their arrest.[54]

As bank robberies captured the headlines throughout 1911 and 1912, legislators decided that enough was enough. In January 1913, a bill was introduced in the state legislature to offer a reward of $1,000, payable from funds controlled by the state banking commissioner, for the apprehension of bank robbers. The bill also appropriated $15,000 to hire men to track them down.[55] According to the *Daily Oklahoman,* "This is in line with legislation asked by the bankers' association of the state as a means of reducing the rapidly growing number of bank robberies in Oklahoma."[56]

The pilfering went into overdrive from May 1914 to January 1915 when fifteen Oklahoma banks incurred losses of $32,050. Thefts were compounded by an estimated $5,000 in damage to bank fixtures, due largely to the use of dynamite. "The majority of the robberies have been of the most daring kind, being committed in daylight," ran an account in the *Oklahoma City Times*. "So successful have the holdup men been that they have become more daring, and already have robbed five banks this month. It is believed the work is being done by an organized gang, members of which are stationed in different sections of the state." Robberies and amounts stolen between May 21, 1914, and January 5, 1915, included the Bank of Millerton (May 21, $1,200), Osage State Bank (June 10, $1,500), Keystone State Bank (September 8, $3,000), Central State Bank at Kiefer (September 30, $6,400), Farmers National Bank at Tupelo (October 6, $1,800), the Bank of Pontotoc (October 14, $2,300), Byars State Bank (October 20, $1,400), Farmers State Bank at Glencoe (November 13, $2,000), Citizens Bank at Wardville (November 20, $800), Prue State Bank (December 16, $800), Carney State Bank (December 29, $2,500), Preston State Bank (January 4, nothing), and the First National Bank at Owasso (January 5, $1,200).[57]

Throughout 1915, the Oklahoma Bankers Association flagship publication, the *Oklahoma Banker*, was packed with accounts of bold break-ins, daylight heists, fast horses, gunplay, and bravado. By 1916, when Oklahoma banks were being robbed at four times the national rate, insurance companies threatened to cancel bank policies.[58] Ocean Accident and Guaranty Corporation, the largest insurer against burglaries, was compelled to follow through on cancellation threats.[59] Governor Lee Cruce was no doubt pleased to have the legislature's blessing to put the criminals behind bars where they belonged.[60]

Governor Cruce's campaign to put bank robbers out of business was not enough to save Pawnee County deputy sheriff Bob Moore. On January 12, 1915, three unmasked bandits robbed the First National Bank of Terlton of a reported $3,000 (later found to be only $300) in currency and silver and forced two bank officers and a customer at gunpoint to march to the place where five horses were tied. Deputy Moore arrived as they were mounting their horses and was shot through the heart when he emerged from a cornfield. Two other men joined the gang and, with their ill-gotten gains lashed to the pommel of a saddle, skedaddled in a hail of bullets and with a posse in hot pursuit. The running battle on horseback left two of the robbers' horses dead and one of the robbers in custody. Only thirty-six years old, the fallen lawman was survived by a wife and four children.[61]

The dust had barely settled from the Terlton bank robbery when the *Daily Oklahoman* published an open letter to the state legislature expressing outrage over Deputy Moore's death in the line of duty. Next came a plea for stronger laws:

Why not, then, legislators, pass a law quickly that will offer huge rewards for the apprehension of bank robbers—a reward so great that every bandit will be quickly caught? Why not pass laws providing the maximum imprisonment—that is, for life, for bank robbers? Let's have the most nearly perfect laws that will protect our brave peace officers, and then another law that will make banking houses safe from the men who work behind the six-shooter or with the nitro-glycerine. . . . Let's have laws so strong that bank robbers will not dare to ply their trade in this state.[62]

Even as citizens mourned Deputy Moore's death and seethed with indignation, two more banks were pillaged on January 13: Garber State Bank, where $2,750 was stolen; and Vera State Bank, where a loss of $1,400 was reported.[63] Because of Bartlesville's proximity to hideouts in the Osage hills, the Bartlesville Clearing House Association hired three gunfighters noted for their marksmanship and fearlessness to stand guard "in such a manner as to give them a view of every person going in or out of the various banks. All are dead shots, both with rifles and six-shooters." In the event that known scoundrels showed up in Bartlesville and approached a bank, "they will be met with guns, and the bark of the Winchester and six-shooter will be heard." Other precautions included stationing automobiles for instantaneous pursuit by posses and alarm systems. Similar precautions were taken in nearby Caney and Coffeyville, Kansas. One banker commented that Bartlesville bankers were not afraid of desperadoes and considered the placement of gunslingers around town as an appropriate supplement to their insurance policies: "While not a bank in the city would lose a dollar if they were robbed, yet we are not going to take a chance and practically invite a raid by not being prepared."[64]

John Hoefer, president of Farmers National Bank in Kaw City, did not need hired gunslingers to make his point. In early April 1915, three robbers rode into town, pillaged his bank, locked him and his assistant cashier in the vault, and lit out for the Osage hills. After emerging from the vault, Hoefer declared that he "would have whipped the whole bunch if they had just laid aside their guns."[65] A concerned citizen in Oklahoma City with a flair for gadgetry suggested installing a trapdoor in the ceiling of bank vaults to drop down and trap thieves once they were inside. He claimed to have such a device in his suburban home and said that it worked splendidly—so splendidly, in fact, that he was anxious to find investors to finance the manufacture of his "life-saving, money-saving, robber-saving mechanism."[66] History records neither his method of testing the device nor his aptitude for entrepreneurship.

The long arm of the law finally caught up with Henry Starr, one of the West's most notorious outlaws. One-quarter Cherokee and full-blood outlaw, Starr distinguished himself as an intelligent and capable person with a magnetic personality who could have made a good living in normal pursuits. But normal pursuits were not his destiny. As a contemporary noted, he "craved the excitement in robbing banks as some men crave alcohol or drugs." Born and raised in the law-challenged Indian Territory in 1873, Starr launched his career in 1892 when a deputy attempted to arrest him for allegedly robbing an express office in Nowata. Shots were exchanged, the deputy was killed, and Starr's life of crime was off and running.[67] Encouragement for his chosen profession came from his uncle, the notorious Sam Starr, and his aunt, Belle Starr, queen of the outlaws, whose thievery and association with the likes of Jesse James and the Younger brothers were all a young man needed to forgo traditional routes to success.

Following a daring raid on the Bank of Carney on December 29, 1914, that netted nearly $3,000 in cash, Starr became the first outlaw to be valued at $1,000, dead or alive, under the new bank robbery law.[68] Undeterred and more than likely flattered, Starr continued to search for easy profits. His quest eventually landed him in Stroud where, between the hours of eight and ten o'clock on the morning of Saturday, March 27, 1915, he and six accomplices committed what the *Chandler Tribune* called the "boldest bank robbery in the history of the great southwest." The desperadoes arrived in Stroud in a covered wagon with four horses in tow, hardly an uncommon sight in a village of immigrants. With their wagon and horses parked at the stockyards two blocks south of the First National Bank, the bandits put their plan into motion.

A sentry was posted in the stockyards while the others split into two groups of three. One group headed north to Main Street and the First National Bank. The other went east along the railroad tracks before turning north toward the Stroud National Bank. Once in position two blocks apart on Main Street, the men signaled to one another and entered the banks simultaneously.

With no warning, customers and bank officers were jerked from their Saturday morning routines to find themselves staring down the gun barrels of Henry Starr and his gang. Hands shot up and safes were duly pillaged. Stuffed money bags in hand, the outlaws at the Stroud National Bank marched their hostages two blocks west and one block south to rendezvous with their partners at the First National Bank.

Toting loot from both banks, the thieves made for the stockyards for an easy getaway. What they did not count on was the quick thinking of a nineteen-year-old boy, Paul Curry, who looked up from his work at his father's grocery store across the street from the First National Bank to see the robbery in progress. Fueled with the passion of youth, he seized a Winchester, rushed out of the store, took aim, and shot one of the bandits, Lewis Estes. The fallen scoundrel alerted Starr to the source of the gunfire. Before he could respond in kind, Starr was struck just below the hip by a bullet from Curry's Winchester. "Before he could rise from the ground," ran a riveting article in the *Chandler Tribune* the following Thursday, "Curry had him covered and Starr gave up any further attempts to effect an escape."[69]

The fallen outlaws were promptly taken to Dr. J. W. Adams's office to have their wounds dressed. Their next stop was the Lincoln County jail in Chandler, where they awaited their fate at the hands of the county's prosecuting attorney, Streeter Speakman.[70] Their partners had long since skipped town, allegedly to the Osage hills. Newspapers gushed with news of the daring holdup, none more poignant than an article in the *Daily Oklahoman:* "Although posses from north, west, and south are searching for the five members of the Starr gang that escaped with approximately $2,600 after the fight that followed the robbery of the two Stroud banks Saturday morning no trace of the fugitives had ben [*sic*] found Sunday night."[71]

Thus ended Henry Starr's career in outlawry—for the time being, anyway. Peace officers who had been tracking outlaws since territorial days declared that the Cherokee badman, writhing in pain in a dank cell in Chandler, was the greatest outlaw in history. The *Daily Oklahoman* relied on their testimonials to provide a postscript for Starr's storied past: "He has robbed more banks and trains and committed more daring crimes in these days of telephones, autos and many railways than the James boys and other notorious outlaws did when communication was poor." Clearly respectful of an old nemesis, one peace officer asserted,

"He has avoided killing unless he was forced to it. He is one of the bravest of the whole list and the kindliest."[72]

Following Starr's death in February 1921 after a gun battle during a bank robbery in Harrison, Arkansas, the journalist Frederick Barde chimed in with an epitaph for an outlaw who "was far above the average bank or train robber": "In all of his career it was his boast that he never killed a man in robbery and never harmed a woman or child. He was the sort of an outlaw that even the officers who trailed him would enjoy sitting down to a meal with him or ride trail with him. The sort of man who breaks the law but still holds to certain ideals that men admire."[73]

As far as Starr was concerned, avoiding bloodshed was a strategy for success in his chosen profession. As he explained to a friend while "scouting" in the Cherokee country, "A man who commits a crime and then shoots an officer who tries to capture him is a fool. The officers never quit hunting you if you kill a man, but they don't pay much attention to you if you just rob a bank or stick up a train. While I am scouting I am going to take good care not to kill a man."[74]

Henry Starr's career brings to mind another of the fabled social outlaws, Bill Doolin, who was killed in a shootout with U.S. deputy marshal Heck Thomas in north central Oklahoma Territory in August 1896. "I had respect for him in many ways," recalled onetime lawman Charles Colcord, "for he was a brave man with many good characteristics." One of those characteristics, generosity, was no secret in the Osage country where, on many occasions, Doolin helped people with gifts of livestock and other necessities of frontier life. Bank of Pawnee president Charley Vandever once told Colcord that he trusted Bill Doolin as much as any of his customers, so much so that he once loaned him $500 on nothing more than his word and was promptly repaid. Doolin returned the favor by preventing his gang on three occasions from robbing the Bank of Pawnee "because of his kindly feeling toward Charley."[75]

Social outlaws of Doolin's and Starr's ilk revealed their kindly feelings in a variety of ways. Starr once admitted to gathering a bundle of mortgages and banknotes that he had plundered from a bank in Caney, Kansas, tying a stone to them, and throwing them into California Creek in northern Oklahoma so that beleaguered farmers would not have to pay them off. The bundle was never recovered and the value was never ascertained, but a man who claimed to have seen it declared it was "twelve inches through."[76]

One wonders what Chandler banker Hugh Johnson and his banking brethren across the state thought about the big-hearted villain languishing in the Lincoln County jail—a man who had held up innumerable banks, was respected by the same lawmen who had been gunning for him for decades, and thought tossing vital bank documents into a creek was a sign of compassion.

Just another day of banking in Oklahoma?

Some men rob with a gun; others rob with a pen. The year after Henry Starr was felled in the streets of Stroud, farmers in Lincoln County formed a voluntary association to bring suits against bankers who charged more than legal maximum rates. Although farmers chalked up a few victories, bankers retaliated by refusing to lend money unless applicants had perfect credit ratings and could provide absolute security, thus putting loans out of reach for those who most needed them.[77] By 1915, there were 7,615 national banks in the United States, and only 1,022 of them charged an average interest of 10 percent per annum or higher on loans. According to Comptroller of the Currency J. S. Williams, no fewer than 317 of those banks were in Texas and 300 were in Oklahoma, routinely saddling farmers with interest rates that were legally defined as usurious.[78] The Oklahoma Bankers Association rallied to bankers' defense and recommended that county banks form associations to defend their policies.[79] From an economic standpoint, high interest rates were to be expected in recently settled areas where risks were high and demand for capital outran the available supply. In Oklahoma and elsewhere, routine business practices and capital accumulation were the prerequisites to lower rates commensurate with those in older states.[80]

Ending one of the most bitter and prolonged legislative battles since statehood, the Glascoe Usury Bill, which aimed to set a maximum interest rate of 10 percent per annum, was defeated in the House by a vote of fifty-two to thirty-eight on March 3, 1915. Claiming that the stringent anti-usury bill would have put two hundred small banks out of business, the Oklahoma Bankers Association credited each lawmaker "who stood by his guns in this fight."[81] Perhaps not surprisingly in a state that still celebrated rugged individualism and tolerated its extreme manifestations, usury laws were only enforced on an individual basis.[82]

Defeat of the Glascoe Usury Bill proved to be little more than a delaying tactic. Pressure from farmers to eliminate usurious lending gained traction in an age of progressive legislation, and, within a year, bankers were battling for a lost cause. The House approved an anti-usury law by a margin of sixty-four to twenty-five, and the Senate followed suit with a vote of twenty-five to twelve. The governor signed the bill on March 4, 1916. The new law limited the maximum legal interest to 10 percent per annum, and penalties required bankers to forfeit twice the amount of interest on loans that exceeded the legal rate.[83] Banks found guilty in the future were denied access to state courts to collect usurious loans.[84] On the eve of the bill's passage, the Oklahoma Bankers Association stood squarely on the principle of supply and demand to argue in vain that legislators should leave banking to bankers. A scathing editorial in the *Oklahoma Banker* left little doubt about bankers' commitment to a free market: "By silly and by selfish and ignorant legislation amateur statesmen have brought around a condition within the state that produces a scarcity of money among those who require financial assistance."[85]

Throughout World War I, bankers in Oklahoma and, indeed, all over the West, showed their patriotism by managing Liberty bond drives that oversubscribed on a regular basis.[86] Predictably, Oklahoma bankers went a step further when they decided to sell war-savings stamps, known in the common vernacular as "baby bonds," in small denominations. Further evidence of their patriotism came at a chamber of commerce meeting in Oklahoma City when business leaders developed the concept of a war stamp savings bank, a special institution for which bankers would volunteer their time and where bond sales would be the only item of business. A building was duly designated at Main and Broadway, and the enterprise was launched with neither liabilities nor expenses.

There was no shortage of fanfare at the opening of the nation's first War Stamp Savings Bank. Downtown took on a festive air the day before the grand opening in March 1918 as the Oklahoma Railway Company festooned trolley catenary wires with flags, merchants competed to see who could come up with the most patriotic window display, and participants in the parade slated for opening day received last-minute instructions. Colonel H. W. Pentecost, grand marshal of the parade, "was kept busy all day assigning them places, and seeing that his aides understood every detail of the gigantic pageant."[87] Citizens turned out en masse to enjoy the festivities and empty their wallets in support of the war effort. The program went statewide, then regional, and finally national, thus showing a skeptical nation what Sooner entrepreneurship in the defense of liberty was all about.[88]

The third Liberty bond campaign was launched nationally on April 6, 1918. "This is Oklahoma City's way of putting it over," ran an account in the chamber of commerce's newsletter, "and the results speak for the efficiency of the plan. There were 11,000 bonds sold in the campaign. Oklahoma City in the first, second and third Liberty Loans, has gone over and will continue to do so in each of the succeeding loans authorized by the Government, which are sure to come."[89] At the end of the month, sixty-one of the state's seventy-seven counties had subscribed to their quotas—not a bad showing, but not quite good enough for true-blue patriots. When the *Daily Oklahoman* promised (threatened?) to publish a list of delinquent counties, the laggards fell into line. Preliminary figures published on May 5 showed not only that all counties had done their duty but also that Oklahoma had exceeded its quota of $29,033,200 with an impressive $35,857,150—enough to make the kaiser choke on his bratwurst.[90]

War bonds were not all that bankers were selling. Even as the Federal Reserve Act of 1913 was pushing banks into conformity with a new ethos of regulation, bankers and businessmen in Oklahoma were doing their best to bring agriculture in line with modern farming practices. "Plainly stated, business backed by science is being hooked to the farm in Oklahoma," wrote Frederick Barde. "For the first time in the history of this stae [sic] an understandable message of how to make an Oklahoma farm pay maximum dividends is being carried straight to the farmer. He is being caught at his plow or in his wood lot and made to listen."[91]

Gone were the days when farmers could afford to eschew the advice of experts as though calloused hands and on-the-farm training were adequate substitutes for science. Demonstration farms, commercial clubs, and the agricultural and mechanical experiment station in Stillwater were equipped to bring state farming practices up to modern standards of productivity. Under the slogan "Pull together for Oklahoma," the Oklahoma Bankers Association joined the bandwagon.[92] Its promotion of increased credit for farm loans and the implementation of scientific management aided the war effort by increasing cereal production by 21 percent, cotton by 45 percent, and potatoes by 20 percent.[93] Barde quoted one farmer who had clearly seen the light:

> I believe the managing of a farm is as much a business as running a bank, mercantile house or operating a railroad. And until the farmer looks upon his occupation as such and studies it with the same degree of care, and with the same object in view to get the very best possible out of it, he will never reach the high mark of success he deserves. I want to tell you that the time is fast coming when a farmer's success will not depend upon the strength of his back or the number of hours he can endure to work in the field without sleep. The time is not far off when the farmer who toils sixteen hours in the field and sleeps the other eight of the twenty-four, is not going to be able to hold his own with the one who puts in a part of the time studying the economical principles of his business, the same as any other business man must do.[94]

In a state heavily dependent on agriculture, it made sense for bankers to promote scientific farming as a surefire way not only to enhance the value of loan collateral but also to foster a positive vision of capitalism in its tug-of-war with radical ideologies such as socialism. The Oklahoma Bankers Association's Agricultural Committee called on bankers to take responsibility for "the country's most fundamental and important industry," not by telling farmers how to farm, but by sharing business expertise.[95] The *Oklahoma Banker* featured tips for farmers on a regular basis. One imagines an editorialist's finger wagging as he admonished his readers to get with the program: "The salvation of Oklahoma's gigantic farming interests is bound up in this movement, and every other interest in Oklahoma, with few exceptions, depends on the prosperity of the farmer. When you enlist in this work, Mr. Banker, you take the best and surest road to success for your own bank."[96]

One banker who needed no convincing of the benefits of scientific farming was Hugh M. Johnson, president of the First National Bank of Chandler. To discourage farmers from relying on a single crop, he offered $75.00 to the woman who could raise the greatest variety of crops. He also offered $25.00 to the farmer who produced the greatest variety of forage. In the spring of 1912, the banker's agricultural contests lured five thousand farmers to Chandler for an exhibition of more than three hundred displays of wise farming techniques.[97] Thus did the symbiosis of banking and farming play out in Lincoln County, much as it did throughout the young state's history, and as it would continue to do in the years to come.

While Oklahoma bankers were extolling scientific farming as the ticket to prosperity, the federal government was trying to boost the economy by enlisting the power of pent-up savings. After forty years of agitation, Congress chose New Year's Day of 1911 to launch postal savings banks. Nationwide, there were 1,703 savings banks, an average of 1 bank for every 52,000 people. Post offices, by contrast, numbered almost 60,000, and their services could easily be expanded to lure savings from mattresses and piggy banks to savings accounts beyond the purview of state banking laws. Estimating that the money in people's pockets was 65 percent of the money in circulation, or about $2 billion, the postmaster general advocated postal savings banks as a conduit between private savings and national banks that would release postal savings deposits into the economy as fast as they came in. "There is every reason to believe that a system of postal savings banks would, to a great extent, call out these private hoards and return them to circulation through the regular banks . . . of the country," wrote Postmaster General Frank H. Hitchcock in his report for fiscal year 1909–10. According to laws governing these economic engines, anyone over ten years old could open an account, and his or her money was free from the interference of relatives or creditors. Married women could open an account without reference to their husbands. Depositors were limited to a single account that could be opened with as little as one dollar, and interest would accrue at the rate of 2 percent per annum.[98]

Early on, each state was authorized to open only one postal savings bank. In Oklahoma, Guymon was the lucky city. The post office was managed entirely by women, and it was located in a corner of the building occupied by the First National Bank of Guymon—a potentially awkward arrangement, as employees of two federally sanctioned institutions, both in the business of banking, now eyed each other from across the lobby.[99] R. B. Quinn, whose office was upstairs in the First National Bank building, expressed the skepticism that many bankers felt as Uncle Sam entered the banking business. "Bankers are not favorably impressed with the new institution," he wrote to the journalist Frederick Barde a few days after the postal savings bank opened, "but the bank here is doing a nice business and small depositors are patronizing it liberally and the indications are that the venture will be a success."[100]

By war's end, the transition in banking from frontier symbols of safety to regulations commensurate with the needs of a new century was nearly complete. Nowhere was the transition more apparent than in the Federal Reserve Act of 1913, a milestone not only in business and banking but also in a culture that was increasingly attuned to sound business principles. The nation had been without central banking since the Second Bank of the United States charter was allowed to expire in the 1830s. With the creation of the Fed, central banking was revived as a mechanism to impose control on the growth of currency and credit and to stabilize their supply. The creation of postal savings banks in 1911 represented another extension of the government's role in the economy. Arguably, the evolution of banking from private, profit-oriented institutions to a centralized system of national banks under federal supervision was the most remarkable achievement in finance of the post-frontier period.[101]

It was in the context of dizzying changes and rampant bank robberies during the war years that Oklahoma state banking commissioner J. D. Lankford committed himself to rooting out incompetent and reckless banking. At the time of his appointment, folks in his hometown of Atoka practically went into mourning at the prospect of losing one of their most valuable citizens to Oklahoma City. But duty called, and it could not have fallen on the shoulders of a more worthy servant: "clean and honest—a man you cannot buy—strong and quiet as the mountains; a man who inherits convictions which are grounded in the Old Book, and a past master in finance, with all the capacity and resource needed for every situation that may develop in his great position as executive head of our State Banking Commission."[102] Toward the end of his term, the latter-day Cincinnatus pointed with justifiable pride to the state's emergence "from what would be termed a state thoroughly infested with financial criminals and incompetents, with lax laws and but little execution of same, toward leadership in all that is clean, practical, and right in banking, as well as in good citizenship."[103]

The economist Thomas Bruce Robb opined in 1921 that general economic conditions in Oklahoma were mimicking those of older states. "It seems fair to assume that certain events of pioneer days will not be repeated," concluded Robb. With a wary eye on Oklahomans' penchant for experimentation, even a jaded economist recognized that a new culture of capitalism was dawning: "In the short space of twenty-five years Oklahoma has been transformed from a wild prairie to a civilized state."[104]

CHAPTER THREE

The Roaring Twenties

> A bank, by virtue of its very nature, is the hub about which business must and does turn; it controls the wheels of industry, it directs the forces of conservatism and sound judgment that make successful business possible—these services and others too numerous and well known to mention make it the Gibraltar on which the prosperity and future hope of business rests.
>
> <div align="right">Rex F. Harlow, <i>Harlow's Weekly</i></div>

Throughout his 1922 gubernatorial campaign, Oklahoma City mayor John Calloway "Jack" Walton promised a party to end all parties in the event of his victory. "When I am elected governor, there will not be any inaugural ball, and there will not be a tea dansant," he promised. "I am going to give an old-fashioned barbecue. It will be a party for all the people, and I want you all to come."[1]

Walton's elevation to the state's highest office was nearly thwarted when businessmen from across the state, fearful that he would bring the same ineptitude he had displayed as mayor of Oklahoma City to the governorship, organized at the Skirvin Hotel in late September 1922 to block his election. "This belief was shared by Democrats and Republicans alike," wrote Charles Colcord, "and finally took form in an organization that sought to accomplish his defeat at any reasonable cost."[2]

Last-ditch scrambling to avert disaster failed to sway the electorate, and the soon-to-be fifth governor of Oklahoma followed through on his promise with a hoedown unrivaled since Andrew Jackson had opened the White House to throngs of supporters who, clad in homespun clothes and unmindful of their muddy boots, heralded frontier democracy with festivities that sent guardians of propriety running for cover.[3] Guests at Jack Walton's inaugural celebration were invited not to the governor's mansion, but to the fairgrounds, where muddy boots did not matter, and where a feast of mythic proportions smoldered in six quarter-mile-long barbecue pits and steamed in four 8,800-gallon coffee percolators. The slaughter preceding the great gorge would have impressed the Olympians of antiquity: 289 head of cattle, 70 hogs, 36 sheep, 2,540 rabbits, 134 possums, 25 squirrels, 15 deer, 3 bears, and fowl too numerous to mention. Exotic fare was measured in poundage. Two thousand pounds of bison sizzled alongside 1,500 pounds of reindeer. Like Noah of biblical lore, a Walton supporter who did not want to leave a species begging donated an antelope.[4] The fragrance wafted across the plains; it was said that "the gourmets of Kansas City and Emporia smacked their lips over the aroma of those 20,000 gallons of coffee."[5] One local newspaper reported: "[The meat] gave forth an odor that tickled the nostrils of those within its area of distribution and made them impatient for the day of the big feed to arrive.... The barbecue is the principal event in the eyes of most of the people, excelling in importance even the inauguration of the new governor."[6]

Some said the governor's inauguration at the fairgrounds would lack dignity, but Walton had an answer—he would take the oath of office twice: once on Monday, January 8, in the state house; and then on Tuesday at the fairgrounds with the people. The solemnity of the first swearing-in was a pale prelude to the extravaganza on Tuesday, January 9, 1923, that roared to life with a parade stretching ten miles across the bleak winter landscape. Floats, marching bands, spirited horses, Native Americans in their finest regalia, and battle flags from the War to End All Wars wound their way through a swarm of hungry celebrants from the stockyards to the fairgrounds. Three teams of oxen pulled a wagon carrying a cowboy band whose members alternated between crooning to the crowd and firing their revolvers. Brigadier General B. H. Markham of the Oklahoma National Guard mounted a trick horse and was unceremoniously dumped when the beast rose on its hind legs and pranced to the music.[7]

Eventually the procession reached the fairgrounds, where the governor was sworn in to the accompaniment of shouts, whoops, and pistol shots. Nearby, 165 tremulous workers, flanked by national guardsmen, greeted the multitude with steaming plates piled high with God's bounty. By sundown, some 50,000 people had had their fill. Serving continued well into the night as revelers danced and sang and ate until they could eat no more. Servers scooped and poured until 125,000 people had sated their bellies.

The *New York Times* did its best to describe the bash to incredulous easterners: "In Oklahoma the pioneer tradition is fresh and recent. She 'steps on her gas' all the time. She is full of the joy of life, the passion for self-expression." Even though frontier ways were beyond reckoning to civilized folk back east, they were certainly worthy of note as modernity came relentlessly on. "It is not necessary to take a strictly moral view of these things," suggested the reporter. "The oil and gas in the Oklahoma nature easily take fire. At any rate, until the last notes of 'Turkey in the Straw' have died away in the state house at Oklahoma City let us rejoice in the barbecue and fiddle, the enjoy-yourself-and-let-the-world-go-hang spirit of 'Jack' Walton's people's party and Oklahoma."[8]

Governor Walton's term ended ten months later less ceremoniously than it began. "Walton had run true to form," concluded Colcord about one of the most divisive state-level entanglements in U.S. history. Walton "had operated even worse than we had expected and had the state in a turmoil. Distrust of the state and its government quickly developed among financial interests throughout the country and money had almost ceased to come into the state."[9] The governor, whose political playbook included proclaiming martial law, attempting to suppress newspapers, and stationing machine guns outside a federal judge's court, was impeached on twenty-three counts. He was convicted and escorted from the governor's office in November 1923. Subsequent attempts to capture his party's nomination in 1934 and 1938 failed.[10] By then, Jack Walton's people's party had seared itself into western lore as a last hurrah from the American frontier—three centuries of hell-for-leather bravado reduced to a monster barbecue on the Oklahoma plains.[11]

Had anyone stopped eating long enough to listen, they might have heard the frontier closing not to the crackle of gunfire or blaring of trumpets, but to the hissing and popping of meat in a pit, and a fading chorus of "Turkey in the Straw."

Governor Walton's cornucopia notwithstanding, trouble was brewing in rural Oklahoma as a quarter century of rising prices for agricultural products, enshrined in collective memory as "the golden age" of American farming, slammed into the post–World War I depression. Saddled with more produce than they could sell now that European farmers were back in business, farmers watched helplessly as prices plummeted and left them unable to service their loans. Farm foreclosures in Oklahoma reached 50 percent between 1926 and 1930—the third highest percentage in the nation—and banks with an abundance of farm loans in their portfolios followed them into the abyss.[12] On the eve of the great unraveling, the number of banks peaked at thirty thousand in 1922, and their assets totaled approximately $52 billion. This compares to twelve thousand commercial banks in 1900 with more than $9 billion in assets. What is more, only about 43 percent of commercial banks, holding less than 50 percent of total assets, were under the full jurisdiction of the federal government. More than six decades after the creation of the national banking system, and a decade and a half since the creation of the Fed, American finance remained hobbled by a dual banking system that tolerated an astonishing number of banks and remained resistant to federal oversight.[13]

Among those who watched helplessly as commodity prices and bank deposits plunged in tandem was Blaine County banker Bert Willis. The progeny of Cherokee Outlet homesteaders, Willis worked as a cowboy before rising to prominence as a banker in Canton, and he had to reach back to the Panic of 1907 for a comparable mood of doom and gloom. "In between 1920 and 1924 there was wailing along the watercourse of the North Canadian River," he wrote in his unpublished 1953 memoir, written at the suggestion of state bank examiner E. H. Kelley and tucked away in the Oklahoma Historical Society's archives ever since. "It was the time of the scratching of the head and the pulling of the hair, although as remembered there were not so many suicides as there were in the last panic."[14]

Nationwide, 5,400 banks suspended operations, 4,500 permanently, between 1921 and 1929. Thousands of others found their capital so impaired by losses that they either closed voluntarily without loss to their creditors or agreed to "shotgun weddings" with larger and stronger institutions.[15] In Bert Willis's northwestern Oklahoma neighborhood, county-seat banks that were either closed by the state banking commissioner or placed in voluntary liquidation in the 1920s included Farmers State Bank of Alva (chartered April 25, 1904, with capital stock of

$10,000, closed due to insolvency March 20, 1926); the Ellis County Bank in Arnett (chartered October 8, 1907, with capital stock of $10,000, closed due to insolvency December 6, 1924); the Bank of Buffalo (chartered June 8, 1907, with capital stock of $10,000, placed in voluntary liquidation December 29, 1921, and assets sold to the First National Bank of Buffalo); Cheyenne State Bank (chartered August 2, 1909, with capital stock of $35,000, placed in voluntary liquidation August 25, 1922); and the Commercial Bank of El Reno (chartered September 12, 1906, with capital stock of $20,000, closed due to insolvency February 25, 1922).[16]

Nearly four thousand banks disappeared nationwide through mergers during the 1920s.[17] Small banks with less than $100,000 in capital were the hardest hit; of these, banks in the South, Midwest, and West whose portfolios bulged with agricultural loans were most vulnerable when farm prices tumbled. Towns with fewer than 2,500 residents experienced 80 percent of the suspensions, and half of those suspensions were in communities with populations under 500. But in regions where regulation was the most lax and where chartering was a no-brainer, there was no shortage of banks to take their place. Iowa, the state with the most bank failures, had one bank for every 1,400 people, while New Jersey, which suffered the fewest failures, had one bank for every 7,500 people.[18] Gazing from his ivory tower at the turmoil below, Professor Charles S. Tippetts saw firsthand what was happening, and he offered a bleak assessment of the dual banking system that was impervious to reform: "The past eight years constitute one of the darkest chapters in all American banking history. . . . One of the chief explanations for this disgraceful debacle may be found in the structure of our dual banking system. It is impossible to create a unified banking system of high standards and sound banking practices as long as each state tries to build up its own banking system at the expense of the national banks."[19]

Meanwhile, the Oklahoma legislature closed a raucous chapter of banking history on March 31, 1923, when it repealed the bank guarantee law. Early on, fears that national banks would lose money as depositors flocked to the security of state banks seemed justified as national banks opted for state charters and deposits in state banks skyrocketed. From September 23 to November 27, 1908, State Banking Commissioner H. H. Smock's report showed an increase of 26 state-chartered banks (from 520 to 546) and an increase in individual deposits of $4,477,823.50. Ominously, eight of those new banks represented conversions from national to state charters.[20] Any hope that national bankers had of offering deposit guarantee to their customers was dashed when Attorney General Charles J. Bonaparte ruled in July 1908 that deposit insurance was beyond the purview of national banks. By then, fifty-seven national banks, assuming that they could participate in the new law, had already paid their assessments into the guaranty fund and gave state officials yet another headache when they demanded reimbursement.[21] Inevitably, the rivalry between state and national banks escalated into a prolonged battle for the hearts, minds, and, above all, money of Oklahoma depositors.

During the law's fifteen years of enforcement, few defended the principle of deposit guarantee more adamantly than Senator Robert L. Owen. He fervently believed that the Oklahoma law not only mitigated abuse by unscrupulous businessmen but also lessened the likelihood of bank panics. "The plan has worked excellently well in Oklahoma," declared the senator in December 1908 from faraway Washington, D.C., "and if any defect should appear in the statute it would be promptly corrected."[22]

Closer to home, Oklahoma's second governor, Lee Cruce, wasted no time in donning Haskell's mantle and expressed his support for deposit guarantee. Less than three years after the law was passed, , the former banker from Ardmore used his first message to the Third Legislature on January 10, 1911, to deny that banking laws were in need of reform. "Our laws have been built around the fundamental idea of protecting the depositor who commits the safety of his money to the keeping of our State bankers," said the governor. With 693 banks reporting assets of $76,394,089.70 as of November 10, 1910, legislators were honor-bound to replace partisan politics with sound business principles, which included support for the bank guaranty law.[23]

In an address on May 23, 1911, to a gathering of 1,500 bankers in Oklahoma City, Governor Cruce made a plea for unity among state and national bankers, with a caveat: "I will stand by all national banks the same as the state banks, but when you strike down the state banks of Oklahoma, you strike down one-half of the capital of this state, and when you draw your swords, you will find the state administration ready to protect the state banks in this state at any cost."[24] Acknowledging that Oklahoma had its fair share of reckless banking, the law-and-order governor called on the state banking board to place dishonest bankers where they belonged—in the state penitentiary. "Unburdened of dishonest bankers, stripped of its incompetent ones, the Oklahoma bank guaranty law will continue to live and be a benefaction to the thousands of trusting depositors in Oklahoma who commit their savings into the keeping of state banks operating under this law."[25]

At the other end of the spectrum were bankers with national charters like O. E. Grecian, president of the First National Bank of McCloud, who decried the proliferation of state banks whose only goal was to turn a fast buck. "Our so-called state guaranty law," complained Grecian, "is, in my opinion, the most vicious ever enacted by a state legislature. One of the worst effects conspicuously apparent is the fact that new state banks are being chartered at an alarming rate, and we all know that there are already entirely too many banks in the state."[26] Nor were principals of state-chartered banks altogether enthused by the bank guaranty law. Bert Willis at the Bank of Canton spoke for many when he suggested that taking the politics out of banking stood a far better chance of ensuring the safety of deposits than forcing bankers to play ball with politicians. "If we had been anything like smart we could have worked out something that would have worked better than that did and been satisfying to the people and wouldn't have cost us nearly so much. But bankers are just human beings and they leave it to others to be smart. Maybe they are too busy taking care of their own business and leave politics to the politicians, little realizing that politics and business are handcuffed together and must go to the same place at the same time."[27] George E. Roberts, a onetime director of the New York mint who went on to become president of the Commercial National Bank of Chicago, was inclined to agree with the Oklahoma bankers' assessments. For him, deposit guaranty was "a crude and imperfect remedy" that opened the floodgates to "reckless and incompetent people" whose numbers and potential for mischief would increase "if they were backed by unlimited credit."[28]

Alarm bells sounded when State Banking Commissioner E. B. Cockrell issued a report showing that state bank deposits dropped by $4,447,193.19 between January 31 and June 30, 1910. The poor showing was particularly disturbing because it came on the heels of two years of steady increases in state bank deposits. Inevitably, critics of deposit guarantee suggested that the decline reflected a loss of confidence in state banks in the wake of the Columbia Bank failure in late 1909, additional failures as other banks reaped the whirlwind, and the subsequent depletion of the guaranty fund.[29]

Disagreements nearly turned violent in May 1911 when A. G. C. Bierer, a stockholder and an attorney for the Bank of Indian Territory in Guthrie, confronted a swarm of officials who dropped by to demand an emergency assessment or face closure.

"You are a set of thieves and burglars, and I dare you to try to close the doors of this bank," declared the defiant banker.

Undaunted, Assistant State Banking Commissioner R. L. Garnett tacked a notice of closure on the cashier's window and said simply, "This bank is closed."

"Like h———l it is," fumed Bierer as he tore down the notice and stuffed it in his pocket.

Bierer had drawn his line in the sand. His unwelcome visitors, including A. C. Cruce, the governor's brother and a representative of the state banking board, and Frank M. Canton, "adjutant general of the Oklahoma National Guard, and one of the quickest and surest crack shots in the state," were left to wonder what to do about a banker who was ready to defend his institution with his bare fists.[30]

By 1912, lawsuits over deposit guarantee were making the headlines. Tempers flared after U.S. district judge John H. Cotteral ordered that state banks that had reorganized under national charters were still liable for assessments. Meanwhile, the Oklahoma Bankers Association was adding its voice to the cacophony by insisting that the legislature undertake a radical revision of the bank guaranty law. First and foremost was the need to take banking out of the hands of politicians and to put it into "the hands of men who are directly associated with the banking business." According to the OBA, "There is no more important business in Oklahoma than the banking business and the greatest care should be taken that it is supervised in an able and just manner. The opportunity to make of this business the football of politics should be forever eliminated."[31]

Debates and diatribes over deposit insurance continued throughout the war years and into the Roaring Twenties. When Governor Walton recovered from his bacchanalian rite of passage to assume the state's highest office, he joined a host of state officials saddled with the unenviable task of satisfying depositors whose accounts were wiped out in the tsunami of bank failures fostered by wild-eyed speculation. Editorial pages seethed with fury toward unscrupulous lenders and lax regulators. "There have been so many crooked banks and so many failures," railed an irate citizen in *Harlow's Weekly*, "that the burden which has been pyramided upon other state banks is insurmountable, and the losses cannot be made good by the guaranty law."[32] After the law was repealed, some demanded that the state issue bonds and use the proceeds to reimburse depositors. Others failed to see the logic in using taxpayer money to pay the debts of failed banks, any more than taxpayers should be liable for the debts of failed merchants.

The invective escalated when a probe launched to investigate the liquidation of state banks uncovered a tangle of improprieties. State auditor C. C. Childers caused an uproar when he expressed doubt that the House of Representatives had the authority to direct the expenditure of state funds on liquidations, even though the money had been appropriated from a fund that both the Senate and House had set aside to cover such expenses. The Byzantine twists and turns in what *Harlow's Weekly* dubbed "Oklahoma's state bank muddle" prompted one editorialist to suggest that something was rotten not in Denmark, but in Oklahoma City: "Why beat around the bush, gentlemen of the banking probe committee? All your investigations point in one direction: to the corruption under your very noses here in Oklahoma City. The wire pullers are here. It is here that the signal is given when a small bank is to be closed."[33]

Nowhere was frustration with failures and liquidations of state banks more forcefully expressed than in *Harlow's Weekly*'s call for stronger laws that would render the need for expensive cleanups unnecessary, or at least highly unlikely: "We need a law to protect present and future depositors more than we need laws to reimburse the past losses of depositors. There is one country where bank failures are unknown. It is said that in China there has not been a bank failure in 500 years. This fact is due to the Chinese law, which provides that when a bank fails the banker is immediately beheaded. The execution takes place first and the investigation of the bank is made afterward."[34]

Debates over deposit guaranty continued well into the 1930s. By then, the jury was in, and the verdict was not good news for this cornerstone of progressivism. States that had enacted some version of deposit guaranty legislation—Oklahoma, Kansas, Texas, Nebraska, Mississippi, South Dakota, North Dakota, and Washington—had all run into trouble and had been forced to suspend or repeal their programs. Launched during the halcyon days before 1920, deposit insurance systems foundered when accumulated reserves failed to stem the tide of farm and bank failures occasioned by the post–World War I depression. Generally speaking, state experiments with deposit insurance foundered because nobody figured out how to control entry into the banking professions or maintain quality standards over bank assets and operations. Passing legislation in a period when bank failures were rare, lawmakers assumed that small premiums would cover losses. They did little or nothing to try to prevent bank failures in the first place.[35]

The *Oklahoma Banker* concluded that deposit insurance, well intentioned though it might be, fostered "loose and incompetent banking." It also forced stockholders of sound banks, and ultimately the public, to pay for the sins of others. "What America needs," asserted an editorial in the *Oklahoma Banker,* "is not the guarantee of bank deposits, but better banking laws which will make the issuing of new bank charters more difficult and which will not encourage competitive banking to the point at which it may endanger the welfare of a community. What we want is not the guarantee of bank deposits against losses incurred by reckless banking, but the end of reckless banking itself."[36]

In Blaine County, Bert Willis and his brothers at the Bank of Canton were hardly surprised to see the bank guaranty law swept into the dustbin of history. "The Willis boys were very much opposed to the law as passed," recalled Bert. "They made their objections loud and long but to no avail. In our minds it was a foregone conclusion that it would end up in failure. We always claimed it was passed purposely for the political banker, for the big shots that were also in banks. Their politics were rotten and their banks were worse."[37]

With memories still fresh of State Banking Commissioner J. D. Lankford's success in curbing abuse, the state bank imbroglio of the 1920s was all the more galling. *Harlow's Weekly* suggested that the mess would have been mitigated if Oklahoma had been blessed with an effective banking commissioner and regulation by the Fed: "If in the past few years we had had both a fearless and honest bank commissioner, at least 90 per cent of the bank failures would never have occurred. If all of the state banks had been under federal bank examiners and had been connected with the federal reserve system, many of the crooked or reckless loans would never have been made and few failures would have occurred." State and national bankers alike no doubt read editorials in *Harlow's Weekly* and the *Oklahoma Banker* with interest tinged with trepidation as their industry lurched toward conformity with sound banking principles—a tall order in a state where violation of banking laws was common and, more often than not, "due more to crooked dealing than bad judgment."[38]

Even as Oklahomans were falling victim to what would one day fall under the rubric of "white collar crime," there was plenty of the old-fashioned variety to keep law enforcement busy. Back in 1896, *McMasters' Weekly* had proclaimed the decline of the "bad man": "The day of the desperado is ended, and monstrosities like [Ben] Thompson, who boasted when in his cups of the number of victims he had slain, will henceforth cease to afflict humanity."[39] Such assessments were clearly premature, more reflective of frontier boosterism than reality. A more realistic view of the mayhem visited on banks was evident a few months after statehood, when a movement to make bank and train robbery punishable by death gained traction in the legislature. A letter-writing campaign supported by bankers and state officials in the spring of 1908 aimed to enlist the organizational skills of the Oklahoma Bankers Association "to rid the new state of some of its most undesirable criminals"—permanently.[40]

Unfortunately, the bandits who roamed the Oklahoma countryside during the Roaring Twenties did not get the message. In 1924 alone, fifty-four bank robberies were committed in Oklahoma, netting the scoundrels a tidy $269,000.[41] Insurance rates on daylight holdups shot from $2.00 to $10.00 per $1,000, and insurers' threats to cancel bank policies were carried out with increasing frequency.[42] Rage over holdups in the Henry Starr mold had been mounting for years. Bankers' pleas for help fell on deaf ears in the wooded east, where hostility toward banks that had fueled agrarian socialism fostered an attitude that bankers were getting what they deserved. Henry Starr, who was admired by lawmen and celebrated for his kindness, once suggested that some of the bankers he had victimized were in the "robbery business, too."[43]

Bankers at the summit of international finance were not faring much better in the court of public opinion. In July 1920, anarchists who, in an earlier age, might have targeted a head of state, detonated a bomb outside the offices of J. P. Morgan & Company at 23 Wall Street in New York.

The partners were unhurt, but thirty-eight bystanders were killed and another four hundred were injured for being in the wrong place at the wrong time when enemies of the lords of finance came calling.[44]

Rarely a week went by when Oklahomans did not read about a bank robbery over their morning coffee. In December 1922, three unmasked men, all apparently under the age of thirty, held up the First State Bank of Avery in Lincoln County and escaped in an automobile with more than $4,000 in currency. The heist began when the men asked cashier John Murphy to change a ten-dollar bill. As he was counting their change, the men drew their revolvers and forced the cashier and his wife, who was standing nearby, into a room where they were bound with baling wire and gagged. Half an hour after the robbers fled the scene, a customer entered the bank and released Mr. and Mrs. Murphy from captivity.[45]

Acting on a tip from onetime outlaw Bud Davis, six officers staked out the First National Bank of Pawhuska. Unfortunately, Davis's description of the marked bank applied to the nearby Liberty National Bank as well. The day after the stakeout, bandits struck the unmarked bank. Complicit in the robbery was Liberty National Bank teller H. C. Hinson, who allegedly directed the robbery from inside the bank. Ed Ellis, who eventually pled guilty to the robbery and stood trial in Pawhuska in March 1928, testified that he had known Hinson for several years and that he was a teller at a bank in Shidler when it was robbed. For this reason, Ellis and his accomplice "were not afraid to plan and execute the robbery with him."[46]

By the mid-1920s, bankers had had enough. Under the auspices of the Oklahoma Bankers Association, twenty-seven vigilance committees were organized throughout the state. Ultimately, the OBA hoped to establish outposts in every county, "systematically and scientifically organized for the express purpose of killing, capturing and convicting if possible, every man who attempts to rob a bank in our state."[47] Membership quotas were established and marksmanship competitions were developed, complete with prizes and an annual pistol and rifle contest in the spring of 1925 at the government range north of Oklahoma City. By November, about one-third of the state was properly organized. The largest organization was in Lincoln County, where 113 men operating from Tyron, Carney, and Chandler stood ready to teach bank robbers "the difference between looking up the barrel of a gun and their old, familiar habit of looking down the barrel of a gun."[48]

As crime raged in the 1920s, the Oklahoma Bankers Association armed and trained bankers statewide to take matters into their own hands. Few were more serious about fighting crime than the Carney unit of the Lincoln County Vigilance Committee, 1925. Courtesy Oklahoma Bankers Association.

Fighting fire with fire turned out to be the right strategy. As the *Oklahoma Banker* went to press in November 1925, fewer than a dozen robberies had been committed since the beginning of the year, and losses were negligible. Inspired by its top crime fighter, Eugene P. Gum, the OBA didn't bother to disguise its contempt for a sluggish legal system and was deadly serious about taking a bite out of crime: "The primary purpose ... of covering every county in the State as quickly as possible, is that the unscrupulous yeggs may understand in the unmistakable language of a high-powered rifle that the bankers of Oklahoma are tired of their nefarious practices and are determined to set up a gravestone at the head of their liefless [sic] forms or drive them at the point of a gun into the penitentiary, where they belong."[49]

Success in curtailing burglaries notwithstanding, America's war on crime filled the pages of the *Oklahoma Banker* through the 1920s and 1930s. Even in a field crowded with brazen bank robbers, none elicited more fear from potential victims than Charles Arthur Floyd. Known to history as Pretty Boy Floyd, Charles was one of seven children whose impoverished father in Georgia dreamed of a better life in Oklahoma. Poverty followed him and his family west, where they scratched a meager living from the soil near Sallisaw, the home of John Steinbeck's fictional Joad family that seared the image of desperate southwestern farmers into the American consciousness. After an unsuccessful go at farming, Floyd turned to crime as his best shot at escaping his squalid surroundings. Adopting Henry Starr's brand of social banditry that bankers found so vexing, Floyd was known to throw money out the window of his getaway cars as a sign of solidarity with people who, like himself, had landed on the losing side of a dog-eat-dog economy.[50]

Advertisements in the *Oklahoma Banker* for target-hardening technologies proliferated, and writers both inside and outside the banking profession weighed in on the scourge of their time. "Thoughtful consideration justifies the conclusion that the American crime war is the greatest issue that has ever presented itself to the American people," wrote U.S. Army lieutenant colonel George Chase Lewis in a guest column in March 1927. In language that seems ripped from today's psychology journals, Lewis pinned the blame on an apathetic public whose "contact with newspaper articles" had desensitized people to the magnitude of the problem. Lewis likened media saturation to "the pound pat of butter that bulks large in the plate but seems invisible when spread throughout the sandwiches." Equally culpable were the "professional uplifters" who were more interested in reforming criminals than "the more vital necessity of protecting the life and property of the healthy, law-abiding, tax-paying citizens."[51] Lewis continued his analysis in the April 1927 issue of the *Oklahoma Banker* to depict popular culture, awash in cars, booze, and moving pictures, as a slippery slope to perdition:

> Unquestionably, one of the most potent sources of crime has been the breaking down of the bonds of parental discipline and the removal of the responsibilities formerly imposed on the young people by habit-forming chores, such as milking, dressmaking, cooking and kindling fires and similar tasks. The mammoth bakeries now make the bread; the department stores supply every type of clothing; the organized dairies deliver milk at the door and public service corporations furnish electric lights and gas heaters by turning a button. The vigorous American youth is thereby relieved of character-building chores and responsibilities. The lax present-day parental control permits the youthful

leisure hours thus gained to be filled with idleness, joy-rides and jazz.[52]

If the war on crime ranked first on bankers' agendas, then their ongoing campaign to improve crop yields ran a close second. The OBA's Agricultural Committee had a stake in every facet of farm and ranch production. In April 1930, the *Oklahoma Banker* offered tips on topics ranging from soil conservation, crop rotation, and marketing to purchasing seed for the spring planting season. And nowhere was Sooner pride more evident than when representatives of the agricultural sector pulled off a coup. When the stock-judging team from the agricultural and mechanical college in Stillwater won first place at the fatstock show in Fort Worth for the fourth consecutive time, the *Oklahoma Banker* praised future farmers who had apparently escaped the seductive lure of pop culture: "It may be, as some folks say, that our colleges are hotbeds of socialism, atheism, whoopee and a few other things; but when it comes to a matter of judging stock, our A. & M. boys, under the able leadership of Prof. Darlow, make the rest of the colleges go way back and sit down."[53]

The OBA's efforts on behalf of agriculture did not stop at editorials. When drought descended on the plains, bankers initiated and funded conservation drives and hired experts to teach principles of scientific management. In 1937, 103 meetings were held in seventeen counties, and 9,464 attendees came away with a deeper understanding of soil conservation. By the end of the year, an estimated 235,218 acres of topsoil were preserved. Land that had been abandoned because of depleted soil was plowed under, often with the advice of a local banker who not only provided financing but also gave intangible assistance in counseling farmers and promoting the program. By 1978, the First National Bank and Trust Company of Oklahoma City would commit $50 million to $60 million of its loan portfolio to agricultural loans—less than the $100 million in loans to petroleum companies, but certainly enough to reflect the importance of agriculture to the state's largest bank.[54]

Even as new forms of production and distribution were pulling Oklahomans into tighter webs of collaboration, competition between banks was fostering a need to advertise like never before. Challenges in the first decades of the twentieth century were legion: bank failures; shaken confidence in the ones left standing; the move toward group and branch banking; and cutthroat competition at home and abroad. "These are some of the present day circumstances," wrote Edwin Bird Wilson, president of Edwin Bird Wilson, Inc., of New York and Chicago, in the September 1931 edition of the *Oklahoma Banker*. "Although history repeats itself and some of the circumstances are repetitions of past experiences, the banking situation today is as new as today's newspaper." Frontier banking, RIP.

Wilson recommended advertising as the modern banker's ticket to clearing up misunderstandings, restoring old friendships, making new friends, earning goodwill, and establishing a brand reflecting sound business principles. Eschewing free publicity as uncontrollable and even ruinous ("What an uncertain staff to lean on!" proclaimed Wilson), Wilson urged bankers to seize control of their messages. "Banks that are strong, banks that are sure of themselves, banks that know their power to help business can settle the question of confidence by giving the public a chance to know the true, unexaggerated vital facts about the banks." For Wilson, the stronger the bank, the greater its moral obligation to help and protect business. Long gone were the days when bankers could rely on symbols of safety to win the public's trust. The competition for customers was too keen to leave anything to chance. What is more, the lure of overseas markets was beckoning capital abroad. "The vast investments of American business in foreign countries make it impossible for big American banks to confine their activities to this country," wrote Wilson.[55] Mass media, chiefly newspapers and magazines, offered the surest route to success in post-frontier banking, both at home and on distant shores.

Meanwhile, advertising in the retail sector was helping to spawn a revolution in purchasing habits with far-reaching implications for banks: installment buying. Unlike their thrifty predecessors who had been weaned on frontier scarcity, citizens-turned-consumers were an impatient lot. They were also increasingly urban: the number of people with nonfarm jobs rose from 18 million in 1900 to 37 million in 1929.[56] A trickle of manufactured goods before World War I became a flood when the hostilities ended. By the twenties, people were increasingly comfortable with buying what they wanted when they wanted it, and a lean bank account was no longer a deal killer. "This is an age of installment buying," asserted D. K. Snyder, assistant cashier of the Drovers National Bank in Kansas City in an address to the National Retail Credit Association in Omaha in November 1927.[57] High-pressure salesmen and ubiquitous advertising were turning a practice that was once associated with low social standing into the new norm. The *Oklahoma Banker* estimated that two out of five American families were "using the easy payment plan, not once but again and again." In the opinion of Oklahoma's favorite son, Will Rogers, Americans were perfecting the art of paying something they did not have for something they did not want.[58]

Both cause and effect of the revolution in consumption was the transition from an economy based on cash to one based on credit. Instant gratification was all the rage, and credit was the new engine. The trend toward consumer loans, apparent in the 1920s and an accepted portal to shopper's paradise in the 1930s, was driven to a large extent by automobile purchases and was accelerated by other kinds of household purchasing. The proportion of bank loans extended to households shot from 9 percent in 1929 to more than 20 percent in 1939. From 1900 to 1929, the total volume of bank credit expanded from $7 billion to $49 billion. This seismic shift in bank loan portfolios from business to household lending set the stage for diversified patterns of credit that shape contemporary banking.[59]

"Credit is the greatest asset to modern business taken from an economical standpoint," claimed D. K. Snyder to his assembly of true believers in Omaha. To facilitate the flow of credit, bankers were forced into the awkward position of prying into the affairs of their customers and then, perhaps even more awkward, divulging information to third parties. Saddled with new expectations, bankers faced a dilemma: should banks release information as a business courtesy, or should they charge a fee? Snyder's position was unequivocal, and perhaps not altogether unexpected in an industry that has raised fee-charging to an art form.

> A bank's only commodity is credit. His stock in trade is information he has obtained through years of effort and expense regarding the individuals and business houses in his community. This information is the most valuable thing he possesses, except the good will of his depositors. . . . The banker of today is a busy man and the one in the bank most capable of answering inquiries intelligently is generally one of the busiest men in the bank,

which is particularly true in small banks. I do not believe I have left any doubt as to my attitude regarding this proposition. I feel that credit inquiries should be paid for.[60]

The revolution in consumption was not without its critics. Even as installment buying brought the fruits of industrial production within the reach of millions, prescient bankers were urging caution. In an annual address to the Oklahoma Bankers Association in May 1927, OBA president E. D. Kilpatrick of Le Flore County claimed that he was not entirely opposed to extending credit for consumer goods. "But I am opposed to it when it is for luxuries, or for necessities, for that matter, when it keeps the buyer's nose to the ground (which it so very often does), and in debt, because there is no telling where it will lead." No doubt raised in the old school of pay-as-you-go, Kilpatrick suggested that debts are the root of much, if not all, evil. One wonders what financial calamities he had witnessed in his corner of southeast Oklahoma. "Installment buying is like dynamite," he concluded. "It is safe when in the hands of those who know how to use it, but very dangerous when in the hands of the unskilled."[61]

Plus ça change.

On August 2, 1920, a branch of the Tenth District Federal Reserve Bank opened for business in the Continental Building at Second and Broadway in Oklahoma City. Immediately upon its establishment, the bank was the largest in the United States "in amount of business done in proportion to its number of members."[62]

The branch's opening came at the end of a prolonged campaign to lure the branch to Oklahoma City that began shortly after passage of the Owen-Glass Federal Reserve Act of 1913. With central banking still in its infancy, delegations from Saint Louis and Kansas City vied for Oklahoma City's support in their bids to become parent cities of the Federal Reserve System. It came as no surprise when Missouri's principal cities were designated as parent cities. But when Oklahoma was split between the Kansas City and Dallas districts, bankers found themselves in the fight of their lives. As reported in the *Daily Oklahoman,* "Amazement was expressed by practically every banker and business man in the state, and as the import of the change was investigated and weighed carefully, leading men of Oklahoma became convinced that a terrific blow had been struck at the commercial and industrial prosperity of Oklahoma."[63] As one banker explained, if Oklahoma's southern counties had remained in the Dallas district, a large share of trade and commerce "would inevitably have followed the forced channels of finance," and commerce that might have accrued to the benefit of Oklahoma would have been siphoned off to the south. "Of course," said the anonymous banker in an interview for the *Daily Oklahoman,* "our banks would have felt the effects first." He went on to elaborate on Oklahoma's brush with disaster in April 1914 when the Federal Reserve Bank announced its plan for establishing districts: "Big business follows the channels of finance. Big factories, mills, and other industrial enterprises can only be successfully established where their needs can be taken care of by big banks. And if the district lines had not been changed Oklahoma City would have been obliged to struggle along in a small way where she can now branch out in a big way, a real financial center so recognized everywhere."[64]

True to form, the Oklahoma Bankers Association rose to the challenge. At its annual convention in May 1914, the OBA adopted resolutions directing Oklahoma's congressional delegates to wield their influence and place the state's banks in Kansas City's jurisdiction. According to OBA secretary W. B. Harrison, "The resolutions were far the most important acts of the convention. They were unanimously adopted, and the bankers were very vigorous in expressing their sentiments. It was a matter in which they were in no way divided. More interest was displayed in this than in any other topic." Included in the OBA's resolutions was a plan to send a committee to Washington, D.C., to lodge a formal protest before the Federal Reserve Board and, come Hell or high water, "correct the mistake that has been made."[65]

In February 1915, reasoned protest backed by evidence found its way into the Federal Reserve Board's deliberations when three delegates from Oklahoma joined Harrison on a trip to Washington, D.C., to plead their case: William Mee, president of the Security Bank of Oklahoma City; Guy Robertson of Lawton; and E. K. Thurmond of Sayre. With the active intervention of Oklahoma senator Robert L. Owen, only five southern counties—Bryan, Atoka, Marshall, Coal, and Johnston—were conceded to the Eleventh District, headquartered in Dallas, in May 1915.[66] McCurtain, Choctaw, and Pushmataha Counties also remained in the Dallas district.[67] On July 1, 145 national banks with aggregate capital and surplus of $6 million and total resources of about $25 million were transferred from the Dallas district to the Kansas City district. The *Daily Oklahoman*'s account of the battle's final skirmish testifies to the resilience of Oklahoma bankers in the face of perceived injustice: "Thus is closed one of the most momentous conflicts in the interest of the state of Oklahoma that has been waged in its little more than a quarter century of struggle and progress."[68]

The battleground then shifted from jurisdictional disputes to the location of branch banks. The three Tenth District contenders were Oklahoma City, Tulsa, and Wichita. Oklahoma City's bid was backed by 696 of the state's 800 banks, while Tulsa's support was limited to its own banks and a few in Muskogee. In a spirit of cooperation that belied the cross-state rivalry, the state's principal cities stood shoulder to shoulder to make sure that Wichita would not snatch the prize. In the end, Wichita's case was hopeless, as it was too close to the parent bank to be a serious contender.[69]

With Wichita out of the running, the Federal Reserve Board summoned delegations from Oklahoma City and Tulsa to Washington, D.C., for a meeting on October 21, 1919. After hearing presentations and reviewing documents, the Federal Reserve Board sent a telegram to Kansas City requesting reports on commercial activity in the southern part of the district. On November 26, the Federal Reserve Board sent letters to Oklahoma banks outside the contending cities to ask for their preferences on the bank's location. The letter read in part: "In order that this Branch may be located with a view to the interests of the territory to be served, the Board desires from you an unbiased statement indicating your preference as between the two cities named."[70]

The referendum turned out to be good news for Oklahoma City. "Oklahoma City seems sure to win the bank now," said Frank P. Johnson, president of the American National Bank and chairman of the Oklahoma City campaign. "More than 200 member banks in the state endorsed Oklahoma City when we presented the petition to the board, and I am certain they will return the same decision now. The vote was more than two to one for us. We have been in close touch with all the banks and can rely upon them fully."[71] The good news hit the streets when the Federal Reserve Board issued a press release announcing Oklahoma City's selection on December 17, 1919.[72]

Cooperation between the cross-state rivals notwithstanding, Oklahoma City reveled in its victory. Headlines blared with the good news on Thursday, December 18, the same day that Frank Johnson used the *Daily Oklahoman* as a bully pulpit to explain the benefits that would accrue to Oklahomans as a result of the Federal Reserve Board's decision: "It means that the money that banks have kept on deposit in the Federal Reserve Bank and other banks outside the state will now be kept in the state. This will provide cheaper money, easier money, more loan money for every point in Oklahoma." Johnson was not bashful about his bank's prominence in the state's finances. He asserted, "Location of the branch in Oklahoma City means that the biggest, strongest, leading bank in Oklahoma City, which is The American National Bank, will be in ever-increasing measure a financial headquarters for the whole state." In case readers were slow to get the point, the American National Bank explained why, exactly, it had emerged as Oklahoma City's financial headquarters: "The American National Bank has won premier place in Oklahoma City. It leads in amount of deposits and number of depositors and is a member of the Federal Reserve system. It is the bank that can most ably serve the interests of bankers throughout the state in connection with the Federal Reserve Bank."[73]

Despite the postwar slump, the new bank's growth was nothing short of phenomenal. As a banker's bank, the institution reigned as a sort of "super bank" that kept hundreds of other banks in the district flush with cash.[74] Rediscount rights were conferred in July 1921, thus enabling the bank to accept applications for loans and rediscounts from member institutions. Other functions included issuing and redeeming currency and engaging in collection and clearing of checks.[75]

Busy as it was, the bank was a quiet place. "The customers seldom come to the bank themselves," ran a story in the *Daily Oklahoman* some twenty years after the bank's founding. "Almost all the business is transacted through various communications—telephone, telegraph, mail, messenger."[76] Numbers belied the serene ambiance: the daily average of items handled in August 1922 was 41,418, an increase of 2,444 over the previous August, and the average daily clearings were $1,758,440.81. *Harlow's Weekly* did not wait for precise figures to laud the bank's rise to national prominence: "While no actual comparative figures are available, it has been reported out of Kansas City that during the month of February, 1923, the number of items handled by the Oklahoma City branch was greater than those handled in either of the parent banks at Atlanta and San Francisco, as well as larger than those handled in the branches at Buffalo, Baltimore, Birmingham, Denver, Detroit, El Paso, Houston, Helena, Jacksonville, Nashville, New Orleans, Little Rock, Louisville, Omaha, Portland, Memphis, Salt Lake City, Seattle, and Spokane."[77]

The only problem was space. When the bank opened on August 2, 1920, it had approximately fifty employees, but that number quickly doubled. Functions were therefore divided between two locations: the banking rooms were in the Continental Building; and the money department was installed in the basement of the American National Bank. Thus did Frank Johnson close ranks with central bankers whose role—metaphorically, at least—was to be the cowboys in control of the herd.[78]

As president of the American National Bank and landlord of the Fed's money department, Frank Johnson was surely on hand when Federal Reserve Board governor W. P. G. Harding came to town in May 1921 to address the Oklahoma Bankers Association convention. On a tour of the bank's dual facilities, he saw firsthand the crowded conditions and recommended construction of a new building. His listeners needed little convincing, and the southeast corner of Third and Harvey was transformed into a construction site for what would be a jewel in Oklahoma City's mushrooming crown.

Diagonally across from the beautiful new home of the Elk's Lodge and directly across from the park adorning the unoccupied portion of government-owned land where the federal building stood, the edifice arose at a cost of $500,000. Office furniture was custom-built by the Tibbs-Dorsey Manufacturing Company, a local firm whose president, P. W. Tibbs, gushed with pride at winning the contract. "We have never built any better work than this," said Tibbs in an interview with *Harlow's Weekly*.[79] Other touches included a beautiful bronze doorway, eight large columns of Belgian black and gold marble, bronze chandeliers, and a gigantic vault—"the latest work in burglar-proof bank vaults and that, aside from the fact that the interior may be smaller than a few others, the construction work, including the two monster doors, are as large or larger than any west of the Mississippi river, and compares favorably with those in New York and Boston." Discretely located at the back of the lobby was a guard with a machine gun seated in a "pill box" made of bulletproof steel and glass who controlled not only the front door, but also the entrance to the work room and vaults at the back.[80] Five hundred tons of steel, 38,000 feet of wiring, a time lock, and a sophisticated

Bankers statewide let out a collective cheer when the Federal Reserve Bank of Kansas City chose Oklahoma City as the location for a branch bank. To accommodate the branch's rapid growth, a building was constructed at the corner of Third and North Harvey Streets in Oklahoma City. Courtesy Western History Collections, University of Oklahoma Libraries.

panel of electric lights were enough to make even the Henry Starrs of the world think twice about a heist.[81]

A holdup while money was in motion was not much of an option. The bank's money truck was fortified with heavy-armor steel from top to bottom and bulletproof glass. Amenities for the driver included a sliver of daylight for the front window and an electric fan for summer weather. Clearly, bankers wrapped in an ever-tighter web of policies and regulations were not quite done with frontier symbols of safety to ensure customers that their money was safe, and that their friendly neighborhood moneymen were here to stay.

Placement of the cornerstone of the splendid new building took place on Saturday, December 7, 1922. To acknowledge the wellsprings of so much of Oklahoma's wealth, Federal Reserve Bank officials decided to enclose something special in it: a phial of oil from what was reputed to be the region's first oil well in Johnstone Park in Bartlesville 145 miles to the northeast. It was still pumping at the rate of five barrels per day when E. L. George, secretary of the Oklahoma City Chamber of Commerce, traveled to Bartlesville to snatch a few drops of the precious liquid.

Known to the oil cognoscenti as Old Faithful, the well hit pay dirt at a depth of 1,300 feet on April 15, 1897, several years before Bartlesville roared into history as the epicenter of the Oklahoma oil boom. The driller, George B. Keeler, obtained the lease from the Cherokee Nation in 1892. As it turned out, Keeler was ahead of his time—the Cudahy Oil Company took over the lease from Keeler five years later and capped the well until 1903 because there was no market for the oil and no railroads to transport it. As Keeler recalled, "This was one of the first leases ever taken for oils or minerals in that nation. It was one of the thirteen leases taken during the year, and each lease covered an area of five square miles."[82] Ever since that cold December day in 1922, Oklahomans could claim, literally and figuratively, that oil lay at the bottom of Oklahoma banking.

"The building is completed," declared the *Daily Oklahoman* on May 6, 1923. "The Oklahoma branch of the federal reserve system is 'open for business' within the four walls of its own physical property; a structure that represents a financial rock of Gibraltar to bankers and business men of Oklahoma, an institution linked to a monetary system that practically guarantees that the American dollar will always be worth 100 cents." Benefits accruing from the branch bank included a more elastic currency; access to funds that were no longer "impounded as useless reserves at far distant points"; a means by which agricultural, commercial, and industrial paper could be converted quickly into currency or credit; and a mechanism by which member banks could convert their reserves into gold.[83]

Right on cue, Oklahoma banks started compiling some impressive numbers. Oklahoma City came in second to Denver, and Tulsa ranked third, among principal cities in the Tenth Federal Reserve District in the accumulation of savings for the twelve months preceding the opening of the new branch bank. Savings, too, were on the rise: in April 1922, savings deposits in Oklahoma City banks totaled $4,679,058; on April 2, 1923, the total was $6,279,367, an increase of $1,600,309.[84] The good news continued in July when the *Blue Book of Southern Progress* ranked Oklahoma's national banks second among southern states in resources, deposits, and number of institutions. The state's 449 national banks had total resources of $377,105,000 and deposits of $310,133,000. "Oklahoma national banks have shown a substantial growth during the six months to date, 1923, in accompanying the general growth of financial channels of the southland," ran an upbeat report in the *Daily Oklahoman* in July 1923.[85] The same source indicated that the aggregate of Oklahoma City bank clearings was approximately $91,619,000 per month—more than comparable figures in ten American cities with larger populations.[86]

Prohibited by the reforms of the 1860s from making mortgage loans because of the threat they posed to liquidity and safety, national banks often ceded the field to building and loan associations. Founded in 1899 and headquartered at the corner of First and Harvey, the Oklahoma City Building and Loan Association, self-branded as "*The HOME Folks,*" put progressive principles to work in facilitating loans for people of modest means. The association opened its books with $4,000 in capital; by 1901, it was servicing loans on thirty-seven homes and had assets of $20,000.[87] Traditional banks, compelled to balance the safety of depositors against the inherent risks of lending, focused on short-term loans (three to five years) to farmers and businessmen. In the spirit of capitalism, building and loan companies found a niche among salaried people who needed long-term loans secured by the properties they were buying, to be repaid in monthly installments. Such loans were especially attractive because they did not require borrowers to renew them at the end of specified periods of time as long as payments were made in a timely manner. An advertisement in the *Oklahoma Banker* in January 1927 stated the building and loan association mission in simple terms: "To furnish a safe and convenient plan for saving money and from the funds thus created, lend money, repayable in monthly installments over a period of years, to those desiring to buy or build a home or pay off mortgages or existing liens."[88] Building and loan companies had been regulated by the state banking commissioner since 1913, when the Fourth Legislature voted in emergency session to place them under state control.[89]

With an impressive asset base of $4,359,016.97 and lending power of $350,000 per month in August 1918, Oklahoma City's three building and loan associations were clearly doing their part to create a city of homeowners. In its newsletter, *Oklahoma,* the Oklahoma City Chamber of Commerce acknowledged that eye-catching neighborhoods were pushing frontier days ever further into history: "For today Oklahoma City is above everything else a city of attractive homes with such an appeal from the residence standpoint as to make people want to live here."[90]

In July 1923, *Harlow's Weekly* estimated that about 60 percent of the homes built in Oklahoma towns of any size were financed by building and loan companies.[91] It was further estimated that, from the early teens to the early twenties, building and loan companies aided thirty thousand families in building homes, helped another twenty thousand to buy homes, and increased the value of real estate lots by $36 million through financing of home construction.[92] The authorized capital stock of Oklahoma's building and loan companies in March 1923 was $184,550,000; shares outstanding were valued at $137,457,500; and the full and prepaid shares totaled $48,974,246.26.[93]

While state banks were scrambling to stay afloat during the twenties, building and loan associations were thriving. According to *Harlow's Weekly*, "Failure of a building and loan association in Oklahoma is never heard of, a tribute both to the prosperity of the state, to the observances of the stringent statutes governing the associations, and to the general management of the associations. The fact that all elements except one, in the building and loan business, are definitely known, eliminates nearly all chances for failure." That one element, of course, was the degree of prosperity in the communities that lenders served. Because so much of building and loan business was a matter of public record, opportunities for fraud were kept to a minimum, "probably lower than in any other line of business."[94]

Competition between banks and building and loan companies, fierce though it was for the lenders, helped spread the opportunity for home ownership down the socioeconomic ladder. *Harlow's Weekly* put it this way:

> Regardless of the present contest, however, the building and loan associations are making wonderful strides forward in their development; with capable and substantial business and financial men at their heads and with corps of efficient salesmen and clerks, there is no doubt but what they are destined to play a bigger part in the future financial and building life of the state than they have even with their activity in the past. An institution that is founded on the basis that the building and loan association is, one that has for its purpose the helping of people of moderate means to secure homes, will hold a powerful place in the considerations and plans of the public during the future years.[95]

As the twenties drew to a close, legislators in the nation's capital were embroiled in debates over one of the most contentious issues in banking policy: group, or branch, banking. Opposition to branching had deep rural roots, and it dated back to Andrew Jackson's visceral hatred of monopolies and legendary campaign against the Second Bank of the United States that he once vowed to kill before it killed him.[96] Weaned on frontier democracy, Jackson and his ilk believed that branching fostered absentee capital, and it ranked alongside elites and monopolies as an evil to be extirpated from the Republic. By the 1870s, Populists were fanning fears of branching even more. It is possible that branching would have stabilized banking at the turn of the twentieth century, but no matter: it reeked of monopoly, and frontier democrats would have none of it. By failing to permit branching by national banks in any state, the federal government ensured that western bankers would not benefit from the national system and could opt instead for more lenient, and often poorly regulated, state laws.

By the 1920s, interest in branch banking was making a comeback, and unit-banking states such as Oklahoma found themselves in the swirl of controversy.[97] Responding to the antitrust sentiments that had shaped Woodrow Wilson's reform agenda in the 1910s, Congress reined in banking power in 1927 with the passage of the McFadden Act, which prohibited interstate expansion by banks. Behind these policies lay an American ideal, honored more in the breach than in the observance, that vigorous competition among small-scale economic units would lead to optimal results in industry and finance. In the end, American industry would find it far easier to circumvent checks on its power than would the banks, which were heavily regulated and subject to political oversight.[98] The McFadden Act also encouraged national banks to extend loans on nonfarm real estate.[99]

Weighing the costs and benefits of the new law, Oklahoma bankers added their voices to the national debate over branch banking. R. W. Hutto, cashier of the Security National Bank in Norman, spoke for a majority of the state's financial leaders in August 1929 who opposed branch banking. "In my judgment," wrote Hutto,

> the power of the Federal Reserve Board will pall into insignificance when our national banking laws permit openly branch ownership. Fixing money rates is an important aspect of this

new situation (branching), but even more important is the fact that credit will be supplied only when and where it is desired by a large group.... I view with alarm the possibility that branch banking will result in the withdrawal of banking resources from small cities and towns and the concentration of them in the nation's larger commercial centers. A system of branch banking will result in the withdrawal of funds from our lesser communities. Large corporations and large financial groups in ... cities will be the beneficiaries of this movement.[100]

On December 11, 1929, Frank P. Johnson entered the fray in an address at the Oklahoma Bankers Association convention in Oklahoma City. Now pushing sixty, he had spent half of his life in banking, and he had witnessed and participated in Oklahoma's transition from frontier to region. He began his remarks with an assertion that he had always been an independent banker and did not own a single share of stock in any bank except his own. He revealed his bookish ways when he cautioned against excessive stress on independence: "Independence does not mean that a man shall live unto himself. The great American war for independence was won by the pooling of men and money by the thirteen colonies. Nearly all military, political and economic crises have been met by pooling of men and money."[101]

Turning his attention to the issue at hand, Johnson employed that same sense of balance to branching and declared that he was not so much an advocate as a student of group banking: "Until the field becomes more clearly defined and the results can be more carefully analyzed, it hardly behooves any of us to take a positive position on the subject at this time." Johnson went on to list objections to group banking cited by former comptroller of the currency Henry M. Dawes. These included excessive government control, the erosion of community, the increasing power of distant banks, and the siphoning of money and credit from small communities to urban centers. Even in the face of such dire prospects, Johnson argued that there might be one compelling argument on behalf of branch banking, discernible in the future but obscured by the glare of present circumstances, that would sweep all the rest "into the discard." Once again, history yielded lessons for those patient enough to listen: "There was every reason why the citizens of Pompeii should remain in their beautiful valley, but Vesuvius belched and the citizens fled to the hills."[102]

One wonders how Johnson's peers greeted his address on a topic of such import. Were some persuaded to give the matter more thought, perhaps even to cast their lot with the opposition? Given the polarization generated by branch banking, many were probably annoyed by his sense of balance and simply stuck to their guns, more convinced than ever that branching would siphon money from rural areas, channel it to the cities, and foster competition tilted in favor of large, lower cost banks.

Whatever their perspectives on branch banking and opinions of Frank Johnson's use of the bully pulpit, none would have disagreed with Rex F. Harlow's tribute to bankers published in *Harlow's Weekly* in September 1923. Harlow's editorial has lost none of its resonance in the decades separating the Roaring Twenties from our own time: "A bank, by virtue of its very nature, is the hub about which business must and does turn; it controls the wheels of industry, it directs the forces of conservatism and sound judgment that make successful business possible—these services and others too numerous and well known to mention make it the Gibraltar on which the prosperity and future hope of business rests."[103]

CHAPTER FOUR

The Dawn of Conservative Banking

> It seems to me that we are at the threshold of a new era in banking. January 1, 1934, will be the dawn of conservative banking. The conservative banker will come into his own, for the hand of the "wild-catter" in banking has been called by the Government. Hereafter, banking is going to be a profession—not merely the vehicle of speculation.
>
> W. J. Barnett, Oklahoma state banking commissioner

Urban growth notwithstanding, agriculture ranked number one in the nascent state's economy. But as modernity steamrolled its way across the land, a new industry muscled its way to the heart of Oklahoma's economy: the "awl b'ness."

Since territorial days, businessmen in Oklahoma City had watched with envy as frontier villages in the Indian Territory prospered from the bounty below. Some, including Charles Colcord and Charles "Gristmill" Jones, invested in eastern oil wells and brought their profits back to Oklahoma City. Monuments such as the Colcord Building, the Commerce and Exchange Building, and the Biltmore Hotel owed a large measure of their financing to Colcord's oil investments. Oklahoma City's building boom would have been far less spectacular without wealth pouring into the region from Tulsa, Bartlesville, Red Fork, Glenn Pool, and similar towns that were blessed with shallow oil deposits.

Yet profits made in the east only whetted western Oklahomans' appetite for wells of their own. Geological reports left little doubt that the oil was there, and visionaries insisted that it was only a matter of time before western Oklahoma would come into its own. But test wells kept coming up dry. The only explanation was that nobody had had the audacity, or the technology, to drill deep enough to find it.[1]

All that changed when the Indian Territory Illuminating Oil Company (ITIO) stepped into the picture. Building on the advice of geologists and three decades of experience in Oklahoma oil production, the ITIO acquired a block of some ten thousand acres in central Oklahoma and began probing for deposits. Part of the land was owned by Vincent and Mary Sudik, a hardworking Bohemian couple of peasant extraction who raised dairy cattle and children on their patch of prairie. Pleased to have some extra money from selling their lease, the Sudiks went about their business, milking their cows, selling their produce, and raising their children, seemingly indifferent to the hubbub on the back forty. Perhaps the Sudiks relished the last few moments of quiet before industry unleashed its fury.

The Sudiks and their cows paid scant attention as hard steel bored relentlessly to depths of four, then five, then six thousand feet at the ITIO Mary Sudik No. 1. On March 26, 1930, at a depth of 6,400 feet and with a roar that blew the top off the derrick and sent the crew and cattle stampeding for cover, gas-driven oil thundered to the surface, filled the sky with an acrid plume, and swamped fertile fields as far as the eye could see. Witnesses must have thought the Apocalypse was at hand as twenty joints of casing sailed into the air before crashing into the derrick.[2] Engineers descended on the eruption to harness the flow and limit the waste and damage, but oil trapped in a pressure cooker for eons would not be easily tamed. "Due to the enormous gas volume," ran a breathless account in the *Daily Oklahoman* on March 29, "the well presents one of the most difficult problems ever confronted by operators in the local area."[3] Many days later, the geyser was spudded in the backyard of a pleasant housewife who was content to tend to her chores as the ground shifted, literally and figuratively, beneath her feet.

The well was promptly dubbed "Wild Mary" after the Bohemian farmwife who was anything but wild. Its fame spread far and wide by media ravenous for sensational stories, and the Oklahoma City oil field was open for business to anyone with the temerity to take it on. When at last the monster was capped, there was hardly a soul to be found who was unaffected by the raw power unleashed on that spring day in

A gusher near Cushing serves as a potent symbol of Oklahoma's mineral wealth. Courtesy Western History Collections, University of Oklahoma Libraries.

Oklahoma. Except, maybe, Mary Sudik. "I can't be bothered," she told reporters who beat a trail to her farmhouse. "I'm busy with my first grandchild."[4]

With oil came a witches' brew of chemicals and contraptions that made roughnecking one of the most dangerous ways to make a living. George Gorton of Cement in Caddo County learned firsthand just how perilous his profession could be. "Fire was just about the most dreaded thing that could happen," wrote Gorton in his memoir, "next to a tornado, in these small southwestern towns like Cement, because they did not have a sufficient water supply or the means for getting it quickly to the site of the fire. Combine this with lack of rain and strong winds and it is easy to see how a major catastrophe was always lurking around the corner."[5]

By the time Oklahoma City affixed its star to the petroleum industry, the stereotype of the swashbuckling wildcatter was embedded in western lore. Ever since the first commercial well in the Indian Territory was drilled west of Chelsea in the Cherokee Nation in November 1889, oilmen had been a familiar sight, hauling the tools of their trade to one promising spot after another in hopes that their next well would be the new El Dorado.[6] During the World War I era, entrepreneurs added a whole new dimension to pioneer independence, and they dodged a bullet when the federal government failed to follow through on threats to nationalize the oil industry.

The trouble started when politicians vowed to bring stability to the oil business. They stirred up a hornet's nest when they alleged that premiums paid for crude oil were too high. "Probability of the federal government taking over the oil industry has alarmed operators and refiners as nothing has done before in years," blared *Harlow's Weekly* under the headline "Disaster Confronting Oil Industry" in the summer of 1918. "But WHY? Who wants to be controlled? Who is seeking control? Isn't the government getting all, and more, oil than it needs? Isn't the price all right? Are there any oil producers or refiners in bankruptcy courts? Isn't the business flourishing?"[7]

Oilmen's contempt for meddlesome politicians was vindicated as Oklahoma's oil production zoomed off the charts to take first place among the states in 1918, 1920, and 1922. "Also," asserted Wesley I. Nunn in *Harlow's Weekly* in February 1923 with more than a hint of bravado, "for the first time in the history of the state, the production of oil became the state's chief industry. That is, the total value of the oil produced for the first time exceeded the total value of all crops produced in the state, and this by a goodly margin, too."[8]

What was good for drillers was good for bankers, but the flood of wealth created problems of its own. In March 1923, Exchange National Bank of Tulsa president James J. McGraw used the *Oklahoma Banker* as a bully pulpit to describe the challenges and opportunities that bankers faced in financing the oil industry. With an eye on nefarious dealings that had long since branded Oklahoma as an outlaw state, McGraw reminded readers that the inherent risks of investing in oil were compounded by investors' yen for quick profits. But times were clearly changing as advances in geology, refining methods, and marketing brought the oil industry into closer conformity with sound business principles. "The day of the fly-by-night company is gone; the day of the usurious financier is gone," wrote McGraw in his epitaph for frontier wildcatting. "Information is available as to management; as to properties; as to indebtedness, which makes it unnecessary for the investor to treat an oil investment as a chance at roulette." McGraw was preaching to the choir when he called on the government to cooperate with the oil industry rather than single it out for attack, either through threats of nationalization or excessive taxation. Relying on logic that has stood the test of time, McGraw predicted that national security would depend increasingly on energy self-sufficiency: "The one nation of the future that will be secure and self-sufficient, is that nation that has an adequate and permanent supply of crude petroleum produced within its own borders and by its own citizens. Those nations that have not the necessary deposits of petroleum within their territories, are moving the heavens to control such deposits in other lands."

McGraw suggested that bankers examine the problem of oil financing from a dual perspective of credit and capital—that is, the character and assets of the borrower, and the proper use of capital in oil production and distribution. McGraw might have overstated the stability of the oil business, but he was certainly on track in predicting that oil would "absorb in the coming years a great measure of the world's capital." Like agriculture, railroads, and steamships, oil was a mainstay of the global economy, and it was up to bankers to see that the industry received the financing it needed. McGraw claimed, "I feel that an examination of the fundamental relations of petroleum to the changing economic world will compel the admission that its absorption of capital is fully justified; and that its future demands will receive the consideration they should have."[9]

Few associate the onset of the Great Depression with large-scale construction projects. But that is exactly what Oklahomans witnessed as the nation careened into a wretched decade that began with Wall Street's nosedive in October 1929. Early on, most Oklahomans assumed that their robust economy would weather the storm that was gathering back east.[10] All one had to do was look out the window at the oil derricks sprouting from the flatlands to realize that Oklahoma was in the catbird seat, uniquely poised to withstand the shock waves of an imploding national economy. In Oklahoma City, there were no better symbols of the state's resilience than the fortress rising at the southeast corner of Robinson Avenue and First Street (present-day Park Avenue) to house the First National Bank and Trust Company and another one across the street, where the Ramsey Tower was adding its own thirty-three stories to the skyline. Competition between the behemoths to see which one would go down in history as the city's first skyscraper captured the public's attention as the Great Skyscraper Race of 1931.[11] As Arthur Ramsey, the son of the building's builder, W. R. Ramsey, recalled many years later, "They had all kinds of races between the two buildings . . . who would finish the steel work first and who would finish the brick and stone work? And the papers would play it up." Such was the rivalry that local gamblers placed odds on which tower would reach the sky first.[12]

Tulsa bankers were buoyed by Federal Reserve Bank of Kansas City chairman M. L. McClure's sanguine outlook. During a tour of the Tenth District to assess economic conditions, he and Federal Reserve governor W. J. Bailey, together with several other officials, enjoyed a respite from their travels at a breakfast hosted by the First National Bank and Trust Company of Tulsa at the Mayo Hotel on October 7, 1930. "Of all the Federal Reserve Districts," asserted McClure, "the Tenth District seems to be the most fortunate and the least affected by the drought and the depression. It is the district that will probably recover quickest." In McClure's estimation, farmers were less affected by the drought than by low commodity prices, and a combination of high unemployment and weak demand for consumer goods was casting a cloud across the business landscape. "But," he said, "conditions here are better than the general average." Citing the self-correcting nature of business cycles,

The Great Skyscraper Race of 1931. In Oklahoma City, the First National Bank Building and the Ramsey Tower reached skyward at the onset of the Great Depression. Courtesy Oklahoma Historical Society.

McClure seemed to be on solid footing in predicting a gradual recovery "through the working of natural laws." He then singled out historic levels of deposits in Tulsa banks as the surest sign that the economic downturn would be short-lived: "Deposits in Tulsa, for instance, at the last call, were greater than ever before in the history of the city. It is much the same everywhere in the district. I would not say that the deposits generally are greater than ever before, but they are greater than they have been for eight or nine years. We have a condition that has not been experienced in any previous depression. There is plenty of money and it is cheap. It is there when business gets ready to use it."[13]

Similar optimism prevailed in the Panhandle, where farmers were downright giddy after a gully washer in late February 1931 produced wheat fields that "never did look prettier than they do now."[14] The upbeat mood made bankers positively hostile to a proposal that $500 in drought relief be sent to each of the Panhandle counties. At a meeting of Cimarron and Texas County bankers, a resolution was adopted that practically dared big-city bureaucrats to send money where it was not needed, *thank you very much*. "And," declared the self-sufficient bankers in a flurry of altruism, "we recommend that these funds be used where they are so badly needed at this time."[15]

Bankers who gathered in Blackwell in September 1932 agreed that business conditions were improving. As evidence, they pointed to the state's corn, cotton, and wheat crops and fair pastures. "Better things definitely are in the offing," said Oklahoma Bankers Association president H. G. Hendricks of Tulsa. "The backbone of the depression probably was reached in June. One of the most important things is the public psychology. I have noticed a decided tone of optimism among men who have studies [*sic*] conditions."[16]

And talk about optimism! "There was not a recession in sight," wrote Blaine County banker Bert Willis, whose Bank of Canton had seen deposits skyrocket from a postwar low of $102,000 to $245,000 in 1929. "We had our weather eye out for one, too, as bankers are always prone to look rather to the dark side. To all intents and purposes everything was running smoothly and the financial stream was filled with big fish, playing around in the deep, cool and pleasant streams and pools of prosperity. We were making money again and the goose was hanging high with a ham hock in every pot and two cars in every garage."[17]

If backers of the First National Bank Building and the Ramsey Tower in Oklahoma City had enough confidence in the future to build skyscrapers and gamblers had the gumption to bet on the race; if a banker of M. L. McClure's stature and experience was reminding Tulsa bankers of how fortunate they were; if Panhandle bankers were thumbing their collective nose at relief funds; if the president of the Oklahoma Bankers

Association thought that the (small *d*) depression had already run its course; and if a Blaine County banker could wax poetic to describe his bank's affluence—then how bad could things really get?

The answer was: plenty. But before Oklahoma joined the rest of the world in its downhill slide, Frank Johnson and his brother, Hugh, gave their adopted state something to crow about. The brother bankers had emigrated from Kosciusko, Mississippi, to the Oklahoma Territory in the 1890s and, after a few false starts that typified frontier entrepreneurship, had affixed their stars to the banking industry. Frank was president of the American National Bank in Oklahoma City, and Hugh was president of the First National Bank of Chandler before moving to Oklahoma City to become president of the First National Bank. After several years of competing from opposite corners of Main and Robinson, the Johnsons merged their institutions in 1927 to become the First National Bank and Trust Company of Oklahoma City. Their crowning achievement was, in the words of pioneer newspaperman Angelo Scott, "the truly wonderful 33-story First National Bank and Trust Company building"—a marvel of design and architecture, a symbol of the confidence that two frontier bankers placed in their adopted state, and a sure bet to win the Great Skyscraper Race of 1931 against what Scott described as "the slim and stately Ramsey Tower, also 33 stories."[18]

The bank building was slated for occupancy on or before October 1, 1931, but construction was not completed until November. On November 28, the transfer of the bank's safety deposit boxes took place under the scrutiny of forty guards armed with automatic weapons and shotguns. Employees were careful to avoid dropping any "private stock" that might have been in the boxes. In the days of Prohibition, an accidental spill might have left quite a mess, not to mention a scandal.[19]

While most of the nation's businesses were running for cover, the First National Bank building opened to the public on December 14, 1931. The structure was 55 percent occupied (an impressive figure in comparison to occupancy rates in the East) when the bank moved into the first four floors and basement. Officers and directors had decided against a gala opening, but plenty of folks showed up anyway for a public viewing. And what a view it was! The building was the fourth-largest structure west of the Mississippi, contained more aluminum than any building in the world, and was crowned with an aviation beacon visible from a distance of a nearly a hundred miles.[20] One stationary beam pointed toward the municipal airport to guide aviators, while the other revolved.[21]

The great banking room on the second floor was a simplified reflection of Italian Renaissance design and architecture. King Tutankhamen's tomb, discovered nine years earlier, influenced the bird and foliage patterns. Saint Genevieve rose marble was used for the wall wainscoting, counters, and the lower sections of the room's giant white columns. Marble for the flooring was quarried near Rome at Tivoli, Italy, brought by steamer to New York City, and shipped by rail to Oklahoma City. Modern amenities included pneumatic tubes to carry messages throughout the bank, a miniature post office where mail was prepared and sorted directly for the trains, and a women's lounge, complete with telephones and a writing alcove.[22]

Dominating the great banking room was a vaulted ceiling featuring a 23-by-84-foot skylight. The lobby opened from street level onto a marble staircase. Four murals by Edgar Spier Cameron—*The Louisiana Transfer, The Sunset Trail,* and two others depicting *The Run of April 22, 1889*—served as testaments to Oklahoma's frontier heritage. Just off the main lobby on the second floor were roomy, comfortable suites, "furnished in taste and simplicity," for the bank's officers: Hugh M. Johnson, chairman of the board; Frank P. Johnson, president; and Charles W. Gunter, chairman of the Executive Committee and vice chairman of the board. A native of LaGrange, Mississippi, and former insurance man, Gunter did not know the Johnsons back in the Magnolia State, but we can be sure that he and the brother bankers found opportunities to celebrate their southern heritage. As one newspaper reported at the time of the First National Bank's opening, "Although each of the trio of financiers has been away from the 'old home state' for many years, Mississippi still remains a 'second home.'"[23] R. A. Vose rounded out the executive team as president of the First National Building Corporation.[24]

On the fourth floor was the directors' room, where the sixty-one men who sat on the First National Bank's board of directors were to hold their sessions. Unlike old-fashioned assembly rooms with conference tables, the boardroom was comfortably furnished in a modernistic style that was in vogue at the time. Nearby on the fourth floor was the trust department. The savings department was located on the first floor. And far below in the basement were a vault with a twenty-eight-ton door and a state-of-the-art security system "planned for the present and future safe keeping of the personal property of Oklahoma City citizens."[25]

Even the Great Skyscraper Race of 1931 could not obscure the gathering storm. From 1930 to 1932, commercial banking nationwide was plagued by a vast increase in suspensions, an even greater contraction in the number of banks, a gradual but steady decline in deposits and commercial loans, an increase in investments in U.S. securities, and a clamoring for liquidity as anxious depositors put whatever they could in savings accounts.[26] Total commercial bank suspensions from 1930 through 1932 reached 5,096 (1,350 in 1930, 2,293 in 1931, and 1,453 in 1932), leaving untold thousands of individuals and businesses with no way to redeem their savings and checking accounts. Commercial bank suspensions were augmented by mergers and consolidations that brought the number of banks lost to a staggering 6,224. The hunt for liquidity produced a vicious circle as bank failures intensified the crisis, and the crisis spawned more bank failures. Savings accounts were vaporized, the money supply nosedived, prices collapsed by a third from peak to trough, and real interest rates shot above 10 percent, crushing institutions and households that happened to be in debt.[27]

Unemployment was the most visible face of the Depression. It peaked at thirteen million in 1933, leaving images of soup lines and squalid refugee camps seared forever into the national consciousness. As the Depression ground on, people who were employed but hanging on by a thread defied their unions' leadership and took to the streets, sometimes in a hail of bullets, to demand higher wages and decent working conditions. Using a tactic pioneered by rubber workers in Ohio, many sat down on the job and refused to budge until either their demands were met or they were hauled off to jail. According to one estimate, 1.5 million workers in a wide range of industries, from longshoremen on the West Coast to teamsters in the Midwest to textile workers in the South, went on strike in 1934.[28]

Oklahoma's favorite son, Will Rogers, captured the mood of an angst-ridden nation in a radio address on October 18, 1931. Immortalized as the "Bacon and Beans and Limousines" speech, the cowboy-philosopher cut straight to the chase before the next speaker, President Herbert Hoover, stepped up the microphone. "The only problem that confronts this country today is at least 7,000,000 people are out of work," declared

Rogers in his signature Oklahoma twang. "That's our only problem. There is no other one before us at all. It's to see that every man that wants to is able to work, is allowed to find a place to go to work, and also to arrange some way of getting a more equal distribution of the wealth in the country."[29]

In Oklahoma City, the mounting crisis was reflected in building permits whose value plunged from $24 million in 1929 to just over $20 million in 1930 to less than $1,600,000 in 1932.[30] The Depression reached its nadir in Oklahoma City in 1933, when building permits totaled a paltry $1,441,894 for the entire year.[31] Bank deposits were another barometer of the misery index. At the First National Bank and Trust Company of Oklahoma City, deposits slid from $65 million in January 1930 to $30 million in 1933, thus forcing the bank to limit credit at a time when people were in dire need of loans.[32] Dwindling deposits came as no surprise as Oklahomans lost their jobs in droves. In March 1930, 33,000 Oklahomans were jobless. That number skyrocketed to 80,000 September 1931 and to 117,000 in August 1932.[33]

Statewide, bank failures were draining the life out of communities. In December 1928, 336 state banks and 325 national banks in Oklahoma reported combined resources of $567,878,087. In 1930, there were 301 state banks and 264 national banks whose resources had declined to $474,506,598. By December 1932, only 253 state banks and 224 national banks remained solvent in Oklahoma, and their combined resources were $327 million. Heavily dependent on livestock, land, and crops for security, bankers were powerless to stop their loan collateral from declining in value by more than 50 percent between 1929 and 1932.[34]

"It was hard to place the blame for the depression, though many tried," wrote Bert Willis, the quintessential country banker who, along with his brothers, always considered the Bank of Canton in Blaine County "as an ordinary small bank." Far from centers of power but close to the Depression's most vulnerable victims, Willis offered an analysis that has an all-too-familiar ring. Lacking in erudition but chock-full of homespun wisdom, Willis's take on the debacle of his day survives as a testament to capitalism's tug-of-war with democracy:

> We don't know that it would have helped if the blame could have been placed, but it would be nice to know, just in case. We smaller fry blamed the big boys for financing the stock market

men, and they in turn blamed the manipulators and managers of the market and the manipulators blamed Wall Street, and thus the merry circle. In my poor way of thinking it was the man that wanted easy money, or maybe it was the gambling spirit, and we are possessed more or less with that. There is always insecurity in fast dealing and fast dealing and quick money seemed to be what the people demanded. It was a vicious circle. Sorter like a dog chasing its tail, always snapping at it, but never getting close enough to bite, and then again what would have happened if he had taken a bite of his tail.[35]

It was not long before the enveloping gloom manifested itself on the city's streets. In January 1931, a food riot broke out in Oklahoma City when three hundred unemployed people carrying a banner emblazoned with the slogan "Don't strike, don't starve, fight" stormed Standard Grocery in a desperate bid for food. Later that year, 576 families were camping in tents along the North Canadian River in what became one of the nation's only city-sponsored shantytowns. To mitigate trespassing and to protect private property, the city council in early 1932 approved construction of a de facto Hooverville near the river between Pennsylvania and Blackwelder Avenues and asked residents either to pay $1.00 or eight hours of labor per month for squatter's rights.[36] In keeping with its philanthropic mission, the Junior League gave $1,000 to the Committee for Relief of Unemployed Women in the fall of 1931, and in June 1932 it launched the Health Center in Walnut Gove. Charitable efforts notwithstanding, hundreds of indigents remained without shelter and slept on the ground when a cold front blasted through the city in November 1932.[37] Now on the last leg of their journey from frontier to region, Oklahomans saw little cause for celebration as they found themselves in just another outpost of pain and misery.

As though they did not have enough to worry about, bankers were besieged by a wave of bank robberies. American banks suffered 310 holdups in the six months ending February 28, 1931, compared with 193 attacks during the same period in the previous year, making for an increase of 61 percent. Moreover, as James E. Baum explained to a sullen group of bankers at an American Bankers Association meeting in Augusta, Georgia, in April 1931, most of the depredations were committed in twelve central and southwestern states. Baum, who was in charge of the ABA's crime investigations, blamed weak and ineffectual laws, disconnected and inadequate police powers, and a lack of security in the nation's banks for the current scourge.

"Bank bandits strike where resistance is weakest," explained the veteran crime fighter, "not only within the banks, but also where police protection is largely in the hands of constables and sheriffs whose work is localized and seldom permits the time or facilities to match present day criminals and their high-powered automobiles and firearms." Baum recommended radio as the most efficient means of communicating with police departments and called upon bankers "to help secure it as standard equipment."[38] Oklahoma City time lock inspector P. N. McKee suggested time locks as the best protection money could buy—even in an age of good roads, fast cars, and automatic weapons. "The holdup artist cannot wait half an hour while this timelock is running down, but the banker can predetermine his requirements and can wait."[39] For a mere $300, McKee's company could furnish a bank with a safe and time lock, delivery included, and install it inside the bank vault.

The Bank of Canton's time lock was of little use when robbers came calling in 1933, "the very peak of hard times." Called to the countryside on insurance business, Bert Willis returned to the bank and was puzzled to find the door locked. He procured his key and opened the door, only to find himself and two customers who had followed him into the bank staring down the barrel of "the biggest gun you ever saw." Then came a gruff voice ordering him and the two bewildered customers to "'stick em up,' and up went six hands so high that they raked the cobwebs off the ceiling." Willis quickly ascertained that three robbers had taken command of the building and had ordered his brother, Oliver, to open the safe. Informed that the time lock was engaged and that the safe could not be opened for an hour, the robbers decided to wait it out and kept their captives subdued at gunpoint.

All were understandably scared, but Bert's niece, Ruth, "was just as mad as she was scared. She could have bit one if she could have got her teeth near him. She kept looking them over very carefully and so much so that the guardian of the inner circle took exception to it and told her to keep her eyes forward and not so much on him or the other two." Right on cue, the timer on the safe expired, and the robbers helped themselves to about $1,300 before seizing Oliver as a hostage and making their getaway. "They let Oliver out about a half mile west of town and vanished in thin air. They never was seen again, and even though we went to several places where they picked up suspicious characters, we never got a trace of them."[40]

To make matters worse, insurance was hard to come by. "In those days it was difficult to get holdup insurance," wrote Willis, no doubt with hard-earned sympathy for the insurance companies. "That was account of robberies taking place so often and this was especially true in country banks." Even if insurance could be obtained, it was prohibitively expensive, and it came with strings attached such as mandatory closings at noon, the installation of expensive equipment, and a requirement that at least two employees remain in the bank at all times—all quite sensible, but mostly unfeasible for small country banks. Bert and his brothers did manage to secure a policy for $1,000, "but even at that we had to pay a high price for it."[41]

Target-hardening technologies and insurance policies were certainly a welcome addition to the banker's arsenal, but they did little to deter Oklahoma's most notorious outlaw: Charles "Pretty Boy" Floyd. In a typical heist, Floyd and his accomplice, George Birdwell, robbed the First State Bank of Stonewall on April 21, 1932. The pair took off with about $600 and two bank officers as hostages to shield them from armed citizens who caught wind of the robbery and gathered at the bank. Within minutes, police radios crackled to life, and heavily armed officers fanned across the countryside to intercept the duo. "It was truly a modern robber chase," ran an account in the *Blackwell Morning Tribune*. "Instead of the clatter of horse hoofs, the whirring of airplane propellers, the burr of high-powered motor cars and the incessant wireless operations filled the air." Two airplanes, one piloted by none other than Wiley Post who led the "aerial posse," were dispatched from Oklahoma City to scour the south central Oklahoma countryside. Another airplane took off from Pauls Valley. Heavily armed officers on the ground and in the air knew all too well that Floyd had vowed never to be taken alive. A confrontation would surely mean a gunfight to the death.[42]

In November 1934, an outraged citizen named Hugh Zimmerman of Omega took to the skies after the First National Bank of Okeene was robbed "by three desperate yeggs." Moments after hearing the news, Zimmerman cranked up his homemade "Model T sky-wagon" and swooped across the plains until he spotted the getaway car. The *Oklahoma Banker* captured the drama: "As soon as he sighted the car he zoomed down within a few feet of it to see if he were following the right prey, and was rewarded by seeing the robbers poke their heads out the car windows and point guns at him." Undaunted, the flying vigilante set his plane down near a filling station and told an attendant to alert the authorities. A high-speed chase on the ground and acrobatics in the air ensued until Zimmerman ran out of gas and had to land. Down below, the robbers evaded capture by pushing their car across a dry creek, slicing through a wire fence, and escaping on another highway. The Oklahoma Banker added its voice to a chorus of tribute for the aviator-turned-lawman: "Too much praise cannot be given Hugh Zimmerman for the courage and cool nerve he exercised in volunteering to follow these robbers and if the gasoline had not given out he could have kept them in sight until the officers effected a capture."[43]

If there was a silver lining in the clouds that hung over those dreary days, it was that most of the money stolen from banks was recovered, and many of the crooks were put in jail. According to a survey conducted by the Oklahoma Bankers Association, only 1 percent of the $62,241 looted in thirty-four robberies in the first eight months of 1932 was never recovered. Fourteen robbers had received prison sentences, two were killed, and numerous others were awaiting trial.[44] Good news, to be sure, but scant consolation to officers who were gunning for Pretty Boy Floyd.

Throughout the early 1930s, bankers used the Oklahoma Banker as a forum to analyze problems and suggest solutions stemming from the meltdown in global finances, and their essays and speeches were often printed in their entirety. In September 1930, R. S. Hecht, president of Hibernia Bank and Trust Company of New Orleans, addressed the general session of the American Bankers Association convention in Cleveland, Ohio. His catalog of banking woes included bank failures, unit banks' struggle to survive against a tide of branch banking, rising agitation in favor of branch banking, and rumblings of change in Federal Reserve policies that, among other things, would liberalize rules governing the eligibility of paper for rediscount. Recognizing that every American had a stake in resolving these problems, Hecht urged his audience to welcome public participation in debates that raged across the land.

Among the most contentious issues was the dual banking system that allowed state and national banks to compete for customers under entirely different systems of regulation. With the ghosts of Jefferson and Jackson howling in protest, there was a rising chorus of support among bankers for bringing all banks under a single jurisdiction "in the interest of economy, efficiency and sound banking uniformity." Drawing an analogy between the federal system of government and state and national banks, Hecht urged caution. "I do not think that analogy is far-fetched," he said. "The states should not surrender all political jurisdiction to the central government, and the local business life of the states should not be made to surrender all control over financial functions to national financial instrumentalities. There are many variations of business conditions from state to state and there are special fiscal requirements of the various states." Moreover, Hecht believed that state and national banks helped each other insofar as they provided models for one another to emulate: "A great many undesirable competitive inequalities have been wiped out by this mutual evolutionary process and further progress along the line of uniformity so far as is desirable is anticipated."[45] Debates notwithstanding, it seems clear that the new culture of capitalism spawned by progressivism at the turn of the century was fostering among bankers what Walter Lippmann recognized in 1914 as "fellowship in interest, a standard of ethics, an esprit de corps, and a decided discipline"—all antidotes to runaway competition, and all evidence that the hell-for-leather ethos of the frontier had given way to bonds of cooperation.[46]

In an address to bankers on December 9, 1930, William A. Erwin, dean of men at Washburn College in Topeka, Kansas, waxed sociological to assess the future of banking. Eschewing a narrow focus on banking issues, Erwin spoke about the economic and social revolution that was churning across the land. The advent of chain stores, the exploding size of business units ("We have right now at least a dozen billion-dollar corporations, and there are more on the way"), democratization of business ownership even as control was devolving into fewer hands, a shift in population from rural to urban areas, increasing mobility as more and more Americans took to the road in privately owned automobiles, chronic unemployment, and troubles on the farm were weaving the American fabric into an entirely new pattern. All these changes were unfolding against the backdrop of a depression of historic proportions. Erwin jumped the gun in seeing good times just around the corner. But he was onto something in his prediction of the Depression's legacy to

Abandoned farm near Felt in Cimarron County, 1939. Courtesy Oklahoma Historical Society.

future generations: "But when it is finally at an end, we will likely find that it also has been contributing its share to the revolution in our economic life."[47]

Erwin did not need to remind his listeners that banking was the mainspring of the economic machine and that it, too, was in a state of upheaval. Billion-dollar corporations were finding their counterparts in billion-dollar banks. Group and chain banking, never far from the center of controversy, were threatening stand-alone (unit) banks with outside capital and marketing muscle. Smaller banks were learning to pool their resources through mergers and consolidations. New types of financial institutions were cropping up to offer services ranging from automobile and industrial financing to investment trusts to provide investors with the twin pillars of prudent investing: security and diversification. Meanwhile, an alarming number of banks were withdrawing from the Federal Reserve System, taking out state charters, and adopting plans and policies that ran counter to the National Banking Act. Finally, banks buffeted by change were being liquidated, either voluntarily or otherwise, and leaving depositors, borrowers, and stockholders in the lurch.

Among the many causes of bank liquidations, Erwin singled out excessive competition as a primary culprit. "It used to be the idea that 'competition is the life of trade,'" opined the college dean, perhaps with an eye on Kansas's frontier legacy. "If that were true, somebody would have to explain why modern business is trying so hard to get rid of it by means of trade agreements, mergers, consolidations and the like. As a matter of fact, we have discovered that competition is the death of business. And surely bankers, in these past few eventful years have been overdone by competition."[48]

As conditions went from bad to worse, the *Oklahoma Banker* welcomed authors with a flair for history to weigh in on the Depression. Alexander D. Noyes, financial editor for the *New York Times* and an authority on the Panic of 1907, placed the Depression in a historical context in an address to the Eastern Savings Conference, held under the auspices of the American Bankers Association, at New York's Hotel Roosevelt on January 28, 1932. For Noyes, the current troubles had much in common with the Panic of 1893 insofar as both events consisted of two distinct panics. Just as the Depression began in the fall of 1929 with a financial breakdown in the U.S. stock market and deepened with a European crisis in 1931, so, too had the Panic of 1893 begun with a crisis in London in the fall of 1890 that eventually manifested itself in the American economy in 1893.[49]

If historical perspective failed to cheer his audience, then maybe his prognostications of better times to come did. Noyes based his predictions on a sanguine assessment of the Federal Reserve System and the beneficial role that the government played in an increasingly global economy:

> Fortunately, there is reason to believe that the time is coming when the United States will resume its proper place. . . . Our government has set the example in the courageous pledging of the public resources to meet the real needs of the situation and stop the ravages of panic. Our banks will follow, and in due course our investors also will come to their senses, and people will begin to understand the real part which the conditions of the day assign to the United States in the recovery from this period of depression.[50]

It took Franklin Delano Roosevelt two days to travel from his home in Hyde Park, New York, to Washington, D.C., for his inauguration as the thirty-second president of the United States. At no time during that tortuous trip was he able to forget the momentous task that awaited him, or the disease that was eating away at the nation's banking system. Upon his arrival on Thursday, March 2, 1933, the weather matched the mood of his fellow citizens—bleak and somber, with a winter rain settling in. By the next day, unwilling to wait for federal action, twenty-two states had already declared banking holidays to alleviate pressure on their beleaguered banks.[51] Among them was Oklahoma, whose governor, the indomitable William H. "Alfalfa Bill" Murray, had decreed a bank holiday in his state on the same day that Roosevelt arrived in Washington, D.C., to assume the mantle of national leadership.[52]

Even as Governor Murray and State Banking Commissioner W. J. Barnett decreed that banks would close from 9:00 A.M., Thursday, March 2, until 9:00 A.M., Monday, March 6, 1933, they and others in positions of authority scrambled to assure Oklahomans that the situation was less dire than it was elsewhere. The three-day holiday affecting the state's 255 state banks and 220 national banks was not forced on the state by the condition of Oklahoma banks—which the duo assured a jittery public was "better than in any time for more than 18 months"—but rather by the moratorium that was declared in Michigan and replicated in other states. "Fortunately," declared Murray and Barnett in a joint statement, "we feel that our Oklahoma banks are particularly free from the load that injured the banks of Michigan and other eastern states; namely, their freedom from loans on real estate and the ownership of industrial stocks and bonds."[53]

Fears were further allayed when First National Bank and Trust Company of Oklahoma City president Frank Johnson's front-page editorial in the *Daily Oklahoman* was published on March 2, the first day of the bank holiday. Under the headline "City's Banks in Splendid Condition," Johnson dipped into his reservoir of historical knowledge to remind readers of another crisis that was mitigated by calm, yet decisive, action: "Many will remember 1907—when all Oklahoma banks closed for a week. In the second week of the holiday the banks opened under the partial payment plan. Thereafter the payments were increased weekly, or twice a week, until normal business was being transacted and nobody lost a dollar.... This is a time for cool heads and courageous leadership. Let every merchant carry on business as usual."[54]

Neither Governor Murray's sanguine outlook nor Frank Johnson's historical perspective was enough to persuade Herbert H. Champlin, president of the First National Bank of Enid, to close his bank. Thanks to Champlin's insistence on plowing earnings into his business, the Champlin Refining Company grew to become the world's largest family-owned oil company engaged in every phase of the business, from drilling and refining to operating service stations. But Champlin, who had been involved in banks long before he went into the oil business, was a banker at heart, and he was determined to stand by his depositors in their hour of need. His disgust with President Hoover's economic policies was but a prelude to his frustration with Roosevelt's and, by extension, with Governor Murray's high-handed management of the banking crisis. Declaring that his bank's national charter put it beyond the state's reach, Champlin became the only banker to defy the governor's edict.

For three days, Governor Murray tried in vain to persuade Champlin to close his bank. On March 4, the exasperated governor dispatched the state militia to Enid to begin a drama that came to symbolize Oklahoma contrariness.

"Everybody knew that they were going to shut the bank down," explained Champlin's great-grandson, Joel Champlin.[55] Folks in Enid knew something else: H. H. Champlin would figure out how to have the last word. According to family lore, they were not disappointed. As an expectant throng milled in front of the bank, Champlin was enjoying a cup of coffee with the national guardsmen who had been dispatched to pry him from his bank. After an amiable chat and perhaps a couple of refills, he asked to be carried through the front door. The guardsmen complied, and photographs of a small-town banker being evicted from his bank at the behest of a power-mad governor seared themselves into the collective memory of a Depression-weary nation.

Not for the first time and certainly not the last, Oklahoma was in the precedent-setting business. According to *Time Magazine,* the incident marked the first bank closure by armed force in the history of American banking.[56] Once planted on terra firma, Champlin addressed the crowd with words that surely caused a ruckus in the governor's mansion and that could still make his great-grandson laugh out loud: "Okay, everybody, you can go home. The state's in charge. The government's in charge, so everybody can just go home. We'll be open—you can have your money as soon as the state will let it go!"

Then as now, bankers seek advantage when they can. "He got a lot of P.R. mileage out of it," concluded Joel Champlin, clearly relishing a chance to tell one of his family's favorite stories. "It must have been good!"[57]

Down the road from Enid in Canton, the Willis brothers were enduring their own Depression-era troubles, and they were probably not surprised to see folks come out in support of their hometown banker. "The whole community was concerned in the affairs of the bank for there is nothing much worse and affects more people than a bank failure," wrote Bert Willis. "It takes years to get over one of those things. Most of the people gladly worked with the banks. Our own customers knew that we were having a hard time of it, because they were having a hard time of it." Like their customers, the Willis brothers were scraping by on modest incomes. Bert's monthly salary was eighty-five dollars, Oliver's was fifty dollars, and Clay refused any salary at all. Willis explained, "Both had outside interests which brought them in a little. As for the bank stock, we all had that, but was [sic] not a money producing asset. In fact it was in danger of not being any asset at all, but a liability."[58]

Theatrics of a different sort played out at the American National Bank of Sapulpa. Lewis Jackson, a major shareholder and bank director, decided that a bit of showmanship might be the ticket to boosting depositors' confidence in their bank. Third-generation banker Bill Berry, chairman of the rebranded American Heritage Bank and member of a family that has been at the center of northeast Oklahoma banking since 1912, explained what happened: "One day, when I guess the bank had a lot of concerned customers in the lobby, Lewis Jackson came in with a suitcase, and had some bills sticking out of the edge where the suitcase was closed. He threw his suitcase up on the teller stand and said, 'Deposit all my money in the bank!'" Bill and his brother, bank president Guy Berry III, chuckled at the memory of a story that might be more apocryphal than factual, but is nonetheless representative of plucky Oklahoma businessmen who steered their banks through the Depression. "This had kind of a calming effect," concluded Bill, "as he was known to be a very successful oil man at the time."[59]

Just as Frank Johnson did his part to ease tensions in Oklahoma City (but not, apparently, in Enid), so, too, did President Roosevelt muster his considerable rhetorical skills to soothe the nation's frayed nerves. In his inaugural address on Saturday, March 4, Roosevelt borrowed a line from Thoreau when he declared, "Let me assert my firm belief that the only thing we have to fear is fear itself."[60] Having dispensed with the pep talk, Roosevelt unleashed a tirade against the nation's money changers that resonates to this day in political lore. Why, he asked rhetorically, was the nation mired in a depression? "Primarily, this is because rulers of the exchange of mankind's goods have failed through their own stubbornness and their own incompetence, have admitted their failure and abdicated.... Practices of the unscrupulous money changers stand indicted." Waxing biblical, Roosevelt thundered on: "The money changers have fled from their high seats in the temple of our civilization." Sharing his listeners' distrust of bankers, the new president called for strict supervision of banking, credit, and investments, and an end to speculation with other people's money as the only way to "return that temple to the ancient truths."[61]

President Roosevelt's bombast found its match in the oratory of Senator Burton K. Wheeler of Montana, who declared, "The best way to restore confidence in the banks would be to take these crooked presidents out of the banks and treat them the same way we treated Al Capone when he failed to pay his income tax."[62]

As the invective rained down from the White House, Congress, the media, and a fed-up public, support mounted for punitive regulations against banks. Lost in the heated rhetoric were the voices of scholars, who perceived bankers more as victims of ill-conceived government policies than as the scoundrels depicted in the court of public opinion. As H. Parker Willis of Columbia University, arguably the most respected academic on banking at the time, noted at the end of a congressional investigation into the causes of the banking crisis: "A fair examination of the facts disclosed by the Senate investigation leaves the feeling that but few persons, relatively, have been examined, and that these, while often 'prominent' are not in themselves representative of either banking or business. We must, accordingly, reject entirely the notion that—so far as these inquiries show—there has been a revelation of demonstrated crookedness on the part of American finance, trade, and banking at large. There has been nothing of the sort."[63]

Voices of reason notwithstanding, the president's pledge to "a new deal" for the American people was electrifying. "America hasn't been as happy in three years as they are today," quipped Will Rogers. "No money, no banks, no work, no nothing, but they know they got a man in there who is wise to Congress, wise to our so-called big men. The whole country is with him."[64] As usual, the plainspoken pundit was right on the money: the new president received 450,000 messages that confirmed Rogers's outlook. Less famous but no less prescient was Bert Willis, whose own Blaine County as well as nearby Kingfisher County voted solidly for Roosevelt, and whose take on the new president's popularity was surely on target:

> It was no surprise for practically every farmer and most business men that were consulted were for the change. They were not so much for anything as they were agin [sic], but they were tired of the depression and were for anyone that had a promise, and it didn't make very much difference what the promise was. They were looking for some one that knew what to do, or at least had some kind of a remedy, whether it was sound or hair-brained. Don't think they stopped to think, just so it was a change and different from what had been experienced.[65]

Roosevelt wasted no time in fulfilling his promise of decisive action. On March 5, 1933, he launched his "Hundred Days" war against the Depression by invoking the Trading with the Enemy Act, passed in 1917 to give the president the power to oversee and restrict trade between the United States and its enemies in times of war and to outlaw the hoarding of gold. As far as Roosevelt was concerned, declaring a nationwide banking holiday was fully justified under the 1917 law. The genius behind Roosevelt's plan, dubious under the Constitution but brilliant in terms of gaining credibility for his fledgling administration, was to extend the scope of the law to the crisis at home. With Congress's blessing, the expansive law confirmed what was already happening throughout the land, including Oklahoma.

Relying on precedent from the Panic of 1907, scrip was used to make up for the dearth of legal tender. Under Hubert Hudson as chairman, Edgar T. Bell as secretary-treasurer, and civic leaders as trustees, a cash reserve association was formed in Oklahoma City. Printed on special safety paper and slightly larger than ordinary currency, the scrip served its purpose for six days. Headquarters to sell and exchange the scrip were set up in the First National Bank Building under the direction of P. E. Pulley. The plan was delayed when President Roosevelt declared that the four-day bank moratorium would begin on Monday, March 6, and called for a nationwide system of clearinghouse coupons as a medium of exchange. Roosevelt's initiative prompted Governor Murray to question the legality of the homegrown scheme, but when Monday and Tuesday passed and no clearinghouse coupons made their appearance, the cash reserve association ignored the governor and opened its office on Wednesday, March 8, for the sale of scrip. It was sold only to reliable firms in blocks of $1,000, and a premium of $10 per $1,000 was charged to meet expenses. Checks were taken in payment only after receiving a check for the deposit at the bank and signed agreements that the purchasers would guarantee the check.

Three hours after the office opened, $34,500 in scrip was in circulation. That number rose to $95,500 at the close of business. By Saturday, $135,294 was greasing the wheels of commerce. About 250 stores accepted it at full value, and soon it was in general use. Until the banks opened on Tuesday, March 14, cash reserve association scrip was the only money in circulation in Oklahoma City. Issued in denominations of $1.00, $5.00, and $10.00, the scrip featured a picture of Oklahoma City's skyline and the slogan "City of Progress." Vestiges of frontier boosterism were evident when the *Daily Oklahoman* praised the scrip plan as one of the most successful emergency measures in the nation.

When real money resumed circulation, scrip poured into the cash reserve association office faster than it had gone out. All of it was redeemed at full face value—all, that is, but $729 that was never claimed. By the time Oklahoma celebrated its fifty-year jubilee on April 22, 1939, celebrating the opening of the Oklahoma country to non-Indian settlement, the last bit of unredeemed scrip reposed in scrapbooks and musty desk drawers. Records remained on file at the First National Bank and Trust Company, and cash reserve association officials burned the redeemed scrip in a ceremony.[66] We can only assume that Oklahoma City's most venerable bank was well represented at the bonfire. Whatever incantations were offered to summon happier days were lost to the smoke and ashes.

Oklahomans were just getting used to their new currency when, on Thursday, March 9, the cascade of change in the nation's banking system went into overdrive. After forty-three minutes of debate in the House and slightly more leisurely consideration later that day in the Senate, Congress passed the Emergency Banking Relief Act of 1933.[67] Title I confirmed the president's authority to declare a bank holiday under the terms of the 1917 Trading with the Enemy Act; Title II gave the comptroller of the currency additional powers to reorganize banks; Title III facilitated the reorganization of weak banks by authorizing them to issue a new class of preferred stock; and Title IV permitted the issue of Federal Reserve notes backed by government obligations rather than gold. Following passage of the act, 4,500 employees at the Bureau of Engraving and Printing began working around the clock to get untethered currency into circulation.[68]

We rely on Walter Bimson, president of the Valley National Bank in Phoenix, Arizona, who earned a reputation as one of the nation's most vocal cheerleaders for renewed lending, to capture a sense of the drama that heralded the dawn of conservative banking when the congressional roll call was broadcast that day on the radio.[69] His memory of that extraordinary moment is preserved in his memoir, *Financing the Frontier: A 50-Year History of the Valley National Bank,* published by the bank in 1950:

> It is a momentous and historic occasion, because this probably means the beginning of a new day in the banking business—and the beginning, may we hope, of the end of the Depression, which has held us and the rest of the world in its cruel grip.... For days, we have been under a strain that is now beginning to show on the faces and in the temper of the officers. I feel weary—very weary—but well, and now even my weariness is forgotten in the tenseness of this moment.[70]

On Sunday, March 12, 1933, President Roosevelt delivered the first of his fireside chats from the upstairs study in the White House. An estimated 60 million Americans turned on their radios to hear the president's prescription for the nation's ills.[71] Not surprisingly, his topic was banking. "I want to talk for a few minutes with the people of the United States about banking," intoned the president in the soothing cadence that would do so much to restore confidence to the battered nation. "I can assure you, that it is safer to keep your money in a reopened bank than under the mattress."[72]

The president's message hit home, and when banks reopened that week, the money flowing into the nation's banks was matched by the confidence that crept back into people's outlooks. An avalanche of federal legislation ensued, all aimed at putting people back to work and putting money in their pockets. Roosevelt had not only turned radio into an integral part of his political arsenal, but he had also shown a disillusioned citizenry that the federal government was on their side, and that regulations emanating from Washington, D.C., were lighting the path to a brighter and more inclusive future. Starting with the first fireside chat, Roosevelt won the nation to his side by offering to help citizens understand their plight and by convincing them to participate in the actions of their government.[73]

Closely related to the banking overhaul was Roosevelt's determination to curb financial abuses, particularly in the securities markets. Writing to Congress on March 29, 1933, the president stated: "What we seek is a return to a clearer understanding of the ancient truth that those who manage banks, corporations, and other agencies handling or using other people's money are trustees acting for others."[74] Within a year, the Securities and Exchange Commission (SEC) was flexing its muscles to make the stock exchange less of a gambling casino and to insist on transparency throughout the securities markets.

A milestone in the effort to pull America from the abyss came at 11:45 on the morning of June 16 when Congress passed the Banking Act of 1933. Better known as the Glass-Steagall Act after its congressional sponsors, Senator Carter Glass (D-Va.) and Representative Henry B. Steagall (D-Ala.), the new legislation embodied structural reforms in the banking system destined to carry the nation's banks to century's end. With the stroke of a pen, a firewall went up to separate commercial banks, which took deposits and made loans, and investment banks, which originated, traded, and distributed securities. Even though most small-town bankers never dabbled in the securities business and were unaffected by Glass-Steagall, the law sent a strong message to Wall Street financiers to stop operating their banks like casinos.[75] But passage was anything but foreordained. "This bill has more lives than a cat," declared President Roosevelt before affixing his signature. "It has been declared dead 14 times in the last few months and it finally came through."[76]

The Glass-Steagall Act provided for a Federal Deposit Insurance Corporation to begin operations on January 1, 1934. "This act was the magic carpet on which the depositors could tread," wrote Bert Willis, "and of all the things of the Roosevelt administration, this one act probably done [sic] more to restore confidence and alleviate the situation and assist in recovery than any other act."[77] Under the auspices of the FDIC, all bank deposits up to $2,500 were to be insured 100 percent. On July 1, deposits up to $10,000 would be fully guaranteed. Seventy-five percent of deposits between $10,000 and $50,000, and 50 percent of larger ones, would be protected under the new insurance regime.[78] The FDIC would start with $500 million in capital acquired from the sale of stock to the Treasury Department and the Federal Reserve banks. Later, banks would be required to contribute a portion of their deposits to the fund. President Roosevelt, whose skepticism of large-scale public works spending was matched by his opposition to the federal guarantee of bank deposits, accepted both only when it became clear that Congress had jumped on the bandwagon.[79]

Oklahomans and their neighbors up and down the plains must have experienced a collective case of déjà vu as the government promised that no citizen would ever lose a penny on insured bank deposits. The *Boise City News* summed up the nation's acceptance of a law that had been pioneered in Oklahoma: "On New year's Day, American banking, prodded by Uncle Sam, turned over a new leaf. On that day, the Glass-Steagall banking law, with its deposit insurance feature, went into effect. As a result, the nation's depositors never again may experience the widespread loss of life savings, forfeiture of homes and general distress which always have trailed in the wake of bank disasters."[80]

All banks that were members of the Federal Reserve System were required to join. Others had the option to join until July 1936, at which time enrollment would be compulsory. In provisions that brought down the curtain on frontier banking once and for all, the Glass-Steagall Act of 1933 weakened the connection between speculation and banking.[81] No longer could banks maintain affiliates to underwrite securities, join in market pools, and engage in stock transactions on behalf of customers. And no longer could the nation's money changers serve on boards of industrial, retail, and commercial companies to manipulate the marketplace with impunity. Adolph A. Berle, a member of the White House brain trust, summed up the new ethos of banking after passage of the

Glass-Steagall Act when he told an audience of bankers that, from now on, they were to be bankers only, eschewing speculation and acting as "responsible heads of their institutions at fixed salaries."[82]

Not everyone was thrilled with the new legislation. Back in Oklahoma, State Banking Commissioner W. J. Barnett was downright skeptical. "The Government has gone into business—it has gone into the banking business," he complained in a fall 1933 speech. "Can any of you ever recall our Government doing anything half-way?" Presumably in the absence of protests, Barnett injected history with a dose of frontier optimism to outline what he believed to be the future of his profession:

> It seems to me that we are at the threshold of a new era in banking. January 1, 1934, will be the dawn of conservative banking. The conservative banker will come into his own, for the hand of the "wild-catter" in banking has been called by the Government. Hereafter, banking is going to be a profession—not merely the vehicle of speculation. I believe as a profession banking holds the greatest promise for men of courage, ability and leadership, and that the success of the individual banker in the future will be determined by his reaction to such a challenge. The spirit of America is the life of America. It has been since the Boston Tea Party. I know the banker of the future will be the spirit of America by being the financial life of America.[83]

The closing of the frontier and the dawn of conservative banking put speculators and entrepreneurs on notice that banking was a profession and no longer simply a route to easy profits. Thanks to state and national banks and building and loan companies, cities were built, industries were lured to Oklahoma, and farms were brought up-to-date with scientific methods of land management, all with the enthusiastic support of the Oklahoma Bankers Association, chambers of commerce, and commercial clubs that did their part to spread the gospel of economic development. Derricks that had belched and spewed toxins across the prairie were tamed, properly financed, and linked to a labyrinth of pipelines to bring heat to people's homes and fuel to their cars. Wealth derived from oil and gas deposits was unevenly distributed, to be sure, but it nevertheless lifted the state from a neglected backwater to a center of commerce and industry.

As frontier scarcity gave way to industrial abundance, bankers acquiesced to installment buying and advertised their services in ever more innovative ways. Billion-dollar corporations were becoming the new norm, and billion-dollar banks were rising to meet their needs. Some looked at their old nemesis, branch banking, as a wave of the future that deserved thoughtful consideration rather than outright condemnation.

President Roosevelt's fireside chats aimed at soothing the nerves of a frayed nation, and broadcasting of congressional hearings on impending bank legislation in 1933 heralded the emergence of radio as a powerful force in shaping public opinion. Some greeted the nascent technology with enthusiasm bordering on mania, claiming that its ability to wrap a far-flung nation in ever-tighter webs of communication mitigated whatever perils it might pose for the common good. Others, convinced that motion pictures had worked enough mischief on popular culture, warned that radio was debasing what was left of cultural refinements, polluting the air with propaganda, and spreading a pall of homogeneity across the land. One thing was certain: radio was but the latest manifestation of mass culture that was forging a new world, and neither bankers nor the customers they served, accustomed to the norms of frontier banking, would be immune from its effects. The daunting challenges that mass culture raised, and the trade-offs listeners found in broadcasting, became staples of American life. Mass communication made the emerging modern world all but impossible to avoid.[84]

Even as businessmen and bankers were learning the most effective uses of mass media, symbols of safety that had lured skeptics to deposit their money in frontier banks were becoming less important in fostering confidence than federal regulations. Designed as a palliative for bank panics, the Federal Reserve System was facilitating the flow of currency and credit in ways that had been impossible during the post–Civil War era. Socialists who had challenged Oklahoma's two-party system and undermined sound business principles were branded as traitors in the wake of the Green Corn Rebellion of 1917. They were further marginalized as the fear of Communism took root after World War I. Even as Socialists were running for cover, bankers were rallying behind the banner of national unity to promote Liberty bonds as the surest way for citizens to stymie aggression in Europe and ensure peace and prosperity at home.

National unity was further reflected in a rising chorus of insistence on uniform banking practices. Long gone were the days of slow travel and spotty communication. Resistance to the revolution in communication and transportation was not an option. Simply put, the United States was no longer a collection of watertight compartments, but rather, an economic unit. "Therefore," wrote S. J. High, president of the American Bankers Association State Bank Division, "it is desirable that finance, trade and industry throughout the country operate along generally uniform or at least consistent lines, so that a contract or an agreement or obligation in connection with business transactions shall mean virtually the same thing in all parts of the country."[85]

Bank robberies, too, were becoming less frequent. Under the leadership of the Oklahoma Bankers Association, armed vigilantes put bank robbers on notice that their freewheeling days were over. In October 1934, James E. Baum of the ABA's Protective Department reported that the number of attacks on banks had fallen by a third nationally since the previous year, the first decrease since 1929. He cited three causes for the downward trend: the killing or imprisonment of professional bank robbers, including John Dillinger and members of his gang as well as Clyde Barrow and George "Machine Gun" Kelly; mandatory time-locking restrictions imposed by the casualty and surety underwriters on July 15, 1933, when they limited coverage on exposed cash; and more adequate protective facilities. Nearly fifty holdups in 1934 were stymied by target-hardening technologies, "proving that it can be done and that protective equipment is available to overcome the bandits' advantage of surprise attack."[86] Men whose weapon of choice was a pen rather than a gun faced increasing oversight, and more certain retribution.

Efforts to guarantee state bank deposits in Oklahoma and other western states by legislative fiat had gone down in flames, only to be resurrected in 1934 when the federal government, under the auspices of the newly created FDIC, responded to a crisis of epic proportions. By then, the total number of banks had declined to half of its 1920 number, and those whose banks survived the Depression had lessons galore to pass on to future generations. Writing in 1953, cowboy-turned-banker Bert Willis dipped into his repertoire of western metaphors to describe his trials as a community banker in Blaine County: "We never did believe in the idea that when a man came in for a shot of encouragement in the arm to shoot him in the pocketbook first. We felt also that we could ride it through if we were good enough riders. In passing let me say that at one time it was my portion to ride bucking bronco's [sic], but let it be said for the record that none of them ever bucked with so much effect as this thing we were riding."[87]

While Bert Willis was hanging onto the toughest bronc he ever rode, private banks were disappearing, and issues of national banknotes were fading into history, even as they earned iconic status on collectors' shelves.[88] Often flying by the seat of their pants to rescue a nation in peril, policy makers of the 1930s created precedents that, for better and worse, have remained as guideposts for later generations. Just as their decisions set the tone for banking policy for much of the twentieth century, so, too, will bankers of later generations chart banking policy for the remainder of the twenty-first.

Through it all, bankers were never far from the action as these and other episodes in banking and commercial history muscled their way into the national narrative. The surest sign that a frontier settlement might blossom into a thriving community was the establishment of a bank, and the more ornate and awe-inspiring, the better. As the frontier became fodder for entertainment, Wild West shows and rodeos were unlikely to include displays of prowess in double-entry accounting or drawing up loan documents. But we can be sure that bankers were behind the scenes, happy to accept deposits and provide some short-term financing, and to secure in their role as pillars of their communities.

Nurtured through a century of mass entertainment, mythic constructions of the West have given us a pantheon of heroes that still resonates in popular culture. Yet even as legends of the past morph into facts of the present, they remind us that there is no "real" history of the West, no history that can neatly excise its popular or legendary representations.[89] So maybe it is time to look beyond the larger-than-life heroes and fast horses that frame our understanding of the frontier. Then, maybe we will decide it is not only cowboys and gunslingers who deserve a voice in western history.

The fact is, frontiersmen were never quite the rugged individualists who populate the West of our imagination. Just as the lone cowboy would have been hard-pressed to bring his cattle to market and the sodbuster ill-equipped to raise his own barn, so, too, were bankers of little use outside the networks of cooperation that facilitated the flow of capital and credit. Those networks both expanded and tightened following the closing of the frontier in the 1890s as an ethos of regulatory compliance settled across the business landscape. Westerners were rugged individualists chiefly in their dreams (and in the dreams of their eastern and foreign admirers). In real life, they were likely to draw paychecks for digging in corporate mines, plowing corporate fields, and tending corporate cattle.[90]

The national community that flourished briefly during the Wilson war state was here to stay. To borrow an axiom from the sociologist Max Weber, who had witnessed the frontier's curtain call during his sojourn through the Indian Territory in 1904, an iron cage of rationality and predictability was putting an end to Oklahoma's penchant for experimentation that had distinguished the frontier from more settled regions. If bankers who witnessed and participated in the closing of the frontier did not exactly mourn its passing, they surely greeted the new culture of capitalism that reached its apogee in the New Deal with ambivalence, wondering how they and their descendants would fare now that Uncle Sam was calling the shots.

The end of their journey from frontier to region did not mean that Oklahomans were forgetting how to take care of themselves. First National Bank and Trust Company of Oklahoma City president Frank Johnson, a quiet and modest man, might not have handled a gun since his days as a military cadet at Mississippi A&M College. The same could not be said about his down-the-street neighbor, W.T. Hales, a real estate developer who owned an imposing mansion at the corner of Northwest Fifteenth Street and Hudson in Oklahoma City's posh Winans District. Papa Hales, as he was known, had made his money trading mules during World War I. He often said that he wanted to build a house big enough that he could drive a team of mules through the front entrance. Judging from the size of his dwelling, his housewarming party must have been quite a show.

Perhaps Frank Johnson's wife, Aida, was entertaining friends in her elegant home at the other end of the block and his daughter, Ethlyn, was grooming her steed for a horse show on the day Papa Hales discovered that the mild-mannered banker had been receiving death threats. No doubt itching for action in his all-too-respectable neighborhood, the onetime mule trader and would-be charioteer told him, "Don't you worry, Frank, I'll take care of you. I'm down at the end of the block, and I keep a gun on me all the time. If anyone comes around you, I'll shoot him!"[91]

Just another day of banking in Oklahoma.

PART II

Depression, Surge, Boom, and Bust

CHAPTER FIVE

The Home Front

> Trends are as inevitable as the tides of the sea. After the Crash in 1929 no human mind could erect a barrier that would check the avalanche and it is reasonable to assume that the climb now so definitely on the way will not be long interrupted even by economic, social or political stupidity.
>
> Walter B. Stephens, president, Oklahoma Bankers Association

Americans who came of age during the 1930s earned distinction as "the greatest generation" for persevering through the Great Depression, turning the tide of war against fascism, and proceeding in the postwar period to fulfill America's promise as a land of opportunity for anyone with the right stuff to succeed. "I am in awe of them, and I feel privileged to have been a witness to their lives and their sacrifices," wrote newsman Tom Brokaw in his paean to people who set the standard for grit and determination. "This is the greatest generation any society has produced."[1] Allowing for social norms that privileged white males, we continue to marvel at the sacrifices they made to ensure a better world for their children. Simply put, the greatest generation summons our deepest admiration. And when life's challenges come our way, who among us does not hope that we can be just as stubborn as they were in beating the odds?

Of course, not all members of the greatest generation were required to take up arms or confront stark poverty or maintain wartime production schedules in the nation's factories. Bankers, too, had their hands full, doing their best to facilitate the flow of currency and credit in the face of challenges that were shaking the foundations of the capitalist system. As key players in economic development, they shouldered the additional responsibility of building their communities over the long term, even as they responded to immediate crises on a daily basis. "It was imperative that we work with the borrower and gave [sic] them a chance to work with us," explained Blaine County banker Bert Willis. "The lesson of adversity is to work with people, whether in private life or in business. Any other attitude would have been fatal. We collected where and when we could, we extended and took additional security where we could and just trusted to the future to right the wrong."[2]

Expressing optimism that was a bit out of fashion in the spring of 1934, Oklahoma Bankers Association president Walter B. Stephens of Hobart discerned better days coming on like a force of nature: "Trends are as inevitable as the tides of the sea. After the Crash in 1929 no human mind could erect a barrier that would check the avalanche and it is reasonable to assume that the climb now so definitely on the way will not be long interrupted even by economic, social or political stupidity."[3] Stephens turned out to be right—economic trends in the 1930s were indeed pointing in the right direction. But that was easier to discern in hindsight than from the bottom of the trough, where he and his ilk were unwittingly staking their claim as members of the greatest generation.

Walter Stephens was not the only banker with an upbeat attitude. A week before the First National Bank and Trust Company of Oklahoma City welcomed the public into its new digs—"as magnificent a rhapsody in glistening stone and gleaming metal as ever graced the golden west"—in December 1931, bank president Frank Johnson was profiled in the *Daily Oklahoman*. His interviewer, coincidentally named T. T. Johnson, spared no hyperbole in describing Oklahoma and Johnson's bank as mirror images that reflected the can-do spirit of the frontier. "The history of this great western house of finance, interwoven as it is with the amazing growth and development of one of the nation's most progressive states, has taken color from pioneers and sons of pioneers, who in less than half a century, have turned virgin plains of buffalo grass into productive farms, Midas oil fields, and cities of glittering towers."[4]

Frank Johnson's gun-toting neighbor on Northwest Fifteenth Street, W. T. Hales, was a member of the bank's board of directors, and he had dropped by for a sneak preview of the First National Bank building when reporter T. T. Johnson arrived for his interview. Neither Frank Johnson nor Hales gave the *Daily Oklahoman* reporter a reason to doubt his claim that the bank trumped Edna Ferber's classic novel of old Oklahoma, *Cimarron,* in epitomizing the growth and development of Oklahoma. Johnson wrote, "In 1931, there they were: the school teacher, who became president of a great bank; the shrewd horse and mule trader, who became a director in that bank and one of the southwest's leading capitalists; and the bank in a frame shack, grown into one of the most magnificent structures in America ... Oklahoma epitomized."[5]

Walter Stephens's optimism was reflected in a trend toward long-term investments. In 1900, 49.9 percent of Oklahoma banks' assets were in loans and discounts, and only 2 percent was placed in investments. By 1920, 64.3 percent of assets were in loans and discounts, and the amount allocated to investments had risen to 8 percent. But in 1935, a dramatic shift in asset allocation was reflected in a ratio of 27.1 percent of bank assets in loans and discounts and 28 percent in long-term investments.[6] Bankers' willingness to allocate an increasing percentage of their assets in investments augured well for community and infrastructure development.

An indication of Oklahoma's prominence in national affairs came in August 1932 when three Oklahomans representing the Tenth Federal Reserve District were invited to President Herbert Hoover's Council of Peace: Waite Phillips, chairman of the board of the First National Bank and Trust Company of Tulsa; Lew Wentz, an oilman from Ponca City; and Frank Johnson of Oklahoma City. Summoned rather ambiguously "for the purpose of organizing a concerted program along the whole economic front," delegates were asked to make recommendations on issues ranging from industry and agriculture to employment, all in an effort to return the nation to prosperity.[7] According to a report from the National Association of Supervisors of State Banks, the nation's 13,902 state banks and 6,373 national banks reported total resources on December 31, 1931, of $63,130,550,964.10 and deposits of $50,214,192,615.59. Association secretary and treasurer R. N. Sims said the figures illustrated "how well the banks of our country have weathered the storm of depression."[8]

As Oklahoma bankers pondered the implications of trends in their profession and did their part to promote good governance, many used the *Oklahoma Banker* as a bully pulpit to express their views of the federal government's reaction to a nation in crisis. For the most part, editorials in the 1930s denounced government intrusion in banking as a threat.[9] "I am for any legislation that will bring about economies in government but cannot subscribe to more appropriations to dole out to the public," opined one banker in March 1932, nearly a year before President Roosevelt took office and raised doling out money to the public to an art form. "You cannot liquidate your indebtedness by borrowing more money," he continued. His opinion of the government's increasing role in business has a familiar ring to contemporary bankers who are enduring their own time of troubles: "The government should go out of business. Thrift, industry and economy must be practiced by the individual as well as the nation as we adjust ourselves to the simple life of the new régime."[10]

In November 1933, it was D. W. Hogan's turn to weigh in on an economy in free fall. At a meeting of the state chamber of commerce, Hogan, president of the City National Bank of Oklahoma City, expressed his opinion that civilization reached its zenith in 1913, when industrial nations bound by a commitment to free trade and laissez-faire economics were producing vibrant commercial cultures and spreading the fruits of industry across the globe. Since then, the United States had devolved from a debtor to a creditor nation, a tragedy compounded by a war to end all wars and a worldwide depression. "It was this financial confusion and bewilderment into which our country was plunged during the dying days of the Hoover Administration that caused the political revolution in the presidential election in the fall of 1932 which resulted in an overwhelming majority for Roosevelt." explained Hogan. After reviewing the revolutionary legislation of 1933, he described the guaranty of bank deposits as "unsound" and the "wild orgy of spending" in 1929 as a prelude to disaster. Nevertheless, he stopped short of condemning an administration that was reacting to a crisis of epic proportions. "We should realize that we are the Government," concluded Hogan. "That this is our city, our state and our nation. We have all our holdings invested in it. It, then, is our plain duty to stand by and support our government. We cannot expect the government to support us."[11]

E. A. Walker, president of the Tradesmen's National Bank of Oklahoma City, waxed biblical in his address at a bankers' convention in Lawton on February 22, 1934. "Be not deceived," intoned the banker-turned-preacher (for the moment, anyway) to his flock of financiers. "God is not mocked; for whatsoever a man soweth, that shall he also reap." In Walker's estimation, the current malaise had its roots in World War I, not only in terms of death and destruction, but also in the socio-economic dislocations spawned by the war and that played out in the Roaring Twenties. In the United States, those dislocations included the massive migration from rural communities to cities, a rising demand for credit as well-paid workers sought housing, and the collapse of the rural economy when the bottom dropped out of farm prices. Walker reserved special opprobrium for salesmen—thoroughly trained, universally optimistic, and determined to lure customers into the consumer nexus through installment buying. "The victims of this super-salesmanship found themselves in the position of owing not only much more than the articles were worth, but far more than they could ever hope to pay." Even as the twenties roared, what Woodrow Wilson called a "vicious circle" and Calvin Coolidge designated as a "profitless prosperity" was leading America down the road to ruin.[12]

Now that the reaping was in full swing, America's cities teemed with the unemployed, and the Roosevelt administration was redefining the relationship between business and government. As though they needed reminding, Walker told his listeners that the federal government could not appropriate money to employ people indefinitely. A more likely remedy for chronic unemployment was to encourage people to return to the countryside and rebuild the self-sufficient communities they had abandoned in pursuit of the good life. "In any State of the Union," declared Walker, "a good farm, properly cultivated and managed, will yield a comfortable living for the farmer and his family."[13]

While E. A. Walker was extolling the virtues of the yeoman farmer, he and his colleagues across Oklahoma were working hard to improve agricultural output. By the late 1930s, their efforts were paying dividends. Shocked by dust storms that were stripping farmlands of their topsoil and searing horrific images into the national consciousness, bankers redoubled their advocacy of scientific farming techniques such as terracing and initiated conservation drives. Realizing that highly educated experts might actually have something to teach self-sufficient farmers, the OBA hired W. H. McPheters, an extension agricultural engineer from Oklahoma A&M College (later Oklahoma A&M University, and later still Oklahoma State University), to educate farmers about soil conservation. Bankers also promoted and financed crop-improvement programs, especially regarding cotton and hybrid strains of wheat. In

A so-called country bank in Arcadia, 1937. Courtesy Western History Collections, University of Oklahoma Libraries.

1937, 9,464 people attended 103 countywide meetings in seventeen counties. By the end of the year, an estimated 235,218 acres of topsoil were preserved through terracing. In 1939, bankers formed the Wheat Improvement Association. During the presidency of R. R. Jackson of Anadarko, the OBA partnered with Oklahoma A&M College and the Millers' Association to finance thirty plots across the state where farmers planted varieties of wheat and tested their crops for quality and yield. When a healthy variety was developed, the OBA recommended it to farmers statewide.

Recognizing the importance of educating the future farmers of America, bankers poured time and money into the 4-H movement and provided scholarships to Oklahoma A&M College for agribusiness programs. Bankers' involvement in agriculture extended to sponsorship of contests, farm tours, and award ceremonies at county fairs for youth accomplishments. To single out a single example of the partnership between bankers and farmers, H. H. Ogden, president of the First National Bank and Trust Company of Muskogee, assisted seventy-three boys in securing purebred Hampshire gilts at a cost of about $2,000. Each participant in the program in 1937 received expert advice on developing a herd of hogs. Eventually, each participant repaid the bank in full for the money and credit that had launched them on their careers in agriculture.[14]

Less successful were attempts to address one of America's most vexing problems: land tenancy. By 1935, an estimated 2,800,000 of the nation's 6,800,000 farmers were tenants, and the average sharecropper's annual income was $312. The problem was even worse in Oklahoma, where an astounding 50 percent of farmland was worked by tenants or sharecroppers. As late as 1940, tenants were hard at work on more than 40 percent of the state's farms.[15] Still, bankers did what they could to lend money to tenants, particularly when it came to getting every possible acre under production to aid in the war effort. One way or another, bankers never wavered from their twofold mission: to generate loans, and to carry debtors as long as they could in keeping with sound business principles.

The Great Depression toppled banks and wiped out fortunes, but it never sullied Tulsa's reputation as the "Oil Capital of the World." Opinions differ on the origins of Tulsa's nickname. It might have entered the common vernacular as early as 1901, when oil was struck at Red Fork a few miles southwest of Tulsa and oilmen descended on the hamlet to seize a piece of the action. Or maybe it was in 1905, when the Sue Bland No. 1 roared to life on Ida Glenn's farm some fifteen miles south of Tulsa, that the designation stuck.

Whenever Tulsa became synonymous with the oil industry, one thing is certain: Tulsa's prominence as an oil center was due in no small measure to a bank with yet another well-deserved moniker—"the Oilman's Bank," the First National Bank and Trust Company of Tulsa, a pioneer in financing oil development and production.[16] Like all Oklahoma banks, the First National Bank and Trust Company of Tulsa had humble beginnings. Capitalized with $10,000, the bank opened as the Tulsa Banking Company on July 29, 1895, in a small, two-story building in the 100 block of Main Street. Principals included cattleman Jay Forsythe; his brother-in-law, B. F. Colley; and his son-in-law, C. W. Brown.[17] In 1897, nearly half of Tulsa's business district, including the bank, was destroyed in a catastrophic fire that prompted Forsythe to spearhead the organization of a volunteer fire department. The bank's safe was unharmed, and Forsythe and his associates reopened later the same day in J. M. Hall's store and remained there for several months while a two-story stone structure was built on the bank's original site.

A restructuring resulted in the injection of additional capital and the appointment of William H. Halsell, a cattleman from Vinita, as the bank's president. The bank received a charter as the First National Bank on January 3, 1899. By 1903, the bank's holdings totaled $117,835. Needing yet more space to accommodate growth, the bank relocated in 1905 to a five-story building—a veritable skyscraper described as the "the finest in the Southwest"—on the corner of Second and Main Streets. Built at a cost of $85,000, the bank featured Tulsa's first elevator and included such amenities as interoffice telephones and drinking fountains on every floor.

The First National Bank's growth paralleled and, indeed, facilitated Tulsa's emergence as the Oil Capital of the World. The bank merged with City National Bank on April 11, 1908, and the Oklahoma National Bank on July 10, 1911. Between mergers in 1910, the First National Bank's deposits grew to $697,979.21, and capital stock mushroomed to $125,000. It quickly outgrew its third building and, on April 19, 1918, moved into a ten-story building at Fourth and Main Streets. The bank's new brick and stone home—complete with an interior finished in marble, a ceiling trimmed in gold, and a special room where women could conduct their business beyond the prying eyes of men—was widely considered as an architectural masterpiece. A safe-deposit vault with a thousand boxes and a sixteen-ton door was in the basement.

Growth continued on December 31, 1920, when the First National Bank merged with the Union National Bank. By then, oilmen whose success is the stuff of legend, including Harry Sinclair, W. G. Skelly, W. K. Warren, and J. Paul Getty, had moved their operations to Tulsa. Tulsa's position as the Oil Capital of the World was cinched when Skelly brought the first International Petroleum Exposition (IPE) to town in 1923. The expo grew from 27 exhibits and attendance of 14,203 in its first year to 628 exhibits and attendance of 194,491 in 1940.

The Oilman's Bank went into overdrive in the late 1920s. On July 30, 1928, it merged with the First Trust and Savings Bank and was renamed the First National Bank and Trust Company of Tulsa to reflect its newly acquired power to manage trusts. It was the only bank in Tulsa to be granted such powers until 1948. Board member and oilman R. Otis McClintock agreed to serve temporarily as president until a permanent appointment could be made. His "temporary" position lasted for thirty-five years and forty-five days. The next merger came on

The International Petroleum Exposition, Tulsa, May 1936. The annual IPE branded Tulsa the Oil Capital of the World. Courtesy Western History Collections, University of Oklahoma Libraries.

June 22, 1929, with Tulsa National Bank. Following the consolidation, the First's resources exceeded $45 million, and its capital was an impressive $2.5 million. Filling the chairman's chair was oilman and philanthropist Waite Phillips, a Tulsan whose contributions to his community were beyond measure.

By 1930, Tulsa was home to 140,000 people and eight hundred oil and gas companies.[18] When the oil and gas cognoscenti wanted to know about the latest in petroleum technology, they flocked to the IPE. But when they wanted to shake hands on a multimillion-dollar oil deal, there was no better place to go than the Mayo Hotel. Opened in 1925, the eighteen-story, six-hundred-room edifice was the brainchild of Cass A. and John D. Mayo, brothers whose first successful project was a furniture store at Fifth and Main Streets. Their hotel, destined to reign as Tulsa's tallest building for only two years, was constructed by architect George Winkler in the Sullivanesque style of the Chicago School.[19]

John Mayo's daughter, Margery Bird, provided a child's perspective of a grand opening that resonates to this day in Tulsa lore. "I remember, that was when photographers had these flashlights—you know, the flash picture?—and my brother and I were scared to death," recalled Mrs. Bird more than eight decades later. "We cowered! My mother said the next day, when it was in the paper, 'Well, that was a good picture of you hiding behind me!'" Constructed of steel that was in ample supply after the armistice ending World War I, the hotel was a veritable fortress. As Mrs. Bird recalled, "There was an excess of steel, come the armistice, and so that was available to them for a foundation. So they always said that hotel was there to stand, having been built on a steel basis."[20]

Like his friend Otis McClintock, John Mayo never intended to remain in his position permanently. But when a manager dropped the ball, Mayo took on management responsibilities and never looked back. "It ended up being where he spent the majority of his life," said Mrs. Bird.[21] Cass Mayo helped his brother manage their varied interests from his office at the nearby Mayo Building, known to most as the Petroleum Building. Notable guests at the Mayo Hotel from 1925 to its closure in 1980 (and before its reopening in 2001) included President John F. Kennedy, Bob Hope, Charles Lindbergh, Babe Ruth, Charlie Chaplin, Mae West, and oilmen too numerous to count.[22]

John Mayo was a close friend of Otis McClintock and a lifelong member of the bank's board of directors. When he died, his son and Margery Bird's brother, Burch Mayo, filled the elder Mayo's seat on the bank board. Asked about the relationship between the hotel and the bank, Bird left no doubt about where her father and uncle received their funding. The First National Bank, she said with a smile, was the fountain "from whence the blessings flowed." The close relationship between the Mayos and the McClintocks ranks among Bird's fondest memories of a life spent at the center of Tulsa's commercial culture. "So having that dual relationship, both business and friend, made for a very interesting life, for me," she recalled. "I can even remember selling war bonds when the bank was at Fourth and Main Street, before the new building [was built] at Fifth and Boston."

Then again, relationships had a way of getting a bit too cozy. Bird, who described herself at the age of ninety-four as "a true antique," dipped into her repertoire of Tulsa lore to recount the time when Miss Jackson, the owner of Tulsa's most exclusive shop, was summoned to the bank to explain why she was behind on her loan payments.

"Well," responded the indignant shopkeeper to her inquisitors, "if some of your wives would pay their bills, I would not be delinquent!"

As to Otis McClintock's succession to presidency of the bank, Mrs. Bird was certain who pulled the strings. "I believe he [McClintock] was selected to become the president of the First National due to Waite Philips. Mr. Philips was very much a man behind the scenes, quiet, but I'm sure he spoke privately and effectively whenever it was necessary."[23]

By late 1932, the Great Depression was venting its full fury on Oklahoma City. To cite a single economic sector, oil refining payrolls dropped 33 percent, prompting the Oklahoma City Chamber of Commerce to counsel its members to "wait out" the storm before proceeding with development plans.[24] When the economy hit rock bottom in 1933, city officials were taking heat from Washington, D.C., for catering more to taxpayers than the unemployed. Accounts indicate that federal relief efforts allowed local officials to feel that they were off the hook.[25]

But when it came to crime, nobody was off the hook. While Pretty Boy Floyd was wreaking havoc in rural banks, a scoundrel wielding a machine gun was reminding wealthy Oklahomans of just how vulnerable they were. On July 22, 1933, George Kelly, best known as "Machine Gun" Kelly for his choice of weaponry, along with Albert L. Bates, burst into the home of oilman Charles F. Urschel in Oklahoma City and brought an abrupt end to his wife's bridge party. Kelly and his accomplice proceeded to abduct Urschel and his guest, Walter Jarrett, at gunpoint while their wives looked on in horror. With memories of the Lindbergh kidnapping still fresh in the nation's collective memory, news of Urshel's abduction by one of America's most notorious outlaws made the headlines nationwide. Urschel remained in captivity in a farmhouse near Paradise, Texas, for more than a week. He was released on July 30 after the kidnappers were paid $200,000 in documented bills. Blindfolded during his captivity, Urschel had the presence of mind to memorize details about his location, including the passing of an airplane at regular intervals, and enabled FBI agents to locate the hideout and, eventually, to put Kelly and his henchmen behind bars.[26]

Another milestone in crime prevention came on October 22, 1934, when Pretty Boy Floyd was gunned down in East Liverpool, Ohio, by FBI agents. With two of America's most notorious bank robbers out of commission, Oklahomans had a better shot at a good night's sleep. Oklahomans with a conscience, however, did not have much of a reprieve.

That same year, Oklahoma became the first of six states where the federal government ousted the local administration. Governor "Alfalfa Bill" Murray's administration was charged with corruption, failure to ask for sufficient funds, inability to meet employment quotas, and refusal to use social service case workers. Federal Emergency Relief Administration (FERA) director Harry Hopkins cited Oklahoma as one of fourteen states to fall short of its duty to provide aid to its own citizens. "I'm thoroughly fed up on states and cities passing the buck to us," raged the irate bureaucrat. "If you don't give two whoops about them [the unemployed] . . . why should we sit up nights in Washington worrying about them?"[27]

For the First National Bank and Trust Company of Oklahoma City, the best form of defense was clearly to go on the offensive. Advertisements in the *Oklahoma Banker,* usually placed in the inside front cover, touted the bank's longevity and commitment to sound banking principles to woo banks into its network of correspondent banks. "Here are a few of the reasons why you should choose the First National Bank and Trust Company as your Oklahoma City correspondent," ran an unambiguous ad in June 1932: "(1) It is safe; (2) Service is kept at a high standard; (3) Geographical location is a convenience; (4) Officers are men you know; (5) Items are cleared and collections made promptly; (6) Credit accommodations are ample."[28] In the next month's issue, the bank reported total resources of $50,780,365.59—hard to resist for bankers throughout Oklahoma who were considering their correspondent banking options.[29] In October, wordsmiths with a flair for catchy slogans and typography had their way. The First National Bank and Trust Company of Oklahoma City was "Not good because it is *big,* but big because it is *good.*"[30]

Not to be outdone, The First National Bank and Trust Company of Tulsa published an advertisement in November 1932 to commemorate the state's silver anniversary. Beneath a drawing of a rosy-cheeked boy and a collage of frontier images, the bank declared that it was twelve years old at statehood in 1907—brash, bold, and, like a healthy twelve-year-old boy, ready to take on the world:

> In Territorial days a boy of twelve was a man. He could ride a horse and rope and tie and brand a steer. He carried a gun,

knew how to shoot as well as a man—and sometimes had to. He was strong and self-reliant. Often he was the head of the family. Outwitting nature and hostile red men and roving outlaws sharpened his thinking ... but at heart he was a boy. And like our boys today, he had his hopes and dreams ... usually he wanted to own a herd of cattle, and later to own a bank.[31]

When the Banking Act of 1933 went into effect, the First National Bank and Trust Company of Oklahoma City included more than half of the banks in Oklahoma in its network of correspondent banks.[32] Meanwhile, advertisements were branding the bank as the only charter member still in existence of the Oklahoma City Clearing House and the one whose president, Frank Johnson, had been elected as the first president of the association. Celebrating its thirtieth year of operation in 1933, the Oklahoma City Clearing House was heir to methods of exchanging checks and settling accounts first proposed by Albert Gallatin, secretary of the treasury under President Thomas Jefferson, and pioneered in the United States in 1853.[33]

The First National Bank and Trust Company of Oklahoma City chose the *Daily Oklahoman's* fiftieth anniversary edition of April 23, 1939, to remind readers that its predecessor, the Oklahoma Bank, was up and running on the day settlers thundered into the land that is now Oklahoma to stake their claims to a new life: "In this our fiftieth year, we pause to express hearty appreciation to our friends and customers who are, in the truest sense, the builders of this bank ... to pledge anew our most sincere efforts to a continuation of the same cordial relations throughout the years to come."[34]

Having lost his only daughter, Ethlyn, to pneumonia in May 1931, Frank Johnson had much to think about on his walks to and from his office at the First National Bank Building in Oklahoma City. Rain or shine, he was a common sight as he walked downtown in the early morning hours. Compromised by poor health, Hugh likely did not accompany his brother on his walks. But others in the neighborhood—R. A. Vose, C. B. Ames, Dennis Flynn, George Sohlberg, and Charles Colcord—were likewise disposed to walking. One imagines a team of city builders, briefcases in hand and a spring in their steps, walking past the sycamores that

Partiers gather in the lobby of the First National Bank Building in Oklahoma City, 1941. Note the covered wagon in the background symbolizing the bank's genesis when the Unassigned Lands were opened to non-Indian settlement in the Land Run of 1889. Courtesy Oklahoma Historical Society.

Frank and his wife, Aida, had planted along Fifteenth Street to remind them of their leafy Mississippi homeland, and turning south on Hudson or Walker toward the business district that they had built.

Angelo Scott had been watching and working with men such as these since his arrival in the Indian Territory as an eighty-niner, and he knew something about their mettle. "I am not an expert in the lore of cities and do not know what manner of men have built other cities," he wrote in his 1939 classic, *The Story of Oklahoma City*. "But I cannot conceive that any other city has ever had, at every stage of its progress, more able, more devoted, more self-sacrificing, indefatigable, and unconquerable men to push it on to triumph over every difficulty than Oklahoma City has had and has today." Comparing those civic leaders to soldiers in the Great War, Scott insisted that "retreat" was not in their vocabulary:

"The men of Oklahoma City have never known when to retreat. They haven't given a single inch. They have fought as one man, shoulder to shoulder, year after year, decade by decade, through sunshine, storm, and near disaster. And they have conquered! Shall we not all salute them!"[35]

Typically, Frank Johnson had to wait for the bank watchman to open the door. His punctuality and the upbeat attitude it signified notwithstanding, he could not fool his contemporaries; they knew that the Depression weighed heavily on him, more so than his brother. "He could not throw off worry like his more complacent brother, Hugh," asserted one reporter. "If the record could be had, the truth would be that Frank Johnson wrestled through months of sleepless nights with the problems of 1930 and 1931." A profile in the *Oklahoma City Times* reveals an archetype of Oklahoma bankers who weathered the Depression—tortured souls whose commitment to their communities never faltered: "Johnson was tied to a wheel from which he could not get loose. Too many business men among those listed as the customers of a bank with $55,897,000 assets depended upon the judgment of the little gray-haired man who sat in his inside office behind a pair of round heavy glasses, smoked his big, black cigars, analyzed balance sheets and made decisions."[36]

Frank Johnson was at the pinnacle of his career when he was pictured on the front cover of the July 1935 edition of the *Oklahoma Banker*, not as president of the state's largest bank, but as an elected member of the Oklahoma Natural Gas Company's board of directors. At the close of business on June 29, 1935, his bank's resources were $55,897,594.50, and capital stock was $5 million. Clearly, the bank reflected Oklahoma's agonizing climb from a depression that set the standard for financial turmoil.[37]

On the morning of Saturday, October 5, 1935, Johnson attended a regular bimonthly bank directors' meeting, and he felt great. William P. Kattigan, a bank employee who took him home after the meeting around 2:00 P.M., later claimed that his boss seemed downright jovial: "I drove him home in my car and he remarked that it was such a beautiful day he would like to take a long motor trip," said Kattigan.[38]

Later that day, Johnson had his chauffeur, Albert Washington, drive him to the home on Northwest Eighteenth Street of his friend First National Bank director Samuel L. Gloyd, whose wife had died that morning. Within thirty minutes of arriving to pay his condolences, Johnson complained that he was not feeling well and asked Washington to take him home. Alarmed, Washington drove his employer home, carried him to his upstairs bedroom, and unfastened his collar.

By then, the heart attack that claimed his life was well under way. Dr. Stratton D. Kernodle was summoned to his bedside, but it was too late. Frank Pearson Johnson died at 10:15 P.M. in the company of his wife, Aida; her friend, Mrs. D. A. Richardson; Dr. Kernodle; and Albert Washington, his faithful chauffeur. Washington later reported that Johnson died in his arms. He was sixty-three.[39]

Frank Johnson's body lay in state at Hahn's Funeral Home. Services were conducted in the Johnson residence by the Reverend Paul S. Wright, pastor of the First Presbyterian Church, prior to Frank's interment in the family mausoleum at Fairlawn Cemetery. As a tribute to the late president of the "financial Gibraltar of the Southwest," banks in Oklahoma City closed at noon.[40]

Frank Johnson's sudden death sent shock waves through Oklahoma's banking community. Predictably, the *Oklahoma Banker* published a lengthy paean to a fallen comrade: "Frank was ever a town booster. His faith in Oklahoma City helped to make it what it is today. His magnificent contributions to the erection of the Commerce Exchange, the YMCA, and the Hightower Building, the Biltmore Hotel and the 33-story First National Bank Building will ever remain a monument to his civic pride. His decisions came after a ton of preparation but when he started down the road he never turned back."[41]

The *Oklahoma News* cut directly to the chase in describing the banker's role in shaping Oklahoma banking: "From his position as president of the largest bank in the state he gained control of many private industrial enterprises and his word was virtually 'law' to many leaders of industrial enterprises." He was credited with exerting sufficient leadership to bring stability to the oil business when "oil came to the city's back door." Other accomplishments catalogued in newspapers and magazines in the wake of Johnson's death included his active participation in the Democratic Party, directorship of the Biltmore Hotel Company at a time when Oklahoma City was struggling to maintain a metropolitan hotel, and leadership positions in the Oklahoma City Building and Loan Company, the Oklahoma Savings and Loan Association, the Oklahoma City Clearing House Association, the Oklahoma City Chamber of Commerce, the Presbyterian Church, the Elks Club, the Oklahoma University Club, and

Sigma Alpha Epsilon Fraternity.[42] "In all these years he lived among us, he went quietly on his way, climbing the ladder of business success without once faltering, and arriving at the topmost rung without any desire for a fanfare of trumpets to announce the fact. . . . He was gentle and kind, firm and fair, strong and wholesome, and he had the confidence of all who knew him."[43]

Friends and associates were quick to chime in with their own tributes. State Treasurer Hubert Bolen recalled that "Frank Johnson was always helpful to the state treasury. Whenever he had a lot of money to pay out, he always put up securities to accommodate us, and it never meant a penny to him. We were always grateful." Scott Ferris, a leader in the Democratic National Committee and Oklahoma Highway Commission, said that the "state of Oklahoma has lost one of its most influential business men. I personally lost one of my best friends. Oklahoma will feel keenly the loss of a man like Frank Johnson." Tradesmen's National Bank president E. A. Walker claimed that "Frank Johnson not only was an outstanding banker in the city, but in the state and country as well. He was a man of the highest character and great industry." Oilman F. C. Hall said simply that he "was one of our foremost citizens. We have lost one of our most valuable men." W. T. Hales, the gun-toting mule trader who lived down the street from the Johnsons, recalled his neighbor as "an energetic and upright man" who "was responsible for many new buildings in this city. We have lost one of the finest and most brilliant men the state ever had." Surely speaking for the entire board of directors of the First National Bank and Trust Company, vice chairman of the board Charles W. Gunter said, "I've watched Johnson's career for more than a quarter of a century, and in my opinion no man has been his equal in financial ability. In addition, he was genuinely an all-around friend."[44]

Politicians who no doubt remembered Frank's late father-in-law, J. P. Allen, as an able mayor from territorial days (1897–99) and loyal member of Governor J. B. A. Robertson's administration (1919–23) added their voices to the approbation. Former mayor Walter C. Dean (1927–31) remembered Johnson as "superior in business ability" and "a complete, honest friend." Mayor John F. Martin (1935–39) mourned the passing of "a man with a superlative knowledge of finance, and a sturdy character behind it."[45] Whoever penned Frank's obituary in *The Investor* took credit for finding a quality that had heretofore escaped notice: "There was one characteristic of this eminent Oklahoma banker that no publicist has, thus far, noted. His door was always open. The path to his desk was free to anyone who wished to travel it. His ear was alert to any proposal, acceptable or unacceptable. Merchants, industrialists, promoters, salesmen—all had their audiences. He never rejected a proposition without hearing it. Perhaps that trait of his business life contributed largely to his almost romantic success."[46]

Johnson's open door was no secret in Oklahoma City's African American community. Roscoe Dunjee, editor of the *Black Dispatch,* noted the passing of not only a pioneer banker but also someone who "for a quarter of a century loaned a sympathetic ear to every worth while [sic] Negro, or Negro organization, striving to press forward in the Sooner capital." Dunjee remembered Frank Johnson as a man who was always fair and never hesitated to extend advice on business, saving, establishing credit, and managing money—all sorely needed in Dunjee's neighborhood. In his lengthy tribute, the editor recalled an incident during the short-lived administration of barbecue-loving governor Jack Walton. The word on the street in the black community was that the Ku Klux Klan was fomenting a movement to oust the inept governor from office. Frank Johnson, along with other businessmen, had decided that banking interests would benefit from Walton's ouster, and he asked Dunjee to support a constitutional amendment that would allow the state legislature to convene without Governor Walton's participation. But Dunjee, principled in an era when African American principles did not count for much, could not in good conscience support an amendment that the Klan was endorsing.

Dunjee's subsequent troubles landed him in jail. The details are not altogether clear from his editorial, but no matter. The point is that he had a sympathetic ear downtown. Dunjee wrote that he would never forget how Frank Johnson had "hurried to the county jail to make a bond, releasing me from a two-hour confinement." Still, Dunjee stuck to his guns and refused to support the amendment. "I was forced to say 'no' to Mr. Johnson, my friend, that morning, but it is a great tribute to his liberalism and fine spirit in that it never made any subsequent difference with my relationship in the bank."[47]

The commitment to (small *d*) democratic ideals that Frank had displayed throughout his eventful life—from his stint as a cadet at Mississippi A&M College and subsequent career as a journalist in Kosciusko to teaching eighth grade in the Oklahoma Territory to the pinnacle of power at the First National Bank and Trust Company of Oklahoma City—never wavered. "Frank Johnson never said 'no' to hundreds of his Negro friends who weep at his bier today," wrote a bereaved Dunjee. "During the past week we have talked with fully a score of black men and women who relate similar stories about his kindly spirit and who know that one who lived in a house by the side of life's highway and was a friend to everybody, has passed across the golden strand."[48]

Charles W. Gunter, vice chairman of the board of the First National Bank and Trust Company of Oklahoma City, said it was unclear who would succeed Johnson as president.[49] As board members settled in for weighty discussions, the media launched into a frenzy of speculation. An article in the *Oklahoma City Times* on October 8 provided a roster of the candidates as well as glimpses, not altogether flattering, of their personalities and qualifications for the job: "Will it be Hugh, two years younger than his brother, slowed down by ill-health and recently pleased to do some traveling and catch up on his loafing? Will it be R. A. Vose, the small, quiet, fellow who is never seen in front but who, next to Frank himself, has been the most potent factor in the affairs of the First for many years?" Apparently, the smart money was not on Vose, because he cared little for "the window position" and was unlikely to take the helm and attendant responsibility. Other contenders included Frank Johnson's son-in-law, Billy Hightower, Kent Hayes, and R. A. Vose's son, C. A., better known as "Chuck." "These three junior officers are being groomed for high places," ran the newspaper speculation. "Their turns probably will come later."[50] The speculation ended on January 14, 1936, when Hugh Johnson was named president.[51] Although less outgoing than his late brother, Hugh came into the position with a wealth of banking experience and financial acumen. In spite of an asthmatic condition that sapped his energy, he maintained the stability and respect that had always been a hallmark of the bank's management team.

On April 28 of Hugh Johnson's second year as president, the state legislature passed the Banking Act of 1937. Its goals were threefold: (1) to provide more effective control over the creation of financial institutions; (2) to prevent bank failures and rehabilitate troubled banks; and (3) to provide for the orderly liquidation of doomed banks. The code of 1937 required the banking commissioner, who was appointed by the governor and served at his pleasure for four years, to have at least five years of bank experience; the assistant banking commissioner was required to have at least three years of experience. The Banking Act of 1937 also created fourteen positions for bank examiners and placed the power to grant charters in the Oklahoma Banking Board, consisting of the banking commissioner and three other people chosen by the governor.[52] Bert Willis, who complemented his responsibilities at the Bank of Canton with a four-year stint in the Oklahoma State Senate, claimed that the new banking code "remedied many evils and made other things clearer and made for better banking. There was quite some opposition to the bill but it passed."[53]

The new regulations made it more difficult to secure a charter, and capital requirements were restructured to reflect the size of communities in which banks operated. Somewhat paradoxically, the banking board refused to issue charters to bankers who failed to furnish deposit insurance protections offered by the FDIC, and the FDIC required a minimum capital structure of $30,000. As a practical matter, therefore, most institutions opened after 1937 needed $30,000 in paid-in capital. Other sections of the code included more stringent requirements for public disclosure and a mandate requiring the banking board to examine banks twice annually. Bank officers found to be incompetent, dishonest, or unwilling to abide by the new rules were to be removed. To prevent the concentration of funds, the code limited the amount a bank could loan to a single person or corporation to 15 percent of its capital and surplus.[54]

The Banking Act of 1937 was a milestone in progressive business legislation, and it signaled that Oklahoma was tying its future ever more firmly to national networks of finance and commerce. But that did not mean that Oklahomans were losing their flair for down-home celebrations. Even the lingering effects of the most serious financial meltdown in modern history and winds of war blowing across Europe and Asia were not enough to dampen enthusiasm for the fiftieth anniversary of the Run of '89. Business leaders across the state began beating their civic drums in early 1939, determined to link past accomplishments to a rosy future.

Adopting the slogan "Tepees to Towers," Oklahoma City held two massive parades in April 1939, one downtown and the other in Capitol Hill, which were enjoyed by an estimated 100,000 people. Determined not to let his sixty-five years slow him down, Mayor Robert A. Hefner rode a horse in both processions. The *Daily Oklahoman* printed 200,000 copies of a special edition on April 23 that ran 292 pages and consumed 870 tons of newsprint, which, if extended in a strip seventeen inches wide, would have covered more than 10,000 miles.[55] Speculating on the next fifty years, the Oklahoma City Chamber of Commerce used the special edition to rekindle the frontier spirit: "As Oklahoma celebrates its 50th anniversary, Oklahoma City stands on the threshold of a new Run—the Run of '39. What our accomplishments will be during the next fifty years we dare not say, but this much is certain, the motivating force behind Oklahoma City's future growth will continue to be the Chamber of Commerce."[56]

In his biennial report to the governor of October 13, 1941, State Banking Commissioner Linwood O. Neal gave official sanction to the upbeat mood. In 1939 and 1940, only two bank failures were reported, "both attributable to embezzlement rather than insolvency": the Bank of Amorita, where a $70,000 shortage was almost completely covered from deposit insurance; and the First State Bank of Stonewall, where deposit insurance also came to the rescue of depositors. At the beginning of 1939, twenty-four banks were in receivership in which liquidation had not been completed. Addition of the two failed banks made for a total of twenty-six banks in receivership for the two years covered in the report. With 90 percent of the state's 183 state banks on a dividend-paying basis as of December 31, 1940, Neal felt justified in reporting satisfactory progress. "Never before to my knowledge have they been in such sound condition," crowed the banking commissioner. "With few exceptions all are setting aside sufficient surpluses, undivided profits and reserves to meet future contingencies. Statistical information discloses that financial institutions of Oklahoma rank near the top in the nation with respect to sound condition."[57]

The fiftieth anniversary hoopla ended, and Oklahomans resumed their anxious vigil over the triumph of fascism in Europe and Japan. As a prelude to the dark days ahead, defense spending skyrocketed. On the eve of open hostilities, the military establishment was spending some $300,000 for vocational and defense training in Oklahoma City. At the urging of the defense industry, savings accounts reached historic highs. Department store purchases soared as wary citizens prepared for the shortages that were surely coming.[58]

But, as businessmen were quick to demonstrate, war clouds often had a silver lining. "In 1939 war broke out in Europe and to all intents and purposes the depression was over," wrote Bert Willis. "Wild and reckless spending was the order of the day and that was what took all the steam out of the depression. Roosevelt had tried hard and long but couldn't wring as much out of the depression in 8 years as the war did in 8 days."[59]

Under the leadership of its president, W. E. "Billy" Hightower, the Oklahoma City Chamber of Commerce pulled out all the stops to bring some of that wild and reckless spending to Oklahoma by luring defense industries to the state. Among Oklahoma's lures were its high percentage of "native born" people, the state's geographic location, a well-developed transportation infrastructure, ample supplies of power and fuel, an absence of industrial labor competition, and plenty of good weather for flying. There was even talk of using Lake Overholser as a training area for seaplanes, a prospect that did not seem so farfetched after Captain R. S. Fogg sat an amphibious craft on the lake to check out its possibilities.[60]

Billy Hightower, a onetime all-American quarterback at Northwestern University in Evanston, Illinois, and a veteran of the American Field Service in World War I, came by his business acumen honestly. His father was C. C. Hightower, one of Altus's founders and southwestern Oklahoma's most prominent bankers.[61] The younger Hightower launched his own banking career on January 6, 1919, when he became a trainee at Frank Johnson's American National Bank. His storybook wedding to Ethlyn Johnson on April 30, 1918, in the third-floor ballroom of the Johnsons' elegant home at 439 Northwest Fifteenth Street, surrounded by palms, ferns, and sweet peas in orchid shades and accompanied by excerpts from D'Hardelot and Wagner, certainly did not hurt his business prospects.[62]

Hightower's rapid rise in the ranks continued when he was elected vice president of the bank on January 1, 1923. He retained that position, as well as a seat on the board of directors, until the historic merger in 1927 between his father-in-law's American National Bank and his uncle Hugh's First National Bank created the First National Bank and Trust Company of Oklahoma City.[63] Devastated by his wife's death from pneumonia in May 1931 and his father-in-law's death from a heart attack in October 1935, Hightower poured his energies into raising his two small children, Frank and Phyllis; pulling his bank through the Depression; and filling out his civic portfolio to promote his state's economic development.

Hightower was one of fourteen business leaders who actively campaigned for military largesse. Meeting at the Oklahoma City Chamber of Commerce on October 16, 1940, the group formed the Industries Foundation of Oklahoma, Inc., a type of trust empowered to acquire land and erect facilities for lease and eventual sale to the federal government. Articles of incorporation were filed on December 10, 1940. The organization was funded when 291 men subscribed $294,500.[64]

Hightower succeeded S. W. Hayes as president of the Oklahoma City Chamber of Commerce in 1941, the same year that Oklahoma's first significant military post established since territorial days was opened southwest of Oklahoma City on land occupied by the Oklahoma City Municipal Airport. Military strategists planned to use the field as a training facility for aerial bombardment and photo reconnaissance. Given the embryonic state of commercial aviation and the scarcity of military funding between the wars, it only made sense for the military to share runways and air traffic control facilities with commercial aviation. Construction began in February 1941 on what was known simply as Air Base Oklahoma City. Its less prosaic appellation, Will Rogers Field, came in the spring and gave Oklahomans one more way to commemorate their favorite son, who had perished in an aircraft accident six years earlier in Alaska.[65]

Business leaders had plenty to crow about when Will Rogers Field was dedicated on June 28, 1941. But even as the development of Will Rogers Field was capturing the public's attention, R. A. Singletary, the Oklahoma City Chamber's manager of governmental relations in Washington, D.C., who was known in business circle as Oklahoma's third senator, caught wind of the Army Air Corps' intention to build three air depots: one on the East Coast, one on the West Coast, and another in the middle. There were also rumors that Douglas Aircraft Company of Santa Monica, California, was looking for a location for a bomber assembly plant. When it became clear that Oklahoma City was in the running—and, better yet, that the air depot would be permanent and require up to 2,500 civilian employees—Oklahomans quickly warmed up to the idea of adding defense work to their state's constellation of economic sectors.

But there was a catch: officials signaled that an assembly plant and an air depot would not be located in the same city. Judging that an air depot might offer more permanency than an assembly plant, Oklahoma City businessmen repaid Tulsans for their support when the Fed was eyeing Oklahoma City as a headquarters for the Tenth District Federal Reserve Bank by casting their lot with their cross-state rival to secure the aircraft assembly plant for eastern Oklahoma.[66] The gambit certainly helped, and on January 31, 1941, Tulsa's selection as the location for a bomber plant was announced. Built at a cost of $15 million, the Tulsa Bomber Plant produced medium and heavy bombers. At its peak, some 24,000 people worked around the clock between 1942 and 1945.[67]

Even as Tulsans were celebrating their good fortune in early 1941, the War Department announced that Cimarron Field west of Oklahoma City would be used as a primary training base. To keep land prices from skyrocketing in the area that might one day blossom into a major air depot, the Oklahoma City Chamber did its best to keep the wraps on its negotiations with the War Department. But as the weeks went by and visitors from Washington, D.C., came and went, people knew something big was in the wind. The speculation ended on March 10, 1941, when Congress passed an appropriation bill for three air depots, one of which was slated for construction in Oklahoma City. President Franklin D. Roosevelt signed the bill on March 18, and on April 8, Assistant Secretary of War Robert U. Patterson signed the project orders. The estimated cost for the Oklahoma City depot was $14,036,215, and civilian employment was expected to grow to 3,500.[68]

The facility was designated on May 21, 1941, as the Midwest Air Depot, Oklahoma City. On July 8, the army awarded a $14,270,000 contract for depot construction to Charles Dunning and Company, Patterson Steel Company, and T. L. James and Company. Founded by T. L. James in Ruston, Louisiana, in 1926, T. L. James and Company, Inc., grew to become James Construction Group, LLC, one of the largest general contractors in the Gulf Coast region. Formal groundbreaking ceremonies were held on July 30, 1941, and the base was officially activated on March 1, 1942. In August, the Oklahoma City Chamber of Commerce asked the War Department to rename the depot in honor of Major General Clarence L. Tinker, an Oklahoman of Osage heritage who had died in June during a bombing raid against Japanese positions on Wake Island. Within a year, the rechristened Tinker Field had a civilian workforce of nearly fifteen thousand. Not long after T. L. James and Company broke ground at Tinker Field, T. L.'s nephew, Dan W. James, bought the Skirvin

Hotel in downtown Oklahoma City. From 1945 to 1963, James and his son, George W., applied their extraordinary people skills to branding the Skirvin Hotel as the go-to place for business deals and festive gatherings.[69] Tinker Field's link with Oklahoma banking families came in 1949 when Dannie Bea James (Dan's daughter and George's sister) married Frank Hightower (Billy's son and Frank and Aida Johnson's grandson). In the ensuing years, expansions at Tinker and Will Rogers Fields and the Tulsa Bomber Plant, together with military spending at other facilities across the state, bore testimony to the bankers and businessmen who fought successfully for Oklahoma's share of military spending.[70]

Luring military facilities to Oklahoma was not the only way that bankers blended business and patriotism. In a replay of the Liberty bond drives that sped the Allies to victory in World War I, Oklahoma financiers played a leading role in five bond issues between 1941 and mid-1944 that brought in $145,323,074 in bonds and stamps, an amount that represented 134 percent of the state's goal of $108 million. Every county in the state exceeded its quota, with Tulsa County leading the charge and Oklahoma County coming in a close second in bond purchases. At the same time, bankers redoubled their efforts to improve crop yields and increase efficiency on the farm. Under the slogan "The Flag on the plow as well as on the battleship and the tank," bankers promoted everything from victory gardens for personal consumption to soil conservation, seed improvement, and silos for storage of excess food. And while the world came apart at the seams, bankers continued to bet on the future farmers of America to make the world a better place. Attention and funding for youth programs paid off when youngsters in the 4-H program purchased $99,500 in war bonds and stamps by June 1942—about as seamless a blend of business and patriotism as one could imagine in those trying days on the home front.[71]

First National Bank and Trust Company of Oklahoma City president Hugh Johnson died in his sleep in the early morning hours of Monday, January 10, 1944, one day before the annual stockholders' meeting. His death at the age of seventy was greeted with less fanfare than his brother's passing nearly a decade earlier. An account in the *Daily Oklahoman* attributed his death to a slight cold, compounded by an attack of influenza the previous week, and rendered fatal by many years of suffering from asthma. Services were conducted in his spacious home at 420

Northwest Fourteenth Street on Wednesday, January 12, and he was laid to rest next to family members in Fairlawn Cemetery.[72]

Once again, the bank was thrown into turmoil. But not for long. Only five days after Hugh's death, Billy Hightower was elevated to the presidency. R. A. Vose, whose association with Frank and Hugh Johnson began in 1904 when he joined the American National Bank's board of directors, was selected as chairman of the board. Vose retained his position as president of the First National Building Corporation and continued at the helm of the Southwestern Cotton Oil Company, the business that had wooed him to the Oklahoma Territory at the turn of the century.[73]

Directors were pleased with the smooth transition. Under the leadership of Billy Hightower and Vose, all things were possible.

Early the next month, Billy Hightower's son, Frank, phoned home with distressing news. Aida, Frank Johnson's widow, had been visiting her grandson in Washington, D.C., where he was preparing for a career in the diplomatic service, when she fell ill. Bewildered and far from home, Frank Hightower did what any young person would do in such circumstances. He called his dad.

Billy Hightower was a take-charge kind of man, and he knew what to do. He summoned his pilot, Roy O. Hunt, to take him and his daughter, Phyllis, to Washington, D.C., in the Lockheed 12 that he co-owned with his friend and associate in oil drilling ventures, Leslie Fain.[74]

Hunt was tired. He had recently logged many miles in the air. And he knew that storms were brewing in the East. He also knew that Billy Hightower was not one to take "no" for an answer.

The first thousand miles or so went without incident. But, sure enough, storm clouds were gathering over the Appalachian Mountains. Fog and rain became sleet. Visibility plunged. Ice formed on the wings. Low on fuel, Hunt dropped altitude and made for the nearest air field.

Four miles northwest of Elkins, West Virginia, and 160 miles short of its destination, the plane slammed into Rich Mountain.[75]

Billy Hightower and his daughter, Roy Hunt and his wife, and copilot George Ruddy died on a wooded hillside in West Virginia on Friday, February 4, 1944. Hightower's friend Leslie Fain was so distressed upon hearing the news that he suffered a fatal heart attack. Frank Johnson's widow, Aida, died a more peaceful death in Washington, D.C., in the company of her grandson, Frank, whose ambition of a career in the Foreign Service was sacrificed to pressing responsibilities at home.

Presidency of the $140 million institution passed to R. A. Vose. Although he had been associated with the bank since becoming a director of the American National Bank in 1904, it was not until his election as chairman of the board on January 15, 1944, that he held a leadership position. As reported in the *Daily Oklahoman,* Vose preferred "to remain in the background as a director." Vose's successor as chairman of the board was L. B. Jackson, a director as well as an oil producer and chairman of the board of the American National Bank of Sapulpa, which he had helped to organize. Mrs. Hugh (Mary) Johnson, still grieving from her husband's death in January and now charged with making funeral arrangements for Billy Hightower and his recently married daughter, Phyllis Penn, was elected to succeed Billy Hightower on the board of directors. A. J. Peters, a vice president, was advanced to executive vice president.[76] Just graduated from Yale University and mourning the loss of his father and sister, twenty-one-year-old Frank Hightower was in no position to join the board of directors. Frank Porter, one of Billy Hightower's closest friends and associates, was chosen to serve in his stead.[77]

Thus ended the Johnson/Hightower era at the First National Bank and Trust Company of Oklahoma City. Taking a cue from Walter B. Stephens, who believed that trends "were as inevitable as the tides of the sea,"[78] Vose and his fellow bankers on the home front might have taken solace that the Depression was over and the tide of war was turning in the Allies' favor. From February 1944 to the bank's demise in the troubled 1980s, the Voses steered the venerable institution through challenges and opportunities beyond the ken of their predecessors. Over the years, they and, indeed, the entire community of Oklahoma bankers never left much doubt about their profession's role as a catalyst of community development, and its importance in shaping state and local history.

CHAPTER SIX

Postwar Oklahoma

> Somewhere down the line, the thought must be brought to our national leaders that there is such a thing as regulating a particular industry to death, and the demise of the free enterprise financial system we have will ultimately be the demise of this country's greatness.
>
> H. E. "Harry" Leonard, Oklahoma state banking commissioner

Anyone who made it through the Great Depression and World War II knew better than to take anything for granted. Americans were so traumatized by the twin scourges of unemployment and deflation that they looked to the federal government to keep up the spending and accepted inflation as the price of security. Postwar administrations were happy to oblige with inflationary programs that included price supports, housing loans, tax reduction, and a wide range of easy-money policies. "We can understand quite readily why it is necessary for the government to have what is called loose money," wrote Blaine County banker Bert Willis. "They have built a big program and it takes money to support the program and the only way to get big money is to have easy money."[1]

Even though government spending dropped to 40 percent of its wartime peak, it was still 4.6 times greater than its five-year prewar average.[2] Once dismissed as radical by apostles of free-market capitalism, John Maynard Keynes's prescription of government spending to stimulate the economy found a vast laboratory in postwar America, where two lessons from the Depression were slowly sinking in: (1) cures are not automatic and recovery is not inevitable; and (2) government spending is crucial to renewed economic growth. Ideological differences notwithstanding, the evidence was unambiguous. Keynesian economics worked. America was on a roll.[3]

The postwar boom—remembered as the "golden age" or "long boom" in English, *les trente glorieuses* in French, and the *Wirtschaftswunder* in German—lasted until the early 1970s, and it saw income per person in most developed countries more than double.[4] At the risk of oversimplification, the good times flowed from a constellation of six factors. First, low levels of production since 1930 had built up substantial demand. Second, six years of bombing and strafing had destroyed facilities that were becoming obsolete, prompting one economist, with due deference to the dead and maimed, to characterize World War II as "a giant program of economically useful demolition."[5] Third, the war broke down barriers to mobility of labor and capital and, in the process, facilitated the development of technologies that could be used for peaceful purposes. Fourth, population reversed its decline to produce a baby boom of historic significance. Fifth, government spending followed the Keynesian model to become a vital component of economic growth. Finally, existing technologies such as electricity were exploited to their full potential by entrepreneurs who took advantage of the government's expansive programs and amassed the wherewithal to succeed.

Entrepreneurship extended to financial services as well, most notably to the fully amortized home mortgage. Ironically, one of the hottest financial instruments, the mortgage-backed security, emerged from the urban riots of the 1960s. It was intended as a safe way for industrial unions to invest their pension funds, but wound up as the vehicle of choice for hot-money investment banks seeking ways to evade geographic and state boundary restrictions on lending.[6] As ownership structures became more flexible and leverage became more available, productivity surged.

New Deal legislation left its legacy in the "mixed economy" in which government served the dual role of business partner and referee, and it spawned a debate about the proper role of government in the economy that has never subsided. Two broad conclusions can be drawn from FDR's sometimes ad hoc attempts to revive the economy. First, the New Deal was not so much a descent into what business leaders assailed as socialism as it was a conservative effort to save capitalism. Emergency banking legislation sought not to dismantle the business system and replace it with something else but rather to amend the system to make it succeed. Second, the New Deal forged a new economic relationship between citizens and their government. Numbers tell the story of the federal government's role in boosting the economy: whereas federal spending of all kinds amounted to about 2 percent of gross national product (GNP) in 1929, it was closer to 25 percent in 1970.[7] For Oklahomans with an eye on history, the success of Keynesianism spelled trouble for rugged individualism, which remained central to American self-identity long after the frontier faded into history. Yet the basis for rugged individualism and its manifestation in laissez-faire economics had long since been eroded by the success of the industrial economy, a fact that was lost on bankers and business leaders who yearned for a return to some golden age that existed more in mythology than history. Long before FDR put Keynesian economics to the test, laissez-faire had shown itself to be an anachronism—a vestige of an America that had ceased to exist, if indeed it ever had.

A classic and successful mix of government spending and private enterprise evolved in the form of the McClellan-Kerr Arkansas River Navigation System. The waterway had its beginnings in 1946 when Congress passed the Rivers and Harbors Act authorizing a nine-foot-deep navigation channel up the Arkansas and Verdigris Rivers to Catoosa, Oklahoma. Congress did not allocate funding for the project until 1956. In 1959, the Oklahoma legislature granted port authorities broad powers to develop, operate, and expand their facilities. To acknowledge the support of Oklahoma senator Robert S. Kerr and Arkansas senator John L. McClellan, Congress named the system after them in January 1971. Official dedication of the $1.2 billion system came when President Richard M. Nixon visited the Port of Catoosa on June 5, 1971.

The navigation system grew until it stretched for 445 miles and included eighteen locks and dams, thus creating a staircase from the Mississippi River to Catoosa. Two ports—one at Catoosa and another at Muskogee—were designated as foreign trade zones. From 1971 to 1990, an average of 7.6 million tons of freight traveled along the navigation system. Tonnage increased to 10.6 million tons in 1994. By century's end, sand, gravel, and rock were the primary cargoes; petroleum products, chemical fertilizers, wheat, coal and coke, iron and steel, soybeans, and various agricultural products filled out the list. Over the years, this audacious project not only provided an outlet for products from America's heartland but also saved billions of dollars in flood damage, provided hydroelectric power for millions, created jobs, and opened up recreational opportunities along its serpentine path.[8]

The halcyon years between 1948 and 1973 were uninterrupted by recessions, let alone depressions. If bank deposits were a reflection of renewed prosperity, then Oklahomans could be assured that their worst days were behind them. According to the American Bankers Association 1945 roll call, the First National Bank and Trust Company of Oklahoma City was the largest bank in the state as of December 31, 1944, with $154,024,878 in deposits and a deposit-based national ranking of 106. Other top-tier Oklahoma banks included the First National Bank and Trust Company of Tulsa, with $118,174,381 in deposits and a ranking of 140; the National Bank of Tulsa, with deposits of $116,975,204 and a ranking of 141; and Liberty National Bank of Oklahoma City, with deposits of $63,115,567 and a ranking of 250.[9] Statewide, there were some 420 stable banks in the 1940s.[10]

Taking center stage in the bullish postwar economy was home construction. Lured by government programs promoting home ownership, GIs returned home to stake their claims to the American Dream, and builders were there to greet them. Bank loans nationwide increased by a whopping $15.4 billion between June 1946 and December 1948, the largest expansion on record.[11] Early fears that too much credit would send inflation off the charts were laid to rest as suburbs spread across the land and industries roared to life. Once early fears of deflation dissipated, state and local governments joined the bandwagon and spurred economic development throughout America.

Oklahoma mirrored the national trend as the state's share of agricultural jobs declined from 33 percent in 1940 to 5 percent in 1970. Meanwhile, manufacturing's share of Oklahoma jobs doubled from 8 to 16 percent. The loss of farm jobs went hand-in-hand with farm consolidation and migration from rural to urban areas. These patterns were most evident in the 1950s, when the number of Oklahoma farms slid from 142,000 to 95,000.[12]

Demographic shifts had a tremendous influence on the banking industry. Country bankers, long accustomed to their role as pillars of their communities, lost influence as urban banks became wealthier in both relative and absolute terms. By 1960, thirty-three cities with more than six thousand people were home to half of Oklahomans, and a quarter of the state's population lived in Oklahoma City and Tulsa. By 1970, 52 percent lived in one of the state's four metropolitan statistical areas (MSAs) as defined by the U.S. census: Oklahoma City, Tulsa, Lawton, and the region around Fort Smith, Arkansas. Meanwhile, banks of all sizes were not only adapting to demographic shifts and changes in marketing and technology but were also competing with government sources of funding. To cite a single example, commercial banks in January 1957 had $84,023,000 in non–real estate loans, while other institutions (mainly the Production Credit Association and the Farmers Home Administration) had $36,080,000 in such loans—not enough to put banks out of business, but enough to give them a run for their money.[13]

If there was a downside to the happy days attending postwar prosperity, it lay in Oklahomans' willingness to turn a blind eye toward vice and corruption. One person who kept his eyes wide open was Albert McRill, a onetime city manager of Oklahoma City and author of a shocking exposé of city governance bearing the alluring title *And Satan Came Also*. Drawing on public service experience dating back to statehood in 1907, McRill opened fire on sacred cows of all descriptions. "Many Oklahoma Cityans would be shocked," wrote McRill, "to read that the underworld of Oklahoma City and County is larger, more destructive, and more powerful politically in 1955, than at any other time in the City's history." And what, exactly, was this seamy underworld that was apparently thriving beneath the radar of law-abiding citizens? "Briefly, it is that enormous array of organized and unorganized law-breakers and the semi-regulated resorts that breed and foster crime and vice, the businesses, legitimate and otherwise, that are avenues for the distribution of liquor and dope and the harboring of prostitutes, the 'pay-off' corrupters of local government, the political machines allied with underworld leaders, and certain powerful business interests that fatten on illicit traffic," explained McRill. As evidence of his allegations, McRill directed readers to look no further than a front-page story in the *Daily Oklahoman* about the "policy racket" in the tenderloin of the Second Ward that had mushroomed into a two-million-dollar-a-year business and showed no signs of abating. Police officers were stymied in their efforts to prevent underground kingpins from deluging their banks with "huge sacks of nickels, dimes and quarters extorted from 10,000 menial toilers whose emotional weaknesses and superstitions make them easy preys to the policy-swindling racket."[14] Queried about authorities' inability to bring racketeers to justice, Chief of Police Roy Bergman said simply, "There is not much we can do to stop them. We try to harass them as much as possible. We try to check them every day and if a known bookie is around we fine him $20, the maximum under our city ordinances."[15]

Competition and an occasional boost from Uncle Sam notwithstanding, most businesses (the legitimate ones, anyway) relied on bank credit during the postwar era. Between 1946 and 1957, the number of loans outstanding at Federal Reserve member banks doubled. In 1957, commercial banks had more than 1.5 million business loans on their books. According to one survey, 40 percent of firms were regular bank borrowers and an additional 35 percent borrowed occasionally. Most business borrowers were small to medium-sized firms. To cite a single illustration of the importance of small businesses in the economy, seven-eighths of bank business loans in 1955 went to firms with less than $250,000 in assets. One study noted that commercial banks were far and away the largest suppliers of funds to small businesses. More than any other group in the financial community, commercial bankers maintained close connections with small business owners as customers and members of their boards of directors. Through daily contact with the activities and problems of small businesses, commercial bankers knew how to help them achieve their goals.[16]

Evidence in the 1950s confirmed what small businessmen and businesswomen had long since accepted as an article of faith: a bank's success depended on gaining and preserving the goodwill of small business. Good customer relations not only accrued to the benefit of the banker's bottom line but also reflected the fact that community development depended on a steady supply of credit to stimulate economic growth. The expansion of bank credit took the form of increasing checking deposits as loan proceeds were credited to borrowers' accounts. Such expansion was possible if banks had enough funds to meet deposit withdrawals and maintain legal reserve requirements.

For its part, the Federal Reserve System fostered the growth of credit in two ways: by reducing reserve requirements and by adding to bank reserves through purchases of Treasury securities on the open market. The public played its part by limiting cash withdrawals to a small proportion of deposit expansion. As a result of all this activity, the dollar volume of checking deposits shot up by 50 percent from 1945 to 1960. The proportion of families with checking accounts rose from about 33 to 57 percent from 1946 to 1960. In 1961, banks reported an astounding 46 million personal checking accounts.[17]

Even as they followed national trends in commercial banking, Oklahoma bankers contributed to economic growth in their state by participating in the formation of the Oklahoma Finance Authority. Beginning in the 1950s, this organization attracted industry to the state by pledging to put up 25 percent of the cost of an industrial development project. Local banks loaned 50 percent of the cost, leaving the developer to front only 25 percent.[18] Meanwhile, Congress got into the act in 1953 when it created the Small Business Administration (SBA) as an independent agency of the federal government. Working closely with commercial banks, the SBA provided counseling services for small businesses and protected free enterprise, all in an effort to foster economic development. With SBA counseling, small businesspeople could position themselves to procure loans. Under certain conditions, the SBA even helped to guarantee them.[19]

When they were not attracting industry and fostering small business growth, Oklahoma bankers were supporting agriculture by opening new departments in the postwar period to serve the unique needs of farmers and ranchers. Bankers also continued a tradition dating back to territorial days of supporting young people in their agricultural endeavors. For inspiration, bankers might have looked east, toward Gettysburg, Pennsylvania, where President Dwight D. Eisenhower's prizewinning herd of Black Angus cattle showcased the benefits of scientific breeding. During and after his presidency, Eisenhower shared his enthusiasm for the cattle business with foreign dignitaries, including Soviet premier Nikita Khrushchev, French president Charles de Gaulle, and Great Britain's wartime prime minister, Winston Churchill.[20]

In midcentury, Future Farmers of America (FFA) and 4-H clubs were frequent recipients of bankers' largesse. Even though the number of farmers was declining, bankers were mindful of agriculture's importance to the state's economy. According to statistics supplied by the American Bankers Association, 410 of Oklahoma's 425 commercial banks in 1970 held farm credit. Although agriculture did not necessarily constitute the bulk of these banks' loan portfolios, it was certainly an important factor in overall lending. "Thus," concluded H. E. "Gene" Rainbolt—president of Federal National Bank of Shawnee and 1970–71 president of the Oklahoma Bankers Association—in November 1970, "a generalization that the economic well being of most of the banks in Oklahoma is directly related to the success and prosperity of individual farmers and agri-business would be true. A further acceptable generalization would be that the prosperity of individual banks depending on the rural economy would be determined by the extent to which they participate with their farm customers."[21]

With only fourteen Production Credit Associations in the state whose interest rates during 1969 "certainly were not cut rate," Rainbolt saw plenty of upside for commercial banks. To increase banks' agricultural loans, the OBA president encouraged bankers to treat farmers and ranchers as they treated their urban customers—that is, as competent businesspeople who were perfectly capable of understanding and implementing sophisticated systems of financial control and reporting. "There is absolutely no reason why banks should have a continuously lessened share of the farm loan business," concluded Rainbolt. "For, in the long run, if we don't make the loans, neither will we get the deposits. At that point, the prosperity of the farmers in our area will be of no consolation for some other institution will reap the benefit."[22]

Rather than dispense advice from the comfort of their offices, country bankers with farming and ranching backgrounds worked directly with their neighbors to improve crop yields. Noting that Oklahoma's farm population declined at an average annual rate of 1.39 percent from 1933 to the mid-1950s and wreaked havoc on rural communities, National Bank of Tulsa assistant vice president Kenneth N. Domnick admonished his fellow bankers to promote efficiency on the farm through modern methods of irrigation and brush control. According to one soil conservation report in March 1952, Oklahoma's beef production stood to increase by $100 million annually if farmers would get to work in transforming the state's ten million acres of post oak and blackjack thickets into productive grassland. One banker who got the message was Clark Chapman, president of the First State Bank of Talihina, whose pasture improvement program was the envy of his neighbors. As he commented in the fall of 1955, "The pasture improvement program in the last ten years has more than doubled the value of all the land in southeastern Oklahoma, and during this time we have only scratched the surface." Union National Bank of Bartlesville chairman Don Tyler, American

National Bank of Bristow vice president Albert Kelly, and First National Bank of Stigler president Homer Carlile were among the growing legion of country bankers who practiced what they preached on their own farms by aerial spraying of chemicals. Ultimately, improving crop yields and pasturage through brush control was the key to transforming large farms that struggled on thin profit margins into smaller and more profitable family farms. According to Domnick, "The additional purchasing power which will result from this expanded and intensified agricultural program will be felt in every community in Oklahoma."[23]

Beneath Oklahoma's fertile farmlands was wealth of a different sort—limestone, lead, zinc, granite, and a host of other minerals with enormous market value. According to the U.S. Bureau of the Census, Oklahoma in 1950 ranked sixth after Texas, Pennsylvania, California, West Virginia, and Louisiana in the total value of its mineral products. As deposits were discovered and prices rose, the cash value of the state's mineral products more than doubled between 1940 and 1950.[24] But there were two sources of wealth that stood head and shoulders above the rest, and they have shaped not only the state's economy but also its culture: oil and gas. With a flair for understatement, an observer at midcentury quipped, "Oklahomans could have eaten without oil, but it's doubtful they would have needed bigger belts."[25]

Figures from 1954 reveal the true engine of Oklahoma's economy in the postwar period, and they come to us from K. S. Adams, chairman of the board of Phillips Petroleum Company, who used the *Oklahoma Banker* as a platform from which to extol the importance of oil and gas to Oklahoma's economy in general and banking in particular. "It is oil, and its twin, natural gas, which have raised Oklahoma above a mere subsistence economy to one of wealth and progress," wrote the oilman in September 1955. "I would be the first to praise agriculture and other flourishing industries in our state; but the fact remains that without oil and gas Oklahoma would never have attained its present rank of 22nd in bank deposits and 25th in population among the nation's states." In 1954, the value of oil and gas reached $570 million, more than all crops and livestock marketed in the previous year. Landowners were paid more than $100 million in royalties, lease rentals, and lease bonuses, 70 percent as much as farmers received for that year's wheat crop. Wages paid to the state's 46,400 production workers totaled $220 million; another $50 million went to the thousands who processed oil in refineries. The petroleum industry's annual purchase of supplies and equipment in Tulsa alone was more than $500 million in 1954. Although Oklahoma ranked fourth nationally in the volume of crude oil production, it ranked second in the number of oil industry employees. "Like a chain reaction, the force is also felt by bankers, retail and wholesale merchants, service personnel, and others who meet the demands of those whose incomes are derived directly or indirectly from the oil and gas business," wrote Adams. What is more, that force was spread across sixty-two counties where oil and gas was produced.[26]

The implications for the banking industry were unambiguous: oil and gas flowing from thousands of wellheads injected cash into Oklahoma banks, and that cash became the basis for loans that kept existing wells in operation and financed new ones. Adams estimated that $300 million was spent on drilling in 1954, and much of it came from Oklahoma banks. He went on to cite a single anecdote to illustrate how far Oklahoma had progressed in terms of financing its own economic development: "This is a far cry from going to London to secure financial backing as a Muskogee group had to do in 1897."[27]

Looking ahead, Adams saw a continuation of the good times. Drillers in 1954 sank 8,800 new wells, and the value of oil and gas produced in Oklahoma had more than trebled since 1940. Meanwhile, new technologies such as water flooding and sand fracturing were increasing the rate of return from old and new wells alike, thus making oil recovery ever more profitable. Meanwhile, major discoveries ranged from western extensions of the Golden Trend oil field in south central Oklahoma to new fields in the Panhandle. Adams cited two regions that would soon figure prominently in the state's oil and gas production: "the Anadarko basin in the northwest and the McAlester basin in the southeast. Geologists believe both of these regions will be profitably productive."[28]

Two clouds on the horizon would have a familiar ring to contemporary drillers: interference from Washington, D.C., and the threat posed by foreign imports. Adams continued, "As bankers, many of you are keenly aware of the highly uncertain risks in financing development of gas for long-term contract commitments when the producer's price—and your repayment—is determined not by the contract but by a Washington agency." When it came to imports, Adams was unequivocal in his warning about excessive dependence on foreign sources of oil: "The nation must not risk a major defense emergency with foreign supplies cut off and with the domestic industry too far behind in producible crude to meet the needs essential to survival."[29] *Plus ça change.*

Adams ended his editorial with a plea for cooperation from Oklahoma bankers in supporting the oil and gas industry—a plea that was heartfelt but perhaps not altogether necessary, as he was basically singing to the choir: "The petroleum industry depends heavily upon the service and cooperation of the state's bankers. It looks to you for large amounts of new capital to meet many of its requirements. It depends upon you to serve its employees and allied businesses. I can report unqualifiedly that the service and cooperation you have given has been of vital help in making the oil and gas business in our state strong and ever-growing. I am sure that we will continue to work together in creating an increasingly prosperous Oklahoma."[30]

House and Home Magazine set the tone for the 1960s with its first issue of the decade: "Never has a decade in America's history started with greater expectations: technology stands at its highest level—pocketbooks are bulging—new frontiers in space, materials, are open before us. This issue is about the promise of those golden years."[31]

Fifty-nine banks were established in Oklahoma between 1950 and 1970, and all but twelve of them opened for business during the expansive, gold-tinted 1960s. Typically, their founders sought to grow their banks in burgeoning suburbs, hoping for holding companies that owned older banks to target them for acquisition. To attract deposits and out-of-state customers, suburban bankers offered promotional gifts (the ever-popular toasters and kitschy piggy banks), held parties in their lobbies, and offered higher rates of interest on large deposits.[32] Drive-in facilities, pioneered in Oklahoma by the First National Bank of Tulsa, were becoming regular stops for customers who were spending much of their lives behind the wheel. As drive-in banking caught on, the Oklahoma legislature interpreted laws against branching literally and insisted that that drive-in facilities be attached to their banks. Deciding to act first and ask forgiveness later, bankers with less rigid interpretations of the state's banking codes attached their drive-in facilities to their bank buildings with cables and phone lines. By the mid-1960s, the thoroughly modern OBA was leading the charge to permit drive-in facilities within three hundred feet, and later one thousand feet, of bank buildings.[33] The decade ended with the construction of Liberty Bank, which became the tallest structure in Oklahoma City. The completion of this behemoth in 1968 launched a construction boom in which older banks supplemented or replaced the towers they had constructed in the 1950s.[34]

While Oklahoma bankers were plotting their end runs around state banking codes, legislators decided it was high time to revise them for the first time since statehood in 1907. The task fell to a group whose members included a committee of state bankers, trust company representatives, and the Special Committee of the Executive Council of the Legislature. To oversee the committee's work and draft new codes, the Oklahoma Bankers Association hired Conn, Mayhue, Kerr, and Harris, a law firm that was headed by one of Oklahoma's most illustrious bankers: Jack T. Conn.

Born and raised in Ada, Conn was one of the state's busiest bankers. In addition to a legal career that put him in charge of numerous cases involving the energy giant Kerr-McGee, Conn was president of the Oklahoma State Bank in Ada, a position that he had held since his father-in-law and former bank president, C. H. Massey, died in October 1951. Conn's expertise in business development pushed him into the presidency of the Ada Chamber of Commerce, fund drives for the Valley View Hospital in Ada, and numerous trips to Oklahoma City in support of highways and roads. In 1957, he was elected as president of the Oklahoma Bankers Association. "Jack Conn was the president of the American Bankers' Association *and* the Oklahoma Bankers' Association," said Denver Davison, a director of Vision Bank of Ada and a longtime admirer of Ada's favorite son. "He was high up in banking, and he was president of the Oklahoma State Bank."[35] With typical self-deprecation, Conn claimed that the OBA did more for him than vice versa. As he wrote in his 1979 memoir, *One Man in His Time,* "While I fear it is true I did little for the OBA, I shall ever be indebted to the Association for what it did for me."[36]

From its inception in 1963 to its completion of what Conn described "a herculean task" in 1965, the banking code revision committee drew heavily on the Model Banking Code of the American Bankers Association; the Oklahoma Statutes; the banking laws of Colorado, New Mexico, and Oregon; and the National Banking Act to bring Oklahoma's codes into the mid-twentieth century. Among the committee's most significant changes was to excise the banking powers of trust companies. Heretofore, trust companies had been authorized to take deposits with or without interest, guarantee special deposits, and operate safe-deposit vaults. As Conn wrote in his memoir, denying these powers to trust companies in the revised code saved Oklahoma from the nemesis of community bankers: statewide branching. Under the McFadden Act, the comptroller of the currency had the right to accord national banks the same privilege to branch as was granted to state banks, and trust companies were permitted to branch under state law. "Had the Code not deleted the deposit rights of trust companies," wrote Conn, "the Comptroller would have been empowered to grant statewide branching to national banks."[37] The revision sailed through, and much to the relief of Jack Conn and his ideological ilk, the battle over branching was left to fight another day.

Conn and his legal team made their final appearances before the Senate and House Banking and Currency Committees in May 1965, and the Banking Code of 1965 became effective on August 31. "On the whole, I am reasonably proud of the Code," wrote Conn in his memoir. "It is far superior to the hodge-podge of laws it replaced, and the Code has stood the best [sic] of time fairly well."[38]

Congress, too, was changing the rules of the game with a slew of legislation. The Bank Holding Company Act of 1956 (subsequently amended) authorized the Federal Reserve Board of Governors to approve the establishment of bank holding companies and prohibited bank holding companies headquartered in one state from acquiring a bank in another state. The law was implemented in part to regulate and control banks that had formed bank holding companies in order to own both banking and nonbanking businesses. Generally speaking, the law prohibited a bank holding company from engaging in most nonbanking activities or acquiring voting securities of certain companies that were not banks.[39] Under the terms of the Bank Merger Act of 1960, Congress sought greater control over bank mergers by requiring premerger approval by one of the three federal banking agencies. Henceforth, the Justice Department would have an advisory role in rulings on whether or not bank mergers were anticompetitive.[40] The Economic Development Administration (EDA), created by Congress in 1965, made loans to build permanent industrial facilities in "redevelopment areas," designated by the secretary of labor in regions with chronic unemployment and low annual incomes. With minimal risk to their bottom lines and confident that their communities would benefit from industry, most Oklahoma bankers were happy to cooperate with the EDA.[41]

Just as commercial bank credit played a major role in financing productive capital formation by the nation's businesses, farms, and government agencies, it also provided financing for millions of families to buy homes, autos, and durable goods that came with postwar prosperity. The extension of bank credit to home mortgages and personal lending that began in the 1930s continued. By 1960, more than 20 percent of all bank credit was going to individual households. From 1945 to 1960, the number of dwellings increased by twenty million; 75 percent of the increase was in owner-occupied homes. Approximately 85 percent of home purchases involved credit, typically in the form of mortgage loans payable in monthly installments over twenty to thirty years. By 1960, home purchasers owed $140 billion in mortgage debt that covered about sixteen million homes.[42]

During the charged year of 1968, Congress passed two pieces of legislation aimed at leveling the playing field for mortgage borrowers: Title VIII of the Civil Rights Act—best known as the Fair Housing Act and passed just one week after the assassination of Dr. Martin Luther King, Jr.—which prohibited discrimination in extending mortgages and home improvement loans; and Title I of the Consumer Credit Protection Act—best known as the Truth-in-Lending Act—one of the toughest and most far-reaching pieces of consumer legislation of the postwar period. Legislation was finally catching up to demands to bring the American Dream within everyone's reach.

With input from the OBA, the Oklahoma legislature created another agency to aid businessmen and their bankers to arrange financing: the Oklahoma Business Development Corporation (OBDC). Up and running in 1973, the OBDC secured operating funds from members who received shares in the corporation, and it encouraged industrial growth by providing new and existing businesses with short-term and intermediate funds for working capital and equipment purchases. Financial institutions interested in joining the OBDC pledged a percentage of their assets to make funds available for loans. OBDC loans were often made in conjunction with regular bank loans. The OBDC was particularly effective in rural areas where funding was scarce.[43]

Even as they took advantage of opportunities to grow their banks, leaders in the banking industry were encouraging their colleagues to get involved in economic development projects. Nobody was surprised to see the multitalented Jack Conn, whose forced resignation from the

The civil rights movement roared to life with the NAACP's Freedom Now march on North Shartel Avenue in Oklahoma City, April 3, 1965. Note the First National Bank Building towering in the background. Courtesy Oklahoma Historical Society.

Oklahoma State Bank in Ada was the prelude to his election as president of Fidelity National Bank and Trust Company in Oklahoma City in the fall of 1964, throw his influence behind redevelopment projects. Speaking at a groundbreaking ceremony for Fidelity Bank's downtown express bank, Conn verbalized what bankers across Oklahoma were doing on a daily basis—participating in projects that would accrue to the benefit of their communities and, by extension, their banks: "Many American cities have been seeking the means to offset the problems of a decaying central business district. Every conclave arrives at the same solution: Community funded building projects are limited by funds and methodical development.... The rejuvenation of any city must depend on businessmen who see the wisdom of making an investment in the future of their local economy. Banks have a responsibility to demonstrate economic leadership."[44]

Bankers also shared a responsibility to encourage community involvement among their younger colleagues. The first annual conference of young bank executives, sponsored by the OBA, was held on December 10, 1970. Shawnee banker H. E. Rainbolt set the tone for the conference when he defined the "Dividends from Involvement," a presentation title that he chose "because of the extreme urgency of our involvement." After castigating bankers who watched from the sidelines as legislation whittled away at their competitive edge, Rainbolt cut to the heart of his message: "Lack of involvement not only stops progress, but also causes loss of the investment we already have." Although Rainbolt saw a wide range of needs and opportunities for involvement, there was one business-building activity that trumped all others: participation in the OBA. "It is a source of support for legislation, community improvement, and can affect all echelons of your environment."[45]

Another way for bankers to demonstrate their community spirit was to promote student internships. On March 15, 1971, incoming OBA president Frank G. Kliewer, Jr., of Cordell offered his thoughts on the OBA's first annual student-intern program, slated to launch that summer. At the top of his list of concerns was the brain drain that was siphoning off Oklahoma's most promising students to other states.

> Most bankers are aware of the problems of attracting intelligent and imaginative young men and women to a career in banking. Much has been written about the problems of management succession in unit banking states. Each year large out-of-state banks come to Oklahoma campuses in search of management talent. Too often they hire our best graduates, or their search is frustrated by the fact that the typical graduating student has already made a career commitment in an area other than banking. Career opportunities in large and small Oklahoma banks must be brought to the attention of college students before they reach graduation.[46]

For Kliewer, one way to entice talented young people into banking careers in Oklahoma was to invite them into the OBA internship program. Interns received stipends of $400 per month and credit at their colleges and universities. During their internships, students could expect to become familiar with a broad range of specialties, including bookkeeping, operations, lending, investing, deposits, reserve management, safe deposits, and marketing. The first order of business was a meeting of interns, bankers, and professors during the third week of May to review the program. Professors and students then met during the last week of June and July to determine students' progress and prepare lists of suggestions for bankers. The program concluded with a group discussion and, finally, a banquet in September.[47]

The postwar era from the end of World War II to the early 1970s was a time of great optimism among Oklahoma bankers. The mixed economy, once heralded as the death knell for laissez-faire capitalism, was increasingly accepted as economic development in a new guise, commensurate with the needs of an industrial and increasingly global economy. Demographic shifts of seismic proportions were providing old banks with opportunities for growth, and new ones were sprouting up to serve the needs of rural communities and suburbs. State and federal programs were opening new opportunities for bankers, even as they leveled the playing field for minorities who were emerging from the revolutionary 1960s more as participants, and less as victims, of the American financial system. The twin engines of Oklahoma's economy, agriculture and energy, were creating a standard of living that previous generations of Oklahomans could never have imagined, and they were fueled by banks, whose success depended on the success of their communities. When they were not showing farmers how to improve crop yields or working with drillers to sink new wells, bankers were leading the charge in economic development projects and helping students and young executives to fulfill their career ambitions. It is no wonder that the postwar era has remained fixed in America's collective memory as a time when all things were possible—as a time when poverty could be eradicated, the world could be made safe for democracy, and astronauts could set foot on the moon. Perhaps it is not only nostalgia that invites us to think of the postwar era as a time when the American Dream was possible for anyone with the gumption to earn it.

With opportunities came challenges, and none was more vexing for bankers than crime. From 1946 to mid-1963, there were no bank robberies in Oklahoma City. Isolated, rural communities were not so fortunate. During the late 1950s and 1960s, thieves struck the First National Bank of Pauls Valley, the First National Bank of Maud, the First State Bank of Harrah, the State National Bank in Depew, the Bank of Red Oak, and the First National Bank of Nash. The crime spree came to Oklahoma City on June 7, 1963, when two robbers looted $26,000 from the First State Bank and Trust Company. This heist was followed by an average of two thefts a year in Oklahoma until October 23, 1968, when a lone gunman seized $12,800 from the May Avenue Bank.[48] "This is getting to be too much," lamented May Avenue Bank president Ben T. Head, whose bank had already lost $27,000 in a robbery in December 1964. "Just like the last time," continued the seething president, "I didn't know a thing about it until someone ran into my office and said that the bank had just been robbed."[49]

Head and his colleagues who thought they were being singled out for misfortune had only to consult crime statistics to realize that something big was in the wind. Nationwide from 1957 to 1967, the three main classifications of bank theft mushroomed: robberies went from 278 to 1,470; burglaries increased from 171 to 600; and larcenies went from 42 to 189. Even more galling were the statistics on injury and death. In 1967 alone, twenty-three people were killed and sixty-one were injured when robbers came calling. The FBI estimated that there were 2,658 external bank crimes in 1968, an increase of 17.7 percent over 1967.[50]

Faced with an avalanche of crimes against banks, Congress passed the Bank Protection Act of 1968. Input came from the four regulatory authorities—the Federal Deposit Insurance Corporation, the Federal Reserve Board, the comptroller of the currency, and the Federal Home Loan Bank Board—and these in turn received advice from law enforcement officers, banks, equipment manufacturers, and trade associations.[51] The act established minimum standards for installing, maintaining, and operating security devices and outlined procedures to discourage theft and assist in the identification and apprehension of thieves. Banks and thrift institutions were required to designate officers to oversee their banks' security programs. Time limits for compliance were mandated, and reports were to be submitted at regular intervals. Institutions that failed to comply with the new law were subject to a civil penalty not to exceed one hundred dollars for each day of violation. Ultimate responsibility for protecting banks lay with their boards of directors. Directors were cautioned against skimping on security devices and relying too heavily on insurance policies to safeguard their assets. Evidence showed that the failure to curb crime through target-hardening technologies led to increases in bank insurance premiums of as much as 200 percent—a false economy at best, and possibly an invitation to disaster.[52]

If the road to hell is indeed paved with good intentions, then the Bank Protection Act of 1968 was but a snowflake in a blizzard of regulations that blew ever stronger in the 1970s, and it made bankers long for the days when moneymen survived by their wits and the goodwill of their customers. "I am tired of being regulated and legislated to death," railed one banker who had had enough of politicians with good intentions. "It takes one of our employees full time trying to keep up with the volume of new rules and regulations passed by some state or federal agency or another.... Let's end some of this nonsense by leaving prudent management up to those responsible within their own banks."[53]

An objective assessment reveals that banking in the 1970s was no more regulated than public utilities, transportation, telecommunications, and perhaps a few other economic sectors. But what was unique about banking was that banks had to pay for their own regulation. Unlike other regulatory agencies, the Federal Reserve System received no congressional funding and relied on member banks to turn over a percentage of their deposits for operating funds. What is more, annual audits performed by the comptroller of the currency were funded by the banks being audited. Banks also had to cover the cost of keeping records and preparing reports, as well as other costs of complying with regulations. And when the Securities and Exchange Commission called, it called collect.

Some compliance and regulatory costs were easier to measure than others. What was the cost of keeping a customer waiting while branch personnel dug through files to answer a question? How much did it cost for a bank officer to prepare for an SEC challenge? "It's not just the number of people or the cost of reporting," explained Jim Hirshfield, controller at Seattle First National Bank (Seafirst), one of several bank officials who, along with the bank's executive vice president Leigh Younes, was tied up in an SEC challenge in December 1974. "It's the terrible priority. If we don't file these reports properly or on time, Leigh Younes or I could go to jail or the Bank could be fined." Day-to-day compliance issues arose in the form of inspectors from an alphabet soup of agencies empowered to collect reports on short notice. One frustrated banker expressed a common complaint that has lost none of its resonance since the seventies: "In a free society, government regulations should extend only so far as necessary to protect the public interest. Rules and regulations should be written in response to economic and social change. But the government moved away from that decades ago. The regulatory agencies believe that they know what is good for society and they have long since taken the lead playing God rather than responding. And that is frightening."[54]

In an address to the OBA New Regulations Workshop in Oklahoma City in December 1975, State Banking Commissioner H. E. Leonard identified three sources of regulation: the law, which aimed to ensure conformity and mitigate chaos; regulatory agencies (the comptroller of the currency, the Federal Reserve Board, the FDIC, and state banking agencies), which were responding to bewildering changes in social and economic relations; and Congress, whose insistence on doing things for people that they apparently could not do for themselves was causing bankers to declare that enough was enough. "I think all of us will agree that this is the area which has nearly gotten out of hand," said Leonard, "and the overreaction of us regulators is 'peanuts' compared to the overreaction of Congress in some of its responses to special interest groups, special situations, specific circumstances." For Leonard, those special interests included "a very, very small group of financial institutions in the East" that had pushed Congress into unwise legislation. "Somewhere down the line," continued the banking commissioner as heads no doubt nodded in unison, "the thought must be brought to our national leaders that there is such a thing as regulating a particular industry to death, and the demise of the free enterprise financial system we have will ultimately be the demise of this country's greatness."[55]

Saddened by his government's apparent desire to bring all banking functions under federal control, Commissioner Leonard imagined that only two letters were available in Congress's dwindling repertoire, now that acronyms littered the financial landscape: "'YM,'—you must do certain things—and regulation 'YC,'—you can't do anything not covered by regulation 'YM.'" Like OBA presidents who prodded members to get involved in business-building activities, Leonard admonished his listeners to engage in politics: "Under our democratic system, your business is in the hands of the government. The stock certificate may be in your name but you run your business in accordance with political edicts. As long as there is a banker that doesn't know his Congressman, and legislator, on a first-name basis, you still have progress to make." He also urged bankers to clean their own houses—to run their banks in such a way as to be beyond criticism. He was hopeful that bankers would decide to regulate themselves, much as physicians and attorneys did through licensing and codes of ethics. "Is your industry ready, willing, able, to regulate itself?" asked Leonard. "Until it is, it's going to get worse before it gets better."[56]

A final challenge to postwar banking was sometimes referred to simply as "the change," and it encompassed the bewildering array of technologies that were redefining the relationship between people and their money. In an address to a gathering of Oklahoma bankers, Roger Guffey, president of the Federal Reserve Bank of Kansas City, focused on electronic funds transfer (EFT) as a tool that gave bankers an edge on their competition, even as it pushed them to the limits of their organizational

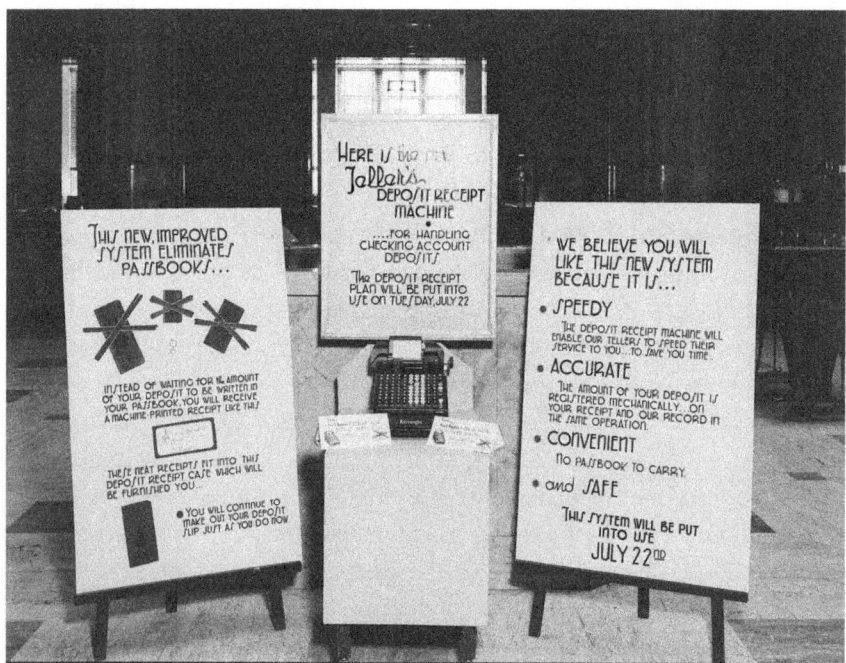

The pace of technological advance quickened with the teller's deposit receipt machine, on display in Oklahoma City, July 1947. Courtesy Oklahoma Historical Society.

A typical bank lobby scene shows tellers equipped with the latest Burroughs adding machines, June 1948. Courtesy Oklahoma Historical Society.

skill. He noted, "As Oklahoma banks and consumers reap the advantages of this marriage of technology and market opportunity, as new services come on line for your customers, other fundamental issues will arise, issues which will put to the test your process of orderly response to change."[57]

First on Guffey's list of issues was the fading distinction between savings and demand accounts. As depositors transferred money from one account to the other at the speed of light, how were banks supposed to calculate interest on savings accounts? And as the transition to electronic technology picked up steam, what would happen to banks' earnings and the ability to generate capital? These questions led inexorably to uncertainties pertaining to reserves. Because reserve requirements for savings deposits were lower than they were for demand deposits, what would become of banks' capacities for investment? How would the Federal Reserve Board conduct an effective monetary policy as money flowed from demand to savings accounts?

Vexing as these questions were, a transcendent issue that surely made old-school bankers squirm in their seats was the erosion of relationships occasioned by technology. "Your marketing plans generally have stressed the development of continuing personal and business relationships with your customers at many points in your service structure," said Guffey. "The new electronic banking technology, however, is essentially an impersonal one. How will you retain the warm, personal flavor of banking relationships in a push-button environment?"[58]

With heads once again nodding in agreement, Guffey criticized Congress for paying more attention to self-imposed deadlines than the potential impact of hastily written legislation. Bent "on getting *something* passed in mid-1976," Congress was rushing to complete three pieces of financial reform legislation: the Financial Institutions Act; the International Banking Act; and the Federal Reserve Reform Act. "There is no doubt in my mind that significant change is warranted and that timing is also essential in response to the massive market changes of the past few years," said the Kansas City banker. "However, the nation can ill afford to see some legislation rushed through just to meet an arbitrary deadline."[59]

Guffey was deeply troubled with Congress's willingness to play politics with the Federal Reserve System. In keeping with "the traditional unwillingness of the American people to tolerate any undue concentration of economic and financial power," the Fed's architects had tried to place the system beyond short-term political influence. But with Congress clamoring to place Federal Reserve presidents under its control, Guffey envisioned a day when the exclusive franchise to create money vested in the Federal Reserve System would be passed into the hands of politicians who also had the authority to spend money. He concluded his remarks with a history lesson—a lesson as cogent in our own time as it was in his, and one that has commanded attention throughout American history during times of financial turmoil: "Economic history is replete with clear lessons of what happens when the 'money creating' process in a nation is taken over by political forces. Initially, more money is created to finance politically desirable projects; then inflation takes over; followed by the printing of more money. Inevitably, rampant inflation so weakens the financial structure that the economy collapses, and very often so does the political structure as well."[60]

Nobody in the banking industry saw any use in pretending that changes were the result of some grand strategy. "I can't think of *any* important public law that resulted from a grand strategy," quipped James Smith, comptroller of the currency under President Gerald Ford. Old-fashioned bankers had entered their twilight, and nobody could predict with any confidence how their successors would manage their new freedom. Their success as mere providers of financial services would henceforth depend on their sensitivity to customers' needs. But bankers have rarely distinguished themselves as early adopters of technology or anything else, for that matter, that threatens the status quo. And time was running out. The barbarians were approaching the gates.[61]

But something else was already inside the gates, and it was nothing less than the scourge of civilization: inflation. Like viruses that have altered the course of history, inflation is invisible to the naked eye. But its effects are visible in the regimes it has toppled and dictatorships it has spawned. To grasp how inflation affected Oklahoma banks in the postwar period, we must retrace our steps to the 1960s and the beginning of a story that is largely forgotten and only dimly understood. It is the story of the Great Inflation.

The story begins with the election of John F. Kennedy as president in 1960. He was swept into office on a tide of postwar prosperity and faith in the power of ideas. The central idea was one that guided domestic as well as foreign policy for nearly three decades: pay any price, and bear any burden, to win the Cold War. Kennedy's economic agenda might have been a bit fuzzy, but he was crystal clear in his conviction that America's economic performance at home was connected to its ability to discredit the Soviet Union and its loathsome ideology. "We must recognize the close relationship between the vitality of our own domestic economy and our position around the world," declared the president at a standard stump speech. "If we stand still here at home, we stand still around the world." At the time, the annual rate of inflation was a negligible 1.4 percent—a nuisance, perhaps, but not enough to dampen Americans' confidence in continuing prosperity. Stable prices meant a strong economy and a secure future.

To guarantee a robust economy, Kennedy and some of America's best and brightest economists focused with laser-like intensity on maintaining full employment, which was pegged by consensus at an unemployment rate of 4 percent. According to the managerial elite, full employment would put an end to recessions and would ensure companies a steady stream of customers for their products and services. Higher costs (including higher labor costs) could be recovered through higher prices. What is more, workers in a full-employment economy could press for higher wages without fear of losing their jobs. A prosperous age was at hand as pesky business cycles, vestiges of a less enlightened age, dropped into the dustbin of history. As late as 1970, Arthur Okun, a Yale economist who served on President Johnson's Council of Economic Advisors from 1964 to 1969 and who chaired it for a year, wrote, "Recessions are now considered to be fundamentally preventable, like airplane crashes and unlike hurricanes."[62]

For a while, deft adjustments in monetary and fiscal policies to ensure low unemployment seemed to be working. The economy expanded 5.3 percent in 1964 and 5.9 percent in 1965. Meanwhile, the unemployment rate dropped to 5 percent by the end of 1964 and to almost 4 percent a year later. And inflation? It hovered at less than 2 percent in both years. In December 1965, no less an authority than *Time* magazine touted Keynesian economics as the secret to steady, stable, noninflationary growth. Then, in "the fifth, and best, consecutive year of the most sizeable, prolonged and widely distributed prosperity in history," the U.S. economy was the envy of the world and, not incidentally, a gigantic thorn in the Soviet Union's side. In a not-so-subtle jab at America's ideological nemeses, *Time* put it this way: "Communists, Marxists and the British Labor Party's radical fringe damned Keynes because he sought to strengthen a system that they wanted to overthrow."[63]

Low unemployment remained the North Star of economic policy for more than a decade. Lacking peripheral vision and supremely confident in their ability to fine-tune business cycles out of existence, policy makers were slow to realize that they had ignited an inflationary spiral. Wages were chasing prices, and prices were chasing wages, with no end in sight. Good intentions notwithstanding, policy makers in the 1960s were in for a rude awakening.

Prescient observers might have sensed trouble when inflation hit 3.5 percent in 1966. But presidents came and went, and none put inflation at the top of their agendas. The rate jumped to 6.2 percent in 1969 and, in the midst of a mild recession, slid back to 5.6 percent in 1970. Then, on August 15, 1971, President Richard Nixon stunned the nation when he announced a ninety-day wage-price freeze as part of a program to let the dollar depreciate and abandon America's commitment to pay foreign governments in gold for the dollars they held. The gambit ended badly, and when controls were lifted, inflation exploded into double digits.

Considering the lessons that might have been gleaned from Johnson's and Nixon's failure to control inflation, it remains a matter of some wonder that President Jimmy Carter fared even worse. By pinning the blame for inflationary spikes on the Vietnam War and oil price explosions—that is, on onetime events that exonerated normal economic policies—policy makers were lulled into complacency. In 1979, the annual inflation rate was running at a blistering 13.3 percent. By 1980, the rate was racing toward 15 percent.[64]

In a classic case of the law of unintended consequences, the obsession with full employment had hardened into ideology, and it unleashed the most corrosive and destabilizing menace of all: inflation.

Now, the barbarians really *were* inside the gates.

Inflationary spikes were still in the future when Oklahoma bankers found themselves in the glare of public attention, and not the kind they wanted. Their troubles began in December 1967 when M. J. Swords, vice president of the Federal Reserve Bank in Kansas City, informed Oklahoma State Banking Commissioner Carl Sebring that State Treasurer Leo Winters was mishandling the state's money. Specifically, Swords accused Treasurer Winters of increasing deposits in the First American Bank and Trust Company of Purcell in order to obtain a personal loan in the amount of $15,000. Both Winters and Sam Ewing, president of the bank, quickly dismissed Swords's accusation as a lie, but the damage was done. Governor Dewey Bartlett appointed a committee to investigate the charges, and subpoenas were issued to seven bankers. One of them was Gene Rainbolt, president of Federal National Bank of Shawnee, and the principal stockholder in the Purcell bank.[65]

When bankers and state officials faced their accusers for the first time on a cold December morning in 1967, none imagined that the imbroglio would grind on to the middle of the next decade—past the summer of love in 1967; past the bloodstained Democratic National Convention in Chicago in 1968; past the mother of all rock concerts at Max Yasgur's farm in upstate New York in 1969; past President Richard Nixon's resignation in the wake of a bungled burglary at the Watergate Hotel in Washington, D.C., that set the standard for political brazenness; and past the peace treaty that signaled the end of America's misadventure in Southeast Asia. Through these and other milestones that seemed to send American history spinning out of control, the question that Oklahomans pondered as they sipped their coffee and read their morning papers was: What was Leo Winters doing with the people's money?

From the beginning, Treasurer Winters denied that he had ever used his office as leverage to force bankers to make loans to him. His statement after the initial hearing was unequivocal: "The attorney general and his team proceeded all day long until he himself admitted that he had exhausted all of his evidence and failed to prove a single thing that violates my trust to the people or that I am ashamed of." He did, however, testify that he had increased state deposits in 173 banks in fifty-nine of Oklahoma's seventy-seven counties, and that some of the banks from which he received loans might have received increases in state deposits.[66]

Hearings were held, subpoenas were issued, investigations were launched, and gallons of ink were spilled to explain what, exactly, Leo Winters was doing with Oklahomans' money. In early 1972, federal investigators got into the act, determined to get to the bottom of the treasury secretary's alleged favoritism in depositing state money in small banks in return for campaign contributions. Winters insisted that the "big bankers"—specifically, the head honchos at the First National Bank and Trust Company and Liberty National Bank in Oklahoma City—were out to destroy him for taking up to $300 million "in idle state funds" out of their coffers and spreading taxpayers' money around the state.[67]

Pressure continued to mount, and in June 1973 Rainbolt and his senior vice president at Federal National Bank, Ben Smith, suspended themselves from active management of the bank pending the outcome of their upcoming trials. "(W.) Ben Smith (Jr.) and I have suspended ourselves as directors and officers of the Federal National Bank," declared a frustrated Rainbolt in a prepared statement, "and we will take the same action with regard to other banks in which we hold office." Rainbolt's announcement came just days after he voluntarily suspended himself from his position as state highway commissioner, a post to which he had been appointed by Governor David Hall.[68]

When the case finally went to trial in April 1974, Treasurer Winters and his codefendants, including Ben Smith of Shawnee, were ready. Their lead counsel, state senator Gene Stipe of McAlester, quickly subpoenaed a host of Republican heavy hitters to testify on behalf of the defendants. Among the sixty-four people summoned to Oklahoma City were former U.S. attorneys general John Mitchell and Richard Kleindienst, U.S. senators Henry Bellmon and Dewey Bartlett, and former Oklahoma governor Raymond Gary. Rainbolt, by then named on a single charge of mail fraud, was to be tried at a later date.[69]

All eyes were riveted on the U.S. District Court in Oklahoma City when, in an abrupt announcement on Thursday, April 4, Judge Wesley E. Brown dropped the charge against Rainbolt. Even as the judge was signing an order dismissing the Rainbolt indictment and announcing a recess so that he could consider some "legal problems," a smiling Leo Winters took the opportunity to announce his candidacy for another term as treasury secretary. "Today is a good day for the people of Oklahoma," declared a beaming defendant whose acquittal seemed all but certain. "I have been planning for some time to announce that I will be a candidate for re-election to the office of state treasurer," continued Winters. "The timing is appropriate for this announcement to be made today."[70] Winters went on to remind his listeners that he had collected more than $70 million in interest on taxpayers' money, an achievement that Gene Stipe had exploited to its full potential in front of the jury. "That figure is more than 10 times the interest collected by all the other treasurers since statehood in 1907," said the justifiably proud treasurer. Following the proceedings, Treasurer Winters walked over to Gene Rainbolt and said simply, "Congratulations."[71]

Later in April, Rainbolt was called as a witness for the defense in ongoing proceedings against Winters. Although he conceded that he had used his personal influence with Winters to obtain state funds for four Oklahoma banks, he vigorously denied that political contributions were expected from the banks in return for state deposits.[72]

In late June 1974, the year-old federal grand jury indictment against State Treasurer Leo Winters and eleven codefendants was dropped.[73] As the cloud lifted and the spectacle faded into a bad memory, Rainbolt resumed active management of his banking interests and ended his yearlong voluntary suspension from the Oklahoma State Highway Commission.[74] The long nightmare was over.

We leave the final word on the Leo Winters banking scandal to Gene Rainbolt's friend and associate, Jim Bowles, who put his accounting skills to work in helping Rainbolt to acquire and manage interests in problem banks between 1971 and 1984. "[Winters] was exonerated," said Bowles. "And let me tell you why he was exonerated. Senator Gene Stipe was his lawyer. And Senator Stipe was a colorful fellow! In any event, they had prepared a chart showing the amount of interest income that had been earned during the tenure of Leo Winters. And when the jury sat and looked at that chart, they were so angry with the predecessors, that they didn't care what Leo had done to get elected. They loved him!"[75]

Then and now and surely for all time, nothing succeeds like success.

Legal troubles notwithstanding, success was very much on Gene Rainbolt's mind as he and other Oklahoma bankers devised strategies to expand their banking assets. In the absence of state laws permitting branch banking, Rainbolt and his ilk had a choice: they could either buy stock in a one-bank holding company and rely on bank performance to increase the value of their investments, or they could spread their bets by investing in multiple one-bank holding companies. Those who chose the latter path to asset appreciation found inspiration—and, more to the point, a winning strategy—in Bert Lance, a Georgia banker whose financial savvy and political connections landed him a job as director of the Office of Management and Budget (OMB) in the administration of a fellow Georgian, President Jimmy Carter. Today, Lance is remembered primarily for two things: resigning from his job at the OMB less than a year after his appointment when questions were raised about his alleged mismanagement of Calhoun First National Bank of Georgia, a bank owned by his wife's family, where he worked his way up the ladder to become president and chairman of the board; and his implication in a scandal involving the Bank of Credit and Commerce International—better known by its acronym, BCCI—a major international bank founded in 1972 by Pakistani financier Agha Hasan Abedi. Some might recall Bert Lance's pithy contribution to the financial lexicon—"If it ain't broke, don't fix it." What has practically vanished without a trace is the down-home banker's strategy for making big-time money in banking. The strategy worked like a charm not only for Lance in Georgia but also for two of Oklahoma's most renowned bankers: Morrison Tucker of Oklahoma City, whose banks eventually failed when his reach turned out to exceed his grasp; and Gene Rainbolt, whose collection of problem banks coalesced in 1989 to form the BancFirst Corporation.

And then came the BCCI scandal. When legislators decided that the banking industry might indeed be broken and rode to the rescue with slew of legislation to fix it, Bert Lance's moneymaking strategy went straight to the dustbin of history. As Oklahoma State University's OBA Chair of Banking and Finance Gary Simpson explained, "He was the guy, the kid in the class, who did a bunch of crazy stuff and got the entire class in trouble. Everybody else was fairly clean, but he's the one who did the crazy stuff and got everybody upset."[76] Collateral damage spread to Oklahoma, where Rainbolt and Tucker were forced to adjust their empire-building strategies. An additional casualty was Oklahoma City banker Tom Loy, who had to abandon his dream of building a banking empire of his own.

Loy left banking in 1999. In early 2000, he launched Metafund, an Oklahoma City–based firm that invests in businesses and projects serving low-income neighborhoods and distressed areas. Still wondering in 2012 about the empire he might have created in the 1980s if Bert Lance and the high-profile BCCI scandal had not tanked his career aspirations, Loy explained the strategy that Morrison Tucker used to his advantage and Gene Rainbolt raised to an art form. "In the late 1970s, you could potentially borrow more than the purchase price of a bank," said Loy. "In essence, you could use the assets of the bank you're acquiring as collateral for the loan. Not only that, you get to use what are called 'compensating balances' to buy down the loan that you are using to buy the bank." And what were compensating balances? Simply put, they were balances that bankers required borrowers to maintain in a checking account at their banks, typically 10 percent or so of the loan balance. Borrowers rarely objected because they had to park their money somewhere, so why not park it at the bank that was lending them money?[77]

"But here's the little known kicker," continued Loy. "Suppose I buy 51 percent of a bank, and borrow all the money to do it. I now control the bank, even though I don't own all of it. I can use compensating balances as a negotiating tool back at the bank. I want that balance to earn me something, and what I want it to earn me is a buy-down on my loan rate."[78]

In subsequent negotiations, a 6 percent interest rate on a loan might drop to 5 percent, or a 5 percent interest rate might drop to 4 percent. The borrower might even convince his banker to ratchet the interest rate down another notch by agreeing to maintain higher compensating balances at the bank. So far, so good. The banker has a new customer who, as the majority shareholder, can grow the bank through robust and professional ownership. The borrower is pleased to receive a favorable interest rate, thanks to compensating balances. And at the end of the day, he walks away with controlling interest in the bank without spending a dime of his own money.

"What's so critical here? What's the trick?" asked Loy. "Think about it. Remember when I said I only bought 51 percent of the bank? The compensating balances are coming from all of the stockholders. So I am getting 100 percent benefit from the compensating balances, because it's my loan. It's not a loan for all the other stockholders. It's just me, the 51 percent owner. So the minority stockholders are, in effect, subsidizing my purchase of their bank, because I own control of it!" Loy continued, "Everybody did it. Morrison Tucker did it. Bert Lance did it. Gene Rainbolt did it. Lots of bank owners did it."[79] Rainbolt's modus operandi differed insofar as he borrowed only the book value of the banks he intended to acquire. When he lacked the capital to supply the remainder of the financing, he assembled investor groups to provide equity for the balance of the purchase price. Controlling stockholders were given no preferential treatment in Rainbolt's deals, as all investors bought their stock at the same price.[80]

Gordon Greer, who joined BancFirst in December 1996 to become chairman of the executive committee, saw nothing unusual in using leverage and compensating balances to acquire banks. "It was a procedure that was not unique, necessarily, to Gene Rainbolt," explained Greer. "He just carried it to a grander scale with a lot more banks involved, and different partners. But it's been done by others on a much smaller scale." What was unique, and what forced Oklahoma bankers to operate the way they did, was the state's prohibition against owning more than one bank under a single charter. "Oklahoma and Kansas and a few other states around here didn't have the ability to do that," continued Greer. "If you were going to own a lot of banks, you had to own a lot of banks. You couldn't do it through a multibank holding company or branching. You had to own banks individually."[81] According to Professor Simpson, Rainbolt had always been a believer in multi-office banking, and his collection of banking interests simply showed that he was ahead of his time. "I'm not saying that he did anything illegal or anything," said Simpson. "That was the way that you did multi-office banking, back in those days. It was done all over the United States."[82]

Bankers who relied on Bert Lance's modus operandi to acquire controlling interest in banks not only increased their own wealth but also built value in the stock of the banks they acquired. Buying controlling interest in banks through leverage and compensating balances was thus a win-win proposition: bankers won by increasing both the number and value of their banking assets, and minority bank stockholders won as the value of their stock increased. "And it was common practice until Bert Lance's little empire started coming apart," said Loy. "People found out about this compensating balance deal. They decided to go after bankers because they perceived an abuse of minority stockholders."[83]

Bert Lance's fall from grace in the wake of the BCCI scandal was problematic for bankers who had replicated his bank-buying strategy, only to find themselves in the glare of public opinion and thwarted in future acquisitions by new regulations and heightened scrutiny. "That was my plan for building a banking empire," said Loy, still wistful some three decades after his dreams came to naught. "I had seen what Morrison Tucker had done with his version. And then I saw what Gene Rainbolt had done to scale—admittedly smaller banks, in Gene's case, but nonetheless, a whole bunch of them! I thought, 'I can do this! I don't have to be independently wealthy to do this. All I have to do is build a solid reputation. And if I build a solid reputation over a few years, I can grow my own Gene Rainbolt–type banking empire!'"[84]

Tom Loy was late to the party, and his empire would have to remain in the realm of unfulfilled dreams. But for bankers such as Tucker and Rainbolt, who had already acquired banking interests through leverage and compensating balances, the game was far from over. It was, however, time to come up with a new strategy.

While Gene Rainbolt and Morrison Tucker were leveraging themselves up to the hilt and using compensating balances to expand their holdings, George Records was putting an entirely different asset-building strategy into play. In the late 1950s, Records went into business with his father-in-law, W. R. "Ross" Johnston, a banker from Shawnee who had relocated to Oklahoma City to expand his business interests. Chief among those interests was Midland Mortgage Company, a firm whose main function was to produce loans and then place them in mortgage-backed securities. Based in the Hightower Building in downtown Oklahoma City, where afternoon treats were available from Frank J. Hightower's famed Cellar Restaurant downstairs, Midland Mortgage Company developed a business model aimed at servicing those loans by collecting payments, paying insurance premiums and taxes, and making remittances to investors. After Ross Johnston died in 1976, Records applied the lessons he had learned under his father-in-law's tutelage to build Midland Mortgage Company into one of America's most successful privately owned enterprises.

As millions of dollars piled up in escrow accounts, Records discovered a problem that most folks might envy: what to do with all that cash? His solution, as bold as it was simple, was for Midland Mortgage Company to open its own bank. A bit of sleuthing revealed that a new savings and loan charter was for sale in Stilwell, a tiny hamlet just west of the Arkansas line in Adair County. Records explained his decision to expand his company into retail banking: "The law provided that organizers of a new stockholder-owned savings and loan association [founding stockholders] could own no more than 10 percent of the stock when it was issued. But the law was silent on anybody else that came along and bought those people out. All I wanted was the charter. I didn't care about the business. I could open branches around the state, which banks couldn't do in those days, because Oklahoma was a unit-banking state. There were no branching restrictions on a savings and loan association. Nobody had ever exploited that opportunity." When Records approached the savings and loan principals in Stilwell, he discovered that their initial capitalization was $500,000. "I made them an offer," recalled Records about his purchase of Adair County Savings and Loan in 1982. "The day their charter was issued, I'd give them $1 million for their charter. So they doubled their money the day they opened up. They were tickled to death, and I got what I wanted, and I only had to pay a $500,000 premium!"[85]

Thus began a new era for Midland Mortgage Company. As the law compelled companies to conduct board meetings in the locations where their charters were issued, Records and his associates were in for some memorable trips. "We had to fly into Siloam Springs, Arkansas," said Records's longtime associate Betty Rodgers-Johnson. She continued:

> We did drive a few times, but that was just nerve-wracking, to go over there for a board meeting. Stilwell, Oklahoma! Oh, those days, that was so wild! We had to have the board meeting where the bank charter was located, and we had to operate that bank over there. We had to go over there once a month for a board meeting, and there was no place to eat—the Circle K, and it was a dull place to eat, and it was a dry county. We actually ate at a church dinner one time, and we were so excited, because we finally had some place good to eat![86]

On September 30, 1982, Records received permission to move the former savings and loan to Oklahoma City and form a bank holding company. Records named it MidFirst Bank, sold his interests in Stilwell, and never looked back.

From war's end to the 1970s, commercial banks were the largest and most diversified type of financial institution in America's high-productivity, high-consumption economy, and they stimulated economic growth in four ways: (1) they extended credit to businesses to purchase capital goods and to families to purchase durable goods; (2) they furnished at least 25 percent of external financing for businesses, including farms, as well as for state and local governments (the proportion rises to more than 30 percent if bank-administered pension and trust-fund investments are included); (3) they provided nearly 50 percent of consumer credit and about 17 percent of home-mortgage funds; and (4) their deposits provided most of the spending money circulating in the economy. Moreover, commercial bank deposits provided an outlet for personal savings, particularly for people who needed safety and liquidity. Nearly 75 percent of Americans held funds in the form of pensions and trust funds that commercial banks managed in order to meet the diverse savings needs of their customers. Assured of safety and liquidity as never before,

American consumers would henceforth direct their attention to matters that had long been the stock-in-trade of economists, but were now fodder for pundits and catalysts for public debate: inflation, unemployment, economic growth, and monetary policy.

The American banking system is a striking example of the spirit of nineteenth-century enterprise, and it rested on the principle that capital can be increased through an extension of credit based on the creation of money. Not that the relationship between credit and money has ever been an easy one, any more than democracy and capitalism have ever reached a point of equilibrium—the "golden mean" that Aristotle and his philosophical brethren were so zealous about. Throughout financial history, efforts to improve banking performance in one sphere have been to the detriment of the other. Indeed, it is no exaggeration to define banking history as a series of alternating efforts to extend abundant credit on the one hand and supply a high quality and stable quantity of money on the other. One pines, as President Harry Truman famously did, for a one-handed economist.[87]

The tug-of-war between money and credit—and between those uneasy bedfellows, capitalism and democracy—became more complicated than ever in an age of galloping technology and overreaching politicians. But that did not preclude some old-fashioned tomfoolery, some of which took the form of run-of-the-mill crime, and some of which required uncommon audacity. The latter reached cosmic proportions in the late 1970s and early 1980s in (you guessed it!) Oklahoma, where oil-patch pioneers were scrambling to find the next El Dorado, and where the mouse that roared turned out to be a little shopping-center bank with imperial ambitions.

CHAPTER SEVEN

Boom

I believe that, beyond lending money, a banker has to encourage and create opportunities. Concern for a customer and a desire to see him succeed are not inconsistent with a sound credit policy.
 Bill P. "Beep" Jennings, chairman of the board, Penn Square Bank

No event looms larger in post–World War II Oklahoma banking than the collapse of Penn Square Bank. In some ways, the shopping-center bank that shook the world fits the profile of manias in financial history that resonate to this day: "tulipomania," which rendered Dutch investors first spellbound and then broke when the bottom fell out of the bulb market in 1637; the orgy of speculation in Louisiana real estate in the early eighteenth century, which ended in a heap of devalued banknotes, bruised the Bourbon monarchy, and added a moniker with a French accent—"millionaire"—to America's financial lexicon; the popping of the South Sea Bubble in 1720, which brought many a wannabe millionaire in Great Britain to ruin; and the California gold rush of 1849, where the American Dream foundered in squalid mining camps and busted boomtowns. Closer to our own time were the dot-com bubble, gestated in the womb of the "new economy" (whatever that was), and the Great Recession of 2008, grounded in the stubborn notion that home prices can only go up.

But really, the rise and fall of Penn Square Bank, described by one chronicler as "a dinky Oklahoma correspondent bank that had turned out to have the fire power of Lee Harvey Oswald,"[1] was in a league of its own and, more to the point, pure Oklahoma—chock-full of hubris that has surfaced throughout the state's history whenever natural resources have beckoned as the new El Dorado. The siren song this time came not from land or oil or precious metals, but rather, natural gas deposits in the Anadarko Basin of western Oklahoma, available for the taking as long as one had the guts and money—or, more likely, someone else's money—to drill to mind-boggling depths. When irrational exuberance turned out to be just that, drillers, investors, and bankers (and, of course, their stockholders and employees) spiraled into a financial freefall not seen since the Great Depression. Collateral damage extended to run-of-the-mill depositors with modest ambitions—say, putting braces on a child's teeth or financing a patio for a ranch-style home in the suburbs. As customers at Penn Square Bank and a growing legion of its correspondent banks from coast to coast cashed their paychecks and made their deposits and signed their loan papers, none suspected that bankers with less modest ambitions were ensconced in offices only a few feet away, pencils sharpened and phone lines humming, preparing to reap the whirlwind.

Two journalists deserve credit for chronicling the rise and fall of Penn Square Bank: Mark Singer, whose *Funny Money* combines the author's insights as a native Oklahoman (albeit a Tulsan with the requisite condescension toward his cross-state cousins) with the caustic wit of a New York journalist; and Phillip L. Zweig, a reporter for the *American Banker* who broke the story with a feature article in April 1982 and eventually distilled months of investigative journalism into *Belly Up: The Collapse of the Penn Square Bank*. In late 2010, Zweig donated his research files—an enormous collection crammed into fourteen storage boxes—to the Oklahoma Historical Society, leaving this author with a sore back and Oklahomans with a portal into a homegrown catastrophe.

Seasoned bankers will find this chapter and the next one to be a tour of familiar territory or, more likely, a bad trip. For those who came on board in the years since the dust settled, the Penn Square Bank fiasco is known more anecdotally than historically, and perhaps as a morality tale hewn from a noxious chapter in Oklahoma history. And for an increasing number of Oklahoma bankers, the collapse of Penn Square Bank is ancient history, no more relevant to present-day concerns than the failure of the Capitol National Bank of Guthrie in 1904, the Rose Anti-Wildcat Banking Bill of 1897, the Panic of 1893, merchant banking in the Indian Territory, or freighting on the Santa Fe Trail.[2] It is hardly original to suggest that Americans have short memories.

Wherever Penn Square Bank lies along one's spectrum of relevance, one thing is certain: forgetting about it is to ignore one of history's few unambiguous lessons. If, as the philosopher George Santayana famously suggested, not learning from history dooms us to repeat it, then let us take a deep breath, revisit the Penn Square Bank story and its ugly aftermath, relearn the lessons, and pledge to remember them.[3] At the outset, I defer to Zweig, who tells us that *anadarko* is an Indian word meaning, "man who eats the honey of the bumble bee."[4] One wonders if any of the protagonists in the Penn Square Bank drama took time to reflect on the etymology of "anadarko"—a honey pot if ever there was one, but one with a vicious sting.

The Arab oil embargo of 1973 is as good a place as any to begin untangling the Penn Square Bank imbroglio. Anxious to flex their muscles in a world addicted to oil, members of the Organization of Petroleum Exporting Countries (OPEC) turned down their spigots and gloated as oil prices quadrupled to spawn what might have been the greatest nonviolent transfer of wealth in human history.[5] As international finance sailed into uncharted territory, the arcane vernacular of economics was, for once, crystal clear: oil producers were running surpluses on their balance sheets, and other countries were not.[6] To pass the time as they sat idling in gas lines, disgruntled Americans flipped on their car radios to hear Merle Haggard croon a mournful dirge that might be the unlikeliest Top 40 hit ever: "If We Make It Through December." The shortage psychology was felt in Washington, D.C., when Congress suddenly woke up to the perils of dependence on foreign oil. A familiar refrain echoed from the halls of power in the nation's capital to the oil fields of Oklahoma and Texas: "Drill, baby, drill!"

But drilling for oil was only part of the answer. As geologists became more familiar with the Anadarko Basin, they realized that vast deposits of natural gas, primarily methane, were trapped in formations more than 15,000 feet below the surface. The Anadarko Basin covers approximately 50,000 square miles and stretches from west central Oklahoma and the Texas Panhandle to Kansas and Colorado. Its sedimentary deposits range in thickness from 2,000 feet in the north and west to 40,000 feet in the south.[7] By the late 1950s, technology had advanced to the point where wells were descending more than two miles in what was entering the driller's vernacular as "the deep gas play," and geologists were confident that even deeper sedimentary layers were ripe for exploration. The only impediment to bringing that gas to the surface rested on a simple equation: the deeper you drilled, the more money you needed. Until the price of gas below 15,000 feet could be deregulated—that is, until its price could be divorced from the price of shallower gas and brought in line with the enormous cost of extracting it—then the riches of the Anadarko Basin would remain where they had been for eons, and Americans would have to look elsewhere for a solution to their energy dilemma.

In the spirit of the free enterprise that has shaped banking and commerce in Oklahoma, one of the state's most daring entrepreneurs took center stage in the campaign to make drilling in the Anadarko Basin economically feasible: Robert Alexander Hefner III. A scion of Oklahoma wildcatters, Hefner was raised in Beverly Hills, California. Early on, he was introduced to activities that later became his passions: playing polo, sailing in the Caribbean, and hunting grouse in the Cotswolds. He arrived in his ancestral state as a freshman at the University of Oklahoma. On his way to a major in geology, he took a course in stratigraphy, which put the fire in his belly to go where no man had gone before: miles deep in the Anadarko Basin.

In 1961, Hefner met Laurence Glover in New York, and through him became acquainted with David O'D. Kennedy. Both of them shared Hefner's interest in drilling for deep gas. By 1963, Hefner was the "H" in the GHK Company, a partnership destined to set the standard for audacity in natural gas exploration. Under the aegis of the GHK Company, Hefner and his partners accumulated leases around Elk City, Oklahoma—the de facto capital of the Anadarko Basin—and set out on their dual quest to secure financing for their drilling ventures and to convince Congress to deregulate the price of deep gas. At its peak, the GHK Company's lease holdings amounted to roughly 200,000 acres, mostly within a hundred-square-mile area surrounding Elk City.[8]

Fueled by visions of what natural gas could do for his country, Hefner made numerous trips to Washington, D.C., to make his case before Congress. Speaking before the Senate Committee on Commerce in his capacity as chairman of the Independent Gas Producers Committee on

November 7, 1973, Hefner left no stone uncovered in his effort to win the hearts and minds of his listeners. His testimony included the energy shortage, pricing structures, estimates of natural gas reserves, the staggering costs of exploration, and of course the clincher: the need to deregulate prices and allow deep gas to find its market value. "Deregulation only of new gas prices is a specific, affirmative and, importantly, a simplifying step which will quickly increase the supply of our most desirable fuel during the critical near term," said the swashbuckling driller as he wound toward his conclusion. Deregulation would not only accrue to the benefit of consumers, promote investment in risky exploration, and enhance environmental quality but also would push America along the path of energy independence.[9]

Hefner struck much the same chord on March 24, 1977, when he testified before the House Committee on Interstate and Foreign Commerce. This time, he brought the GHK Company's experience to bear on the potential of the deep gas play to mitigate America's potentially ruinous dependence on foreign sources of energy. "My experience in the deep Anadarko Basin," declared Hefner to what was surely a rapt audience, "has led to my firm belief that the potential natural gas resources remaining to be discovered in the Deep Anadarko Basin (below 15,000 feet) are of crucial importance to the nation's energy resource base and thus to our national energy policy."[10]

Clearly comfortable in the political arena, Hefner found common cause with the Democratic ticket during the 1976 presidential campaign and served as chairman of the Oil and Gas Men for Carter.[11] "He seemed to be everywhere, whether you were on the House or Senate side, or at the White House," recalled one observer. "He was a likable fellow, who seemed to be interested in this one particular subject. He was pretty effective; he came across as a pretty competent guy."[12]

In November 1978, Hefner played to a larger audience when he was interviewed for a *National Geographic* article, "Natural Gas: The Search Goes On." Unfazed by the technology required to extract oil from formations nearly five miles beneath the surface, Hefner posed with a drilling rig towering in the background. With his blond mane rippling in an Oklahoma breeze, the man coming to be known as "Mr. Deep Gas" coolly offered his prediction of an energy-independent America. "We think we'll find between 70 and 360 trillion cubic feet of gas in the

Anadarko between 15,000 and 40,000 feet," he said. "We're as sure as 150 million dollars in research and exploration can make us. We're even predicting gas production below 50,000 feet, with better technology."[13]

In his contributions to trade and technical publications, Hefner extolled new technologies and pricing structures that were accruing to the benefit of the GHK Company and, by extension, the nation. "Deep gas offers U.S. industry a way to back out foreign oil at a cost that will generally be either equal to or lower than oil," he wrote in the March 1979 issue of *Petroleum Engineer International*. "This will have the dual effect of reducing inflation while improving our environment—a truly noble national goal."[14] The next month, Hefner coauthored an article in the *Review of Regional Economics and Business* with Neil J. Dikeman, Jr., interim director of the University of Oklahoma's Center for Economic and Management Research, to report on the staggering amount of natural gas below 15,000 feet in the Anadarko Basin and its potential impact on Oklahoma's economy. Using sophisticated models that only an economist could love, Hefner and Dikeman described a bonanza in the making: "The gas which will be produced in 1982 will have an output value of approximately $2.9 billion. Due to the multiplier effect, this volume of output will create outputs in other industries of approximately $1.7 billion. An estimated $1.3 billion in additional output will occur in Oklahoma."[15]

In the swirl of controversy over President Jimmy Carter's proposed gas tax in the late 1970s, Robert Hefner found plenty of support for his conviction that natural gas, and not new taxes, was the solution to America's energy needs. Dismissing fears that America would freeze in the dark unless Congress could be compelled to levy a gas tax, the *Wall Street Journal* on April 27, 1977, admonished President Carter to brush up on his geology. In the process, he would realize that natural gas deposits were far from depleted and that drilling for it should be encouraged through price deregulation. Estimates of U.S. natural gas reserves ranged from 20,000 to 50,000 trillion cubic feet—that is, "enough to last between 1,000 and 2,500 years at current consumption."[16]

On the eve of Ronald Reagan's inauguration as president, *60 Minutes* correspondent Harry Reasoner interviewed energy experts who came to the same conclusion about America's energy crisis: there *was* no energy crisis except, perhaps, the one fostered by wastefulness, mismanagement, and shortsightedness. Then Congressman David Stockman, who was about to become President-elect Reagan's advisor on economics and energy, cited studies indicating that natural gas could replace two to four million barrels per day of imported oil in the coming decade. Not surprisingly, Robert Hefner was tapped for his expertise in natural gas supplies. "What I like to say," said Hefner as his movie-star looks were beamed to viewers across America, "and I believe this completely, is that natural gas is the bridge fuel to 21st century energy technologies. And so, there's no question in my mind that we can get well into the next century with natural gas until we've developed the other sorts of energy systems that we—there's no question we will develop in the 21st century."[17]

President Carter's signing of the Natural Gas Policy Act (NGPA) on November 9, 1978, was greeted with toasting and cheering throughout the oil patch. The legislation that Hefner and his brethren had worked so hard to push through had three fundamental goals: (1) to create a single natural gas market; (2) to equalize supply and demand; and (3) to allow market forces to establish the wellhead price of natural gas.[18] With the stroke of a pen, price controls on gas below 15,000 feet were lifted. Even though the new law was not slated to go into effect until November 1, 1979, oil companies were building into their pipeline contracts an overwhelming incentive for producers to bring as many wells as possible on stream.[19]

And thus, the Anadarko Basin was open for business. To paraphrase the journalist Mark Singer, it was as though Washington, D.C., had pointed its finger at western Oklahoma and singled out its residents to become rich.[20] They complied, and the scramble was on.

One more event conspired to push the deep gas play into overdrive. It was heralded by more saber rattling from the Middle East, this time in the form of a revolution that toppled Shah Mohammad Reza Pahlavi of Iran on January 16, 1979, and elevated to power a theocratic regime bent on the destruction of America, excoriated by Ayatollah Khomeini as "the great Satan." Thus began a nightmarish stream of televised images—of Old Glory and presidential effigies engulfed in flame; of black-clad imams clutching their Korans and enjoining the faithful to resist the seduction of Western ways; of throngs of bearded zealots chanting "death to America!" But nothing was more poignant, and nothing was more deeply seared into America's collective consciousness, than the footage of fifty-two blindfolded hostages marched at gunpoint from the American embassy in Tehran and paraded before a roiling mob. CBS anchor Walter Cronkite became the unofficial scorekeeper for a game that nobody wanted to play by closing his newscasts with a tally of how many days the hostages had languished in captivity.

Once again, Americans were forced to acknowledge their vulnerability to foreign energy supplies. And once again, America's oil and gas industry was summoned to the rescue. But this time, Robert Alexander Hefner III was leading the charge.

Both cause and effect of the energy boom that was gathering steam in the Anadarko Basin was bankers' increasing willingness to fund drilling ventures. At the international level, political turmoil was no longer a deal killer for bankers eager to boost their income-earning assets by making energy loans to developing countries. Top American banks that decided the reward was worth the risk included Chase Manhattan, whose projected total capital investment in the petroleum industry worldwide in 1980 was $51 billion. By 1985, bank executives planned to double their commitment to energy lending to $119 billion.[21]

Closer to home, President Carter was playing the role of counselor-in-chief with his suggestion that a malaise was casting a pall across the land, and the specter of a "national catastrophe" resulting from dependence on foreign oil was fueling predictions that oil would rise to eighty dollars and maybe even ninety dollars a barrel by 1990. Bankers answered the clarion call by tailoring their lending policies to accommodate the demand for domestic oil production. Some loans went abroad to help non-OPEC members ramp up their production and thereby pay for their own oil imports. "Petrodollars" entered the financial lexicon as money poured from U.S. banks in the form of loans to foreign customers to pay for imports; those countries used the money not only to pay for OPEC oil but also to finance economic development and service their debts to American banks. As interest on loans to developing countries piled up, bankers did not have to ponder very long what to do with their windfall: lend it!

As money cycled and recycled between U.S. banks and OPEC members and nonmembers, some of America's top banks perceived energy lending as the ticket to prosperity. One of those banks was Continental Illinois National Bank of Chicago, the seventh-biggest bank in America. Its chairman, Roger Anderson, came to Continental Illinois in 1946 after four years in the navy, where he had acquired a taste for disciplines well suited to banking: accounting, controls, budgets, and statistics.[22] A dry and prim man fond of shapeless suits and prone to banalities in his speeches, Anderson was an unlikely candidate for leading his bank to the pinnacle of global finance. But beneath his drab exterior was an ambition to lend enough money to earn Continental Illinois a seat at the table with the likes of Chase Manhattan, Citibank, and Bank of America.[23]

Under Roger Anderson's stewardship, Continental Illinois retained the services of McKinsey and Company, a management consulting firm that touted 15 percent annual growth rates and a concept known as "decentralization by market segment." This rather inelegant turn of phrase referred to the strategy of segmenting markets, pushing lending authority down to the lowest possible levels in the organization, and encouraging officers to act independently in their specialized markets. McKinsey and Company also recommended that big banks become more aggressive in soliciting business from their correspondent banks—that is, participating in loans that were too big for small, regional banks to handle on their own.[24] Bankers' moneymaking predilections were thus reinforced by McKinsey and Company's foolproof strategy, and loan officers were dispatched from Chicago to roam the West like latter-day gunslingers—young, ambitious, competitive, and above all, willing to take risks.

The strategy paid off. Between 1975 and 1980, Continental Illinois hit its 15 percent annual growth target, and operating profits almost doubled. In terms of its energy portfolio, the bank became ever more aggressive in lending directly to oil companies and buying energy loans from other banks. It was all enough to make business journalists and analysts sit up and take notice. In the estimation of many, it was one of the best-managed companies in the country.[25] Almost two years into its McKinsey and Company makeover, the prestigious *Dun's Review* in 1978 singled out Continental Illinois for its stellar management policies; others included Boeing, Caterpillar, General Electric, and Schlumberger. Business overseas was booming as well. Loans in Asia, Africa, and Latin America doubled. In 1981 alone, assets in Latin America grew by a billion dollars.[26]

Perhaps most impressive of all was the way that Roger Anderson succeeded not so much by the sweat of his own brow as by the sweat of other and equally ambitious brows. As noted in *Institutional Investor*, "He truly believed that he could set broad goals and then let the people out in the field do the rest—trusting that their entrepreneurial instincts would keep them and the bank out of trouble."[27] Freed from the tedium of bureaucracy back in Chicago, young and hungry loan officers scoured the land for opportunities to test their mettle in the prestigious oil and gas division. One officer quipped, "Oil and gas was to lending officers what a SWAT team is to a cop."[28] In August 1984, *Institutional Investor*'s editorial board named Roger Anderson the banker of the year—an accolade meant not to acknowledge his success, but rather, his role in bringing down Continental Illinois.[29]

While Chase Manhattan was financing foreign oil ventures and Roger Anderson's troops were scouting for business in America's heartland, Seattle First National Bank was looking to expand beyond its traditional niches in lumber, fishing, and aerospace, none of which were doing very well in the doldrums of the 1970s. Even though the bank's managers knew next to nothing about energy lending, they decided that oil and gas might be a perfect match for America's nineteenth-largest bank. Contrary to its image as a conservative lending institution, Seafirst, as it was generally known, was aggressive to the point of recklessness in pursuing a 15 percent annual growth rate. At the helm of this financial dynamo were a vice chairman who fell asleep during important meetings, a senior vice president with a flair for exotic fashion, and a chairman who entertained on the roof of the fifty-story corporate headquarters and flew his party guests in by helicopter.[30]

The man chosen to head up Seafirst's energy department, John R. Boyd, was described as a super-salesman and a smooth talker who kept everyone in stitches. "He was probably one of the funniest people I ever met," recalled one banker who knew him. "When the going got serious or tough, he'd bend the thing around so it was funny, and he got his way out of it." Sometimes his humor backfired. Such was the case when he returned from a trip to Abu Dhabi sporting the duds of a traditional Arab sheik and strolled into a meeting of the World Banking Credit Committee. They threw him out. Boyd was also a master of good-buddy banking, and he had a room filled with gifts that he kept on hand for special clients. The lucky ones wound up with a $150 carved duck decoy from Eddie Bauer—just the thing for the banker who has everything.[31]

Like Continental Illinois, Chase Manhattan and Seafirst were in thrall to McKinsey and Company's formula for success—a formula that signaled the dawn of a new day. Bankers were no longer, well, *bankers,* the denizens of musty buildings and wearers of green eyeshades. They were now providers of *financial services,* masters of electronics and holding companies and global capital flows. Perched atop glistening towers of glass and steel and fueled by a yeasty brew of personal ambition and corporate strategy, they answered their country's call for energy independence by making loans to domestic oil and gas companies and participating in loans with correspondent banks that lacked the capital to go it alone. And what better place to flex their financial muscles than the Anadarko Basin of western Oklahoma, where seasoned drillers like Robert Hefner had the guts and technological wherewithal to enlist deep gas in the cause of America's renewal.

The stage was set for a historic convergence of interests. Anything could happen. Something certainly did.

The big problem with financing expensive drilling ventures in Oklahoma was that the banks were too small. Until banking laws were overhauled in the 1980s, Oklahoma was a unit-banking state, meaning that banks were restricted to a single office. The state's archaic banking structure dated back to the formation of its banking laws at the turn of the twentieth century, when hardscrabble Populists in the William Jennings Bryan mold resurrected the ghost of Thomas Jefferson with their suspicion of banks in cahoots with eastern moneymen. Even after the Twin Territories were united in a single state in 1907 and firmly entwined in national networks of banking and commerce, few regions of the United States exhibited more opposition to big banks and more support for antitrust laws than Oklahoma. Grassroots populism, mirrored in Oklahoma's constitution as well as its prohibition against multibank holding companies and branch banking, fostered hundreds of small banks and kept them from becoming large. By the 1970s, Oklahoma and its ideological twin, Texas, were home to some two thousand banks, representing more than 13 percent of the national total.[32]

Another problem in securing financing for drilling ventures has to do with the nature of the oil and gas industry. Simply put, how is a banker supposed to value oil and gas for the purpose of establishing collateral? Drillers can dazzle their bankers with complex equations and geological maps until the proverbial cows come home, but at the end of the day, the value of their properties is basically a petroleum geologist's best guess—not the strongest plank to stand on in a loan committee meeting.

Until the twin dilemmas of large-scale financing and valuation of mineral properties in capital-poor Oklahoma could be solved, all the guts and whiz-bang technology in the world would be insufficient to unlock the wealth buried 15,000 feet deep in the Anadarko Basin.

Problems are often opportunities in disguise, and in this case, opportunity came knocking in the form of Penn Square Bank. Chartered by the comptroller of the currency as Penn Square National Bank of Oklahoma City on February 12, 1960, the bank's organizers included William P. "Beep" Jennings, president of the Bank of Healdton in southern Oklahoma.[33] As the only child of a small-town banker, Beep Jennings was weaned on community banking, and he combined his professional responsibilities with volunteer work, which included a stint as president of the state chamber of commerce. He left Penn Square Bank in 1964 and went to work at Fidelity Bank in downtown Oklahoma City, where he served as an executive vice president and chief lending officer. Longing to run his own show, Jennings returned to Penn Square Bank in the mid-1970s as a co-owner with Larry Rooney and Stanley Lee.[34] Each owned a quarter of the bank's stock; the rest was parceled out among stockholders. As chairman of the Penn Square Bank board of directors, Beep Jennings—fifty-one years old, affable, optimistic, good-natured, and perhaps less hardnosed than he thought he was—settled in for the duration.[35]

It was hard not to conclude that Jennings's star was on the rise, and people were taking notice. "As a bank business developer, Bill has no superior," wrote Jack T. Conn in his memoir. "He was an excellent executive vice president of Fidelity, and the incredible growth of Penn Square under his management adds more laurels."[36] According to State Banking Commissioner Robert Empie, "If you were having a dinner party of some size, you'd want Beep as your emcee, *and he knows the oil business.*" Perhaps ominously, Empie continued, "But he's not a detail man, or an operations man."[37]

Whatever his qualifications as a bank business developer or executive vice president or emcee or oilman, one thing is certain: Beep Jennings's remarks to the bank's shareholders in January 1976 gave no evidence of the mayhem to come: "While our growth in 1975 has been impressive, the principal emphasis in 1976 will be toward quality and safety. In a period of declining loan demand, which is the rather universal forecast for the coming year, banks must be cautious not to lower lending standards in an effort to hold or increase earnings. The past high earnings rate of 1.5 percent on average total assets in 1975 may possibly be reduced in 1976 in the interest of soundness and liquidity."[38]

And then one morning, Beep Jennings announced at an eight o'clock meeting that he wanted to start an oil and gas department at Penn Square Bank. At the time, assets were about $40 million, and the bank's loan portfolio included only one oil and gas loan. Contrary to Empie's assessment, nobody, including Beep Jennings, knew much about oil and gas lending.

Much later, Jennings explained his concept that was by no means original, but had yet to be tested in a really big way: a bank did not have to lend on its own assets if it could loan on another bank's assets.[39] Better yet, why not tap into the pecuniary interests of money center banks, where officers with visions of 15 percent annual growth rates dancing in their heads were already on the lookout for loan participations? In the evolving vernacular of the oil patch, banks with lots of capital were "upstream," whereas banks with less capital such as Penn Square Bank were "downstream," and both monikers could be molded into verbs and perhaps other linguistic forms not yet imagined. If correspondent relationships with upstream banks could be exploited to their full potential, then Penn Square Bank, perched expectantly downstream like a fly fisherman in a mountain brook, would reap the benefits of loan origination and servicing fees—all at minimal risk to shareholders, and all at maximum benefit to the bank's asset base, which in 1977 was not quite $70 million.[40]

Beep Jennings's brainstorm, plagiarized though it was, had yet to morph into policy when he hired William George "Bill" Patterson in 1977. Patterson's thin résumé as an assistant cashier at the First National Bank and Trust Company of Oklahoma City was no impediment to a professional boost at Penn Square Bank. Jennings had known the young man from Bartlesville for years. What is more, Patterson had recently married his way into Panhandle royalty by taking as his bride the daughter of the president of the First National Bank of Amarillo, whose family was close to the Jenningses. Nor were Patterson's youthful antics as a Sigma Chi at the University of Oklahoma a deal killer, even though his nickname, "Monkey Brains," followed him into adult life as a distinctly unbanker-like moniker.[41]

Beep Jennings found Patterson winsome. In the estimate of pop psychologists of the day, Patterson was the son that Jennings, the father of five daughters, never had. During his first year on the job, Patterson's diligence and winning ways gave credence to his reputation as a man who "could sell snowmobiles to Okies."[42] Before long, it was a sure bet that Bill Patterson—handsome, hardworking, and, like John R. Boyd at Seafirst, always up for a good time—stood to make Penn Square Bank a pile of money.

Patterson had been at Penn Square Bank only about a year when Jennings put him in charge of oil and gas lending. By then, Americans had had their fill of Koran-clutching zealots and were more anxious than ever to burn their own fuel. Merle Haggard's woeful tune "If We Make It Through December" had dropped a few notches on the Top 40 hit list, but it still captured the mood of an angst-ridden nation. What President Carter branded as "a national malaise" was felt by Robert Hefner, and his tireless writing and lobbying and mugging for the cameras on behalf of deregulating deep gas were vindicated with the passage of the Natural Gas Policy Act on November 9, 1978. In anticipation of the law going into effect in late 1979, pipeline companies were loading their contracts with incentives for drillers to ramp up their production. And all the while, corporate gunslingers with a license to deal were prowling the Southwest in search of oil and gas loans to participate in and drillers to finance.

A perfect storm was in the making. Few suspected that Penn Square Bank, its bland, three-story edifice poking between trendy shops and eateries, would become its epicenter. Fewer still suspected that a Sigma Chi known as Monkey Brains would be the one to set it all in motion.

Frank Murphy was president of the bank when Beep Jennings and his partners bought their majority stake. A self-described "country boy" from Chelsea, Oklahoma, Murphy presided over steady growth and conservative lending, and he was a stickler for sound collateral and proper documentation. Not surprisingly for this modest and cordial man, he took an instant dislike to Jennings's protégé for what he perceived as insubordination.[43] Any reservations Murphy had about his go-it-alone style were silenced in March 1981 when Patterson was promoted to executive vice president in charge of energy lending.

With 16,182 shares representing 7.2 percent of the stock, Patterson became one of the principal owners of First Penn Corporation, the bank's parent company.[44] Gifted with the power of persuasion and granted the clout to go with it, Patterson threw his considerable energy into shaping the oil and gas division to the contours of his own blustery style. It was early 1979, and twenty-two-dollar-a-barrel oil was a few months from its run-in with Iranian mullahs and their anti-Western bravado. Nevertheless, all the signs pointed to a surge in oil and gas prices, particularly now that deep gas prices were heading toward deregulation.

When the word hit the streets that Penn Square Bank was serious about financing drillers, some of Oklahoma's most renowned entrepreneurs made their way to Patterson's office. What they found when they got there was a high-energy loan officer who refused to let paperwork get in the way of a lucrative deal and a master of delegation who never let a secretary's lack of formal education prevent her promotion to the ranks of the money managers. According to a former bank officer, "You could walk in the door without a financial statement or any formal written proposal, and if what you outlined verbally sounded feasible you could sit down and sign your name to a note and maybe some oil and gas mortgages all prepared in blank." One bank officer claimed that most of Penn Square's loan documents were signed in blank. At one point, only three loan officers and a small support staff were managing a billion-dollar portfolio. Overdrafts and sloppiness became commonplace. In a pinch (or, as was often the case, in a swank bar), deals were scratched on cocktail napkins.[45]

Joel Champlin of Enid recalled the story of a friend who dropped by Bill Patterson's office in search of funding for a drilling operation. Just out of college and untutored in the fine art of financing, the young man arrived to see a room full of prominent bankers, including some from Continental Illinois of Chicago, who had come to sop up their part of the gravy train. Reassured by the presence of rock-solid bankers, Champlin's friend screwed up his courage and told Patterson that it would be nice to have $500,000, but that he could probably make do with $100,000.[46]

"Son," said Patterson, perhaps sizing up his young visitor to discern his Greek lineage in college, "you can't do *shit* with five hundred thousand! How about *five million?* What could you do with *that?*" Speechless, the young man declined and made for the door. "Here I am, and I didn't have a dime, and this guy was willing to loan me five million, and I'm just a kid out of college! I said 'no.' It scared me. Anybody who would loan me that was crazy!"[47]

As Patterson was hitting his stride in what amounted to an independent fiefdom, Penn Square Bank's assets grew from $90.82 million on December 31, 1978, to $141.48 million a year later. The growth was impressive—so impressive, in fact, that the comptroller of the currency conducted a special examination in early 1980 and declared the bank to be "a matter of special supervisory concern."[48] Specific problems included rapid growth of loans and assets, insufficient liquidity, inadequate capital, an increase in classified assets, violations of banking laws, and a preponderance of loans concentrated in the oil and gas division. National bank examiner Bill Chambers showed a flair for metaphor when he put Penn Square Bank on a watch list of the most closely monitored and poorly managed banks in the country and accused its management of operating on "the ragged edge of acceptability." A Washington official did some rough calculations and came to a stunning conclusion: Penn Square's growth rate put it on track to become the third-largest bank in the country by the end of the century. Awestruck, a senior official in the comptroller of the currency's office in Washington, D.C., remarked to a colleague, "There's something in Oklahoma City that's growing. It's weird. It's just weird."[49]

Closer to home, Penn Square Bank's competitors agreed. Gayla Sherry was managing the draft collections department at Liberty Bank and Trust Company of Oklahoma City during the go-go days of the early 1980s, and she was plenty busy with oil and gas drafts. But neither she nor her colleagues could keep up with Penn Square Bank's blistering pace, particularly when the headhunters showed up to woo her staff with big-time salaries. As she recalled,

> As Penn Square grew, astronomically, really, in the late seventies and early eighties, most of us at Liberty were kind of scratching our heads and saying, "What's going on? They're growing too fast!" And they would raid our staff. I had several employees leave the draft collections department to work there. And I always had this gut feeling that something's not right, because they were offering salaries that were double what Liberty was paying. Liberty was very progressive, I should say, in salaries—they were very competitive. And so, for them, at Penn Square, to offer twice the amount, I just thought, "This is weird." I just had

a sense that it was a house built on sand, instead of rock. It just never seemed to back up.[50]

The comptroller's and Sherry's concerns flew beneath the radar of Bill Patterson's most frequent visitors, including Robert Hefner, a.k.a. Mr. Deep Gas, whose first loan was a modest $300,000 and was made at a time when his finances were severely strained. Hefner was destined to push the limits of a concept known as "debtor's leverage," which goes something like this: if you owe the bank $100,000, you lose sleep; if you owe the bank $10 million, the banker loses sleep.

Mr. Deep Gas's audacity found its match in another frequent visitor to Patterson's welcoming office: Carl Swan. It was said that just being in Swan's circle of acquaintances was enough to boost one's credibility, much like belonging to the right club confers status on its members. Unlike the debonair Robert Hefner, Swan earned his keep in the oil patch as a roughneck and mudman, and his workingman's journey to the inner circle conferred dignity on his wealth. By the mid-1970s, Swan was a rich man, and few doubted that he would follow through on his pledge to parlay his modest millions into a billion.[51] On his way to that billion, Swan met J. D. Allen, a man who rose from humble origins in Ringling, Oklahoma, to rub shoulders with the likes of Las Vegas showman Wayne Newton and several American presidents. His international travels took him to London, where he was probably as close as the average Brit would ever get to J. R. Ewing of *Dallas* fame. Along their way to becoming two of Penn Square Bank's largest customers, Allen and Swan launched the Longhorn Oil and Gas Company as a vehicle to strike it rich in the Anadarko Basin. In light of the chicanery that was propelling their chosen bank into a league of its own, it was perhaps more than coincidence that J. D. Allen hailed from the only town in southern Oklahoma named for a circus.

Bill Patterson's knack for wooing local business was nothing compared to the attention he lavished on out-of-town bankers who arrived at Penn Square Bank from upstream. One of them was John R. Lytle, a lifelong Chicagoan who spent his career at Continental Illinois and was placed in charge of the bank's midcontinent oil and gas division in 1977. By the time the Continental Illinois won its accolades from *Dun's Review* in 1978, the bank was meeting Chairman Roger Anderson's goal of 15 percent annual growth in assets, largely by becoming a significant player in energy lending. About $1 billion of its loan participations floated upstream from Penn Square Bank and helped Continental Illinois realize an all-time record net income of $254.6 million in 1981.[52] In their brief but exhilarating dance at the pinnacle of energy lending, John Lytle formed close friendships with Jennings and Patterson—friendships destined to be among the first casualties of Penn Square Bank's demise in the summer of 1982.

Where John Lytle was conventional, his counterpart at Seafirst, John R. Boyd, would have felt right at home in the Sigma Chi house at OU. Much as Bill Patterson had a reputation as a party animal, Boyd, clearly a youngish forty and known among his colleagues as "the Bill Patterson of the West," was a trickster. He liked to appear bare-chested at office parties, a cigarette dangling from his mouth and a drink in each hand. He was known to chomp on cigars (particularly hand-rolled Jamaican Macanudos) and, sporting hats in the style of Chairman Mao, chat on the phone with business clients. In a later age, Skype and videoconferencing might have been his undoing. Boyd was a regular at the Rainier Club, where he lingered over lunch with his clients, bought a half dozen of his prized cigars on the company tab, and strolled back to work with a handful. He had a subscription to the *New York Times,* but rather than read it and perhaps acquire some tips on business deportment, he stacked them unread against his wall like timber at a Pacific Northwest logging operation.[53]

On Seafirst's way to $400 million in Penn Square Bank loan participations, the fun-loving Boyd added a new expression to the financial lexicon: "dump-truck banking." It happened when "Wild Bill" Patterson, as he was affectionately known, and some associates arrived in Seattle in Penn Square Bank's Rockwell Commander jet (one of two aircraft requisitioned for the trip) "filled with good lookin' young dollies" for the 1981 Christmas bash.[54] Also along for the ride was documentation representing some $100 million in loans that Penn Square Bank needed to unload before the end of the 1981 accounting period.

"Here come the guys from Oklahoma!" Boyd bellowed as Patterson and his crew swaggered into the dining room. "They practice the dump truck theory of banking," continued the banker-turned-emcee. "They pile loans into a dump truck, bring them to Seattle, pick up cash and dump it back at Penn Square."[55]

As it turned out, those loans were the sorriest batch of bad paper Seafirst had ever bought from Penn Square Bank. According to former Seafirst officers queried for a four-part series published in the *Seattle-Post Intelligencer* in the summer of 1983 under the heading "The Wrecking of Seafirst," the Christmas 1981 loans had already been sold to Continental Illinois National Bank and a few other banks of its stature. When their shoddiness came to light at Continental, the upstream bankers decided to ship them back downstream.[56] Like a school of determined salmon, Wild Bill and his brigade loaded up the rejects, hopped on another upstream current, and churned their way to Seattle.

Seafirst's 1981 Christmas bash was about eight months in the future when Meg Sipperly, a Long Island native and corporate loan officer at Chase Manhattan Bank in New York, made her first trip to Oklahoma City. Long before her name switched from Sipperly to Salyer and she was elected in 2008 as the Sixth Ward's councilperson for Oklahoma City, Meg graduated from Mount Holyoke College and was recruited by Chase Manhattan's international banking department.

"It was my dream, probably, to be running the Paris office of Chase Bank," said Salyer. But destiny had other plans, and she found herself commuting not to the Champs Elysées, but to the West Coast—until, that is, she received a fateful call from one of her senior officers.

"You know that trip you're planning to Seattle? You need to cancel it. You're going to Amarillo and Oklahoma City." Wondering how she had managed to cross someone so early in her career, Salyer made her first trip to Oklahoma City in April 1981. Her first meeting was with Penn Square Bank president Frank Murphy and Bob Kotarski, head of the bank's correspondent lending division. By the time she caught a plane back to New York, her briefcase bulged with six credit participation opportunities totaling $7.5 million. "And that was the beginning of what was about a year-and-a- half relationship with Penn Square," said Salyer. "In that eighteen-month time frame, our portfolio went from zero to about $300 million." At its peak, Chase Manhattan's Penn Square Bank portfolio represented about 190 individual loans; in that group was a much smaller number of customers who took out multiple loans.[57]

As Chase Manhattan's loan-participation portfolio increased in size, so did the frequency of Salyer's trips to Oklahoma City. "Essentially, Penn Square was the *only* account that I was working on, and I wasn't alone," she said. "I had a couple of junior officers assisting, and as we got toward the end of things, I had a couple of direct peers that were working on it as well." More than three decades after earning her banking spurs in Oklahoma, Salyer's memories of the adrenaline rush she felt as a young woman in charge of a multimillion-dollar account remained as vivid as ever. "It was an *incredibly* exciting, *very* (no pun intended!) high-energy, *very* intense, time. I was working seven days a week. We were meeting with clients *all the time*."[58]

Chase Manhattan Bank's involvement in energy lending dated back to the glory days of Rockefeller's empire. But now, spurred on by McKinsey and Company's no-holds-barred strategy for success and lured by the goings-on in the Anadarko Basin, Chase Manhattan gave Salyer broad latitude to participate in Penn Square Bank's application of an ancient business practice: merchant banking. "This kind of a set up had operated all over the world," explained Salyer, "where somebody that had resources partnered with somebody that had access to somebody that needed those resources, and you put those parties together, and by doing that, you earned a fee." Collecting fees from upstream bankers was thus a new twist on a time-honored tradition—a tradition that Beep Jennings was honing to the contours of a red-hot business climate.[59]

Like so many success stories that turn to bust, the energy boom of the early 1980s was supported by a compelling narrative: daily doses of America-bashing images from the Middle East; entrepreneurship deployed in the interest of America's energy independence; technology that made drilling for deep gas possible; oil prices climbing to the stratosphere; deregulated deep gas left to find its market value; state banking legislation that pushed small banks into the embrace of large ones with piles of capital; and most of all, the distinct possibility, perhaps inevitability, of getting rich. But according to Salyer, most people wanted to make their money legitimately. "It is my firm belief," explained Salyer, the conviction in her voice still resonant after three decades of thinking about it, "that most of the people that were clients of that bank, that were borrowers at that bank, were legitimate, honest people trying to create a business or trying to stay in a business, in a climate that was receptive to that happening."[60]

As the pace of activity ramped up to warp speed, the facts on the ground seemed to support the narrative that had taken up residence in Oklahoma's collective consciousness. Scrambling to execute Chase

Manhattan's strategy in a booming economy, Salyer had no reason to question the constellation of factors that was accruing to the common good. "It was a circumstance of timing and strategy that all came together," she said.[61]

Neither Salyer nor most of the people who lived through and made money in those giddy days could have anticipated Chase Manhattan Bank's annual report for 1982, the shocking message of which was too much for even the most skilled spinmeister to soften. The report began, "It is with mixed feelings that we review the performance of the Corporation in 1982. On the one hand, it was a difficult year for the Chase. We absorbed substantial losses—the result of our well-publicized problems relating to Drysdale Government Securities, Inc., and to loans acquired through the Penn Square Bank, N.A., which failed in July." In 1982, Chase Manhattan charged off $75 million in energy-related loans acquired through Penn Square Bank. "The future value of this portfolio obviously will be affected by conditions prevailing in the energy market," continued the somber letter to stockholders. "But the $75 million charged off represented our best estimate at year-end 1982 of losses incurred."[62]

It seemed like everyone was having trouble with estimates.

Continental Illinois, Seafirst, and Chase Manhattan were not the only institutions enamored of banking with the guys from Oklahoma. Three others—Northern Trust, Michigan National Corporation, and Hibernia—joined the party as "spillover banks" whenever the Big Three decided that they, too, needed some help. Meanwhile, Robert Hefner kept up his punishing pace of advocacy on behalf of deep gas. On April 23, 1981, he was granted a hearing before the Senate Subcommittee on Energy Regulation. "I urge the Subcommittee to give our industry the chance to produce the energy America needs to achieve non-inflationary, steadily improving, real economic growth," concluded Hefner to listeners who surely appreciated his celebrity status.[63]

Hefner was back in Washington, D.C., on November 6, 1981, to make a statement before the Senate Committee on Energy and Natural Resources. This time, he made three key points: (1) the Natural Gas Policy Act was "not just working well, it is prompting the largest natural gas drilling boom in the history of the industry"; (2) "the NGPA is providing or can provide, if properly implemented, maximum incentives for production of all of the natural gas in the United States remaining to be found"; and (3) speculative problems, including inflation and high interests rates, were hampering production. "Our industry is one of the great success stories in America today," declared Hefner. "To stay that way we need exactly what our customers need: stable costs, reasonable credit, and a buoyant economy."[64] Even as controversy raged over further decontrols of natural gas aimed at bringing its price closer to the energy equivalent of crude oil, Hefner stuck to his guns, insisting that three-quarters of the nation's gas-bearing sediments lay below fifteen thousand feet. As he said in an October 1981 story in Fortune, "We've got to focus capital where we can find the giant, Prudhoe Bay-type reserves."[65]

By then, neither congressmen nor bankers—and certainly not drillers!—needed convincing that the deep gas play in the Anadarko Basin was the real McCoy. In the early morning hours of January 28, 1981, two perennial oil-patch losers, Clark Ellison and Buddy Appleby, awoke to the news that they were overnight millionaires.[66] The Tomcat No. 1, an exploratory well about three miles north of Eakly in Caddo County, Oklahoma, in which the two men held a 7 percent interest, had rumbled and belched its way to glory as one of the biggest strikes ever. The operator, Ports of Call Oil Company of Oklahoma City, had been aiming for the Hunton formation at a depth of 20,000 feet. But pay dirt happened to be at 15,335 feet in the sandstone and shale deposits comprising the Springer formation, leaving plenty of leeway to qualify for deregulated deep gas prices.[67]

The first sign that something big was afoot was when the drilling mud disappeared into the hole. With a deafening roar that rendered communication all but impossible and left no time to engage the rig's giant stack of blowout preventers, the crew scrambled for cover as the well blew out and spewed natural gas into the air at a rate of more than 100 million cubic feet per day. With deep gas selling for ten dollars per thousand cubic feet, millions of dollars' worth of sweet natural gas a day was sending vapor and noxious fumes cascading across cotton fields and peanut patches, prompting authorities in Eakly to make plans for an evacuation. For days after the blowout, residents waited anxiously for wind shifts to signal a hasty departure. Gathering at the recreation center, they greeted each other with the cheerful query, "You ready to go?"[68]

For Ellison and Appleby, who had lost their wives and fortunes and most of their dignity in years of unsuccessful ventures, the Tomcat No. 1

stood to make them about $50,000 a day, or nearly $1.5 million a month. The Washington Gas Light Company's 19 percent interest in the well transformed a standard gas distribution company into a player in the big leagues. Within days, its stock price surged from $18.50 to more than $40.00. Lease bonuses that had been in the range of $500 an acre shot up to $3,000 an acre—if, that is, unleased acreage could be found. One local farmer who agreed to lease his thirty acres got a check for nearly $1 million. Never mind that the rush of gas at the Tomcat No. 1 caused the collapse of some of the shale layers in the Springer formation at the bottom of the hole and shut off the flow, leaving owners of mineral interests with much to fret about and Ports of Call Oil Company with a major headache.[69] As John Lehr of the Tulsa-based fund Samson Properties quipped in an interview with *Oil and Gas Investor* in December 1981, "The hardest problem in the Anadarko today is how to say 'no' to investors with money to spend."[70]

And so the stars lined up to produce a boom that struck at the heart of what it means to be an Oklahoman. Statistics are one way to measure the frenzy that gripped western Oklahoma in those heady days: the price of Oklahoma crude oil increased tenfold between 1972 and 1981; natural gas prices, unshackled from their chains, shot up; and employment in the oil patch grew from around 34,000 jobs in the early 1970s to a peak of 102,000 in 1981.[71] At the same time, personal income zoomed off the charts. According to the Oklahoma Commerce Department's Bureau of Economic Analysis, from 1979 to 1981 Oklahoma was second only to Alaska in its percentage increase in personal income. "There was a very rapid growth in mining," declared bureau spokesman David Cartwright, who clearly had a flair for understatement. Not only was Oklahoma's percentage increase in total personal income the second highest in the nation; its percentage increase in per capita personal income also gave the state a number two ranking—again, topped only by Alaska. During those giddy years, earnings in the oil and gas industry went from $1,491,000,000 in 1979 to $3,304,000,000 in 1982. Wholesale trade shot up 54 percent, and machine manufacturing increased 51 percent.[72]

Prosperity in the oil patch meant big business for oil-field suppliers. According to Denver-based Petroleum Information Corporation, industry revenues rose from $16.1 billion in 1979 to $31.7 billion in 1981 for an increase of 97 percent. During that same time period, revenues of eight of the largest oil-field supply companies surged 56 percent, and their profits climbed 102 percent. Few expected the oil-field industry's torrid growth to continue indefinitely. But nearly everyone thought it would last long enough, surely through 1982 and perhaps into the mid-1980s, to justify ramping up production of drilling rigs and rock bits and other tools of the trade. Rig builders turned out 1,100 rigs in 1981, adding 30 percent to the national total in a single twelve-month period. In early 1982, they were confident that they would find customers to buy an additional 1,400. Rosy predictions had the added effect of luring hundreds of entrepreneurs into the oil-field supply business. Between 1979 and 1981, more than four hundred new oil-field companies, operating from garages and machine shops from Texas to the Rocky Mountains, joined the International Association of Drilling Contractors, all bent on striking it rich in the "awl b'ness."[73]

Cities that had the good fortune to sit on top of the bounty felt the effects of the boom in their sales tax revenues. From 1977 to 1982, revenues went from $866,548.40 to $5,660,996.11 in Elk City, from $763,859.48 to $3,123,059.28 in Clinton, and from $609,579.10 to $1,920,886.51 in Weatherford.[74] At the peak of the boom in late 1981, Elk City was home to six banks, leaving plenty of options for depositing the money raining in from the eight hundred or so rigs then drilling in Oklahoma.[75] But if you were looking for a place to put your head down for the night, the options dwindled. Bob McCormack, a veteran banker from Duncan whose company, McCormack & Associates, Inc., has provided consulting services to banks since 1985, recalled Elk City as ground zero of the drilling frenzy. "I remember, in those days, Elk City people were renting out a place in their garage for somebody to put a cot for $800 a month," said McCormack.[76] Duncan certainly felt the heat, but not to the extent as Elk City and its bustling neighbors to the north.

Never far from the action were Robert Hefner the proselytizer and Bill Patterson the moneylender, each captivated by what the Anadarko Basin had to offer, and each daring to go where lesser mortals feared to tread. Basking in their glow like a watchful parent was Penn Square Bank chairman Beep Jennings, whose model of correspondent banking with upstream banks had catapulted his bank to a position of leadership in oil and gas lending. As he told journalist Mark Singer, "I believe that, beyond lending money, a banker has to encourage and create opportunities. Concern for a customer and a desire to see him succeed are not inconsistent with a sound credit policy. I think I'm a damn good credit man and I'm a damn good collector."[77]

The deep gas play in the late 1970s and early 1980s unleashed a testosterone-charged era of what Gayla Sherry and her incredulous colleagues dubbed "yeehaw banking" (a southwestern version of dump-truck banking that captured the fancy of John Boyd and his gang in Seattle).[78] Inspired by predictions that oil prices would soar into the hundreds of dollars a barrel, drillers and their bankers succumbed to hubris on a fantastic scale, and it found expression in western bravado and iconic imagery that form the deepest strata of American culture. Nowhere was their get-rich-quick ethos more deeply ingrained than in Oklahoma. Oil wells spudded in the Indian Territory to become the genesis of empires; trespassing on federal land that rendered Oklahoma the only state in the Union to be identified with land-grabbing ne'er-do-wells (Sooners, that is); Indian land fraud that enriched the few and forever besmirched Oklahoma's claim as a crucible of democracy; scrambles to charter the first bank in town, and never mind the capital; real estate bubbles that turned paupers into princes and, sometimes, back into paupers; gushers that put millions in people's pockets and a glossy sheen on untold acres of prime farmland—these and other experiences that shaped Oklahoma history continue to flow like an underground aquifer through the state's culture. With guts and money (that is, other people's money) and a push from the gods of good fortune, the American Dream could become the American Reality—in this case, with an Oklahoma accent. Seen in its historical context, the Anadarko Basin boom was simply the latest—but surely not the last—journey to the Promised Land.

But numbers cannot begin to describe the dreamscape that drew pilgrims by the thousands to those arid plains. At the time of this writing in 2014, you could still bring tears to an Oklahoma oilie's eyes by asking him or (less likely but certainly possible) her to recall the boom times: sleepy villages transformed into dynamos of buying and leasing and drilling; hairdressers and plumbers and schoolteachers mortgaging their homes to cash in on the "awl b'ness"; cocktail banter about penny oil stocks and off-the-chart leasing bonuses; hardscrabble ranchers driving their wives to dinner in sleek new Cadillacs; fistfights breaking out in county courthouses as landmen (and women) wrestled for ponderous deed books that recorded every transaction visited upon every scrap of land in those blessed environs; and pickup truck bumpers proudly displaying a whole new genre of oil-field witticism—"Oilfield Trash and Proud of It," and that all-time favorite, "Please Don't Tell My Mother I'm Working in the Oil Patch. She Thinks I'm a Piano Player in a Whorehouse."

Oh, the joy of easy money! The delight, after generations of mundane toil, in finding the key to prosperity in the flatlands of western Oklahoma, their plainness the perfect camouflage for the treasures below!

Like Icarus in his mythic flight from the Labyrinth, Oklahomans were soaring toward the sun on wings made of wax. Who among them, or us, could have foreseen the day when bumper stickers on dented and weathered pickup trucks would signal the end of the party and, metaphorically, the unfortunate boy's plummet into the sea: "Lord, Please Give Us Another Boom. We Promise Not to Piss It Away This Time."

CHAPTER EIGHT

And Bust

"The dead rats just kept floating to the top of the punch bowl."
Steve Plunk, national bank examiner

Anadarko Basin fever seemed to be catching on everywhere—everywhere, that is, except the comptroller of the currency's office in Dallas, where regional administrator Clifton Poole and his colleagues were watching a disaster in the making. The examination of Penn Square Bank conducted in early 1980 was not the first, and certainly not the last, in a series of steps undertaken by federal officials aimed at curbing the bank's excesses. In June 1980, Penn Square Bank directors were required to submit periodic reports to the regional office in Dallas. In a foretaste of what lay in store for the high-flying bankers, they were summoned to a meeting in Clifton Poole's office on June 19. The meeting started badly and deteriorated when Poole ordered the directors to cease and desist the practices that were branding their bank as a renegade. For the rest of the year, letters flew and phone lines hummed between Oklahoma City and Dallas, but not even stern warnings from the comptroller's office could put a damper on the bank's growth. In its annual report for the year ending December 31, 1980, Penn Square Bank reported growth in assets of $288.26 million over the prior year, an increase of 103.7 percent.[1]

An examination conducted between January 5 and February 27, 1981, revealed further deterioration in the bank's overall condition. On

June 23, Clifton Poole notified the FDIC of the bank's precarious condition, prompting that agency to participate in examinations for "contingency purposes."[2] In its spring 1981 report card issued on July 1, the comptroller's office in Dallas noted that the "overall deterioration in the loan portfolio is of significant concern to this examination due to this institution's overall cash management and liquidity problems." The report went on to accuse directors and senior management of failing to prudently supervise the bank's activities and, in a replay of the showdown a year earlier, summoned them to another meeting in Dallas. In a no-holds-barred face-off on July 29, Poole told Jennings and his colleagues that they were "flirting with disaster" by failing to comply with nine of ten items listed in the "administrative agreement" reached the previous summer.[3] Once again, harsh words were exchanged; once again, Penn Square Bank directors stuck to their unorthodox growth strategy. The sparring continued for the rest of 1981, with the comptroller's office doing what it could to enforce compliance and the bank continuing to book loans. Penn Square Bank's annual report for 1981 showed a 36.7 percent increase in asset growth to a dizzying $394.16 million.[4]

Chairman Beep Jennings was beaming. As he noted in the annual report, "Since 1974 assets and stockholders' equity have increased more than tenfold, while deposits are more than 12 times their level eight years ago."[5] Such was the momentum in Bill Patterson's energy-lending department that, between September 30, 1981, and April 1982, the bank generated $900 million in loans.[6] Clearly dismayed by the juggernaut next door, one suburban banker near Penn Square Bank remarked, "This is crazy. It just can't last."[7]

While officialdom tried unsuccessfully to bring Penn Square Bank to heel, it was business as usual in Bill Patterson's energy-lending division, which was anything but usual. In the tsunami of press reports that later attended the bank's closing in July 1982, analogies were drawn between the bank and the Sigma Chi house at OU. The main differences were that bankers wore suits (most of the time, anyway) and had more money. Patterson's attire kept his staff guessing—one day it was a Tyrolean outfit, complete with a plumed hat and lederhosen, and on another day it was the tattered garb of a hobo. He pushed the limits of political correctness by strolling through the bank one day wearing a Nazi helmet emblazoned with swastikas.[8] One imagines reams of loan papers hitting the floor as stunned secretaries let go their cargo to gawk at their boss disguised as a storm trooper.

Quitting time, and sometimes pre-quitting time, was often heralded with the popping of champagne corks and rounds for everyone. On a really good day, when the streams to New York and Chicago and Seattle were teaming with loan participations, toasts and ribald banker banter were interrupted by Bill Patterson's call to action: "Let's rodeo!" There followed a quick trip to Las Vegas—the bank's jets were handy for that—where the revelry ramped up a notch and Patterson might be spotted wearing his signature Mickey Mouse ears.[9]

Joel Champlin of Enid never experienced the fun and games, but he was happy to recount stories of friends who had ringside seats at the bacchanalia. "And I have some friends who said that the amazing thing about Patterson was that he would go, go, go all the time," said Champlin. "One New Years, they took a jet, and they started in New York, and they partied, and they flew to Chicago, and then they flew to Denver, and then they flew . . ." Champlin's voice trailed off as he struggled to describe a party scene that, even at a distance of three decades, continues to boggle the mind and defy the imagination. "And he was drinking Champagne out of cowboy boots," said Champlin at last, "and he was putting them back on. So he was just a fun guy, incredible amount of energy—go, go, go the whole time!"[10]

Celebrations closer to home often wound up at Cowboys, a watering hole in Oklahoma City favored by hard-partying bankers, where the reveler-in-chief quaffed beer from his boots and reenacted Sigma Chi food fights, leaving the waitstaff with a mess, the bank with an ever-increasing expense account, and upstream bankers in town for business meetings with enduring impressions of Oklahoma. "There's no way we'll ever do business with this guy," remarked an officer from Manufacturers Hanover Trust Company in New York who stopped in at Cowboys for a drink and witnessed Bill Patterson in action. This time, Patterson's fun and games fell flat, and Manufacturers Hanover Trust Company saved a pile of money.[11]

Patterson's antics seem all the more extraordinary insofar as they played out under the purview of Penn Square Bank president Eldon Beller. Like his predecessor, Frank Murphy, Beller fit the stereotype of the conservative banker. His tenure as president of Penn Square Bank began in April 1981, and it followed a stellar career as executive vice president and chief lending officer under the tight-fisted Chuck Vose, Sr., at the First National Bank and Trust Company of Oklahoma City.[12] "He was a Vose man," declared Arvest Bank senior vice president G. P. Johnson Hightower, who was in his late twenties and working in the First's national accounts division at the time of Beller's departure. "He was going to, by God, tow the company line! He grew up the old-fashioned way." Hightower and his colleagues were understandably shocked when Beller took his old-school credentials from the state's largest and most profitable bank to Penn Square. In all likelihood, Beller's decision had something to do with a salary that was twice his earnings at the First.[13]

But that might not be the whole story. "My thought was, why would Beep Jennings hire Eldon Beller, and what in the world would prompt Eldon Beller to go there?" asked Hightower rhetorically. "Well," he continued, "I kind of think that Beep hired Eldon because he was a hard-line, old-fashioned banker. I guess [Jennings] thought he could control the Monk."

"You're talking about Bill Patterson?" I asked.

"Yep," said Hightower.

Scouting for business in the Midwest and Southeast in the early 1980s, Hightower relied mainly on hearsay to chronicle the rise and fall of Penn Square Bank. "I had little children, I was on the road a week every month, and my business was all national except for national clients that had local offices. I didn't even hear that much, except stories of big parties, drinking whisky out of boots, and throwing quail at Cowboys." Still, Hightower heard enough to perceive the logic in Jennings's decision to woo Eldon Beller from the First. "I think he needed an authority figure, who was an old-line banker. But, it was obviously too late. Eldon was the kind of guy you would immediately have respect for. I mean, you wouldn't want him to see you walking into the office at 8:05 or something. You'd never be late!"[14]

Meanwhile, back in the trenches at Penn Square Bank clerks and secretaries were no more successful than national bank examiners in following the paper trail. But then, some of the secretaries might have been preoccupied. John Mabrey, senior executive vice president and chief administration officer at Citizens Security Bank in Bixby, was a bank examiner in 1979 and spent six weeks divining the secrets of Penn Square Bank's success. "One of Bill Patterson's secretaries had a $60,000 unsecured loan," recalled Mabrey. "She'd used the money to buy a Mercedes. I asked, 'Why didn't you take the Mercedes as collateral?'" And the answer? "Well, she's going to pay the loan back, so we really don't need the collateral."[15]

Tension mounted between the oil and gas division and the note cage as the books careened out of balance by some $30 million. In what one officer described as a shell game in which nobody could locate the pea, loans were stuffed in cardboard boxes and shipped upstream to Continental Illinois, and the people on the receiving end did not even bother to look at them. They just said, "Leave them here. We'll wire you the money."[16] Such was Continental Illinois's faith in its winning strategy and modern-day gunslingers that nobody noticed when its loans at Penn Square Bank hit $1,056,000,000—six times its lending limit to one borrower.[17]

As more and more bad loans cropped up, Patterson hit on an ingenious way to keep them off the books: simply advance interest on past-due accounts, much like Chase Manhattan and Continental Illinois did with loans to third world countries. As this practice became more common, the need arose to come up with a new moniker, and "upstreaming of interest" was coined as one more assault on the English language. Another maneuver was to roll interest on one loan into a new loan as a way to pay the interest on the new one. In a particularly clever sleight of hand, loans were made to one company or partnership to pay off the notes or overdrafts to another company or partnership owned by the same company.[18] And so on.

Some bankers were jealous of Penn Square Bank's track record and became more aggressive in their lending policies. Others, stodgier and perhaps trained in old-school methods of bookkeeping, tried to discipline their errant competitor. Liberty National Bank and Trust Company of Oklahoma City stopped accepting Penn Square Bank's letters of credit, and the First National Bank and Trust Company of Oklahoma City forced the shopping-center bank to secure its Fed funds lines.[19] But nothing, it seemed, could stop Penn Square Bank from stealing customers from its competitors by offering deals of a lifetime.

Nick Berry, a former artist with Jordan and Associates in Oklahoma City, was asked to produce a series of advertisements for the company's red-hot client. "The Jordan and Associates account executive was explicit in his instructions," said Berry. "He told me to put them together like

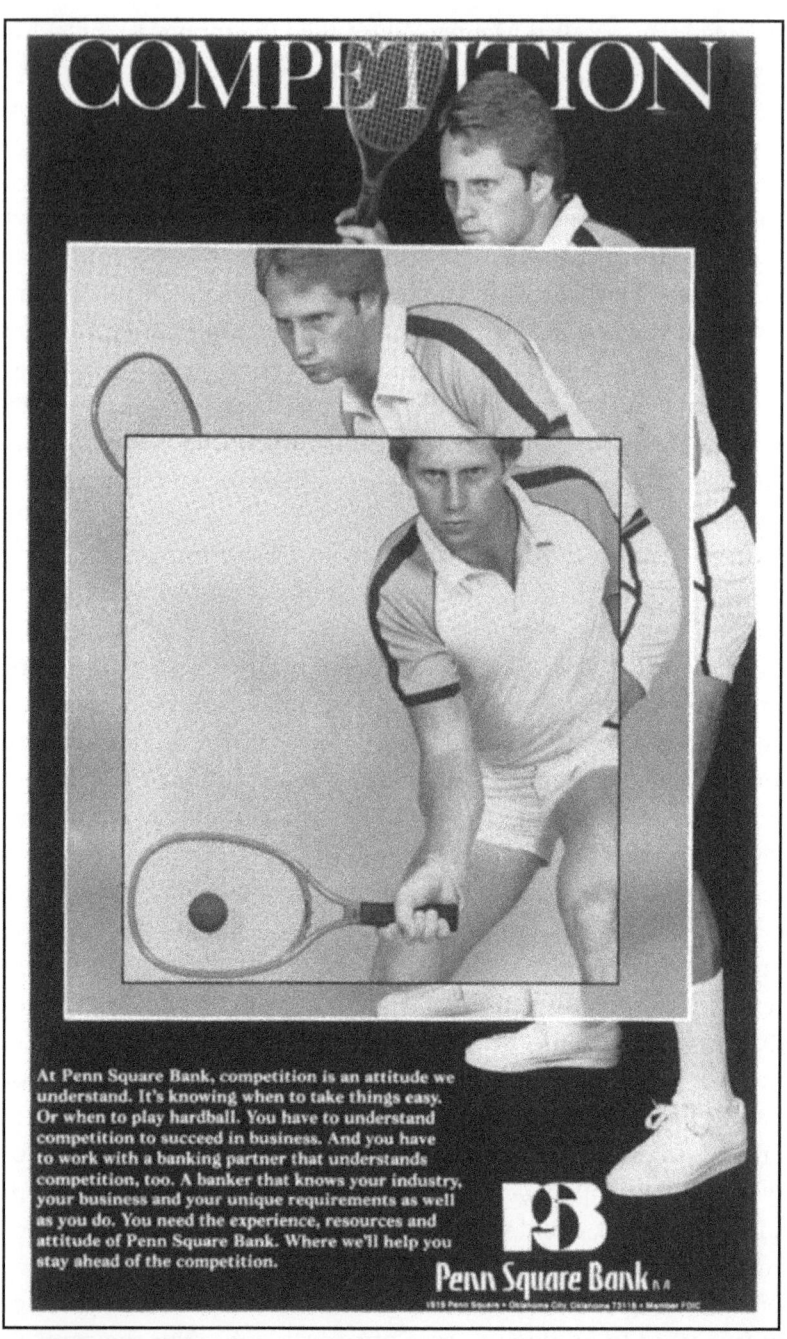

A series of advertisements designed by Nick Berry of Jordan and Associates in Oklahoma City branded Penn Square Bank as a dynamo of energy lending, 1981. Courtesy Nick Berry Penn Square Bank Advertisement Collection.

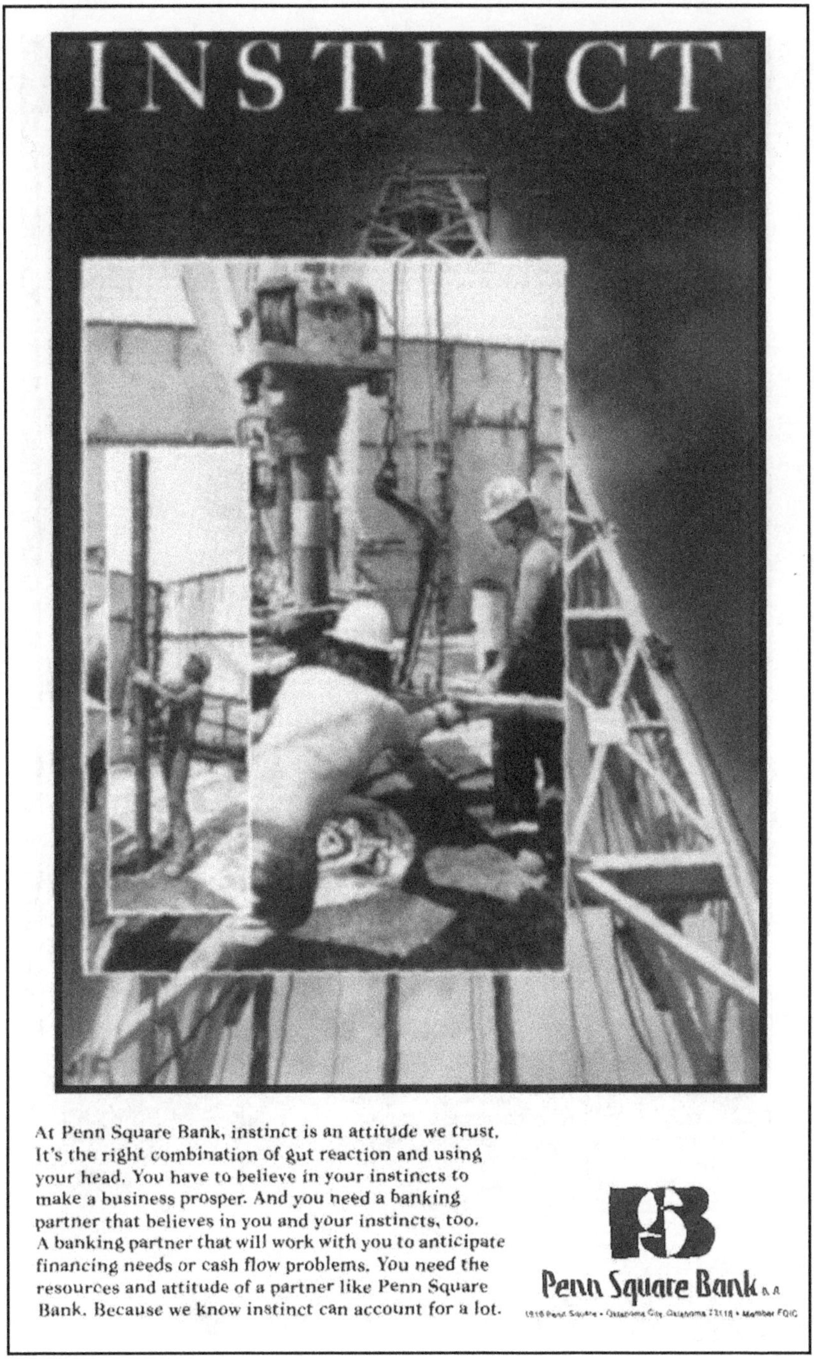

INSTINCT

At Penn Square Bank, instinct is an attitude we trust. It's the right combination of gut reaction and using your head. You have to believe in your instincts to make a business prosper. And you need a banking partner that believes in you and your instincts, too. A banking partner that will work with you to anticipate financing needs or cash flow problems. You need the resources and attitude of a partner like Penn Square Bank. Because we know instinct can account for a lot.

they were in motion, and to make sure they expressed a sense of power." Berry recalled the early 1980s as a period of "excess, decadence, and over-indulgence," an ethos that was on display every day in the upscale neighborhood of Nichols Hills just north of the bank. "I remember seeing some men sporting mink coats," continued Berry. "And it wasn't unusual to see a Ferrari or Rolls Royce cruising down the street. One Rolls that I saw regularly was orange!"[20]

Fancy cars were all the rage as John Mabrey puzzled over the books. He and his examination team left the bank on a Friday afternoon and were astonished when they returned the following Monday to find that an unusual remodeling job had taken place over the weekend. "They had cut a wall out and driven a Rolls Royce in the lobby, and put the wall back up!" exclaimed Mabrey, still incredulous at a remove of thirty-plus years. The deal was simple: Deposit $1 million and leave it in the bank for five years, and the car was yours. "That's while the examiners were there!" continued Mabrey. "Instead of interest, they would give you a Rolls Royce. That was crazy! They did it while the examiners were there! They could have waited two weeks, and we wouldn't have known about it."[21]

Mabrey and his colleagues filed their reports, but to no avail. "We would write up the report and send it on, but they wouldn't really do much about it," said Mabrey. "Everything was going along so good."[22] Mabrey paused to reflect on his six-week experience of watching a disaster in the making—a disaster that nobody was inclined to stop.

By the time Phillip L. Zweig arrived in the Southwest from New York to cover the deep gas play for the *American Banker,* the boom was somewhere near its crescendo, and there was no shortage of newsworthy stories. But as he wound his way from bankers' offices in Dallas to towering rigs and bustling boomtowns in the Anadarko Basin, he was beginning to suspect that something was amiss in the gas boom's financial underpinnings. Before he left New York, he had studied statistics on Oklahoma banks published by Sheshunoff Information Services, and one bank whose name made easterners think it was in Pennsylvania was notable for its extraordinary asset growth rate. Nestled next to Shelly's Tall Girl Shop and swabbed with a drab whitewash, the bank's low operating expenses indicated that it was booking and monitoring a lot of loans with very few people. Zweig's interest was piqued, but he did not give the bank much thought as he transitioned from New York highrises to the wide vistas of Oklahoma.

In the course of Zweig's conversations and interviews, the bank kept coming up, and when it did, eyes rolled and brows furrowed and sentences dangled. Revealing a flair for understatement, Zweig acknowledged that bankers "are not comfortable talking about other banks, particularly those that might be in trouble."[23] The peripatetic Zweig also found that the glow was fading from the oil-boom euphoria. Oil-field service companies were having a tough time collecting their money from contractors, and bankers were beginning to reminisce about other booms that had ended badly. The easy-come-easy-go attitude is probably encoded in the genes of native Oklahomans, but it was enough to give a New York journalist pause for reflection.

From Dallas high-rises to Oklahoma gas rigs, an implacable logic was taking hold, and it confirmed economics' designation as "the dismal science." Frenzied natural gas production, OPEC's diminishing clout in manipulating fuel prices, and slackening demand attending the new conservation ethos were conspiring to produce an oversupply of natural gas and to push prices ever lower. As the chief financial officer of one deep gas producer explained, pipeline companies were becoming overextended on their take-or-pay contracts. Simply put, they were committed to buying more gas, deep and shallow, than they could possibly sell.

Like the proverbial canary in the coal mine, the stock market foretold dark days to come. By October 1981, prices of most oil and gas common stocks were down 30 percent from the previous year. According to lease broker Steve Knox, "The whole Ponzi scheme stopped in January."[24]

So maybe the real story was not in western Oklahoma, but rather, in the offices of a place called Penn Square Bank. Zweig's reportorial radar went on high alert when bank officials met his initial inquiries with stonewalling—an unpardonable sin to any journalist, and a sure sign that he was onto something. Board chairman Beep Jennings became downright belligerent when Zweig asked him about his bank's loan losses in 1981. Such financial information is a matter of public record and was easily obtainable from the FDIC, but it did not appear in the bank's annual report. "Get them yourself!" snapped Jennings to the startled reporter. Which he did, discovering that Penn Square Bank's loan losses had risen more than tenfold over the previous year. Even more shocking than the losses was the purpose for borrowing the money in the first place. The bank's money was spent not on oil and gas production, but rather, to purchase racehorses.[25] Zweig revealed his reportorial zeal in his method of finding out where bank examiners were staying. Knowing the amount of their expense accounts, he looked for motels in the metro area that fit their budgets. Sure enough, Zweig narrowed his search until he found motels swarming with guys in suits.[26]

Comparing the coverage of troubled banks to a high-wire balancing act, Zweig knew he had to tread lightly. Overt criticism could trigger a run on the bank, and excessive restraint would compromise his responsibilities as a journalist and might put depositors at risk. But Zweig's commitment to ethical journalism was not enough to keep Jennings from summoning a special meeting of Penn Square Bank's board of directors on April 2, 1982, to discuss how to handle the gadfly from New York. Enraged by inquiries that he castigated as flat-out accusatory, Jennings referred to the reporter's facts as "highly inaccurate and in some cases absurd." Bank president Eldon Beller noted that he had spoken to Preston Morrow in the comptroller of the currency's office and had given him an unambiguous message: if Zweig "continued to make inaccurate and harmful statements about the Bank to third parties, which could harm the bank, he [Mr. Beller] would expect the Comptroller's Office to assist us at our request." By then, Jennings had heard enough. He closed the meeting by admonishing the board to maintain "a low-key approach" when Phil Zweig came calling.[27]

After checking and rechecking his facts and consulting with his editors back in New York, Zweig broke the story on April 26 with a four-thousand-word article in the *American Banker* under the title "Oklahoma's Penn Square Bank, Maverick Oil Patch Lender: Some Say It's Bet Too Heavily on Energy." Referring in his opening paragraph to Penn Square Bank's reputation as Continental Illinois's loan production office in Oklahoma City, Zweig cut directly to the chase: the bank was up to its eyeballs in loan participations, and sinking deeper. He explained, "Having sold more than $2 billion in participations—almost seven times the $300 million in loans the bank now has on its own books—Penn Square may well have originated more loans relative to its own portfolio than any other bank in the nation. The volume of participations relative to loans varies considerably from bank to bank, but it is certainly unusual for outstanding participations to exceed net loans."[28]

The news got worse. Nationwide, drilling rigs were being idled as declining prices for oil and gas could no longer support the enormous costs of operating them. This was particularly bad news for Penn Square Bank, whose "huge volume of participations, rapid growth, highly aggressive lending practices, some acknowledged snafus in loan documentation, and a dramatic rise in charge-offs in 1981 have made it the object of some sharp criticism in Oklahoma banking circles." Meanwhile, some of the bank's most highly leveraged borrowers, including Robert Hefner, Carl Andersen, Jr., and Carl Swan were "believed to be experiencing serious cash flow difficulties." Older banks downtown were increasingly wary of Penn Square Bank's strategy of earning fee income rather than holding assets. Despite Chairman Jennings's declaration that no correspondent "has ever lost a penny on a Penn Square loan," upstream bankers were signaling that the volume of their loan participations exceeded their comfort level "because of what they called the customary 'moral obligation' of a loan originator to buy back loans that go bad, particularly loans sold downstream."[29]

Beep Jennings, characterized as "an old-school entrepreneur," dismissed criticisms of his bank as plain old jealousy and insisted that the $4.2 million in 1981 charge-offs represented a onetime write-off of bad real estate loans, not energy credits, much of which he expected to recover. Zweig wrote, "Taking a short puff on his ever-present cigar, Mr. Jennings asserts that his institution has been a boon to the expansion of the capital-intensive oil and gas industry in Oklahoma, a state he describes as relatively cash-poor despite its robust energy economy." "Our growth," explained Jennings to the prying reporter, "appears so dramatic because we started with such a small base. By moving into an active posture early, and concentrating efforts on independent producers, perhaps when other banks were not, we established an original base of producers who are our very best salesmen. Word gets out pretty quickly that Penn Square is interested in the oilman."[30]

Early on, the local press did not seem to pay much attention to Zweig's article. Perhaps suspecting, as Oklahomans are apt to do, that New York journalists are incapable of getting anything right west of the Hudson River, the *Sunday Oklahoman* and the *Oklahoma City Journal Record* published articles in May and June of 1982 portraying Penn Square Bank as a community-oriented bank with a winning formula. On May 2, the *Sunday Oklahoman* credited Beep Jennings with orchestrating a revolution in energy lending. Before Penn Square Bank came on the scene, energy lending, at least in central Oklahoma, had been the almost exclusive preserve of the First National Bank and Trust Company of Oklahoma City. True, Liberty Bank and Fidelity Bank were coming on strong, and the First Continental Bank in Del City had broken the $140 million mark in assets to become the ninth-largest bank in the Oklahoma City area. But nobody could match Penn Square Bank and its practice of marketing energy loans to larger banks. Boasting that his bank was selling 80 percent of its energy loans to upstream banks, Jennings laid claim to a distinguished tradition pioneered by merchant bankers in England. Orthodox bankers had doubts about Penn Square Bank's notoriety as Continental Illinois's loan production office in the oil patch, but no matter. By March 31, 1982, Penn Square Bank was ranked as the fourth-largest bank in the Oklahoma City metropolitan area and among the top ten banks in the state. The *Sunday Oklahoman* mentioned Zweig's article briefly and almost dismissively—more as a foil for Beep Jennings's bravado than an indication of impropriety.

On June 6, it was the *Oklahoma City Journal Record*'s turn to report on Beep Jennings's financial savvy. In a speech to the Kiwanis Club of Oklahoma City, Jennings dispensed free advice to folks wondering what to do about economic problems that were beginning to cast a pall on Oklahoma's energy boom: "Put hay in the barn, tighten belts and learn to make do." As heads around the room no doubt bobbed in unison, Jennings cautioned his listeners not to expect much of a drop in interest rates. He then touched on a favorite theme in business circles: congressional ineptitude. "Congress," intoned the bank chairman to more bobbing of heads, "has the lowest credibility, in regard to fiscal policy, that it has ever had." He asserted that inflation was more to be feared than unemployment ("Ask the people of Germany. They know what inflation can do.") and, in an abrupt change of pace, urged his listeners to do their part for historic preservation. Beyond their aesthetic value, said Jennings, restored buildings make "good economic sense—these building restorations not only preserve history, but are useful economically."[31]

While Beep Jennings was playing to the home crowd, his colleagues upstream were showing signs of stress. Fielding questions about a precipitous drop in the stock price of Continental Illinois's parent company, Continental Illinois Corporation, occasioned by problems in the bank's burgeoning energy loan portfolio, Chairman Roger Anderson put on his game face. "Sometimes we have seen these worries enlarged out of proportion, especially when memory fails to recall banking's proved ability to cope with and reconcile them," he explained in an interview in the *Chicago Tribune* the day after Zweig's article was published in the *American Banker*. Perhaps to bolster his own confidence, he concluded, "Our loans are very well grounded."[32]

The noose tightened a month later when the *Wall Street Journal* weighed in on the effects of Continental Illinois's aggressive lending. Once a favorite of analysts and business school graduates alike, Continental Illinois was sinking under the weight of problem loans. Of special concern were energy loans. With about 15 percent of its total loan portfolio in oil and gas, Continental Illinois was betting much more on energy than most banks outside the Southwest. Charge-offs against earnings in 1981 were nearly triple the average rate of the previous five years. Lawrence Fuller, a bank analyst with Drexel Burnham Lambert, Inc., put it this way: "They have been very aggressive, and it is costing them now."[33]

In signs that the times were truly changing, Detroit was beginning to roll out fewer gas guzzlers, and consumers were climbing aboard the conservation bandwagon in increasing numbers—good news for the planet, but bad news for bankers who were counting on high energy prices to fuel their lending sprees.[34] Morgan Guaranty Trust Company discerned a "fundamental shift in the demand for and supply of oil" that could have brought a drop of 25 to 30 percent in the price of oil in 1982–83. This seismic shift spelled trouble not only for oil exporting countries but also for domestic companies whose fortunes were increasingly tied to international markets.[35]

By the late spring of 1982, a pall of uncertainty was hovering above the oil patch, and its shadow reached to the whitewashed dynamo in the Penn Square Shopping Center. Perhaps it was some consolation that bankers had company in their impending fall from grace. For months, federal snoops had been prowling the back roads of Oklahoma and nabbing county commissioners on the take. In what became the largest scandal of its kind in American history, county commissioners by the score were exposed for their habit, long since accepted as a cost of doing business in just about all of Oklahoma's seventy-seven counties, of receiving kickbacks and bribes in the manner of third world kingpins. Much to Oklahomans' chagrin, the *Economist* on November 7, 1981, blew the lid off what came to be known simply as the county commissioner scandal—hardly the makings of a state PR campaign.[36]

Meg Salyer was Chase Manhattan Bank's designated hitter for structuring loan participations with Penn Square Bank, and she has pinpointed the moment when the wheels started coming off the bus. She and some Chase associates had scheduled a dinner with two of Penn Square Bank's most frequent borrowers: Frank Mahan (who earned the distinction of being one of the few people who could get kicked out of Junior's, a popular venue for Oklahoma oilies) and William E. "Billy" Rowsey, homegrown Okies who had combined their resources in the fall of 1979 to form a drilling concern, Mahan & Rowsey, Inc.[37] "The Mahan-Rowsey is probably the first largish credit that we had an opportunity to look at," said Salyer.

> So, the two of them came to New York with Bill Patterson and—I can't think who else from the bank—but, you know, one or two from Penn Square, and we had dinner in New York with, I think, two senior vice presidents of Chase. There was at least one v.p., myself, and then several others. Frank Mahan was so rude at that dinner that two people got up and left. And the next day, you know, I just said I wouldn't ever have anything to do with him. It was not a relationship that I managed or had anything to do with.

Searching for a way to summarize her thoughts, Salyer borrowed a line from Mark Singer's *Funny Money*. "This place is evil," said Salyer and one of Singer's interviewees.[38]

Salyer was dumfounded by a business boom that was quickly morphing into a morality tale, and she found herself staring up at the underbelly of American business. "Most of these were normal people operating on the facts and circumstances at the time, involved in a crazy, heady . . ." Her voice trailed off as she reflected on the experience, now thirty years distant. "Did people drink wine out of their shoes from time to time? Yes! Did people throw quail out of their pockets? Yes! It was probably all partly just a relief from the incredible, crazy tension. Was everybody minting money? Yes! And then the cards began to come down, and there was a lot of scrambling to place blame."[39]

The beginning of the end of Penn Square Bank can be dated to April 19, 1982—a week before Phillip Zweig's article was published—when the comptroller of the currency launched his final examination. The long-suffering regional administrator Clifton Poole quickly notified his superiors in Washington, D.C., that "potentially serious problems" were coming to light.[40] More examiners with expertise in energy loans were brought in from Houston, Dallas, and other cities to lend their assistance, prompting one Penn Square Bank employee to remark, "They were like rabbits. They seemed to multiply overnight."[41] Simultaneously, examiners supervising the big three correspondent banks—Continental Illinois, Chase Manhattan, and Seafirst—were advised of the "poor quality" of loans and the likelihood of significant losses. A banker who examined Penn Square Bank loans after its collapse commented, "The collateral was misfiled or not filed. It was just horribly documented. There wasn't a good loan in the lot."[42] So much for Bill Patterson's mantra: "There are no bad deals. Every deal can be corrected with money."[43]

In May, an energy loan expert was sent to Chicago to assist with an assessment of Continental Illinois's portfolio. Back in Oklahoma City, as many as thirty borrowers were identified on June 16 as possible violators of Penn Square Bank's legal lending limits, and employees were cautioned against extending additional credit to them.[44] And on June 28, large depositors began withdrawing their funds.

The last day of June 1982 was a busy one, both in Oklahoma City and Washington, D.C. It was then that the comptroller asked FDIC chairman William M. Isaac to summon a meeting to discuss the imminent failure of Penn Square Bank. Isaac responded by dispatching ten examination and liquidation personnel to Oklahoma City. The bank's shoddy paperwork, including some three thousand improperly documented loans, made their task all but impossible. Ugly words circulating among regulators in Washington, D.C.—"insider loans," "cozy relationships," "kickbacks," "altered documents," and "criminal referrals"—foretold lawsuits to come.[45] The comptroller also issued a notice of the charges against Penn Square Bank and a temporary cease and desist order requiring bank officials to take immediate action to rehabilitate their bank. To retain liquidity, the bank tapped the Federal Reserve for $20 million. On the advice of an unnamed advisor, the GHK Company started pulling its money out.[46]

The next day, Phillip Zweig answered a call from a source whom he had come to refer to as "Deep Vault"—someone who had been of invaluable help in researching his April 26 article in the *American Banker* and whose secrecy reminded him of Deep Throat, the informant who helped Bob Woodward and Carl Bernstein break the Watergate scandal for the *Washington Post* in the early 1970s. "It's time for you to pack your bags," said Deep Vault, no doubt in a conspiratorial whisper. "Things are really bad here."[47]

On July 2, Chairman Jennings called a special meeting of the Penn Square Bank board of directors. In a series of sessions, punctuated by recesses, that lasted most of the day, the directors came face to face with the consequences of the bank's runaway growth. Jennings began by summarizing his meeting the previous day with representatives of the comptroller's office and by reminding officers that they were no longer permitted to authorize loans or pay overdrafts. If anyone was surprised to hear that Bill Patterson had been suspended, the minutes do not show it. Jennings also reviewed the goings-on upstream, where representatives from Continental Illinois, Chase Manhattan, and Seafirst were enduring their own trials by fire at the hands of officials from the comptroller of the currency's office. About twenty Penn Square Bank shareholders, surely wondering if they were throwing good money after bad, had signed subscriptions for additional capital stock. Marion C. Bauman, regulatory counsel from McAfee and Taft, P.C., explained the FDIC's process for taking over a bank and assured his listeners at the board of directors meeting that depositors would be protected to the extent allowed by law. There was some discussion about whether or not the bank was technically insolvent. National bank examiner Steve Plunk was mentioned as one of the people who thought it was. Late in the day, Chairman Jennings closed the meeting by alerting board members to the probability of more meetings over the Fourth of July weekend.[48] It is safe to assume that nobody was surprised.

More than four years later, Shirley Vint, manager of Penn Square Bank's wire-transfer department at the time of the failure, testified in court that July 2, 1982, the bank was "a madhouse." Her testimony was part of a consolidated trial of lawsuits stemming from Penn Square Bank's failure.

One of the participants in the trial was Downriver Community Federal Credit Union of Ecorse, Michigan, which held $4 million worth of CDs in the bank. The credit union had instructed its money broker to have a $1 million certificate wired out of the bank when it matured on July 2. Needless to say, the certificate was not wired out that day. While directors were shielded behind closed doors, Vint was fielding phone calls "in the hundreds." The Federal Reserve funds wire machine, which implemented wire transfers, was inoperable almost as soon as the bank opened on July 2. Employees in her department were told not to use the machine until further notice from the Federal Reserve. Transfers had to be performed using a code and required authorization from Vice President Bert Davis and one other bank officer. The rest piled up on Vint's desk. "Our biggest depositor had moved all his money out the day before," said Vint. "You didn't have to be a genius to figure out what was happening."[49]

Throughout what turned out to be Penn Square Bank's final examination, which began in late March 1982, Steve Plunk and his team were under pressure to follow the lead of the previous examination team—described by Plunk as "the dream team" because of its members' extraordinary acumen in sniffing out financial wrongdoing—and to give Penn Square Bank a clean bill of health. But within days of arriving at the bank, Plunk's interest was piqued by a balance sheet account labeled "Other." Upon inquiry, he discovered that the account was reserved for interest paid on behalf of borrowers who could not service their loans. Stunned, Plunk demanded to know who the borrowers were. "They were pretty much the core people at Penn Square," said Plunk. The list not only included bank directors but also read like a Who's Who of major players in the Anadarko Basin. "Basically, those loans were past due," continued Plunk, the incredulity in his voice undiminished by the passage of three decades. "And they were past due for a substantial period."[50]

Plunk's radar went on high alert, and no amount of pressure from his home office in Dallas or the increasingly hostile bank directors and officers in Oklahoma City could derail him and his team from getting some answers. His challenges were compounded because, as a native of Tennessee, he was targeted as an outsider who did not understand energy lending. Nevertheless, his team was less than two weeks into the examination when Plunk informed Clifton Poole in Dallas that he was ready to declare the bank insolvent. As a former field examiner, Poole knew that the thirty-one-year-old Steve Plunk was onto something big, and he distinguished himself as the only person in a position of authority who supported the examination team's findings. After a five-minute conversation with his subordinate, Poole was ready to alert the higher-ups in the comptroller of the currency's office in Washington, D.C., that Penn Square Bank was in serious trouble. "The ball was in motion," said Plunk. "And it just spiraled from that point on."[51]

Plunk considered himself fortunate to be able to focus with laser-like intensity on the financials. "All I needed to know was, did they have more bad loans than they had capital? And I kept that narrow focus. That was probably the most fortunate part during that whole thing. I didn't ponder their repercussions, or what it was going to do to the world, or what it was going to do to [Federal Reserve chairman Paul] Volcker. I just said, do they have more bad loans than they have capital? And I was convinced they did." Plunk was alarmed when bank officers, including President Eldon Beller, either stonewalled or deflected his questions to the renegade loan officer. "I couldn't really get a lot of information out of the officers," said Plunk. "They didn't know, or they didn't want to report anything without talking to Bill Patterson."[52]

Inevitably, Plunk's persistence landed him in Patterson's office (that is, when the peripatetic loan officer was actually *in* his office), where he found an increasingly agitated executive whose patience with the bank examiners was wearing thin. Plunk showed up one day with a stack of loan documents that he wanted to review with him. "I could not keep him focused," said Plunk. "He would jump up on the couch, point at a map of Oklahoma, and tell me how many oil and gas reserves there were!"[53]

Their relationship hit rock bottom when Patterson threatened to pull some strings at Continental Illinois Bank to get Plunk fired. "I could call them, and they could get you fired," said Patterson. And Plunk's response? "Well, besides that, Bill, how is this loan going to pay?"[54]

Steve Plunk never met Phil Zweig, but he thought that his reporting was accurate, and he credited his articles in the *American Banker* for signaling the beginning of the end. "He was having almost a daily article in the *American Banker*," recalled Plunk, who was placed under a gag order and prohibited from talking to the press. Pressured from all sides, Penn Square Bank entered what Plunk described as a deathwatch. "The dead rats just kept floating to the top of the punch bowl," said Plunk. Like the harried Shirley Vint in the bank's wire-transfer department, Plunk characterized the bank's final hours as "a madhouse."[55]

As Penn Square Bank officials scrambled to keep their house of cards from collapsing, Gene Rainbolt, then president of Federal National Bank of Shawnee—whose banking interests would one day coalesce into the BancFirst Corporation—perceived an opportunity to add to his holdings. His son, David, had been working at Republic Bank in Dallas, and he returned to Oklahoma to help his father manage his investments just as the economy was starting to cool. His first assignment was to represent his father's management services company, Thunderbird Financial Corporation, at a meeting to bid on Penn Square Bank's assets. David showed up with little confidence that Sid Carroll of the FDIC would accept his five-million-dollar bid for a bank whose assets were valued at upwards of a half-billion dollars.

"Let's say there were 15 or 20 bidders," recalled David about a meeting that took place just before the July Fourth holiday of 1982. "In any event, we are in there, and Sid walks in, and he said, 'We discovered information that would preclude us from doing a purchase and assumption in this thing, and we are going to liquidate the bank. Close it.' They sent us all back home."[56]

While Penn Square Bank directors were circling their wagons, Shirley Vint was scrambling to stave off chaos in the wire-transfer department, Steve Plunk was reporting misconduct on a colossal scale, and David Rainbolt was reporting to his father on the stillborn bidding, members of the Federal Reserve Board of Governors in Washington, D.C., were rearranging their plans for the Fourth of July weekend. At 2:45 P.M., Friday, July 2, the first in a series of emergency meetings was convened to discuss the fiasco going down in Oklahoma City. Towering above his colleagues, the cigar-smoking Fed chairman Paul Volcker wanted to know what others thought about the decision made by the FDIC and comptroller of the currency to arrange an immediate takeover of Penn Square Bank. A verbatim passage from the minutes of that charged meeting reads as follows:

> The bank was reportedly in danger of imminent failure because of sizable loans, including participation loans, that might not be collectible, coupled with significant deposit outflows. The bank, with nearly $500 million in deposits at the end of 1981, had made

more than $2 billion in loans to oil and gas exploration companies in the region and then sold participations in those loans to banks throughout the country, including some money center banks. With the downturn in prices for energy-related products, many borrowers now were unable to repay the loans. Also, the bank had made commitments for additional loans, but it was believed many of those commitments had not yet been funded.[57]

Officials recognized that the bank might need a loan from the Federal Reserve to operate for the rest of the day, with the understanding that a takeover would be arranged over the weekend. A sticking point was whether or not the Fed should extend credit under the circumstances. One board member questioned why the bank was not closed immediately rather than at the close of business. The answer, self-evident to those who had been working the case, was that the comptroller of the currency had not yet completed the bank exam and was not ready to declare it insolvent. The board finally agreed that the Federal Reserve Bank of Kansas City could lend money to Penn Square Bank "provided acceptable collateral was pledged."[58]

Discussions resumed at 4:30 P.M. on Saturday. By then, it was becoming clear that arranging a takeover would be difficult as long as federal examiners were unable to determine what portion of the bank's loan portfolio was uncollectible. Moreover, allegations of fraud made potential acquirers reluctant to assume the bank's liabilities. More officials from the FDIC and the comptroller of the currency's office joined the meeting, including FDIC chairman William M. Isaac, who reported that the FDIC was closing the bank because it saw little chance of finding a merger partner. There was a great deal of concern about uninsured depositors and the damage that the closing would do to public confidence in the financial system.[59] The bad news continued on Sunday, when the board of governors learned that potential acquirers were still spooked and that examiners were still a long way from determining the extent of bad loans. The best the comptroller of the currency could do was promise to prepare a statement of the bank's condition prior to its opening for business on Tuesday, July 6.[60]

The moment of truth arrived at 2:00 P.M. Monday, when staff reported that fears concerning loan losses and unknown contingent liabilities had derailed efforts to arrange a takeover of Penn Square Bank, either by a single institution or a consortium. The meeting recessed until 5:00 P.M. so that discussions could be held with officers of the comptroller of the currency and the FDIC. When the meeting resumed, Chairman Volcker reported that the comptroller of the currency and the FDIC "foresaw no possibility of arranging a takeover of Penn Square Bank. Because no other alternative proved feasible, the Comptroller would declare the bank insolvent and close it later this evening, with no immediate payout to the uninsured depositors."[61] Ultimately, the FDIC projected that, after collection of insurance from the bonding agents and settlement of all suits and claims against Penn Square Bank, uninsured depositors might be reimbursed at no less than 80 percent of their claims.

Oblivious to the goings-on in faraway Washington, D.C., Gayla Sherry, then manager of the draft collections department at Liberty Bank and Trust Company of Oklahoma City, was spending a quiet evening with her husband. Her experience no doubt reflected countless others on that steamy holiday weekend—a weekend of fireworks and family gatherings, of afternoons spent splashing in tepid swimming pools, and of savoring a respite from the rhythms of workaday life.

"I remember there was a full moon, and I don't know what that meant," recalled Sherry nearly three decades later. "But of course, it was hot in July. And I remember sitting out in the back yard with my husband, and we were having a drink, looking at the moon, and talking about it. And I remember saying, 'They're never going to close it. It won't happen.'"[62]

That evening, Comptroller of the Currency Todd Conover called national bank examiner Steve Plunk in Oklahoma City and went through a scripted prelude to declaring the bank insolvent. Having dispensed with the formalities, Conover told Plunk, "I have become satisfied that the bank is insolvent. I have appointed the FDIC as receiver. Please advise the bank that we are closing it and appointing the FDIC as receiver effective at 7:05 P.M., Central Daylight Savings Time."[63]

Headlines on Tuesday, July 6, blared with news of the FDIC's seizure of Penn Square Bank and its 28,000 accounts. In his prepared statement, Comptroller of the Currency Todd Conover said that "at closure the bank held total assets of approximately $525 million and total deposits of $470 million." He assured depositors with less than $100,000 that they would get their money; corporate depositors and others with accounts

Penn Square Bank's closing by the FDIC on July 5, 1982, was both cause and effect of the worst economic downturn in the oil patch since the Great Depression. Courtesy Oklahoma Historical Society.

exceeding $100,000 would be considered as claims against the failed bank.[64] The failure was the fourth-largest commercial bank failure in the history of the FDIC, the twenty-first bank failure in the United States in 1982, and the largest Oklahoma bank to fail since the Great Depression.[65]

History lessons and statistics meant little to depositors, who congregated at the bank to catch a glimpse of their financial futures. A young man, clad in a maroon bathing suit and sporting a slight sunburn from the Fourth of July weekend, leaned against his pickup truck and stared vacantly at the bank. He asked a reporter if he would have to wait in line to get his money. When told that he did not need to sleep in his truck, he replied angrily, "You don't have $100,000 in this stupid bank." Four young men wearing cowboy hats parked their white Continental in front of the bank. Asked by a reporter if they were affiliated, one man in the front seat replied tersely, "No comment." He then buried his face in his hands and cried. A policeman stood guard at the entrance, while TV cameramen photographed the lengthening line of depositors. An ambulance, its lights flashing, drove onto the sidewalk outside the oil and gas division offices where Bill Patterson had erected his ill-fated empire. According to a member of the ambulance service, he and his crew had been summoned as a precaution. The driver commented, "We'll sure be needed before the day is over."[66]

Bankers whom Phillip Zweig interviewed for the *American Banker* were by no means shocked by the failure, although some were surprised that the FDIC had resorted to an outright liquidation. Penn Square Bank's poor management and renegade lending practices were no secret among the banking cognoscenti. "Everybody knew that Penn Square was horrible," recalled BancFirst president David Rainbolt. "I mean, I don't think that anyone expected the entire economy was collapsing, because it was just Penn Square Bank, and it was notoriously sloppy. They just thought it was a bad bank. And it didn't take much of a cooling in the economy to take Penn Square Bank out. It just took a little bit of the bloom falling off the rose—that was enough to do in Penn Square Bank. It had no resilience, because it was so sloppy and mismanaged."[67]

Just down the road from Beep Jennings's hometown of Healdton, Bob McCormack, who was then working at Security National Bank of Duncan, watched in disbelief as Wild Bill Patterson steered his bank off the cliff. "Everybody that I knew and talked to—we all knew it wouldn't work," said McCormack. "It couldn't last. It was just going too far, too fast. The price of oil, as I recall, went up to forty-four dollars a barrel. And they were sort of operating under the premise that it was just going to keep going up and hit a hundred dollars a barrel. And if that had happened, they'd still be here today! I don't know, but the next thing you knew, oil was fourteen dollars a barrel. And that's when everything started coming unwound."[68]

The downward slide in oil prices was mirrored in deterioration in the natural gas market—bad news in the gas patch, and fatal to the great enabler in Penn Square Shopping Center. Nobody at the time wanted to talk about Penn Square Bank for fear of being accused of bad-mouthing a competitor, spreading rumors, suffering from sour grapes—or a combination of all three. "They are now becoming more talkative," wrote Zweig a few days after the FDIC takeover, "and the specifics of these practices are beginning to emerge. The facts make the rumors pale in comparison, according to many local banking sources."[69]

Some were relieved that maybe, just maybe, they had dodged a cannonball. Gayla Sherry recalled her bosses' alarm as their oil and gas customers peeled off from her bank to do business at Penn Square—and then, when the cards came tumbling down, doing an abrupt about-face.

"Occasionally, they would ask me, as the manager of the department, 'What's going on? Are we not offering them the best services? Are we charging too much? Why are we losing customers to Penn Square?' But I'll never forget, the day after Penn Square failed, those same managers and executives came to me and said, 'We weren't doing anything like them, were we?' So, it shifted from, 'What's going on with them? Do we need to change and be like them?' to, 'Oh, gee, I hope we weren't like them!'"[70]

Even those who might have seen it coming were unaware that Pandora's box had become unhinged. Mick Thompson, a banker from Poteau who would be appointed as state banking commissioner in 1992, was serving as a Democratic representative in the state legislature at the time of the FDIC takeover. Even chairing the Banking and Finance Committee was not enough to alert Thompson to the looming catastrophe. "I would say, the legislature, and most of the bankers in Oklahoma, did not realize the impact," he said. "It was not that big a deal—we thought. A lot of banks were in trouble. But the ripple effect of Penn Square—" Thompson paused to reflect on a shopping-center bank's demise that was about to transform Oklahoma banking. "We didn't realize there was going to be that kind of effect," he said finally, "not only in Oklahoma, but nationally. It was after the fact that we saw it was going to be a big deal."[71]

In an editorial in the August 1982 edition of the *Oklahoma Banker*, the Oklahoma Bankers Association put the best face on a dire situation. The OBA praised government officials and journalists for mitigating panic with "timely, responsible, and reassuring comments." Of utmost importance was the fact that Penn Square Bank was unique in its exposure to the energy market. "OBA officials and bankers across the state continued to point out that typical Oklahoma banks have loan portfolios which are widely diversified, thereby insulating those banks to the cycles of any one industry." In a sure sign of stability, bankers pointed out that the state's banks ranked in the top five in the nation in earnings in 1981. Touting the health of their industry and fielding members' questions at a rapid clip, the OBA was a source of calm in a tumultuous summer. The editorial closed with a plea for professionalism that people had come to expect of their bankers: "As events resulting from the failure of Penn Square Bank begin to unfold over the coming months, it is imperative that members of Oklahoma's banking community continue to act with prudence, responsibility and professionalism in dealing with this unique and unfortunate situation."[72]

Congress wasted little time in opening a formal inquiry into the failure. In the summer of 1982, bank directors, senior officers, and representatives of Penn Square Bank's accounting firms—Peat, Marwick, Mitchell & Company and Arthur Young & Company—testified before the House Banking, Finance, and Urban Affairs Committee. Others who testified included Clifton Poole; Roy E. Jackson, the FDIC's regional director; and Robert Hefner, whose previous hearings in the nation's capital had been much more enjoyable. In days of grueling testimony, the outrageous practices that had fueled Penn Square Bank's growth came to light: the notorious "upstreaming of interest"; sloppy and/or missing documentation on multimillion-dollar loans; loans that exceeded legal lending limits to individuals and companies; and, of course, the tangled sinews binding Penn Square Bank to its upstream, big-city correspondents. According to former president Eldon Beller, there was no way to control the bank's oil and gas division as long as Bill Patterson was reporting directly to Chairman Beep Jennings. "I never had complete control over Bill Patterson and oil and gas," said the disgraced bank president. In case committee members were slow to catch on, Beller commented, "The growth of the bank was so dynamic that it outstripped personnel and physical plant."[73]

The drama was replayed in December when hearings were held before the U.S. Senate Committee on Banking, Housing, and Urban Affairs.[74]

Just as there are several ways to measure the boom, so, too, are there ways to measure the bust. The clearest indication that the boom had turned to bust lay in the declining number of drilling rigs operating in Oklahoma. Hughes Tool Company, one of the world's largest oil-field service operators, began keeping track of rotary rigs in the 1930s, and its reports were acknowledged as a reliable bellwether—some might say the Bible—of domestic drilling activity.[75] According to its tally reported in the *Sunday Oklahoman,* Oklahoma suffered a precipitous drop in active rigs in 1982, from 882 on January 25 to 448 on September 13.[76] For the week ending October 8, Oklahoma led the nation in active rigs idled; the state was down 3.6 percent from the previous week for a total of 366, compared to 380 the week before. This dismal showing represented a 54.7 percent drop from 809 active rigs in Oklahoma during the same week in 1981.[77]

The decline in drilling in Oklahoma mirrored the nationwide trend: on August 16, 1982, there were 2,645 rotary rigs in operation, down from the record of 4,530 in late 1981.[78]

Matters went from bad to worse as the operators who remained in business contended with falling prices. According to Hans Helmerich of Tulsa-based Helmerich and Payne, gas that sold for ten dollars per thousand cubic feet (mcf) in late 1981 was going for five dollars to six dollars by September 1982. "That changes so many factors and has a domino effect," he said. "Whereas last year, deep gas looked like a blockbuster economically, this year it has 60 percent of the attractiveness it had. The economics of a field are changed."[79] Helmerich's fellow Tulsan and independent oilman Wayne Swearingen of Swearingen Management Associates blamed the troubles on a toxic brew of low natural gas prices, cost overruns on deep drilling, and reduced demand for gas. As he noted in a newspaper interview, "I doubt there is a section anywhere else in the United States that has been more severely hurt by that combination of factors than the section below 15,000 feet in western Oklahoma."[80] For Robert A. Hefner III, the downturn was nothing less than apocalyptic: "For our business," said the veteran driller in an interview for the *New York Times*, "this has been worse than the crash of 1929." By the spring of 1983, the GHK Company was receiving about five dollars per mcf of natural gas—about half the anticipated price. Of the company's twenty-three exploratory gas wells operating in 1982, only one was still in operation.[81]

Bad news for drillers translated into equally bad news for oil-field supply companies. Michael Rogers, who had recently been hired as a human resources manager for Thunderbird Financial Corporation, was in the audience when Keith May, a former national bank examiner who had gone on to serve as a commercial loan officer at Fidelity Bank, spoke to a group of bankers in August 1982. "Nobody's paying anybody," said May to his stunned listeners. "There's gridlock in the oil patch."[82]

Spending for oil and gas exploration in 1982 in the United States was off 25 percent from the previous year, down to $24 billion, and oil-field goods and service companies were bracing for a staggering loss of $8 billion. "Our part of the business has been in free fall," said John D. Platt, chairman of Geosource, a maker of geophysical equipment and provider of seismic services, in September 1982. "Every month since January, in division after division, we've had business outlooks that have been too optimistic. You almost have to wait until a month is over before you decide what to do the next."[83]

In a survey of twenty-seven oil-field supply firms in late 1982, the *Oklahoma City Journal Record* found that, with only one exception, companies had suffered a complete reversal from a year earlier in terms of sales, payroll, and—perhaps most importantly—hope.[84] "It's the pits," said John Haggin, executive vice president of the Association of Oilwell Servicing Contractors. "The people that are in real trouble are the ones that are highly leveraged. They are in bad shape, particularly with the financing company. It's scary to see the fate of the drillers and well service contractors."[85] Drilling contractors that bought rigs with borrowed money in 1981 were particularly hard hit. Less drilling meant less demand for rigs, and many contractors were unable to meet their interest payments. Of an estimated 5,400 land rigs in the United States, fewer than half were in use by the fall of 1982. The layoffs, as reported by *Business Week* in September 1982, were nothing short of horrific: 4,000 at Halliburton, 7,000 at Dresser Industries, 2,250 at Smith International, and 2,500 at Hughes Tool Company.[86]

In a related measure of the busted economy, the downturn in drilling hit communities in the Anadarko Basin fast and hard. City sales tax revenues in the three largest cities tell the story of vanishing resources. From 1982 to March 1984, city sales tax revenues dropped from $5,660,996.11 to $225,470.70 in Elk City, from $3,123,059.28 to $235,685.37 in Clinton, and from $1,920,886.51 to $124,421.53 in Weatherford.[87] At the same time, bankruptcies among oil and gas companies were zooming off the charts. "We've been setting new records each month," said Steve Livshee, chief deputy clerk for the Bankruptcy Court for the Western District of Oklahoma in April 1983. According to Sam Hammons, onetime director of the state's energy department, for every company that had declared bankruptcy, "there are five others teetering on the brink. What we're seeing is a classic boom and bust. We're in a horrendous squeeze."[88] Speaking to what must have been a somber crowd at the Fifth Annual Oil and Gas Conference in Oklahoma City in September 1983, William D. Neary, senior partner in the Dallas law firm of Thompson and Knight, reported that oil and gas bankruptcies were "four times more prevalent in 1983 than at any other time in memory." One of Neary's clients was the GHK Company, one of several Oklahoma companies that were trying to reach workout agreements with their creditors as an alternative to declaring bankruptcy. "You can have enough creditors that it is impossible to deal with them all," explained Neary. "But Texas and Oklahoma are way ahead in their willingness to seek a voluntary settlement."[89]

No matter how settlements were reached, one thing was certain: the bust signaled the end of the million-dollar handshake that had always been a source of pride among Oklahoma oilies. "The oil business has traditionally been a handshake business," explained Joe McEuen, head of Sterling Pipe and Supply Company of Oklahoma City, a few months after the debacle. "Now, everything has to be documented. You have to dot every 'i' and cross every 't' before a deal can be made." McEuen, clearly educated in the handshake school of business, pointed his finger directly at Penn Square Bank for destroying a time-honored tradition. "There was a new psychology after Penn Square went under that made everyone more cautious," he said. "That has caused a tremendous shortage of cash right now that everyone is having to deal with."[90]

Contrary to popular opinion, not all banks in Oklahoma were caught in the maelstrom. "Bill Jennings was a friend of mine," said Gene Rainbolt. "But, prior to Penn Square's failure, we refused to accept their certificates of deposit as collateral for loans. We were *so* aware of the exceptions that they were doing in their lending."[91]

"It didn't affect us at all," said Brian Shipp, president of Idabel National Bank. Nestled in the southeastern corner of McCurtain County, Shipp's bank relied on timber, tourism, and agriculture to bolster its loan portfolio. Energy lending, then as now, might as well be taking place on another planet. "Most of the local banks, to my knowledge, don't do a lot of lending outside their market area," continued Shipp. "So the oil bust didn't affect us. Nor did the oil boom! I have read the books about Penn Square, and the bankers drinking Champagne out of cowboy boots. That did not exist around here."[92]

Farmers State Bank of Quinton board chairman Bill Jordan agreed. "Really, it didn't have any effect on our bank, per se," he said. "Being a small, community bank, we weren't really big enough to be involved in the oil and gas loans, at that particular time." But in terms of banking culture, Penn Square Bank's implosion released a tidal wave over the industry; when it receded, nothing was the same. "I think as a result of that, we got a lot more conservative," continued Jordan as his associates nodded their heads in unison. According to executive vice president

Laura Miller, Farmers State Bank's problems appeared in the form of plummeting prices for cattle and real estate. "We had a lot of loan losses," she said. "And we were very conservative for awhile there. Everybody was tightening their belts." Longtime board member, bank customer, and Quinton's most celebrated chuck wagon racer, Jerry Fowler, chimed in with his own memory of the bad old days of belt tightening. "She got real tight on me!" he exclaimed, pointing at Laura Miller from across the room. Laughter ensued as Fowler, sporting a cowboy hat and red kerchief, continued in his signature southeast Oklahoma drawl, "I remember those times! I remember those times! It got *real personal!*"[93]

Steve Baggerly, president of the Bank of the Panhandle in Guymon, described banks such as his, which were never awash in energy loans, but whose trust-based business cultures provided scant cover when regulators came calling. He explained, "The crisis in the late eighties and early nineties changed the face of banking, and it changed the relationship between the customer and the banker. The days of going in and getting an unsecured loan because, you know, 'I know Michael Hightower, he's a good guy, he's always paid, so he wants $10,000, sure, no problem.' Michael wasn't any different in '83 than he was in '79, the bank wasn't really different, but the regulators were not going to have that type of relationship anymore. They were going to demand information."[94]

Charlie Butler, president of the First National Bank of Hooker, insisted that "the character issue still repays the loans." But after Penn Square Bank went down, the regulators would have none of it. Asked what regulators thought about "character loans," Butler answered without hesitation, "They had no idea what you're talking about." The veteran banker summed up the seismic shift in lending practices in a single sentence: "There's not many handshake deals anymore."[95]

Nor were there many human resources managers interested in hiring people with Penn Square Bank on their résumés. "I considered it a stain on their record," said Michael Rogers, who earned his banking spurs at Thunderbird Financial Corporation and later, United Community Corporation before the company blossomed into the BancFirst Corporation in 1989. "Should you hire a person with a Penn Square background, or not? That was the question."[96]

Given the extent of Penn Square Bank's unorthodox lending practices, nobody was surprised to find lawsuits sprouting like weeds, and keeping track of them became something of a cottage industry. A detailed account of litigation that spanned the 1980s lies beyond the scope of this work, but a few highlights should suffice to illustrate the consequences of the bank's failure for Oklahoma's legal system.

In the spring of 1983, the FDIC prepared two class action lawsuits on behalf of depositors who lost millions in the Penn Square Bank collapse. Of particular concern to the FDIC were about 150 credit unions that lost $111 million in uninsured funds, all of it in certificates of deposit larger than the $100,000 maximum insured by the FDIC. Savings and loans were in a similar predicament—much of their holdings in Penn Square Bank were in uninsured CDs. Federal regulators, who first estimated that $190 million of the bank's deposits were uninsured, later upped that figure to $250 million.[97]

In January 1984, former Penn Square Bank vice president Thomas S. Orr waived a grand jury indictment and pled guilty to tax evasion and fraud, in part for arranging money for racehorse sales and then profiting by serving as a broker for those deals. U.S. attorney William S. Price called Orr's admission "the first breakthrough and the first major step in the investigation" of Penn Square Bank's demise.[98] In June, the FDIC's lawsuits finally made it to the litigation stage. In its sixty-six-page, $138 million suit, the FDIC estimated that the losses from "several years of alleged negligent and reckless practices at the bank" would reach $90 million, plus interest. The lawsuit sought to recover the loss and $50 million in punitive damages from six bank officials and directors: Beep Jennings, Eldon Beller, Bill Patterson, Carl Swan, and directors John R. Preston and C. F. Kimberling. As noted in the *Oklahoman and Times,* "The lawsuit adopts many of the allegations made in hundreds of earlier lawsuits filed across the nation since the bank failed. Those suits have been filed by borrowers, uninsured depositors and investors in Oklahoma oil and gas ventures financed through Penn Square Bank."[99]

In July 1984, Bill Patterson was named in a thirty-four-count (later reduced to twenty-five-count) federal indictment charging him with wire fraud, misapplying bank funds, and making false entries.[100] Jurors were asked to decide who was the real Bill Patterson: was he "an egotistic master of deceit who built a house of cards with bad loans," or was he the fall guy in "a treacherous, insidious plot" designed to offer him up as a scapegoat for Penn Square Bank's fall from grace?[101] His acquittal on September 27, shocking to many, hinged on the issue of intent. As one juror, who requested anonymity, explained after the trial, evidence of Patterson's alleged intent to defraud Penn Square Bank or any other bank "just wasn't there." As he left the courtroom with the help of one of his attorneys, all the weeping and choking Bill Patterson could say was, "Nobody knows what I've been through the past two years. I'm just so tired I can hardly stand up." He went home, went to sleep, and awoke to the news that a Chicago grand jury had issued a sixteen-count indictment against him for the damage he had inflicted on Continental Illinois National Bank.[102]

The litigation continued in August 1986 when an overloaded court system consolidated lawsuits into a five-phase legal proceeding. Claims against bank officers and directors, in addition to claims against the FDIC for its own alleged wrongdoing, were tried first. Lawsuits not requiring a jury were considered in later phases.[103] Among the most damaging testimonies was that of national bank examiner Steve Plunk, who cited upstreaming of interest as the most serious problem the bank had in terms of threatening its solvency. "I had never seen anything like it," said Plunk.[104] The bank examiner further testified that former president Eldon Beller lied to examiners when he was confronted about making interest payments on behalf of customers who were unable to do so.[105] Further damaging testimony came in the form of allegations that Penn Square Bank officials were guilty of fraud in presenting false financial statements to asset management firms and credit unions that held certificates of deposit at the bank. "Penn Square Bank made material misstatements and omissions," said Tom Dann, attorney for plaintiff Downriver Community Federal Credit Union of Ecorse, Michigan. "Either they knew the financial statement was false, or they recklessly misrepresented its financial condition, knowing they didn't have a basis to know if it was true or not."[106]

While the legal system groaned under the weight of lawsuits, ordinary people revealed yet another measure of declining fortunes as they cut their losses and figured out how to get on with their lives. One of the first businesses to go was oil and gas exploration leasing. In 1981, the Anadarko Indian Agency auctioned off a lease for a record-breaking $11,000 an acre. And then came the bust. "At our last sale, we had 79 tracts to lease but only sold 12," said agency administrator Bill Titchywy. "The money is just not there anymore to buy the land. Basically, the bottom has fallen out."[107] But not all auctioneers were ready to throw in the towel. Equipment auctions, where anything from hydraulic cranes and tractors to chain saws, became a familiar sight along Oklahoma highways in the early 1980s. "More and more people are interested in cash today," said Ray Patterson, owner of Ray Patterson and Associates of Frederick and secretary of the Oklahoma State Auctioneers Association.[108]

Business was also on an upswing for charity workers as legions of unemployed oil-field workers abandoned the dreams that brought them to western Oklahoma and stood in line for handouts. A tearful caseworker at a Salvation Army kitchen in Oklahoma City commented in August 1982 that "sometimes we have to turn the pot over in our kitchen to show them we have no food left." The American Red Cross in Stillwater made a public request for more food for the needy, prompting churches in the area to join the bandwagon. As a Red Cross spokesman explained in August 1982, "Throughout Oklahoma and the country church groups are being asked to get more involved in charity. As the government reduces spending on social programs and as more and more people become jobless, the church is often a last resort for a needy family."[109]

While the auction business was booming and charity workers scrambled to keep up with demand, Tim Haynes, owner of Haynes Wrecker Service in Elk City, was experiencing a bust in his side business—renting U-Haul trailers. "I'd say that 75 percent of the people are moving out of state," he said in July 1982. L. L. Himelic, manager of an Elk City apartment complex, noticed a slackening of demand for housing. At the height of the boom, he had only to call the first person on his waiting list to fill a vacated apartment. As the economy cooled, several calls were necessary to find a renter. Elk City assistant police chief Randy Smith, who had contended with increased vandalism during the boom times, noted that people were moving away from the area. Smith had a personal reason to regret the loss of population—all four of his rental houses in nearby Sayre were vacant. On the upside, fewer squatters were camped along the highway, and there were not as many arrests for public intoxication. The exodus was also evident in state parks that had been home to oil-field workers unable to find accommodations in town.[110] "We were overrun with tent people all trying to get on in the oil fields," said Foss State Park superintendent R. L. Pyron. "It was like *The Grapes of Wrath* in reverse—Oklahoma began looking like California did to the Okies in the dust bowl days."[111] Superintendent Pyron guessed that people who lost their jobs and could no longer afford the camping fees simply left when their time limits ran out.

"This was a booming town," said Clarence Lewis, a service station attendant in Sayre in August 1982. "Money wasn't no object around here for four or five years. Now people are broke. If you don't believe it, look at this." He pointed to a clipboard full of charge slips. "All credit. People used to pay in cash." Shop owner Gloria Larson of Burns Flat was likewise concerned about the post-boom future. "I'm scared that when the oil boom is gone, this will be a ghost town," she said. Her fears were borne out by the Oklahoma Employment Securities Commission's report that unemployment in Washita County doubled from 1981 to 1982.[112]

Among the recently unemployed Anadarko Basin workers was Jimmy Lane, a native of Tennessee who came to Oklahoma via Texas aboard a Greyhound bus. "You could just hang your name on the wall and they'd come to the bar and find you," said Lane at the nearly empty Calmez Hotel in Clinton, where he was staying in October 1982. "People were everywhere; you'd see guys walking down the street with backpacks. They were sleeping in the halls and on the floor. You couldn't find a place to stay; now there's just eight rooms rented in this whole hotel." Robert Glomski, Lane's roommate at the Calmez and a native of Michigan who came to Clinton by way of Wyoming and Texas, exhibited the kind of pluck one would expect from an itinerant oil-field worker. "We've heard there's work at Hobbs, N.M., and the Texas Panhandle," he said. "I'll keep after it somewhere as long as I've got 10 fingers. When I lose a finger, that's it."[113]

But the return to earth was not entirely bad news, particularly for longtime residents who had seen enough of runaway growth and inflated expectations. "About 50 percent of the out-of-staters have split since the slowdown," said Burns Flat bartender Roger Lee. "All the locals will be damn glad when it's over, that I can tell you."[114]

If there was a silver lining to the bust of the 1980s, it lay in the sense of humor that has seen Oklahomans through hard times, and will surely do so again and again. The humor this time flowed from the pen of songwriter Nita Lee, a Logan County housewife who, with the help of her son and daughter, penned a ballad to commemorate the good ole boys at Penn Square Bank, whose ambitions took them to the pinnacle of their entrepreneurial dreams and left them high and dry when the chickens came home to roost. It was the summer of 1982, and everywhere she looked, banks were busting and businesses were folding, lawyers were suing, drillers were cussing, and roustabouts were packing their bags and hitting the highway. The underbelly of the American Dream was exposed for all to see, and it was not a pretty sight. But Nita Lee, recently returned from a recording studio in Nashville, found opportunity where others saw only despair and became the hottest item on local radio stations with the rowdy tune "Who Said the South Wouldn't Rise Again?"

"The whole thing was just something to laugh about," she said. "It's the fall of something and it's kind of sad, but the American people have always been able to find the humor in something."[115]

Jokes and anecdotes, and at least one commemorative tune, survive as the most persistent reminders of the Penn Square Bank debacle. Yet as the seasons pass, fewer people remain to share them, and they have fewer listeners to shake their heads in wonder and perhaps chime in with their own stories. Other booms and busts have come and gone, and the iconic histories of Penn Square Bank—Mark Singer's *Funny Money,* and Phillip Zweig's *Belly Up*—are left to gather dust in library stacks and on bankers' bookshelves. In a world of e-books and iPads, Penn Square Bank's slide to oblivion might one day be complete.

All the more reason, then, to revisit the bank's meteoric rise and catastrophic fall, not only for their obvious value as a morality tale, but also because the bank's collapse in July 1982 signaled a paradigm shift that reverberated far beyond Oklahoma. That sultry July Fourth weekend marked the beginning of a depression in the oil patch unrivaled since the 1930s. Banks teetered, and some sank, under the weight of unwise loan participations. Character lending succumbed to blizzards of documents and armies of regulators. And as we will see in the following chapters, Oklahoma's archaic unit-banking laws came under fire, and were eventually overhauled altogether, as bankers scrambled to remain solvent. Banks whose balance sheets were hopelessly mired in bad paper became easy prey for stronger ones whose management had avoided the seductive lure of easy money. The lucky ones survived as branches of more prudent banks. But many bankers suffered the indignity of watching as FDIC officials shut down their banks, parceled out whatever they could salvage from the wreckage to depositors and creditors, and left vacant buildings as monuments to imperial ambitions.

But some bankers simply minded their own business. "We didn't get hooked up in buying any of the participations from any of the banks that were getting into the oil-related business," said Don Clark, who went to work for First State Bank of Anadarko in 1957 and was named president in 1981. "We stayed conservative, and we took care of our customers, and did the things we knew how to do. And even today, 42 percent of our loan portfolio is in ag." Don's wife, Kitty, who joined the bank's board of directors in 1988, agreed: "The oil and gas business was not the expertise here. We're an agricultural community. You don't loan money on something that you don't have expertise in." Laughter ensued as Don added a postscript to his wife's story: "I never wanted to make a loan on something I didn't know something about!" The First State Bank of Anadarko's conservatism paid off when the FDIC closed the nearby First National Bank of Gracemont and put it on the auction block. "We bought it from the FDIC, because the bank failed, and we were the high bidder on it," explained Don of his foray into mergers and acquisitions. "And it did not fail because of local loans," he continued, speaking slowly and deliberately to make sure I got it right. "The bank there bought participations and made loans outside our local community."[116]

Down in McCurtain County, Idabel National Bank felt nary a ripple from the goings-on in Oklahoma City and other towns whose bankers had joined Beep Jennings's journey to the Promised Land. "We have not had any booms, but we haven't had any busts either," said Brian Shipp. "From a banking standpoint, that's good. I'd rather—" Shipp paused to reflect on his bank's routine, rather mundane by some standards, of providing financial services to its community, and on McCurtain County's lack of experience with bank failures. "You know," he said finally, "the busts can put you out of business. So, you can do without the booms if it means staying in business and living to play another day."[117]

The last word on the rise and fall of Penn Square Bank goes to Citizens Security Bank of Bixby president and CEO Carlisle Mabrey III. Other than the cultural shift that obliterated character lending and heralded a thorough realignment of banking relationships, Citizens Security Bank's experience was limited to collateral damage in the form of plummeting prices for real estate and agricultural products. Mabrey credited his family's tradition of conservative lending for avoiding the get-rich-quick schemes that led so many to ruin.

"I'm going to say, Dad's conservatism, along with our board, the older folks on our board, who had been through some ups and downs, kept us from getting into serious trouble," explained Carlisle as his brother John nodded his head in agreement. "What's the deal? The conservatives keep their heads when everybody else around you is losing theirs! That's kind of the way it was!"[118]

And, perhaps, that is still the way it is.

PART III

Road to Recovery

CHAPTER NINE

The Rest of the Story

> We must have sound federal policies in dealing with bank problems. Those policies should be fair to everyone.
>
> U.S. senator David L. Boren, in a letter to a constituent

To understand the scope of the damage that Penn Square Bank inflicted on American banking, one need look no further than the FDIC's annual report for 1983, which introduced its section on the largest FDIC pay-off in the agency's history with quantitative measures of the meltdown: "A major continuing liquidation involves the Penn Square Bank, N.A., of Oklahoma City, which failed July 5, 1982, resulting in the largest deposit payoff in FDIC history. Of the Bank's $465 million in deposits, only about $200 million were insured and immediately available to their owners." To pay insured depositors, the FDIC established a special entity: the Deposit Insurance National Bank (DINB). By June 1983, the FDIC estimated that depositors in Penn Square Bank might expect to recover only 65 percent of their deposits in excess of the insurance limit. The estimate was subject to revision and depended "on future collections from the liquidation of Penn Square assets and the outcome of a large number of legal actions." As of the end of 1983, the FDIC had collected $500.4 million in principal and interest on loans, securities, and other assets. Out of the total, $235.1 million was paid to the holders of loan participations, $5.7 million repaid secured advances from the Federal Reserve to Penn Square, $16.9 million was paid to owners of pledged deposits, and approximately $87.6 million was paid to uninsured depositors and other creditors holding receiver's certificates for proven claims. The FDIC invested excess collections in Treasury bills totaling approximately $133.6 million.[1]

The Penn Square Bank failure also figured prominently in its correspondent banks' annual reports for 1982. Continental Illinois reported that income before security transactions declined from $260.3 million in 1981 to $84.3 million in 1982, primarily due to sharply increased provisions for credit losses: "Both the earnings decline and the increased provision reflect a steep rise in problem credits, principally the result of the combined impact of weak economic conditions worldwide on many customers and loan participations purchased from the former Penn Square Bank, NA, of Oklahoma City."[2] Seafirst's annual report began with a blunt declaration: "Without a doubt, 1982 was the most difficult year in Seafirst Corporation's history." Net loan losses zoomed from $32.4 million in 1981 to $186.2 million in 1982 and included $125.2 million in charge-offs for Penn Square Bank and other energy loans.[3] More bad news was expected from the nearly $400 million in Seafirst's dabbling in dump-truck banking. At year-end 1982, Chase Manhattan Bank of New York estimated its losses from Penn Square Bank loans at $75 million. Readers of the annual report were cautioned that the value of the portfolio would "be affected by conditions prevailing in the energy market."[4]

The annual report writer from Chase Manhattan was wise to be cautious. In December 1984, *Forbes* reported that the bank's losses were closer to $146 million. As the red ink spread, Chase Manhattan officials decided that enough was enough. Under pressure from two multimillion-dollar shareholder derivative suits over Penn Square Bank, they took the extraordinary step of suing six former officers "for negligence and breach of duty." Evidently, legal expenses, bad publicity, and a hit to company morale were acceptable prices to pay for making a point. "It's highly unusual and questionable," said Dennis Block of New York's Weil, Gotshall & Manges about the lawsuits. "I can't think of any situation where a bank or any company tried to collect from its employees for ordinary negligence."[5] Clearly, theirs was no ordinary negligence.

Continental Illinois, Seafirst, and Chase Manhattan were not the only banks sucked into the maelstrom. In February 1984, Michigan National Corporation omitted its first-quarter dividend and announced new charge-offs of $7.7 million related to the collapse of Penn Square Bank. The new charge-offs brought the bank's total losses stemming from the failure to $87.5 million.[6] Hibernia National Bank in New Orleans was on the hook and went all the way to the Tenth U.S. Circuit Court in Denver in May 1984 to request status as a "preferred claimant" against assets that were then held by the FDIC. The court upheld a lower court order in denying the request. According to the court, Penn Square Bank assets that fell under FDIC control included nearly $26.4 million in promissory notes involving eighty-four loans in which participating interests of between 47 and 100 percent were sold to Hibernia.[7]

The contagion spread to credit unions. About 150 of them, including one at the U.S. House of Representatives, stood to lose $20 million, representing 20 percent of their $106.3 million in uninsured deposits held at Penn Square Bank. Savings and loan associations, too, stood to lose a pile of money. A few days after Penn Square Bank was closed, the Federal Home Loan Bank Board, charged with regulating savings and loan associations, refused to comment on the problems that were surely coming.[8] Money brokers who placed their clients' funds in Penn Square Bank's high-yielding certificates of deposit were hard hit as well. Thomas Higgins of Los Angeles–based Professional Asset Management testified during phase one of the consolidated Penn Square Bank trial in September 1986 that his firm's clients dropped from 1,172 to 653, and its portfolio dropped from $1.6 billion to $824 million as a direct result of the bank's failure. Even though the losses were "incremental" and the firm eventually returned to profitability, Higgins insisted that the profits it lost "went away and are never coming back."[9]

Penn Square Bank was an equal-opportunity wrecking ball. Those caught in its arc as it bashed its way across America ran the gamut from middle-class professionals looking to grow their nest eggs to masters of finance whose reach, it turned out, exceeded their grasp. But nowhere did the havoc wrought by the little shopping-center bank come closer to tanking the financial system than at Continental Illinois National Bank of Chicago, where charge-offs in the neighborhood of $1 billion in 1982 were a warm-up for what was to become the largest rescue of a financial institution in American history. Milestones along the road to rescue included stern warnings from the comptroller of the currency in July 1982 that bank officers needed to review and strengthen their lending policies; forced resignations in August of John R. Lytle, the vice president in charge of energy lending, and others tainted by scandal; and the bank's recognition in July 1983 that nonperforming loans had ballooned to $2.1 billion.[10] Lionized by *Dun's Review* in 1978 as one of America's best run companies, Continental Illinois was about to take center stage in the too-big-to-fail debate.[11]

As Continental Illinois officers lurched from one crisis to the next under the watchful eyes of federal regulators, true believers in the cause of deregulation were making strides in their crusade to dismantle decades of regulation and return America to its roots—real or imagined—in laissez-faire capitalism, a movement that began under President Carter's tenure and gained steam with Ronald Reagan's election to the presidency in 1980. Touting deregulation as a panacea for the nation's economic ills, major banks won the freedom to charge whatever they wanted on loans and for their services, and to pay what they chose in interest on their deposits. They were venturing into such activities as stockbrokerage and financial futures trading and campaigning to enter a wide array of businesses heretofore barred to commercial banks, including real estate, insurance, and underwriting securities.[12] Meanwhile, banks were lobbying for permission to set up branches across state lines and to form ever-larger units through mergers and acquisitions. Changes in banking laws notwithstanding, one thing seemed certain: no amount of deregulation—or regulation, for that matter—could postpone Continental Illinois's day of reckoning forever.

By early 1984, loan officers at Continental Illinois were displaying a latent talent for conservative lending. Higher-ups were doing their best to salvage what they could from bankrupt customers and were hoping to benefit from an economic recovery that was gaining traction. Recovery came, but not for Continental Illinois. As one Chicago executive remarked, "It took a while to sink in that Continental could really go under. Then [early in 1984], when companies saw there was some risk, they got their money out."[13] Old-timers caught a whiff of the 1930s, when the Reconstruction Finance Corporation bought $50 million of the bank's preferred stock to save it from collapse.[14] Even worse than the loss of money was the damage done to the bank's reputation and, by extension, to the integrity of the banking system. James P. McCollom, author of the definitive book on the rise and fall of Continental Illinois, suggested that the bank "could cover the lost money, but the banking industry could not cover the fact of a huge error, a misjudgment, one that reflected on the wisdom of all of them."[15] On March 30, Chemical Bank bought Continental Illinois's credit card business for $1 billion—a good move in terms of increasing capital, but one bound to give investors and depositors, not to mention officialdom in Washington, the jitters.[16]

Some surely wondered if the end was at hand when the bank became the butt of jokes. "If I had known how easy it was to get a loan from Continental Illinois," quipped Chrysler head Lee Iacocca—the beneficiary of federal largesse at his own ailing company—to the Economic Club of Chicago, "I would never have gone to the government."[17] The audience howled.

For two years, Continental Illinois had been operating under the Penn Square Bank cloud, and rumors spread like wildfire. The rumor mill, already churning with stories of Japanese buyouts and grim conclaves of federal officials, went into overdrive on May 9 when Reuters released a brief but explosive report "of the impending bankruptcy of the Continental Illinois Bank, the nation's seventh largest." The story went global, and by the close of business that day, the bank had lost a billion dollars in deposits.[18]

As foreign investors continued to withdraw their money, on May 11 the bank borrowed $3.6 billion from the Federal Reserve Bank of Chicago to stay solvent. Officials insisted that they had $17 billion in collateral to back the borrowing.[19] Over the ensuing Mother's Day weekend, emergency calls were made to banks across the country. By Monday, sixteen major banks, with backing from the Federal Reserve Board, offered Continental Illinois $4.5 billion in available credit for thirty days. At the same time, Standard and Poor's lowered the bank's debt rating.[20] By then, the lid was off the story, and bank officials came face to face with the revolution in communications. A story that began as a private affair fueled by gossip careened from the financial pages to national television, where the likes of Dan Rather, Tom Brokaw, and Peter Jennings made a complex story simple: Continental Illinois was going down.[21]

A turning point came on May 17, when the FDIC injected $1.5 billion in capital into Continental Illinois and other banks anted up an additional $500 million. The Federal Reserve and the FDIC further guaranteed that no depositors, no matter how large, would lose a penny of their deposits in the beleaguered bank.[22] Oklahomans with an eye on history might have experienced a moment of déjà vu in recalling

Governor Charles N. Haskell's promise that depositors in state-chartered banks would never lose a penny thanks to the Oklahoma Bank Guaranty Law of 1908—a cornerstone of his progressive agenda, and the nation's first experiment in deposit guarantee since New York State's safety fund system was in effect from 1829 to 1842.[23]

On May 17, the $4.5 billion in credit that had been extended by sixteen major banks was increased to $5.5 billion, with twenty-eight banks participating.[24] The next day, Moody's followed Standard and Poor's lead and lowered the debt rating of Continental Illinois's parent company.[25] From mid-May to July, Continental sold off $5 billion in assets and low-interest loans to raise needed capital. Under intense pressure to liberalize the state's banking laws, the Illinois House of Representatives in Springfield passed a bill to allow out-of-state banks to acquire Continental Illinois, but there were no takers. Legions of reporters roamed downtown Chicago searching for shards of news, determined to scoop what might be the biggest story of their careers. The city hummed with water-cooler conversations. Rumors flared up, died, and made way for new ones. The *Wall Street Journal* reported on July 17 that Continental had lost half its deposits; the run had exceeded $14 billion. Finally, on July 18, it was game over: the *New York Times* broke the complete story of the meeting in Washington the day before, when FDIC chairman William Isaac, members of his staff, and a committee of Continental directors defined a plan under which the FDIC would take over 80 percent of the bank's stock.[26] That same day, Federal Reserve loans to offset deposit outflows topped $5 billion. Two days later, Continental Illinois National Bank was, for all intents and purposes, nationalized.[27]

Chairman Isaac fended off criticism that the federal government had overstepped its bounds. He insisted that the decision to rescue Continental Illinois was made "in a specific context" and was the proper course of action. "We had a very large, very complex and rapidly moving problem and we had to take steps to get it stabilized," said Isaac. "There were a lot of rumors floating around, a lot of funds leaving the bank. We needed to assess the bank's true condition."[28] Federal Reserve Board chairman Paul Volcker agreed and insisted that the rescue was necessary to safeguard the integrity of the banking system. "We are certainly going to try our hardest—and we have powerful tools at our disposal—to provide a continuation of banking services and avoid that kind of shock to the system," he said.[29]

Predictably, the rescue plan ignited a firestorm of controversy about the proper role of government in the economy. In his ongoing defense of the government's extraordinary actions, FDIC chairman Isaac dismissed claims that Continental Illinois had effectively been nationalized. "Not one nickel of taxpayer money is in this transaction," said Isaac. "As soon as we see this bank is back on its feet . . . the FDIC will sell its interest in this bank. The FDIC will not . . . be running this bank."[30] Another FDIC official chimed in a bit more forcefully: "The FDIC is not going to be running this damned bank. The new management will." Others were not so sure. Said Merrill Lynch analyst James Wooden, "What we have in essence is a nationalized bank." One Wall Street analyst commented that the FDIC was willing to let smaller banks go under but rescued Continental Illinois because it was simply too big to fail. "You put it in a category like Chrysler," he said in reference to another government bailout that remained a matter of fierce controversy. "You don't save every bank, but you do save Continental." William Cline of the Institute for International Economics peered into the future and did not like what he saw. "The whole Continental episode puts a cloud over banking," he said. Cline went on to predict that the bailout would "heighten both public and shareholder apprehension about private banks."[31]

On Capitol Hill, Representative Fernand St. Germain (D-R.I.), chairman of the House Banking Committee, said that the bailout "raises the greatest array of questions in the history of the federal bank regulatory system." Senate Majority Leader Howard H. Baker insisted that the rescue "is going to force us to review our attitude toward the entire banking system, and specifically government regulation and insurance." Back in Chicago, David G. Taylor, chairman of the bank's parent company, Continental Illinois Corporation, voiced what might have been the prevailing opinion at ground zero of the historic bailout: "This is not the go-it-alone path we aspired to, but at this point it is the best course open to us."[32] As a condition of the rescue plan, Taylor was on his way out. And in spite of gallons of ink, hours of testimony, and mountains of reports and documents, the sixty-four-dollar question remained unanswered: how had a little shopping-center bank in Oklahoma City managed to set in motion such a frightful train of events? Congressman St. Germain, the ranking banking industry legislator, summed up the common wisdom: "Very frankly, these city slickers got taken in by country bumpkins. It's unbelievable and scary, scary, scary."[33]

Chagrined that some of their own had been catalysts for the disaster, Oklahomans weighed in on the debate. James Baker, a financial analyst from Oklahoma City, spoke for Oklahoma's community bankers in criticizing the government's double standard for large and small banks. "I think it's blatantly unfair when the federal government decides to save the large money center banks and not save community banks," he said. Asserting that size was no guarantor of safety, Baker criticized policies that created an uneven playing field for the nation's banks: "Continental Illinois proves there is no correlation between the size and soundness of a bank. The community banks in this country are in much better shape than the money center banks."[34]

Nobody was more troubled by the government's action than Oklahoma senator David L. Boren, who used the *Oklahoma City Journal Record* as a bully pulpit to criticize the FDIC for not acting sooner when Penn Square Bank was floundering. "In hindsight," said the youthful Democrat from Seminole, "if the FDIC had taken care of Penn Square, they probably never would have had to rescue Continental Illinois." During that charged summer of 1984, Boren was engaged in a dialogue with the FDIC concerning its handling of the Penn Square Bank failure in July 1982 as well as the failure of the First Continental Bank and Trust Company of Del City, which had been closed on May 11 and then reopened under new ownership. As part of his efforts, Boren was working closely with U.S. representative Mickey Edwards, a Republican from Oklahoma City, to introduce legislation to "make the FDIC more accountable." For Senator Boren, the Continental Illinois bailout raised two questions that struck at the heart of the American banking system in the 1980s: (1) was the market discipline espoused by proponents of deregulation applicable only to small banks?; and (2) should depositors be expected to take risks that did not apply to stockholders and management? Quoting financial guru Louis Rukeyser, Senator Boren suggested that the government rescue of Continental Illinois had exposed the truth about late twentieth-century banking—"the bigger they are, the softer they fall."[35]

Senator Boren relished the opportunity to take his concerns directly to his constituents. His sense of fairness was evident in his response on August 6, 1984, to a letter from Oklahoma Historical Society archivist William D. Welge about the FDIC's handling of the Continental Illinois National Bank failure. Although his letter to the senator has apparently been lost, it is clear from the senator's response that Welge took a dim view of the bailout. Senator Boren did too, and he promised to give the matter his utmost consideration in the U.S. Senate. "I am giving this problem very close attention," wrote Senator Boren to a vexed Welge. "Congressional action may be necessary if we cannot get the Comptroller of the Currency and the FDIC to voluntarily agree to such a policy of equity for all banks and depositors." In what was surely one of many letters written to constituents who were troubled by the direction their government was taking, Senator Boren made a point that has lost none of its resonance in nearly three decades of controversial banking policies and legislation: "We must have sound federal policies in dealing with bank problems. Those policies should be fair to everyone."[36]

Adam Smith, the eighteenth-century Scotsman whose *Wealth of Nations* was the foundational text for modern economics, proposed a definition of banks that, by 1980, was a hopeless anachronism. A bank, wrote Smith, "agglomerates the transaction balances of the community to lend at interest to its commercial enterprise." Fast-forward two and a half centuries since the publishing of Smith's seminal book, and you have financial institutions that find money where they can. Their funds are no longer limited to the agglomeration of deposits. The banker's bottom line shifted as legislators opened more avenues for banks to make their money and deploy their resources. In the ensuing scramble to develop products and services, bankers entered into competition with other financial institutions, including insurance companies, stockbrokers, mutual funds, originators and packagers of mortgages, and vendors of electronic payments services.[37]

As traditional banking that had worked just fine for generations slid into the dustbin of history, some predicted that Congress would eventually tear down remaining barriers between commerce and finance and allow banks to own industrial companies and/or to be owned by them.[38] Oklahoma City businessman Tom Loy, who launched his career in banking in 1975 as a protégé of Oklahoma City banker Morrison Tucker before launching his own company, Metafund, in 2000, characterized changes in the late 1970s and early 1980s as nothing short of revolutionary. With a keen sense of history, Loy cited two catalysts: rising interest rates and inflation. "In the mid to late seventies," said Loy, "something started that is, in my strong historical opinion, the most significant set of events, circumstances, perfect storm—whatever you want to call it—to happen after the Great Depression. And that was, starting in the mid-seventies, interest rates and inflation started skyrocketing."[39]

Competition in the financial-services industry was doing what it was supposed to do insofar as it fostered innovation and creative thinking. But when market interest rates rose above the regulated rates that banks could pay on savings and time accounts, commercial bankers went into panic mode. Spurred on by Federal Reserve Board chairman Paul Volcker's iron-fisted control of the money supply, interest rates peaked at 21.5 percent in the late 1970s.[40] "We had rampant inflation, at that time, and he was doing all he could to break inflation," recalled Gordon Greer, who was then working at Liberty Bank in Oklahoma City. "It was difficult! It was pretty hard to make money when you have to pay 20 percent for the money that you borrow. Inflation and high interest rates hurt a lot of people. It was really difficult on municipalities and others that had to borrow money and pay high rates of interest. It was not a pleasant time."[41] Volcker's jeremiad against inflation found expression in a campaign with a convenient acronym: "Whip Inflation Now," or "WIN." "They had little smiley-face buttons they were giving out all over the country that said, 'WIN,'" recalled Loy. "Whip Inflation Now. I don't know how you do it with smiley-face buttons, and nobody else seemed to know how to do it with anything else other than smiley-face buttons, until Paul Volcker came along."[42]

But bankers were not smiling. Wooed by the higher rates offered at other depository institutions as well as nonbank banks such as money-market mutual funds, depositors abandoned commercial banks in droves and took their money elsewhere. Alarmed by the prospect of a shrinking banking sector, the Fed coaxed Congress into a series of deregulatory measures.[43] Congress signaled its intention to make commercial banks more competitive when it passed the Depository Institutions Deregulation and Monetary Control Act (DIDMCA) of 1980. The DIDMCA set the tone for a wave of deregulatory measures that crystallized on both sides of the Atlantic under the leadership of the free market's most dedicated apostles: U.S. president Ronald Reagan, and British prime minister Margaret Thatcher. Under the auspices of the newly created Depository Institutions Deregulation Committee, the DIDMCA included three fundamental changes in U.S. commercial banking law: (1) it allowed bankers to create accounts that could pay market interest rates; (2) it phased out Regulation Q that, since the banking reforms of the 1930s, had established ceilings on the rates commercial banks could pay on time and savings accounts; and (3) it increased deposit insurance from $40,000 to $100,000 per account.[44]

In short order, NOW (negotiable order of withdrawal) accounts, pioneered in Massachusetts and authorized nationwide in 1981, and ATS (automatic transfer system) accounts came on the market. The NOW account was essentially a checking account that paid market interest rates. With an ATS account, NOW account balances were moved into interest-bearing overnight accounts and redeposited each morning.[45] The next deregulatory milestone came when Congress lifted restrictions on the interest rates that banks could pay depositors on their checking accounts. As a result, Super NOW accounts hit the streets in January 1983, leaving depositors to scramble for the highest rates they could find and bankers to struggle as never before in their efforts to attract and keep their customers.[46]

Spawned by a combination of high interest rates, an inflationary spiral, technology, and a fickle Congress bent on regulating banks even as it tried to make commercial banks more competitive through deregulation, NOW, ATS, and Super NOW accounts were game changers, and they were harbingers of changes to come as deregulatory zeal swept across the land. For the cigar-chomping Paul Volcker, it was all a bit too much. "I liked the old comfortable world," he said as he snuffed out a stogie in a giant pewter ashtray, "where there were specialized institutions."[47] In 1980, it was too soon to tell how the paradigm shift would affect Oklahoma banking. But there could be little doubt that the effects, and the consequences, would be huge.

Changes that were revolutionizing the banking industry were to a large extent driven by rapid-fire advances in technology that had everyone hustling to stay ahead of the curve. Change was also coming from banking legislation rooted in the idealism of the 1960s and aimed more at achieving social goals than imposing limits. Laws against discrimination in lending (no "redlining") and imperatives to clarify interest rates that people would pay on their loans (truth in lending) and receive on their savings accounts (truth in savings) signaled that the playing field was leveling as never before. Perhaps the most challenging legislation for bankers to swallow was the Community Reinvestment Act (CRA, title VIII of the Housing and Community Development Act of 1977), which required banks to document lending to low- and middle-income areas, develop community outreach programs, and expand services to those neighborhoods.[48] It also denied the powers of merger and acquisition to banks that were not sufficiently responsive to lending needs in their hometowns.[49]

Among those who were fed up with Congress's good intentions was Jack T. Conn. Although he had stood at the helm of Fidelity Bank of Oklahoma City since the fall of 1964, Conn never forgot his roots as a community banker in Ada. He spoke for many Oklahoma bankers when he singled out the Community Reinvestment Act of 1977 as a particularly odious instance of congressional meddling whose acronym, CRA, "would be more accurate if it ended in 'P.'" As the veteran banker noted way back in 1964, "If bankers relax their vigilance, they do so in the words of Hugh Johnson: 'This is just like mounting the guillotine on the infinitesimal gamble the ax won't work.'"[50]

In the spring of 1983, more changes were signaled when the Senate Banking and Currency Committee held hearings on a cornerstone of New Deal legislation: the Glass-Steagall Act of 1933. Named for its authors—Senator Carter Glass of Virginia, an influential member of the Senate Banking and Currency Committee, and Henry Steagall of Alabama, chairman of the House Banking and Currency Committee—the law separated banking and securities businesses by prohibiting banks from engaging in securities underwriting.[51] The legislation aimed at making banks less vulnerable to failure and made sense in the crisis atmosphere of the Great Depression. But over the years, the law was relaxed through waivers authorized by the Federal Reserve System.[52] In the wave of deregulation that swept Ronald Reagan into office in 1980, free-market zealots put Glass-Steagall in their cross hairs and advocated revision or, better yet, outright repeal. Specifically, the Reagan administration was proposing an expansion of bank holding company activities in three primary areas: (1) insurance underwriting and brokerage; (2) real estate investment, development, and brokerage; and (3) securities activities, including underwriting state and local revenue bonds and offering mutual fund services.[53] There was no doubt about it: Adam Smith's definition of banks was on a one-way trip to oblivion.

No matter how adept bankers were at managing change, there was no getting around a harsh reality: their industry was in crisis. In the first eight and a half months of 1984, fifty-five banks nationwide collapsed—

more than during all of 1983 and the most since the last year of the Great Depression. In May and again in July, massive infusions of federal money had been required to keep Continental Illinois, at one time among the ten largest banks in America, from failing. A few weeks later, the nation's largest savings institution, the Financial Corporation of America, turned to the government to staunch an outflow of depositors' money. Sepia-tinted images of Depression-era bank runs did not quite capture the zeitgeist of the computer age, when telexes and money managers began to set the pace for global capital flows. "Yet the stakes, for individual investors and for the nation, are just as high," wrote M.I.T. economist Lester C. Thurow in September 1984. "Banks are still the central cog in the complex, interdependent machinery that moves money around—essential to the development of new products and industries that create economic growth. A threat to the soundness of our private banking system is an economic nightmare."[54]

The crisis came at an awkward time for proponents of deregulation. Even as laissez-faire zealots were slashing and burning their way through the regulatory thicket, the very institutions they sought to unshackle were turning to the federal government for salvation. Thurow blamed a constellation of factors, "including the ignorance and stupidity of our leaders, both in private banking and in the Federal regulatory agencies," for the turmoil of the 1980s.[55] Topping his list was fierce competition spawned by changing definitions of banking that compelled banks to take extraordinary risks (with other people's money, of course) to avoid unwanted takeovers. Another problem that grew more menacing by the day was the staggering amount of debt owed American banks by developing countries with less-than-sterling credit ratings. Mexico, Brazil, Venezuela, Argentina, and Nigeria were the time bombs ticking the loudest. Through October 1983, banks had to reschedule $75 billion worth of foreign debt, which was at least ten times as much as in any previous year in history.[56] Then there was the alphabet soup of agencies—six, to be exact—charged with keeping banks within the law and away from unsound practices, but often tripping over one another instead of operating from the same playbook. Throw in congressional dillydallying and nonstop media hype, and you had the makings of a perfect storm. "What is missing so far," wrote Thurow, "is any sense that our leaders have developed a coherent plan to resolve the crisis. The feeling of nervousness and uncertainty still hovers over the banking system."[57]

To illustrate the "bad luck, bad management and bad regulation" that riddled American banking, Thurow pointed straight to Continental Illinois officers and their banking brethren who depended on energy loans from Penn Square Bank to further their ambitions, professional and otherwise. "Neither Continental nor any of the other banks that acquired smaller amounts appears to have considered that the price of a barrel of oil might plummet or that a bank the size of Penn Square could not properly analyze and supervise the huge numbers of energy loans it had made." Thurow went on to cite the chicanery and stupidity that hastened Penn Square Bank's demise and left it with "negative net equity"—in layman's terms, broke. The bag left in Continental Illinois's possession was the biggest, and when nobody could be induced to take it over, the FDIC seized ownership of 80 percent of the shareholder equity "in what is essentially a new Continental bank."[58]

Thurow questioned a system that forced taxpayers to absorb losses from bad loans but kept them from seeing any of the benefits from successful bailouts. Then again, Americans could count themselves lucky—Continental Illinois did not tank the banking system, countries that might have defaulted on their debt did not, and the sun still rose in the East. "It has often been said that is takes a crisis to move American policy makers to action," he concluded. "We have had the crisis."[59]

Professor Thurow had plenty of company in his apprehension over the state of American banking. Throughout the mid-1980s, financial professionals and academics used the national press to play the blame game and to promote their ideas for reform. FDIC chairman William M. Isaac supported a proposal to reorganize federal agencies along functional lines. "This country needs a strong, independent central bank," wrote Isaac in January 1984, a year and a half after Penn Square Bank's demise and several months before the FDIC takeover of Continental Illinois. "For the central bank to conduct monetary policy intelligently, it must have full access to all information pertinent to the financial system (and all other major industries). The central bank is also entitled to a voice in major policy decisions affecting the financial system."[60] George Champion, chairman of Chase Manhattan from 1961 to 1969, agreed that fundamental changes were necessary and blamed bankers and regulators for eroding confidence in the banking system. "In my opinion," wrote Champion in June 1984, "major changes are needed to be undertaken not only by the banker but by those agencies charged with the responsibility of bank examination if we are to have a healthy system."⁶¹ A partial solution would be to transfer the examination of member banks from the Federal Reserve Bank to the FDIC, with a directive that both the Office of the Comptroller of the Currency (OCC) and the FDIC take steps to improve the quality of bank examinations. In Champion's opinion, confidence in banking would be restored not by federal intervention, but rather, by bankers and the agencies that regulated them.

Auditors, too, were feeling the heat of heightened scrutiny. As watchdogs, they were responsible for nipping problems in the bud. Yet banks' cost cutting on audits and competition for clients between auditing firms were undermining confidence in the profession at a time when accurate assessments of banks' conditions were more important than ever. To illustrate the plight of auditors, reformers cited Peat, Marwick, Mitchell and Company's inept audit of Penn Square Bank shortly before its spectacular failure. In his testimony before a congressional committee, national bank examiner Steve Plunk complained that Peat, Marwick auditors tested only 15 percent of the bank's loan portfolio.

New York bank consultant David Cates suggested that auditors often fail to spot potential problems because they rely on a "snapshot" of the books. By not anticipating future loan growth based on past trends, auditors risked approving loan-loss reserves that are inadequate to accommodate a rapid increase in high-risk loans. With a focus on the wrong snapshot, even dump-truck banking might float beneath an auditor's radar. "They missed the fact that Penn Square's loan portfolio was exploding like a super nova in space," declared Cates. And all too often, auditors looked askance at potential problems rather than risk losing a client. "Auditors rarely sell their souls," quipped New York University accounting professor Lee Seidler, "but they sometimes do shade their souls." Fourteen months after the FDIC took over Penn Square Bank, the Michigan National Bank of Detroit filed suit against Peat, Marwick and asked for $41 million in damages from worthless energy loans purchased from the disgraced bank. In all, five Penn Square Bank creditors sued the accounting firm.⁶²

Citing deposit insurance as a culprit in prodding banks toward excessive risk taking, Stanford University economist Michael J. Boskin came down hard on the Continental Illinois rescue: "Continental Illinois Corp.'s bailout by the Federal Reserve and the Federal Deposit Insurance Corp. is offensive both because of public officials' disingenuous statements suggesting that taxpayers won't foot the bill and because the bailout is being used as propaganda in the attempt to re-regulate banking." For Boskin, deposit insurance had been extended far beyond its original purpose, which was to do what the Oklahoma legislature, at Governor Haskell's prodding, had done in 1908: guarantee small depositors that their money was safe. The proper course of action was not to bury banks in restrictive legislation but rather to clarify the extent of deposit insurance, provide greater information, and prevent the extension of deposit insurance to other financial assets so that unwary taxpayers would not be left "holding a hidden, but large and growing, bag."[63]

Within days of the historic bailout, the comptroller of the currency revealed another impediment to keeping banks on the straight and narrow when it revised its guidelines for loan participations. Although the guideline circular cited "recent abuses" as the reason for the clarification, officials denied that the timing of the circular had anything to do with Penn Square Bank's loan participations and the losses incurred by its upstream banks. (Dump-truck and yeehaw banking were conspicuous by their absence.) John Noonan, director of commercial examinations in the comptroller's office, warned banks of consequences for noncompliance with the revised guidelines, ranging from citations in their examination reports to cease and desist orders for the worst offenders.[64]

Editors of the prestigious daily newspaper the *American Banker* attributed banking woes to legal confusion in the financial industry. Even Congress was unable to agree on definitions of key terms in the financial lexicon, including such basic ones as "broker," "savings and loans," "savings banks," and "insurance activity." Simply put, the compartmentalization of financial activities dating back to the Great Depression was breaking down. Factors contributing to a brave new world of financial services since the 1970s included sustained high levels of inflation, heightened awareness among businesses and individuals alike of the importance of maximizing return on capital, and the burgeoning sophistication of communications and computer technology. Such pressures resulted in more flexibility in the kinds of services offered by financial institutions and vastly increased their geographic reach. "The point has arrived," asserted the *American Banker* in April 1984, "that national policy for financial regulators, depository institutions, service corporations affiliated with such institutions, and holding companies owning such firms is becoming indecipherable except to a handful of attorneys who are schooled in the intricacies of the history of these developments." The *American Banker* called on Congress to alleviate "the confused and litigious status of federal law affecting the structure of the financial services industry, its regulators, and regulatees."[65]

A contrary view came from New York University economics professor Jonas Prager. Wary of knee-jerk legislation from a Congress bent on doing *something,* he cautioned legislators to keep their hands off the financial system, particularly as banks were moving inexorably toward a more competitive environment. Prager explained, "Legislative stagnation on the federal level is preferable to action, especially when a brief survey of federal banking legislation will indicate that rarely has the public benefited from laws ostensibly fashioned to protect its interests."[66]

Even though they adhered to the contours of modernity, debates over the definition of banking in the 1980s pointed straight back to the conundrum that had bedeviled the nation's founders, and that had shaped Oklahoma banking in the days of merchant banking in the nineteenth century: how to reconcile capitalist enterprise with the freedoms enshrined in democracy. By the mid-1980s, banks were selling insurance, stocks, and even cut-rate merchandise, all in an environment of dizzying deregulation, and all consistent with free-market principles. While big-city bankers were banging on the doors of Congress and state legislatures, demanding the freedom to plunge even further into new businesses, old-school bankers were ducking for cover, convinced that everything they had dreaded with the demise of relationship banking, from corporate raiding and sales of junk bonds to greenmailing and asset stripping, was coming to pass. Seemingly overnight, companies were playthings of the stock market and potential takeover targets, subject to the caprices of investors, money managers, leveraged buyout firms, and takeover artists.[67]

Even as the American model of a stock market–based economy was blossoming into full flower, cooler heads knew that banking remained fundamentally different from other industries buffeted by the impartial winds of the marketplace. "Deregulation of banking is potentially dangerous," wrote Robert A. Bennett in the *New York Times* in February 1984, "not just for the institutions that might get caught up in turbulent markets for financial services, but for the nation." The FDIC rescue of Continental Illinois was still several months in the future when Henry Kaufman, an economist and managing director of Salomon Brothers, put the matter in its simplest terms: "When you encourage the entrepreneurial drive of the banks, the only way that drive can be disciplined is by allowing banks that have behaved improperly to fail. This is a key issue. Are we willing as a society to have major institutions that hold savings and temporary funds fail so that the proper discipline can be exerted on them?"[68]

Kaufman, whose firm competed with commercial banks, was probably biased. Not so with Federal Reserve Board chairman Paul Volcker, who spoke for many in calling for a pause in the rush to deregulate so that Americans could figure out what they wanted their banking system to be. Both men were alarmed at the piecemeal fashion in which changes were being made in the financial system, and both called for a consensus on an overall blueprint for change. On the other side of the debate were those who, like FDIC chairman William Isaac and Walter B. Wriston of Citicorp, wanted to sweep away the remaining cobwebs of regulation and open financial institutions to even greater competition. "My experience," said Wriston, "has been you either move forward or you die—it's true in all biology."[69]

Maybe so. Yet few relished the prospect of reverting to a Darwinian state of nature. As George M. Salem, a bank stock analyst at A. G. Becker Paribas Inc., commented, "Bankers want to be protected but yet they want a lot of freedom." Wherever one stood on the continuum between capitalism and democracy, one thing seemed clear: if policy makers continued to believe in protection for banks and their depositors, there had to be some form of regulation in effect to temper banks' activities. William Cline put it this way: "The counterpart of Government insurance is some degree of Government regulation because, if the Government merely provides safeguards, it would tend to create excessive risk taking by the banks. The central question is where one strikes the proper balance between differing levels of regulation."[70]

Looming in the background in all these debates was the specter of Penn Square Bank—an institution that clothed itself in the mantle of free-market capitalism and proceeded to squander other people's money on speculative ventures, leaving untold thousands of innocent bystanders caught in the collateral damage to wonder what happened to their seat at the table. Alan Meltzer of the Carnegie-Mellon Institute, whose views would resonate in a later time of banking troubles, articulated the position of many who were—and are—offended by the too-big-to-fail argument:

"You can't have deregulation without people accepting the risk. There has to be an understanding that if banks get into trouble, they have to pay the consequences. You can't have a system where the banks are free to take as much risk as they choose and then dump the losses on the taxpayer."[71]

By late 1982, business failures nationwide were on track for a record year. According to Dun and Bradstreet, commercial and industrial failures hit a near-record of 689 in the week ending November 4, 1982. The tally of bankruptcies was slightly lower than the fifty-year high of 696 bankruptcies reached in the week ending August 26. The surge in corporate failures pushed the forty-four-week total to 21,597 for a weekly average of 491. This compared with only 14,499 failures reported during the same period in 1981. No matter their size, companies across America were starved for business. "What companies need is cash flow and there has not been the sales growth that would generate it," said Purdue University professor William C. Dunkelberg.[72]

Oklahoma mirrored the national trend toward lowered expectations. An August 1982 survey conducted by the Oklahoma State University Office of Business and Economic Research predicted an anemic growth rate of 1.6 percent over 1981. "The continuing slump in Oklahoma's economy during the summer months has lowered expectations for the state's performance in 1982," ran the gloomy report. "Contributing to the lower forecast are the flat performances of the construction and oil and gas sectors of the economy, and the declines being experienced by the larger manufacturing sector."[73]

Plagued by an oversupply of natural gas, energy experts gazed into their crystal balls in late 1982 and saw different futures, none of which were cause for optimism. Tulsa consultant Wayne Swearingen predicted that the worst would be over in twenty-four months, while William Talley, his counterpart in Oklahoma City, saw no end in sight to the glut in supply and pricing woes.[74] Meanwhile, Hughes Tool Company continued to report on the decline in active rotary rigs. On September 26, 1983, the count stood at 248 active rigs in Oklahoma, down from 409 a year earlier.[75]

More barometers of an ailing economy came from Will Bowman of the Oklahoma Employment Securities Commission, who reported a precipitous drop in state tax collections. Other indicators included unemployment at historic highs (sixty thousand Oklahomans were out

A Helmerich and Payne rig probed four and a half miles deep, five miles south of Elk City in the Anadarko Basin, to become Oklahoma's deepest well and the second deepest well in the world. Courtesy Oklahoma Historical Society.

of work in the late fall of 1982), a doubling of demand for emergency assistance, and a 33 percent increase in applications for food stamps. Bowman had no reason to expect a rise in consumer purchasing to stimulate the economy. He reported, "With unemployment at 10 percent nationally and in some areas 20, the situation is quite desperate for many people."[76]

Speaking on "The Deindustrialization of America" at a conference on high technology hosted by Oklahoma City University in January 1983, Boston College economics professor Barry Bluestone suggested that the Sunbelt, a mecca for northern workers during the oil and gas boom, was losing its glow. But maybe there was an upside. "The 1980s has to be a decade not unlike the 1930s in terms of public policy," said Bluestone. "In the 1930s, we went through vast experimentation. We tried ideas which were absurd, but also ideas that have become the bedrock of American social policy."[77] One suspects that Oklahomans, usually optimistic and always keen to find the humor in things, found something to think about in the Boston professor's vision of a revitalized public sector.

Bad news for business meant bad news for banks. Between 1934 and the 1980s, bankers lived up to their reputation for stodginess. Failures were infrequent; the few that did fail were mostly small banks undone by crop failures or insider tomfoolery. Risky loans were the exception rather than the rule, and most bankers were content with a stable "spread" of 3 to 4 percent between their cost of funds and the interest rates they charged their borrowers. At the end of the day, most bankers were left with a satisfactory profit margin, even with allowances for general and administrative expenses and loan losses. Government was right to play referee by making charters hard to get and by limiting the interest rates bankers could pay depositors. After all, stable and profitable banks were good for everyone.[78]

But all that changed in the early 1980s, and the change was reflected in the declining value of bank stocks. According to a Salomon Brothers survey released in the summer of 1982, bank stocks were about the worst investment anyone could make in the second quarter of that year. An investor who picked the Standard and Poor's financial common stock index would have lost 10.4 percent of his investment; anyone selecting the Salomon Brothers' twenty-two-bank index would have come out only slightly better with a 6 percent loss.[79] FDIC chairman William Isaac, still reeling from his agency's takeover of Penn Square Bank, reported that the number of problem banks had soared from 220 to 320 by October of that dismal year. Continental Illinois's troubles were still on the horizon when the chairman said that the number of problem banks was bound to grow as loan losses piled up and competition fostered by deregulation forced financial institutions into trouble.[80]

Nowhere was Isaac's prediction more prescient than in Oklahoma, where bank failures set the tone for a decade that many would just as soon forget. As American Heritage Bank of Sapulpa chairman Bill Berry put it in April 2012, "The 1980s were so bad in the overall banking business in Oklahoma—I mean, half the banks went broke!—that it makes the current financial crisis seem like peanuts!" Bill's brother and bank president Guy Berry revised that percentage downward to closer to a fourth, but the point was taken. "I think there were 130 bank failures," he said. "We started out with 520, so a fourth of the banks, approximately, went broke. Everybody had some degree of trouble."[81]

A random sample of newspaper clippings from the mid-1980s tells the story of an industry in crisis—of banks caught in a vice of business failures and rapid-fire changes in the financial landscape. The flip side of failures—mergers and acquisitions that enabled failed banks to open their doors as branches of the acquiring bank—is described in the next chapter as part of a dizzying array of changes wrought by technological advances and Reagan-era deregulation that completely redrew the financial landscape. For now, we focus on the grim statistics of the 1980s as evidence that economics sometimes lives up to its billing as "the dismal science."

We begin with the closing of the First Continental Bank of Del City on May 11, 1984—the twenty-eighth of the year nationwide, and one of three closed that week. The others were the National Bank of Carmel in California with $70.8 million in deposits and the Mississippi Bank in Jackson with $167.6 million in deposits. In the absence of a merger partner, the FDIC implemented its modified deposit payoff program at the First Continental Bank of Del City, under which another bank was used as an agent for the FDIC and paid off insured deposits to customers almost as if a merger had taken place.[82] The bank reopened on May 14 as the United Del City Bank. In a sign of good faith to frazzled customers, bank employees handed out cookies and punch and piles of printed materials at the door on opening day. Most agreed with Doyle and Bobbie Kirby, customers who accepted FDIC assurances that their money was safe. "If what they say is true, why should we be worried?" asked Mrs. Kirby.[83]

What the Kirbys and other depositors in the festive bank lobby might not have known was that Oklahoma state banking commissioner Robert Empie had recently issued cease and desist orders to several state banks, including the First Continental Bank of Del City (reopened as United Del City Bank), and told them to clean up their acts or face the consequences. Although Commissioner Empie was responsible only for state-chartered banks, he said in an interview with the *Miami (Oklahoma) News-Record* that several national banks in the state were also operating under cease and desist orders.[84]

In October 1985, it was Farmers State Bank of Afton's turn to close its doors—the tenth failure in 1985, and one that prompted Empie to confer with Governor George Nigh about what he feared was a syndrome developing in Oklahoma banks. Empie said that he closed the bank in Afton after its capital was depleted through what he called "notoriously imprudent lending practices."[85] Security Bank and Trust Company in Miami, with deposits of $93 million, bought the failed bank's good assets. That same month, Empie closed the Bank of Canton (founded in 1902) in Blaine County, with deposits of $18 million. "The reason (for the closing) was an excessive concentration of credit to weak borrowers in the agricultural sector," said the banking commissioner.[86] A group of fifteen investors cherry-picked its good loans and deposits and reopened as the Community State Bank of Canton. Banker and memoirist Bert Willis was surely rolling in his grave as the bank that he and his brothers had steered through good times and bad succumbed to the banking bust of the 1980s.

In 1985, Oklahoma's thirteen bank failures put the state in second place behind Kansas in the nationwide ranking. Finance professor Gary Simpson said that he expected between fifteen and twenty banks, mostly of the small and weak variety, to fail in 1986. On the bright side, the demise of such banks posed little threat to the economy; banks that failed in 1985 held $292 million in deposits, representing just 1 percent of the total deposits held in the state's commercial banks. In a financial version of survival of the fittest, more failures could even lead to a strengthening of the state's financial base. "While the experience of 1985 should not be taken lightly," said Simpson, "bank failures in Oklahoma have perhaps received more attention than they deserve. Nationwide, over 100 banks failed in 1985, with many of the Midwestern states suffering agricultural credit problems similar to Oklahoma's."[87]

Nevertheless, it never paid to be too sanguine about a bank failure. Nearly three decades after the 1980s shakeout, veteran Oklahoma City banker Gayla Sherry put the bank failures in historical perspective. "I think the image of banking was probably the biggest loser," she said.[88] She credited the media and regulatory agencies for doing a good job in reassuring the public that the world was not coming to an end. But even though the average consumer suffered little more than inconvenience from the spate of bank failures, the public's confidence in the banking system had been breached. Regardless of their size, bank failures demolish consumer confidence, and even in the best of circumstances, a failed bank's loans are virtually impossible to place in another institution. As bank historian Martin Mayer famously wrote, "They have a stench of death about them."[89]

Sure enough, 1986 proved to be a banner year for bank failures. By Thanksgiving, fifteen banks had closed, prompting the FDIC—one of Oklahoma's few growth industries—to draw up plans for hiring public accounting firms to help with examinations. FDIC spokesman Alan Whitney said that if the plan worked in Oklahoma, it would be expanded "fairly quickly" outside the Southwest. Closure of the Bank of Commerce in Norman with $38 million in deposits on November 20 brought the number of bank closings nationwide to 126—a post-Depression record.[90] The year ended with Cordell National Bank's failure on December 4 with $72 million in deposits, bringing the total number of failed banks since July 5, 1982, to thirty-eight.[91] About 40 percent of failed institutions nationwide were farm banks. An additional 1,400 banks across the country had the dubious distinction of being on the FDIC's problem list.[92]

Banking woes also showed up in plunging profits. During the first half of 1986, Sheshunoff Information Services of Austin, Texas, reported that Oklahoma's 529 commercial banks lost a collective $64.2 million after earning $84.7 million during the same period in 1985. Moreover, key indicators of bank health showed Oklahoma banks to be "among the worst performing in the country in 1985." In its percentage of nonperforming loans (i.e., loans that were ninety days past due and not accruing interest), Oklahoma ranked fourth behind other energy-producing states—Wyoming, Montana, and Alaska.[93]

More of the same ensued in the first quarter of 1987 as nine more banks closed their doors. To keep track of the wreckage, the *Daily Oklahoman* published a regular feature, updated as information became available, that included an outline of the state with numbered dots representing communities in which a bank had failed and a listing of failed banks, their deposits, and the dates they were closed. Included in the doomsday roster of early 1987 were the Security National Bank in Norman (January 8—$174 million), the First National Bank of Rush Springs (January 15—$12.6 million), the First National Bank of Skiatook (January 15—$15.5 million), the National Bank of Frederick (January 22—$22.4 million), People's State Bank and Trust of Holdenville (January 29—$19.3 million), the Community Bank of Seiling (February 11—$5.4 million), the First City Bank of Atoka (February 12—$12.4 million), the First National Bank of Sapulpa (March 5—$7.5 million), and the Expressway Bank of Oklahoma City (March 12—$17.6 million).[94] To aid state banks, Governor Henry Bellmon proposed a two-pronged plan to arrange for a bank consortium to buy assets of failed banks from the FDIC and use state funds to buy preferred stock of failing banks to enable them to receive FDIC assistance.[95] Even though his plan failed in the legislature, Bellmon counted on Oklahoma's congressional delegation—David Boren (D-Seminole) and James Inhofe (R-Tulsa)—for help. They made headway in crafting legislation that compelled the FDIC to establish pools of capital to save ailing banks.[96]

Nobody was encouraged by a study conducted by the Federal Reserve Bank of Kansas City in the spring of 1987 that blamed management, and not general economic conditions, for the sorry state of Oklahoma banking from 1980 through 1986. The study's focus on so-called phoenix banks (i.e., those that had returned to profitability) revealed solutions that remained within the grasp of management but that all too often eluded their reach. According to the study, "Poor economic conditions were a factor in asset problems for half of all phoenix banks, but most often such conditions were secondary to incompetent management practices."[97]

Gayla Sherry left Liberty Bank and Trust Company of Oklahoma City after its merger with the First National Bank of Tulsa and joined the Federal Reserve Bank of Kansas City's branch in Oklahoma City in early 1988. Ensconced in the Fed's business development department, she had a ground-eye view of a shakeout that seemed to have no end in sight. Any thoughts she entertained about enjoying a reprieve from bank failures were put to rest during her first day on the job when she had the unpleasant task of circulating a memo about the failure of Union Bank in Oklahoma City. "Even by '88 and into '89, there were still many banks failing," she said. "It seemed like ... gosh, it seemed like there were several a week! It was kind of like, okay, it's Friday, who's failing?" But then, like everyone else, she got used to it. With apologies for seeming insensitive, Sherry described bank failures as little more than items on her to-do list. "By the time I joined the Fed—and this sounds kind of crass—but the process of banks failing, and the assets being taken by somebody else, was almost just routine, because there were so many. The bank kept its same routing number, the checks would still clear, we would still send cash out, and they would still deposit cash back with us. So, it just was kind of a routine process of just changing the name on the records. Sometimes there were management changes, but not always."[98]

But the decade of the 1980s was not all doom and gloom. In a tradition dating back to land runs and lotteries and success stories that branded Oklahoma as a place for unabashed optimists, good news was muscling its way into the maelstrom. Even as T-shirts blared a downbeat slogan—"Oklahoma, Home of the FDIC"—a few intrepid bankers were touting prosperity as the state's best-kept secret.

"We were the biggest bank in Dewey County, and we went through the eighties when a lot of banks closed, and our deposits increased by $10 million," said Jim Pittman, vice chairman of the First National Bank of Seiling. "We were conservative. I think we charged off five loans in ten years. Our income was really good during those ten years when a lot of banks were just the opposite. You know, they struggled and so forth. That was our biggest growth, percentage-wise, that we have ever had." At a time when most Oklahoma bankers were running for cover, Bowers Financial Services ranked the First National Bank of Seiling thirty-third on its list of America's safest banks. Asked to explain his bank's success in bucking the trend, Jim's son and bank president, Kirk, the fourth-generation Pittman to run the bank, shrugged and said simply, "All these other banks were failing or being bought, and people were moving their money to our bank, because of its conservative nature. That got around." For the Pittmans, conservatism in the eighties meant four things: avoiding the drilling mania; maintaining a loan-to-deposit ratio of 10 percent; maintaining a capital base of 15 to 20 percent of assets; and offering more jumbo CDs than any bank in the region. Long before online banking became all the rage, customers from as far away as Woodward, Fairview, and Canton were making the trek to Seiling. Well into the new millennium, Kirk Pittman remained rightfully proud of his bank's and, by extension, his family's commitment to conservative banking principles. "To me, that was due to faith in the bank, and the faith people had in our family, at that time," he said.[99]

Down in Oklahoma City, Founders Bank and Trust Company chairman Wayne Stone relied on similar principles to report a profit of $1.4 million in 1986. "The bank has always had a conservative approach to business," said the upbeat banker. "We've always associated ourselves with the right kind of customers. The worst is behind Founders."[100]

Eddie Jackson, president of Lincoln National Bank, which managed a .54 percent return on assets (ROA) in 1986 in its second year in existence, agreed. "This is the best region in the country if you want to talk future," he said. The small-town banker's philosophy was simple: "Get to know your customers. Don't loan money to people you don't know. The people need to have some tie to our service area. And then you become their total bank and grow with them."[101]

Community Bank of Oklahoma City executive vice president and chief financial officer Morris Permenter attributed his bank's success to "good personnel and an excellent loan review policy," both of which are critical to any bank's success. "We try to be conservative," he said. "Every loan has a risk to it, so we apply a lower percentage rate to those loans with lower risk."[102]

The conservative, proceed-cautiously approach also paid off for Nichols Hills Bank and Trust Company of Oklahoma City. "We never have set the world on fire," said Kenneth Lawson, Jr., president of the bank whose former neighbors in the nearby Penn Square Shopping Center did, "but we take our business very seriously."[103]

Of the forty-seven failures that began with Penn Square Bank on July 5, 1982, and ended with the Expressway Bank of Oklahoma City on March 12, 1987, none resonated further and wider than that of the First National Bank and Trust Company of Oklahoma City. Stung by a hefty percentage of nonperforming loans attending the oil and gas bust, the bank reported a loss of $45.4 million for the first quarter of 1986. Assets dropped to $1.9 billion, and primary capital was an abysmal 5.4 percent. Matters went from bad to worse when losses incurred in 1985 were revised upward to $66.6 million. Underwhelmed by the bank's performance and angered by management's stonewalling, federal regulators put Chairman of the Board Charles A. Vose, Sr., squarely in their cross hairs. Few insiders were shocked when, on September 1, 1985, Vose tendered his resignation as chairman of the board and chief executive officer. Edward C. Joullian III, who was then serving as a bank director, was named as chairman of both the bank and the holding company. Kenneth W. Townsend, a longtime bank employee, became the First's acting chief executive officer. For the time being, both Charles A. Vose, Sr., and his son, Chuck, were to remain as directors of the holding company, and the Vose family retained its 24 percent ownership. The elder Vose, then eighty-four years old, kept an office at the First until his death on December 10, 1986.[104]

Queried about Vose's "voluntary resignation," Townsend waxed diplomatic to say only that there had been "some conversations with regulators" prior to the announcement.[105] Yet it was an open secret that Vose's leadership was largely to blame for the bank's plight. Gerald R. Marshall, a former president of Liberty National Bank and Trust Company of Oklahoma City, who later became a senior vice president at the First National Bank of Dallas (later Bank of America), served as president of the First in the 1970s. Citing the senior Vose's toxic relationship with regulators, Marshall's take on Vose's resignation and the subsequent scramble to find a new chief executive probably gets closer to the truth: "There isn't any doubt about it," he said in reference to regulators in charge of the headhunting expedition. "They told him that they would not approve a new CEO that had ever even met Mr. Vose."[106]

G. P. Johnson Hightower—a great-grandson of First National Bank cofounder and president Frank P. Johnson, great-grandnephew of cofounder and president Hugh M. Johnson, and grandson of president W. E. "Billy" Hightower—carved his name into the family banking tree in March 1978 when he entered the First's management training program. When he left for a position at BOK Oklahoma City (formerly, Fidelity National Bank and Trust Company) in April 1986, the end game was in full swing, and he had plenty of company in his dash for the exit. Queried about management's role in the impending debacle, Hightower confirmed Gerald Marshall's recollection of the senior Vose's hostility toward regulators: "When management thumbs their nose at the regulators for about four decades, somebody's going to get back at somebody!"[107] Retribution toward stonewalling management played out in aggressive classification of loans that, in a less hostile environment, might have been accorded a smidgen of leniency. But as the First careened toward its bitter end, leniency was the last thing on regulators' minds.

Out of time, short on options, and under heightened regulatory supervision, the comptroller of the currency entered negotiations with First Interstate Bank of Los Angeles, a multistate banking company with assets of $49.6 billion as of March 31, 1986, to take over the failed institution. Such was the magnitude of the pending transaction that the FDIC paid First Interstate Bank a whopping $72 million to close the deal.[108] Oklahoma was once again in the precedent-setting business. Never before had a "negative premium" been paid to the buyer of a failed bank.[109]

On July 14, the comptroller of the currency declared the bank insolvent, and plans for a speedy rescue went into high gear. There was no public announcement of the closing, but none doubted that history was in the making. Escalators from the ground floor to the great banking room sputtered to a halt. Out-of-order signs were placed on the night depository slot and the automatic teller machines. Reporters clustered outside the front door.[110] Shortly before 6:00 P.M., police and Oklahoma County sheriff's deputies marched solemnly into the bank. Moments later, FDIC representatives descended on the premises in groups of two and three until their number swelled to fifty. In a choreography repeated throughout the oil patch in those dark days, the number crunchers fanned out in preplanned positions, some disappearing into the financial center on the ground floor, and others making for elevators and escalators. Finally, James G. Cairns, Jr., former president of People's National Bank in Seattle, Washington, and now president, chairman of the board, and CEO of the First Interstate Bank of Oklahoma City, appeared before the multitudes to announce what they already knew—the bank had been closed and sold.[111]

G. P. Johnson Hightower, the last of the Johnson/Hightower family to serve the onetime Rock of Gibraltar, was watching television when his childhood friend, Pete Everest, called to say he was sorry. "I was watching the news with a tear in my eye," recalled Hightower. "I was the only one at home."[112] Shock waves quickly spread from Oklahoma City to towns throughout the state. Charles McCall, chairman of the board of Atoka State Bank (later, Ameristate Bank of Atoka), was working alongside his father, C. A. "Barney" McCall, when the news reached southeastern

Oklahoma. The younger McCall remembered the bombshell like it was yesterday. "They were the main data processor for small country banks all over the state of Oklahoma," he said. But the relationship between the First National Bank and its small-town correspondent banks went far beyond data processing. "Who would have ever thought that the First National Bank would go under? I would have never thought that," continued McCall, the emotion in his voice still resonant some three decades later. "You know, that was just a bank that we all looked to. What's First National going to do? That's what we need to consider doing, whatever First National did."[113]

Cairns's appointment had been cleared with the regional director of national banks in Dallas following examinations in 1985 that resulted not only in the imposition of capital and policy requirements but also in the departure of Charles A. Vose, Sr., and his son, Charles A., Jr., both of whom took much of the heat for the First National Bank's failure.[114] Whatever the Vose legacy, their leadership following the deaths of the bank's first three presidents—Frank P. Johnson, his brother Hugh, and Frank's son-in-law, W. E. "Billy" Hightower—earned them a place in Oklahoma banking history. Their exit from the banking business was surely hastened by an oil bust that was severe by any standards, even for a state accustomed to a boom-and-bust economy.

With Cairns at the helm, the First Interstate Bank of Oklahoma City opened for business at 8:00 A.M. on Tuesday, July 15, 1986. The next day, a full-page advertisement was published in the *Daily Oklahoman* over Cairns's signature aimed at reassuring a rattled public that the bank was in good hands. His message ended with a nod to the bank's storied past: "For most of its 97 year history, the record of the First National Bank and Trust Company of Oklahoma City was one of enviable accomplishment. Such a record didn't just happen; it was the direct result of the dedicated efforts of individuals. It is from this legacy that we continue to draw inspiration. It is this legacy that forms the bedrock upon which future records of achievement will be built. We are proud to unite these positive aspects of this unique history. We're charting new directions in a changing world. Won't you join us?"[115]

For better or worse, interstate banking had come to stay. A cartoon in the *Daily Oklahoman* depicted the First Interstate Bank of Oklahoma City rising phoenix-like from the charred remains of the First National.[116] One wonders if anyone with a sense of history was there to reflect on other perilous episodes that had threatened the First National Bank and its predecessors and competitors: the panic of 1893, when bank founder T. M. Richardson's quick thinking saved the bank from ruin; the panic of 1907, a calamity of such magnitude that it spawned an overhaul of the banking system through the Federal Reserve Act of 1913; the incineration that gutted the Lee Hotel in 1908, home of Frank Johnson's American National Bank, which merged with his brother Hugh's State National Bank to form the First National Bank in 1927; the wave of agrarian socialism during the World War I era, which posed unsettling alternatives to free-market capitalism; bank failures stemming from speculation in oil and real estate; brazen holdups enshrined in western lore, curtailed when the OBA sent gun-toting vigilantes across the state to settle the score; and, of course, the Great Depression of the 1930s. The debacle of 1986 had plenty of precedent in a state known for its tenacity.

Under Joullian's chairmanship, the board of directors had offered Cairns a substantial salary with expectations of great things to come. What they got was disappointment. Prospects brightened when First Interstate Bank sent thirty-nine-year-old John Dean to take his place. By the fourth quarter of 1986, the Los Angeles–based bank was returning to profitability.

Yet traditions born of another era had little place in the innovations that First Interstate Bank applied to rescue a failed bank and revive a sagging economy. As of this writing in 2014, all that survives of "the financial Gibraltar of the Southwest" is a great banking room to bear testimony to its storied past. Tragically, sections of marble have been pillaged and fixtures have been carted off. Tenants in offices far above the great banking room complain of out-of-state landlords with little respect for an outdated building. Plans to open a pub, perhaps even a restaurant, come and go, but the years pass and the great banking room remains empty and eerily silent. Even the Beacon Club, a favorite venue for handshake deals and celebratory feasts, was relocated to the Oklahoma Tower, leaving the First National Bank Building with more empty space and Oklahoma Cityans with one less link to the commercial culture that spawned a sprawling city, and no memories of an aviation beacon that once lit up the western sky. The story of banking in Oklahoma from 1907 to 2000 was far from over, but its final chapters would have to be written without the First.

CHAPTER TEN

The Change

> The thing that has not changed in a small community is that community banks and customer service are still the number one priority.
>   Linda Christensen, Bank of the West, Thomas, Oklahoma

Bank failures were not the only story of the 1980s. Between the fall of Penn Square Bank in July 1982 and the century's end, changes wrought by technology and deregulation were spawning a paradigm shift in financial services that fundamentally altered people's relationship with their money and, on many levels, with each other. For better or worse, old-fashioned banking was either on life support or flatlining altogether. Depression-era regulations were falling by the wayside as bankers lobbied successfully to expand their range of activities. Capital lost all respect for state and national borders and sloshed around the globe at the click of a computer mouse. Social changes reflected in statistics compiled by the Equal Employment Opportunity Commission (EEOC) and released by the American Bankers Association showed that the number of women holding managerial and professional positions in the nation's largest commercial banks grew by 65 percent between 1975 and 1984. Minorities were close behind: during the same time period, their representation in the three highest banking levels grew at a rate of 50 percent. "As these figures indicate, women and minorities are making significant progress up the corporate ladder of banking," said Mark Pabst, chairman of the ABA Human Resources Division. "The banking industry of today is more challenging and competitive than ever, and because of that we are attracting some of the nation's brightest minds to the industry, including many women and minorities."[1]

The fraction of American households that did not have a bank account passed one-quarter in 1996 and was rising. In a disturbing sign that not everyone was part of the global banking village, the storefront check-cashing shop trailed only mutual funds and financial planning as the most rapidly growing sector of the financial-services industry. As of 1995, there were 6,000 such shops in the United States, up from 2,150 in 1985, and they cashed upwards of 200 million checks worth more than $60 billion. Check-cashing shops tended to pop up in neighborhoods without grocery stores and ATMs (automated teller machines). They also gave customers who could not wait for payday a handy way to pay their bills, albeit at punishing interest rates. Such establishments spread to the suburbs, where more and more people were opting out of traditional banking.[2]

Down on the farm, the laws of supply and demand foretold higher prices stemming from the drought-reduced harvest of 1980. Yet a perfect storm of bad economic news was pushing farms and the banks they depended on to the brink: declining grain prices as worldwide demand for U.S. grains and oilseeds declined and harvests worldwide hit record levels; sluggish demand for livestock products, even as production was peaking; inflation that outstripped the rise in farm asset values; and interest rates that climbed through the roof and kept on rising. According to Gary Benjamin with the Federal Reserve Bank of Chicago, "The possibility of three consecutive years of depressed earnings indicates that more farmers will have to liquidate assets to meet debt service and/or family living expenses. Their ability to do so will depend on how well the value of land, which accounts for the bulk of farm sector assets, holds up in the face of the prolonged slide in farm income."[3] Those who experienced the farm crisis of the 1980s remember the convoys of tractors and combines snaking their way to state capitols to demand a fair price for their produce, the vigorous debates in the halls of Congress over the plight of the family farm, and the stillborn efforts to galvanize independent-minded farmers into collective action. Such efforts were certainly well intentioned and sometimes even heroic, but they were inadequate to alleviate problems that were destined to get worse before they got better. The crisis ebbed as land values rose in the 1990s. Yet anyone with experience in agriculture knew better than to predict an end to troubles on the farm.

Meanwhile, banks continued to navigate their way through changes that were reaching warp speed. Included in what bankers had long since dubbed simply "the change" were rapid-fire advances in technology, competition from nonbank institutions and the resulting rush to market bank services as never before, new kinds of accounts and services, and cultural shifts that forced even the stodgiest of bankers to implement new policies and procedures. NOW accounts were giving people their first taste of interest-bearing accounts on which checks could be written. ATMs became ubiquitous and were preferable to standing in teller lines to cash checks and make deposits. By 1996, there were roughly 120,000 ATMs installed in the United States, and cardholders were making nine billion withdrawals a year.[4]

The profusion of financial products and whiz-bang technology spawned more of the same, and customers became conspicuous by their absence in bank lobbies as online banking became all the rage—a boon for the harried bank patron, but a loss for people who valued face-to-face communication that made trips to the corner bank occasions to socialize. Stock Exchange Bank of Woodward president Bruce Benbrook spoke for many of his fellow bankers in lamenting the loss of personal contact with customers, particularly with the younger ones who were growing up in the fast new age of technology. He explained, "As years go by, the younger and younger people get more and more used to not going in a bank. They never go. They have a paycheck automatically deposited, they go to ATMs, they do their banking at home. The older customers, they still love to come in and visit with you and say 'hey.' They love to make a trip to the bank and visit with people. But like I said, the younger generation, every year that goes by, I think that's less and less of a factor."[5]

Beginning in the 1980s, state prohibitions against branch banking toppled like dominoes to leave Texas and Oklahoma as two of the last bastions of unit banking (meaning that a bank had to restrict its services to a single location) until they, too, fell in line with the zeitgeist of the century's final decades. Oklahomans could take perverse pride that their state was a catalyst for interstate banking. One of earliest mergers to cross state lines, made possible when Washington State legislators gave it the green light, was organized in 1982 to allow Bank of America to take over Seafirst Bank, which had come up short in its experiment in dump-truck banking with the guys from Oklahoma.[6] By the 1990s, unit banking was well on its way to obsolescence. Financial behemoths were muscling their way into big cities and small towns alike, forcing bankers of all descriptions to rethink their strategies for survival.

As though bankers did not have enough to worry about in the 1980s, scandal reared its ugly head on March 10, 1987, when Governor Henry Bellmon suspended State Banking Commissioner Robert Y. Empie for "incompetence, malfeasance, and neglect of duty." Coming on the heels of the county commissioner scandal that branded Oklahoma as a haven for insider dealing and brazen thievery, Empie's suspension gave Oklahomans one more reason to question their leaders' fitness for office. As Governor Bellmon explained to his shell-shocked constituents, not ousting the banking commissioner "might have had the effect of lessening people's confidence in the (banking) system."[7]

News of the firing came as a shock to bankers throughout the state as well as heads of both bank trade associations—OBA executive vice president Robert E. "Bob" Harris and Community Bankers Association executive manager James P. McKeown. "We're surprised, and we're shocked," said Harris upon hearing the news. McKeown agreed. "I think the community banks across the state will be quite surprised and find it very difficult to believe that commissioner Empie, whom they consider a friend and has served the state probably during its most difficult banking era, has in fact abused his position," said McKeown.[8]

"That's news to me," said John T. Hannah, a Muskogee banker and member of the state banking board. "I wasn't aware that this was coming about or that this had happened." Murlin Derebery of Shawnee was likewise caught off guard and insisted that none of the state banking board members he had queried about the summary sacking saw it coming. "It caught us all by surprise," he said. In his executive order attending the firing, Governor Bellmon accused Empie of holding or controlling more than fifty thousand shares of stock in United Oklahoma Bank, which was one of the banks regulated by the commissioner, and where Empie had served as president from 1963 to 1979. United Oklahoma Bank chairman and CEO Morrison G. Tucker said he was unsure about Empie's ownership of stock in the bank. "I cannot comment on that," he said. "That would be a private matter." But it was no secret that United

Oklahoma Bank was in dire straits. After losing $3.9 million in 1985, the bank lost $21.3 million in the first nine months of 1986 and was seeking special assistance from the FDIC.[9] If the banking commissioner was indeed using his information and influence to try to sell his stock, he would have been in violation of state law.

Empie denied wrongdoing and chalked the imbroglio up to politics as usual, precipitated no doubt by the extraordinary number of bank failures during his tenure as commissioner. "There is a written agenda behind this," he said. "The governor wants me out very quickly and I have been hearing rumors of this now for nearly three months." Declaring that everything he knew about United Oklahoma Bank came from the morning paper, Empie dismissed charges that he stood to profit from insider information. As he commented wryly for the *Tulsa World,* "You did not have to be bank commissioner to read the newspaper."[10]

In the end, Governor Bellmon retracted his accusations, and Commissioner Empie was able to retire with dignity and pass the baton to his deputy, Wayne Osborn, a seventeen-year veteran of the agency who served as banking commissioner until 1992. He and his successor, Mick Thompson, who was executive vice president of Central National Bank in Poteau from 1977 to 1990, had their hands full in restoring people's confidence in the banking system and steering Oklahoma banks from the crisis-ridden eighties to prosperity in the nineties.[11]

Such were the issues and challenges attending the twilight of the old millennium and the dawning of the new. Oklahoma's challenges were compounded by a need to get beyond the boom-and-bust cycle of its petroleum-based economy and to attract new capital into the state. Even though they were understandably wary of making new loans, Oklahoma bankers knew they had to do their part to reverse the outflow of capital that attended the bust of the early eighties and to promote investment in their communities. As University of Oklahoma finance professor Donald G. Simonson wrote in June 1986, "Oklahoma's problem is how to replace that lost investment spending with other economic activity." For Simonson, the solution lay in a combination of private-sector initiatives and government programs to stimulate business development. "Future employment and income for the state," wrote Dr. Simonson, "depends on the rate of investment spending now and in the near future."[12]

For a down-to-earth take on the nation's economic challenges, we turn to Will Rogers, whose transcendent wisdom lost none of its prescience between his time and century's end. "An economist's guess," quipped the Cherokee cowboy with a twinkle in his eye, "is liable to be as good as anybody else's."[13]

Other than farmers, none took the crisis in American agriculture in the 1980s more seriously than U.S. senator David Boren. In an interview with the *Oklahoma Banker* in September 1982, Boren cited figures indicating the depth of the crisis: farm purchasing power in 1982 was projected to be $100 million lower than in 1932, the worst year of the Depression; farm debt between 1961 and 1981 rose from $28 billion to $200 billion, even as net farm income, in constant terms, grew from $11.9 billion to only $23 billion; interest costs in 1981 were a staggering $19 billion; and the value of farmland was declining for the first time in twenty-eight years. "Agriculture is the nation's largest industry," declared the Democrat from Seminole. "Two out of every three American jobs are associated with agriculture. When the agriculture industry cannot pay its bills from current cash flow for the third year in a row, the entire economy will be affected, just as we are seeing today." Echoing a familiar refrain, Boren blamed low prices, high interest rates (a staggering 15 to 20 percent of farmers' operating capital), which had increased 130 percent between 1978 and 1981, and declining exports for farmers' sagging fortunes. He admonished farmers to stay in touch with their legislators and bankers to do what they could to help their borrowers stay afloat. Boren reminded bankers that, as opinion leaders in their communities, they were uniquely positioned "to educate the rest of the community about the economics of agriculture."[14]

According to Frank W. Naylor, undersecretary for small community and rural development at the U.S. Department of Agriculture, farm credit problems were showing signs of easing in late 1983. "There'll be no shortage of credit next year for most farmers," he said. "But all lenders to farmers are going to be looking more closely at their farm loans and making sure crop and livestock producers have sound operating plans for 1984."[15] But for First National Bank of Frederick chairman and past OBA president Bill Crawford, the sanguine view from Washington, D.C., did not square with what he was experiencing in Oklahoma. Testifying at a special hearing on the farm crisis in early 1985, Crawford cited four factors as causes of a "cost-price squeeze" that was forcing record numbers of farmers to throw in the towel: high interest rates, low commodity prices, unusually poor weather conditions, and high production costs. Nationwide, 85 percent of borrowers had seen deterioration in their financial condition over the previous year; in Oklahoma, an estimated 90 percent of full-time farmers lost money in 1984. As royalties from oil and gas production declined from their peak in the red-hot days of the early eighties, farmers lost their buffer against hard times, prompting some observers to predict that one of every four farmers would be out of business by 1988. Crawford spoke for many bankers in calling on Congress to balance the federal budget as a prerequisite to alleviating the crisis in agriculture: "When the federal government brings spending in line with revenues, you'll begin to see an easing in the credit markets, and then interest rates will slide . . . and with that, a weakening of the dollar in foreign markets."[16]

The continuing drop in land values left farmers with less equity to pledge against their loans and bankers with little incentive to increase their agricultural loan portfolios.[17] In a survey of agricultural banks conducted by the American Bankers Association, respondents estimated that 7 percent of their farm borrowers would be discontinued between June 1985 and June 1986. Almost two out of three banks in the early reporting sample reported an overall decrease in their portfolio quality.[18] Writing in the Federal Reserve Bank's *Economic Review*, research officer and economist Mark Drabenstott cited the most striking toll of 1985: the mounting number of distressed farms, rural merchants, and farm lenders. "Farm business failures and farm lender closings occurred at a rate not witnessed since the Great Depression," he wrote.[19] Drabenstott's expectation of more of the same in 1986 proved to be prescient when the Federal Reserve Bank in Kansas City showed a 50 percent decline in Oklahoma farmland values in less than four years, even as interest rates remained at historic highs and prices for agricultural products continued their downward slide.[20]

To find relief for their financial woes, farmers and ranchers in Kay, Noble, and Osage Counties depend on American AgCredit. Founded in 1916, American AgCredit provides financial services to agricultural and rural customers in Oklahoma as well as California, Colorado, New Mexico, Nevada, and Kansas.[21] One of American AgCredit's branch offices is just down the street from the Pioneer Woman Museum in Ponca City.

"When you hear the farm credit system, that's a nationwide organization," explained American AgCredit of Ponca City vice president Felix Hensley. "Farm credit associations specialize in agricultural lending. That's all we do. And we have competitive interest rates. When you couple that with some other programs that we offer for our stockholders, it's a pretty inviting program that we have for the individuals." Hensley's associate, vice president Kent Crain, explained the somewhat surprising term "stockholder": "As a part of the loan origination, they become a stockholder." Dividends, or patronage, are paid annually and are based on the size of a stockholder's loans. Thus, if the cooperative declares a 1 percent patronage payment, a stockholder with an average outstanding loan balance of $100,000 would receive $1,000.[22]

Hensley and Crain remembered the 1980s as a time when commodity prices dropped from record highs in the 1970s to abysmal lows in the 1980s. Seemingly overnight, the price of wheat went from six to two dollars a bushel. As commodity prices fell through the floor, inflated land values plummeted by as much as 60 or 70 percent. "Everyone in the eighties suffered," said Hensley. "There wasn't anyone that the farm crisis of the eighties did not impact, one way or the other." Strapped for cash and desperate for interest rate relief, borrowers came scampering to farm credit offices in Ponca City and elsewhere across the state. "Back when interest rates at commercial banks here in the eighties got up to 19, 20, 21 percent, we were down pretty low," explained Hensley. "Our all-time high was 13 percent." Asked why American AgCredit was able to offer such low rates compared to commercial banks, Hensley boiled it down to a single word: stability. Asked to elaborate, he described the farm credit system as extraordinarily well capitalized and utterly attuned to the unique needs of agricultural borrowers. "And that's part of being a member-owned farmer and rancher co-op," explained Hensley. "We're here for the farmers and ranchers, whereas your commercial banks—a lot of your commercial banks are profit oriented."[23]

Then again, plenty of commercial banks did their part to alleviate the crisis on the farm. To help farm families make wise decisions and choose alternatives, many bankers threw their support behind IFMAPS—the Intensive Financial Management and Planning Support program. Launched in March 1985 and sponsored by Oklahoma State University's Department of Economics, the Oklahoma Cooperative Extension

Service, and the Extension Service of the USDA, IFMAPS aimed to help farm families improve their financial management skills, assess their farms' financial health, implement financial strategies, and communicate effectively with their creditors.

IFMAPS was not a panacea for farm troubles, but it was certainly a step in the right direction, and it represented a tradition dating back to territorial days of bankers working with farmers to improve their production and manage their finances. A letter written in the 1980s from a banker who sponsored an IFMAPS workshop might have been written at the dawn of Oklahoma agriculture, when bankers and farmers forged an alliance that strengthened with the passage of time and the advent of new technologies: "We think there is a very basic change in philosophy regarding the American farmer. The traditional view of farming as a way of life is giving way to the realization that farming is a business. The two most pressing needs are accurate accounting and reasonable forecasting. The IFMAPS program targets these needs: The workshops provide a basic introduction to terminology, as well as a preparation and analysis of financial documents. The individual assistance program can provide the immediate in-depth help many of our farmers need!"[24]

By the early 1990s, the worst of the crisis was over. Commodity prices were rising and interest rates were dropping from their astronomical highs, leaving famers will less burdensome debt loads and more money to invest in their farms. Improved bottom lines had the effect of luring investors to the countryside and fueled a rise in farmland values. In a stunning reversal from the early and mid-1980s, improving conditions on the farm attracted foreign buyers, chiefly from Japan, Germany, Brazil, Canada, and the United Kingdom. "Even though the amount of foreign investment is small," said American Society of Farm Managers and Rural Appraisers (ASFMRA) president Layton C. Hoysler, "their interest should tell us a great deal about the worthiness of investing in farmland."[25] Rural conditions were improving so much that, by the mid-1990s, bankers were targeting young people who had been leaving the farm in droves to fatten their agricultural loan portfolios. A key tool was the Oklahoma Beginning Farmer Loan Program, a joint initiative of the Oklahoma Department of Agriculture and the Oklahoma Development Finance Authority (ODFA), which used tax exemptions to offer low-interest loans to aspiring farmers. Dennis Buss, president of the Service Bank of Tonkawa and chairman of the OBA Agriculture Committee, encouraged bankers to take advantage of the loans' tax-exempt status. "If you could use the program together with other loan programs, like those of the Farmers Home Administration, I'd say it (the Beginning Farmer Program) would be an excellent tool."[26]

When they were not helping farmers to improve their bottom lines, bankers were steering their institutions through "the change"—a kaleidoscopic swirl of technological marvels and Reagan-era deregulation that was collapsing brick-and-mortar banks and electronics into an efficient and user-friendly means of delivering financial services. The three primary ingredients of the change in banking at century's end were electronic funds transfer, the proliferation of nonbank banks, and the advent of multibank holding companies and branch banking. Separately, each of these changes was mind-boggling. When they coalesced, they were nothing short of revolutionary.

The First National Bank and Trust Company of Tulsa was a trailblazer in electronic banking clear back in 1937, when an automatic deposit machine was installed in the bank lobby. The device operated on an electric eye beam. When a deposit was inserted in a chute, the beam was broken and a bell was sounded to assure the depositor that the deposit had been accepted.[27] Even though subsequent gadgetry represented quantum leaps in technology, the aim was always to provide customer convenience and efficient bank operations.

Beginning in the early 1970s, electronic delivery systems made their debut in the form of ATMs, followed by the automated clearing house (ACH) in 1972.[28] The Bank, N.A. (formerly the National Bank of McAlester), heralded the arrival of ATMs with a contest to name the two machines installed in its facilities in 1979. The winners were MAT (Money Any Time) and PAT (Pay Any Time). Some financial institutions found economies of scale by joining forces. In Muskogee, three banks and two savings and loans combined to house and install ATMs in the four quadrants of town. "It would be cost prohibitive for our bank to install and operate ATMs because they are very expensive," said Harry Leonard of the First National Bank and Trust Company of Muskogee. To woo customers to their kiosks, a few banks resorted to the tried-and-true method of offering premiums, and not just piggy banks. The Exchange National Bank of Perry installed two machines: one at the bank and the other at the Perry Plaza Shopping Center near Interstate 35. "It was slow getting started," said bank vice president Norma Jerome. "We spent a lot of time getting our customers educated. In one promotion, we gave away free portraits if they came in to see the ATM demonstration. It was a big success."[29] Jerome added that even older customers were starting to use the machines—a sure sign that high tech had arrived in Perry to stay. But for a real trendsetter, we turn to the Stroud National Bank, the first bank in the nation to install an ATM on a turnpike, and the first one to install a machine in a McDonald's restaurant. First Lady Shirley Bellmon joined bank officials Kim Wheeler and Glen E. Wheeler for the ATM dedication on July 16, 1987. "We don't know how many transactions to expect," said Kim Wheeler, "although three people tried to use it during a five-minute period when the machine was being installed."[30] History is silent on whether or not Mrs. Bellmon and the bankers feasted on Big Macs and fries to celebrate Stroud's foray into electronic banking.

While communities were embracing new ways of banking, some bankers decided that the convenience of ATMs was not worth the time and hassle of operating them. Lincoln Bank and Trust Company in Ardmore was the first bank to have an off-line, or stand-alone, ATM facility. It opened in 1976 and was housed in a kiosk in a shopping-center parking lot. "We also were the first to get out of the ATM business," said bank chairman and president John W. Grissom. "It just wasn't viable for us. We found it was expensive to operate and we encountered security problems." For American National Bank of Bristow president Tracy Kelly, it all boiled down to the needs of customers. "Today's applications of technology doesn't [sic] always apply to the community bank," said the veteran banker after conducting marketing studies to determine the feasibility of ATMs in Bristow. As it turned out, Bristow was not ready for them. "While the community bank is certainly wanting to provide convenience for the customer, sometimes there just isn't a need," continued Kelly. "Each bank has to study and decide what is right for their community."[31]

ATMs were the vanguard of in-home banking, an integrated structure aimed at allowing people to access account information, pay their bills, read monthly statements, fill out loan applications, and compare interest rates from various banks from the comfort of their homes. Tests of evolving technologies around the country indicated that Americans were ready and willing to alter their banking habits, particularly when bank CEOs signaled their enthusiastic support of technology and customers were given the chance to accept change at their own pace rather than have it forced upon them. As Catherine L. Bond wrote in the *Oklahoma Banker* in October 1986, consumers are inherently selfish and are interested in how something will directly affect them. "The entire marketing program should be built on this premise," she wrote.[32] Still, proponents of electronic banking knew where to look for early adopters. "The evolving home information industry is likely to be further stimulated as the youth of today, with their 'computer-is-friendly' attitude, arrive full force in the marketplace," wrote John F. Fisher, senior vice president of BancOne Corporation of Columbus, Ohio. "Clearly, the pace of acceptance is geared to a worldwide society much more willing to push buttons than pencils."[33]

Nowhere were the pros and cons of technology more hotly debated than in community banks, where resistance stemmed from suspicions that the playing field was tilting in favor of large institutions. To quell such fears, finance professor Don Simonson countered the "shakeout theory"—that technology throws the competitive balance toward the biggest players—with his "divisibility theory." Applied to the banking industry, this theory suggested that technology might give small banks a leg up in competing with larger ones. Even in the early 1980s, microcomputers were enabling small businesses to stay flexible and responsive to customers' needs at minimal cost. The most significant small bank advantage lay in its capacity to avoid the risks of investing in computing hardware and software. "Electronic banking renders the brick and mortar branching systems of big regional money center banks less competitive," claimed Simonson.[34] By enabling banks to tailor their systems to suit local needs, computer technology promised to be more of a friend than a foe to the community banker.

Overall, Oklahomans' attitude about ATMs in particular and electronic banking services in general was upbeat, and they did their part to usher in the brave new age of banking. In 1975, there were fewer than a hundred ATMs installed throughout Oklahoma. By 1984, that number had mushroomed to 650; nationally, at least 4,500 financial institutions were involved one way or another with ATM programs. In Oklahoma, approximately 35 million transactions were performed on EFT systems in 1984 for an average of 136,719 per day and a volume of nearly $2 billion. The average card usage was just under three per month, compared to the national average of 1.1 per month.[35] A decade later, Bank IV vice president Cheryl Bond said that about 35,000 customers were using her bank's debit cards, known as Visa cash services cards. "The customer support of this product may be the strongest for any bank product I've seen in recent years," said Mark Graham, Bank IV executive vice president and director of retail banking.[36] Graham spoke for many when he said that customers who became accustomed to using debit cards would never bank anywhere that did not offer them.

By 1994, costs had fallen to the point where community banks could add check imaging to their repertoires of high-tech services. Imaging systems were designed to capture electronic pictures of paper checks, and they allowed banks to save money and staff time in statement preparation and mailing and to simplify account research. "The key to the whole thing is going to be cost-effectiveness," said Alva State Bank and Trust Company cashier Todd Holder. American National Bank of Lawton senior vice president and cashier John Rogers claimed that his bank ventured into check imaging to improve its processing and to better serve its customers. His bank's first image statements were mailed in March 1994, likely earning it distinction as Oklahoma's pioneer in check imaging. PNB Financial Corporation, a Kingfisher-based holding company, joined the bandwagon when it installed a check-imaging system in its nine locations. Banks that were not quite ready to install their own systems could rely on C-Teq, an Oklahoma City–based check and data processing firm that planned to roll out an imaging service in August 1994. C-Teq president and CEO Anne Johnstone expected at least fifteen banks with assets up to $400 million to sign up for the new service.[37]

Clearly, the smart money was on the gradual replacement of checks with electronic transactions and check imaging. Yet even the most vocal advocates of electronic banking knew better than to write off customer service as a vestige of old-fashioned banking. "The thing that has not changed in a small community," said veteran Custer County banker Linda Christensen, "is that community banks and customer service are still the number one priority."[38] Big-city bankers tended to agree. "It doesn't matter how automated you can do anything," said Arvest Bank's G. P. Johnson Hightower. "People still want to deal with people."[39]

The promise of electronic banking was matched by concerns about computer security, defined in July 1982 by behavioral science management consultant Peter H. Hackbert of Norman as "the protection of data from accidental or intentional disclosure, destruction or modification."⁴⁰ Acknowledging that most industrial organizations could not survive without their computers, Hackbert admonished bank managers to develop a comprehensive plan to ensure the integrity and accuracy of their data, protect and conserve corporate assets, and guard against unforeseen circumstances and disasters. As banks have all too often learned the hard way, an effectively implemented computer security program eliminates the intuitive guesswork that bankers have traditionally relied on to safeguard their information and, of course, to protect other people's money.

In an effort to help its members stay ahead of the curve, the Oklahoma Bankers Association focused on "new age banking" at its May 1983 annual convention in Tulsa. "The challenge to change, to adjust is not easy in banking, or in any other industry," asserted a conference announcement in the *Oklahoma Banker*. "But the ability to change breeds success and strength." To foster success and build stronger banks, the OBA held workshops on microcomputers and the regulatory process aimed at helping conference attendees "rethink their traditional roles."⁴¹

By the end of the eighties, the question was no longer whether or not to move with the technological tide; it was to figure out the best way to go about it. By one estimate in late 1989, more than 50 percent of banks in Oklahoma were using third parties for data processing. Those that maintained their own data processing, or operated with a mixture of in-house services and off-site computer systems, included Barnsdall State Bank, the First National Bank of Geary, Choctaw State Bank, and the First State Bank and Trust Company of Shawnee. Barnsdall State Bank cashier Jimmie Price spoke for many when he explained, "By having an in-house computer system, we have faster access to our files and can go to the computer and look up any file we need at any time." Larry Deets of First Data Management Company of Oklahoma City said that the trend over the past decade had been toward in-house data processing. "Whichever alternative a bank chooses," he said, "it should enhance the banks' goals of achieving efficiency and profitability and accomplish other objectives the bank has made."⁴²

As the century entered its last decade, the winds of change had given bankers a dizzying array of financial tools, from ATMs and ACHs to desktop check printing, software for practically anything, automated bill payment, twenty-four-hour information lines, and digital imaging of paper documents. In late 1991, the American Bankers Association estimated that 70 percent of banks with assets under $300 million were using personal computers. The tally increased to 90 percent for banks with assets between $300 million and $1 billion, and 97 percent for banks with assets of more than $5 billion.[43] One cannot help but wonder which banks were not on the technology bandwagon, and how on earth they accomplished anything.

Both cause and effect of the change in banking was the proliferation of so-called nonbank banks. One had to look no further than Sears, Roebuck and Company's purchase of Dean Witter and American Express's purchase of Shearson Loeb Rhoades (both in 1981) to form Shearson/American Express for signs that jurisdictional walls were crumbling and hybrid institutions were the wave of the future. In a survey conducted in November 1984 of the 2,235 CEOs of all commercial banks in the United States with assets in excess of $100 million, 93 percent of respondents predicted that Sears would be "a major competitive threat" in the markets in 1990; respondents perceived that other threats would be Merrill Lynch (83 percent) and American Express (77 percent).[44] By February 1985, the comptroller of the currency had approved applications for nonbank bank charters in twenty-one states for sixty applicants. Oklahoma bankers could at least be grateful that no applications had been approved for nonbank banks in their state, but few doubted that they were on their way. As lawsuits over which institutions could call themselves banks and which could not littered the financial landscape, the OBA stuck by its guns, insisting that the comptroller of the currency was authorized under the National Banking Act to approve only one of two types of banks: a full service national bank or a national bank with only trust powers. As evidence of its opposition to nonbank banks and commitment to its members, the OBA sponsored a bill in the state legislature to permit only banks that both accepted demand deposits and offered commercial loans to operate in Oklahoma.[45]

What banks needed as never before was a strategic plan to improve their public image, increase their use of new technology in bank operations, and increase their profitability. The planning imperative was all the more urgent as bank-bashing journalists prowled for bankers who had run afoul of fair-lending laws or mutual fund disclosures.[46] Among those who answered the clarion call to guide banks through the change were Ed Wertzberger and Bill Browning of Arthur Andersen and Company in Oklahoma City. Amid doom-and-gloom predictions that the nation's banks would decrease from fourteen thousand in the mid-eighties to fewer than ten thousand by 1990, the duo touted "strategic management" as the ticket to better banking. "A social force presently encompassing the entire industry is the declining faith of the public in financial institutions," wrote Wertzberger and Browning in the *Oklahoma Banker*. "The rash of highly-publicized bank failures in the past few years has the public concerned for the safety of their deposits. To counter this situation many banks are attempting to project a stronger image of financial strength and security." Quoting G. K. Chesterton—"It's not that they cannot solve the problem, it's that they cannot see the problem"—Wertzberger and Browning came to the rescue with flow charts and diagrams to deconstruct management structures as the first step in molding them to the contours of the new age. What they and like-minded consultants hoped to leave behind were fiercely competitive bankers—technologically savvy and fully in tune with the needs of their customers.[47]

Sometimes, the most effective defense is attack. To retain customers and recapture money that had been flowing out of banks and into institutions that offered a wide array of financial services, bankers began to hire securities firms to broker common stocks, bonds, options, futures, and other investments that had heretofore been beyond the purview of the stodgy corner bank. "I see a tidal wave of money flowing back into community banks and financial institutions," said James Baker, founder of a securities firm that was contracting with Oklahoma banks to offer securities services, in November 1982. "It is critical that Oklahoma institutions recapture money that has been flowing out. The Penn Square Bank insolvency has created a climate that reduced the amount of money flowing in. We have become as capital short as we were before the oil boom."[48]

Another strategy to remain competitive came in the form of Super NOW accounts, which were essentially checking accounts that paid interest in the range of 8 to 9 percent as long as minimum balances were maintained. Most bankers welcomed the freedom to compete with brokerage houses, even though most expected that money flowing into the new accounts would come mainly from money that was already in their banks in the form of demand-checking accounts. Nevertheless, in the first two weeks after the new savings instruments were introduced in mid-December 1982, banks and savings and loans recovered an estimated $10 billion from brokerage houses—a sure sign that bank customers wanted to remain loyal to their banks but, at the same time, reap the benefits flowing from deregulation.[49] Customer loyalty to their banks was reflected in a mid-1987 study that examined the competitive structure of the Oklahoma financial-services industry from the perspective of households. Among the findings was that consumers held positive attitudes toward their banks. In spite of the boom-to-bust roller coaster ride they had so recently endured, most respondents thought their deposits were secure and still relied on their banks as their primary sources of financial services.[50]

In the new age of banking, nobody could rely on products and services to sell themselves. To compete with nonbank banks, bankers had to jettison outmoded marketing concepts and embrace the fine art of communications. "Banks must not only say who they are," wrote Landor Associates president and CEO John Diefenbach. "They must say what they offer. And they must say it in a 'tone' modulated to appeal to very specific market segments."[51] Financial professionals had only to look at other industries, from retail and consumer products to food services, travel, and health care providers for examples of effective marketing. A step in the right direction came in early 1983 when the OBA developed television commercials and print advertisements for member banks aimed at reclaiming their industry from the doldrums of the early 1980s and at publicizing their increasing array of services and tradition of community investment. Adopting the campaign slogan (in all caps, in case viewers and readers were slow to get the point) "DO YOUR BANKING AT A BANK . . . YOUR LOCAL OKLAHOMA BANK," the OBA campaign mimicked others that were building steam across the country.[52]

As evidence of bankers' newfound appreciation for salesmanship, the Bank Marketing Association released results in late 1985 of a survey of 1,100 banks that measured expenditures in five categories of marketing: advertising, public relations, sales promotion, staff sales training, and marketing research. From 1983 to 1984, U.S. banks increased their median expenditures by 7.1 percent. Perhaps not surprisingly, banks with assets in excess of $100 million increased their marketing expenses the most (11.5%), while smaller banks lagged behind with a 2.1 percent increase.[53] Nevertheless, there was clearly a trend toward aggressive marketing, and it continued unabated through the 1980s and 1990s. "Financial institutions are making measured progress in building their sales programs," said Tom J. Hefter, president of the Financial Institutions Marketing Association (FIMA) in early 1987. "The result is existing customers are using more services. In other words, more financial institutions are involved in sales as a part of a relationship marketing effort compared to outside sales programs designed to pull in new business."[54]

Marketing campaigns were matched by a renewed commitment to customer service, an aspect of American business that, according to many, had fallen on hard times. There was plenty of blame to go around for the dip in customer service, but one thing was certain: banks that ignored their customers' complaints did so at their peril. Carl Lewis, a senior analyst for the Fort Worth–based consulting firm Sisk Company, Inc., admonished bankers to see themselves as others saw them by putting themselves in the customer's place. Lewis's signs of poor customer service derived in part from the conflict between galloping technology and people's efforts to keep up, and they were as commonsense as they were ubiquitous: perceptions of feeling ignored, cheated, or overcharged; losing privacy; receiving inadequate information about a product or service; and being kept waiting for no apparent reason. Ultimately, customer service meant putting the "I," "we," and "us" back in communications with customers. Lewis's message has lost none of its urgency since the late 1980s: "It is actions by people that most often determine whether service is perceived as good or bad."[55]

Other customer service initiatives in the 1990s included focusing on the needs of small businesses and offering mutual funds to their customers. Blanche Ross, vice president of Oklahoma Bank and Trust in Clinton, spoke for many in touting the popularity of mutual funds. "I think it's gone real well," she said in April 1993. "Generally, investors like the higher yields, and flexibility of mutual funds." Teri Nance, assistant vice president of brokerage services at WestStar Bank in Bartlesville, said that mutual funds were selling better than annuities at her bank. "People like the fact [that] mutual funds not only provide returns on their investment but also offer the opportunity for the original investment to grow."[56]

Inextricably linked to technological advances and competition fostered by nonbank banks was the third ingredient of the change: branch banking. For years, Congress had been an arena for debates about the limitations imposed on banks by the McFadden Act of 1927 and the Banking

Acts of 1933 (best known as Glass-Steagall) and 1935—all vestiges of the Great Depression aimed at separating traditional banking from market-related activities, and all eventually scrapped in an era of deregulation and runaway technology.[57] Across the land, state legislatures saw the handwriting on the wall and came up with ways to allow local banks to coalesce into larger, more muscular institutions that could withstand the pressure from money center banks that was surely coming.

In the 1970s, there was an overwhelming consensus among bankers and academics that branching made sense on economic grounds, and most states were loosening restrictions on growth and acquisitions within their own boundaries. In states that allowed some form of branching, banks were able to diversify risk, coordinate their responses to economic shocks, and allocate capital across regions.[58] By the fall of 1983, multibank holding companies were permitted in forty states, and the movement to unleash interstate competition was building to a crescendo.[59] As the main policeman of big bank mergers, the Federal Reserve Board hastened the arrival of interstate banking by permitting banks to engage in market-related activities as long as the ensuing revenues were not a major contributor to their overall operations.[60] With interstate banking in sight, it turned out that size really mattered. According to consultant John Mingo of Golembe Associates, "The driving rule is what's the biggest merger I can get away with on legal grounds if the economics and vibrations are right."[61]

Intrastate branching (as opposed to interstate banking), of course, was nothing new. Historically, the lion's share of bank profits came from paying below-market interest rates to savers. To attract those lucrative deposits, commercial banks built branches, and their numbers exploded from 1,000 in 1920 to more than 4,000 in 1946 to about 10,000 in 1960.[62] By 1982, the nation's 15,000 banks were operating about 42,000 branches. At the same time, bank operating costs were rising at an explosive annual rate of 14 percent, even as the cheap deposits that had subsidized bank growth were disappearing with the elimination of interest rate ceilings. Pushed by a combination of declining profits and rising costs and lured by the expansive potential of technology, banks were poised for a shakeout of historic proportions.[63]

But not everyone was on board. In a state rooted in prairie populism and wary of big business, it is hardly surprising to find Oklahoma as one of the last holdouts in allowing banks to expand their market reach by establishing branches.⁶⁴ Gary Simpson arrived at Oklahoma State University as an assistant professor of finance in 1978 to encounter a strong unit-banking culture. "It's amazing, but back in those days, people pretty much did business with banks very close to where they did business and lived," he said. "Of course, there was no branching to speak of, at that time, so you pretty much were limited to your local bank, unless you wanted to drive several miles." During a former four-year stint as an FDIC bank examiner, Simpson was trained to question so-called out-of-market loans. Why, after all, would someone drive to a bank in another community to obtain a loan unless there were problems at home?⁶⁵

Weaned on rugged individualism and wary of eastern moneymen and their nefarious ways, most Oklahoma bankers drew a line in the sand—or more accurately, around their state—when it came to branch banking. As late as 1982, holding companies in Oklahoma were restricted to owning a single bank, and no bank was allowed to operate more than one office more than a thousand feet from the bank headquarters. Yet even in a state whose constitution drew on William Jennings Bryan's fiery brand of Populism in the 1890s and whose first governor, Charles Haskell, staked his reputation on deposit guarantee, the stars were beginning to align in favor of branch banking and multibank holding companies. To promote of more liberal legislation that would enable weak banks and savings and loan companies to merge into healthier institutions, more than two hundred Oklahoma bankers broke with tradition and signed up to support changes in the state's banking laws. In anticipation of more liberal laws, banks in Seiling, Skiatook, and Weatherford applied for federal charters in September 1982. "We are positioning for interstate banking and multibank holding companies," said Dale Mitchell, a former top official with the First National Bank and Trust Company of Oklahoma City who owned controlling interest in the Bank of Commerce and the Gilcrease Bank in Tulsa. Other prominent financiers who were rising to meet the future included George Records, Morrison Tucker, Gene Rainbolt, Ronald Grubb, and Chuck Vose and his son, Chuck, Jr. Peering into his crystal ball, Mitchell spoke for other leaders in Oklahoma banking when he said, "We can keep growing as our customers grow, and we can keep them longer. We need to develop a strategy to keep our good customers and control our destiny."⁶⁶

As multibank holding companies and branch banking gained traction across the country, community bankers in Oklahoma had signaled their displeasure in 1974 by creating the Independent Bankers of Oklahoma. First National Bank of Midwest City president R. S. "Bob" Amis was elected as the association's first chairman, and First Mustang State Bank president Gary Huckabay was elected as vice chairman. Citing polls indicating that 84 percent of bankers in Oklahoma wanted to retain the state's prohibitions against branch banking and multibank holding companies, Amis took issue with the Oklahoma Bankers Association's neutrality. "Thus," said Amis, "a majority of Oklahoma banks are without continuous representation on the very issues most vital to their survival. By forming their own state organization, the independent bankers feel they can assist the OBA in this divisive area. Branching or its alternative, the multibank holding company, would be merely a 'hunting license' for expansion-minded banks with no benefit to the public."[67]

According to Craig Buford, president and CEO of the Community Bankers Association of Oklahoma, which succeeded the original group, the acrimony over banking structure in the 1970s never entirely dissipated, and it continued to fuel community bankers' suspicions of big-city banks. "It became a very heated and controversial issue," said Buford, "and across the country, a lot of states formed a community-banker type organization."[68] Gary Simpson recalled clashes between bankers that reverberated far beyond boardrooms. "It's what you would expect, right?" asked Simpson rhetorically. "You've got basically a unit-banking state that's converting into a multi-office state, and people with those franchises, those charters, in small towns, were scared to death that they were going to have Bank of America across the street from them. So they were very much anti-multi-office banking, whether you do it through holding companies or you do it through branches."[69]

The founding of the BancFirst Corporation was far in the future when David Rainbolt returned to Oklahoma from a stint with Republic Bank in Dallas to help his father, Gene, manage his banking interests. He was just settling back into his home state as the associations' fight over the future of Oklahoma banking was turning ugly. "By '82 and '83, the OBA was beginning to be conflicted," said David. "About half of their membership wanted [branching], and half of them didn't. Over the course of the eighties, the OBA became more expansionary, and the Community Bankers Association—the independent bankers of Oklahoma—remained very, very anti-expansionary. It was just chin-to-chin war over the structure, with the independent bankers of Oklahoma."[70]

But clearly, the tide was rising against the holdouts. Eventually, community bankers who belonged to the rebranded Community Bankers Association of Oklahoma, along with other state associations and the Washington, D.C.–based Independent Community Bankers of America (ICBA), surrendered to the inevitability of branching and focused on promoting legislation that would level the playing field for community banking and defend against costly and burdensome regulations. Other benefits of membership included training programs, assistance with legal and compliance issues, and references for service providers deemed to be the best in their fields.[71]

Even though their cause was lost, community bankers who experienced the sea change in banking law remained proud that they fought the good fight, and they credited themselves with easing Oklahoma's transition to multibank holding companies and branch banking. "We didn't win the legislation in the end," said Buford, "but what we did was slow the process down, and by slowing the process down, we maintained our franchise value, and as branching came in, it came in slowly, and it gave everybody time to get ready for it."[72]

The OBA and the CBAO have long since buried the hatchet over banking structure, and they are connected through overlapping boards of directors and common goals. Still, the OBA was by far the larger and more influential of the two associations, and there remained an undercurrent of frustration among community bankers with laws that shattered Oklahoma's unit-banking structure and leveled the field in the direction of large banks on the prowl for acquisitions.

The tug-of-war over branch banking and multibank holding companies entered its twilight in June 1983 when the Oklahoma legislature passed the first of several laws aimed at restructuring the state's banking industry. For Mick Thompson, memories of those heady days remained crystal clear at a remove of three decades. When he was elected as a Democratic state representative in 1976, Thompson was making a name for himself as a no-nonsense banker at Central National Bank in Poteau. During his eight years in the legislature, he served as chairman of the Banking and Finance Committee, was majority floor leader from 1983 to 1984, and was a member of the Appropriations and Budget Committee. As a state legislator and longtime community banker, he was both witness to and participant in the paradigm shift in Oklahoma bank structure. Thompson described the end of unit banking this way:

> The thing that we did—that I would say was a milestone in banking—was that we passed the first multibank holding company/branch banking laws. Prior to that, Oklahoma had no branching at all. It was a huge fight, because community banks felt like they were protecting their charters, and the value of their charters. The large banks felt like they needed to have branching activity, and be able to branch in some of these other areas that were growth areas. I think, probably, if we hadn't had the issues in the eighties, with bank failures, and hadn't had the problems with Penn Square, we probably would not have even taken it on, much less could have passed, those kind of changes in banking.[73]

Thompson denied that the overhaul in banking laws was the result of scientific reasoning. Community banks were in danger, pure and simple, and something had to be done. Working late into the night, Thompson and his fellow legislators came up with the idea of permitting one branch within 1,500 feet of the main office and another within 25 miles. "It was really a bunch of committee members, one night, trying to figure out what we could pass," said Thompson, mindful throughout those hard-nosed deliberations that limited branching would accrue to the benefit of his own banking interests in Poteau. "And it was kind of like, 1,500 feet and 25 miles sounded like a good deal!" Additional pressure came from lobbyists who roamed the state capitol. "I think we called it the 'Lobbyist Full Employment Act,'" said Thompson, "because both sides employed a tremendous amount of lobbyists to either pass or kill this issue."[74]

Among the most effective lobbyists for liberalized banking laws was former Elgin banker and State Banking Commissioner H. E. "Harry" Leonard. He was working alongside his son, Mike, at the First National Bank of Muskogee as debates raged and tempers flared over branch banking. "They had tried to pass branch banking several times, but it was always the big banks versus the small banks," recalled Mike Leonard. "The big banks wanted it, and the small banks were afraid of it." Wary of the clout that big banks would exert if community bankers refused to acknowledge a paradigm shift in the making, Harry Leonard put his reputation on the line to help craft branching laws. And then he took his message on the road to become a full-time ambassador for branch banking.

"Dad basically took off about a year from the bank and traveled the state, soliciting bankers' support to get branch banking passed," continued Leonard. "The reason he could do that was because, having been state banking commissioner, he had a reputation for fairness. When Dad told people something they knew what he was telling them was the truth. He had confidence and respect. And he's probably one of the few people who could have done that. Dad really didn't have a dog in that hunt. He just knew, for the state of Oklahoma, and for banking, it had to happen. And his philosophy was, let's make it happen the right way."[75]

Joining Harry Leonard in his crusade was a youthful David Rainbolt, whose efforts to expand his father's banking interests were stymied by Oklahoma's archaic laws pertaining to bank structure. As far as Rainbolt was concerned, influence peddling was less effective in fostering change than the crisis mentality that reached fever pitch in the early 1980s. "It's amazing how unified everybody was in such a short amount of time," he said. "It wasn't anybody's speech. It wasn't anybody's influence. It wasn't enlightenment. It was desperation! We hit the same wall at the same time."[76]

The first nail in the coffin of the state's unit banking was House Bill 1123, which provided for revisions to Section 415 of Title 6 of the Oklahoma Statutes.[77] Bipartisan support for the bill was evident in the lopsided tallies: 73–23 in the House, and 32–12 in the Senate.[78] Supported by Governor George Nigh and slated to go into effect on October 1, 1983, the bill permitted banks to establish up to two branches, with three main caveats: branches had to be either (1) within the corporate city limits where the main bank was located; (2) within twenty-five miles of the main bank if the town it branched to did not have a bank; or (3) within five miles of the main bank in counties with populations of 500,000 (i.e., Oklahoma County). Branches could be established by merger, de novo, or both. To assuage independent bankers, the bill required a majority of directors of each bank within a multibank holding company to be from the bank's local area.[79] An additional restriction, deemed "silly" and "ridiculous" by State Banking Commissioner Robert Empie, prevented detached facilities from being established within 330 feet (defined as the distance measured by a straight line between the nearest exterior walls) of a competing bank or one of its branch offices.[80] No acquisition or merger where "control" was taken could be consummated without prior approval of the Federal Reserve Board.[81]

Last-ditch efforts to derail the legislation took the form of constitutional challenges that made their way to state attorney general Mike Turpen's office. On September 13—just two weeks before House Bill 1123 was to go into effect—Turpen and assistant attorney general George Barr ruled that the law "does not, on its face, violate (the) Oklahoma Constitution."[82] With that, the sluice gates opened, and one of America's last holdouts abandoned unit banking and affixed its star to the banner of branch banking and multibank holding companies.

The ink was barely dry on the historic law when James A. Pickel, president of Vector Specialized Construction, Inc., and business manager of Elliott and Gann Architects of Oklahoma City, was dispensing advice to bankers on how to adapt to branch banking. Topping Pickel's list of priorities were developing a comprehensive plan aimed at defining objectives, designing new facilities to meet those objectives, and establishing a budget to maximize return on investment. "To define your objectives, determine the correct design, and develop an honest budget will require a thorough examination of your marketplace and your bank," wrote Pickel in November 1983. "But the end results should be worth the effort since your bank will be in a better position to compete and grow in today's financial environment."[83]

Adaptation took on a frenzied pace as revisions to the original law attempted to keep up with the cascade of bank failures. In 1985, banks were allowed to branch statewide by acquiring failed and/or failing banks. Revisions in 1986 allowed banks to establish branches by acquiring up to two banks and converting them into branches. However, the acquired banks had to be outside the corporate city limits of the acquirer but within a fifty-mile radius. At the same time, the special branching provision that applied only to densely populated Oklahoma County was eliminated.[84] As noted by OBA vice president and general counsel Laura N. Pringle, "The 1986 legislation particularly seeks to address problems occasioned by the current economic climate and also to allow natural growth within a newly enlarged market area by branching."[85] In 1988, branching law was amended to allow statewide branching by acquisition of healthy banks. A revision in 1990 allowed branching by acquisition of savings and loan associations, individual branches of savings and loan associations, and individual branches of banks.[86]

Early on, fears that big banks would swallow little ones in a Darwinian fight for survival were put to rest as major Oklahoma banks looked to each other for broadened asset and deposit base and small banks paired off. More farfetched anxieties that a Japanese bank might open up across the street were likewise laid to rest.[87] Gene Rainbolt was not surprised by the form that mergers were taking less than a year after House Bill 1123 was passed. "Never did I think there would be a mass acquisition of the rural banks," he said. "The large banks are not inclined to take on dissimilar businesses."[88] Mick Thompson, who was appointed as state banking commissioner in 1992, claimed that small-town bankers who were most afraid of predatory takeovers were the same people who wound up opening branches in metro areas. "Very seldom did a metro area [bank] go to a small town," said Thompson. "So it had the reverse effect. But bigger banks could buy some of these failed banks and keep facilities in their communities. That was the real purpose that we were driving at."[89]

The largest banking consolidation in early 1984, approved by the Federal Reserve Board on April 26, was the merger between Liberty National Corporation of Oklahoma City, which owned Liberty National Bank, and First Tulsa Bancorporation, which owned the First National Bank of Tulsa. The resulting institution was a holding company called Banks of Mid-America with assets of about $3.2 billion. As Banks of Mid-America chairman J. W. McLean explained, "There will always be a role for the smaller community banks—even though historically large return on assets will be more difficult to maintain as deregulation forces new product development, increased cost of funding, and much, much more competition. Of course, Oklahoma is very early in its experience with a multibanking structure. While there have been some consolidations, it is fortunate that there has not been the 'rush' experienced earlier in other states."[90]

Other mergers in the spring of 1984, either planned or contemplated, further allayed fears that small Oklahoma banks were ripe for takeover by behemoths in Oklahoma City and Tulsa and confirmed the tendency of banks of similar size to join forces and achieve economies of scale: BancOklahoma Corporation and Fidelity of Oklahoma, Inc.;

United Oklahoma Bankshares and American Bank and Trust Company of Edmond; Nichols Hills Bank and Central National Bank and Trust of Enid; First National Bank of Bartlesville and Exchange National Bank of Tulsa; First National Bank of Enid and Fairview State Bank; Sheridan Bank and Trust Company and American National Bank, both of Lawton; and Union Bank of Bartlesville and Dewey Bank.[91] Nichols Hills Bank president Homer Paul voiced the outlook of many bankers when he described the merger of his bank and Central National Bank of Enid. "This is not a time in banking to be frivolous or adventuresome," he said with a flair for understatement in a decade of record bank failures. "We are planning a deliberate and conservative approach in our attempt to provide for future consumer needs." Paul's focus as he moved to complete the merger was on the needs of his customers. "Our whole motivation is to provide more and better services for them," he said.[92]

Meanwhile, Liberty National Bank's troubles were far from over, and they were causing headaches for its partner in the Banks of Mid-America, the First National Bank of Tulsa. Of the ten largest banks in the Oklahoma City metro area in 1982, eight had folded or had been replaced by 1988. The only survivors were Liberty and Guaranty Banks. Rumors that Liberty would soon join the casualty list were fueled by reports of diminishing capital, excessive debt, and unpaid preferred stock dividends. In early 1988, at least one store in Oklahoma City posted a sign on its door with a dire message: checks drawn on Liberty National Bank would no longer be accepted.[93]

Incensed to discover that the only solution might be a takeover by a Pittsburgh-based investment company, Oklahoma City oilman and philanthropist John E. Kirkpatrick stepped up to the plate and offered to recapitalize the bank to the tune of $20 million. "We may have to wait another five or ten years to buy that yacht we have talked about," said John to his wife, Eleanor. True to character, Eleanor responded, "I guess I can wait five or ten years to buy a yacht."[94] Other investors, including Walter Helmerich III from Tulsa and T. Boone Pickens from Amarillo, fell in line, and what became known as the Oklahoma Plan shifted into high gear. At a meeting in Tulsa on June 14, 1988, the Banks of Mid-America's board of directors approved the plan whose goal was to maintain local control of Liberty National Bank of Oklahoma City and the First National Bank of Tulsa.[95] The plan was completed in October 1988 with a capital infusion of $75,200,000 into the Banks of Mid-

America. Asked if he was planning a party to celebrate his success, Kirkpatrick responded, "No, I'm not much for celebrations, but I did sleep better."[96]

By the 1990s, bank customers were growing accustomed to seeing banks in multiple locations. One of those banks was the Bank of Oklahoma (BOK), an institution whose roots went back to formation of the Exchange National Bank of Tulsa in 1910, and whose investors in the early days included such luminaries as Harry F. Sinclair, who eventually rose to the bank's presidency. The bank's survival during the Great Depression was due in no small measure to two other luminaries, H. G. Barnard and J. A. Chapman, who pumped $6.5 million of their own wealth into the bank. Thanks to their foresight, the Exchange National Bank of Tulsa, reorganized in 1933 as the National Bank of Tulsa, helped its hometown to earn its moniker as the Oil Capital of the World. The National Bank of Tulsa became the Bank of Oklahoma in 1975, only to find its fortunes on the skids during the bust of the 1980s. It was placed into FDIC receivership in 1990. A year later, Tulsa businessman George Kaiser stepped up to the plate and acquired controlling interest in the bank. At the time, the BOK was a $2 billion bank and operated from twenty branches in Oklahoma.[97] Under the leadership of Chairman George Kaiser and president and CEO Stan Lybarger, the BOK's explosive growth remained consistent with the principals' commitment to community banking. Asked to comment on the BOK's success in becoming the largest bank in the state with record earnings in 2010, Lybarger said simply, "Banks that experienced the downturn in the 1980s and managed to survive did not repeat the mistakes of those times." "And," he added as Kaiser nodded his head in agreement, "it's been fun!"[98]

Not that all mergers turned into happy marriages. G. P. Johnson Hightower's brief stint as a vice president at BOK Oklahoma City (formerly, Fidelity National Bank and Trust Company of Oklahoma City) in the late 1980s left him with a lingering distaste for Tulsans with a condescending attitude. "The old Fidelity had been bought by BOK," said Hightower. "I was there for fifty weeks, and decided to get out of that deal." Queried about the banking version of a cross-state rivalry that dated back to territorial days, Hightower acknowledged that Fidelity was carrying lots of bad assets when BOK signaled its interest in acquiring it. Several top BOK executives had counseled against the takeover. Nevertheless, Hightower had reason to believe that BOK Oklahoma

City became the scapegoat for the BOK's problems. No sooner was the deal consummated than local management started feeling pressure from the home office. "Management from Tulsa sent over several guys to run some of the divisions," continued Hightower. "And they kind of put them on top of our heads. Consequently, the Oklahoma City management of BOK Oklahoma City was kind of run out into the streets."[99]

Kaiser and Lybarger were not the only bankers with a creative streak. Idabel National Bank's Homeland store branch opened in November 1992 to become the first supermarket bank in Oklahoma. A month later, Liberty Bank of Midwest City opened a branch at a Max Saver Foods Store. Liberty Bank of Tulsa joined the bandwagon with an in-store branch, and the Bank of Oklahoma announced plans to relocate five of its branches to Albertson's stores in Oklahoma City and Tulsa. Vane Lucas of the Bank of Oklahoma put it this way: "I think in the past, the traditional idea when putting up a branch was to build it and hope people come. In this (supermarket banking), you build it where people are already coming."[100] Gene Walker, senior vice president of The Bank, N.A., of McAlester, claimed that his branch in a Wal-Mart supercenter achieved its twelve-month goal for consumer loans in the first five months of operation in 1993. "Imagine having a Wal-Mart store as your lobby," he said. "There is no way this opportunity can be duplicated." According to bankers who were operating in the retail giant in late 1994, Wal-Mart locations were drawing as many as fifty thousand customers a week.[101]

Allowing Oklahoma banks to expand their reach in the midst of a severe recession was one thing; the prospect of opening state borders to predatory financial institutions, whether banks or nonbank banks, was something else altogether. With a wary eye on mergers and acquisitions, which were gaining momentum nationwide, the OBA circled its wagons and resisted congressional legislation that would remove the last barriers to interstate banking.[102] At the other end of the spectrum was Governor George Nigh, who believed that interstate banking would lure money into Oklahoma's beleaguered economy.[103] As tempers flared and fears of foreign invasion mounted, one did not have to look far for signs that interstate banking was poised for assault. By the summer of 1985, Kansas was the only border state in which legislation had not been introduced to permit regional interstate banking—a region that included Oklahoma. In her series of legislative updates in the *Oklahoma Banker*, Laura Pringle promised OBA members that their organization would continue to oppose interstate banking and would insist on enforcement of restrictions on nonbank banks in Oklahoma: "Efforts to monitor interstate banking developments will continue to include reviews of permissive legislation and loophole-closing bills in other states as well as Congressional action and litigation developments."[104]

The inevitable opening of interstate banking came in 1986 when the state legislature passed two separate bills: Senate Bill 553, signed into law by the governor on May 7, and Senate Bill 502, part of which called for an interim study on interstate banking, which amended the first bill in the final days of the legislative session in June. Pringle explained that the new law permitted out-of-state bank holding companies to acquire control of banks that had either failed, were in the process of failing, or were subsidiaries of insolvent bank holding companies that were restricted in paying dividends. There was no limit on the number of such acquisitions that could be made by an out-of-state holding company, but no out-of-state bank was permitted to acquire an Oklahoma bank.

In any event, there was a clear preference for in-state buyers. All out-of-state acquisitions required approval by the Federal Reserve Board. In giving the nod to an acquisition, the Fed had to make three determinations: (1) the in-state bank or banks being acquired had to have been in existence on May 7, 1986, or have been operating for five years; (2) notice of the acquisition had to have been published and sent to stockholders; and (3) the board and a majority of the shares of the bank or its Oklahoma bank holding company had to have approved the acquisition. Pringle's conclusion, couched in legalese that mutes the enormity of the change, served notice that a new age was dawning in Oklahoma banking: "To the extent that federal law now addresses expansion across state lines and permits expansion within the state, Oklahoma's limitations and approval processes will not be enforceable. Likewise, unless protections for state limitations are included in any further permissive federal legislation for interstate banking, our statute will be preempted to the extent federal law addresses these issues."[105]

Thus did Oklahoma, only three years removed from allowing branching within its borders, cast its lot with interstate banking. Just two months after passage of the historic legislation, the First National Bank and Trust Company of Oklahoma City was acquired by First Interstate Bank of Los

Angeles to become the first major bank in Oklahoma to operate under out-of-state control. Whatever one's perspective on interstate branching and multibank holding companies, two things are certain: both changes were rendered inevitable by the revolution in technology and the rush to deregulate, and both have had an immeasurable impact on our relationship with our money and the people who handle it.

CHAPTER ELEVEN

Great Expectations

The bankers of this decade will be better bankers. They must be better bankers. Never before have we faced greater competition.

             Ronald P. Edwards, Bank of Tulsa

It seems unfortunate to wind toward the conclusion to this history of Oklahoma banking on a downbeat message. Even as bankers scrambled to adapt to change and resurrect their tarnished image, stories that grabbed the headlines in the 1980s and early 1990s—the Penn Square Bank debacle, problems on the farm, and, of course, a spate of bank failures unrivaled since the Great Depression—kept them on the defensive and left their customers hankering for good news. Yet it would be nothing short of historical malpractice to gloss over the Olympian-scale thievery and wrongdoing that tainted financial institutions of all descriptions, and whose dimensions will never be known with precision: the collapse of the savings and loan industry.

 Savings and loan associations, known in the common vernacular as thrifts, laid claim to a noble tradition of putting people of modest means in their own homes and safeguarding their modest assets. "Savings and loans existed to put folks into houses—that's what they were for," explained Mark White of Osage Federal Bank in Pawhuska. "If you wanted a home loan in the twenties, thirties, forties, fifties, sixties, even in the seventies, primarily you went to a savings and loan. That's what they specialized in, whereas a commercial bank does commercial lending.

The lines between banks and savings and loans started blurring about twenty or thirty years ago . . . to the extent now that there are basically no real differences between a savings and loan and a bank."[1]

Because their reason for existence and modus operandi once distinguished savings and loans from banks, a synopsis of their obliteration serves as yet another cautionary tale of how not to handle other people's money. Unlike bankers who treated their banks as community resources, the perpetrators of the savings and loan looting treated thrift institutions with callous and often criminal disregard for customers. In a report to the FDIC, a bushy-haired bank stock analyst named Jonathan Gray described the damage done by American Diversified Savings and Loan in California. His description, mathematically dubious but colorful nonetheless, provides an apt metaphor for greed on steroids: "A company with $11 million in assets lost $800 million. With perhaps $500,000 in equity, it destroyed $800 million of insured deposits, a kill ratio of 1,600 to 1. . . . This anecdote is tantamount to a news report that a drunken motorist has wiped out the entire city of Pittsburgh."[2]

Untold gallons of ink were spilled on the savings and loan fiasco before it faded from collective memory in the 1990s and vanished altogether in the new millennium. At the risk of oversimplifying this tragic chapter in financial history, the episode can be attributed to four regulatory relaxations that contributed to a raid on taxpayers that has been eclipsed by, well, subsequent raids on taxpayers. Those exemplars of Reagan-era deregulation began with the Garn–St. Germain Act of 1982, signed into law by the regulation-adverse president with the comment, "I think we hit a home run."[3] Thus did President Reagan launch his jeremiad against financial regulations with a sense of mission unrivaled since Andrew Jackson settled into the White House in 1828 bent on wrecking the Second Bank of the United States—which, of course, he famously did.[4] The Garn–St. Germain Act of 1982 was intended to relax regulations on the savings and loan industry so that it could grow out of problems attending the change in banking and profusion of investment opportunities. But, to paraphrase songwriter Bob Dylan's manifesto, what it really did was allow men to rob not with a gun, but with a pen.

First on the list of dozens of regulatory relaxations following the Garn–St. Germain Act of 1982 was the easing of capital standards for savings and loan associations. According to the Federal Home Loan Bank of San Francisco, the new rules meant that a person with $2 million in hand could start a savings and loan and attract $1.3 billion of insured deposits—$99.85 of other people's money for every 15¢ of the individual's own—to invest as he or she pleased. Second, changes in the rules for rescuing insolvent savings and loans through merger permitted the acquiring institution to capitalize "goodwill" which is, of course, an intangible asset. Booking goodwill as an asset allowed savings and loans to acquire vastly more deposits. Because goodwill could be depreciated over forty years, the relaxed rule was as good as hanging a sign over the door reading "FRAUD ENCOURAGED HERE." Third, rules pertaining to "loss deferral" allowed savings and loans to sell loans on which they showed a loss and amortize the loss over the life of the loan. Finally, so-called appraised equity value gave savings and loans license to credit themselves with increases in the appraised value of properties and assign that credit to capital.[5]

Freed from the tedium of financing homes, savings and loan executives let out a collective cheer when Congress gave them the green light to buy so-called junk bonds—that is, bonds whose extraordinarily high yields reflected their extraordinarily high risk. Reigning supreme in the high-flying world of high-risk bonds was Drexel Burnham Lambert's Michael Milken, dubbed the "Junk Bond King" for pioneering the creation of junk bond pools and selling them on the open market. "Michael Milken at Drexel Burnham Lambert made junk bonds famous," explained Oklahoma City businessman Tom Loy. "He made them famous by giving them free credibility and a liquid market. Drexel Burnham Lambert got a market for them, because not only were there individuals out there who would invest in these pools, to some extent, but Congress let the savings and loan industry invest in junk bonds." And the result? "That was one of the dumbest congressional ideas of all time!" declared Loy. Congress "let savings and loans make all kinds of ridiculous investments that they had no business investing in."[6]

To add fuel to the fire, deposit insurance—pioneered in 1908 by Governor Charles Haskell and Populist legislators in the brand-new state of Oklahoma—enabled savings and loan proprietors to draw deposits from the public after they were hopelessly insolvent.[7] Once they no longer had their own money in their institutions, they had license to gamble with depositors' money in ventures that set the standard for audacity. If they won, they could keep their gains. If they lost, the government would make good on depositors' losses. With odds like that, you had to have a screw loose (or, perhaps, a smidgen of moral intelligence) to sit on the sidelines.

With the law on their side and piles of risk-free money to be made, savings and loan associations, whose aggregate assets reached about $1 trillion in 1984, departed from their historic mission of financing home ownership and morphed into casinos. Federal Home Loan Bank Board chairman Edwin J. Gray, perhaps feeling a bit repressed in his drab banker suits, revealed a yen for the wild side when he likened the new breed of thrift executive to the daring crop-duster pilot—a far cry from the old-style, conservative gardener who was content to tend his deposits and keep his boots firmly planted in the soil. "It's fun, it's profitable," gushed Joseph W. Bandura, president and chief executive officer of the Nassau Savings and Loan in Princeton, New Jersey, as he guided his institution into the terra incognita of construction loans in the summer of 1984. But now that his thrift's construction projects numbered sixty-one, the seasoned executive, his brown hair permed into tight curls, had a caveat for the faint of heart: "Construction loans are risky, there's no doubt about it. You're going to take your lumps along the way." Ronald A. Seagraves, president of the Security Savings and Loan Association in nearby Vineland, New Jersey, clearly preferred crop dusting to gardening, particularly now that Washington had signaled its forbearance by rescuing Continental Illinois. "You can't be a traditional thrift anymore, there's no earnings in the balance sheet," he said. Dreaming of how to grow his thrift's $850 million in assets into real money in a period of high interest rates, Seagraves asserted, "You have to go outside the traditional lines of business, into such fields as loan development, high-volume mortgage-banking, things that will bring abnormal fee income or returns."[8]

To borrow from national bank examiner Steve Plunk's description of Penn Square Bank's final days, the dead rats just kept floating to the top of the punch bowl. Most of those rats found their way to the Federal Savings and Loan Insurance Corporation (FSLIC), the agency charged with insuring savings and loan deposit accounts. "Billions and billions and billions of dollars were lost," said Loy. "The FSLIC rolled over on its back and put its little legs up in the air and breathed its last breath. And the commercial banking industry took it on the chin, along with taxpayers, to take over the FSLIC and merge it into the FDIC."[9]

To orchestrate what was becoming the costliest bailout in U.S. history, Congress passed the Financial Institutions Reform, Recovery and

Enforcement Act (FIRREA). Signed into law on August 9, 1989, by President George H. W. Bush, FIRREA established the Resolution Trust Corporation (RTC) to sell properties seized from failed savings and loans. By June 30, 1990—less than a year into its historic rescue operation—the RTC had seized 247 institutions with assets of $65 billion and either liquidated or sold an additional 207.[10] Ramping up his original estimate that $50 billion would suffice to clean up the mess, Treasury Secretary Nicholas F. Brady warned Congress that the RTC was in danger of running out of funds by the end of 1990 and might require a heftier budget—say, $89 to $132 billion. But really, an open-ended rescue operation would be preferable. According to the panicked treasury secretary, providing a specific amount might mean "having to face the prospect of returning at relatively short intervals as markets change and, with them, the estimates."[11]

Given the scope of federal agencies' financial obligations and contingent liabilities, some feared a catastrophic breakdown of the entire financial system. Ronald Utt, vice president of the U.S. Chamber of Commerce Foundation (formerly, the National Chamber Foundation) and a former employee at the White House Office of Management and Budget, offered the chilling prospect that the savings and loan debacle was the tip of the iceberg. In his downbeat assessment, taxpayers could be on the hook for bailouts in the trillions of dollars. Chiding lawmakers for being disingenuous with the public and taxpayers for wishful thinking, Utt recommended an Omnibus Credit Solution Act "to fundamentally restructure these many programs in order to reduce taxpayer exposure to costly program failures."[12]

In June 1990, the RTC's list of real estate for sale hit the streets, and it made readers' eyes pop: 35,908 properties were on the block, and they carried an aggregate book value of $14.9 billion. RTC officials conceded that the volume of real estate disposals was so staggering that procedural shortcuts were inevitable. Equally inevitably, they would open the door to waste and fraud of mind-boggling proportions. "It gets all the way down to hiring people to trim the grass," said RTC inspector general John J. Adair.[13] Further up the food chain, Neil Bush, an oil and gas developer in Colorado and, more to the point, the son of President Bush, was fending off accusations that he had abused his position on the board of Silverado Banking, Savings and Loan Association of Denver by making inappropriate (and unpaid) loans to his business associates. According to regulators, "Bush did everything in his power to bring about a regulatory violation. Bush's conduct was clearly contrary to generally accepted standards of prudent operation."[14]

Citing parallels between the savings and loan debacle and the subprime mortgage meltdown of 2008, OSU's Gary Simpson suggested that America's more recent experience was not nearly as bad as it could have been: "People complain about what happened over the past five years. That could have been a lot worse. I mean, you saw some dishonest people, or unscrupulous people, come into the marketplace over the past five years, but actually, not to the extent that we saw during the savings and loan period."[15]

It was all too much for Tulsan Jess Wade. He spoke for many in his rant to the editor in the *Tulsa Tribune* just a couple of years before the venerable newspaper fell victim to changing times and ceased publication. "This whole mess is the ultimate sting operation and we, as American taxpayers, are the patsies. And if that isn't hard enough to swallow, we don't get so much as an apology from the administration, past or present. They won't admit culpability. They'll simply ask us to reread their lips, then expect us to roll over and pay until we're dead."[16]

To the extent that Oklahomans participated in the looting, they were complicit in nothing less than a national tragedy. In the second quarter of 1989, Continental Federal Savings and Loan of Oklahoma City's loss of $52,990,000 earned it distinction as one of the nation's twenty-five worst performing thrifts. According to Bauer Financial Reports, those underperforming thrifts lost more than $3 billion during the quarter. An earlier report from the Office of Thrift Supervision on second-quarter thrift performance, dated August 22, 1989, noted that 939 thrifts nationwide suffered an aggregate loss of $4.9 billion—*in one quarter!*[17]

Then again, bad news for thrifts meant good news for banks that were still standing, particularly after the 1990 revision in state law allowing banks to establish branches by acquiring savings and loan associations and/or their branches.[18] Among those beneficiaries was Stillwater National Bank and Trust Company (rebranded Bank SNB in November 2013). Since 1973, CEO Robert McCormick and his team had taken what was then the third-largest bank in Stillwater with $20 million in assets and transformed it into a dynamo commanding 65 percent of market share. By the time the bank went public in March 1993, the Stillwater market was tapped out, and McCormick had to look elsewhere for growth opportunities. He found them in Oklahoma City, Tulsa, and Chickasha, where the FSLIC was auctioning off assets of the defunct Continental Federal Savings and Loan. "Those three got us to Oklahoma City and Tulsa," explained G. P. Johnson Hightower, who was a senior vice president at Bank SNB before accepting a position with Arvest Bank in early 2014. "So, it was kind of game on."[19]

With assets of $1.43 billion, deposits of $1.1 billion, and 171,292 deposit accounts, Tulsa-based Sooner Federal Savings Association was Oklahoma's largest thrift. It came under the control of federal regulators in November 1989. Within six months, Chairman George Bragg was waxing optimistic about the prospect of a speedy takeover by a healthier institution. "Sooner's in really good shape," said Bragg. "It should be an easy resolution." Speaking from her office in Washington, D.C., RTC spokeswoman Kate Spears was not so sure. Even though the bidding process for Sooner Federal and other insolvent institutions was under way, potential buyers would need plenty of time to review financial records and attend bidders' meetings.[20] Other Oklahoma institutions placed in receivership whose assets were up for auction in June 1990 (and their deposits) included Duncan Savings and Loan Association ($133.5 million), American Home Savings and Loan Association in Edmond ($78.2 million), First Federal Savings and Loan Association of Seminole ($32.9 million), and Great Plains Savings Association of Weatherford ($69.6 million).[21] A hint of scandal made the headlines in early 1991 when Tulsa mortgage banker Gary B. Hobbs was indicted on forty-five counts of bank fraud, embezzlement, and money laundering in the failed Cross Roads Savings and Loan of Checotah. Authorities seized his Tulsa home (valued at $850,000), a 1988 Mercedes Benz 300 TE station wagon, a 1989 Cadillac Fleetwood, and a lady's diamond and sapphire ring worth $41,730. Proceeds from selling the seized items went to the RTC.[22] History is silent on what happened when the amorous Mr. Hobbs came clean with the ring's recipient.

Like flaming stars on the brink of extinction, once-noble contributors to American prosperity had become the loci of red-hot, unbridled gambling before drowning in an ocean of bad debt. Outraged by a Congress bent on asking bankers to pick up the tab, OBA president Roger Beverage put it this way: "If there ever was a 'great bank robbery' in Washington, this is it. It's bad enough that bankers are being asked to step up to the plate, again, and bail out their savings and loan competitors. What makes it worse is that bankers are the only ones of whom this financial burden is being demanded, and it's highly likely that they'll get nothing in exchange for the 'privilege' of paying a big part of the tab."[23]

One by one, savings and loan associations succumbed to the wiles of big-city aviators who dazzled depositors with their prowess in the cockpit, even as they carted money out the cargo door. Tragically, their perfidy was hidden in plain sight, aided and abetted by a government that had reneged on its responsibility to ensure liberty and justice for *all*. And, in a pattern that has become an all-too-familiar postscript to the popping of speculative bubbles, taxpayers were asked to join bankers in cleaning up the mess.

Chalk up a win for capitalism in its tug-of-war with democracy.

The savings and loan debacle was in full swing when President Ronald Reagan passed the conservative mantle to his vice president, George H.W. Bush. The former navy pilot's tax-cutting, small-government rhetoric warmed the hearts of Republicans and enough Democrats to ensure his victory over Massachusetts governor Michael Dukakis in the election of 1988. If voters were asked to recall the campaign's defining moments, two would surely pop to the top of the list: a distinctly unmacho Michael Dukakis driving a tank and, in the process, tanking his candidacy; and six words that would come back to haunt George Bush and tank his presidency—"Read my lips. No new taxes." Whatever Bush accomplished as president was not enough to placate voters who took his no-new-taxes pledge seriously. His chances of serving a second term sank lower when the longest period of economic expansion since the Kennedy/Johnson prosperity of the 1960s ran out of steam in July 1990. Three metrics suffice to describe an economy that was once again on the skids: inflation hit 6.1 percent in late 1990; unemployment climbed to 7.4 percent in 1992; and the budget deficit doubled from $152 billion in 1989 to $290 billion in 1992.[24]

Bad news at the national level was still on the horizon as Oklahomans heaved a collective sigh of relief at the dawning of the new decade. "Thank God. Another decade has passed," declared Ronald P. Edwards, president and chief executive officer of the Bank of Tulsa. Edwards spoke for many when he described the 1980s as "a roller coaster" whose violent swings came from a combination of overreliance on energy and a dearth of policing in financial services. With a not-so-subtle reference to a certain shopping-center bank nestled next to Shelley's Tall Girl Shop in Oklahoma City, Edwards lamented "an overall freewheeling attitude" that had taken root in Oklahoma's banking industry. "Now we face the opportunity of the 90s," he wrote. "The economic roller coaster that careened so rapidly downhill has now started on a slow, gradual ascent. Everything isn't great but it's getting better." Readers surely nodded their heads in agreement as they reached the conclusion of the Tulsa banker's January 1990 editorial in the *Oklahoma Banker.* "The past decade has taught us some very tough lessons, but lessons well learned. The bankers of this decade will be better bankers. They must be better bankers. Never before have we faced greater competition." The competition included credit unions and brokerages, but especially thrift institutions that were benefiting from federal bailouts. Admonishing bankers to heed the lessons of the 1980s in general and the thrift industry in particular, Edwards waxed optimistic about the 1990s: "The coming decade can be one of great opportunity. The past years have been a stern taskmaster, but the lessons taught will serve the wise pupils beyond the next decade and into the next century."[25]

Edwards's sanguine outlook found confirmation in the Federal Reserve Bank of Kansas City's prediction of modest growth in 1990. Those predictions included a narrowing gap between Oklahoma and the rest of the nation. Evidence came from renewed stability in the energy sector, a continuing rebound in manufacturing, and improvements in agriculture stemming from strong farm incomes and stabilization of farm debt. According to Federal Reserve Bank of Kansas City senior economist Alan Barkema, "The farm sector's reduced debt load suggests that the industry is far more resilient to any financial shocks that may lie ahead." In terms of banking, the Fed's Charles Morris asserted that the performance of Oklahoma banks mirrored the improving health of the state economy. "Although profits at Oklahoma banks are still low," said Morris, "they have risen sharply in the past two years." As evidence, the Fed's economists cited Oklahoma banks' average return on assets, which rose from -0.73 percent in 1986 to 0.02 percent in 1988, mainly due to improved performance in their loan-loss provisions.[26]

Robert C. Dauffenbach, director of the Oklahoma State University Office of Business and Economic Research, was equally sanguine about the 1990s. "Despite obvious difficulties, I still have some good feelings about the 1980s," he said. "Oklahomans sucked in their guts and came up with the bucks that did not allow us to fall behind and perhaps moved us ahead. We are seeing more work on bridges, roads, pollution, etc. It's not a one-time thing, it is continuous." According to F&M Bank of Tulsa president Bruce Raines, "Oklahoma has a great outlook in the 1990s. The economy is growing again." Economic indicators included a growth rate in personal income that was expected to exceed the national average, an uptick in wage and salary employment, and rapidly dropping rates in unemployment. By most accounts, the state was losing its reliance on energy as an economic driver and becoming more diversified. Moreover, commodities could be produced in Oklahoma cheaply and without sacrificing quality. The only clouds on the horizon, persistent sluggishness in construction and financial industries, were not enough to deflate Bruce Raines's enthusiasm. "Banks will continue to do what they've always done," he said. "They are leaders in economic development as they work and cooperate with community groups. They help attract new industry and help communities expand and grow." With memories of the 1980s still fresh, Dauffenbach urged banks to overcome their fears and "open their vaults." "The bad times are behind us," he said. "We had to be cautious and prudent—and we still need to—but the risk of an economic downturn is behind us."[27]

Few were more optimistic than Bruce Benbrook, whose tenure as OBA president in 1990 earned him distinction as the youngest president in the association's history. A third generation banker, Benbrook assumed the titles of chairman, president, and chief executive officer of the Stock Exchange Bank of Woodward after the untimely death of his father in 1981. "My grandfather, A. M. Benbrook, served as president from 1922 to 1959, and then my father, Temple Benbrook, served as president of this bank from 1959 to 1981," explained Benbrook.[28]

"Our state is on the road to recovery," he said at the outset of his term as OBA president. "However it can only happen if bankers endorse and support economic development programs. It is important for the Association to get involved on the state level and for the bankers to be involved in their local communities." As president, Benbrook focused on building a strong educational system and encouraging OBA members to get involved on community, state, and federal levels. In all his leadership positions, Benbrook was mindful of the truism that "a good leader is one who knows where he is going, how to get there and how to persuade enough people to go along to make it successful."[29]

In 1991, Persian War jitters and a drop in consumer spending signaled a sputtering economy. According to a consumer attitude survey conducted by the University of Michigan, Americans were apprehensive about lagging incomes, troubles in the financial industry, cutbacks in public services by states and municipalities, and that perpetual measure of well-being—job security. Nevertheless, banks nationwide were doing their part to recover from the doldrums. Characterizing the recovery as "slow and uneven across the nation," Federal Reserve Board chairman Alan Greenspan reported that banking firms were gaining increased access to capital markets and were in a better position to lend as credit demands picked up. "As banks make further strides in bolstering their capital positions," said Greenspan, "they will become better able to take advantage of opportunities to add profitable loans to their balance sheets."[30]

Economist Robert Dauffenbach claimed that Oklahoma was faring better than the nation. "Oklahoma was not as affected by the national recession as some states were," he said. "That can be attributed to the state's diversification and the fact that we had already endured an economic trauma in the mid '80s." Michael Applegate, OSU professor of economics and manager of the Oklahoma State Econometric Model, reported positive growth of about 1 percent in the state's economy. Ken Scoggins, president of Investment Performance, Inc., predicted that bank earnings would continue to increase. "Banks have more earning assets as a percentage of total assets than a year ago," said Scoggins. "While the nation's economic recovery seems sluggish, Oklahoma can expect to see slow, steady growth for the next couple of years. And that is just what Oklahoma needs."[31] At year-end 1991, Oklahoma's bank profits earned it a ranking of 22 among the 50 states and the District of Columbia. Of the 414 banks in the state, 9 out of 10 were profitable.[32]

The positive news continued in 1992 as commercial bank deposits in Oklahoma surged toward $24.3 billion. To alleviate apprehensions about job security, the state's midyear unemployment rate of 6.6 percent compared favorably to a 7.8 percent rate at the national level, the highest rate in eight years. Gains in retail and residential construction were evident in the first two quarters of 1992, when investment in new and expanding manufactures exceeded total 1991 investments by 65 percent. By late 1992, there was a consensus among economists that growth would be slow, manufacturing would continue to increase, business profits would improve, and inflation would remain negligible—all good news for bankers, and all pointing to a state and national economy geared for doing business in an expanding global marketplace in 1993.[33]

Any doubts that Oklahoma banking was on an upswing were put to rest when the American Bankers Association included several state banks on its 1991 lists of the most profitable banks in the nation, based on return on average equity capital and pretax income per employee. Listed in the ABA's top one hundred small community banks were Republic Bank of Norman, the Bank of Commerce in Chouteau, the First National Bank of Lindsay, the First National Bank of Okeene, Meno Guaranty Bank, the Bank of Locust Grove, the Bank of Union, Hopeton State Bank, First Bank and Trust of Fort Gibson, the First National Bank of Konawa, First Bank of Apache, the Bank of Commerce in McLoud, Okemah National Bank, Farmers and Merchants National Bank of Fairview, and the First State Bank of Gould. Listed among the one hundred most profitable large community banks were the First State Bank of Harrah, Alva State Bank and Trust Company, Sand Springs State Bank, Central National Bank of Alva, and First Bank and Trust Company in Duncan.[34]

According to the FDIC, state banks reported a 35.7 percent increase in annual net income to a record $340 million for 1992. The previous record was $321 million in 1981 and compared to profits of $251 million in 1991. Ken Fergeson, chairman and CEO of the National Bank of Commerce in Altus and 1992–93 OBA chairman, attributed the improvement to effective Federal Reserve policies and "bankers simply working smarter." Improving asset quality was reflected in a drop in nonperforming assets of 23 percent in 1992 to $490 million, down from $639 million a year earlier. Collectively, Oklahoma banks' 1.2 percent return on assets in January 1993 compared favorably to banks in the southwest region (Texas, Louisiana, Arkansas, New Mexico, and Oklahoma) that reported a 1.15 percent aggregate return on assets. The national aggregate return on assets was .96 percent. Gary Simpson pointed to growth in all loan categories as a reflection of a strengthening economy. "These numbers simply substantiate our findings that the Oklahoma banking industry is extremely sound," said Simpson. Other FDIC data for 1992 provided conclusive evidence of gains since 1991: total assets of $30.4 billion, up 7.7 percent from $28 billion; deposits of $26.6 billion, up 7 percent from $24.8 billion; equity capital of $2.58 billion, up 12.7 percent from $2.29 billion; and net interest income of $1.16 billion, up 15 percent from $1 billion.[35]

Oklahoma banks continued to show strength in 1993. In the second quarter (April–June), the state's 386 banks reported more than $100 million in net profits, 13.5 percent higher than 1992 second-quarter net profits of $89 million. Through the first six months of 1993, profits totaled $229 million, up 30.11 percent from a $176 million in the first half of 1992. Other second-quarter measures showed similar gains over the first two quarters of 1992: bank assets stood at $30.5 billion, up 6.7 percent from $28.6 billion; return on assets was 1.53 percent, up from 1.25 percent; deposits were up 6 percent, to $26.6 billion; and nonperforming assets continued to drop, falling 28 percent to $404 million.[36] In December 1993, the FDIC reported that Oklahoma banks earned profits of $321 million in the first nine months of 1993—up 19.8 percent from 1992, and clearly on target to shatter the full-year profit record.[37] Meanwhile, a combination of mergers, acquisitions, and branching conspired to diminish the number of Oklahoma banks by 4.2 percent from 403 a year earlier. On March 31, 1993, there were 392 commercial banks in Oklahoma. That number dropped to about 370 at year-end 1993.[38]

Improving bank performance in the early 1990s did little to mitigate bankers' perennial complaint about regulations concocted in faraway Washington, D.C. Waxing nostalgic after thirty-five years in the banking industry, Glenn P. "Red" Ward lamented the wave of regulations that flowed from the Penn Square Bank debacle and were draining the romance from his profession. "No one can argue against regulations if imposed consistently and equitably," he wrote in a spirit of accommodation. "But they have not been."[39]

None doubted that more regulations were on tap as Congress came to grips with the savings and loan bailout, a debacle that Gary Simpson predicted would cost taxpayers $300 billion in the 1990s.[40] One of Congress's get-tough-on-crime responses was the Crime Control Act of 1990, which, among other things, increased the maximum jail time for nearly every bank fraud and embezzlement case. According to OBA vice president and general counsel Mary Beth Guard, the most disturbing aspect of the new law was its invitation to the private sector to wage war on fraud. Toward that end, private parties were given the opportunity to file confidential declarations with the U.S. attorney general or his designate relating to violations that might spawn civil penalties. "This Act represents a disturbing return to lynch mob justice," wrote Guard. "With temptation posed by the potential of large monetary gains and few safeguards against abuse, there will doubtlessly be at least a few false declarations filed." Guard predicted that the attorney general's mandated reports on declarations filed, rewards paid, and convictions obtained "ought to make for interesting reading indeed."[41]

Knee-jerk regulations attending the savings and loan bailout included a hidden cost: the social return that taxpayers rightfully expected for the increased taxes that they had to bear. As Dave Morris wrote in an editorial in the *Tulsa Tribune*, "Having socialized the responsibility for this disaster, taxpayers now should have the right to demand a social return for our money." At a minimum, Morris suggested that the bailout should strengthen local economies and expand affordable housing. Voicing a concern destined to resurface some two decades later in the wake of another financial fiasco, Gary Simpson lamented the inevitability that commercial banks would be required to pay the social costs of the savings and loan bailout, even as they would be forced to submit to increasing regulation. "Unfortunately, for commercial banks, the idea of having the banks provide the social return is politically expedient," he wrote. "It is, of course, grossly unfair." Simpson then issued a call to arms. "Many people do not know the difference between an investment banking firm, an S&L and a commercial bank, making the commercial banking industry's task of persuasion much tougher. Nevertheless, bankers must step forward and forcefully make their case."[42]

Sadly, not many bankers were prepared for what was coming down the pike. According to Greg Pitzer of Arthur Andersen and Company in Oklahoma City, 99 percent of Oklahoma banks in the early 1990s did not have a compliance program, a shortcoming that would be of interest to regulators when they showed up in bankers' lobbies to perform their examinations. Wayne Barnes of Professional Bank Systems put it this way: "So just like insurance, a compliance system is not profitable, but when you need it, you're glad you have it." The compliance officer's job not only was difficult and required constant training but was usually a part-time position, with no additional pay and little support from senior management.[43]

Bankers reserved special opprobrium for two of the most burdensome regulations: the Community Reinvestment Act of 1977 and FIRREA of 1989. The CRA required commercial banks to extend loans to low-income borrowers, consistent with safe and sound banking practices. A CRA rating was assigned to banks according to results of regulatory exams and analysis of their lending records. Scores were "outstanding," "satisfactory," "needs to improve," or "substantial noncompliance." From 1990 through 2007, 16.3 percent of banks were outstanding, 79.5 percent were satisfactory, 3.8 percent needed to improve, and 0.4 percent fell into the substantial noncompliance rating. Those ratings became matters of public record, and regulators relied on them when they considered bank applications for new branches, mergers, or acquisitions.[44]

Clearly, bankers ignored CRA ratings at their peril. According to Wayne Barnes, bankers' most common mistakes in the early 1990s were disregard for truth-in-lending laws and senior management's lack of involvement in the CRA process. "Many banks are not finding what their community's needs are, not addressing those needs, and not defining and documenting the CRA process," he said.[45] In keeping with the law of unintended consequences, the CRA has been blamed for increasing the supply of and the demand for mortgages that served as catalysts for the subprime mortgage disaster of 2008.[46] Other regulations stemming from the heightened social consciousness of the 1960s included the Fair Housing Act of 1968, the Equal Credit Opportunity Act (Regulation B) of 1974, and the Home Mortgage Disclosure Act (Regulation C) of 1975 (amended between 1988 and 1991).[47] In June 1993, Congress and bank regulators increased their focus on perceived lending discrimination. In letters to every bank and thrift institution in the land, federal regulatory agency heads made clear that examiners would enforce their lending laws. The ABA and OBA did their part by helping banks to address the issue.[48]

The second regulation that kept bankers up at night was FIRREA, already noted as the law that created the Resolution Trust Corporation, the centerpiece of Congress's savings and loan bailout. The law also transferred thrift regulatory authority from the Federal Home Loan Bank Board to the Office of Thrift Supervision. According to OBA executive vice president Roger Beverage (formerly president, before paid and volunteer titles were changed), the OBA was actively involved in shaping the bill. "During the entire process, we continually monitored the bill's development and communicated with bankers and legislators about the bill's progression through the legislative process," said Beverage. The OBA's Mary Beth Guard summarized the effects of the new legislation:

"This will create a more level playing field between savings and loans and commercial banks." FIRREA left little doubt that bankers needed to mind their business as never before. Among other provisions, FIRREA increased costs for FDIC insurance premiums (up to 80 percent over the two years following the bill's passage), increased exposure for banks and bankers to civil money penalties (up to a maximum of $1 million per day in some instances), increased regulatory authority over banks, and increased requirements attending the Community Reinvestment Act and Home Mortgage Disclosure Act. "Slowly and surely, though, we will see financial service providers looking more and more alike," said Bruce Benbrook.[49] Roger Beverage was more emphatic. "This bill has changed the lives of commercial bankers forever," he said. "The savings and loan industry as banks have known it and as it used to exist is gone. The irony is a new, stronger competitor may well emerge as the 'financial services business' continues down its path of consolidation. The regulatory process has been strengthened, and federal regulators now have more power and authority than ever before."[50]

For most bankers, enough was enough. In a survey conducted by the American Bankers Association, a whopping 93 percent of bankers surveyed chose regulatory burdens as their most daunting challenges. The Community Reinvestment Act was deemed the most burdensome regulation, followed by truth-in-savings and truth-in-lending requirements. In what was perhaps the most troubling finding, one in four bankers said they had seriously considered surrendering their bank charters because of regulatory burdens.[51] According to a study commissioned by the Herbert V. Prochnow Educational Foundation of the Graduate School of Banking at the University of Wisconsin-Madison, banking regulations were "confusing consumers and crippling their ability to make informed decisions" while costing banks "the equivalent of 19 percent of net income" and placing small and independent community banks at a competitive disadvantage.[52]

In early 1993, the OBA joined the Community Bankers Association of Oklahoma and bankers nationwide in a grassroots campaign under the no-nonsense slogan "Cut the red tape!" "Our goal is two-fold," explained Beverage. "We want to reduce the amount of bank paperwork that's required but, equally important, we want to change the perspective of lawmakers in Washington so they will stop requiring banks to live by additional, nonsensical regulations that have nothing to do with safety and soundness."[53] OBA chairman Ken Fergeson hailed the campaign as long overdue and desperately needed. "It is indeed possible to protect safety and soundness without piling on meaningless and costly paperwork, and without choking off credit to customers, small businesses and communities as a whole," he said. "Striking a balance is the aim of what our campaign is all about."[54]

To confirm that hard-nosed lobbying can achieve results, bankers spent 1993 counting their victories. In August, the industry's red tape relief bill (S. 265) in Congress continued to add cosponsors—up to 261 in the House and 50 in the Senate. The next month, the Senate Banking Committee reported to the full Senate a bill (S. 1275) containing twenty-one banking regulatory reduction provisions, most of which were taken from the red tape relief bill. The bill included President Clinton's program to spur community development lending.[55] On November 28, the U.S. House of Representatives passed H.R. 3474, a bill that included a number of regulatory relief measures. Passage of the bill came during a rare Sunday session just before Congress adjourned for the rest of the year, and it contained more than thirty provisions to reduce red tape and paperwork imposed on banks by the FDIC Improvement Act of 1991 (FDICIA). The Senate counterpart to H.R. 3474 was expected to be heard after Congress reconvened in late January 1994. "This come-from-behind victory shows that our campaign to educate lawmakers about the connection between too much paperwork and not enough bank credit has been a success," said ABA executive vice president Donald G. Ogilvie. "At the beginning of this year, many thought the idea of such legislation being enacted was a pipe dream. Today, it's within reach." Joe Williams, president of the American Heritage Bank in El Reno and Ken Fergeson's successor as OBA chairman, brought the message home. "When this process started about two years ago, no one in Washington gave bankers much of a chance," he said. "But Oklahoma bankers helped lead the way. Very early in the year we were able to persuade several of the eight members of (the Oklahoma) delegation that this legislation was desperately needed. Without this kind of grassroots activity, this never could have happened."[56]

Agreement on cutting the red tape was one thing; agreement on branch banking was something else altogether. Throughout the early 1990s, bankers continued to debate the pros and cons of branching, an issue that flared up throughout the twentieth century. As the new millennium approached, it showed no signs of abating.

Wherever one stood on this hot-button issue, there was no denying that branch banking laws had opened the floodgates to consolidation on a colossal scale. "There has been a dramatic decrease in the number of banks in Oklahoma," said Larry Briggs—president of the First National Bank in Holdenville and a past president of the OBA—in late 1990. "We've gone from 540 banks in 1982 to 422 today." State Banking Commissioner Wayne Osborn believed that consolidation was accruing to the benefit of the banking business, particularly in the shakeout attending the Penn Square Bank failure in July 1982. "The consolidation of the industry has been good," he said. "It has allowed banks to offer even better services to the public at less cost to the industry." Gene Rainbolt welcomed branching as the wave of the future. "The industry," he said simply, "needs less cost of operation." Nowhere were the benefits of branching more apparent than the BancFirst Corporation. Operating from its support center in the historic Tradesmen's National Bank Building in Oklahoma City, the company's growth came largely from bank acquisitions. In December 1990, BancFirst operated twenty-five offices in seventeen communities and boasted $683 million in assets. "Our goal is to handle more dollars at each location at less dollars of cost," continued Rainbolt. "If we reduce costs, we have a better chance of being around as the industry evolves." Stillwater National Bank and Trust Company president and CEO Robert McCormick, Jr., was not so sure, mainly because most bankers were still reeling from the 1980s. "Most banks have been so focused on getting their own house in order that the changes in structure have not interested but a few of us," he said.[57]

Although laws pertaining to branch banking and multibank holding companies had changed considerably since their original overhaul in October 1983, Oklahoma's banks still had a way to go to catch up to the rest of the country. Proponents of further liberalization insisted that branching allowed banks to compete more effectively with nonbank banks, which could branch statewide with no limitations. Evidence of unfair advantages were not hard to find. According to the American Bankers Association, commercial banks' market share of financial assets declined from 41 percent in the mid-1970s to 30 percent in 1990, while other financial institutions increased their market share from 37 percent

Chartered in 1989, the BancFirst Corporation chose the historic Tradesmen's National Bank Building in Oklahoma City to serve as the support center for its sprawling network of community banks. Courtesy Oklahoma Historical Society.

to 50 percent. Branching also eased the burden on consumers as the savings and loan crisis continued to take its toll. According to Briggs, "It allows banks to branch anywhere by purchasing failed or failing banks and savings and loans or branches of these institutions. It has solved the problem of getting rid of these institutions; provided a customer base already in place; reduced the number of institutions, not the number of facilities; and has been a more effective use of capital and personnel."[58]

Wherever one stood on branch banking, there was no denying that more changes were on the way. As Gene Rainbolt noted with an eye on future acquisitions, "Changes in branch banking law are an inevitable consequence given the rapidly changing global environment." Briggs cited three variables that determined whether or not there were viable alternatives to branching: (1) how would it affect stock value? (2) how would it affect the bottom line? and (3) how would it affect the marketability of bank stock? First Mustang State Bank chairman, president and CEO Gary Huckabay believed that banks would benefit from legislation that would help banks capture a bigger percentage of deposit dollars and help them compete with nonbank banks. For Liberty National Bank and Trust Company of Oklahoma City chairman, president, and CEO Charles "Chuck" Nelson, the changes could not come fast enough. "As long as we're content to leave an unlevel playing field, the more our market share will shrink," he said. "We're losing market share at a phenomenal rate because other financial service providers have unlimited statewide branching and products we can't offer."[59]

From 1990 to mid-1992, there were approximately thirty mergers and acquisitions in Oklahoma. "What is left in Oklahoma is a good core of banks which are making money," said Mark Brackin, president and chief executive officer of the Broadhurst Financial Group in Tulsa. "Bankers can now focus outward and work on the revenue side." Arthur Anderson and Company and the Bank Administration Institute copublished a report predicting a 24 percent decline in the number of banks nationwide by 2000. The report also predicted the number of banks with more than $1 billion in assets would grow 26 percent to 310, and that 7 of those banks would have more than $100 billion in assets.[60]

Many bankers cited new market entrance, growth potential, and economies of scale as key variables in determining what type of institution to merge with or purchase. One of those bankers was Tracy Kelly, chairman of the American National Bank of Bristow, who acquired and then merged three banks. "We decided to purchase the banks and run them as branches because they give us an opportunity to expand our market base," he said. "Thus we become less vulnerable to specific economies of towns or individual areas. We get the best utilization of capital and the technology available to us makes branching more feasible than keeping the free-standing banks." Upon completion of a merger, the focus was twofold: keeping employees happy and maintaining a high level of customer service. "The best thing for the customer is the best thing for the industry," said Kelly. "As long as we keep the customer uppermost in our mind, we can identify the needs of customers and serve them."[61]

Successful mergers and happy customers did not bring an end to debates over bank structure. Controversy continued to swirl in June 1993 when more than 170 bankers gathered in Oklahoma City to discuss the OBA's position on branch banking. The consensus was that no change should be made to existing de novo branching law. On July 1, State Banking Commissioner Mick Thompson stepped into the fray when he issued an emergency rule to continue branching restrictions on state-chartered savings and loans as a way of limiting branching by nationally chartered banks to restrictions set out in state law. Predictably, challenges were quick to follow: the First National Bank and Trust Company of Vinita filed an application with the Office of the Comptroller of the Currency for a de novo branch in Grove; the First Heritage National Bank of Davis sought the OCC's permission to establish a bank in Ada; and the Bank of Southern Oklahoma, N.A., in Madill applied for a new branch in Ardmore. Each of these applications appeared to be in violation of Commissioner Thompson's emergency order. The state banking board and the OBA board of directors wasted little time in voting to oppose all three applications for de novo branches.[62]

Clearly, the last vestiges of unit banking would not pass quietly into the night.

Less visible than headline-grabbing mergers, acquisitions, and branching were three aspects of financial services that remained of vital importance in the waning days of the twentieth century: correspondent banking, bank holding companies, and international banking.

Correspondent banking was rooted in colonial America. It arose in response to the need for redemption centers for banknotes, and it enabled banks of various sizes and levels of expertise to forge relationships and better serve their customers. Early on, small banks deposited large sums of money in their larger correspondent banks; in return for those deposits, the larger banks provided services ranging from cash-letter processing to bank stock loans.

Technology changed everything. "Years ago the primary tie between respondent and correspondent banks was cash-letter processing and loan participation services," explained Bill Shewey, senior vice president of Central National Bank and Trust of Enid. "Now there is definitely an orientation toward more automated services." More changes came in the 1980s as regulators perceived the downside of correspondent banking. As F&M Bank of Tulsa senior vice president Chris Conn explained, "When the bank failures began, regulators got tougher on banks keeping deposits. Correspondent banks were forced to become much more cautious, especially in the area of bank stock loans."[63]

Just as services and levels of expertise vary between correspondent banks, so, too, do approaches to cultivating and maintaining those relationships. "We visit the banks and then go back time and time again," explained CNB Enid senior vice president Theo Fite. "Making bank visits is a way to build strong relationships." Fite estimated that he and his colleague at CNB Enid, Bill Shewey, stayed on the road approximately 50 percent of the time. "We truly view these people as our neighbors and friends," added Shewey.[64]

Under heightened regulatory scrutiny and swamped by technology that would soon blossom into the online revolution, correspondent banking was shedding its good-ole-boy image and taking on the attributes of sophisticated networking. "Correspondent banking is a fascinating area," said Mike Sterkel, senior vice president of Boatmen's National Bank of Oklahoma City. "It is a great challenge to be on the leading edge of technology. Correspondent banks must stay abreast of many developments and figure out new ways to better serve customers." Services in the mid-1990s already included a bewildering variety of electronic funds transfer capabilities, and they were bound to grow with the advent of new technologies. But that did not mean the end of old-fashioned relationships. "The respondent/correspondent relationship is still very vital," said D. B. Green, president and chief executive officer of State National Bank of Marlow. "Years ago, banks had one major correspondent banker. You kept big balances in the bank and it made sure your needs were taken care of. Today, that relationship is not as personal."[65]

An aspect of banking that was both cause and effect of consolidation was the bank holding company. Originally designed as vehicles to repurchase large blocks of stock or finance acquisitions, bank holding companies assumed purchase liabilities with pretax dollars by offsetting bank earnings and holding company debt expenses through consolidation of income and obligations. As Marion Bauman, an attorney with McAfee and Taft, P.C. in Oklahoma City, explained, "Using the bank holding company structure to finance an acquisition can save an amount in taxes equal to ½ or ⅔ of the debt incurred to buy the bank, allowing the debt to be paid off faster." Other advantages of the bank holding company structure included improved management and ownership control, enhanced capital planning and financial flexibility, increased product and service expansion opportunities, geographic expansion techniques, and greater operational flexibility. In terms of product and service expansion, holding companies could engage in personal or real property leasing, management and consultation services, industrial banking, real estate and personal property appraisal services, underwriting services dealing with securities and commodities, tax planning and preparation services, collections, and credit bureau services. Their popularity in Oklahoma was evident in figures supplied by the Federal Reserve Bank of Kansas City's Oklahoma City branch: as of October 9, 1992, 298 of Oklahoma's 406 banks belonged to a bank holding company. As of November 1, 1992, there were 269 holding companies operating in the state.[66]

Many bankers were most enthused about the economies of scale offered by the bank holding company structure. "We have found it cost-effective to standardize and consolidate several functions, including employee benefits and human resources, insurance, loan review, audit, compliance and data processing," said Terrence Cooksey, president of Security Corporation in Duncan, whose banks included Exchange National Bank and Trust Company of Ardmore, Cache Road National Bank of Lawton, and American National Bank and Security National Bank and Trust Company of Duncan.[67]

Benefits notwithstanding, the bank holding company structure was saddled with a few disadvantages. In the mid-1990s, the initial cost of setting one up ran as high as $25,000. According to Bauman, the annual cost of maintaining them was about $2,000, and they added a level of regulatory reporting and supervision. Still, bankers in the 1990s had little reason to doubt the advantages of bank holding companies. As Terrence

Cooksey explained, "Today, with the big emphasis on capital, one thing that will drive acquisitions, mergers and consolidations is it can be done better with capital concentrated in one place rather than spread out among banks."[68]

As rapid-fire advances in technology wrapped the globe in ever-tighter webs of communication, Oklahoma bankers had to factor international competition into their strategic plans. Predictably, opinions differed on the scope and nature of the competition. "The globalization of the industry has greatly increased competition," declared Professor Simpson in March 1991. For Simpson, American banks suffered from three disadvantages: their size vis à vis foreign banks; the prospect of being outnumbered by the competition; and the difficulty of matching overseas competitors' level of service. At the other end of the spectrum was State Banking Commissioner Wayne Osborn, who dismissed international bank competition as basically a nonissue. "International banks coming into Oklahoma is not going to create any major competition as far as costs are concerned," he said. "The products offered by U.S. and foreign banks cost roughly the same. We have to offer better products because consumers continue to demand them, not necessarily because we face competition from foreign banks."[69]

Either way, there was not much doubt that international banks were making headway in U.S. markets. Information compiled by the American Bankers Association in the early 1990s revealed some sobering statistics: foreign banks held almost $700 billion in assets in the United States, representing 23 percent of all U.S. banking assets, up from 15.5 percent in 1982; the largest U.S. bank ranked twenty-fourth on a list of the world's top banks (in 1983, two of the top three world banks were American); and U.S. banks accounted for less than 3 percent of the assets of the top thirty banks at the end of 1988, down from 16.5 percent as recently as 1983. Louis Ederington, the Oklahoma Bankers Professor of Finance at the University of Oklahoma, predicted that competition would stiffen in the coming years as foreign banks leveraged their lower costs of capital and deposits to muscle their way deeper into the American economy. In a chain reaction that would reverberate in states like Oklahoma, regional banks would respond to competitive pressures by moving their business to middle markets represented by small- and medium-sized companies. "That means community banks will face more competition from super regional banks," said Ederington. "So I don't see much good coming out of foreign bank competition for the banking community." Finally, just as technology was beginning to reduce face-to-face communication that lay at the heart of community banking, so, too, was globalization threatening to erode banking relationships. First National Bank of Tulsa senior vice president Rebecca Holland spoke for many when she quipped, "It would be a serious loss to lose the concept of having home town banks."[70]

By the early 1990s, Congress seemed to be moving toward a relaxation of banking regulations as a way of leveling the playing field. But that was scant comfort for bankers in America's heartland. "I believe any regulatory changes made will be aimed at benefitting money center banks and will not help community banks," said Ederington. Besides, relaxed regulations would not be much of a panacea as long as Americans continued to borrow more money than they saved. The bottom line was that neither bankers nor their customers were prepared for international competition that would surely intensify as the new millennium came relentlessly on. Bank consultant George Ozan summed up the challenge: "It's time to learn now how to compete, not when the situation arrives . . . and it eventually will."[71]

Of all the changes that gathered momentum in the 1990s, none was more welcome than the changing face—literally—of the banking profession.

As president and chief executive officer of Washita State Bank in Burns Flat, Virginia Meadows was one of only eleven Oklahoma women who served as the head of one of the state's 421 commercial banks in late 1990. As a twenty-five-year veteran of banking, Meadows did not have an easy climb to the corner office. "When I first became a bank officer in the early 70s, there were few women bank officers and many times I was the only female at bank meetings," she recalled. "At first I was generally ignored, but not being a quiet person, I made my presence felt. Soon I felt accepted as an equal." It was not only in small towns that women had to fight for a seat in the boardroom. The First National Bank in Oklahoma City's board of directors interviewed Michelle Skipper two years before deciding to offer her the top job. "When they interviewed me, they didn't think Oklahoma City was ready for a woman bank president although they said I was qualified," she said.[72]

During and after their climb to the top, women had to learn to balance their work and family lives in a pressure cooker once known derisively as "the mommy track." Skipper, who worked an average of twenty extra hours a week when her three children were small, recalled her mad dash to the day-care center before it closed at six o'clock. "After work, I had to rush to the center to pick up the kids, cook supper and then after the kids went to bed, I worked on bank business again." On the upside, Skipper raised independent children who knew how to take care of themselves and learned what it took to succeed. First National Bank of Geary president Betty Duncan was similarly pressured to fill the dual role of mother and chief executive. Her solution to scheduling conflicts was to insist on attending parent-teacher conferences before 8:00 A.M. and after 5:00 P.M.[73]

Lora Woodall, president, chief executive officer, and chairman of Helena National Bank, learned the banking business from the ground up, and the lessons were not gender-specific. With her grandfather serving on the bank board and her father working as cashier when she was a preteen, Woodall worked as the bank's janitor for twenty-five cents an hour. "My dad was my first mentor," she recalled many years after assuming her leadership position. "He taught me to do things right, treat people right, provide good friendly service, have a good bank to do business with, and always remember anything you do in the bank is confidential. That was important because Helena is a small town and everyone knows everyone."[74]

Central National Bank of Alva president Marilyn Myers told a similar tale of learning the ropes from a respected mentor—in her case, W. D. Myers, Sr., her grandfather and a legend in northwestern Oklahoma. "I still have people coming in, even in the nineties—" Myers's voice trailed off as she recalled an old-timer's story of screwing up his courage to request an auto loan from her no-nonsense grandfather. Myers recounted the man telling her, "I wanted to buy a car, and my dad said I didn't need it, but I wanted one, and your grandpa loaned me, like, $35.00 or something, and he said, 'You come in whenever you can and pay it off.' I came in and paid that off, and I'll never forget that he had enough trust in me to loan me that money, because times were really tough."[75]

City National Bank of Lawton board chair Roma Lee Porter, who began working at the bank when she was fifteen and whose son and daughter were on the payroll in 2010, learned early on the wisdom of loaning money to people you know and businesses you understand. Situated on the edge of the Anadarko Basin, City National Bank was under pressure to join the energy-lending bandwagon in the red-hot 1980s. "Our president back then was Bob Lawrence," recalled Porter. "He was an accountant. And Bob Lawrence said, 'I didn't make any oil loans, because I didn't know anything about oil!'"[76]

With women filling a scant 1 percent of top Oklahoma banking positions in late 1990, the glass ceiling remained pretty much intact. But at least a few cracks were starting to show.

Both cause and effect of increasing gender equality was a groundswell of support for putting an end, once and for all, to discriminatory practices in the workplace. Sexual discrimination, child care, AIDS, and substance abuse topped the list of social issues that were forcing their way into the public sphere and compelling employers to rewrite their employee handbooks.

Banks' vulnerability to sexual discrimination lawsuits dated back to the civil rights movement of the 1960s. Under Title VII of the Civil Rights Act of 1964, employers were barred from discriminating on the basis of gender in hiring, firing, and disciplining their employees. The law also made it unlawful to use gender as the basis for compensation and conditions or privileges of employment. Additional support for women came from the Federal Equal Pay Act of 1963, which made it unlawful to pay male employees more than their female counterparts for equal work or for jobs requiring equal skills. Oklahoma's fair-employment laws completed the trifecta of federal and state statutes aimed at eliminating gender discrimination in the workplace. Unfortunately, new laws did not necessarily translate into new realities. Well into the 1990s and beyond, equal pay for equal work remained a rallying cry for women who worked as hard as men, but who continued to receive less pay for their efforts.

Two Oklahoma banks deserve credit for developing affirmative action plans that addressed the equal pay for equal work issue: F&M Bank of Tulsa, whose job evaluation system mandated pay equality, and Liberty National Bank and Trust Company in Oklahoma City, which required annual evaluations of every job in the bank to ensure equity between jobs. "We are a pay for performance company," declared Dan Shelton, senior vice president of the Human Resources Department. Businesses that lacked the resources to perform extensive compensation studies were eligible for technical assistance in evaluating their compensation policies pursuant to the Pay Equity Technical Assistance Act.[77]

Another and even thornier dimension of gender discrimination was sexual harassment, defined as unwelcomed sexual advances, requests for sexual favors, or other verbal or physical conduct of a sexual nature. Specific guidelines were established by the Equal Employment Opportunity Commission. Employers looking for ways to nip sexual harassment in the bud followed the advice of University of Michigan social psychologist James Grubner, who advised top company brass to take several commonsense steps: (1) make sure to develop effective policies; (2) go beyond posting company policies and explain the procedures for filing complaints, and post a standard form to fill out; (3) educate staff on the specifics of sexual harassment; (4) take complaints seriously; and (5) create an office atmosphere that discourages improper behavior.[78] Brad Windsor, a vice president at Midwest National Bank in Midwest City, was a step ahead of the game in advising employees who wanted to report instances of sexual harassment to report immediately to their supervisors. Employees who were hesitant to talk to their supervisors had the option of placing written complaints in a suggestion box. "The suggestion box is placed near the time clock," Windsor said. "It is located in a private place and is locked."[79]

For women with families, sexual discrimination might have been less of a day-to-day concern than child care. The Oklahoma State Data Center projected that, in 1995 there would be almost 800,000 children, from infants to fourteen-year-olds, in need of child care. Several commercial banks stood in the vanguard of the movement to assist employees with their parenting responsibilities. Programs ran the gamut from referral services, sick child care, dependent care reimbursement, and subsidies to employees with children for on-site day care centers, flextime, and job-sharing arrangements. The Oklahoma City branch of the Federal Reserve Bank provided its employees with information on child care providers and referral agencies. "This is just one more service we can provide our bank employees," said Cherie Sykes, a staff analyst in the bank's personnel department. "It gives them a head start on finding a day care center they are happy with."[80] First National Bank and Trust Company of Tulsa arranged for a local day-care center to provide a 10 percent discount for bank employees. "Of course, employees don't have to take their children there," said Diana Morrow, vice president of the Human Resources Division, "but it is available if employees want it. Many of the employees have taken advantage of it."[81] Informal arrangements such as flextime and job sharing took many forms, including coming to work earlier or later, taking time off in the middle of the day, and job sharing between two employees with similar child care responsibilities.

A particularly vexing issue stemmed from a disease that emerged in the 1980s and blossomed into a full-blown epidemic by the 1990s: HIV infection and its manifestation in Acquired Immune Deficiency Syndrome, or AIDS. From January 1983 to August 31, 1990, 962 AIDS cases were reported in Oklahoma. Oklahoma's toll was only a fraction of the 143,286 cases reported nationwide from 1981 to July 1990. But, given the difficulty of diagnosis and social stigma attached to the disease, cases were no doubt underreported. According to OBA legal counsel Mary Beth Guard, banks needed to have an AIDS policy in place to balance the rights of the infected person with the rights of his or her coworkers. "If a bank waits until an employee contracts the disease to establish a policy," said Guard, "the bank could be deemed to have discriminated against the employee because the policy could be seen as targeting that individual and how to treat that individual."[82] John Harkess, medical director of the AIDS Division of the Oklahoma State Department of Health, agreed that employers should be prepared, preferably with policies developed elsewhere to ensure objectivity and avoid charges of discrimination.[83] Infected persons were protected under the Americans with Disabilities Act of July 1990, a law that granted them the same rights as handicapped individuals under Title VII of the Civil Rights Act.

A problem of an entirely different nature was substance abuse. An estimated 10 percent of corporate America's labor force went to work in the 1990s with illegal substances coursing through their veins. The threat posed by substance abuse was twofold: (1) employees might resort to theft or embezzlement to feed their addictions; and (2) workplaces often experienced decreased productivity as measured by absenteeism, tardiness, excessive sick leave, accidents, ineffective and flawed supervision, complaints from customers, and errors in judgment. To minimize the catastrophic effects of substance abuse, F&M Bank and First National Bank, both of Tulsa, and Liberty National Bank and Trust Company in Oklahoma City offered employee assistance programs and access to trained counselors. The banks paid a portion of the cost and required employees who used the services to pay fees on a graduated scale.[84]

In addressing the social concerns of the 1990s, the banker's bottom line was simple: find ways to increase productivity through employee benefits and a nurturing work environment; and create an employee manual whose policies and procedures were commensurate with state and federal laws and conducive to building a healthy and profitable bank.

In July 1992, Oklahoma bankers paused from their exertions to reflect on the tenth anniversary of the FDIC's closure of Penn Square Bank. Some reminisced about the glory days of the late 1970s and early 1980s, when oil and gas wells were spudded with numbing regularity and bank charter applications piled up like pancakes on the state banking commissioner's desk, waiting to be processed. Bob Harris, a onetime executive vice president of the OBA who went on to become president of the Texas Bankers Association, recalled a time when forty-two bank charters were pending. A former Penn Square Bank employee described what it was like to be at the epicenter of the historic boom: "There was electricity in the air. We worked hard, made good money, and had expensive dinners and many nights of happy hours."[85]

And then, at 7:05 P.M., Monday, July 5, 1982, national bank examiner Steve Plunk, whose team of examiners had uncovered wrongdoing on a scale that dwarfed anything they had ever seen in their collective years of examining banks, listened as Comptroller of the Currency Todd Conover read his scripted prelude to shutting the bank down. Thirty years later, Plunk still carried the transcript in his briefcase as a talisman of an event that shook Oklahoma banking to its core.[86]

"July 5, 1982—" Bob Harris paused to reflect on the mayhem to come, and the fact that so few saw it coming. "The state crashed that day," he said at length, "and no one knew it." Ed Keller, chairman and chief executive officer of Fourth National Bank of Tulsa and the 1982 OBA president, recalled the Penn Square Bank debacle as the most significant event in Oklahoma, and possibly even the nation's, banking history.[87]

Without making excuses for fiduciary misconduct, many pointed to the Natural Gas Policy Act of 1978 as the catalyst for the Penn Square Bank debacle. Spooked by turmoil in the Middle East and convinced that natural gas was in short supply, Congress deregulated the price of deep gas (below fifteen thousand feet). Producers in gas-rich Oklahoma took the bait, and the scramble was on. "That caused the banking community, and not just Penn Square, to have big eyes in terms of what reserves were worth," said Bob Alexander, president of Alexander Energy Corporation and chairman of the Oklahoma Natural Gas Policy Commission. Chiming in with his own 1980s story, Alexander recalled an encounter with a Penn Square Bank official on an airplane. After exchanging pleasantries, the official promptly granted Alexander an unsolicited million-dollar line of credit on the back of a calling card. Deregulation of deep gas, concluded Alexander with a flair for understatement, "caused a drilling boom in which people never really paid attention to what they were doing."[88]

State Banking Commissioner Wayne Osborn had a simpler explanation: greed. "The reason was greed as much as anything else," said the plainspoken commissioner. "They got into such a growth mode. They were paying excessive rates for funds, certificates of deposit and lending funds out without a whole lot of credit evaluation."[89]

Whatever the catalyst, the effects were game changers in Oklahoma's and, to a large extent, the nation's banking industry. Professor Gary Simpson described a ripple effect that spared nobody in its destructive arc across the banking industry. Four years after the FDIC's closure of Penn Square Bank, it was the First National Bank and Trust Company of Oklahoma City's turn to reap the whirlwind. "People thought, 'My God, if it can happen to the First National Bank of Oklahoma City, anything can happen!'"[90]

With memories of Penn Square Bank still fresh and a savings and loan crisis with no end game in sight, Congress passed FIRREA in 1989 and the FDIC Improvement Act in 1991. While most were willing to accept regulations aimed at ensuring the safety and soundness of financial institutions, most thought the pendulum was swinging too far. As OBA vice president and general counsel Mary Beth Guard noted, "The response (to Penn Square Bank) with respect to safety and soundness was appropriate to a certain extent, but it's being carried overboard." Inevitably, bankers passed higher costs of compliance and FDIC insurance premiums on to their customers. "It costs more to have a bank account," said Guard. "It costs more to get a loan." The domino effect continued as regulators learned to scrutinize cash flow and collateral as never before, FDIC officials rewrote their playbook on asset sales and liquidations, and customers learned to take nothing for granted. "The public has a new awareness that they have a responsibility to understand the quality of the bank that they put their money in, especially if it's over $100,000," said Chuck Nelson, president and chief executive officer of Liberty Bancorporation, Inc. "That's the biggest single change since Penn Square, when you get down to it."[91]

Maybe. But it would be hard to beat multibank holding companies and branch banking for first place on a list of post–Penn Square Bank changes. Conceived in desperation and enacted in the nick of time, liberalized banking laws spawned by Penn Square Bank dropped the curtain on unit banking—a cornerstone of Progressive-era legislation, but a hopeless anachronism at century's end. "Low and behold, the banking industry was willing to pass new laws," recalled David Rainbolt. "The banking industry needed to allow its good banks to be merged with its bad banks."[92] What Rainbolt left unsaid was his own role in lobbying for changes in bank structure that so many banks needed to survive.

Bob Harris, described by Gary Simpson as "a very polished, professional, impressive guy" who might have succeeded as a politician, was Roger Beverage's predecessor as head of the OBA.[93] He arrived in Oklahoma City from Lincoln, Nebraska, where he had served as head of the Nebraska Bankers Association, just in time to get a ringside seat at Penn Square Bank's final months. "Bob got here just in time for Penn Square," said fellow Nebraskan Beverage. "He spent a lot of time on television and giving interviews by the local media about what the failure of Penn Square meant. He was famous for emphasizing that the FDIC insurance system really works. Unfortunately, that was the first time we've had, nationwide, to really defend the FDIC system, because we hadn't had many bank failures, and certainly none of the magnitude of Penn Square."[94]

Harris claimed that he was interviewed in the media three hundred times in the weeks following the bank's failure. On the occasion of the tenth anniversary of the FDIC takeover, he recalled the beginning of the paradigm shift in Oklahoma banking: "We received the message a significant number of Oklahoma banks were about to fail. The banking system didn't have the capacity to absorb the failures so it was vital we had interstate banking. The OBA held an emergency board meeting and three weeks later entered a bill for interstate banking in the Oklahoma Legislature. The governor signed it 27 hours later."[95] When he was not mugging for the cameras, Harris was frantically bringing bankers and businesspeople to the table to orchestrate nothing less than the rescue of Oklahoma's banking industry. "He was very down to earth, and he was very popular with the bankers and with the public, and people in the state legislature," recalled Simpson. "He was trying to pull things together, and interact with people in the legislature, just trying to figure out what was going to happen to us. Oklahoma was the epicenter of all these things."[96]

In the ensuing years, the state's bank structure laws were brought in line with laws that had long since upended the banking industry in the rest of the country. In the process, the public got a crash course in the goings-on behind the teller cage. Jon Davis, who was serving in 1982 as the deputy managing officer of the Federal Reserve branch in Oklahoma City, remembered the summer of '82 as a wake-up call for media that had never shown much interest in the banking system. "The media attention has been good," he said. "I believe it is important for consumers to understand the banking system." With the benefit of hindsight, Davis could say with assurance that the banking system emerged from the tortuous 1980s as stronger on all counts. "As a result of Penn Square, bankers are more cautious in regards to lending practices. They look at collateral and cash flow more carefully." A former Penn Square Bank employee suggested that the lessons of '82 extended to bank boards of directors: "Boards of directors for banks realized their responsibilities were not simply a once-a-month tea party to get cash in little envelopes and play 'banker' for an afternoon." Steve Plunk, who was in charge of the bank examination team that put an end to Penn Square Bank's lending binge, eventually landed upstairs as president of Liberty Bank and Trust Company of Tulsa. "I believe regulators are more aggressive now," he said in July 1992. "They don't just key in on the symptoms, but on the causes—excessive growth, detrimental loan to capital ratios, etc. When a bank is in trouble, they move in during the early stages." Robert Empie, vice chairman of Union Bank and Trust in Oklahoma City and a former state banking commissioner, agreed. "Examiners are now extremely critical of banks which have participations in loans when the bank doesn't fully understand and have documentation on every aspect of the loan," he said.[97]

There was a touch of pathos in former Penn Square Bank chairman Bill "Beep" Jennings's memory of the day the bank failed as "without a doubt, the worst day of my life—worse than anything in World War II." He credited a strong faith in God, and himself, for helping him through his dark night of the soul. "I have regrets about the bank," he continued, "regrets that I permitted a strong concentration of loan in the oil and gas industry, but that was prompted by an earnest desire to create a positive economic environment for the state of Oklahoma." At the time of the collapse, 80 percent of Penn Square Bank's lending activity was concentrated in loans to the oil and gas industry. Although he was never charged with a crime, Jennings figured he must have been "the most investigated man in the state"—and possibly the most sued one, as one lawsuit after another listed him as a defendant. Ten years and one quadruple bypass surgery later, the self-described "tough ole coot" maintained his family's ownership of the Bank of Healdton, where his banking career began. Ever the Oklahoma booster, he and an old air force buddy were growing trees, wholesaling them to nurseries, and building a tree-planting machine that would allow two people to plant up to a thousand trees a day, all in the service of Oklahoma's economic development.[98]

Roger Beverage succeeded Bob Harris as executive vice president of the OBA in March 1988—too late to experience the fiasco up close and personal, but in plenty of time to grasp the significance of the event and its long-term consequences.[99] "The bankers who survived in Oklahoma have fought through an incredible series of events since 1982," he said. "It has been an education you couldn't buy anywhere. To say bankers were shell shocked is an understatement. However, they have come to terms with the changing environment of the financial services industry."[100]

Gordon Greer left Liberty Bank in Oklahoma City in 1989 to join Bank IV in Wichita, Kansas. "When I left in '89, I was stunned by how good the economy was in Wichita," said Greer. "It was unbelievable! It was like going to a different world!" Even though plenty of Kansans were involved in the energy industry, Greer found a level of professionalism that kept people from getting carried away by all the hype. Greer continued:

> One of the problems in Oklahoma was that we had all these Johnny-come-latelies in the seventies and eighties that were able to get financing. We had disc jockeys, and real estate salesmen, and people who didn't know anything about the oil and gas business. There was a proliferation of people chasing that rain-

bow in Oklahoma in the late seventies and early eighties, and, you know, a lot of banks, for some reason or another, financed them. The snowball just kept rolling down the hill and kept getting bigger and bigger and bigger, and then all of a sudden, it all blew up on everybody.[101]

G. P. Johnson Hightower, then working as a loan officer at the First National Bank and Trust Company of Oklahoma City, blamed investment tax allowances for enticing people with more money than business sense to his and other lenders' offices. "Those were the days, in the late seventies and early eighties, when doctors and other investors were being promoted all over the place with the tax advantages of investing in oil and gas deals," recalled Hightower. "So, we'd loan money to doctors thinking, 'Well, gee whiz, that oil well isn't going to have to be successful for me to get paid back, because those guys are getting a bunch of surgical fees anyway!'"[102]

But Oklahoma bankers had learned their lesson. As the 1980s faded to a bad memory and the 1990s shaped up as something akin to a golden age, bankers knew that they needed a new modus operandi to prosper in the competitive world of stringent regulations and runaway technology. "There was a change," recalled Professor Simpson. "You got the more professional banker. You got the fellow who was going to ask about cash flows and financial statements more often. And you got people who were more concerned about things like interest rate risk. They were managing banks in a more technical, technological, analytical framework." But change came at a price, and it was reflected in a loss of camaraderie that had always been a hallmark of the banking profession. "Attendance at the Oklahoma Bankers Association conventions started to change," said Simpson about one barometer of changing times. "You didn't see as many people from the larger banks there. And you didn't see as many people there, as many CEOs. It became somewhat of a small bank phenomenon. Basically, the way I read it, the people who were managing banks didn't have time to be out socializing. They saw their jobs as much more demanding. There were more things to get taken care of."[103] Sadly, more and more bankers were coming to the realization that banking was not as much fun as it once was. Consumed with spreadsheets and harried by regulators, bankers greeted the 1990s with renewed optimism, even as they mourned the loosening bonds of collegiality.

To describe changes that roiled the banking industry in the 1970s and 1980s, Oklahoma City businessman Tom Loy, who complemented his business career by teaching banking history for the OBA and other organizations, offered the metaphor of the perfect storm whose first rumblings were felt in 1973 when OPEC clamped down on oil production. Then came the inflationary spiral that the Nixon administration tried, famously and unsuccessfully, to squelch with wage and price controls. Predictably, inflation went into overdrive when controls were lifted. Subsequent attempts to "Whip Inflation Now" with smiley-face buttons failed to make much headway. It was left to Federal Reserve Board chairman Paul Volcker, appointed in the fall of 1979 by President Jimmy Carter and reappointed by President Ronald Reagan, to battle inflation through control of the money supply. Like a physician willing to risk killing a cancer patient by administering ever-stronger doses of chemotherapy in hopes of curing her, Volcker upped interest rates until his patient, the United States of America, nearly flatlined.

The good news was that inflation was finally whipped. The bad news was that the economy went into a tailspin. As the storm reached its full fury, bankers and bank regulators came to understand what interest rate risk was all about. "We had guys who had been bank regulators or bank examiners for twenty years, forty years, and they had never seen interest rates do this," said Loy. "They had never known a post–Regulation Q world. So this was as new to them as it was to kids coming out of college!" None doubted that Penn Square Bank's troubles were brought on by out-of-control lending in a red-hot market. And yet, seen in its historical context, that bank's failure, together with scores of other failures that made for smaller headlines, reflected a paradigm shift that caught everybody flat-footed. Then came the Internet, and all bets were off. By then, two stormy decades had revolutionized the banking industry.

"Did the Internet have a huge influence? Absolutely!" declared Loy. "But that's 1990. By 1990 or '91, the landscape of the banking world in this country and beyond had just changed enormously."[104]

The summer of 1992 brought another milestone to Oklahoma banking: the retirement of State Banking Commissioner Wayne Osborn, effective on August 31. His tenure from 1987 to 1992 capped a twenty-two-year tenure with the state banking department. "Wayne always tried to help banks find solutions to their problems," said attorney Marion Bauman of McAfee and Taft, P.C. in Oklahoma City. "And he was extremely good at it." Sid Carroll, assistant regional director of the FDIC's Dallas office and a veteran of Oklahoma bank auctions, was similarly impressed with Osborn's track record. "I think his major accomplishment was he maintained the stability of Oklahoma's banking industry," said Carroll. "He led with a firm but just hand." Osborn left office with the satisfaction of knowing that his successor would inherit a good working relationship with the Federal Reserve Bank and the FDIC, a heightened respect from Oklahoma bankers, and a smorgasbord of new responsibilities. Asked about his plans for retirement, Osborn played coy and said he was keeping his options open. "I don't have any plans," he said. "Maybe sit back and relax for a while. However, my wife says that will last 30 minutes or so."[105]

Osborn's successor was Mick Thompson, a senior vice president at Central National Bank of Poteau whose public service experience included eight years in the state legislature (1976–84). During his tenure as state representative, he became chairman of the House Banking and Finance Committee and House majority leader.[106] "I was there about the time that Penn Square failed," said Thompson. "That was quite an experience!"[107]

In 1984, Thompson decided not to seek reelection because of family considerations and his promotion to senior vice president at Central National Bank back in Poteau. Public service called again in 1988 when he was elected as chairman of the Oklahoma Development Finance Authority, a public trust that, by the time of his election, had issued nearly $2 billion in revenue bonds to finance business, government, and finance projects. With experience in both politics and banking, he was a natural choice as Governor David Walters's legislative liaison. When Osborn announced his retirement, there was not much doubt about who would be his successor. "Mick has a very strong banking background and a very strong state government background and will be a strong candidate," said Governor Walters on the eve of Thompson's appointment as state banking commissioner.[108]

Thompson's appointment was duly approved, and his four-year term began on September 1, 1992, the day after Osborn departed for his richly deserved retirement. "The State Banking Department has done an outstanding job through some tough times," said Thompson as he assumed his new office. "The banking industry is healthier now and the department can focus on other things."[109]

A milestone that passed with little fanfare came a year later with the closing of the FDIC field office in Oklahoma City. The FDIC—known sardonically as Oklahoma's only growth industry in the 1980s—employed 226 employees in its Oklahoma City field office, and they sprang into action every time a failed bank's assets were put up for auction. Such was the pace of the state's economic recovery that, by the summer of 1993, the FDIC's liquidation work was mostly done, and it was time to close up shop. The office was set to close on October 31. "This is a terrific sign for the Oklahoma banking industry," said a beaming Ken Fergeson. "Notwithstanding the excellent numbers reported for the Oklahoma banking industry for 1992 and particularly the fourth quarter, the closing of this office is more symbolic of the banking industry's comeback."[110] Fergeson's enthusiasm was picked up by bankers and banking officials throughout the region. Everyone was happy that the FDIC had been there in their time of need. But they were happier to see it go.

During its residence in Oklahoma City, the field office handled more than 200,000 individual assets valued at $6.5 billion from 142 institutions. Activity peaked in 1987, a bleak year that saw thirty-three bank failures and two open assistance transactions. Ken Blinco, managing director of the field office, estimated that eight hundred people were working at that time. As employees wound down their business and prepared for other assignments, the office was still concluding the affairs of ninety-five failed bank estates with about four thousand assets valued at $190 million. Any failed bank matters remaining after October 31 would be handled by the FDIC's consolidated field office in Addison, Texas.[111]

It was thus with renewed optimism—perhaps even great expectations—that Oklahoma bankers approached the end of the millennium. Responding to a survey conducted by the OBA's flagship publication, the *Oklahoma Banker,* Bank of Cushing president John Bryant expressed the opinion of many when he opined, "The 'pioneer' heritage of the people of Oklahoma has provided the impetus to work through the difficult times and conditions."[112]

CHAPTER TWELVE

Toward the New Millennium

> Local bankers are keenly aware that the growth of their banks depends upon the economic viability of their trade area. Their success is measured by the economic well-being of those they serve.
>
> Jack T. Conn, chairman and CEO, Fidelity National Bank and Trust Company of Oklahoma City

To measure perceptions of banking and bankers and, it was hoped, to help the industry improve its image, the American Bankers Association commissioned two Gallup surveys, one aimed at consumers, and the other aimed at bank employees. Results were released at the ABA's annual convention in San Francisco on October 7, 1995. For the consumer survey, Gallup researchers contacted one thousand heads of household about their perceptions of banks. Although most consumers reported that banks were their primary financial institutions and were satisfied with their own bank's services, the survey responses made for tough reading. Thomas G. Strohm, chair of the ABA Communications Council, put it this way: "While we did think there would be areas of discontent, I don't think any of us thought we would find such a disconnect between consumer expectations and perceptions."[1]

The survey assumed four drivers of customer satisfaction: (1) caring about and involvement in the community; (2) commitment to meeting consumers' financial needs; (3) flexibility in meeting customers' needs;

and (4) objectivity in making loans. Results revealed disappointment on all four measures. Thirty-one percent of respondents believed that bankers actually cared about, and were actively involved in, their communities. An identical percentage of customers strongly agreed that banks were committed to meeting their financial needs. Only 29 percent strongly believed that banks were flexible in meeting their financial needs, and even fewer—27 percent—strongly believed that banks were objective in their loan decisions. With less than a third of respondents expressing satisfaction with their banks, Strohm conceded that bankers faced an uphill climb to change popular perceptions of their industry. "I think we, as an industry, must consider the fact that we are the ones who need to change," said Strohm. The industry's challenges were compounded by responses indicating a lack of confidence in the industry as a whole and a woeful ignorance of basic banking functions and services. A slim 23 percent of consumers believed that the banking system was financially healthy. Thirty-six percent thought that mutual funds purchased at banks were FDIC-insured, and 39 percent thought that taxpayers paid for FDIC deposit insurance.[2]

The other survey included responses from 2,184 employees across the country, and it showed bank principals that they had more work to do at the office. Sixty-six percent of respondents strongly believed that their banks were meeting the needs of their customers; 71 percent strongly agreed that their banks cared about their communities; 41 percent strongly agreed that banks were flexible in meeting customer needs; and just 50 percent strongly believed that banks were objective in making loan decisions. Perhaps most damning of all, only 53 percent of bank employees strongly agreed with the statement "I feel wanted as an employee at my bank."[3]

Three years later, survey results took a turn for the better. In an annual survey conducted for the *American Banker,* Gallup researchers turned in the industry's best showing since the surveys began in 1984. Eighty-five percent of respondents rated the U.S. banking and financial system as healthy. Only 11 percent thought the industry was unhealthy, and the rest were undecided. According to industry watchers, changing ways of doing business, such as selling nontraditional products by telephone, had not hurt public confidence. In other survey results, 25 percent of respondents rated the banking and financial system as "very healthy," and 60 percent rated the system as "fairly healthy." Thirty-seven percent—

the highest score since 1986—said they had "a great deal of confidence" in the system's safety and security.[4]

Oklahoma banking in the late 1990s exemplified the national trend toward renewed confidence in the nation's financial system. And nobody exemplified Oklahoma banking more than Jack T. Conn, who had retired from Fidelity National Bank and Trust Company of Oklahoma City in 1983 and died in 1991. He would not have been surprised to see his colleagues usher out the twentieth century in much the same way that their forebears had greeted it—confident in the future and responsive to the needs of their communities. "Local bankers are keenly aware that the growth of their banks depends upon the economic viability of their trade area," wrote Conn in his 1979 memoir. "Their success is measured by the economic well-being of those they serve."[5]

Another titan of Oklahoma banking who radiated confidence in his industry was State Banking Commissioner Mick Thompson. The former state representative and banker from Poteau was appointed to the state's highest banking office by Governor David Walters in 1992, was reappointed by Governor Frank Keating in 1996 and 2000, and remained in his position well into the new millennium. At the time of his appointment, the Oklahoma Banking Department was not self-funded and relied on appropriations from the legislature to fulfill its mission, which was primarily to regulate state-chartered banks, credit unions, trust companies, savings and loans, money order companies, and money transmitters.[6] Weaned on community banking in southeastern Oklahoma, Thompson could not understand why banks had to remit assessments to the general revenue fund and then receive part of those funds back to fund operations. "My contention was, that's a tax on the banks, because they're keeping 30 or 40 percent of what the banks paid," explained Thompson. "And so, I said, 'Look, they already pay all of their corporate tax. They pay all their other taxes. They shouldn't be supplementing general revenue with their assessments, especially if they're supposed to be for regulations. We don't need it, and the banks shouldn't pay it.'" Thompson stuck to his guns until he gained control of his departmental budget. But his challenges had only begun. The agency was not nationally accredited, salaries were mediocre, and examiners rarely stuck around for very long. "Once we'd get them trained, the FDIC or the Fed would hire them," said Thompson. "The overall condition of the department was pretty antiquated."[7]

Just two years into his tenure as state banking commissioner, Thompson was making extraordinary headway in positioning his agency for the twenty-first century. He was behind the agency's move to less costly office space, which was smaller than its previous location but was better suited to its needs. He streamlined the bank examination process, put all examiners through Total Quality Management training, and equipped field examiners with new computers. Office operations were upgraded with state-of-the-art technology, and the fees it charged for services were reduced, even as salaries were raised. As Thompson noted, "We think we should always look for ways to operate efficiently because it is the bankers' assessments that run the department, and we should be good stewards of that money."[8] In 1994 alone, six nationally chartered banks were converted to state charters. Thompson was particularly proud of his agency's accreditation by the Conference of State Bank Supervisors—an accomplishment that put his agency on a par with state banking departments nationwide.

Bank failures plummeted nationally in 1994, dipping to less than one-tenth of the number of failures recorded five years earlier. According to the American Bankers Association, only thirteen institutions with total assets of $1.6 billion and insured by the Bank Insurance Fund failed in 1994. That was down from 41 failures in 1993 and 169 in 1990.[9] Oklahoma mirrored the national trend in declining bank failures. There were none in 1993 and 1994, and, according to Commissioner Thompson, none were expected in 1995.[10]

For the first three quarters of 1994, Oklahoma banks' net income neared $280 million. Lending rose 14 percent as assets, deposits, and equity capital all continued in their upward trajectory.[11] Sheshunoff Information Services ranked the state sixteenth in the nation in bank loan growth. With outstanding loan growth of 9.2 percent, Oklahoma ranked well above the national average 6.1 percent.[12] By year-end 1994, Oklahoma banks reported total loan growth of 13.7 percent to an all-time record of $17.1 billion. BancFirst CEO David Rainbolt, who succeeded American Heritage Bank of El Reno president and CEO Joe Williams in April to become the OBA's 101st chairman, spoke for many when he singled out bulging loan portfolios as a particularly good omen. "Loan growth continued to be strong, which is a good sign for future earnings," said Rainbolt. "The economy has improved, and with property values stabilized, bankers feel more comfortable lending against real estate. However," he continued on a note of caution, "we've got to assume that sometime in the not too distant future, loan loss provisions again will rise to normal levels."[13]

No less enthusiastic were regulators. According to FDIC assistant regional director Sid Carroll, "There's nothing out there that scares us, (and) we've seen no evidence of weakened credit underwriting standards." Mick Thompson reserved his praise for the OBA and its chairman, David Rainbolt. "We've been able to accomplish a lot of things with the help of the bankers," said the commissioner. "David Rainbolt and the OBA's leadership have been instrumental in this effort, and our efforts at improving communication with bankers are ongoing."[14]

In faraway Washington, D.C., Congress was responding to years of bank lobbying by peeling off some of the red tape that it had been strapping on banks. The Riegle Community Development and Regulatory Improvement Act of 1994 contained more than fifty provisions to reduce regulatory burdens for bankers and their customers. David Rainbolt revealed a flair for understatement when he commented on the fruits of the "Cut the Red Tape" campaign: "The industry was united in support of this effort, and that consistent message was sent over and over again to Washington. It finally bore fruit." The other landmark legislation was the Riegle-Neal Interstate Banking and Branching Efficiency Act, which authorized full interstate banking in one year and interstate branching by acquisition and merger to start in 1997. The act preserved key states' rights to control bank entry and to set their own rules governing activities of out-of-state banks. At the same time, U.S. attorney general Janet Reno left no doubt that the federal government would come down hard on discriminatory lending. "For those who thumb their nose at us, I promise vigorous enforcement," declared the no-nonsense attorney general. "These actions demonstrate we will tackle lending discrimination wherever and in whatever form it appears. No loan is exempt, no bank is immune."[15]

Back in Oklahoma, Commissioner Thompson reminded bankers to be prepared for stiff competition from credit unions: "Credit Unions are expanding rapidly in Oklahoma. One of my concerns is that while state law does not authorize a community credit union charter, federal law does. This kind of credit union defines its 'common bond' as a specified geographical area, and it can be any location."[16]

Despite a dip in earnings, bank performance remained strong in the first quarter of 1995. Steve Burrage, president and CEO of the First National Bank of Antlers and 1995–96 OBA chairman, struck an upbeat chord in a midyear assessment: "Overall, Oklahoma banks are in very sound condition. Their capital ratios are still high. They had a strong increase in lending as compared to the first quarter of 1994, and the loan to deposit ratio continued to increase, as did bank assets." Other positive signs included declines in past-due and noncurrent loans from the fourth quarter of 1994 and healthy returns on assets. What is more, nearly half of Oklahoma banks (47.3 percent) reported earnings gains during the first quarter of 1995. Meanwhile, the FDIC reported a decline in the number of commercial banks, from 360 at the end of the first quarter 1994 to 348 as of March 31, 1995.[17] Fewer banks came as good news to William Keeton, senior economist with the Federal Reserve Bank of Kansas City. Rather than signaling weakness in the banking system, Keeton spoke for many when he claimed that consolidation was leading to a leaner and safer industry in which small and well-managed banks could continue to rely on flexibility and familiarity with local markets to serve their communities.[18]

With solid reports coming in from the second quarter of 1995, Steve Burrage based his optimism on fact that banks were making their money by lending. "They're no longer making money off their investment portfolios," he said. "Although our interest margins are shrinking, we still have a good spread. Banks are looking to make good loans because that's where they make money." The only sector that did not report double digit increases in second-quarter lending compared to 1994 was agriculture.[19]

On June 30, 1995, Oklahoma banks reported total assets of $33.7 billion, up from $33.1 billion at year-end 1994, and total loans of $18.1 billion, up from $17.1 billion at year-end 1994. There were 346 banks in the state as of June 30, 1995, down from 350 at year-end 1994. Although OSU professor Gary Simpson was optimistic about the future of commercial banking, he cautioned bankers to be on the lookout for declining loan quality. "We're not seeing it yet in Oklahoma, but in other parts of the country loan quality is starting to deteriorate," he wrote in the *Oklahoma Economic Outlook,* an annual report published by the OSU College of Business Administration. "That's one of the things we need to watch for and make sure it doesn't happen here." Turning to the output of goods and services, OSU professor of economics Gerald Lage predicted that growth in Oklahoma's gross state product was on target to equal or exceed the growth in U.S. gross domestic product for the first time since the early 1980s: "We may have more moderate, but steady, growth, smoothing out the large ups and downs in the economy. We may not see the peaks we used to—but we won't see the downside, either."[20] Bank profits soared from $90 million in the second quarter to $99 million in the third quarter of 1995.[21]

Allowing for a dip in the mid-1990s, the five-year trend in bank profitability was clear: $251 million in 1991; $339 million in 1992; $398 million in 1993; $350 million in 1994; and $360 million in 1995.[22] Burrage attributed earnings growth to ever-improving credit quality. At the same time, past-due and noncurrent loans, charge-offs, and loan-loss provisions were all moving back toward historically normal levels.[23] As 1995 drew to a close, there were only two clouds on the banking horizon: deterioration in agricultural lending, and revisions to the Community Reinvestment Act that reminded bankers to heed Attorney General Reno's warning of dire consequences for noncompliance.[24]

Elation over a rebounding economy was muted on April 19, 1995, when a homegrown terrorist named Timothy McVeigh detonated a bomb in the Alfred P. Murrah Federal Building in downtown Oklahoma City. McVeigh's horror show claimed 168 lives, injured more than 680 people, and destroyed or damaged 324 buildings within a sixteen-block radius of the explosion. Oklahoma City's claim to the most destructive act of terrorism in U.S. history would last until September 11, 2001, when terrorists of another ilk put New York City and Washington, D.C., in their cross hairs and changed the course of history.

In 1996, community bankers were heartened to see some of their own on the American Bankers Association's list of top-performing banks with assets under $100 million. Measured according to five-year returns on assets and other key metrics, the list included the Bank of Locust Grove, Lakeside Bank of Salina, the Bank of Commerce in McLoud, the Northwest Bank in Oklahoma City, and the Bank of Commerce in Chouteau.[25]

According to the FDIC's reporting for the second quarter of 1996, Oklahoma's 340 commercial banks had net earnings totaling $98 million, up 8.9 percent from $90 million for the same quarter of 1995. For the first half of the year, bank profits totaled $196 million, up 12.7 percent from 1995. Even though problems persisted in the agricultural sector and there was an uptick in noncurrent loans, bank performance in midyear 1996 continued to show steady improvements over the same period in 1995. Total loans and leases stood at $19.06 billion, up 6 percent; total assets stood at $35.1 billion, up 4.2 percent; deposits were up $1.6 billion to $29.5 billion; and equity capital reached $3.25 billion, up 3.9 percent. The FDIC's report reflected continuing consolidation, although at a more modest pace than in previous years. The number of Oklahoma commercial banks declined from 346 in mid-1995 to 340 in the second quarter of 1996.[26]

The good news continued through the third quarter and on to the end of the year. With real estate and commercial lending leading the charge, Oklahoma bank profits in 1996 rose by $15 million from the previous year. Although their number had declined from 342 to 332 in 1996, the state's commercial banks posted total net income of $370 million for the year, up 4.3 percent from $355 million in 1995. Other comparisons between 1995 and 1996 were similarly upbeat. Total lending rose 6.8 percent during 1996 to almost $20 billion, with a 9.8 percent jump in real estate loans and an 8.3 percent increase in commercial and industrial loans; total assets grew 4.6 percent to $36.1 billion; total deposits stood at almost $30.1 billion, up 4.3 percent; and equity capital stood at $3.38 billion, up 3.6 percent.[27]

All signs pointed to more of the same in 1997. "The Oklahoma banking industry should be very profitable in 1997," wrote Professor Simpson in the 1997 *Oklahoma Economic Outlook* section on banking. "Commercial banks will have ample liquidity for loans over the next year. The question is whether a sufficient amount of quality loan requests will be available." At the same time, the trend toward consolidation continued apace. "A few new banks were chartered in 1997," continued Simpson, "but the strong long-run trend is to have a small number of large banking firms and approximately 100 small geographic or product niche banks."[28]

Second-quarter 1997 figures conformed to Simpson's rosy predictions. According to the FDIC, the state's commercial banks posted $103 million in net earnings, up 4.9 percent from the second quarter of 1996. Moreover, 67 percent of Oklahoma banks enjoyed earnings gains in the second quarter. Loans were up in major categories, including real estate, commercial, industrial, and individual lending; only farm lending lagged behind. Profits at midyear totaled $201 million, $5 million above total for first half of 1996. Other indicators of bank performance showed similar gains over the second quarter of 1996. Total assets stood at $37.1 billion, up 5.8 percent; total deposits stood at $30.05 billion, up $499 million; and equity capital increased a hefty 33.2 percent to $4.3 billion. The number of commercial banks continued to decline, from 340 at midyear 1996 to 326 at midyear 1997.[29]

The big story of the year was the merger of Boatmen's National Bank of Oklahoma City into NationsBank. This resulted in a "migration" of Boatmen's holdings from Oklahoma's statistics to those for North Carolina and had a negative impact on the way profits, loans, and deposits were reported. Although the merger was officially completed in the first quarter, the operational conversion from Boatmen's branding, systems, and services to NationsBank was completed in the third quarter. Such were the consequences of this change in reporting that the FDIC launched a review of its reporting methods to see how each state's assets and deposits might be more accurately reported. Nonetheless, Oklahoma's commercial banks posted $100 million in net earnings in the third quarter, up from $96 million, or 4 percent, from the same quarter of 1996. Bank profits were down slightly, from $291 million in the third quarter of 1996 to $284 million a year later.[30]

Changes in FDIC reporting in 1997 rendered year-to-year comparisons difficult. Under the change, the FDIC credited profits, loans, and deposits of interstate branches to its statistics for the state where branches' headquarters were located. Nevertheless, year-end results showed a continuing string of successful years. Oklahoma's banking industry in 1997 improved its return on assets by 10 percent while generating $370 million in net earnings. Commercial banks had an average return on assets of 1.16 percent for 1997, up from 1.06 percent in 1996. Only 2.5 percent of banks were unprofitable in 1997, down from 4.22 percent in 1996. Moreover, 68.7 percent of banks realized earnings gains in 1997 compared to 63.55 percent in the prior year. On December 31, total loans and leases stood at $19.1 billion, assets totaled $34.1 billion, deposits totaled $28 billion, and equity capital stood at $3.3 billion. The year ended with 320 banks statewide.[31]

Nobody was more pleased with bank performance in 1997 than OBA president Roger Beverage. Incredibly, Congress had managed to adjourn without enacting legislation that was harmful to banks. Measuring legislative success by a lack of action was not exactly great news, but as far as Beverage was concerned, it was certainly "better than a kick in the seats." In terms of a more active agenda in the nation's capital, Beverage heaped praise on Congress for finally getting around to addressing the thorny issues of credit unions and the unfair advantage they enjoyed vis-à-vis commercial banks. "For years, no one wanted to talk about taxing large credit unions," wrote Beverage in the *Oklahoma Banker.* "Now it's a subject that is being actively discussed in Washington and elsewhere." The OBA executive pointed to the five new charter applications filed between mid-1996 and year-end 1997 as evidence of renewed interest in banking. Noting that 1997 marked the OBA's hundredth anniversary, Beverage expressed gratitude that more bankers were getting involved in the politics of their profession: "As we begin the next century of operation, more bankers are involved in the Association, bringing a wide variety of thoughts and ideas to the table about how we can help you and your bank be more profitable."[32]

A snapshot of Oklahoma's economy in general and banking in particular in mid-1997 showed nary a trace of the troubles that had plagued banks in the 1980s. The average size of banks had increased from $68.7 million in 1991 to $113.9 million; commercial banks remained the dominant depository institutions, holding 80 percent of deposits (14 insured savings associations held another 10.8 percent and 102 credit unions held the remaining 9.2 percent); the state's employment growth rate was predicted surpass that of the nation, with 30,000 jobs expected to be created in 1998; and real per capita income was on track to increase by 2.4 percent. These and other positive indicators were enough for Professor Gary Simpson to predict continued economic growth. "We've settled into a pattern where we're earning a little over one percent return on assets, and I think we'll see that this year as well," he wrote in the 1998 *Oklahoma Economic Outlook*. Simpson's only concern was the rather remote possibility that the economic crisis in Asia might affect Oklahoma's economy. Given the extent of global integration, some effects were all but inevitable, but they were unlikely to show up until after 1998.[33]

As predicted, bank earnings remained strong in the first half of 1998. Oklahoma's 317 commercial banks (down from 326 in mid-1997) reported net income of $207 million. That total was 3 percent higher than the $201 million in bank earnings in first half of 1997. Declines in some categories were attributed to the FDIC's decision in 1997 to assign the holdings of interstate branches to the states where branches' headquarters were chartered. Changes in key indicators since the first quarter of 1998 were thus somewhat misleading in terms of measuring bank performance: total state bank assets stood at $34.9 billion (down $87 million); and deposits totaled $28.8 billion (down $446 million). Equity capital stood at $3.4 billion, and banks' return on equity was 12.11 percent.[34]

Although earnings in the fourth quarter of 1998 dropped from $87 million to $79 million, the state's 310 commercial banks (down from 320 a year earlier due to mergers) posted year-end net earnings of $386 million, up 4.9 percent from 1997. Meanwhile, total assets grew by 4.6 percent to $35.6 billion, and deposits increased by $713 million to $28.7 billion. Equity capital increased 5 percent in 1998 to $3.48 billion. An impressive 65.70 percent of banks reported earnings gains in 1998, while 4.85 percent of banks were unprofitable.[35]

The number of Oklahoma's commercial banks continued its downward slide to 305 by mid-1999. Still, net earnings topped $200 million. Comparisons to the first half of 1998 continued to indicate a healthy banking sector: assets totaled $38.84 billion, up from $34.9 billion; deposits totaled $30.7 billion, up from $28.8 billion; equity capital stood at $3.6 billion, up from $3.43 billion; and return on equity was 11.46 percent, down slightly from 12.25 percent in mid-1998. The percentage of banks reporting earnings gains dropped from 62.5 percent in mid-1998 to 46.6 percent in mid-1999, while 5.24 percent of banks were unprofitable compared to 3.47 percent the year before.[36]

The millennium ended on an upbeat note for the nation's banks. Commercial banks nationwide set a new earnings record for the eighth straight year, with $71.7 billion in profits. The industry's return on assets in 1999 also rose to an all-time high of 1.31 percent. Oklahoma's commercial banks, now numbering 300, reported profits in 1999 totaling $418 million. By comparison, profits in 1997 and 1998 were $368 million and $381 million, respectively. Assets totaled $39.6 billion (up 11 percent from 1998), and deposits reached $31 billion (up 8 percent from the prior year). Equity capital increased $124 million to $3.6 billion, and return on assets was 1.09 percent, down slightly from 1.11 percent in 1998.[37]

The news got even better in Oklahoma City, where urban renewal projects launched in 1993 under MAPS (Metropolitan Area Projects) were breathing life into a moribund downtown business district. Financed by a combination of new taxes and private dollars, the city's visionary capital improvement program ran the gamut of new and upgraded sports, recreation, entertainment, cultural, and convention facilities.[38] Credit for the bold initiative went to Mayor Ron Norick, the Greater Oklahoma City Chamber of Commerce, and business leaders such as Ken Townsend and Ray Ackerman. "Every company CEO was pulling all senior management into big meetings," recalled G. P. Johnson Hightower about the genesis of MAPS in the early 1990s. "MAPS passed in 1993, after a hell of a lot of lobbying," he continued. "So I'm saying, we still went into the early nineties in a desperate situation. And by the mid to late nineties, things were getting a little more fun, and business was getting better."[39]

Positive trends notwithstanding, clouds appeared on the horizon in early 2000 in the form of declining returns on assets. Weiss Ratings, Inc., reported in mid-2000 that banks' return on assets dropped from 1.32 percent in mid-1999 to 1.15 percent, the lowest level in four years. "This sudden drop in bank profitability . . . is especially worrisome considering the industry actually enjoyed a record profit during the first quarter," said Weiss Ratings chairman Martin Weiss. "This decline in profitability is yet another sign that the banking industry's good fortunes have peaked. Expect more declines in the months ahead." Several Oklahoma banks and thrifts bucked the trend and earned sterling marks from the ratings agency: the First National Bank and Trust of McAlester (ROA 1.43 percent, net income $2.9 million); Oklahoma Bank and Trust of Clinton (ROA 1.87 percent, net income $947,000); Fort Sill National Bank (ROA 1.92 percent, net income $1.5 million); First National Bank of Altus (ROA 1.17 percent, net income $918,000); and First National Bank and Trust of Chickasha (ROA 1.33 percent, net income $957,000). Other Oklahoma banks and thrifts were chagrined to find themselves categorized among the nation's weakest financial institutions: First National Bank of Nowata (ROA –2.78 percent, net income –$1.2 million); McCurtain County National Bank, Broken Bow (ROA –2.23 percent, net income –$962,000); Metrobank N.A., Oklahoma City (ROA –2.65 percent, net income –$505,000); First Bank of Cleveland (ROA –1.15 percent, net income –$131,000); and Community State Bank of Hennessey (ROA 0.72 percent, net income $68,000).[40]

Weiss's prediction of declining fortunes came at the tail end of what Oklahoma bankers recalled as a golden age of banking. "In the golden age of the nineties, banks made money," said finance professor Gary Simpson. "They were profitable. And I am not saying it was easy for them, or handed to them on a platter. I think they earned it, because they had become much more cost-conscious, much more bottom-line conscious, much more analytical. And then, of course, they had diversification. Almost everybody had branches by then. So you had some diversification to help even things out." In terms of banks' loan portfolios, diversification meant less dependence on businesses and more dependence on real estate. "For somebody like me, and for people who had been working in banks, the movement to real estate lending was stunning," continued Simpson. "A few years ago, banks tended to think of their big customers as businesses. They were financing commerce. Now, they were financing real estate. If you look at the numbers, you'll see real estate is the dominant category. In the nineties, I think banks used that concept to become more profitable."[41]

While many bankers were basking in the glow of a golden age, Oklahoma's largest industry—agriculture—was suffering from an economic double whammy: drought and low commodity prices. These ancient scourges were creating a domino effect that was undermining the agricultural economy and threatening real estate values and profits on Main Street. In August 1998, the FDIC signaled its alarm by issuing a letter imploring bankers to work closely with their agricultural customers. "In supervising institutions impacted by the drought, the FDIC will take into consideration the unusual circumstances these institutions face," wrote FDIC director Nicholas J. Ketcha, Jr., in a letter to FDIC-supervised institutions. "The FDIC recognizes that efforts to work with borrowers in communities under stress can be consistent with safe and sound banking practices as well as in the public interest." As of late August, the state had lost an estimated $3 billion in wages and revenues. The state agricultural department was predicting a total of $2 billion or more in losses to Oklahoma's agricultural economy.[42]

"Everyone is short on money," said Todd Huckabay, president of the Bank of the Wichitas in Snyder. The dreaded domino effect was coming into play in his part of the state as declining prices for cattle and wheat wreaked havoc on the real estate market. Down the road in Altus, Dennis Vernon of the First National Bank was most concerned about the cotton and peanut crops. Problems on the farm were impacting most everybody in farm-related businesses, including fuel and fertilizer suppliers, mechanics, and auto dealers. And like Huckabay, Vernon was beginning to see a downturn in the real estate markets. Far to the east, problems stemming from low commodity prices and a shortage of feed for livestock were exacerbated by forest fires. "Right now, we're trying to help our ranchers find money to pay for hay," said Antlers banker and former OBA chairman Steve Burrage. Burrage and his agricultural customers were counting on a hay hotline established by the governor to procure hay at little or no cost. Other farm products that suffered as the drought wore relentlessly on included wheat, peaches, soybeans, and corn.[43]

Inevitably, the drought's effects were manifested in defeatist attitudes and a corresponding slackening of demand for loans. "Yes, there is a definite effect (of the drought) to not have people out this summer," said Jeff Morris with Landmark Bank in Ada. "Because it is so hot and dry, we're seeing less activity, no boat loans or other summer loans." Given the scope of the problem, bankers and their customers were grateful for any help that might come their way. As far as some folks were concerned during the grueling summer of '98, the best way for the government to help was to get out of the way. "We applaud the FDIC for their recent actions," said Scott Dewald, executive director of the Oklahoma Cattlemen's Association. "We view this as the federal regulator getting out of the way and allowing banks to do what they do best: help people, producers and our entire economy."[44]

Effects of the drought persisted well into 1999. Jack Carson, information officer for the Oklahoma Department of Agriculture, insisted that commodity prices had not been this low since World War II. Wheat yields in northwestern Oklahoma were up, but a combination of low prices and invasive weeds was forcing producers to rely on government subsidies to prop up their operations. Larry DeWitt, chair of the OBA's Agriculture Committee and an assistant vice president at Farmers Exchange Bank in Cherokee, expressed mixed feelings about subsidies. Even though they enabled farmers to make it through hard times, they rubbed against the grain of rural values. "We're lived with subsidies since the 1940s and I think there has to be something else," said DeWitt. "I think management is a key. Producers must be able to control overhead costs to increase or realize a profit." For many northwestern farmers, "something else" was other grain crops such as soybeans, milo, and cotton—that is, anything that might help farmers pay down their loans and keep their land. The silver lining in mid-1999 was a rising price for cattle. That came as good news to Doug Tippens, executive vice president of American Heritage Bank in El Reno, who doubled as a rancher. "Cattle are the only bright spot in the business right now," said Tippens. "The cattle deal is how we're going to make it out of this thing."[45]

Rising beef prices were not enough to lift agriculture out of the doldrums. According to the American Bankers Association's *1999 Farm Credit Survey Report,* banks were using government loan guarantees and were borrowing money from the Federal Home Loan Banks to keep farmers and ranchers in business. At the same time, banks were working with their customers to restructure debt, provide credit for operating expenses, and offer financial services that were sorely needed in rural communities. For the purposes of its survey, the ABA defined farm banks as those with more than $2.5 million in farm production and farm real estate loans or more than 50 percent of their loan portfolios in farm lending. As evidence of the close relationship between banking and agriculture, 98 percent of the 481 farm banks surveyed asserted that they did not turn down any creditworthy applications due to lack of loanable funds.[46]

Inevitably, the combination of drought and Oklahoma's infamous winds spawned what farmers feared most: wildfires. By October 2000, the Oklahoma Farm Bureau estimated that more than 100,000 acres had been scorched. As revenue losses soared past $600 million, ranchers searched in vain for grazing land. Scott Bulling, the bureau's director of commodity marketing services, broadcast a frantic plea for anyone with grazing land for horses and cattle to contact him so that messages could be posted online. But for some farmers, and even cattlemen, who had glimpsed light at the end of the tunnel in 1999, it was too little and too late. Larry DeWitt claimed that he knew several farmers who had chosen to exit agriculture altogether. "My customers depend so much on cattle grazing wheat that if they don't have it—they don't have a farm," he said. "Many ranchers are choosing to get out while they still can, before they start eating equity." Those who toughed it out could count on government subsidies and loan guarantees. But as long as commodity prices were tumbling and energy costs were rising, a permanent solution to problems on the farm remained elusive. "It's hard to say where we'll go from here," concluded DeWitt. "Many farmers just want to get through this harvest. It's inevitable that we're going to lose some farmers, but some should make if through. These will be the ones with little debt."[47]

Roger Beverage's guarded optimism that Congress might one day enable banks to compete more effectively with credit unions was premature. Well into the late 1990s, bankers across the land railed against a tax code that enabled the nation's twelve thousand credit unions to pay nary a cent in federal taxes. Building on what amounted to a federal subsidy, credit unions had extraordinary latitude to woo customers away from banks with high rates on savings accounts and low interest rates on loans and credit cards. "This issue is about *fairness* in that competitive arena," declared a belligerent Roger Beverage in February 1998. "Think about it: if you paid just $1 in federal income tax in 1997, you paid more that all 12,000 credit unions combined."[48] Another way to look at it was that the average bank in 1995 paid $500,000 in federal income taxes. And credit unions? Zero.

A report issued jointly by the Credit Union National Association (CUNA) and the Consumer Federation of America (CFA) added fuel to the fire with the claim that consumers stood to gain "billions" overall by taking their business away from banks. According to the report, the gap between bank and credit union credit card rates was so large that shifting balances from bank to credit union credit cards would lower annual interest payments by about $8 billion. What is more, without losing their federal deposit insurance protection, savers could earn up to $16 billion more in annual interest on their savings deposits. The American Bankers Association issued a heated rebuttal to the CUNA/CFA report and offered statistics of its own, but to little avail.[49] Not for the first time and certainly not for the last, bankers felt shortchanged by the legislative process, and they were left to fight a rearguard action to defend their industry from what they perceived as unfair competition.

Competition from nonbank banks and unfriendly legislation were not all that bankers had to worry about at century's end. Memories of the golden age of banking notwithstanding, newspaper headlines in the 1990s reveal an astonishing variety and alarming extent of bank fraud. A random sample of headline-grabbing cases in the *Oklahoman* is by no means scientific, but it does serve to reveal the flip side of technologically driven convenience in opportunities to scam the system.

Our sample begins in Tulsa in the spring of 1993 when Jerry N. Wood, a senior vice president for Shearson Lehman Brothers, was charged with obtaining checks meant for his clients and depositing them in his personal checking account. Over a three-year period, the duplicitous Mr. Wood allegedly deposited $1.24 million in his account at the Bank of Oklahoma. State senator Penny Williams (D-Tulsa) was one of two dozen clients bilked by their stockbroker. She lost $162,000; other clients' losses ranged from $10,000 to $179,000. "Shearson has been made a victim of Wood's actions," declared attorney Jim Hodges.[50] Similar shenanigans were uncovered on the other side of the state when Woodward investment broker Ronald M. Harris pled guilty to bank fraud by misusing up to $1 million of his clients' money. Facing up to thirty years behind bars and a $1 million fine, Harris admitted to making unauthorized deposits.[51] Harris had not served very much of his five-year sentence when he was ordered to pay more than $800,000 in damages to Vada Dressen, a widow from Mooreland whose husband's retirement funds had been misappropriated. In her civil lawsuit, Dressen alleged that Harris had converted $49,000 of her late husband's retirement account for his own use. An investigation into Harris's modus operandi revealed that he had preyed on vulnerable clients and bilked them of their retirement funds and life savings through church and community ties.[52]

The Bank of Oklahoma in Tulsa made the news again when Roy L. Corn, a former Texaco financial analyst, was busted for depositing oil company checks in his own account at a BOK branch. The embezzlement began in May 1992 when Corn opened an account under the auspices of the Texaco Refining and Marketing Softball League and listed himself as the sole signer. Corn launched his crime spree by writing relatively small checks to himself. The first three totaled less than $7,000. But after a few months, he cast caution to the winds and entered the big leagues (not the sporting variety) with a single Texaco check on October 16, 1992, in the amount of $45,652.99. Clearly not one to display gratitude to a generous employer, Corn was only two credit hours shy of earning his degree in accounting, paid for by Texaco, when his scheme unraveled in April 1996. Federal agents calculated the bank's total loss at $448,910. By then, Corn was unemployed and living in San Francisco. He broke down crying as he pled guilty before U.S. district judge Sven Erik Holmes.[53]

Mayhem struck Christiansen Aviation in Tulsa in the form of bank fraud perpetrated by the owner's office manager, Linda Carol Priest. According to the indictment charging her on more than one hundred counts of bank fraud, the scheme worked something like this: Priest, who doubled as the company's bookkeeper, paid checks to vendors, and when they were returned, she destroyed them. Then, Priest created duplicate vendor payment checks for each vendor and deposited those checks into two accounts that she held at Spirit Bank in Sapulpa and another account at Liberty Bank and Trust Company in Tulsa.

So how could someone deposit checks into her own accounts when the payees were clearly listed? That's what owner Bill Christiansen wanted to know. "It's total incompetency on the banks' part," he fumed. "It's unbelievable that she did it time and time and time again." Even more galling was the fact that the bank failed to catch her; it was only when another employee tipped him off that Christensen accused Priest of embezzlement. In his bank's defense (but not, apparently, to Christiansen's satisfaction), Spirit Bank president Fred Gibson offered a candid assessment of modern banking: "The modern trend in banking is convenience and speed for the customer's benefit," he said. "We process literally thousands of checks every day. With the bigger banks, it's in the millions. For anyone to think we can look at every single signature when there are 10 cars lined up in the drive-through lane, come on."[54]

Chicanery of a different sort played out in Muskogee when J. N. Flint, a former Coal County commissioner, pled guilty to a federal charge of bank fraud while his son, J. Don Flint, pled guilty to growing seven hundred marijuana plants. The elder Flint admitted to defrauding Farmers State Bank of Allen by using cattle as collateral for a loan, even though his son had pledged the same cattle as collateral for a loan from First American Bank in Stonewall. Farmers State Bank lost $45,500 as a result of the fraud. The father-son team's multiple transgressions came to light after Sheriff Tony Taylor and state drug agents took a helicopter ride and spotted marijuana plants growing on the Flints' farm. The Flints were arrested on August 15, 1997. On the bright side, the younger Flint had a green thumb. Sheriff Taylor swore that some of his plants were eighteen feet tall.[55]

It was cars, and not cattle, that led an Ardmore auto dealer down the road to perdition. Between December 1996 and May 1997, James Dan McCaskill received loans from Exchange Bank of Ardmore for cars he did not own. It turned out that the cars actually belonged to employees and another car dealership. A plea agreement showed that McCaskill defrauded the bank out of approximately $260,000. As of late 1998, McCaskill was making restitution and was free on bond while a presentence investigation was under way.[56]

Two California entrepreneurs set the standard for audacity by setting up a phantom bank in Anadarko. First Americans Bank was shoehorned into two rooms between a smoke shop and a bingo hall at the Apache Tribe's community center. Advertising their bank as an "on-shore, off-shore" bank, the principals—Ronald G. Sparks of Sonora and Owen K. Stephenson of Sausalito—promised to hide transactions from federal snoops by operating under a charter from the sovereign Apache Tribe of Oklahoma. Before the duo's duplicity came to light, people nationwide deposited more than $7 million in the operation. Even the bank's president, Brian Condon of Orlando, Florida, became a victim of sorts when he was hired to run the bank in June 1997. "There was no bank," declared the bewildered moneyman when the case made its way to trial. "I was hired to run the software and promote the façade of a bank." Rather than becoming a source of capital that could then be loaned to tribal citizens, depositors' money wound up in accounts at a bank in Lawton that were controlled by (no surprise here) Sparks and Stephenson. Denton A. Harper of Cyril, whose lack of a high school diploma and dearth of banking experience were no impediment to becoming the tribe's banking commissioner, and fellow tribal official Martin Bitseedy signed the charter in 1997. Harper's radar went on high alert when funding failed to materialize, and he resigned his position less than a week after signing the charter. Stephenson urged him to reconsider, insisting that there was money to be made on the ground floor of First Americans Bank, but to no avail. "That's OK," Stephenson said, "we have your signature and we'll just use somebody else."[57]

The case ground on into 2000. Accounts indicate that depositors in First Americans Bank were dissatisfied with the U.S. banking and tax systems, and they were delighted when bank principals did not require social security numbers and other minutiae representing an overreaching government. The SEC found and promptly froze about $2.1 million in assets that were deposited in Local Oklahoma Bank (formerly Citizens Bank) as well as other banks and brokerage institutions. Frozen assets were used to reimburse victims of the swindle, who were identified through the criminal case. Justice prevailed when Sparks was sentenced to eleven years and three months in prison and Condon was sentenced to 120 days of home confinement, followed by five years' probation. As of April 2000, Stephenson was on the lam, his whereabouts unknown.[58] There was no word on how depositors felt about federal busybodies who had recovered as least some of their money.

Sheila A. Williston of Miami was indicted by a grand jury in July 1999 for altering her royalty checks by $50,800 and then cashing them. She received the checks as a member of the Cheyenne Tribe, deposited them in the First National Bank of Miami, and then withdrew the funds. The indictment revealed Williston as a party girl—she spent $5,000 on cocaine and heroin, $3,000 on a trip to Branson, Missouri, and $1,000 on liquor.[59]

A witches' brew of charges, including bank fraud, concealing assets in a 1996 federal bankruptcy, money laundering, and perjury were brought against John and Mary Ann Adams, former owners of a farm equipment company in Medford. A grand jury alleged that the couple defrauded the Bank of Kremlin by hiding more than $90,000 in assets when property was sold to repay the Adamses' debts. John was charged separately with nine counts of concealing bankruptcy assets, including firearms and land. Both husband and wife faced up to thirty years in prison if convicted of bank fraud.[60]

It was bankers' turn to reap the whirlwind when two conspirators pled guilty to bank fraud charges and a third pled guilty to a single charge of making false entries in a bank record. The primary culprits were John Hudson, the former majority owner of banks in Tipton, Hammon, Blanchard, Willow, and Granite; and Jack Butler Rackley, the former president and board chairman of the Tipton Bank and former director of banks in Hammon and Blanchard. The third member of the trio, Larry Baresel, was Hudson's law partner and a former director of banks in Tipton and Hammon. A twenty-two-count indictment charged the southern Oklahoma bankers with participating in a scheme in which straw men were used to obtain loans benefitting Hudson through banks that he controlled. According to assistant U.S. attorney Joe Heaton, the crimes carried a maximum of five years in prison and a $250,000 fine.[61]

Sports fans were disturbed to discover that Terry Miller, a 1970s Heisman Trophy candidate from Oklahoma State University, pled guilty to bank fraud in Muskogee. The former Cowboy running back, whose subsequent NFL career included stints in Buffalo and Seattle, made no attempt to elude his charges. Standing before U.S. district judge Frank Seay in Muskogee federal court, Miller apologized to the people he had hurt and promised to do everything in his power to atone for his misdeeds. "He is truly one of the bravest clients I've ever represented," said Miller's attorney, Steve Stidham, after Miller was sentenced to two years in prison and ordered to pay $179,000 in restitution to the bank in McAlester that he had defrauded. "That probably comes from facing NFL linebackers for five years."[62]

Lola Faye Denton, the owner of an exotic wildlife park southwest of Elk City, was indicted on six felony counts, including making false statements to Washita State Bank in Burns Flat and bankruptcy fraud. Her park, Bear Creek Wildlife, Inc., was created in 1989, and it afforded western Oklahomans an opportunity to get up close and personal with zebras, ostriches, and other creatures not normally seen in those environs. Their opportunity was short-lived, as Denton and her company declared separate bankruptcies in 1993. According to the indictment, Denton lied about her assets when she received two loans in 1990 totaling $630,000 from the aforementioned bank. Perhaps her affection for African fauna skewed her assessment of their value. Among those assets was a fictitious person who purportedly owed her the hefty sum of $250,000. She was also accused of diverting more than $87,000 from her business loans to personal use.[63]

Our unscientific, yet illuminating sample of bank fraud ends where it began, in Tulsa, with the dreary tale of a funeral home executive gone astray. In October 2000, Elijah Thomas Dunlap, Jr., faced a twenty-three-count federal indictment that included allegations of wire fraud, bank fraud, and committing fraud that included interstate travel. Dunlap's troubles began in 1994 when, as chief executive officer of Dunlap Funeral Services, he had entered into agreements to buy several funeral homes as well as prepaid funeral trust accounts from three other funeral services. During ensuing negotiations with companies in Massachusetts and Texas to finance the deal, officials were disturbed to find that Dunlap had declared bankruptcy several years earlier. Understandably cautious, they asked him to pony up $400,000 of his own money to help fund the acquisitions. With "great humility and embarrassment," Dunlap admitted that he repaid a loan from Stillwater National Bank and Trust Company by causing the transfer of more than $400,000 (no coincidence here) from an account that included prepaid funeral benefit funds. He further admitted to using prepaid funeral benefit trust funds to purchase a $381,249.53 certificate of deposit from another bank and taking $72,000 out of a Stillwater National Bank account without the permission of his company's board of directors or the people whose funeral trust funds were used. Dunlap's fortunes sank even further when he was accused of forging the signature of his father, E. T. Dunlap, in 1997 to obtain a loan. Clearly, whatever lessons his father had to offer in the area of moral integrity had fallen on deaf ears. For twenty years, the elder Dunlap served as chancellor for the Oklahoma State Regents for Higher Education. Dunlap's attorney, Stephen Jones, expected his client to serve three to four years in prison.[64]

To quantify the problem of check fraud in late 2000, Brent Yarbrough, president of the Oklahoma chapter of the International Association of Financial Crime Investigators, cited federal studies (as figures for Oklahoma were unavailable) to offer some sobering statistics. Nationwide, check fraud cost $58 billion in 1995. That number rose to $89 billion in 1999; estimates for 2000 were approaching $101 billion. The American Bankers Association projected a 2.5 percent annual growth rate in check fraud at the outset of the new millennium. Yarbrough blamed easy access to sophisticated computer and printing technologies from giant retailers such as Wal-Mart and small office supply stores for the upswing in check fraud. "Imagination is the limit to check fraud anymore," he said.[65]

By mid-1997, Oklahoma's rural banks were outpacing their urban counterparts in requiring thumbprints from noncustomers before cashing their checks. The Oklahoma Bankers Association began promoting thumbprinting in 1996. According to the OBA's Ryan Humphrey, banks were adopting the technology at the rate of about one bank per week. "Banks that enact this program are showing their customers that they are doing everything they can to provide security and safety to their checking accounts," said Humphrey, who estimated Oklahoma's annual losses to check fraud at about $10 million. "It's real easy to get a fake ID and steal someone's checks, and the real purpose of this is to deter fraud."[66]

An indication of how hard it was, and is, to measure check fraud comes from comparing Brent Yarbrough's estimates (above) with the findings of a 1997 survey conducted by the American Bankers Association. Whereas the government studies that Yarbrough cited put damages in the tens of billions of dollars in the mid-to-late 1990s and careening north of $100 billion in 2000, ABA surveys determined that the country's commercial banks were being defrauded at the rate of about $1 billion per year—not exactly small change, but certainly nothing on the scale that the federal government was reporting. Large banks ($5 billion or more in assets) were the hardest hit by check fraud in 1997, and they predicted an annual increase of about 17.5 percent in fraudulent activity.[67] Again, the problem was clearly getting worse, but at that predicted rate, it would have taken many years for check fraud to reach the proportions reported in government studies. To further muddy the waters, the *Oklahoma Banker* reported in February 1999 that check fraud on the national level had grown into a $12.6 billion problem. Everyone agreed on at least two things: the extraordinary ingenuity of fraud practitioners; and employee training as the most effective method of curtailing their activities. What everyone could not agree on, however, was the extent and growth of the problem. One suspects underreporting in ABA surveys and overreporting in federal studies. The truth was perhaps somewhere in between. But no matter how the numbers shook out, it was not good news for bankers.

Whatever the extent of bank fraud and its rate of growth, one thing was certain: bank employees ignored it at their peril. For Sources Technologies president Miles Busby, high-tech ammo certainly needed to be in a bank's arsenal, but nothing could replace tellers as the first and most critical line of defense. Topping his list of the ten most important internal and external security measures was good old-fashioned vigilance: "Train tellers to look at the check, not at the person presenting the check. The check, not the person, is the item to be verified."[68]

While con artists were plying their trade in ever more ingenious ways, old-fashioned bank robbers were making a comeback. According to figures released by the FBI in the summer of 2000, robberies statewide had increased by 50 percent since 1999. Of twenty-one robberies committed in 2000, fifteen were perpetrated in the Oklahoma City metro area. FBI special agent Gary Johnson said that the concentration of robberies in Oklahoma City stemmed from a crime ring. "Obviously, there's a much larger increase within Oklahoma City than that which has occurred throughout the state," said Johnson. "Fortunately, we've been able to track down many of the suspects in connection with the robberies." On an even brighter note, nobody had been hurt, thanks in part to special training by FBI agents and heightened awareness on the part of employees. As was the case with bank fraud, experts claimed that high-tech deterrence against theft was not much use if employees were oblivious to their surroundings. "In every area of potential security risk, the key factor is awareness among bank employees," said FBI special agent Chuck Choney, who conducted training sessions for employees. First Fidelity Bank of Oklahoma City security officer Merleta Motley credited FBI training packets with helping employees get through a heist safely when her bank was robbed in April 2000. Dennis Murphy, senior vice president of BancFirst in McCloud, said that his bank would utilize visitor logs and a "temporarily closed" sign to help protect employees and patrons in the event of a robbery. "We're committed to doing everything we can to make sure every person that walks into our bank is safe and secure for the duration of their visit," he said.[69]

In the 1980s, the mouse that roared heralded the end of Penn Square Bank and the beginning of banking troubles unseen since the 1930s. A decade later, the mouse was no longer roaring. Instead, it had latched itself to a computer. And then, everything changed.

But not right away. When the Internet first came on the scene and bankers had to make room on their desks for unwieldy personal computers, they were not sure what to make of them. As late as mid-1995, David Whittaker, vice president and assistant director of legal services at the Bank of Oklahoma, N.A., in Tulsa, thought that the future of electronic banking was in commercial networks. As an America Online subscriber, he was dazzled by gadgetry that enabled him to access legal documents and communicate with peers across the nation. Because of security concerns, Whittaker doubted that customers could ever be convinced to transfer money and manage their credit cards online. Across the state in Guymon, Brian Anderson at City National Bank and Trust Company opined that the Internet might be an ideal tool for large banks to use to advertise their services, but that was about it. "As far as a small-town community bank goes, I don't think it will be useful at all (for advertising services and performing transactions)," he said. "For the large ones—Boatmen's, Bank of Oklahoma, etc.—it will be a very important tool." Anderson went on to say that many of his banker friends objected to online services because their older customers wanted nothing to do with computers. Then again, baby boomers were in their peak earning years and might be more likely to experiment with new technologies.

"And that's great," he said before adding with a hint of prescience, "but wait until *their* kids get older."[70]

What a difference a few months makes. In the spring of 1996, a communications company in McLean, Virginia, estimated that about 240 banks in North America, and perhaps 500 worldwide, were offering online services.[71] At about the same time, 93 percent of banks responding to a Grant Thornton LLP survey of 750 community banks believed that they needed to employ technology to remain competitive in the new millennium.[72] Perhaps the only surprise was that 7 percent remained unconvinced. To measure the flip side of online banking, the Raddon Financial Group conducted a nationwide survey of consumers and financial-service providers. Results showed an enormous potential for banking with a personal computer and an increasing awareness of the virtually limitless capabilities offered by ATM cards. After a free, three-month trial, 73 percent of those surveyed said they would pay a monthly fee for PC banking with a bill payment function. Meanwhile, *USA Today* reported that people without computers might soon have devices allowing Internet access through their televisions. Companies in the race to provide Internet access via TV were targeting the estimated two-thirds of American households that had televisions, but no computers.[73]

In May 1998, the *Oklahoma Banker* cited U.S. Department of Commerce estimates that 4.5 million households were using online banking. By 2000, that number was expected to skyrocket to 16 million. A revolution was in the making, and as the new millennium approached, it commanded an increasing amount of ink in the *Oklahoma Banker*. Chuck Hall, executive vice president of the Exchange National Bank and Trust Company of Perry, captured the zeitgeist of the late 1990s in language that Oklahomans could understand: "I truly feel like I have a sense of what pioneers felt like when they headed out west for a new beginning. It's exciting, in my opinion, to live in this day and age when technologies are developing so rapidly. The success stories will be from those banks that grasp these new technically advanced products and put them to work in their market."[74]

A sampling of Oklahoma banks that were jumping on the bandwagon reveals an impressive array of innovative initiatives aimed at harnessing the new technology to enhance customer service. Hall expected to attract five hundred Internet banking customers by the end of 1998. Basic services were free, but customers were charged a small fee for the bill-pay feature. Jeff Bates, assistant vice president of Exchange Bank and Trust Company in Ardmore, set up his bank's website and helped organize Internet demonstrations to the community. Such was their success that he hoped to make them monthly events. "Our image is one of 'out front' in the industry," said the tech-savvy Bates. "We have had more interest in the bank since we got on-line [sic]. There is no question that it has opened doors." Terry Almon, senior vice president of Stillwater National Bank and Trust Company's Tulsa branch, said that her bank was testing the waters by using its website primarily for marketing. Plans called for offering online services at no charge to customers. "We realize that our competition is not down the street anymore," she said in April 1996. "It's where the best services are, whether that be in New York City, San Francisco, or Tokyo."[75] Or maybe, Tulsa.

The First National Bank in Heavener's website was unique in that it was designed and maintained by students from the local high school. Security National Bank and Trust Company of Norman's website featured a tool that customers could use to apply for credit cards. The First National Bank of Pryor laid claim to being the first bank in the country to offer online aircraft financing. UMB Financial Corporation, the holding company for UMB Oklahoma Bank in Oklahoma City, provided an interactive planning tool called the "Investor Profile Calculator," which targeted web surfers searching for investment vehicles to suit their ages, goals, and tolerance for risk.[76]

In a state where coming in first has always carried a certain cachet, RCB Bank in Claremore earned distinction as a pioneer in offering true Internet service, meaning that customers could access their accounts via the Internet without special software and without dialing a telephone number. RCB Bank's history goes back to January 1936, when it opened in Claremore as Rogers County Bank. The bank ended its first year with a profit and repeated that performance every year through century's end. "That's my bank!" was adopted as the official slogan in the 1970s and came to signify the company's defining characteristics: Relationships; Community; and Boldness. In 1990, branching outside Rogers County occasioned the name change to RCB Bank.[77]

RCB Bank president Ted McGuire was not sure that Internet service would bring a short-term payoff, but he knew about his bank's reputation for boldness, and he was sure that online banking was the wave of the future. "While this may not be a big money-maker right now, as time goes by, more and more people are going to want to use this technology," said McGuire. "We are looking to the future. In the years to come RCB is going to be on the leading edge of this technology." Interviewed for a March 1997 issue of the *Oklahoma Banker,* CFO Tom Bayless said that the new service, Safenet Home Banking, allowed customers to check account balances, reconcile accounts, find out if checks had cleared, transfer money between accounts, and even view imaged checks online. Before going public with the service, RCB Bank used its employees as guinea pigs to identify problems and work out bugs. Even when customers were allowed to open accounts, RCB Bank held off on a big marketing push to make absolutely sure that no unpleasant surprises were in store for its pioneering customers. Bayless expected about 5 percent of RCB Bank customers to sign up at first. "But next year, that number will probably jump to 20 percent, and in 10 years, who knows?"[78]

BancFirst launched its Internet initiative in the fall of 1997 and, after testing it with customers, unveiled its service in the spring of 1998. In keeping with its extraordinary commitment to employee education, BancFirst held training sessions across the state to inform employees of the features and benefits of the bank's online services. Executive vice president Jay Hannah said that the bank planned to make mortgage calculators and financial planning services available via the Internet. "I think the challenge for bankers will be to determine additional features of interest to our customers," said Hannah.[79]

Another challenge was the safety and security of transactions, and it was met head on with a combination of firewalls and passwords. Cookies—not the baked variety, but rather, electronic information-gathering devices aimed at identifying computers being used—posed a particularly insidious threat to unwary citizens of the Internet, dubbed "netizens" in online vernacular. And of course, there was always good, old-fashioned vigilance, just as important in cyberspace as it was in detecting malfeasance in the office and thwarting robberies in the lobby. According to Terry Almon, Stillwater National Bank cautioned its customers to check their online statements for unusual transactions that might indicate an unauthorized user. "We've not had a case (of intrusion) yet," said Almon, "but we're certainly keeping an eye on it."[80]

According to a study conducted by the OCC, bank websites permitting online banking transactions grew from an estimated 103 at the end of 1997 to 258 by June 1998, an annualized rate of more than 300 percent. Even so, the number of banks offering transactional services remained small, with about 4 percent of all banks, and 6 percent of national banks, pushing the technology envelope. Trends suggested that 15 percent of the nation's banks would be offering transactional Internet services by the end of 1999. The banks that offered online banking services accounted for 40 percent of all banking assets, and national banks offering online banking accounted for 61 percent of all national bank assets. This reflected the sizeable number of large banks with online services. Twenty-seven banks with more than $10 billion in assets—42 percent of the total for that asset group—offered transactional Internet banking services. Customers, however, remained wary. The same OCC report showed that only 4 percent of households conducted their banking business online, even though about 40 percent of bank customers held accounts at banks with Internet services. Given the discrepancy between users and the availability of services, it did not take much imagination to see enormous potential in online banking.[81] A central tenet of sociology was at work: first comes the technology; and then, like ripples building to a tidal wave, comes the paradigm shift in cultural acceptance.

Online banking gained traction with a subsequent OCC report based on information gleaned from national bank examiners in August and September 1999. The verdict was in: banks with online services were typically more profitable than those without. The only exceptions were the smallest institutions. Like the early bird that gets the worm, early adopters of new technologies found validation for their pioneering ways in their bottom lines. Jonathan Fiechter, the OCC's senior deputy comptroller for economic policy and international affairs, put it this way: "While it is too early for Internet services to have much of an effect on bank performance measures, it does appear that banks that were early adopters of Internet banking have adopted a more aggressive business strategy, including an emphasis on fee-generating activities." Although the number of households using online banking remained relatively small, businesses with an eye on cost savings were making the switch in significant numbers.[82]

Leading the charge toward cultural acceptance of new technologies at the turn of the new century were people aged twenty-one to thirty-six, known collectively as "Generation X." So-called Gen Xers tended to be far more technologically savvy than their parents' generation, and they had no time to waste. To gain so much as a nanosecond of their famously short attention spans, marketing professionals learned to disseminate fast-paced, MTV-style messages that often had a surreal quality about them. But for purveyors of online banking services, learning new tricks was worth the effort, because none bought into nontraditional financial services with more gusto than Gen Xers. "You have to pull the segment by age and make certain assumptions," said Jan Garrett, marketing officer for Guaranty Bank and Trust Company of Oklahoma City. "These people are smarter, better educated and keen on technology. We also know that convenience and efficiency are very important to them, and we're not just talking about an ATM. You must have an array of services available." Oklahoma City businessman Tom Loy, then director of the (Jack T.) Conn Graduate School of Community Banking at Oklahoma City University, knew from classroom experience that Gen Xers were in the vanguard of online banking: "There are people who do not want to set foot in a traditional bank. These are e-people, they want to do everything electronically—video tellers, Internet access to their accounts and the like."[83]

Guymon banker Brian Anderson got it partially right. Baby boomers' kids did indeed get older. When they did, they spawned a revolution.

During the countdown to the year 2000, fears mounted that the revolution might be derailed by a colossal software glitch. The problem boiled down to an oversight: in their laser-like focus on pushing the technological envelope, software pioneers forgot to make allowances for the twenty-first century. As the years passed, people who thought about such things realized that computer systems might not know what to do when "19" morphed into "20." By the late 1990s, arcane concerns that techies shared around water coolers and in their computer labs were beginning to seep into very public conversations. Software had become the engine that ran the world, and a glitch of this magnitude could no longer be overlooked. A full-blown crisis was looming whose scope was anybody's guess. Expectations ran the gamut from mild disruptions to the end of civilization as we knew it. A catchy acronym—Y2K—was on everybody's lips. People across the globe flipped over their calendars with trepidation, fearing that the inexorable march of time was about to push civilization off a cliff.

As software engineers whose predecessors had unwittingly unleashed a monster came to the rescue, Y2K preparation became something of a growth industry. In a pace that became more frenzied with each passing day, institutions of all sizes and degrees of complexity girded for battle with the dreaded millennium bug. Federal agencies required banks to prepare analyses of Y2K's anticipated impact on their operations. Untold millions of dollars were spent and gallons of ink spilled to prepare for the new century. A Red Cross Y2K checklist, published in the *Oklahoman* on December 10, 1999, and replicated in one form or another around the world, gave a hint of the gathering storm and the anxiety that people felt in the closing hours of the second millennium:

- Stock disaster supplies to last several days.
- Have some extra cash or traveler's checks on hand.
- Keep your automobile gas tank above half-full.
- Plan to use alternative cooking devices. But don't use flames or grills inside.
- Have extra blankets, coats, hats and gloves.
- Have flashlights, batteries.
- Be prepared to relocate to a shelter for warmth.
- If you use a generator, connect items directly to it; don't connect it to your home's electrical system.

The Red Cross checklist foretold mayhem to come. All the more interesting, then, to reflect on two caveats in the same article: don't bunker in yet; and by all means, be reasonable. "We don't feel it's going to be that big of a deal," said Gary Jackson, executive assistant to the state's Y2K task force chairman, General Steve Cortright of the Oklahoma National Guard. "There may be a few glitches but nothing of any magnitude." Debbie Hampton, deputy executive director for the American Red Cross of Central Oklahoma, simply asked her fellow citizens to check on their elderly neighbors: "Just be a good neighbor, invite them to your home (that night) so they are not alone."[84]

Thankfully, the years of preparation paid off. Most folks were indeed reasonable, although some were a bit sheepish to find that all the sound and fury signified, well, not much. It is comforting to think that a few people invited frightened neighbors over on December 31, 1999, either to celebrate the New Year/Millennium or to brace for crashing computers and chaos of biblical proportions.

The year 2000 dawned with a few technological hiccups, but nothing on the scale of the Apocalypse. Life continued in its hurried and fretful pace, and Y2K faded, as such things are wont to do, to a shady corner of our collective memory until it vanished altogether after 9/11. Now, *that* was a game changer.

For Tom Loy, the end of the millennium was a time to look not to the future, but to history, and to ponder its lessons at a less frenzied clip. As director of OCU's Conn Graduate School of Community Banking and an instructor at banking seminars nationwide, Loy fretted about Gen Xers' dearth of historical consciousness, and he aimed to do something about it by including banking and financial history in his curricula.

"I recently posed the following short oral quiz to the students at several banking schools," wrote the veteran teacher in a 1995 article in the *Oklahoma Banker.* "(1) What was the Penn Square debacle? (2) What happened on October 6, 1979? (3) What were WPPSS ('Whoops') bonds? (4) What happened to the First Pennsylvania Bank in 1980? (5) What caused the S&L crisis of the 1980s?"[85]

The results were not encouraging. Ninety percent of students from all over the United States had never heard of Penn Square Bank. Nobody knew what transpired on October 6, 1979. About 20 percent of Loy's students knew what WPPSS bonds were—an encouraging sign, to be sure, but perhaps less so when you consider that these people were investment *professionals.* One of two hundred students knew something about First Penny (as First Pennsylvania Bank was known among the banking cognoscenti), and that person (a male) just happened to be from (you guessed it) Pennsylvania. As for the savings and loan crisis, all Loy got were blank stares and "highly uneducated guesses" about the causes of one of the most significant financial events in American history.

"In total shock, I terminated the quizzes," wrote a discouraged Loy.[86]

So were tech-savvy but history-deficient Gen Xers to blame for their lack of historical consciousness? Should they be summarily punished, perhaps by confiscating their computers and cell phones (no iPads and smartphones in those days) or short-circuiting their televisions? No, said Loy. Far from it. Maybe, just maybe, the blame lay closer to home. Maybe older and supposedly wiser folks were to blame for failing to educate the financiers and opinion leaders of tomorrow.

"The Baby Boomer generation and our parents' generation are failing to teach the lessons of banking history to Generation Xers," wrote Loy. "In fact, we're not only failing to teach the lessons of history, we're apparently failing to teach much of the history itself, let alone any lessons there from."[87]

To quote Shakespeare's Cassius as Caesar's ambitions threaten to wreck the Republic,

> The fault, dear Brutus, is not in our stars,
> But in ourselves, that we are underlings.[88]

Epilogue

Crossroads of Communities

> A good bank has to have heart. And that is what the community bank really champions: a *caring* attitude—wanting to improve the lot of your people. It sounds kind of paternalistic, but with a bank charter, you have more than just a business. You have what I call a ministry.
>
> Tracy Kelly, Spirit Bank of Bristow

There are two reasons to end this book in 2000. The first one is obvious: 2000 marked the end of a millennium. That is a big deal, and it was too much of a milestone to ignore.

The other reason is less obvious and actually more important, and it is best understood by means of metaphor. Just as stage lighting makes it difficult for actors to see their audiences, so, too, does temporal proximity to events make it hard for us to know what is truly significant in the kaleidoscope of everyday life, let alone to situate occurrences in a historical context. Stuck in what I call "the glare of the present," we perceive and more or less understand our immediate circumstances. But beyond our little specks of light, our vision fails us. The late Zhou Enlai, vice premier of the People's Republic of China in the bad old days of Communism, was famously asked to comment on the significance of the French Revolution. "It's too soon to tell," he said.

For the following concluding thoughts, I rely on two sources: public broadcasting (NPR and the *NewsHour* on PBS) and mainstream print media; and bankers and businesspeople across Oklahoma who welcomed me into their offices from 2009 through 2013 to share their reflections on the business of banking. I leave it to readers to situate these concluding thoughts in the context of the foregoing narrative, which ends in the same spirit in which it began, with bankers at the crossroads of their communities.

For obvious reasons, there was no way to interview every banker in the state. Nor can I possibly share every scrap of wisdom that I gleaned from dozens of interviews. What I can do is draw large enough samples from my reams of field notes and interviews to represent Oklahoma bankers fairly and accurately. If I have failed in any significant way, I will surely hear about it, and I will know where to start the third and final book in what morphed from a single book (what was I *thinking?*) into a trilogy on Oklahoma banking and commerce. Stay tuned.

The Great Recession of 2008 was gathering strength just as I was beginning my research on Oklahoma banking. It is remembered as the worst financial storm since the 1930s, and its effects were felt worldwide in teetering and sometimes collapsing financial institutions, bank bailouts, and stock market downturns. Perhaps the most visible face of the crisis was in the housing market. Ignoring the wisdom that if something seems too good to be true, it probably is, prospective home buyers by the millions signed up for mortgages without reading the fine print and then slept soundly in their new homes, blissfully certain that housing values could only go up. Beginning in 2007, those same millions woke up to the startling realization that they had miscalculated. It turned out that home values could, indeed, go down. An ugly term—"subprime mortgage"—entered the financial lexicon to describe loans taken out by folks who should never have qualified for them but did anyway. Banks that lured customers with glitzy, tech-savvy marketing campaigns felt the heat as their promises turned out to be lies. Sinking in tandem with housing prices was a theory, known in some circles as the Great Moderation, that had been gaining traction since the end of the so-called Volcker recession of the early 1980s. According to this theory, America had seen the end of volatile business cycles and had arrived in a Promised Land of long expansions, punctuated by brief and mercifully mild recessions.[1] Not for the first time and surely not the last, the Promised Land receded beyond the horizon like a mirage on a hot Oklahoma highway.

As the storm reached its full fury, the U.S. economy imploded in a triple whammy of evictions, foreclosures, and prolonged unemployment. By one reckoning, household net worth dropped $12.3 *trillion* from the onset of the recession to early 2012. People who managed to keep a sense of humor blithely referred to their 401(k)s as 201(k)s.[2] The pain was further felt in business failures and a slackening of economic activity. Troubles in the United States contributed in no small measure to the European sovereign-debt crisis.

The clouds eventually parted, much as they did in the wake of other financial storms surveyed in this book: the Panic of 1907; the post–World War I recession; the Great Depression; and the energy bust of the 1980s. And yet, as of this writing in 2014, the final chapters of the Great Recession remain to be written. By the time they are written and perhaps read by at least some of us, it will probably be too late to avoid the next crisis. Nowhere is our metaphor of actors blinded by stage lighting more apropos than in finance. Americans' obsession with quarterly reporting and culture of instant gratification leave us woefully unprepared to absorb the lessons of history, let alone apply those lessons to what might be coming down the pike.

Financial analysts acknowledge that the crisis had many causes, including too much borrowing, foolish investments, and misguided regulations. But at its core, the troubles of 2008 resulted from a lack of transparency. As Frank Partnoy and Jesse Eisinger argued in the January–February 2013 issue of the *Atlantic,* the reason no one wanted to lend or trade with banks was simple: nobody could understand the risks banks were taking. There was simply no way to know from a bank's disclosure statements whether it was a prudently managed institution or, as was the case with so many venerable banks, a ticking time bomb, ready to explode at the first hint of trouble. And don't depend on champions of reform to make bank accounting less opaque. Former SEC chairman Arthur Levitt lamented that none of the post-2008 remedies had "significantly diminished the likelihood of financial crises." He went so far as to compare big banks to Enron, the energy, commodities, and services behemoth that tanked in December 2001 when its hidden risks came to light. When asked if he trusted bank accounting, former Financial Accounting Standards Board member Ed Trott said simply, "Absolutely not."[3]

To test their suspicion of big banks, Partnoy and Eisinger shined their analytical lights on Wells Fargo, surely the most iconic of American banks. Since its inception in the heady days of the California gold rush, Wells Fargo has branded itself as a bastion of dependability and financial security. Perched atop gold-laden stagecoaches with their carbines at the ready, gunslingers in the service of Wells Fargo dared outlaws to pop out from behind their rocks and face them in the open. Reassured by images of foam-flecked horses thundering across the West, people knew the bank's paper drafts were as solid as the gold it shipped around the nation. In an age of smartphones and online banking, Wells Fargo's brand continued to resonate in the West of our imagination—a place where a man's handshake sufficed to seal a million-dollar deal, and where it was easy to tell the good guys from the rascals.

That clarity, to the extent that it ever existed in pure form, has vanished altogether in the company's annual reports. What Partnoy and Eisinger found were details about the bank's businesses that ranged from the incomprehensible to the disturbing. Waxing poetic, they characterized a Wells Fargo annual report as the financial equivalent to Dante's descent into hell. Perhaps, they suggested, the report's authors should take a page from the medieval poet and provide a warning to inquisitive readers: "Abandon all hope, ye who enter here."[4]

The authors soldiered on to find a glossary of terms that obscured far more than they revealed. As profits from traditional lending and brokering activities were squeezed, banks resorted to increasingly complex trading activities and financial instruments to make money. Their sheer volume made the bank look less like a bank and more like a casino. Dante's innermost circle of hell lay in the bank's attempts to assign "fair value" to its assets and liabilities. This was where readers who made it this far discovered variable-interest entities. Known to the cognoscenti as VIEs, these entities were created to borrow money and buy assets. According to Partnoy and Eisinger, every major bank had substantial positions in VIEs, and they were conspicuous by their absence in banks' reporting. As of late 2011, Wells Fargo reported "significant continuing involvement" with variable-interest entities to the tune of $1.46 *trillion*.[5]

To paraphrase the late senator Everett Dirksen, a trillion here and a trillion there, and pretty soon, you're talking about serious money. You're also talking about an erosion of trust in the nation's banks, which is sure to deteriorate further unless popular support for genuine reform can be mobilized. As Partnoy and Eisinger concluded on a downbeat note,

"Without such a mobilization, all of us will remain in the dark, neither understanding nor trusting the banks. And the rot will spread."[6]

As bad paper accumulated and asset values plunged during the Great Recession, Congress came to the rescue with a milestone in banking reform: the 2010 Wall Street Reform and Consumer Protection Act, introduced in the House of Representatives by Barney Frank (D-Mass.) and in the Senate by Chris Dodd (D-Conn.), and known in banking vernacular simply as Dodd-Frank. Enacted (coincidentally, as far as I know) as I was making my tour of Oklahoma banks, the law consumed 848 pages and required regulators to create so many new rules (not fully defined in the legislation itself) that it was expected to mushroom to 30,000 pages of legal minutiae when fully codified. By contrast, the Glass-Steagall Act of 1933, arguably the most influential piece of financial legislation in the twentieth century, ran to a paltry 37 pages. Andrew Haldane, the Bank of England's executive director for financial stability, hit the nail on the head when he said, "Dodd-Frank makes Glass-Steagall look like throat-clearing."[7]

Passing banking legislation was one thing; implementing it was something else altogether. Long after Dodd-Frank became the law of the land, its implementation remained stymied by Wall Street bankers bent on maintaining the status quo. Reformers met them and their lobbyists head on with increasingly strident demands for more transparency, tighter regulations, and more certain punishment for wrongdoing. In a rerun of 1980s debates attending the federal government's rescue of Continental Illinois National Bank, a rising chorus of reformers declared that too-big-to-fail banks were indeed too big and needed to be broken up. None were more outspoken than Elizabeth Warren. A native Oklahoman, daughter of a janitor, former Harvard Law professor, and one-time candidate to head up the Consumer Financial Protection Bureau before she was elected to the U.S. Senate from her adopted state of Massachusetts, Warren grilled regulators in early 2013 for not dragging any Wall Street bankers into court. "You know," she said, "I just want to note on this. There are district attorneys and U.S. attorneys who are out there every day squeezing ordinary citizens on sometimes very thin grounds. And taking them to trial in order to make an example, as they put it. I'm really concerned that too big to fail has become too big for trial. That just seems wrong to me."[8]

To allow smaller banks to flourish and protect the nation from costly bailouts, Senator Sherrod Brown (D-Ohio) was cosponsoring a bill with Senator David Vitter (R-La.) in early 2013 to set a hard cap on the size of the nation's half dozen megabanks. "It's not just that they are too big to fail," said Brown. "They really are too big to understand and too big to manage. They are certainly too big to regulate. And they have only gotten bigger since the financial crisis."[9] Brown sounded like an old-fashioned Populist in his appeal to bring too-big-to-fail banks to heel, saying that doing so would "help Main Street community banks compete with Wall Street megabanks."[10]

Ongoing investigations, lawsuits, and rulings gave reformers a glimmer of hope that their efforts might not be in vain. In January 2013, the Office of the Comptroller of the Currency and the Federal Reserve announced jointly that Wells Fargo, JPMorgan Chase, and Bank of America were among ten banks that would forfeit $8.5 billion to settle complaints that they had wrongfully foreclosed on homeowners who should have been allowed to stay in their homes. In a separate case, Bank of America agreed to pay $10.3 billion to government-backed mortgage financier Fannie Mae to settle claims related to mortgages that had gone sour during the housing crash.[11]

Bank of America's reputation reached a new low when whistleblowers revealed that higher-ups had instructed them to hasten foreclosures by falsifying records in their computer systems and removing documents from homeowners' files to make it look like a borrower had not qualified for a permanent loan modification. Employing the proverbial carrot-and-stick approach, managers punished employees for failing to meet foreclosure quotas and rewarded them with bonus checks and gift cards to Target and Bed Bath & Beyond when they met them. "This is not surprising, but absolutely sickening," said Peggy Mears, organizer for the Home Defenders League. "Maybe finally our courts and elected officials will stand with communities over Wall Street and prosecute, and then lock up, these criminals."[12]

Records were shattered in November 2013 when JPMorgan Chase and Company agreed to pay $13 billion in penalties and acknowledged that it misled investors about the quality of mortgage-backed securities prior to 2008. "Without a doubt, the conduct uncovered in this investigation helped sow the seeds of the mortgage meltdown," said U.S. attorney general Eric Holder. "JPMorgan was not the only financial institution during this period to knowingly bundle toxic loans and sell them to unsuspecting investors, but that is no excuse for the firm's behavior."[13] In another indication that reforms were gaining traction, the Federal Reserve Board, the Federal Deposit Insurance Corporation, the Securities and Exchange Commission, the Commodity Futures Trading Commission, and the Office of the Comptroller of the Currency voted in December 2013 to adopt the so-called Volcker Rule, banning the largest banks from trading for their own profit in most cases.[14]

Landmark rulings notwithstanding, big-city bankers and reformers remained at loggerheads well into 2014, and full implementation of Dodd-Frank seemed further away than ever. Nevertheless, aside from untold acres of felled trees, Dodd-Frank had many consequences, some intended and some not. One consequence (again, more than likely coincidental) accrued to my benefit. Dodd-Frank gave me something to ask bankers about.

"The number one threat to banking today, in my opinion, is regulatory," said Mike Leonard, chairman of the former First National Bank of Muskogee, rebranded Firstar Bank—with branches in Tulsa, Roland, Sallisaw, and Fort Smith, Arkansas—in 2012. "In my opinion, Congress does not understand that banks need to make a profit to stay around." Like bankers across Oklahoma, Leonard was forced to increase his staff to keep up with the paperwork. "A senior vice president of our organization does full-time compliance work," continued Leonard. "That is an add-on to my cost that I did not have four years ago. And we are getting ready to hire him an assistant. So I will have two full-time compliance people, just to keep up with all this, and stay compliant with all these rules and regulations." Leonard's invective escalated when he described Congress's insistence on regulating the profits that banks could make on overdraft protection, debit cards, and other services that customers expect from their banks. "We're still trying to service our customers," said a frustrated Leonard. "We're still growing. Good things are still happening to us. But is it getting harder to make money in the banking business? Absolutely!"[15]

"Any time you talk about regulations, you're going to solicit a high level of complaint from bankers, because bankers feel like we are overly regulated," said Idabel National Bank president Brian Shipp. "And some of that, honestly, is probably true. They have a tendency to name regulations by letter. Reg Z, for instance, is truth-in-lending. Well now, they've started going to Reg AA and Reg BB and Reg CC and Reg DD, and it's more of a psychological issue. It's like, they've got so many regulations, they've started over in the alphabet!"[16]

"But I think, actually, that's been going on for all the years I've been in this business," said veteran banker G. P. Johnson Hightower. "There's just a lot more of it." For emphasis, Hightower walked behind his desk, reached in a drawer, and fished out a stack of exams that he had to pass with numbing regularity to satisfy compliance mandates. He then dropped them on his desk with resounding thuds, one by one, as he recited an alphabet soup of regulation titles. "And it's more complicated," he continued, "and those regulators and politicians up there keep complicating everything they pass by layering up on it!"[17]

First State Bank of Anadarko president and CEO Don Clark agreed. "I think it's overregulated," he said. "They make all these regulations for large banks, and community banks have to follow all those rules and regulations and guidelines. We just got through having an exam, and I asked one of the examiners, how much longer can a bank like this exist, with all the regulations coming out of Washington?" Don's wife, Kitty, shook her head as her husband struggled to express the frustration they both felt toward regulations that were strangling the bank that Don had served for more than a half century. "Small banks, community banks, are going to fade away if something is not done," he said finally. "There is a need for the larger banks, but the small, community banks are the backbone of the community."[18]

Paul Freeman, CEO of the First National Bank of Texhoma in Texas County, was mystified by a Congress that drew no distinction between Main Street and Wall Street. "The regulatory pressures and burdens placed on my customers are enormous," he said. "You know, the amount of money we have to spend just to stay compliant is ridiculous. And you know, there are just a lot of regs coming down that were caused by Wall Street and some of the major—" Freeman's voice trailed off as he searched for a way to describe big-city bankers who wreaked so much havoc in the economy, before finally saying, "the bad players in the industry." He continued, "And there are not many bad players, but they were big enough that—we're all paying for that." Topping Freeman's list of frustrations was his bank's inability to make a profit from home loans due to regulatory burdens. "The bottom line is, we either continue to do home loans and lose money, or we get out of it. And who's going to finance a home in Texhoma, Oklahoma? That's a real bind."[19]

First State Bank of Boise City president Tim Barnes exhibited a flair for understatement when he described the change in banking since he went into the business in the 1970s: "It was quite a bit simpler, in a way. We didn't have quite as much paperwork to do back then." And then came 2008. Like Paul Freeman in neighboring Texas County, Barnes was fed up with making home loans. "In fact, the regulations on home loans have gotten so bad, and are so demanding, that we have quit making those kinds of loans because we don't really have a lot of demand for it, and it takes almost a full-time person to do it." Asked about regulations cooked up in Washington, D.C., that treated all banks alike, Barnes offered a straightforward explanation that I had come to expect from straight-shooting Oklahoma bankers: "I think we've got a mess up there."[20]

Lee Stidham at People's National Bank of Checotah was similarly baffled by the huge net that Congress was throwing to snare renegade bankers—a net that captured Wells Fargo and Lehman Brothers along with his bank in McIntosh County, Oklahoma. "They have gotten to the point where they have gotten mad at the banks in the last few years," said Stidham as Mike, his son and a fellow bank officer, and bank CEO Robert Jennings nodded their heads in agreement. "They hated us! We were never able to convince them in Washington that anything this small can operate! They just can't understand that!"[21] Our conversation continued down the street at the local diner—that is, after my hosts greeted just about everybody in the place, asked them about friends and family, and dished out affectionate backslaps on the way to our booth.

Chickasha Bank and Trust Company president Lindel Pettigrew was particularly vexed by the proliferation of agencies whose vast authority was not matched by oversight of their decisions. "I don't remember exactly how many direct assignments that they have coming out of Dodd-Frank, but they are numerous," he said. "Dodd-Frank also created the new Consumer Finance Protection Agency, and that agency is just now starting to come online and issue regulations. The danger we see about that is, the director of the Consumer Financial Protection Bureau has rule-making authority with no oversight board. It's hard to know what will ultimately come from that." Equally troubling for the Chickasha banker were compliance costs that were hammering his bank's profitability. "There seems to be a lot of talk about concern for the consumer," said Pettigrew. "But every time I get a new regulation, I've got to make whatever adjustments I have to make in our operations, and I am going to pass that cost on to the consumer. And so, it's hard to know what some of these people in Washington are thinking when they pass some of these laws."[22]

First United Bank of Durant chairman John Massey cited overzealous regulators as particularly noxious symbols of changing times. "I've had a great relationship with regulators," said the former state representative and senator and onetime chairman of the Oklahoma State Regents for Higher Education. Yet others have not been so fortunate. Rather than trusting bankers who had long since demonstrated their integrity to operate their banks responsibly, regulators all too often classified loans and let the chips fall where they may. "And so what happens is, they classify a loan," continued Massey. "You can argue with them all day, and they're going to classify it. And the last time I got in an argument, I was wrong!"[23] Feeling suddenly small in front of Massey's massive desk, I had to admire any regulator with the brass to argue with this titan of southeast Oklahoma banking.

State Banking Commissioner Mick Thompson used his bully pulpit to alert officials in Washington to the perils of overregulation. "I think the biggest thing that is really worrying our banks, or concerning to our banks, is the actual implementation of the Dodd-Frank bill," said the plainspoken commissioner. "I told the chairman this: it's the biggest consolidation bill there has ever been for community banking. They say that it's not going to affect community banking. Well, I don't buy that. I have never seen something like this that didn't affect community banking."[24] Sharing Thompson's bully pulpit was OBA president and CEO Roger Beverage. "The OBA maintained a continuous position of opposing the passage of Dodd-Frank because the board of directors, our government relations council, and our officers believed it would impose an inordinate amount of cost on community banks," he said. "We argued for our [congressional] delegation to oppose the bill, which they did, at every opportunity. There was not one time when any one member of the delegation voted *other than* the OBA's position on Dodd-Frank. And there aren't a lot of states that can make that statement."[25]

For Ben Walkingstick at the Union National Bank of Chandler, it all became too much. Once again by coincidence, I drove up and down Main Street Chandler several times before I figured out that the Union

National Bank's signage had been changed—earlier that week!—to announce its new owner: the BancFirst Corporation. "That's one of the reasons why I retired and sold the bank—increased regulations," said Walkingstick as I took measure of the hunting trophies that seemed to be glaring disapprovingly in my direction. "And for a small bank our size, just the cost of complying with all the regulations that are coming down the pipeline now—it's very difficult. I felt it was time for me to sell the bank. If I didn't think the taxes were going to go back up like they have been in the past, I would not have sold my bank. I really wouldn't."[26]

Of course, you did not have to be a small-town banker to fret over the deluge of post-2008 regulations. For BancFirst president and CEO David Rainbolt, the Dodd-Frank law was a game changer in terms of his bank's growth strategy. But in his case, tough times for small banks meant opportunities for his. "Beginning in 2008, things changed. There were loan losses. There were new regulations that increased expenses. Loan demand was down. Rates were approaching zero. All of a sudden, bankers who had no interest in selling were interested in selling. And then really, with the passage of the Dodd-Frank Law, and probably the certainty, eventually, of higher taxes on both capital gains and corporate income taxes being an inevitability—that changed potential sellers' permanent expectations, and prices came down dramatically. *Dramatically.*"[27]

Sociological reasoning led me to generalize from my sample of Oklahoma bankers to reach three conclusions that, honestly, were not all that hard to figure out: (1) bankers resented regulations that treated their banks the same as they treated Wall Street megabanks; (2) they thought it was grossly unfair to be required to pay for regulations aimed at solving problems they did not cause; and (3) they feared that community banks would continue to fall by the wayside as an increasing number of bankers were following Ben Walkingstick's lead and calling it quits.

Concern about federal regulation of the banking industry was nothing new. For precedent, I quote from a letter written by American National Bank of Oklahoma City president Frank P. Johnson dated April 22, 1913, the twenty-fourth anniversary of the Run of '89, which opened the Unassigned Lands to non-Indian settlement.[28] As we have seen, Frank Johnson merged the American National Bank with his brother Hugh's First National Bank in 1927 to create the First National Bank and Trust Company of Oklahoma City.[29] Johnson addressed his letter to his successor, whoever that might be, as president of the American National Bank in 2013. Discovered in the Century Chest buried in the First Lutheran Church of Oklahoma City on April 22, 1913, Johnson's letter survives as portal into a crossroads of American banking history, when pioneer banking was fading into history and federal control of the nation's financial system was coming into focus. "You will be more of a clerk than I am," wrote Johnson. "The government of the United States will be a much stronger factor in the banking business than it is today and you will exercise authority within narrow limits of official control. All the banks of your section will be tied together in one business group with governmental recognition, and your duties and powers will be laid out along the lines of strict business principles as understood by the ablest bankers in your group, and these in turn will be controlled by a great central government bank that will be as strong as the nation itself."[30]

Increasing regulation of the banking industry leads straight to a theme that pervades this book: existential threats notwithstanding, Oklahoma's community banks have retained their franchise value. To flesh out this theme, I needed a definition of community banking. For that, I deferred once again to the experts.

"We see whatever we do in a community as an investment in that community," said Citizens Bank of Ada senior vice president and chief operating officer Scott Estes. "The better Ada does, the better the bank will do. The bank can't do well if Ada doesn't do well. Sometimes, when you have an outside ownership, they're not as interested in Ada as they are in just the business. So, there's that connection—it's one way to separate the local ownership from ownership that's outside of the area."[31]

Bank of the Panhandle chairman and CEO Steve Baggerly struck a similar chord when he described "the Wal-Mart effect" in Texas County. "Wal-Mart won't give a thousand dollars to Circle of Friends, or any other entity, without their picture being taken," said Baggerly. "They're going to have their picture in the paper. We hardly ever have ours in the paper. Maybe that's bad PR. I don't do it to get my picture in the paper. I do it because it's the right thing to do. If we're making money out of this community, we're going to put it back."[32]

Jim Pittman of the First National Bank of Seiling practically answered my question about the meaning of community banking before I had a chance to ask it: "Locally owned and locally operated." At the time of our interview in June 2011, members of the fifth generation of Pittmans were employed at FNB Seiling. As I learned in dozens of interviews, that was far from unusual among Oklahoma's community banks, many of whose charters dated back to the early statehood and territorial eras. "Here, we feel like we know our customers personally," continued Pittman. "They're not just a number. We know where they live, and know about them. And they have been very loyal. We've had a lot of loyal customers."[33]

Handing the baton to fourth and fifth generations of Oklahoma bankers and maintaining the same community spirit that inspired their ancestors has been common, but never easy. "It gets harder and harder," said American Heritage Bank of Sapulpa chairman Bill Berry, whose son-in-law and niece represented the fourth generation of Berry bankers at the time of our interview in April 2012. "It's just like any other independent business. It's hard to keep everybody's interest going in the same direction. Your family gets bigger and bigger with each passing generation." Bill's brother and bank president Guy Berry agreed. "Our bank started in 1905," he said, "and our great uncle came here in 1912. So this year, it's been one hundred years. It's kind of hard to stay in the same business for a hundred years!"[34]

"I think community spirit is common to banking," said National Bank of Commerce of Altus chairman Ken Fergeson. "I have traveled all over the United States, talking to bankers, and they all want their towns to grow and prosper. One way you do that, of course, is making sure that charitable and social organizations do the best that they can for the community. Bankers are very innovative. They are good at promoting."[35]

First Security Bank of Beaver president Chris Berry did not have time to talk to me about community banking when I arrived for our interview on a Friday afternoon. He greeted me in the lobby, apologized profusely for having to leave early, and scooted out the back door. Something about flipping burgers down in Balko.

"Sorry about that, Dr. Hightower," said an employee as my interview went up in a cloud of exhaust. "Do you want me to call Pauline Hodges?"

"Well, sure," I stammered. I had no clue who Ms. Hodges was or what she might have to say, but I was relieved to have a plan B as employees prepared to shut down for the weekend.

The employee nodded and disappeared into an office with a cell phone to her ear. Five minutes later, a smartly dressed woman came in through the same back door that Chris had used to make his getaway, stuck out her hand, and introduced herself as Pauline Hodges. She apologized for her friend's hasty exit and led me to a conference room, where I spent an hour in thrall to the Panhandle's most renowned historian and educator. The next time I saw Pauline was on Ken Burns's masterful PBS documentary *The Dust Bowl,* where she and other veterans of the dirty thirties shared their experiences of the biggest ecological catastrophe in American history.[36] Talk about a plan B!

Heeding his father's admonition "to leave the woodpile higher than you found it," Spirit Bank of Bristow chairman Tracy Kelly spoke about the banker's obligation to serve the people. "It's not trickery or chicanery," insisted the veteran banker whose late-in-life blindness had robbed him of his sight but not, apparently, his vision. "It's just that you serve the people the way you would like to be served." And there was more from a banker whose lessons came largely from the school of hard knocks. "A good bank has to have heart. And that is what the community bank really champions: a *caring* attitude—wanting to improve the lot of your people. It sounds kind of paternalistic, but with a bank charter, you have more than just a business. You have what I call a ministry."[37] Like ministries, banks are built on trust, a primary casualty of the subprime mortgage crisis. To borrow from Australian economist John Quiggin, the trust betrayed by Wall Street megabanks, yet fostered by Tracy Kelly's brand of community banks, "can only be restored through personal knowledge of particular borrowers, the kind that is built up through a long business relationship."[38]

For the late Clark Bass, banking was all about establishing relationships with customers. "Clark was a very creative banker," said Bruce Hall, senior trust officer and director of the First National Bank and Trust Company of McAlester, who had cut his banking teeth as Bass's protégé.

> He told all of his young loan officers, which I had the pleasure to be years ago, that, if a man came in to borrow $6,000 to buy a car, and you didn't think that he could afford to do that, then you try to loan him $3,000 so he could buy a $3,000 car. Don't turn him down completely. If he can afford a $3,000 car, loan him the money to buy the $3,000 car. In addition to that, we used to run ads in those days that we made loans for $100 and above, and so, people who were creditworthy didn't have to go

to the short loan companies to borrow money at high interest rates. They could do it with the bank and establish a bank relationship. We made a lot of small loans to a lot of people and helped a lot of people.[39]

Ameristate Bank chairman Charles McCall relished the chance to talk about his father, C. A. "Barney" McCall, whose tenure at Atoka State Bank dated back to the 1930s and ended with his death in November 2002, the year after the bank set up a branch in nearby Antlers and rebranded itself as Ameristate Bank. "My dad bought the bank in '67, and he stayed here and worked here," said McCall. "Up to the last six months before he died, he was always here. He was kind of the Wal-Mart greeter. Even though he got out of lending, he was the board chairman for many years, after he got out of lending. He knew so many people in Atoka, and he always enjoyed visiting with people. And people would just come in and see him, talk to him."[40]

Veteran banker and consultant Bob McCormack of Duncan was thinking along the same lines when he described his father's funeral. For years, McCormack's family had banked in Elgin, where Harry Leonard served as president of the local bank before his appointment as state banking commissioner.[41] "When I was seventeen years old," said McCormack, "my father was killed in an accident, and so we were all gathered up at my grandparents' house, and had notified all the relatives and that sort of thing. And my grandmother said, 'Has anyone called Harry?'" McCormack was puzzled at the time, but a career spent in the company of Oklahoma bankers cleared up the mystery. "That's community banking personified," he said with a smile, "that after the family, the banker is the next guy that we would call with news like that."[42]

No less important than community spirit is sensitivity to customers' needs. Sometimes, that meant steering clear of get-rich-quick schemes. Central National Bank of Alva chairman Marilyn Myers credited her bank's conservatism for wooing customers when her bank took over the Bank of Woodward after the oil bust of the 1980s. "I think they appreciated, when we came in, that we were very conservative, and not willing to do all those wildcat type things," she said. Senior vice president and director of operations Clint Elliott credited the Myers family's community spirit for the bank's success and, not incidentally, for keeping him on the job for over forty years. "Times were never easy in northwestern

Oklahoma," said Elliott. "We reached out to community needs throughout the years. Everybody that came in was part of their larger family."[43]

For Mike Leonard, customers' needs dovetailed with community banks' imperative to generate fee-based income to offset the soaring costs of regulatory compliance. "You've got to find other sources of income, which is what we are doing, and we have to continue to do," said Leonard. Beginning in January 2012 just a few months before it was rebranded as Firstar Bank, the First National Bank of Muskogee started offering reverse mortgages whereby senior homeowners used a portion of their home's equity as loan collateral. Such loans generally did not have to be repaid until the surviving homeowner moved out of the property or died. At that time, the estate had approximately six months to repay the balance of the reverse mortgage or sell the home to pay off the balance. "We can do anything—stocks, bonds, financial planning, life insurance, and estate planning," continued Leonard. "So that is a product line that not only brings in fee income, but it also makes sure that I can be the one-stop shop for all our customers. They don't have to go to a broker for that part of their business, and then that broker's taking all my business away from me. I can do it all for my customers." And doing it all for customers was, for Leonard, what community banking was all about—not only in Muskogee, but also in Tulsa, where the Muskogee bank's branch was luring big-city customers with the promise of small-town banking spirit:

> Community banking to me is to know your customers, a lot more so than you do in the metropolitan areas. You can't do loans on a handshake anymore, but you still do an awful lot of character lending. You know your customers; you know their parents; you know their grandparents; they have lived here for a long time; they're going to be around; they're not going anywhere; you see them on the street. It is a lot more satisfying for me, anyway, to be a community banker, and to develop those personal relationships, or those relationships with customers, than it is to be a major metropolitan banker.[44]

Stock Exchange Bank of Woodward president and CEO Bruce Benbrook had his own take on the two primary challenges that community bankers faced: globalization and excessive regulation. "I think the greatest challenge from a community banker's standpoint is the global economy," said the third-generation banker. "It's a different world. To compete, we have to be able to provide the products and services that the biggest banks in the country do because they can provide it to our customers over the Internet and numerous other ways. It is an extreme challenge for a community bank, to make it work. We are the only bank in Woodward that's headquartered here. And the other element of that is we continue to get more and more regulations out of Washington that make it extremely difficult for community banks." Following our interview, Benbrook took me on a tour of Woodward to showcase some of the improvements that he and his bank (one in the same, really) had prodded to completion. Lunch at a local diner included the handshaking and backslapping that was part of the routine whenever I was invited to stick around after one of my bank visits. On my drive back to Oklahoma City, Benbrook's comment as we concluded our interview was ringing in my ears: "As long as we can continue to make a difference in the positive growth of our community, then I'll certainly be there doing that!"[45]

Osage Federal Bank of Pawhuska president and CEO Mark White, who divided his time between offices in Bartlesville and Pawhuska (and, I might add, kept an impressive collection of piggy banks in his Pawhuska office), drew a sharp distinction between commercial banks and so-called wholesale businesses, which he described as the equivalent of a car dealer who makes loans, puts them together, and sells them upstream. "We don't do that," he said flatly. "We work directly with customers, and the people we know—they're good people. They take care of us, and we take care of them. It's kind of a mutual situation."[46]

Oklahoma banks did not have to be small to exude community spirit. At year-end 2013, the BancFirst Corporation reported total assets of $6.04 billion, ranking it at the pinnacle of state-chartered banks. Based in its support center in the historic Tradesmen's National Bank Building in Oklahoma City, the company operated from ninety-eight banking locations in fifty-two communities throughout the state.[47] Even so, company patriarch Gene Rainbolt and his son, David, continued to make community development a cornerstone of their business philosophy. Lauding his son's success in relying on local autonomy to build what is known in BancFirst's lexicon as "a super community bank," Rainbolt paraphrased his son's favorite expression. "I think it's David's phrase," said Gene

Rainbolt, "that our objective is to build Oklahoma, one community at a time."[48] At the time of this writing in 2014, BancFirst's objective was evident in television ads touting the unique attributes of communities whose banks had joined the BancFirst bandwagon and had never looked back.

There is a final theme to consider, and it informs this book as well as my previous one, *Banking in Oklahoma before Statehood*. Simply put, it is the dynamic tension between capitalism and democracy.

Unlike bankers' attitudes toward the regulatory state and the meaning of community banking, this theme offers no easy assessments. It is a theme that saw its first stirrings in the backwaters of northwestern Europe with the sprouting of seafaring empires and that roared to life in the nineteenth century as mighty fortunes coexisted all too easily with pestilential poverty. Following the hoopla attending statehood in 1907, Oklahoma brought its frontier persona into the twentieth century to provide a crucible, unique in its particulars but not so different from other crucibles in the grand sweep of history, in which that tension was revealed in fascinating ways. The tension crystallized in banks, where the challenge has always been to serve the public interest, even as the profit imperative inherent in capitalism tends inexorably to encourage risky behavior and favor the few against the many.

How that tension plays out in the years to come is anybody's guess, but one thing is certain: Oklahoma bankers will be close to the action, greasing the wheels of commerce by extending credit and controlling the money supply and doing their part in the production, acquisition, and distribution of goods and services that make communal life possible.

Notes

PREFACE

1. Martin Mayer, *The Bankers: The Next Generation* (New York: Truman Talley Books, 1997), 361.
2. Joyce Appleby, *The Relentless Revolution: A History of Capitalism* (New York: W. W. Norton, 2010), 434.

CHAPTER 1

Epigraph: "Deposits Guaranty Wins West," *Guthrie Daily Leader,* August 29, 1908.

1. Charles Wayne Ellinger, "The Drive for Statehood in Oklahoma, 1889–1906," *Chronicles of Oklahoma* 41, no. 1 (Spring 1963): 23.
2. Roosevelt quoted in Charles Wayne Ellinger, "Congressional Viewpoint toward the Admission of Oklahoma as a State: 1902–1906," *Chronicles of Oklahoma* 58, no. 3 (Fall 1980): 288–89.
3. Ibid., 294.
4. Ellinger, "Drive for Statehood," 26. The Single Statehood Press Association was organized in November 1901 under the leadership of R. E. Stafford of the *Daily Oklahoman.*
5. Ibid., 22.
6. Adams quoted in Irvin Hurst, *The 46th Star: A History of Oklahoma's Constitutional Convention and Early Statehood* (Oklahoma City: Western Heritage Books, 1980), 18.
7. Ibid., 31; Norbert R. Mahnken, "William Jennings Bryan in Oklahoma," *Nebraska History* 31, no. 4 (December 1950): 269; Edwin C. McReynolds, *Oklahoma: A History of the Sooner State* (Norman: University of Oklahoma Press, 1954), 317.
8. Roy P. Stewart, *Born Grown: An Oklahoma City History* (Oklahoma City: Fidelity Bank, N.A., 1974), 170.

9. Hurst, *The 46th Star,* 29; "Barbecue at an Inaugural," unsourced newspaper article, November 9, 1907, Scrapbook, July 8, 1907–May 16, 1908, box 43, vol. 19, 92, in Frederick Samuel Barde Collection, 1890–1916, Research Division, Oklahoma Historical Society, Oklahoma City (hereafter cited as Barde Collection).

10. Mahnken, "Bryan in Oklahoma," 269.

11. Hurst, *The 46th Star,* 32. For detailed accounts of the marriage of east and west, see Muriel H. Wright, "The Wedding of Oklahoma and Miss Indian Territory," *Chronicles of Oklahoma* 35, no. 3 (Fall 1957): 255–60; "Inaugural Day Plans Maturing," *Guthrie Daily Leader,* November 11, 1907; and "Oklahoma a State," *Beaver Herald,* November 21, 1907. Founded in 1886, the *Beaver Herald* branded itself as the Oklahoma Territory's oldest newspaper.

12. Lynne Pierson Doti and Larry Schweikart, *Banking in the American West: From the Gold Rush to Deregulation* (Norman: University of Oklahoma Press, 1991), 52.

13. O. M. W. Sprague, "The American Crisis of 1907," *Economic Journal* 18 (September 1908): 354–55.

14. Robert F. Bruner and Sean D. Carr, *The Panic of 1907: Lessons Learned from the Market's Perfect Storm* (Hoboken, N.J.: Wiley, 2007), 7.

15. Sprague, "American Crisis," 355.

16. Arthur M. Schlesinger, Jr., gen. ed., *The Almanac of American History* (New York: Putnam, 1983), 412–13.

17. Alfred D. Chandler, "The Beginnings of 'Big Business' in American Industry," *Business History Review* 33 (Spring 1959): 20.

18. Bruner and Carr, *Panic of 1907,* 38–41.

19. Sprague, "American Crisis," 357.

20. Charles P. Kindleberger and Robert Z. Aliber, *Manias, Panics, and Crashes: A History of Financial Crises* (Basingstoke, UK: Palgrave MacMillan, 2005), 28.

21. Sprague, "American Crisis," 360.

22. Alexander D. Noyes, "A Year after the Panic of 1907," *Quarterly Journal of Economics* 23 (February 1909): 188.

23. Liaquat Ahamed, *Lords of Finance: The Bankers Who Broke the World* (New York: Penguin, 2009), 53–54; Ron Chernow, *The Death of the Banker: The Decline and Fall of the Great Financial Dynasties and the Triumph of the Small Investor* (New York: Vintage Books, 1997), 105.

24. Untitled newspaper submission, October 28, 1932, folder 9, box 4, Fred L. Wenner Collection, University of Oklahoma Western History Collections, Norman, Oklahoma (hereafter cited as Wenner Collection).

25. Johnson quoted in "Local Banks Have Much Money," *Daily Oklahoman,* October 23, 1907. Frank P. Johnson was the author's paternal great-grandfather.

26. Loren C. Gatch, "An' the west jes' smiled: Oklahoma Banking and the Panic of 1907," *Chronicles of Oklahoma* 87, no. 1 (Spring 2009): 6–7.

27. "Governor's Proclamation," *Blackwell Times-Record,* October 31, 1907.

28. "Greatly Improved Condition Prevails All Over Country," *Shawnee Daily Herald,* October 29, 1907.

29. Untitled newspaper submission, October 28, 1932, folder 9, box 4, Wenner Collection.

30. H. H. Smock was appointed as the state's first bank commissioner on November 16, 1907, and served in that capacity until his resignation on January 1, 1909. See *Fifth Biennial Report of the Bank Commissioner of the State of Oklahoma* (Oklahoma City: Harlow, December 31, 1916), Oklahoma State Banking Department Collection, Oklahoma City (hereafter cited as Oklahoma State Banking Department Collection).

31. Proclamation of Charles H. Filson, Acting Governor of Oklahoma Territory, October 28, 1907, folder 9, box 4; "Old Time Residents Recall Hectic Day in State History," unsourced newspaper article, n.d., folder 1, box 7, both in Wenner Collection.

32. Untitled newspaper submission, October 28, 1932, folder 9, box 4; "Old Time Residents Recall Hectic Day in State History," both in Wenner Collection.

33. Gatch, "An' the west jes' smiled," 13–17; Norbert R. Mahnken, "No Oklahoman Lost a Penny: Oklahoma's State Bank Guarantee Law, 1907–1923," *Chronicles of Oklahoma* 71, no. 1 (Spring 1993): 47.

34. James M. Smallwood, *An Oklahoma Adventure of Banks and Bankers* (Norman: University of Oklahoma Press, 1979), 53–55.

35. A. Piatt Andrew, "Substitutes for Cash in the Panic of 1907," *Quarterly Journal of Economics* 22, no. 4 (1908): 505.

36. "Governor's Proclamation," *Blackwell Times-Record*, October 31, 1907.

37. Gatch, "An' the west jes' smiled," 8–9.

38. Andrew, "Substitutes for Cash," 516.

39. Ibid., 497–98; Smallwood, *Oklahoma Adventure*, 53–55.

40. "Bank Holiday Was Taken in Stride," *Daily Oklahoman*, April 23, 1939.

41. Noyes, "A Year after the Panic," 186–87.

42. A. Piatt Andrew, "Hoarding in the Panic of 1907," *Quarterly Journal of Economics* 22, no. 2 (1908): 298. *Sauve qui peut* translates roughly from the French as "save yourself if you can."

43. Andrew, "Substitutes for Cash," 497–98.

44. Johnson and Hogan quoted in "Acting Governor Proclaims Legal Holiday for Week," *Daily Oklahoman*, August 23, 1931, folder 9, box 4, Wenner Collection.

45. Hugh Rockoff, "Banking and Finance, 1789–1914," in *The Cambridge Economic History of the United States*, ed. Stanley L. Engerman and Robert E. Gallman, vol. 2, *The Long Nineteenth Century* (Cambridge: Cambridge University Press, 2000), 672–73.

46. Doti and Schweikart, *Banking in the American West*, 74.

47. Sprague quoted in Rockoff, "Banking and Finance," 674.

48. Aldrich quoted in Chernow, *Death of the Banker*, 106.

49. Noyes, "A Year after the Panic," 190–206.

50. Branch president quoted in ibid., 211.

51. Ben S. Bernanke, "The Crisis as a Classic Financial Panic," speech delivered at Fourteenth Jacques Polak Annual Research Conference, Washington, D.C., November 8, 2013, http://www.federalreserve.gov/newsevents/speech/bernanke20131108a.htm.

52. Smallwood, *Oklahoma Adventure*, 56.

53. "Finance Has Had Big Part in Building Great State," *Daily Oklahoman*, April 23, 1939.

54. Mahnken, "No Oklahoman Lost a Penny," 48.

55. "'Jim Crow' Bills Are In," unsourced newspaper article, December 3, 1907, Scrapbook, July 8, 1907–May 16, 1908, box 43, vol. 19, 112–15, Barde Collection; Hurst, *The 46th Star*, 52. In keeping with the South's enthrallment to the reign of Jim Crow, debate in both houses resulted in Oklahoma's first law: the segregation of railroad waiting rooms and cars. Railroads were granted sixty days to arrange separate accommodations. They were also required to display copies of the law. For many years, framed copies of Senate Bill No. 1 were a familiar site in railroad coaches and depots.

56. "House in First Night Session," *Guthrie Daily Leader*, December 18, 1907.

57. "For Insuring Deposits," unsourced newspaper article, December 10, 1907, Scrapbook, July 8, 1907–May 16, 1908, box 43, vol. 19, 117, Barde Collection.

58. Thomas Bruce Robb, *The Guaranty of Bank Deposits* (New York: Houghton Mifflin, 1921), 23; "Oklahoma Bank Bill Passed," unsourced newspaper article, December 17, 1907, Scrapbook, July 8, 1907–May 16, 1908, box 43, vol. 19, 121, Barde Collection.

59. "Guaranty Deposits," *Guthrie Daily Leader,* December 18, 1907.

60. "New State's Bank Law," unsourced newspaper article, December 18, 1907, Scrapbook, July 8, 1907–May 16, 1908, box 43, vol. 19, 121, Barde Collection.

61. "Oklahoma Nationals Worried," unsourced article, December 28, 1907, Scrapbook, July 8, 1907–May 16, 1908, box 43, vol. 19, 125, Barde Collection.

62. "To Guarantee Deposits," unsourced article, November 29, 1907, Scrapbook, July 8, 1907–May 16, 1908, box 43, vol. 19, 108, in Barde Collection.

63. Robb, *Guaranty of Bank Deposits,* 23. See also Hurst, *The 46th Star,* 53.

64. A. Piatt Andrew, "The Crux of the Currency Question," *Yale Review,* n.s., 2 (July 1913): 600.

65. *"Plus ça change, c'est plus la même chose"* translates into English roughly as, "the more things change, the more they stay the same"—much wordier, and far less lyrical, than the French expression.

66. Chaplain quoted in Mahnken, "Bryan in Oklahoma," 270; Murray quoted in Hurst, *The 46th Star,* 29.

67. Robert D. Lewallen, "'Let the People Rule': William Jennings Bryan and the Oklahoma Constitution," *Chronicles of Oklahoma* 73, no. 3 (Fall 1995): 295; Smallwood, *Oklahoma Adventure,* 56–57.

68. Lewallen, "'Let the People Rule,'" 293.

69. Nebraska statesman quoted in Ben Haller, Jr., *A History of Banking in Nebraska, 1854–1990* (Lincoln: Nebraska Bankers Association, 1990), 210.

70. Ibid., 208–10. For descriptions of bank guarantee legislation throughout the United States, see Robb, *Guaranty of Bank Deposits.*

71. Charles W. Calomiris, *U.S. Bank Deregulation in Historical Perspective* (Cambridge: Cambridge University Press, 2000), 58.

72. Robb, *Guaranty of Bank Deposits,* 25.

73. Eastern newspapers quoted in "Deposits Guaranty Wins West," *Guthrie Daily Leader,* August 29, 1908.

74. "Guaranty of Deposits," unsourced newspaper article, n.d., folder 26, box 2, Barde Collection.

75. Robb, *Guaranty of Bank Deposits,* 35.

76. Ibid., 41.

77. Hurst, *The 46th Star,* 57–58.

78. "Judge Huston Holds that Bank Law Protecting Depositors of New State Is Constitutional," unsourced newspaper article, dated by hand February 20, 1908, folder 26, box 2, Barde Collection.

79. "Must Obey New Law," unsourced newspaper article, April 17, 1908, Scrapbook, July 8, 1907–May 16, 1908, box 43, vol. 19, 189, Barde Collection; Hurst, *The 46th Star,* 109.

80. Cane quoted in "He Exempts National Banks," unsourced newspaper article, April 20, 1908, Scrapbook, July 8, 1907–May 16, 1908, box 43, vol. 19, 190, Barde Collection.

81. "Bonaparte's About . . . ," unsourced newspaper article, dated by hand August 6, 1908, folder 26, box 2, Barde Collection.

82. "Haskell Says Ruling Augurs for the State," unsourced newspaper article, August 3, 1908, folder 26, box 2, Barde Collection.

83. Untitled newspaper submission beginning, "Discussion of the Oklahoma bank guaranty deposit law," n.d., folder 27, box 2, Barde Collection; Hurst, *The 46th Star*, 108–14.

84. Robb, *Guaranty of Bank Deposits*, 44.

85. Ibid., 45; Mahnken, "No Oklahoman Lost a Penny," 50.

86. Robb, *Guaranty of Bank Deposits*, 44.

87. Ibid., 46.

88. "Discussion of the Oklahoma bank guaranty deposit law."

89. "Help Was Offered by Other Bankers," unsourced newspaper article, dated by hand October 20, 1909, folder 28, box 2, Barde Collection.

90. Johnson quoted in ibid. A. M. Young was appointed as the state's second bank commissioner on January 1, 1909, and served in that capacity until his resignation on June 1, 1910. See *Fifth Biennial Report of the Bank Commissioner of the State of Oklahoma*, Oklahoma State Banking Department Collection.

91. Johnson quoted in "Help Was Offered by Other Bankers."

92. Robb, *Guaranty of Bank Deposits*, 49.

93. "First Money Deposited in Canvas Tent," *Daily Oklahoman*, April 23, 1939.

94. "Discussion of the Oklahoma bank guaranty deposit law."

95. Ibid.; Mahnken, "No Oklahoman Lost a Penny," 51.

96. "They've 'Explained,'" unsourced newspaper article, dated by hand October 19, 1909, folder 26, box 2, Barde Collection.

97. Blaise quoted in "Farmers National, Tulsa, Failure," *Oklahoma Banker* (January 1910), 201.

98. "Two Bankers Are Indicted," *Oklahoma State Capital*, February 17, 1911; "Norton Is Under Arrest," *Oklahoma State Capital*, February 18, 1911.

99. Mahnken, "No Oklahoman Lost a Penny," 54.

100. Robb, *Guaranty of Bank Deposits*, 66; Stewart, *Born Grown*, 68.

101. Examples of Putnam's real estate ads can be found in *Oklahoma City Times*, June 14 and July 2, 1909.

102. George Gorton, *A "Big-Ass Boy" in the Oil Fields: My Adventures 1918–28* (New Berlin, Wis.: Napco Graphic Arts, 1975), 102.

103. Robb, *Guaranty of Bank Deposits*, 67.

104. Mahnken, "No Oklahoman Lost a Penny," 54.

105. Robb, *Guaranty of Bank Deposits*, 66.

106. Angelo C. Scott, *The Story of Oklahoma City* (Oklahoma City: Times-Journal Publishing, 1939), 96.

107. Fred L. Wenner, "How the Capital was Moved from Guthrie," n.d., folder 5, box 4, Wenner Collection.

108. After staking a claim near Britton and opening the Young Ladies' Seminary in Oklahoma City, Alice Beitman (later Mrs. A. S. Heaney) helped organize Oklahoma City's first public schools, served her adopted city as a teacher, and cofounded chapters of the Women's Christian Temperance Union (WCTU) in Britton and Oklahoma City. Flush with cash from real estate deals in Wichita in the late 1880s, her husband financed construction of the New England Apartments at 101 N.E. Third Street in Oklahoma City. See Mrs. A. S. Heaney, interview by Harry M. Dreyer, March 5, 1937, vol. 41, 15, Indian-Pioneer Papers, Western History Collections, University of Oklahoma, Norman (http://digital.libraries.ou.edu/whc/pioneer/).

109. James R. Scales and Danney Goble, *Oklahoma Politics: A History* (Norman: University of Oklahoma Press, 1982), 49.

110. Mrs. A. S. Heaney interview, 15.

111. "Czar Charles Issues his Imperial Ukase at New State Capital," *Oklahoma State Capital,* June 14, 1910.

112. Hurst, *The 46th Star,* 129–43.

113. Scott, *Story of Oklahoma City,* 115.

114. Howard L. Meredith and George H. Shirk, "Oklahoma City: Growth and Reconstruction, 1889–1939," *Chronicles of Oklahoma* 55, no. 3 (Fall 1977): 303. Meredith and Shirk mistakenly identify F. P. Johnson as "E. P." Johnson.

115. Robb, *Guaranty of Bank Deposits,* 70.

116. Meredith and Shirk, "Oklahoma City," 303.

117. Stewart, *Born Grown,* 197.

118. Mahnken, "No Oklahoman Lost a Penny," 55.

119. Irvin Hurst speech, n.d., Living Legend Library, Oklahoma Oral History Collection, Oklahoma Historical Society, Oklahoma City.

120. "Oklahoma Opens War on 'Blue Sky' Money Grabbers," *St. Louis Post-Dispatch,* June 3, 1911, folder 26, box 2, Barde Collection.

121. J. D. Lankford was appointed as the state's fourth bank commissioner on March 2, 1911, was reappointed on March 19, 1915, and remained in office until 1919. Departmental appropriations from July 1, 1915, to July 1, 1917, are reported in *Fifth Biennial Report of the Bank Commissioner of the State of Oklahoma,* Oklahoma State Banking Department Collection. On February 3, 1925, the Honorable Robert L. Williams spoke on the legacy of James Dwight Lankford at the annual meeting of the Oklahoma Historical Society on the occasion of accepting the portrait of Lankford for the Society. See Robert L. Williams, "James Dwight Lankford," *Chronicles of Oklahoma* 3, no. 1 (April 1925): 86–89.

122. J. D. Lankford to the State Bankers of Oklahoma, March 28, 1911, folder 27, box 2, Barde Collection.

123. "Proclamation that Announced Fight," *St. Louis Post-Dispatch,* n.d., folder 26, box 2, Barde Collection.

124. J. D. Lankford to Officers and Directors of all State Banks, July 1, 1915, First State Bank of Boise City Corporate Files, Boise City, Oklahoma.

125. Robb, *Guaranty of Bank Deposits,* 72.

126. Mahnken "No Oklahoman Lost a Penny," 53–56; Colcord quoted in Charles Francis Colcord, *The Autobiography of Charles Francis Colcord, 1859–1934* (Tulsa: privately printed, 1970), 215–16.

127. *Proceedings of the Fifteenth Annual Convention of the Oklahoma Bankers' Association,* quoted in Robb, *Guaranty of Bank Deposits,* 41.

128. "Bankers Demand Guaranty Report Before Payment," unsourced newspaper article, April 8, 1911, folder 26, box 2, Barde Collection.

129. Mahnken "No Oklahoman Lost a Penny," 60.

130. "Insurance of Deposits Not So Pleasant," *Daily Oklahoman,* April 23, 1939.

131. Mahnken, "No Oklahoman Lost a Penny," 62.

132. "'The King Is Dead'—Welcome Gov. Lee Cruce," *Oklahoma State Capital,* June 10, 1911.

133. Hurst, *The 46th Star,* 168.

134. Haskell quoted in Hurst, *The 46th Star,* 163.

135. Gorton, *"Big-Ass Boy" in the Oil Fields,* 120–25.

136. *Encyclopedia of Oklahoma History and Culture,* s.v. "Good Roads Association," by Dianna Everett, http://digital.library.okstate.edu/encyclopedia/entries/G/GO009.html.

137. "Rival Counties, Stand Up," unsourced newspaper article, October 23, 1909, Scrapbook, August 1, 1909–February 9, 1911, box 45, vol. 22, 50, Barde Collection. Hugh M. Johnson was the author's paternal great-granduncle.

138. Johnson quoted in "Oklahoma for Good Roads," unsourced newspaper article, October 14, 1909, Scrapbook, August 1, 1909–February 9, 1911, box 45, vol. 22, 54, Barde Collection.

139. Robb, *Guaranty of Bank Deposits,* 95–96. The table is from Robb.

140. Scott, *Story of Oklahoma City,* 187.

CHAPTER 2

Epigraph: "Investing Public Is Not Prejudiced by Character of Oklahoma's Laws," unsourced newspaper article, November 28, 1908, folder 34, box 6, Barde Collection.

1. Bruner and Carr, *Panic of 1907,* 143.
2. Rockoff, "Banking and Finance," 673.
3. Bruner and Carr, *Panic of 1907,* 145.
4. Ahamed, *Lords of Finance,* 54–56.
5. Ibid., 56; "Aldrich Presents Plan of New Finance System," *Oklahoma State Capital,* January 18, 1911.
6. Bruner and Carr, *Panic of 1907,* 145–48.
7. *Encyclopedia of Oklahoma History and Culture,* s.v. "Owen, Robert Latham (1856–1947)," by Kenny L. Brown, http://digital.library.okstate.edu/encyclopedia/entries/O/OW003.html.
8. *Encyclopedia of Oklahoma History and Culture,* s.v. "Weaver, Claude (1867–1954)," by Carolyn G. Hanneman, http://digital.library.okstate.edu/encyclopedia/entries/W/WE003.html.
9. McLean quoted in Jeffrey Marshall, "Twixt Booms and Panics: Banking in the Gilded Age," in *Banking's Past, Financial Services' Future,* ed. William Zimmerman (New York: American Banker, 1986), 32.
10. Milton Friedman and Anna Jacobson Schwartz, *A Monetary History of the United States, 1867–1960* (Princeton: Princeton University Press, 1971), 189.
11. Rockoff, "Banking and Finance," 673–75.
12. Frank A. Vanderlip, "The Aldrich Plan for Banking Legislation: An Address by the Honorable Frank A. Vanderlip, President of the National City Bank, New York, before The Commercial Club of Chicago" (Madison: Wisconsin Library Services, n.d., ca. 1911), 15. Based on references in the text, the address was probably given about 1911.
13. "Aldrich's Proposed 'Mechanism,'" *Daily Oklahoman,* January 12, 1911. *Fromage* is French for cheese.
14. Friedman and Schwartz, *Monetary History,* 193.
15. H. W. Brands, *American Colossus: The Triumph of Capitalism, 1865–1900* (New York: Anchor Books, 2010), 618–19.
16. "Oklahoma City Society Spends Four Days Before Moving Picture Cameras," unsourced newspaper article, August 1913, Johnson-Hightower Family Archives, Oklahoma City (hereafter cited as Johnson-Hightower Family Archives). Ethlyn (the author's paternal grandmother) was the only child of Frank and Aida Johnson (the author's paternal great-grandparents). She died of pneumonia on May 5, 1931, and was survived by her husband,

W. E. "Billy" Hightower (the author's paternal grandfather), and their children, Frank (the author's father), and Phyllis (the author's aunt). Mourning a death in the banking family, the *Oklahoma Banker* commemorated her passing with praise for her participation in the Junior League of Oklahoma City's philanthropic endeavors. She had been elected to the league's presidency, but death robbed her of the opportunity to serve. Many remembered the one-time movie starlet for her prowess with horses: "Mrs. Hightower was fond of horses and owned some fine ones that placed first or well toward the top in many of the horse shows." See "Mrs. W. E. Hightower Passes On," *Oklahoma Banker* (May 1931), 32.

17. Advertisement for "The Hit of the Season," *Oklahoma City Times,* August 14, 1913.

18. "Great Crowds Go To See Pictures," *Daily Oklahoman,* August 14, 1913.

19. "Vivacity and Grace in Home Made Movie," *Daily Oklahoman,* August 12, 1913.

20. For an account of Frank P. and Hugh M. Johnson's achievements in business and banking, see Michael J. Hightower, "Brother Bankers: Frank P. and Hugh M. Johnson, Founders of the First National Bank and Trust Company of Oklahoma City," *Chronicles of Oklahoma* 88, no. 4 (Winter 2010–11): 388–415.

21. Oscar Ameringer, *If You Don't Weaken,* foreword by Carl Sandburg (New York: Henry Holt, 1940), 228. When it was published in 1940, *If You Don't Weaken* was compared favorably in the national press to such iconic memoirs as *The Education of Henry Adams* and *The Autobiography of Lincoln Steffens.* See *Encyclopedia of Oklahoma History and Culture,* s.v. "Ameringer, Oscar (1870–1943)," by John Thompson, http://digital.library.okstate.edu/encyclopedia/entries/A/AM014.html; H. L. Meredith, "Oscar Ameringer and the Concept of Agrarian Socialism," *Chronicles of Oklahoma* 45, no. 1 (Spring 1967): 77–83; and Michael Kazin, *American Dreamers: How the Left Changed a Nation* (New York: Vintage Books, 2012), 114–18.

22. *Encyclopedia of Oklahoma History and Culture,* s.v. "Ameringer, Oscar."

23. John Thompson, *Closing the Frontier: Radical Response in Oklahoma, 1889–1923* (Norman: University of Oklahoma Press, 1986), 61.

24. James R. Green, *Grass-Roots Socialism: Radical Movements in the Southwest, 1895–1943* (Baton Rouge: Louisiana State University Press, 1978), 5–7.

25. *Encyclopedia of Oklahoma History and Culture,* s.v. "Farmers' Alliance," by Gilbert C. Fite, http://digital.library.okstate.edu/encyclopedia/entries/F/FA017.html.

26. Scales and Goble, *Oklahoma Politics,* 64.

27. Green, *Grass-Roots Socialism,* 124.

28. *Encyclopedia of Oklahoma History and Culture,* s.v. "Ameringer, Oscar"; Howard Zinn, *The Twentieth Century: A People's History* (New York: HarperPerennial, 2003), 55.

29. Garin Burbank, *When Farmers Voted Red: The Gospel of Socialism in the Oklahoma Countryside, 1910–1924* (Westport, Conn.: Greenwood Press, 1976), 7.

30. Green, *Grass-Roots Socialism,* 39–40.

31. Zinn, *Twentieth Century,* 55.

32. Scales and Goble, *Oklahoma Politics,* 66; Thompson, *Closing the Frontier,* 100.

33. Green, *Grass-Roots Socialism,* 71.

34. James M. Smallwood, "Partners in Progress: Banking and Agribusiness in Oklahoma," in *Banking in the West,* ed. Larry Schweikart (Manhattan, Kans.: Sunflower University Press, 1984), 13.

35. "The Landless Man and the Tenant Farmer," *Harlow's Weekly,* January 15, 1919.

36. Green, *Grass-Roots Socialism,* 72.

37. Williams's study quoted in Thompson, *Closing the Frontier,* 103.

38. Burbank, *When Farmers Voted Red,* 56–57.

39. Advertisement, Madill National Bank, *Marshall County News-Democrat,* May 11, 18, and 25, 1916; Green, *Grass-Roots Socialism,* 69; Burbank, *When Farmers Voted Red,* 6.
40. Scales and Goble, *Oklahoma Politics,* 88.
41. "Arrest Socialists on Conspiracy Charge," *Ada Star-Democrat,* August 3, 1917.
42. "Uprising of the Clans," *Ada Star-Democrat,* August 10, 1917.
43. Scales and Goble, *Oklahoma Politics,* 88–89.
44. "The Banking Situation in Oklahoma," *Harlow's Weekly,* October 12, 1912.
45. "Bank Deposits Indicate Prosperity," *Harlow's Weekly,* November 23, 1912.
46. "Deposits in Fifteen Oklahoma City Banks at Highest Point in Five Years," *Daily Oklahoman,* April 20, 1913.
47. Ibid.
48. News brief, *Oklahoma Banker* (September 1911), 92–93.
49. "Investing Public Is Not Prejudiced by Character of Oklahoma's Laws."
50. "Capital Fears Oklahoma," unsourced newspaper article, May 18, 1908, Scrapbook, May 16–December 30, 1908, box 44, vol. 20, 1, Barde Collection.
51. "Resolutions of The Tulsa Commercial Club," April 27, 1908, folder 34, box 6, Barde Collection.
52. "Commercial Clubs of State Resolve to Run Out Political Demagogues," unsourced newspaper article, August 7, 1908, folder 34, box 6, Barde Collection.
53. "Bank Robbers at Ocheleta [sic]," *Oklahoma State Capital,* January 12, 1911.
54. "Mead Bank Is Robbed of All," *Oklahoma State Capital,* February 26, 1911.
55. Smallwood, *Oklahoma Adventure,* 72–73.
56. "Reward for Bank Robbers Provided," *Daily Oklahoman,* January 17, 1913.
57. "Robbed Banks of $32,050," *Oklahoma City Times,* January 14, 1915, folder 20, box 7, Barde Collection.
58. Scales and Goble, *Oklahoma Politics,* 82.
59. "When Will It Stop?," *Oklahoma Banker* (February 1916), 238.
60. *Encyclopedia of Oklahoma History and Culture,* s.v. "Cruce, Lee (1863–1933)," by Linda D. Wilson, http://digital.library.okstate.edu/encyclopedia/entries/C/CR020.html.
61. "Deputy Killed in Daylight Raid on Bank at Terlton," *Daily Oklahoman,* January 13, 1915, folder 20, box 7, Barde Collection.
62. "Open Letter to the Legislature," *Daily Oklahoman,* January 13, 1915, folder 20, box 7, Barde Collection.
63. "Robbed Banks of $32,050."
64. "Gun Men on Strict Guard," unsourced newspaper article, n.d., folder 20, box 7, Barde Collection.
65. Hoefer quoted in "Kaw Bank Robbed," *Oklahoma Banker* (April 1915), 293; "Three Bandits Secure $2,015 in Daylight Holdup of Kaw City Bank," *Mangum Weekly Star,* April 15, 1915.
66. "Bank Burglary Blocked," *Oklahoma Banker* (April 1915), 303.
67. Gorton, *"Big-Ass Boy" in the Oil Fields,* 84.
68. "Puts Price on Head of Starr," *Mangum Weekly Star,* March 4, 1915.
69. "Stroud Visited by Bank Robbers," *Chandler Tribune,* April 1, 1915.
70. "Five Bandits Are Still at Large," *Daily Oklahoman,* March 30, 1915.
71. "Twenty Years of Outlaw Activity Ended for Starr," *Daily Oklahoman,* March 29, 1915. Other accounts put amount stolen in Stroud at $5,815.
72. "Twenty Years of Outlaw Activity Ended for Starr."

73. "The Last of Romantic Outlaws," newspaper submission, n.d., folder 37, box 26, Barde Collection.

74. Untitled newspaper submission beginning, "Henry Starr, Cherokee outlaw, has asked that he be pardoned from the Colorado State Penitentiary," September 27, n.d., folder 37, box 26, Barde Collection.

75. Colcord, *Autobiography*, 174–75.

76. "Starr Is Alleged to Have Thrown Away Bank Paper," *Daily Oklahoman*, April 4, 1915.

77. Smallwood, *Oklahoma Adventure*, 67.

78. Scales and Goble, *Oklahoma Politics*, 81; Burbank, *When Farmers Voted Red*, 18.

79. News brief, *Oklahoma Banker* (November 1913), 141.

80. Robb, *Guaranty of Bank Deposits*, 81–82.

81. Smallwood, "Partners in Progress," 13; "Usury Bill Defeated 52 to 38," *Oklahoma Banker* (March 1915), 261.

82. Smallwood, *Oklahoma Adventure*, 67.

83. Smallwood, "Partners in Progress," 13.

84. Robb, *Guaranty of Bank Deposits*, 81.

85. "What Next?," *Oklahoma Banker* (February 1916), 238. The law was set to take effect on May 21. See "Opinion on New Usury Law," *Oklahoma Banker* (March 1916), 270–74; and "Governor Signs Usury Bill," *Oklahoma Banker* (March 1916), 274.

86. Doti and Schweikart, *Banking in the American West*, 96.

87. "First War Savings Bank in Nation Completed; Huge Parade Tomorrow," *Daily Oklahoman*, March 10, 1918.

88. Smallwood, *Oklahoma Adventure*, 79.

89. "Over the Top," *Oklahoma*, April 1918, official publication of the Oklahoma City Chamber of Commerce, Research Division, Oklahoma Historical Society, Oklahoma City (hereafter cited as OHS Oklahoma City Chamber of Commerce Collection).

90. "Every County in Oklahoma Oversubscribes Bond Quota; State Total Now $35,857,150," *Daily Oklahoman*, May 5, 1918.

91. "Mixing Brains with the Soil of Oklahoma," *Harlow's Weekly*, May 24, 1913.

92. "What the Banker Must Do," *Oklahoma Banker* (November 1913), 134.

93. Smallwood, *Oklahoma Adventure*, 79.

94. Farmer quoted in "Mixing Brains with the Soil of Oklahoma."

95. "Why the Bankers Are Working with the Farmers," *Oklahoma Banker* (December 1913), 188–90.

96. "Means Salvation of Oklahoma," *Oklahoma Banker* (November 1913), 135.

97. "The Good Old Days: 75 Years Ago," *Oklahoma Banker* (April 1987), 24.

98. Hitchcock quoted in "Uncle Sam To Be Head of 48 Banks," unsourced newspaper article, n.d., folder 1, box 11, Barde Collection.

99. Unsourced newspaper submission beginning, "The first and only United States postal savings bank in Oklahoma is at Guymon," January 21, 1911, folder 1, box 11, Barde Collection.

100. R. B. Quinn to F. S. Barde, January 6, 1911, folder 1, box 11, Barde Collection.

101. Kindleberger and Aliber, *Manias, Panics, and Crashes*, 76.

102. ". . . Is Honored," unsourced newspaper article, February 27, 1911, folder 26, box 2, Barde Collection.

103. Robb, *Guaranty of Bank Deposits*, 105. Romans regarded Lucius Quinctius Cincinnatus (519–430 BCE?) as a model of virtue and simplicity. He worked on his farm until he was called to serve Rome as dictator, an office he resigned after completing his duty to the state.

His resignation and return to private life has been cited as an example of good leadership, public service, civic virtue, and modesty. Lankford never rose to the position of dictator, and he was a banker, not a farmer. But he was certainly admired by the people who knew him best as an honest and capable small-town banker who could resist temptations in the state capital.

104. Robb, *Guaranty of Bank Deposits,* 197.

CHAPTER 3

Epigraph: "Banks Serve and Grow or Do Not Live," *Harlow's Weekly,* September 8, 1923.

1. Walton quoted in "Walton 'Makes Good' on Promise to Give People Great Party," *Daily Oklahoman,* January 10, 1923. Walton served as mayor of Oklahoma City from April 7, 1919, to January 9, 1923. See "Previous Mayors," on City of Oklahoma City website, http://www.okc.gov/council/mayor/previous.html.

2. Colcord, *Autobiography,* 217.

3. See Margaret Bayard Smith's letter to Mrs. Kirkpatrick, dated March 11, 1829, White House Historical Association website, s.v. "A Letter of Margaret Bayard Smith to Mrs. Kirkpatrick," http://www.whitehousehistory.org/whha_classroom/classroom_documents-1828_g.html.); and Jon Meacham, *American Lion: Andrew Jackson in the White House* (New York: Random House, 2008).

4. William Warren Rogers, "'I Want You All to Come': John C. Walton and America's Greatest Barbecue," *Chronicles of Oklahoma* 75, no. 1 (Spring 1997): 24–25.

5. Under the headline, "Jack Walton's People's Party," the *New York Times* published an account of the great barbecue on January 10, 1923. The story was reproduced in its entirety by *Harlow's Weekly,* the *Tulsa Tribune,* and the *Okmulgee Times.* See "In the Trail of the Barbecue," *Harlow's Weekly,* January 20, 1923.

6. Newspaper quoted in Rogers, "'I Want You All to Come,'" 25.

7. Ibid., 25–27.

8. *New York Times* quoted in "In the Trail of the Barbecue."

9. Colcord, *Autobiography,* 218.

10. Ibid.; Rogers, "'I Want You All to Come,'" 30.

11. "In the Trail of the Barbecue."

12. *Encyclopedia of Oklahoma History and Culture,* s.v. "Banking Industry," by Lynne Pierson Doti, http://digital.library.okstate.edu/encyclopedia/entries/B/BA011.html.

13. Ned Eichler, *The Thrift Debacle* (Berkeley: University of California Press, 1989), 4.

14. Bert Willis, "And Your Old Men Shall Dream Dreams," unpublished memoir, 1953, folder 6, box 7, 61, E. H. Kelley Collection, Research Division, Oklahoma Historical Society, Oklahoma City (hereafter cited as Kelley Collection).

15. Paul B. Trescott, *Financing American Enterprise: The Story of Commercial Banking* (New York: Harper and Row, 1963), 110.

16. Farmers State Bank of Alva, box 4, Ellis County Bank in Arnett, box 8, Bank of Buffalo, box 18, Cheyenne State Bank, box 23, Commercial Bank of El Reno, box 38, Closed Bank Files, Oklahoma Department of Libraries, Oklahoma City.

17. Trescott, *Financing American Enterprise,* 110.

18. Paul Studenski and Herman E. Krooss, *Financial History of the United States* (New York: McGraw-Hill, 1963), 335.

19. Tippetts quoted in Eichler, *Thrift Debacle,* 5.

20. "Bank Deposits Still Grow," unsourced newspaper article, folder 26, box 2, Barde Collection.

21. "State Bankers Meet December 7," unsourced newspaper article, folder 26, box 2, November 27, 1908, Barde Collection.

22. "Owen Defends Guaranty Law," unsourced newspaper article, folder 26, box 2, December 21, 1908, Barde Collection.

23. "Message to the Members of the Third Legislature in Regular Session Assembled," in *Inaugural Address, January 9, 1911, and First Message of Governor Lee Cruce to the Third Legislature of Oklahoma, January 10, 1911*, 9, folder 24, box 7, Barde Collection.

24. "Extracts from Addresses delivered by Governor Cruce before 1500 Bankers in Oklahoma City, May 23, 1911," in *Governor Cruce Defends State Guaranty Laws*, compliments of First State Bank of Oklahoma City, n.d., 6–7, folder 24, box 7, Barde Collection.

25. Letter from Lee Cruce, in *Governor Cruce Defends State Guaranty Laws*, 3, folder 24, box 7, Barde Collection.

26. Grecian quoted in "Oklahoma Banks Show Up Fallacy," unsourced newspaper article, October 27, 1908, folder 26, box 2, Barde Collection.

27. Willis, "And Your Old Men Shall Dream Dreams," 66.

28. Roberts quoted in "Defects of the Deposit Guaranty Scheme," unsourced newspaper article, n.d., folder 26, box 2, Barde Collection.

29. "Confidence Is Shattered Now," unsourced newspaper article, n.d., folder 26, box 2, Barde Collection. E. B. Cockrell was appointed as the state's third banking commissioner on June 1, 1910, and served in that capacity until his resignation on March 2, 1911. See *Fifth Biennial Report of the Bank Commissioner of the State of Oklahoma*, Oklahoma State Banking Department Collection.

30. "Dares Officials to Shut Up Bank," unsourced newspaper article, May 20, 1911, folder 26, box 2, Barde Collection.

31. "Oklahoma Banker Attacks State Law," unsourced newspaper article, n.d., folder 26, box 2, Barde Collection.

32. "Oklahoma's State Bank Muddle," *Harlow's Weekly*, February 3, 1923.

33. "Bank Probe Committee Has Troubles," *Harlow's Weekly*, May 12, 1923.

34. "Oklahoma's State Bank Muddle."

35. Trescott, *Financing American Enterprise*, 161–62.

36. "Is the Guaranty of Deposits Unsound?," *Oklahoma Banker* (December 1932), 8.

37. Willis, "And Your Old Men Shall Dream Dreams," 68.

38. "Oklahoma's State Bank Muddle."

39. "Decline of the 'Bad Man,'" *McMasters' Weekly*, April 4, 1896. *McMaster's Weekly*, the successor to *Oklahoma Magazine*, boasted on its masthead that it was "The Spokesman of the Common People."

40. "Death for Bank Robbers," unsourced newspaper article, April 1, 1908, Scrapbook, July 8, 1907–May 16, 1908, box 43, vol. 19, 178, Barde Collection.

41. "The Vigilant Movement in Oklahoma," *Oklahoma Banker* (November 1925), 20.

42. "Organization of Viligantees [sic] in Okfuskee County," *Oklahoma Banker* (July 1925), 36.

43. Burbank, *When Farmers Voted Red*, 141.

44. Ahamed, *Lords of Finance*, 211.

45. "Rob Lincoln County Bank," *Indian Journal* (Eufaula), December 22, 1922.

46. "Officers Waited but Tip Failed," *Blackwell Morning Tribune*, March 14, 1928.

47. "Organization of Viligantees [sic] in Okfuskee County," 36.
48. "The Vigilant Movement in Oklahoma," 20.
49. Ibid., 19. The etymology of "yegg" takes us back to the turn of the twentieth century when a Californian by the name of John Yegg spawned a new breed of criminal. Yegg, a drifter with a distaste for honest work, came across a report about burglar-proof safes circulated by the Treasury Department. Yegg was particularly interested in nitroglycerine, and he had plenty of time on his hands to become an expert in its properties. Under his tutelage, hoboes across the land known as "yeggmen" relied on explosives to commit brazen bank robberies. "Yegg" eventually entered the common vernacular as a catchall term for desperadoes who had little regard for human life. Their pillaging became the bane of law enforcement and, predictably, fodder for legend. See "A Bank Burglars' Union," *New York Times,* September 15, 1901.
50. For the best biography of Pretty Boy Floyd, see Michael Wallis, *Pretty Boy: The Life and Times of Charles Arthur Floyd* (New York: St. Martin's Press, 1992).
51. "America's Crime War," pt. 1, *Oklahoma Banker* (March 1927), 25.
52. Ibid., pt. 2, *Oklahoma Banker* (April 1927), 30.
53. "Oklahoma Wins Again," *Oklahoma Banker* (April 1930), 31.
54. Smallwood, "Partners in Progress," 15–20. These figures were provided by Charles A. Vose II, president of the First National Bank and Trust Company of Oklahoma City, in an interview on May 30, 1978. The interview was archived at the OBA.
55. "The New Importance of Commercial Bank Advertising," *Oklahoma Banker* (September 1931), 15–17.
56. Trescott, *Financing American Enterprise,* 190.
57. "An Age of Installment Buying," *Oklahoma Banker* (December 1927), 23.
58. "Instalment [sic] Selling Proves Itself as Good Merchandising," *Oklahoma Banker* (July 1932), 17.
59. Trescott, *Financing American Enterprise,* 168–92.
60. "An Age of Installment Buying," 23–24.
61. "President's Address," *Oklahoma Banker* (May 1927), 24–25.
62. The entire saga of Oklahoma City's successful campaign to lure a branch of the Federal Reserve Bank was published in "Oklahoma City's New Federal Reserve Bank," *Harlow's Weekly,* April 28, 1923.
63. "National Banks of Southern Counties Placed in Kansas City Reserve District Today," *Daily Oklahoman,* July 1, 1915. A map showing an early designation of Federal Reserve districts was published in the *Daily Oklahoman,* April 7, 1914. The Tenth District, headquartered in Kansas City, included 835 national banks in Kansas, Nebraska, Colorado, Wyoming, and parts of Missouri, Oklahoma, and New Mexico. The Eleventh District, headquartered in Dallas, included 726 national banks in Texas, parts of New Mexico and Oklahoma that were not included in the Tenth District, part of Louisiana not included in the Sixth District (headquartered in Atlanta), and southeastern Arizona.
64. "National Banks of Southern Counties Placed in Kansas City."
65. Harrison quoted in "Banks to Appeal to Reserve Chief," *Daily Oklahoman,* May 17, 1914.
66. "Oklahoma City's New Federal Reserve Bank."
67. "Federal Reserve Bank Is Big Banker's Institution," *Daily Oklahoman,* April 23, 1939, Banks and Banking—Oklahoma, Vertical Files, Research Division, Oklahoma Historical Society, Oklahoma City (hereafter cited as OHS Banks and Banking Vertical Files).

68. "National Banks of Southern Counties Placed in Kansas City."

69. "Oklahoma City's New Federal Reserve Bank"; "The Reserve Bank Award," *Daily Oklahoman*, November 3, 1919.

70. Tim Todd, *Confidence Restored: The History of the Tenth District's Federal Reserve Bank* (Kansas City, Mo.: Public Affairs Department, Federal Reserve Bank of Kansas City, 2008), 123.

71. Johnson quoted in "Bank Decision Submitted to Vote in State," *Daily Oklahoman*, November 30, 1919.

72. Todd, *Confidence Restored*, 123.

73. "Bank Will Be Located Here Board Orders," *Daily Oklahoman*, December 18, 1919; Johnson quoted in advertisement/public service announcement, "Federal Reserve Bank Comes to Oklahoma City," *Daily Oklahoman*, December 18, 1919.

74. "Federal Reserve Bank Is Big Banker's Institution."

75. "Oklahoma City's New Federal Reserve Bank"; Smallwood, *Oklahoma Adventure*, 88.

76. "Federal Reserve Bank Is Big Banker's Institution."

77. "Oklahoma City's New Federal Reserve Bank."

78. Niall Ferguson, *The Ascent of Money: A Financial History of the World* (New York: Penguin, 2008), 174.

79. Tibbs quoted in "Oklahoma City's New Federal Reserve Bank."

80. "Federal Reserve Bank Is Big Banker's Institution."

81. "Oklahoma City's New Federal Reserve Bank."

82. Keeler quoted in "Oil from 'Old Faithful,' Oklahoma's Pioneer Producer, to Be Placed in Bank Cornerstone," *Daily Oklahoman*, December 3, 1922.

83. "Oklahoma's Financial Rock of Gibraltar," *Daily Oklahoman*, May 6, 1923.

84. "Oklahoma City Banks Second in Savings in Tenth Reserve District," *Oklahoma Banker* (April 1923), 17.

85. *Blue Book of Southern Progress* cited in "Federal Banks of State Rank High in South," *Daily Oklahoman*, July 22, 1923.

86. "Bank Clearings Here Nearing Top in South," *Daily Oklahoman*, July 22, 1923.

87. Stewart, *Born Grown*, 59.

88. Advertisement, *Oklahoma Banker* (January 1927), 6.

89. "Work of Oklahoma Fourth Legislature," *Mangum Weekly Star*, July 24, 1913.

90. "Building and Loan Companies Show Healthy Growth," *Oklahoma*, August 1918, OHS Oklahoma City Chamber of Commerce Collection.

91. "Building and Loan Associations in Oklahoma Maintain Supremacy," *Harlow's Weekly*, July 28, 1923.

92. "Building and Loan Companies Thrive," *Harlow's Weekly*, February 3, 1923.

93. "How Building and Loan Companies Grow," *Harlow's Weekly*, March 10, 1923.

94. "Building and Loan Companies Thrive."

95. "Building and Loan Associations in Oklahoma Maintain Supremacy."

96. Bartlett Naylor, "Bankers Spilled Blood in Nation's Early Years," in Zimmerman, *Banking's Past, Financial Services' Future*, 18–20; Meacham, *American Lion*, 201.

97. Smallwood, *Oklahoma Adventure*, 95.

98. Chernow, *Death of the Banker*, 53.

99. Friedman and Schwartz, *Monetary History*, 244.

100. Hutto quoted in Smallwood, *Oklahoma Adventure*, 96–98.

101. "Group Banking and Its Application to Oklahoma," *Oklahoma Banker* (January 1930), 17.
102. Ibid.
103. "Banks Serve and Grow or Do Not Live."

CHAPTER 4

Epigraph: "The Situation Confronting Our Banks," *Oklahoma Banker* (October 1933), 12.

1. C. B. Glasscock, *Then Came Oil: The Story of the Last Frontier* (Westport, Conn.: Hyperion Press, 1976), 288–95.
2. "One Producer Completed as Two Go Wild," *Daily Oklahoman,* March 27, 1930.
3. "City's Greatest Well Still Running Wild; Smaller One Subdued," *Daily Oklahoman,* March 29, 1930.
4. Sudik quoted in Glasscock, *Then Came Oil,* 297.
5. Gorton, *"Big-Ass Boy" in the Oil Fields,* 60.
6. Glasscock, *Then Came Oil,* 114–15.
7. "Disaster Confronting Oil Industry," *Harlow's Weekly,* July 17, 1918.
8. "The Oil Industry in Oklahoma," *Harlow's Weekly,* February 10, 1923.
9. "Financing the Oil Industry," *Oklahoma Banker* (March 1923), 12–17.
10. William H. Mullins, "In the Midst of Adversity: The City, the Governor, and the FERA, Part I," *Chronicles of Oklahoma* 76, no. 4 (Winter 1998–99): 375.
11. Meredith and Shirk, "Oklahoma City," 306; Max Nichols and David R. "Dusty" Martin, *Continuing an Oklahoma Banking Tradition* (Oklahoma City: First Interstate Bank of Oklahoma, N.A., 1989), 40. A fascinating account of the construction of the First National Building and the Ramsey Tower can be found in Bill Moore, "Race to the Top: The Great Skyscraper Race of 1931," *Oklahoma Gazette* 19 (November 6, 1997): 17–20. For a sweeping retrospective of Oklahoma City's first half century, see *Daily Oklahoman,* April 23, 1939.
12. Moore, "Race to the Top," 18–20. The great race ended on October 3, 1931, when the Ramsey Tower was completed almost a month ahead of the First National Bank Building. Stockholders in the First National Bank could take solace that, at a height of 456 feet, their building was the tallest one in the state.
13. McClure quoted in "Tenth Federal Reserve in Exceptional Position," *Oklahoma Banker* (October 1930), 23.
14. "Glorious Rain Pleased Farmers of Panhandle," *Guymon Panhandle Herald,* February 26, 1931.
15. "No Relief Fund Is Needed Here," *Guymon Panhandle Herald,* February 26, 1931.
16. Hendricks quoted in "Bankers Are in Optimistic Mood," *Blackwell Morning Tribune,* September 6, 1932.
17. Willis, "And Your Old Men Shall Dream Dreams," 70–71.
18. Scott, *The Story of Oklahoma City,* 189.
19. "Oklahoma City's Skyscraper Now Being Erected," *Oklahoma Banker* (August 1930), 16; Moore, "Race to the Top," 19.
20. "First National of Oklahoma City in New Quarters," *Oklahoma Banker* (December 1931), 11.
21. "Beacon to Flash 75 Miles in State," *Blackwell Sunday Tribune,* September 6, 1931.
22. "First National of Oklahoma City in New Quarters," 11–12; Moore, "Race to the Top," 20.

23. Unsourced newspaper articles, n.d., Johnson-Hightower Family Archives.
24. "First National of Oklahoma City in New Quarters," 11; Moore, "Race to the Top," 20.
25. "First National of Oklahoma City in New Quarters," 11–13.
26. Studenski and Krooss, *Financial History*, 370–71.
27. Ibid.; Robert L. Heilbroner, *The Economic Transformation of America*, in collaboration with Aaron Singer (New York: Harcourt Brace Jovanovich, 1977), 175; Niall Ferguson, *Civilization: The West and the Rest* (New York: Penguin, 2011), 230–31.
28. Heilbroner, *Economic Transformation*, 200; Zinn, *Twentieth Century*, 123.
29. Rogers spoke at the President's Organization on Unemployment Relief radio broadcast. See Will Rogers, "Bacon and Beans and Limousines," on Unsinkable Cork website, http://unsinkablecork.com/willrogers/wrspeech.htm.
30. Mullins, "In the Midst of Adversity, Part I," 375.
31. William H. Mullins, "In the Midst of Adversity: The City, the Governor, and the FERA, Part II," *Chronicles of Oklahoma* 77, no. 1 (Spring 1999): 60.
32. Smallwood, *Oklahoma Adventure*, 104.
33. Mullins, "In the Midst of Adversity, Part I," 380.
34. Smallwood, *Oklahoma Adventure*, 106–107.
35. Willis, "And Your Old Men Shall Dream Dreams," 77–79.
36. Mullins, "In the Midst of Adversity, Part I," 380–84.
37. Ibid., 381.
38. Baum quoted in "Crimes against Banks Mounting Rapidly," *Oklahoma Banker* (April 1931), 27.
39. "Bank Robberies," *Oklahoma Banker* (March 1932), 17.
40. Willis, "And Your Old Men Shall Dream Dreams," 93–96.
41. Ibid., 96–97.
42. "Floyd and his Lone Aide Loot another Bank," *Blackwell Morning Tribune*, April 22, 1932.
43. "The Flying Vigilante," *Oklahoma Banker* (November 1934), 12.
44. "Laws Hinder Bank Bandits," *Blackwell Sunday Tribune*, September 4, 1932.
45. "Problems We Bankers Must Meet," *Oklahoma Banker* (November 1930), 12.
46. Walter Lippmann, *Drift and Mastery: An Attempt to Diagnose the Current Unrest* (Madison: University of Wisconsin Press, 1985), 43.
47. "The Outlook for Banking," *Oklahoma Banker* (December 1930), 21–25.
48. Ibid.
49. Noyes, "A Year after the Panic," 185–212.
50. "How Deep Is the Present Depression?" *Oklahoma Banker* (February 1932), 13–14.
51. Robert M. Garsson, "'The Ballyhoo Years' End in a Crash and a Hangover," in Zimmerman, *Banking's Past, Financial Services' Future*, 33.
52. "Bank Holiday Was Taken in Stride."
53. Murray and Barnett quoted in "State Banks Safe, Holiday Is Precaution," *Daily Oklahoman*, March 2, 1933.
54. "City's Banks in Splendid Condition," *Daily Oklahoman*, March 2, 1933.
55. Joel Champlin, interview by author, April 27, 2011, Enid, Oklahoma, Michael J. Hightower Oklahoma Bank and Commerce Oral History Collection. Research Division. Oklahoma Historical Society, Oklahoma City (hereafter cited as Hightower Oral History Collection).

56. *Time* cited in Henry B. Bass, "Herbert Hiram Champlin," *Chronicles of Oklahoma* 33, no. 1 (Spring 1955): 48.
57. Champlin interview.
58. Willis, "And Your Old Men Shall Dream Dreams," 111.
59. Bill and Guy Berry, interview by author, April 18, 2012, Sapulpa, Oklahoma, Hightower Oral History Collection.
60. Roosevelt quoted in Schlesinger, *Almanac*, 461. The economist John Maynard Keynes made a similar, though certainly less lyrical, reference to the psychological dimensions of the Great Depression when he spoke of a "failure in the immaterial devices of the mind." See Ferguson, *Ascent of Money*, 159.
61. Roosevelt quoted in Garsson, "'The Ballyhoo Years' End," 33.
62. Wheeler quoted in Richard M. Salsman, "Bankers as Scapegoats for Government-Created Banking Crises in U.S. History," in *The Crisis in American Banking*, ed. Lawrence H. White (New York: New York University Press, 1993), 100.
63. H. Parker Willis quoted in Salsman, "Bankers as Scapegoats," 100–101.
64. Rogers quoted in Heilbroner, *Economic Transformation*, 190–91.
65. Willis, "And Your Old Men Shall Dream Dreams," 100.
66. "Bank Holiday Was Taken in Stride."
67. On Tuesday, March 7, Federal Reserve official Walter Wyatt was summoned to the White House to draft a banking bill. In the absence of a specific mandate from the administration, Wyatt worked feverishly over twenty-four hours to draft a bill. "There wasn't anybody in that entire Brains Trust, apparently, that had given any thought—they certainly had no plans—or any real study to the problem created by this banking situation," recalled Wyatt in an oral history many years later. House leaders rushed the Emergency Banking Relief Act through their chamber in record time in spite of the fact that they had been given only one copy of the bill. See Tony Badger, "FDR: A Model for Obama?," *Nation* (January 26, 2009), 20.
68. Garsson, "'The Ballyhoo Years' End," 42–43.
69. Trescott, *Financing American Enterprise*, 210.
70. Bimson quoted in Garsson, "'The Ballyhoo Years' End," 43.
71. Heilbroner, *Economic Transformation*, 191.
72. Roosevelt quoted in Heilbroner, *Economic Transformation*, 43.
73. Bruce Lenthall, *Radio's America: The Great Depression and the Rise of Modern Mass Culture* (Chicago: University of Chicago Press, 2007), 125.
74. Roosevelt quoted in Heilbroner, *Economic Transformation*, 192.
75. Chernow, *Death of the Banker*, 43; Studenski and Krooss, *Financial History*, 368–69.
76. Roosevelt quoted in Garsson, "'The Ballyhoo Years' End," 44.
77. Willis, "And Your Old Men Shall Dream Dreams," 106.
78. "In Bank Law, New Year Brings New Deal to Nation's Depositors," *Boise City News*, January 11, 1934.
79. Badger, "FDR: A Model for Obama?," 22.
80. "In Bank Law, New Year Brings New Deal to Nation's Depositors."
81. Studenski and Krooss, *Financial History*, 395–96.
82. Berle quoted in Badger, "FDR: A Model for Obama?," 22.
83. "The Situation Confronting Our Banks," 11–12.
84. Lenthall, *Radio's America*, 15.
85. "Bankers in National Move for Uniform Financial Practices," *(Boise City) Cimarron News*, May 3, 1929.

86. "Decrease in Crimes against Banks," *Oklahoma Banker* (October 1934), 20.

87. Willis, "And Your Old Men Shall Dream Dreams," 83.

88. Trescott, *Financing American Enterprise,* 208. Hanging in my office in Charlottesville is a framed twenty-dollar bill signed by my great-grandfather, F. P. Johnson, in his capacity as president of the First National Bank and Trust Company of Oklahoma City.

89. Ann Fabian, "History for the Masses: Commercializing the Western Past," in *Under an Open Sky: Rethinking America's Western Past,* ed. William Cronon, George Miles, and Jay Gitlin (New York: W. W. Norton, 1992), 234.

90. Brands, *American Colossus,* 169.

91. Dannie Bea Hightower, interview by author, June 28 and 29, 2008, Harbor Springs, Michigan, Hightower Oral History Collection. Hightower's late husband and the author's father, Frank J. Hightower, was Frank P. Johnson's grandson.

CHAPTER 5

Epigraph: "A Summary of the Past Year's Work and Current Issues of Banking," *Oklahoma Banker* (May 1934), 7–8.

1. Tom Brokaw, *The Greatest Generation* (New York: Dell Publishing, 1998), xxx.

2. Willis, "And Your Old Men Shall Dream Dreams," 91–92.

3. "A Summary of the Past Year's Work and Current Issues of Banking," 6–7.

4. "First National's Amazing Progress Parallels State Record," *Daily Oklahoman,* December 7, 1931.

5. Ibid.

6. Smallwood, *Oklahoma Adventure,* 124–25.

7. "The Nation's Business and Industrial Committee," *Oklahoma Banker* (August 1932), 17–18.

8. Sims quoted in "American Banks Are in Good Condition," *Oklahoma Banker* (August 1932), 18.

9. Doti and Schweikart, *Banking in the American West,* 125.

10. "Glass-Steagall Bill," *Oklahoma Banker* (March 1932), 7.

11. "The Situation and the Outlook," *Oklahoma Banker* (November 1933), 3–5.

12. "The Cause of the Depression," *Oklahoma Banker* (March 1934), 3–11. Walker was quoting from Galatians 6:7.

13. Ibid.

14. Smallwood, *Oklahoma Adventure,* 121–22.

15. Smallwood, "Partners in Progress," 17; Zinn, *Twentieth Century,* 124–25.

16. Susan Dornblaser, *Liberty and Tulsa: Making History Together for 100 Years, 1895–1995* (Tulsa: Liberty Bank and Trust Company, N.A., 1995), 14.

17. Ibid., 1–2; Smallwood, *Oklahoma Adventure,* 26–27; Angie Debo, *Tulsa: From Creek Town to Oil Capital* (Norman: University of Oklahoma Press, 1943), 69, 78.

18. Dornblaser, *Liberty and Tulsa,* 8–20.

19. "History," on Mayo Hotel website, http://www.themayohotel.com/hotel_history.php.

20. Margery Bird (née Mayo; now deceased), interview by author, July 16, 2010, Tulsa, Oklahoma, Hightower Oral History Collection. Mrs. Bird was in her nineties at the time of her interview and died before this book went to press.

21. Ibid.

22. "History," on Mayo Hotel website.

23. Bird interview.
24. Mullins, "In the Midst of Adversity, Part I," 375.
25. Mullins, "In the Midst of Adversity, Part II," 61.
26. *Encyclopedia of Oklahoma History and Culture,* s.v. "Urschel Kidnapping," by Larry O'Dell, http://digital.library.okstate.edu/encyclopedia/entries/U/UR009.html.
27. Hopkins quoted in Mullins, "In the Midst of Adversity, Part II," 62, 69.
28. Advertisement, *Oklahoma Banker* (June 1932), inside front cover.
29. Advertisement, *Oklahoma Banker* (July 1932), inside front cover.
30. Advertisement, *Oklahoma Banker* (October 1932), inside front cover.
31. Advertisement, *Oklahoma Banker* (November 1932), inside front cover. The First National Bank and Trust Company of Tulsa opened its doors as the Tulsa Banking Company on July 29, 1895.
32. Advertisement, *Oklahoma Banker* (July 1933), inside front cover.
33. Advertisement, *Oklahoma Banker* (February 1933), inside front cover.
34. "Fifty Years Forward," *Daily Oklahoman,* April 23, 1939.
35. Scott, *Story of Oklahoma City,* 190.
36. "The Tiny Times," *Oklahoma City Times,* October 8, 1935.
37. Front cover, Frank P. Johnson photo; inside front cover, FNB Oklahoma City advertisement, *Oklahoma Banker* (July 1935).
38. Kattigan quoted in "Banking Chief Dies at Home; Ill Half Hour," *Daily Oklahoman,* October 6, 1935; Dannie Bea Hightower interview, Hightower Oral History Collection.
39. "Banking Chief Dies at Home; Ill Half Hour."
40. "Frank Johnson, Banking Leader, Dies," *Oklahoma Banker* (October 1935), 26; "Johnson Rites in Home Today to Be Simple," *Oklahoman City Times,* October 7, 1935.
41. "Frank Johnson, Banking Leader, Dies."
42. "Banker Frank P. Johnson Dies," *Oklahoma News,* October 6, 1935.
43. Unsourced newspaper article, n.d., Johnson-Hightower Family Archives.
44. "Tribute Paid to Banker by City Leaders," *Daily Oklahoman,* October 7, 1935.
45. Ibid. The mayors' terms of office can be found in "Previous Mayors," on City of Oklahoma City website, http://www.okc.gov/council/mayor/previous.html.
46. "Frank P. Johnson Dies after Witnessing Rich Fruits of His Ambition," *Investor,* October 1935, 4.
47. "A Tear at the Bier of Frank P. Johnson," *Oklahoma City Black Dispatch,* October 10, 1935.
48. Ibid. For a synopsis of Frank Johnson's career, see "Johnson's Rise to Business Fame an Oklahoma Saga," *Daily Oklahoman,* October 6, 1935.
49. "Banking Chief Dies at Home; Ill Half Hour."
50. "The Tiny Times."
51. Nichols and Martin, *Continuing an Oklahoma Banking Tradition,* 46.
52. Smallwood, *Oklahoma Adventure,* 125–28.
53. Willis, "And Your Old Men Shall Dream Dreams," 114.
54. Smallwood, *Oklahoma Adventure,* 125–28.
55. Stewart, *Born Grown,* 247.
56. "From Teepees to Towers," *Daily Oklahoman,* April 23, 1939.
57. Linwood O. Neal to Governor Leon C. Phillips, October 13, 1941, box 9, Kelley Collection.
58. Stewart, *Born Grown,* 248–49.
59. Willis, "And Your Old Men Shall Dream Dreams," 130.

60. Stewart, *Born Grown*, 250.

61. Michael J. Hightower, "The Businessman's Frontier: C. C. Hightower, Commerce, and Old Greer County, 1891–1903," *Chronicles of Oklahoma* 86, no. 1 (Spring 2008): 4–31.

62. "Society Calendar," *Daily Oklahoman*, May 2, 1918; photo and caption of Mrs. Wilbur Edward Hightower, *Oklahoma City Times*, May 4, 1918; unsourced newspaper article, n.d., Johnson-Hightower Family Archives. Many years after the storybook wedding, the Johnsons' ballroom was converted to a playroom and, later still, a clubroom to accommodate the social proclivities of two precocious teenagers—my brother, Johnson, and the author, that is—who were more interested in playing pool and swilling beer than elegant flower arrangements. By then, D'Hardelot's "Because" and the bridal chorus from Wagner's *Lohengrin* were less likely to be heard than selections from the Who and the Grateful Dead and whatever else could be culled from an impressive collection of eight-track tapes.

63. Nichols and Martin, *Continuing an Oklahoma Banking Tradition*, 25–27. Hightower graduated from Northwestern University with a Bachelor of Science degree in 1915 and bragging rights as one of the school's most accomplished athletes. He was attending law school at the University of Oklahoma when hostilities broke out in Europe. Unwilling to wait for the United States to enter the conflict, he and three friends sailed for France and enlisted for a year in the French army's American Field Service. Hightower was an ambulance driver on the Verdun front during the legendary drive to capture Hill 304, better known as "Dead Man's Hill," and on the Saint Mihiel front. He returned to his homeland when the United States declared war, and he enlisted in the navy, where he was commissioned as an ensign before the war ended. Unsourced newspaper article, n.d., Johnson-Hightower Family Archives.

64. Stewart, *Born Grown*, 253–54.

65. Keith Tolman, "Will Rogers Field: The Life and Death of a World War II Airbase," *Chronicles of Oklahoma* 79, no. 1 (Spring 2001): 5–10.

66. Stewart, *Born Grown*, 254.

67. *Encyclopedia of Oklahoma History and Culture*, s.v. "World War II," by Brad Agnew, http://digital.library.okstate.edu/encyclopedia/entries/W/WO025.html.

68. Stewart, *Born Grown*, 256.

69. For a comprehensive history of the Skirvin Hotel, see Jack Money and Steve Lackmeyer, *Skirvin* (Oklahoma City: Full Circle, 2009).

70. McReynolds, *Oklahoma: A History*, 380–81; George W. James (now deceased), interview by author, August 14, 2013, Harbor Springs, Michigan, Hightower Oral History Collection; James Construction Group, http://www.jcgllc.com/old-web-replaced7-6-09/history.htm; Tinker Air Force Base, http://www.tinker.af.mil/shared/media/document/AFD-110725-004.pdf. T. L. James was the author's maternal great-granduncle, Dan W. James was the author's maternal grandfather, George W. James was the author's maternal uncle, and Dannie Bea James (later Mrs. Frank J. Hightower) is the author's mother.

71. Smallwood, *Oklahoma Adventure*, 130–34.

72. "Hugh Johnson Service Is Set for Wednesday," *Daily Oklahoman*, January 11, 1944.

73. Nichols and Martin, *Continuing an Oklahoma Banking Tradition*, 55–56.

74. Leslie Fain's wife, Winnie Mae, was the daughter of Chickasha oilman F. C. Hall, onetime owner of legendary aircraft the *Winnie Mae*, which was named for his daughter. The *Winnie Mae* entered aviation history when Hall's personal pilot, Wiley Post, accompanied by navigator Harold Gatty, piloted it around the world in June 1931 in a record-setting eight days, fifteen hours, and fifty-one minutes. Post subsequently acquired the *Winnie Mae* from

Hall and flew it solo around the world in July 1933. See *Encyclopedia of Oklahoma History and Culture,* s.v. *"Winnie Mae,"* by Jon D. May, http://digital.library.okstate.edu/encyclopedia/entries/W/WI030.html.

75. "W. E. Hightower, City Bank Chief, Dies with 4 Others in West Virginia Air Crash," *Daily Oklahoman,* February 5, 1944; Nichols and Martin, *Continuing an Oklahoma Banking Tradition,* 56. Roy Hunt was a famous speed and acrobatic flier, and his wife was a licensed pilot. This brief account of the crash of February 1944 is taken from the aforementioned sources and stories that have haunted the Hightower and Vose families for generations.

76. "Vose Is Named First National Bank President," *Daily Oklahoman,* February 20, 1944.

77. Dannie Bea Hightower interview, February 16, 2009, Oklahoma City, Hightower Oral History Collection.

78. "A Summary of the Past Year's Work and Current Issues of Banking," 6–7.

CHAPTER 6

Epigraph: "A State Bank Commissioner's View of Federal Regulation of Banks," *Oklahoma Banker* (January 1976), 7.

1. Willis, "And Your Old Men Shall Dream Dreams," 132.

2. Studenski and Kroos, *Financial History,* 461.

3. For a fascinating account of the ideological clash between John Maynard Keynes and his Austria nemesis, Friedrich von Hayek, see Nicholas Wapshott, *Keynes Hayek: The Clash that Defined Modern Economics* (New York: W. W. Norton, 2012).

4. John Quiggin, *Zombie Economics: How Dead Ideas Still Walk among Us* (Princeton, N.J.: Princeton University Press, 2010), 7.

5. Eichler, *Thrift Debacle,* 17.

6. Rick Perlstein, "That Seventies Show," *Nation* (November 8, 2010), 32.

7. Heilbroner, *Economic Transformation,* 186, 198.

8. *Encyclopedia of Oklahoma History and Culture,* s.v. "McClellan-Kerr Arkansas River Navigation System," by Larry O'Dell, http://digital.library.okstate.edu/encyclopedia/entries/M/MC009.html.

9. "Oklahoma's Listing in 1945 Roll Call," *Oklahoma Banker* (March 1945), 24.

10. Smallwood, *Oklahoma Adventure,* 146.

11. Studenski and Kroos, *Financial History,* 481.

12. *Encyclopedia of Oklahoma History and Culture,* s.v. "Oklahoma Economy," by Larkin Warner, http://digital.library.okstate.edu/encyclopedia/entries/O/OK041.html.

13. Smallwood, *Oklahoma Adventure,* 147–48.

14. Albert McRill, *And Satan Came Also: An Inside Story of a City's Social and Political History* (Oklahoma City: Britton Publishing, 1955), 252–54.

15. Bergman quoted in "Bookies Flourishing, City Police Know It," *Daily Oklahoman,* August 27, 1955.

16. Trescott, *Financing American Enterprise,* 221.

17. Ibid., 234.

18. *Encyclopedia of Oklahoma History and Culture,* s.v. "Banking Industry."

19. "About SBA," on U.S. Small Business Administration website, http://www.sba.gov/aboutsba/index.html; Smallwood, *Oklahoma Adventure,* 153.

20. U.S. Department of the Interior, National Park Service, Eisenhower National Historic Site pamphlet, Eisenhower National Historic Site Collection, Gettysburg, Pennsylvania.

The Eisenhower home and farm headquarters are located next to the Gettysburg National Military Park and are open to the public.

21. "President's Message," *Oklahoma Banker* (November 1970), 7.

22. Ibid.

23. "Brush Control: Its Effect on Oklahoma's Economy," *Oklahoma Banker* (November 1955), 7–10.

24. McReynolds, *Oklahoma: A History,* 406–407.

25. "The Impact of Oil on Oklahoma's Economy," *Oklahoma Banker* (September 1955), 6.

26. Ibid., 6–7.

27. Ibid., 7.

28. Ibid., 7–8.

29. Ibid., 8.

30. Ibid.

31. *House and Home Magazine* quoted in Ned Eichler, *The Merchant Builders* (Cambridge, Mass.: MIT Press, 1982), 133.

32. *Encyclopedia of Oklahoma History and Culture,* s.v. "Banking Industry"; Smallwood, *Oklahoma Adventure,* 172.

33. Smallwood, *Oklahoma Adventure,* 158.

34. *Encyclopedia of Oklahoma History and Culture,* s.v. "Banking Industry."

35. Jim Hamby and Denver Davison, interview by author, July 19, 2010, Ada, Oklahoma, Hightower Oral History Collection. Jack Conn was elected and installed as president of the American Bankers Association on October 26, 1966, at the ABA's 92nd General Convention in San Francisco. See Jack T. Conn, *One Man in His Time,* ed. Odie B. Faulk (Oklahoma City: Western Heritage Books, 1979), 435.

36. Conn, *One Man in His Time,* 165.

37. Ibid., 294–95.

38. Ibid., 295.

39. Fraser Federal Reserve Archive, Bank Holding Company Act of 1956, http://fraser.stlouisfed.org/docs/historical/congressional/1956_bankholdact_publiclaw511.pdf.

40. Fraser Federal Reserve Archive, Bank Merger Act of 1960, http://fraser.stlouisfed.org/docs/historical/congressional/bank-merger-1960.pdf.

41. Smallwood, *Oklahoma Adventure,* 153–54.

42. Trescott, *Financing American Enterprise,* 228–29.

43. Smallwood, *Oklahoma Adventure,* 152–53.

44. "Jack T. Conn Calls for Banks to Encourage Local Businessmen in Downtown Rejuvenation Projects," *Oklahoma Banker* (June 1967), 40.

45. "Young Banker's Theme: Involvement," *Oklahoma Banker* (January 1971), 14.

46. Kliewer quoted in "Summer-Interns Return to Campus," *Oklahoma Banker* (October 1971), 6–7.

47. Ibid., 7.

48. Smallwood, *Oklahoma Adventure,* 165–66.

49. Head quoted in ibid., 166.

50. "Synopsis of the Final Bank Protection Regulations," *Oklahoma Banker* (February 1969), 7.

51. "The Bank Protection Act," *Oklahoma Banker* (January 1969), 36.

52. "Synopsis of the Final Bank Protection Regulations," 8.

53. Anonymous banker quoted in "A State Bank Commissioner's View of Federal Regulation of Banks," 5.

54. Hirshfield and anonymous banker quoted in "The Red Tape Blues: Government Regulation of Banking," *Oklahoma Banker* (November 1976), 8, 22–26.

55. "A State Bank Commissioner's View of Federal Regulation of Banks," 7.

56. Ibid.

57. "Managing the Change in Banking," *Oklahoma Banker* (July 1976), 13.

58. Ibid., 20.

59. Ibid.

60. Ibid., 22.

61. Smith quoted in Martin Mayer, *The Money Bazaars: Understanding the Banking Revolution around Us* (New York: E. P. Dutton, 1984), 33.

62. Robert J. Samuelson, *The Great Inflation and Its Aftermath: The Past and Future of American Affluence* (New York: Random House, 2010), 4, 50–55.

63. "The Economy: 'We Are All Keynesians Now,'" *Time* (December 31, 1965), 64, 66.

64. Samuelson, *Great Inflation*, 4, 64–69.

65. "Winters to Defend Himself in Hearing Opening Today," *Daily Oklahoman*, December 7, 1967.

66. Winters quoted in "Winters Probe to Wait Week," *Daily Oklahoman*, December 8, 1967.

67. Winters quoted in "U.S. Investigates Leo Winters' Finances," *Daily Oklahoman*, February 9, 1972.

68. "Two Bankers Initiate Own Suspensions," *Daily Oklahoman*, June 13, 1973.

69. "Winters Subpoenas Former Gov. Gary," *Daily Oklahoman*, March 27, 1974; "Winters, Smith Trial Opens Today," *Shawnee News-Star*, April 2, 1974.

70. Winters quoted in "Indictment Against Rainbolt Dismissed," *Shawnee News-Star*, April 5, 1974.

71. Winters quoted in "Rainbolt Sheds Indictment, May Testify in Winters Case," *Daily Oklahoman*, April 5, 1974.

72. "No Deposit Deals Made, Rainbolt Says," *Daily Oklahoman*, April 18, 1974.

73. "U.S. Drops Case against Winters," *Daily Oklahoman*, June 26, 1974; "Winters Freed of Charge of Bank Fund Misuse," *Shawnee News-Star*, June 26, 1974.

74. "Rainbolt Starts Panel Job Again," *Daily Oklahoman*, June 4, 1974.

75. Jim Bowles, interview by author, April 10, 2012, Shawnee, Oklahoma, Hightower Oral History Collection.

76. Gary Simpson, interview by author, November 9, 2012, Stillwater, Oklahoma, Hightower Oral History Collection.

77. Tom Loy, interview by author, November 5, 2012, Oklahoma City, Hightower Oral History Collection.

78. Ibid.

79. Ibid.

80. H. E. "Gene" Rainbolt, correspondence with author, February 3, 2014.

81. Gordon Greer, interview by author, November 13, 2012, Tulsa, Oklahoma, Hightower Oral History Collection.

82. Simpson interview.

83. Loy interview.

84. Ibid.

85. George and Nancy Records, interview by author, June 4, 2009, Oklahoma City, Hightower Oral History Collection.

86. Betty Rodgers-Johnson, interview by author, February 13, 2009, Oklahoma City, Hightower Oral History Collection. For a history of the Records and Johnston families and their contributions to Oklahoma banking, see Michael J. Hightower, *Frontier Families: The Records and Johnstons in American History* (Oklahoma City: Cottonwood Press, 2010).

87. Trescott, *Financing American Enterprise,* 236–37, 264.

CHAPTER 7

Epigraph: Jennings quoted in Mark Singer, *Funny Money* (New York: Knopf, 1985), 196.

1. James P. McCollom, *The Continental Affair: The Rise and Fall of the Continental Illinois Bank* (New York: Dodd, Mead, 1987), 17.

2. See Michael J. Hightower, *Banking in Oklahoma before Statehood* (Norman: University of Oklahoma Press, 2013).

3. Santayana's oft-quoted passage can be found in "Flux and Constancy in Human Nature," chapter 12 of *Reason in Common Sense,* one of five volumes published from 1905 to 1906 that express the Spanish-born American philosopher's outlook on morality. His comment reads as follows: "Progress, far from consisting in change, depends on retentiveness. When change is absolute there remains no being to improve and no direction is set for possible improvement: and when experience is not retained, as among savages, infancy is perpetual. *Those who cannot remember the past are condemned to repeat it*" (emphasis added). See George Santayana, *The Life of Reason, or the Phases of Human Progress: Reason in Common Sense* (London: Constable, 1906), 284.

4. Phillip L. Zweig, *Belly Up: The Collapse of the Penn Square Bank* (New York: Crown, 1985), 5.

5. Steven A. Schneider, *The Oil Price Revolution* (Baltimore: Johns Hopkins University Press, 1983), 103. See also Judith Stein, *Pivotal Decade: How the United States Traded Factories for Financing in the Seventies* (New Haven, Conn.: Yale University Press, 2010).

6. Darrell Delamaide, *Debt Shock: The Full Story of the World Credit Crisis* (New York: Doubleday, 1984), 34.

7. *Oklahoma Encyclopedia of History and Culture,* s.v. "Anadarko Basin," by Bobby D. Weaver, http://digital.library.okstate.edu/encyclopedia/entries/A/AN003.html.

8. Zweig, *Belly Up,* 11; Singer, *Funny Money,* 35–36, 76–77.

9. Testimony of Robert A. Hefner, III, Chairman of the Independent Gas Producers Committee, Hearings before the Committee on Commerce, United States Senate, Ninety-Third Congress, First Session, on November 7, 1973, box 10, Phillip L. Zweig Penn Square Bank Collection, Research Division, Oklahoma Historical Society, Oklahoma City (hereafter cited as Zweig Collection).

10. Testimony of Robert A. Hefner III, Managing Partner, the GHK Company and Gasanadarko, Ltd., before U.S. House of Representatives, Committee on Interstate and Foreign Commerce, Subcommittee on Energy and Power, March 24, 1977, box 10, Zweig Collection.

11. Singer, *Funny Money,* 79.

12. Zweig, *Belly Up,* 51.

13. "Natural Gas: The Search Goes On," *National Geographic* (November 1978), 632–51, box 10, Zweig Collection.

14. "Deep Drilling in the Anadarko Basin," *Petroleum Engineer International,* March 1979, box 9, Zweig Collection.

15. Robert A. Hefner III and Neil J. Dikeman, Jr., "The Economic Impact of Deep Gas Well Drilling in the Oklahoma Sector of the Deep Anadarko Basin," *Review of Regional Economics and Business* (April 1979), 9, box 5, Zweig Collection.

16. "1,001 Years of Natural Gas," *Wall Street Journal,* April 27, 1977, box 3, Zweig Collection.

17. Hefner quoted in "What Energy Crisis?," transcript of CBS's *60 Minutes,* December 28, 1980, box 9, Zweig Collection.

18. "The History of Regulation: The Natural Gas Policy Act of 1978," on NaturalGas.org website, http://www.naturalgas.org/regulation/history.asp#gasact1978.

19. Zweig, *Belly Up,* 91.

20. Singer, *Funny Money,* 79.

21. "Banks Take on Energy Financing," *American Banker,* February 28, 1980, box 2, Zweig Collection.

22. McCollom, *Continental Affair,* 38–39.

23. "Banker of the Year: Roger Anderson of Continental Illinois National Bank," *Institutional Investor* (August 1984), 69, box 10, Zweig Collection.

24. Zweig, *Belly Up,* 74–75.

25. "Chilling Specter at Continental," *New York Times,* May 20, 1984, box 8, Zweig Collection.

26. McCollom, *Continental Affair,* 195, 239.

27. "Banker of the Year: Roger Anderson of Continental Illinois National Bank."

28. Zweig, *Belly Up,* 73.

29. "Banker of the Year: Roger Anderson of Continental Illinois National Bank."

30. "The Wrecking of Seafirst: A Handful of Executives Bring Down the Bank," *Seattle Post-Intelligencer,* July 11, 1983, box 6, Zweig Collection.

31. Ibid.

32. Zweig, *Belly Up,* 32–33.

33. "The Rise and Fall of Oklahoma City's Penn Square Bank," *Daily Oklahoman,* August 1, 1982, box 10, Zweig Collection.

34. Conn, *One Man in His Time,* 481.

35. Singer, *Funny Money,* 13–17.

36. Conn, *One Man in His Time,* 481.

37. Empie quoted in "The Swinger Who Broke Penn Square Bank," *Fortune* (August 1982), 122–23, box 4, Zweig Collection. Emphasis added.

38. Chairman of the Board's Comments to Shareholders Annual Meeting, January 19, 1976, box 12, Zweig Collection.

39. Singer, *Funny Money,* 19–20.

40. "The Rise and Fall of Oklahoma City's Penn Square Bank."

41. Bill Patterson declined to be interviewed for this book.

42. Singer, *Funny Money,* 59–53; "The Swinger Who Broke Penn Square Bank," 122.

43. Singer, *Funny Money,* 62.

44. "The Swinger Who Broke Penn Square Bank," 122.

45. Former bank officer quoted in Zweig, *Belly Up,* 118–19.

46. Champlin interview.

47. Ibid.

48. "The Rise and Fall of Oklahoma City's Penn Square Bank."

49. Chambers and comptroller official quoted in Zweig, *Belly Up*, 121–22.

50. Gayla Sherry, interview by author, March 9, 2011, Oklahoma City, Hightower Oral History Collection.

51. Singer, *Funny Money*, 48–51.

52. "Chilling Specter at Continental."

53. "The Wrecking of Seafirst: A Handful of Executives Bring Down the Bank."

54. "The Wrecking of Seafirst: Seafirst's 'Truckloads' of Bad Loans," *Seattle Post-Intelligencer*, July 14, 1983, box 6, Zweig Collection.

55. Boyd quoted in Zweig, *Belly Up*, 262.

56. "The Wrecking of Seafirst: Seafirst's 'Truckloads' of Bad Loans."

57. Meg Salyer, interview by author, April 23, 2012, Oklahoma City, Hightower Oral History Collection. Following the death of Frank J. Hightower in October 2000, Meg Salyer and her then husband, Chris, bought the Johnson (later, Hightower) home in Heritage Hills, Oklahoma City.

58. Ibid.

59. Ibid.

60. Ibid.

61. Ibid.

62. "Letter to Stockholders," *The Chase Manhattan Corporation Annual Report 1982*, 3, box 3, Zweig Collection.

63. Statement of Robert A. Hefner, III, before the Subcommittee on Energy Regulation, Energy and Natural Resources Committee, United States Senate, First Session, 97th Congress, April 23, 1981, box 2, Zweig Collection.

64. Summary of Statement of Robert A. Hefner, III, before the Committee on Energy and Natural Resources, United States Senate, First Session, 97th Congress, November 6, 1981, box 2, Zweig Collection.

65. Hefner quoted in "The Blazing Battle to Free Natural Gas," *Fortune* (October 19, 1981), 154, box 10, Zweig Collection.

66. "After a Lifetime of Dry Holes, Oil Partners Strike It Rich with Oklahoma Gas Well," *Wall Street Journal*, February 17, 1981, box 10, Zweig Collection.

67. "With Tom Cat # 1, All's Well for Washington Gas Light Co.," *Washington Post*, April 27, 1981; "Deep in the Anadarko," *Oil and Gas Investor* (December 1981), 14, both in box 10, Zweig Collection.

68. "Deep in the Anadarko"; "Eakly Residents Crack Jokes, But Poise for Flight," *Daily Oklahoman*, January 30, 1981, box 10, Zweig Collection. See also "Lucky Wind Eases Gas Worries," *Daily Oklahoman*, January 31, 1981, box 10, Zweig Collection.

69. "With Tom Cat # 1, All's Well for Washington Gas Light Co."

70. Lehr quoted in "Deep in the Anadarko."

71. *Encyclopedia of Oklahoma History and Culture*, s.v. "Oklahoma Economy."

72. "Oil Boom Put State Near Top in Increase of Personal Income," *Daily Oklahoman*, September 6, 1983, box 11, Zweig Collection. Personal income is the income received by persons from all sources, including income from the government, and is measured before deduction of personal income taxes and other personal taxes.

73. "Oil-Field Suppliers: The Crash after a Boom—An Uncertain Future," *Business Week*, September 27, 1982, 66, box 10, Zweig Collection.

74. "Oil Boom's Gone but Optimism Returns in Western Oklahoma," *Sunday Oklahoman*, April 8, 1984, box 12, Zweig Collection.

75. "In the Oil Patch: Spirit Links Past and Present," *Daily Oklahoman,* December 27, 1981, box 10, Zweig Collection; "Deep in the Anadarko."
76. Bob McCormack, interview by author, June 22, 2011, Duncan, Oklahoma, Hightower Oral History Collection.
77. Jennings quoted in Singer, *Funny Money,* 196.
78. Sherry interview.

CHAPTER 8

Epigraph: Steve Plunk, interview by author, August 3, 2012, Oklahoma City, Hightower Oral History Collection.

1. Zweig, *Belly Up,* 135; "The Rise and Fall of Oklahoma City's Penn Square Bank."
2. "The Rise and Fall of Oklahoma City's Penn Square Bank."
3. Zweig, *Belly Up,* 219–21.
4. "The Rise and Fall of Oklahoma City's Penn Square Bank."
5. Jennings quoted in "Bank's Oil Lending Gets It in Big Time," *Sunday Oklahoman,* May 2, 1982.
6. "The Rise and Fall of Oklahoma City's Penn Square Bank."
7. Zweig, *Belly Up,* 241.
8. "The Swinger Who Broke Penn Square Bank," 124; Singer, *Funny Money,* 120.
9. Zweig, *Belly Up,* 203.
10. Champlin interview.
11. "The Swinger Who Broke Penn Square Bank," 123–24.
12. "The Rise and Fall of Oklahoma City's Penn Square Bank."
13. Singer, *Funny Money,* 114–16; G. P. Johnson Hightower, interview by author, October 17 and 22, 2013, Oklahoma City, Hightower Oral History Collection. G. P. Johnson Hightower is the author's brother.
14. G. P. Johnson Hightower interview.
15. Carlisle and John Mabrey, interview by author, October 11, 2011, Bixby, Oklahoma, Hightower Oral History Collection.
16. Zweig, *Belly Up,* 202, 207.
17. McCollom, *Continental Affair,* 263.
18. Zweig, *Belly Up,* 246–48.
19. Ibid., 204.
20. Nick Berry, interview by author, September 5 and 6, 2013, Oklahoma City, Hightower Oral History Collection.
21. Mabrey interview; Zweig, *Belly Up,* 224.
22. Mabrey interview.
23. Phillip L. Zweig, "On the Job: Covering Penn Square," *Columbia Journalism Review* (January–February 1983): 24, box 2, Zweig Collection.
24. Knox quoted in Zweig, *Belly Up,* 268–69.
25. "On the Job: Covering Penn Square," 24.
26. Greer interview.
27. Minutes of an Informal, Special Meeting of the Board of Directors of Penn Square Bank, N.A., April 2, 1982, box 6, Zweig Collection.
28. "Oklahoma's Penn Square Bank, Maverick Oil Patch Lender: Some Say It's Bet Too Heavily on Energy," *American Banker,* April 26, 1982.
29. Ibid.

30. Ibid.

31. "Bank's Oil Lending Gets It in Big Time"; Jennings quoted in "Time to 'Put Hay in the Barn,' Tighten Belts, Says Jennings," *Oklahoma City Journal Record,* June 6, 1982, box 10, Zweig Collection.

32. Anderson quoted in "Continental Chief Sees Loan Problems," *Chicago Tribune,* April 27, 1982, box 5, Zweig Collection.

33. Fuller quoted in "Big Continental Illinois Is Suffering the Effects of Aggressive Lending," *Wall Street Journal,* June 1, 1982, box 5, Zweig Collection.

34. "Energy Experts Warn of Oil Glut Complacency," *American Banker,* June 23, 1981, box 2, Zweig Collection.

35. Morgan Guaranty Trust Company, news release, March 19, 1982, box 9, Zweig Collection.

36. "Oklahoma: Not Quite Okay," *Economist,* November 7, 1981, 26, box 12, Zweig Collection.

37. Singer, *Funny Money,* 14.

38. Salyer interview.

39. Ibid.

40. Poole quoted in "The Rise and Fall of Oklahoma City's Penn Square Bank."

41. Zweig, *Belly Up,* 349.

42. "The Wrecking of Seafirst: Seafirst's 'Truckloads' of Bad Loans."

43. Ibid.; Patterson quoted in "The Swinger Who Broke Penn Square Bank," 124.

44. "The Rise and Fall of Oklahoma City's Penn Square Bank."

45. "The Swinger Who Broke Penn Square Bank," 122.

46. "The Rise and Fall of Oklahoma City's Penn Square Bank."

47. "On the Job: Covering Penn Square," 24.

48. Minutes of the Special Meeting of the Board of Directors of Penn Square Bank, N.A., July 2, 1982, box 2, Zweig Collection.

49. Vint quoted in "Bank's Final Day Called Madhouse," *Daily Oklahoman,* October 29, 1986, OHS Banks and Banking Vertical Files.

50. Plunk interview.

51. Ibid.

52. Ibid.

53. Ibid.

54. Ibid.

55. Ibid.

56. David Rainbolt, interview by author, June 21, 2011, Oklahoma City, Hightower Oral History Collection.

57. Minutes of the Board of Governors of the Federal Reserve System, Friday, July 2, 1982, 2:45 P.M., box 1, Zweig Collection.

58. Ibid.

59. Ibid., Saturday, July 3, 1982, 4:30 P.M., box 1, Zweig Collection.

60. Ibid., Sunday, July 4, 1982, 12:30 P.M., box 1, Zweig Collection.

61. Ibid., Monday, July 5, 1982, 2:00 P.M., box 1, Zweig Collection.

62. Sherry interview.

63. Conover quoted in Zweig, *Belly Up,* 404. At the time of our interview in August 2012, Plunk still carried the transcript in his briefcase. Plunk interview.

64. Conover quoted in "Penn Square Bank Declared Insolvent," *Daily Oklahoman,* July 6, 1982, OHS Banks and Banking Vertical Files.

65. Ibid.; "Okla. Failure Is 4th Largest," *American Banker,* July 7, 1982. The top three bank failures in FDIC history were: (1) Franklin National Bank, New York, N.Y., 1974, deposits of $1,444,982,000; (2) United States National Bank, San Diego, Calif., 1973, deposits of $931,954,000; and (3) Banco Credit y Ahorro Ponceno, Ponce, Puerto Rico, 1978, deposits of $607,600,000.

66. "Mood Is Sullen and Depressing," *American Banker,* July 7, 1982.

67. David Rainbolt interview.

68. McCormack interview.

69. "Oklahoma Bankers Say They Saw Failure of Energy Lender Coming," *American Banker,* July 8, 1982.

70. Sherry interview.

71. Mick Thompson, interview by author, February 6, 2012, Oklahoma City, Hightower Oral History Collection.

72. "FDIC Liquidates Penn Square Bank," *Oklahoma Banker* (August 1982), 16.

73. Beller quoted in "Hearings Begin on Penn Square," *American Banker,* August 17, 1982.

74. "Highlights of Penn Square Bank Failure," *Sunday Oklahoman,* November 23, 1986, OHS Banks and Banking Vertical Files.

75. "Rotary Rig Count Charts the Booms and Busts of Drilling," *Daily Oklahoman,* December 14, 1983, box 11, Zweig Collection.

76. "Anadarko Basin Shows Resistance to Drilling Slowdown," *Sunday Oklahoman,* September 19, 1982, box 10, Zweig Collection.

77. Hughes Tool Co. figures reported in "Oklahoma Led Nation in Number of Rigs Idled During Week," *Oklahoma City Journal Record,* October 12, 1982, box 4, Zweig Collection.

78. Hughes Tool Co. figures reported in "1982 Could Become Second Best Year in Drilling History," *Oklahoma City Journal Record,* August 31, 1982, box 10, Zweig Collection.

79. Helmerich quoted in "Anadarko Basin Shows Resistance to Drilling Slowdown."

80. Swearingen quoted in "Drilling Slump Hitting State Hard," *Sunday Oklahoman,* October 10, 1982, box 4, Zweig Collection.

81. Hefner quoted in "Gas Slump in Oklahoma: Debts Engulf Many Drillers," *New York Times,* April 26, 1983, box 12, Zweig Collection.

82. Michael Rogers, interview by author, October 18, 2011, Oklahoma City, Hightower Oral History Collection. In the late 1970s, Keith May was also the administrative head of a banking group at Fidelity composed of loan and correspondent banking divisions. See Conn, *One Man in His Time,* 517.

83. Platt quoted in "Oil-Field Suppliers: The Crash after the Boom—An Uncertain Future," 66.

84. "The Famine after the Feast in Servicing: Slowdown Survivors Candidly Comment on the 1982 Crash," *Oklahoma City Journal Record,* November 18, 1982, box 11, Zweig Collection.

85. Haggin quoted in "For Well Service Industry, 'It's the Pits'," *Oklahoma City Journal Record,* November 18, 1982, box 11, Zweig Collection.

86. "Oil-Field Suppliers: The Crash after the Boom—An Uncertain Future," 67.

87. "Oil Boom's Gone but Optimism Returns."

88. Livshee and Hammons quoted in "Gas Slump in Oklahoma."

89. Neary quoted in "Oil, Gas Bankruptcies on the Rise in '83, Attorney Says," *Oklahoma City Journal Record,* October 1, 1983, box 8, Zweig Collection.

90. McEuen quoted in "Handshake No Longer Enough," *Tulsa Tribune,* October 7, 1982, box 10, Zweig Collection.

91. H. E. "Gene" Rainbolt, interview by author, October 18, 2011, Oklahoma City, Hightower Oral History Collection.

92. Brian Shipp, interview by author, October 26, 2011, Idabel, Oklahoma, Hightower Oral History Collection.

93. Bill Jordan, Kelly Jordan, Laura Miller, and Jerry Fowler, interview by author, October 24, 2011, Quinton, Oklahoma, Hightower Oral History Collection.

94. Steve Baggerly, interview by author, August 18, 2011, Guymon, Oklahoma, Hightower Oral History Collection.

95. Charlie and Charlotte Butler, interview by author, August 19, 2011, Hooker, Oklahoma, Hightower Oral History Collection.

96. Rogers interview.

97. "FDIC Preparing Penn Bank Suits," *Daily Oklahoman,* March 30, 1983.

98. Price quoted in "Penn Bank Exec Guilty," *Oklahoma City Times,* January 12, 1984, box 8, Zweig Collection.

99. "$138 Million Suit Names Penn Bank Officials," *Oklahoman and Times,* June 30, 1984, OHS Banks and Banking Vertical Files.

100. "Penn Square Bank Official Indicted," *Daily Oklahoman,* July 18, 1984, box 12, Zweig Collection.

101. "Jury to Decide if Former Penn Banker 'Master of Deceit' or Victim of Plot," *Daily Oklahoman,* September 11, 1984, OHS Banks and Banking Vertical Files.

102. "Patterson Acquitted; Chicago Charges Filed," *Daily Oklahoman,* September 28, 1984, OHS Banks and Banking Vertical Files.

103. "Penn Cases Ready for Trial," *Sunday Oklahoman,* August 10, 1986, OHS Banks and Banking Vertical Files.

104. Plunk quoted in "Upstreaming Interest Alarmed Examiner," *Oklahoma City Journal Record,* August 27, 1986, box 1, Zweig Collection.

105. "Witness Says Banker Lied about Interest," *Daily Oklahoman,* August 29, 1986, box 1, Zweig Collection.

106. Dann quoted in "Jurors to Consider Question of Fraud," *Daily Oklahoman,* September 19, 1986, box 1, Zweig Collection.

107. Titchywy quoted in "Bottom Falls Out of Lease Sales; Two Auctioneers Throw in Towel," *Sunday Oklahoman,* August 1, 1982, box 10, Zweig Collection.

108. Patterson quoted in "Auctions Growing in Popularity as Way of Liquidating for Cash," *Sunday Oklahoman,* September 19, 1982, box 11, Zweig Collection.

109. "With Dreams of Prosperity Going Sour, New Arrivals Turning to Charity," *Daily Oklahoman,* August 29, 1982, box 10, Zweig Collection.

110. "Oil Boomtown Cools Off: Elk City Leveling Off Period Underway," *Oklahoma City Journal Record,* July 23, 1982, box 10, Zweig Collection.

111. Pyron quoted in "Oilies' Numbers Dwindling at Western Oklahoma Parks," *Daily Oklahoman,* August 21, 1982, box 10, Zweig Collection.

112. "Oil Boom Towns Not So Booming," *Daily Oklahoman,* August 1, 1982, box 10, Zweig Collection.

113. Lane and Glomski quoted in "Oilfield Worker Layoffs on the Rise as Anadarko Basin Boom Winds Down," *Sunday Oklahoman,* October 17, 1982, box 4, Zweig Collection.

114. R. Lee quoted in "Oil Boom Towns Not So Booming."

115. N. Lee quoted in "Penn Bank Failure Becomes Grist for Songster," *Daily Oklahoman,* August 29, 1982, box 10, Zweig Collection.

116. Don and Kitty Clark, interview by author, January 23, 2012, Anadarko, Oklahoma, Hightower Oral History Collection.
117. Shipp interview.
118. Mabrey interview.

CHAPTER 9

Epigraph: David L. Boren to William D. Welge, August 6, 1984, OHS Banks and Banking Vertical Files.

1. Federal Deposit Insurance Corporation, *1983 Annual Report: 50 Years of Confidence*, 14, box 6, Zweig Collection.
2. Continental Illinois Corporation, Continental Illinois National Bank and Trust Company of Chicago, *1982 Annual Report and Form 10-K*, 2, box 4, Zweig Collection.
3. Seafirst Corporation, *Annual Report for the Year Ended December 31, 1982*, 2, box 3, Zweig Collection.
4. The Chase Manhattan Corporation, *Annual Report 1982*, 3, box 3, Zweig Collection.
5. Block quoted in "The Best Defense," *Forbes* (December 3, 1984), 210, box 8, Zweig Collection.
6. "Michigan National Omits Its Dividend, Discloses Charge-Offs," *Wall Street Journal*, February 28, 1984, box 12, Zweig Collection.
7. "Hibernia Bank Loses Appeal of Penn Ruling," *American Banker*, May 10, 1984, box 12, Zweig Collection.
8. "150 Credit Unions Big Losers in Crash of Oklahoma Bank," *Washington Post*, July 9, 1982, box 8, Zweig Collection.
9. Higgins quoted in "Penn Square Bank's Failure Caused Big Losses for Broker, Expert Says," *Daily Oklahoman*, September 25, 1986, OHS Banks and Banking Vertical Files.
10. "Chilling Specter at Continental."
11. Ibid.; McCollom, *Continental Affair*, 195.
12. "Chilling Specter at Continental."
13. "Continental's Blow to a Safer Banking System," *Fortune*, June 11, 1984, 93, box 8, Zweig Collection.
14. "In Chicago, the Gloom Lifts," *New York Times*, July 27, 1984, box 8, Zweig Collection.
15. McCollom, *Continental Affair*, 276.
16. Ibid., 324; "The Events Leading to Continental's Rescue," *New York Times*, July 27, 1984, box 8, Zweig Collection.
17. Iacocca quoted in McCollom, *Continental Affair*, 282.
18. Ibid., 18, 21.
19. "The Events Leading to Continental's Rescue."
20. "A Bank in Trouble," *Chicago Tribune*, May 20, 1984, box 8, Zweig Collection.
21. McCollom, *Continental Affair*, 141.
22. "Chronology of a Banking Crisis," *New York Times*, May 20, 1984, box 8, Zweig Collection.
23. See chapter one, "A Brand-New State."
24. "Chronology of a Banking Crisis."
25. "A Bank in Trouble."
26. McCollom, *Continental Affair*, 342, 348.

27. "The Continental Bailout," *Newsweek*, July 30, 1984, 86, box 10, Zweig Collection.
28. Isaac quoted in "Chilling Specter at Continental."
29. Volcker quoted in "Federal Reserve Head Defends Bailout of Illinois Bank," *Daily Oklahoman*, July 31, 1984, box 8, Zweig Collection.
30. Isaac quoted in "FDIC Saves Continental," *Daily Oklahoman*, July 27, 1984, OHS Banks and Banking Vertical Files.
31. Wooden, Cline, and others quoted in "The Continental Bailout," 86–87.
32. St. Germain, Baker, and Taylor quoted in "FDIC Saves Continental."
33. St. Germain quoted in McCollom, *Continental Affair*, 252.
34. Baker quoted in "Chicago Bank's Rescue by Fed 'Blatantly Unfair,'" *Oklahoma City Journal Record*, July 27, 1984, box 8, Zweig Collection.
35. Boren quoted in "Penn Bank Bailout Might Have Saved Continental," *Oklahoma City Journal Record*, July 31, 1984, box 12, Zweig Collection.
36. Boren to Welge, August 6, 1984.
37. Smith quoted in Mayer, *Bankers*, 189–92.
38. Chernow, *Death of the Banker*, 70.
39. Loy interview.
40. Salsman, "Bankers as Scapegoats," 104–105.
41. Greer interview.
42. Loy interview.
43. Calomiris, *U.S. Bank Deregulation*, xiv.
44. David S. Holland, *When Regulation Was Too Successful—The Sixth Decade of Deposit Insurance: A History of the Troubles of the U.S. Banking Industry in the 1980s and Early 1990s* (Westport, Conn.: Praeger, 1998), 131. Regulation Q is a Federal Reserve Board regulation that prohibited banks from being able to pay interest on deposits within checking accounts. Regulation Q was enacted in accordance to the Glass-Steagall Act of 1933, to limit loan sharking and other such unseemly actions. In addition, it motivated consumers to release funds from these accounts and put them into money market funds. See "Regulation Q," on Investopedia website, http://www.investopedia.com/terms/r/regulationq.asp.
45. Jill M. Hendrickson, *Regulation and Instability in U.S. Commercial Banking: A History of Crises* (New York: Palgrave MacMillan, 2011), 180.
46. Mayer, *Money Bazaars*, 67.
47. Volcker quoted in ibid., 11.
48. Hendrickson, *Regulation and Instability*, 214–15; Mayer, *Bankers*, 433.
49. Mayer, *Bankers*, 9.
50. Johnson quoted in Conn, *One Man in His Time*, 301.
51. "New Deal Bank Act Turns 50," *New York Times*, June 17, 1983, box 8, Zweig Collection.
52. Mayer, *Bankers*, 27.
53. "The Sun Sets on Glass-Steagall," *Oklahoma Banker* (April 1983), 24–25.
54. "America's Banks in Crisis," *New York Times Magazine*, September 23, 1984, 48, box 8, Zweig Collection.
55. Ibid.
56. Ibid., 74; see also "Doomsday for Banking Industry?," *Tulsa World*, January 15, 1984, box 8, Zweig Collection.
57. "America's Banks in Crisis," 72.
58. Ibid., 72–73.
59. Ibid., 108.

60. "Who Should Supervise the Banks?," *Wall Street Journal*, January 16, 1984, box 8, Zweig Collection.
61. "Regulators and Bankers Are to Blame," *New York Times*, June 10, 1984, box 8, Zweig Collection.
62. "Auditors Feel the Heat of a New Scrutiny," *New York Times*, May 13, 1984, box 12, Zweig Collection.
63. "Going Overboard on Bank Bailouts," *Wall Street Journal*, August 23, 1984, box 8, Zweig Collection.
64. "New Loan Participation Rules," *American Banker*, August 16, 1984, box 8, Zweig Collection.
65. "Sorting Out the Legal Confusion in the U.S. Financial Industry," *American Banker*, April 27, 1984, box 11, Zweig Collection.
66. "Congress Eyes the Banks," *Wall Street Journal*, July 27, 1984, box 8, Zweig Collection.
67. Chernow, *Death of the Banker*, 65.
68. Kaufman quoted in "A Banking Puzzle: Mixing Freedom and Protection," *New York Times*, February 19, 1984, box 8, Zweig Collection.
69. Wriston quoted in ibid.
70. Salem and Cline quoted in ibid.
71. Meltzer quoted in ibid.
72. Dunkelberg quoted in "Business Failures Near 50-Year High," *Oklahoma City Journal Record*, November 11, 1982, box 4, Zweig Collection.
73. "Expectations for State's Economy Cut in New OSU Study," *Daily Oklahoman*, August 27, 1982, box 6, Zweig Collection.
74. "Two Experts Disagree on Natural Gas Glut's End," *Sunday Oklahoman*, October 31, 1982, box 4, Zweig Collection.
75. Hughes Tool Co. figures reported in "Active Rotary Rigs," *Daily Oklahoman*, October 2, 1983, box 12, Zweig Collection.
76. Bowman quoted in "Dim Outlook Seen for State Economy this Winter," *Oklahoma City Journal Record*, November 13, 1982, box 4, Zweig Collection.
77. Bluestone quoted in "Sunbelt Losing its Glow, Economics Professor Says," *Oklahoma City Journal Record*, January 15, 1983, box 12, Zweig Collection.
78. Mayer, *Bankers*, 16.
79. "Bank Stocks Proved Terrible Investment in Second Quarter," *American Banker*, August 2, 1982, box 6, Zweig Collection.
80. "FDIC Says Problem Banks Increase from 220 to 320," *Daily Oklahoman*, October 20, 1982, box 4, Zweig Collection.
81. Bill and Guy Berry interview.
82. "Bank Closing Just One of Many," *Daily Oklahoman*, May 15, 1984, box 11, Zweig Collection.
83. "Bank Customers Met with Cookies," *Daily Oklahoman*, May 15, 1984, box 11, Zweig Collection.
84. "Several Oklahoma Banks Receive Warnings," *Miami News-Record*, June 17, 1984, OHS Banks and Banking Vertical Files.
85. Empie quoted in "State Banking Industry Still OK, Official Says," *Daily Oklahoman*, October 18, 1985, OHS Banks and Banking Vertical Files.
86. Empie quoted in "Bank of Canton Ordered Closed," *Daily Oklahoman*, October 11, 1985, OHS Banks and Banking Vertical Files.

87. Simpson quoted in "Continued Failures of Small, Weak Banks Forecast," *Daily Oklahoman,* January 17, 1986, OHS Banks and Banking Vertical Files.

88. Sherry interview.

89. Mayer, *Bankers,* 13.

90. "Bank Failures Spur FDIC Plan to Hire Outside Examiners," *Daily Oklahoman,* November 22, 1986, OHS Banks and Banking Vertical Files.

91. "Oklahoma Bank Failures 1982–1987," *Daily Oklahoman,* March 13, 1987, OHS Banks and Banking Vertical Files. The *Daily Oklahoman's* tally of failed banks, published as warranted, is a handy reference and is used throughout this section.

92. "Bank Failures Spur FDIC Plan to Hire Outside Examiners," *Daily Oklahoman,* November 22, 1986, OHS Banks and Banking Vertical Files.

93. "Oklahoma Banks Lose $64 million in First Half of '86," *Daily Oklahoman,* October 30, 1986, OHS Banks and Banking Vertical Files.

94. "Oklahoma Bank Failures 1982–1987."

95. "Bellmon Bank Plan Flops," *Daily Oklahoman,* August 7, 1987, OHS Banks and Banking Vertical Files.

96. "Boren, Inhofe Propose Help for Failing Banks," unsourced newspaper article, March 28, 1987, OHS Banks and Banking Vertical Files.

97. "Study Blames Bad Management for Bank Problems," *Daily Oklahoman,* May 2, 1987, OHS Banks and Banking Vertical Files.

98. Sherry interview.

99. Jim and Kirk Pittman, interview by author, June 23, 2011, Seiling, Oklahoma, Hightower Oral History Collection.

100. Stone quoted in "Good News: Some Banks Prosper despite Slump," *Oklahoma Gazette,* April 8, 1987, 32, OHS Banks and Banking Vertical Files.

101. Jackson quoted in ibid.

102. Permenter quoted in ibid.

103. Lawson quoted in ibid.

104. Nichols and Martin, *Continuing an Oklahoma Banking Tradition,* 75–76.

105. Townsend quoted in "Joullian New Chairman of First National Bank," *Saturday Oklahoman and Times,* September 14, 1985, OHS Banks and Banking Vertical Files.

106. Gerald R. Marshall, interview by author, March 11, 2011, Oklahoma City, Hightower Oral History Collection.

107. G. P. Johnson Hightower interview.

108. "Multi-State Bank Reopens First's Doors," *Daily Oklahoman,* July 16, 1986, OHS Banks and Banking Vertical Files. By comparison, the combined assets of Oklahoma's roughly five hundred banks were in the range of $32 billion.

109. Nichols and Martin, *Continuing an Oklahoma Banking Tradition,* 76.

110. "City Bank's Closing Expected by Many," *Daily Oklahoman,* July 15, 1986, OHS Banks and Banking Vertical Files.

111. Ibid.; "Multi-State Bank Reopens First's Doors," *Daily Oklahoman,* July 16, 1986, OHS Banks and Banking Vertical Files.

112. G. P. Johnson Hightower interview.

113. Charles McCall, interview by author, October 25, 2011, Atoka, Oklahoma, Hightower Oral History Collection.

114. "Seattle Banker Named Chief Executive at First National," *Daily Oklahoman,* January 7, 1986, OHS Banks and Banking Vertical Files.

115. "First Interstate Bank of Oklahoma City: We're bringing down the curtain on one ERA ... and raising it on another," *Daily Oklahoman,* July 16, 1986, OHS Banks and Banking Vertical Files.

116. "Rising out of the Ashes," cartoon, *Daily Oklahoman,* n.d., OHS Banks and Banking Vertical Files.

CHAPTER 10

Epigraph: Matt Jackson and Linda Christensen, interview by author, August 17, 2011, Thomas, Oklahoma, Hightower Oral History Collection.

1. Pabst quoted in "Women Command Key Positions in Banking," *Oklahoma Banker* (April 1985), 28.
2. Mayer, *Bankers,* 451–52.
3. "Ag Outlook Remains Bleak," *Oklahoma Banker* (September 1982), 29.
4. Mayer, *Bankers,* 141.
5. Bruce Benbrook, interview by author, August 24, 2010, Woodward, Oklahoma, Hightower Oral History Collection.
6. Mayer, *Bankers,* 247.
7. Bellmon quoted in "Bellmon Fires Bank Commissioner," *Daily Oklahoman,* March 11, 1987, OHS Banks and Banking Vertical Files.
8. Harris and McKeown quoted in "Commissioner's Ouster Shocks Bank Groups," *Tulsa World,* March 11, 1987, OHS Banks and Banking Vertical Files.
9. Hannah, Derebery, and Tucker quoted in "State Bankers React to Empie Firing," *Tulsa World,* March 11, 1987, OHS Banks and Banking Vertical Files.
10. Empie quoted in "Bank Official Empie Ousted by Governor," *Tulsa World,* March 11, 1987, OHS Banks and Banking Vertical Files.
11. "Osborn to Retire as Bank Commissioner," *Oklahoma Banker* (August 1992), 17; "Thompson Named Bank Commissioner," *Oklahoma Banker* (September 1992), 24.
12. "Oklahoma's Economy: Making the Transition," *Oklahoma Banker* (June 1986), 17.
13. "Will Rogers Quotes," on Brainy Quote website, http://www.brainyquote.com/quotes/authors/w/will_rogers_3.html.
14. "Boren on Agriculture," *Oklahoma Banker* (September 1982), 4–5.
15. Naylor quoted in "Credit Crush on Farmers Eases, Bankers Say," *New York Times,* December 21, 1983, box 4, Zweig Collection.
16. "Ag Picture Growing Dimmer, Says Crawford," *Oklahoma Banker* (March 1985), 15, 24.
17. "Ag Credit Conditions Deteriorate," *Oklahoma Banker* (July 1985), 14.
18. "Ag Bankers Report Credit Tightening," *Oklahoma Banker* (January 1986), 24.
19. Drabenstott's comments in *Economic Review* excerpted in "Farm Business Failures Mount," *Oklahoma Banker* (March 1986), 11.
20. "IFMAPS—Today's Help for Agriculture's Future," *Oklahoma Banker* (September 1986), 6.
21. American AgCredit, http://www.agloan.com/.
22. Kent Crain and Felix Hensley, interview by author, March 16, 2011, Ponca City, Oklahoma, Hightower Oral History Collection, and follow-up correspondence, July 15 and August 26, 2013, via phone and email.
23. Ibid.

24. "IFMAPS—Today's Help for Agriculture's Future," 7.

25. Hoysler quoted in "Farmland Values Continue to Rebound," *Oklahoma Banker* (March 1990), 28.

26. Buss quoted in "State Program Encourages Banks to Loan to Young Farmers," *Oklahoma Banker* (December 24, 1993), 3.

27. "ATMs: Headache vs. Heaven," *Oklahoma Banker* (November 1987), 14.

28. "In-home Banking Today and Tomorrow," *Oklahoma Banker* (November 1982), 10.

29. Leonard and Jerome quoted in "ATMs: Headache vs. Heaven," 14–15.

30. Wheeler quoted in "Stroud Bank Makes History," *Oklahoma Banker* (August 1987), 10.

31. Grissom and Kelly quoted in "ATMs: Headache vs. Heaven," 15.

32. "Electronic Banking Cannot Live on Technology Alone!!!," *Oklahoma Banker* (October 1986), 19.

33. "In-home Banking Today and Tomorrow," 43.

34. "Technology: Friend or Foe of the Community Bank?," *Oklahoma Banker* (July 1983), 5.

35. "Oklahoma Electronic Banking: 10 Years of Growth," *Oklahoma Banker* (August 1985), 16.

36. Graham quoted in "Debit Card Service Gaining Ground in State," *Oklahoma Banker* (February 18, 1994), 1.

37. "Check Imaging Makes Debut in State Banks," *Oklahoma Banker* (June 10, 1994), 1, 3.

38. Jackson and Christensen interview.

39. G. P. Johnson Hightower interview.

40. "Enter Computer Security," *Oklahoma Banker* (July 1982), 4.

41. "New Age Banking," *Oklahoma Banker* (April 1983), 4.

42. Price and Deets quoted in "The Computerization of the Banking Industry," *Oklahoma Banker* (September 1989), 13–14.

43. "The Winds of Change: Financial Innovations Sweep Banking into the 21st Century," *Oklahoma Banker* (November 1991), 11.

44. "CEOs Expect Non-bank Acquisitions," *Oklahoma Banker* (March 1985), 38.

45. "Non-Bank Bank Congestion," *Oklahoma Banker* (February 1985), 10, 11, 24.

46. "Journalists Beat Up Banks as Bashing Continues," *Oklahoma Banker* (February 4, 1994), 5.

47. "Strategic Management: Coping with a Changing Environment," *Oklahoma Banker* (September 1985), 7, 28.

48. Baker quoted in "Banks Making Inroad Into Trading of Stock," *Sunday Oklahoman*, November 21, 1982, box 4, Zweig Collection.

49. "Banks, Savings Firms Launch New Era in Interest-Paying Checking Accounts," *Daily Oklahoman*, January 2, 1983, box 12, Zweig Collection.

50. "The Competitive Structure of the Financial Services Industry: A Focus on Banking," *Oklahoma Banker* (March 1989), 12–13.

51. "Financial Services: The Inarticulate Industry?," *Oklahoma Banker* (July 1986), 14.

52. "OBA Ad Campaign Promotes Banking," *Oklahoma Banker* (February 1983), 14.

53. "Banks Spending More on Marketing," *Oklahoma Banker* (December 1985), 20.

54. Hefter quoted in "Financial Institutions Becoming More Sales Oriented," *Oklahoma Banker* (February 1987), 27.

55. "Quality Customer Service—An Old Idea Becomes an Industry Buzz Phrase," *Oklahoma Banker* (October 1988), 14.

56. "Banks in '93 Will Focus on Small Business Needs," *Oklahoma Banker* (February 5, 1993), 9; Ross and Nance quoted in "Oklahoma Banks Increasingly Offer Mutual Funds to Their Customers," *Oklahoma Banker* (April 2, 1993), 9.

57. Mayer, *Bankers,* 428.

58. Calomiris, *U.S. Bank Deregulation,* 58.

59. "Winning Strategies for Interstate Banking," *Fortune* (September 19, 1983), 104, box 8, Zweig Collection.

60. Mayer, *Bankers,* 428–29.

61. Mingo quoted in "Winning Strategies for Interstate Banking."

62. Trescott, *Financing American Enterprise,* 269.

63. "Winning Strategies for Interstate Banking," 106–20.

64. Hendrickson, *Regulation and Instability,* 172.

65. Simpson interview.

66. Mitchell quoted in "Bankers Getting Set for State Branching," *Sunday Oklahoman,* September 19, 1982, box 11, Zweig Collection.

67. Amis quoted in "Oklahoma Independent Bankers Form Statewide Association," *Oklahoma Banker* (August 1974), 9.

68. Craig Buford, interview by author, August 10, 2011, Oklahoma City, Hightower Oral History Collection.

69. Simpson interview.

70. David Rainbolt interview.

71. Community Bankers Association of Oklahoma website, http://www.cba-ok.org/.

72. Buford interview.

73. Thompson interview; "Thompson Named Bank Commissioner," *Oklahoma Banker* (September 1992), 24.

74. Thompson interview.

75. Mike Leonard, interview by author, April 17, 2012, Muskogee, Oklahoma, Hightower Oral History Collection.

76. David Rainbolt interview.

77. "Branching and Multibank Options in Oklahoma," *Oklahoma Banker* (September 1983), 10.

78. "Empie: Branch Limit 'Ridiculous,'" *Oklahoma City Journal Record,* June 17, 1983, box 4, Zweig Collection.

79. "Branch Banking: Its Impact on Oklahoma's Banking Industry," *Oklahoma Banker* (December 1990), 8; "Oklahoma Legislature Passes Sweeping Bank Restructure Bill," *American Banker,* June 17, 1983, box 12, Zweig Collection.

80. "Empie: Branch Limit 'Ridiculous'"; "Branching and Multibank Options in Oklahoma," 10.

81. "Branching and Multibank Options in Oklahoma," 11.

82. Turpen and Barr quoted in "Multi-Bank Holding Law Ruled Constitutional," *Oklahoma City Journal Record,* September 14, 1983, box 12, Zweig Collection.

83. "Branch Bank Planning: A Place to Start," *Oklahoma Banker* (November 1983), 38.

84. "Branch Banking: Its Impact on Oklahoma's Banking Industry," 8.

85. "The New Branching Law," *Oklahoma Banker* (May 1986), 22.

86. "Branch Banking: Its Impact on Oklahoma's Banking Industry," 8.

87. Simpson interview.

88. Gene Rainbolt quoted in "Banks Haven't Gone Fishing for Smaller Ones Despite Liberalization of State Banking Law," Oklahoma Bankers Special Edition, *Oklahoma City Journal Record,* May 5, 1984, box 11, Zweig Collection.

89. Thompson interview.

90. McLean quoted in "Banks Haven't Gone Fishing for Smaller Ones Despite Liberalization of State Banking Law."

91. Ibid.

92. Paul quoted in "Merger of Nichols Hills, Enid Banks 'Successful,'" *Oklahoma City Journal Record,* May 5, 1984, box 11, Zweig Collection.

93. "Liberty Bank Combats Rumors," *Daily Oklahoman,* January 7, 1988.

94. John and Eleanor Kirkpatrick quoted in Max J. Nichols, *John and Eleanor: A Sense of Community* (Tulsa: Council Oak Books, 1995), 252–53.

95. "Banks of Mid-America Adopts 'Oklahoma Plan,'" *Oklahoma City Journal Record,* June 15, 1988.

96. Kirkpatrick quoted in Nichols, *John and Eleanor,* 257.

97. "Bank of Oklahoma Celebrates 100 Years," *Tulsa World,* November 14, 2010.

98. George Kaiser and Stan Lybarger, interview by author, August 2, 2012, Tulsa, Oklahoma, Hightower Oral History Collection.

99. G. P. Johnson Hightower interview.

100. Lucas quoted in "Supermarket Banking Brings New Bank Marketing Style to State," *Oklahoma Banker* (January 22, 1993), 1.

101. Walker quoted in "In-Store Branching Makes More In-roads in Oklahoma," *Oklahoma Banker* (November 11, 1994), 7.

102. "OBA Fights Nationwide Interstate Banking Measure," *Oklahoma Banker* (August 1985), 11.

103. "Bankers Still Divided over Interstate Banking Idea," *Tulsa World,* April 25, 1986, OHS Banks and Banking Vertical Files.

104. "Regional Banking Laws," *Oklahoma Banker* (July 1985), 5.

105. "Oklahoma's Interstate Banking Legislation," *Oklahoma Banker* (August 1986), 7.

CHAPTER 11

Epigraph: "Guest Editorial," *Oklahoma Banker* (January 1990), 5.

1. Mark White, interview by author, March 17, 2011, Pawhuska, Oklahoma, Hightower Oral History Collection.

2. Gray quoted in Martin Mayer, *The Greatest-Ever Bank Robbery: The Collapse of the Savings and Loan Industry* (New York: Scribner's, 1990), 9.

3. Reagan quoted in Mayer, *Bankers,* 30.

4. Eichler, *Thrift Debacle,* 73.

5. Mayer, *Bankers,* 376–81.

6. Loy interview.

7. Mayer, *Greatest-Ever Bank Robbery,* 20. See also chapter one of this book, "A Brand-New State."

8. Bandura and Seagraves quoted in "Another Crisis Engulfs the Thrifts," *New York Times,* July 22, 1984, box 11, Zweig Collection.

9. Loy interview.

10. "Fewer, Bigger S&Ls to Be Seized," *Tulsa Tribune,* July 19, 1990.

11. Brady quoted in "S&L Bailout Running Out of Bucks," *Tulsa Tribune*, June 14, 1990.

12. Utt quoted in "Thrift Bailout in Trillions?," *Tulsa Tribune*, July 5, 1990.

13. Adair quoted in "S&L Bailout Said to Invite Fraud," *Tulsa Tribune*, June 21, 1990.

14. Unnamed regulator quoted in "Regulators Considering Suit against Neil Bush," *Tulsa Tribune*, July 11, 1990; "Regulators May Disclose Thrift Charges," *Tulsa Tribune*, June 26, 1990.

15. Simpson interview.

16. "Failed Thrifts' Costs Anger Reader," *Tulsa Tribune*, June 12, 1990.

17. Bauer Financial Reports and Office of Thrift Supervision cited in "25 Worst Performing Thrift Institutions Lost More Than $3 Billion in Second Quarter 1989," *Oklahoma Banker* (November 1989), 18.

18. "Branch Banking: Its Impact on Oklahoma's Banking Industry," 8.

19. G. P. Johnson Hightower interview.

20. Bragg quoted in "Sooner Federal Sale Possible by Fall," *Tulsa Tribune*, June 21, 1990.

21. "Four Oklahoma S&Ls Among 59 Offered for Sale," *Tulsa Tribune*, June 28, 1990.

22. "Man Accused of Fraud in Failed Checotah S&L," *Oklahoman*, February 8, 1991.

23. Beverage quoted in "Bankers Brace for Costly S&L Bailout," *Oklahoma Banker* (September 29, 1995), 1.

24. Wapshott, *Keynes Hayek*, 271.

25. "Guest Editorial," *Oklahoma Banker* (January 1990), 5.

26. Barkema and Morris quoted in "Fed Predicts Economy Will Expand in 1990," *Oklahoma Banker* (January 1990), 21.

27. Dauffenbach and Raines quoted in "Oklahoma Economy Continues to Expand," *Oklahoma Banker* (September 1990), 18–19.

28. Benbrook interview.

29. Benbrook quoted in "Bruce Benbrook: A Leader for the 90s," *Oklahoma Banker* (May 1990), 9.

30. Greenspan quoted in "Economic Indicators Reveal Uncertain Economic Direction for United States," *Oklahoma Banker* (September 1991), 15.

31. Dauffenbach and Scoggins quoted in ibid.

32. "Oklahoma Banking Industry Moves Forward," *Oklahoma Banker* (December 1991), 8.

33. "National, State Economies Level," *Oklahoma Banker* (September 1992), 8–9.

34. "Oklahoma's Community Banks Listed Among Nation's Most Profitable," *Oklahoma Banker* (October 1992), 8.

35. Fergeson and Simpson quoted in "State Banks Report Record '92 Profits," *Oklahoma Banker* (March 19, 1993), 1.

36. "State Banks Post $101 Million Second Quarter Profit," *Oklahoma Banker* (September 17, 1993), 1.

37. "1993 Brought Change, Success to Industry," *Oklahoma Banker* (January 7, 1994), 13.

38. Ibid; "State Banks Post $101 Million Second Quarter Profit."

39. "All the Romance Has Gone Out of Banking," *Oklahoma Banker* (March 1988), 14.

40. "Guest Editorial," *Oklahoma Banker* (July 1990), 6.

41. "Congressional Response to the S&L Debacle: The Crime Control Act of 1990," *Oklahoma Banker* (June 1991), 22, 25.

42. Morris editorial in *Tulsa Tribune* cited in "Guest Editorial," *Oklahoma Banker* (July 1990), 6–7.

43. Barnes quoted in "Compliance: The Big Picture," *Oklahoma Banker* (September 1990), 8–10.
44. Hendrickson, *Regulation and Instability,* 214–15.
45. Barnes quoted in "Compliance: The Big Picture," 8.
46. Hendrickson, *Regulation and Instability,* 214–15.
47. "Summary of Fair Lending Laws," *Oklahoma Banker* (January 7, 1994), 8.
48. "1993 Brought Change, Success to Industry," 12.
49. Beverage, Guard, and Benbrook quoted in "FIRREA in Progress," *Oklahoma Banker* (March 1990), 5–7.
50. Beverage quoted in ibid., 7. For a detailed listing of FIRREA provisions that affected Oklahoma banks, see "FIRREA Provisions Impacting Oklahoma Banks," *Oklahoma Banker* (March 1990), 8–9.
51. "CRA, Truth in Savings Rated Most Burdensome Regulations," *Oklahoma Banker* (March 19, 1993), 13.
52. "Banking Regulations Hurting Consumers, New Study Finds," *Oklahoma Banker* (April 2, 1993), 22.
53. Beverage quoted in "Let Banks Get Back to Business—Cut the Red Tape," *Oklahoma Banker* (December 1992), 13.
54. Fergeson quoted in "Bankers Unite for Reg Burden Relief," *Oklahoma Banker* (February 5, 1993), 1.
55. "1993 Brought Change, Success to Industry," 12–13.
56. Ogilvie and Williams quoted in "Red Tape Relief Measure Passes House," *Oklahoma Banker* (December 10, 1993), 1, 3.
57. Briggs, Osborn, Gene Rainbolt, and McCormick quoted in "Branch Banking—Its Impact on Oklahoma's Banking Industry," *Oklahoma Banker* (December 1990), 8–10.
58. Briggs quoted in ibid., 9.
59. Gene Rainbolt and Nelson quoted in ibid., 9–10.
60. Brackin quoted in "Mergers and Acquisitions Affect the Banking Industry," *Oklahoma Banker* (June 1992), 16; "Oklahoma Banking Industry Moves Forward," 8, 17.
61. Kelly quoted in "Mergers and Acquisitions Affect the Banking Industry," 16.
62. "1993 Brought Change, Success to Industry," 12.
63. Shewey and Conn quoted in "Correspondent Banking—Sailing into the Twenty-First Century," *Oklahoma Banker* (September 1992), 10.
64. Fite and Shewey quoted in ibid., 10–11.
65. Sterkel and Green quoted in ibid., 11.
66. Bauman quoted in "Making Effective, Profitable Use of Bank Holding Companies," *Oklahoma Banker* (December 1992), 8.
67. Cooksey quoted in ibid., 9.
68. Ibid.
69. Simpson and Osborn quoted in "International Bank Competition and Its Affect [sic] on Oklahoma Banks," *Oklahoma Banker* (March 1991), 8.
70. Ederington and Holland quoted in ibid., 9.
71. Ederington and Ozan quoted in ibid.
72. Meadows and Skipper quoted in "Oklahoma Women CEOs and Presidents: Worth their Weight in Gold," *Oklahoma Banker* (October 1990), 8.
73. Skipper and Duncan quoted in ibid.
74. Woodall quoted in ibid., 9.

75. Marilyn Myers and Clint Elliott, interview by author, November 17, 2010, Alva, Oklahoma, Hightower Oral History Collection.

76. Roma Lee Porter, William Paul Ellwanger, and Teresa Heater, interview by author, August 23, 2010, Lawton, Oklahoma, Hightower Oral History Collection.

77. Shelton quoted in "Social Issues Affecting the Banking Industry," *Oklahoma Banker* (November 1990), 10.

78. Ibid., 11.

79. Windsor quoted in ibid.

80. Sykes quoted in ibid.

81. Morrow quoted in ibid., 12.

82. Guard quoted in ibid.

83. Ibid.

84. Ibid., 12–13.

85. "10th Anniversary, Penn Square Bank Failure: The Recovery," *Oklahoma Banker* (July 1992), 22.

86. Plunk interview.

87. Harris quoted in "10th Anniversary," 22.

88. Alexander quoted in "Energy Laws Cited as Reason in Bank's Fall," *Sunday Oklahoman,* July 5, 1992.

89. Osborn quoted in "Bank Collapse Triggered Push for Tighter Law," *Sunday Oklahoman,* July 5, 1992.

90. Simpson interview.

91. Guard and Nelson quoted in "Bank Collapse Triggered Push for Tighter Law."

92. David Rainbolt interview.

93. Simpson interview.

94. Roger Beverage, interview by author, June 21, 2011, Oklahoma City, Hightower Oral History Collection.

95. Harris quoted in "10th Anniversary," 22.

96. Simpson interview.

97. Davis, bank employee, Plunk, and Empie quoted in "10th Anniversary," 23.

98. "Bank's Ex-chairman Recalls 'The Worst Day of My Life,'" *Sunday Oklahoman,* July 5, 1992.

99. Beverage interview.

100. Beverage quoted in "10th Anniversary," 23.

101. Greer interview.

102. G. P. Johnson Hightower interview.

103. Simpson interview.

104. Loy interview.

105. Bauman, Carroll, and Osborn quoted in "Osborn to Retire as Bank Commissioner," *Oklahoma Banker* (August 1992), 17.

106. "Aide Possible Pick for Banking Post," *Sunday Oklahoman,* July 5, 1992.

107. Thompson interview.

108. Walters quoted in "Aide Possible Pick for Banking Post."

109. Thompson quoted in "Thompson Named Bank Commissioner," *Oklahoma Banker* (September 1992), 24.

110. Fergeson quoted in "FDIC Liquidation Office in OKC to Shut Down," *Oklahoma Banker* (May 14, 1993), 1.

111. Ibid.

112. Bryant quoted in "Attitudes and Perceptions: How Oklahoma Bankers View their Industry," *Oklahoma Banker* (March 1991), 11.

CHAPTER 12

Epigraph: Conn, *One Man in His Time,* 165.

1. Strohm quoted in "Survey Reveals Image Problems," *Oklahoma Banker* (October 13, 1995), 6.

2. Ibid.

3. Ibid.

4. "Confidence in Banking Industry Hits All-Time High," *Oklahoma Banker* (January 16, 1998), 16.

5. Conn, *One Man in His Time,* 165.

6. "Who We Regulate" on Oklahoma Banking Department website, http://www.ok.gov/banking/Who_We_Regulate/index.html. See also *Oklahoma Banking Department 2011 Annual Report,* Oklahoma State Banking Department Collection.

7. Thompson interview.

8. Thompson quoted in "State Banking Dept. Makes Strides in '94," *Oklahoma Banker* (January 6, 1995), 1.

9. "Bank Failures Plummet Nationally in 1994," *Oklahoma Banker* (January 20, 1995), 6.

10. "Regulators Speak Favorably of State's Banking Industry," *Oklahoma Banker* (February 17, 1995), 6.

11. "Past Year Largely Upbeat for Banking Industry," *Oklahoma Banker* (January 6, 1995), 1.

12. "Oklahoma Loan Growth Outpaces National Rate, Sheshunoff Reports," *Oklahoma Banker* (February 3, 1995), 11.

13. David Rainbolt quoted in "94 Bank Profits Top $350 million," *Oklahoma Banker* (March 31, 1995,) 1.

14. Carroll and Thompson quoted in "Regulators Speak Favorably of State's Banking Industry," 6.

15. David Rainbolt and Reno quoted in "Past Year Largely Upbeat for Banking Industry," 1, 12.

16. Thompson quoted in "Regulators Speak Favorably of State's Banking Industry."

17. Burrage quoted in "State Profits Top $80 Million in 1st Quarter," *Oklahoma Banker* (June 23, 1995), 2.

18. "Fed Economist Sees Solid Future for Oklahoma Banks," *Oklahoma Banker* (October 25, 1996), 7.

19. Burrage quoted in "State's Second Quarter Profits Total $90 Million," *Oklahoma Banker* (September 15, 1995), 1.

20. "Strong Profits, Lending Forecast for Oklahoma Banks in '96," *Oklahoma Banker* (February 2, 1996), 1, 14. Simpson and Lage quotes on page 14.

21. "Third Quarter Oklahoma Profits Top '94 Level," *Oklahoma Banker* (December 22, 1995), 1.

22. "Strong Fourth Quarter Keys Growth in '95 Earnings," *Oklahoma Banker* (March 29, 1996), 1.

23. "Third Quarter Oklahoma Profits Top '94 Level," 2.

24. Hendrickson, *Regulation and Instability,* 214–15.

25. "Oklahoma Banks Ranked among Nation's Top Performers," *Oklahoma Banker* (August 16, 1996), 15.

26. "Second Quarter Oklahoma Bank Earnings Increase 9 percent," *Oklahoma Banker* (September 13, 1996), 4, 23.

27. "State Bank Earnings Reached $370 Million Mark in 1996," *Oklahoma Banker* (March 28, 1997), 5.

28. Simpson's comments in *Oklahoma Economic Outlook* cited in "Another Profitable Year Forecast for State's Banks," *Oklahoma Banker* (January 31, 1997), 1, 5.

29. "Quarterly Numbers Show Continued Earnings Growth," *Oklahoma Banker* (September 26, 1997), 1, 5.

30. "Oklahoma Bank Profits Rise in 3rd Quarter," *Oklahoma Banker* (December 19, 1997), 4.

31. "Early Figures Show Oklahoma Banks Continued Profitable Trend in 1997," *Oklahoma Banker* (March 27, 1998), 4.

32. "1997 Has Been a Good Year for Oklahoma's Banks," *Oklahoma Banker* (December 19, 1997), 2.

33. Simpson's comments in *Oklahoma Economic Outlook* cited in "Strong Lending, Profits Forecast for Oklahoma Banks," *Oklahoma Banker* (January 30, 1998), 1, 4.

34. "State Earnings Remain Strong in 2nd Quarter," *Oklahoma Banker* (October 1998), 4.

35. "Oklahoma Bank Earnings Drop in Fourth Quarter," *Oklahoma Banker* (April 1999), 4.

36. "Oklahoma Bank Earnings Top $200 million in first half of '99," *Oklahoma Banker* (October 1999), 7.

37. "FDIC Reports 10 Percent Increase in State's Bank Earnings," *Oklahoma Banker* (April 2000), 5.

38. See "MAPS" on City of Oklahoma City website, http://www.okc.gov/maps/index.html.

39. G. P. Johnson Hightower interview.

40. Weiss quoted in "Days Not Rosy for All Banks," *Oklahoman,* November 2, 2000.

41. Simpson interview.

42. Ketcha quoted in "Oklahoma Economy Drying Out with Drought," *Oklahoma Banker* (September 1998), 1.

43. Huckabay and Burrage quoted in ibid., 1, 12.

44. Morris and Dewald quoted in ibid., 12.

45. DeWitt and Tippens quoted in "Oklahoma Ag Industry Still Ailing," *Oklahoma Banker* (August 1999), 8.

46. "Ag Lenders Keep Working with Customers Despite Worsening Conditions, Report Shows," *Oklahoma Banker* (February 2000), 24.

47. DeWitt quoted in "Seeking Greener Pastures," *Oklahoma Banker* (October 2000), 4.

48. "Decision Marks Beginning of Battle with Credit Unions," *Oklahoma Banker* (February 27, 1998), 2.

49. "Credit Unions Fail to Tell the Whole Story When Making Comparisons with Banks," *Oklahoma Banker* (June 7, 1996), 1, 23–24.

50. Hodges quoted in "Broker Accused of Fraud, Forging Checks in Tulsa," *Daily Oklahoman,* May 19, 1993.

51. "Woodward Man Admits Bank Fraud," *Daily Oklahoman,* March 4, 1999.

52. "Jailed Broker Told to Pay Widow," *Daily Oklahoman*, October 20, 1999.
53. "Tulsan Admits Bank Fraud," *Daily Oklahoman*, December 18, 1997.
54. Christiansen and Gibson quoted in "Company Owner Blames Two Banks in Alleged Scam," *Daily Oklahoman*, June 5, 1998.
55. "Ex-Coal County Commissioner, Son Plead Guilty," *Daily Oklahoman*, October 30, 1998.
56. "Ardmore Dealer Admits Fraud," *Daily Oklahoman*, December 3, 1998.
57. Condon and Stephenson quoted in "Bank's Ex-President Joins Fraud Trial," *Daily Oklahoman*, April 23, 1999.
58. "Bank Scam Victims Due Part Payback," *Daily Oklahoman*, April 1, 2000.
59. "Woman Indicted in Check Case," *Daily Oklahoman*, July 10, 1999.
60. "Couple Indicted in Federal Fraud Case," *Daily Oklahoman*, July 13, 1999.
61. "Bankers Plead Guilty to Fraud," *Daily Oklahoman*, September 14, 1999.
62. Stidham quoted in "Terry Miller Sentenced for Bank Fraud," *Daily Oklahoman*, September 15, 1999.
63. "Park Owner Indicted," *Daily Oklahoman*, January 21, 2000.
64. "Former Executive Admits Funeral Fraud," *Daily Oklahoman*, October 12, 2000.
65. Yarbrough quoted in "Check Fraud Figures on the Rise," *Daily Oklahoman*, October 5, 2000.
66. Humphrey quoted in "Banks Become All Thumbs for Check IDs," *Daily Oklahoman*, June 15, 1997.
67. "Check Fraud at U.S. Banks Exceeds $1 Billion in 1997," *Oklahoma Banker* (January 1999), 19.
68. Busby quoted in "Computer-Generated Check Fraud Costing U.S. Banks $12.6 Billion," *Oklahoma Banker* (February 1999), 8.
69. Johnson, Choney, and Murphy quoted in "State Bank Robbery Stats Released for 2000," *Oklahoma Banker* (August 2000), 4–5.
70. Anderson quoted in "Oklahoma Bankers See Potential Benefits in On-Line Services," *Oklahoma Banker* (June 23, 1955), 9.
71. "Growing Number of Oklahoma Banks Launch Web Sites," *Oklahoma Banker* (April 18, 1996), 13.
72. "Community Banks Look to Boost Technology Investment," *Oklahoma Banker* (April 18, 1996), 14.
73. "Survey Finds Wider Consumer Acceptance of On-Line Banking," *Oklahoma Banker* (July 19, 1996), 20.
74. Hall quoted in "Oklahoma Banks Begin to Offer True Internet Banking," *Oklahoma Banker* (May 1998), 8.
75. Bates and Almon quoted in "Growing Number of Oklahoma Banks Launch Web Sites," 13. In the early days of the Internet, "online" was typically hyphenated. Similarly, "website" was usually divided into two words. In the fast new age of online banking, there was no time to bother with hyphens and spaces.
76. Ibid., 13–14.
77. "About: History," on RCB Bank website, https://rcbbank.com/pages/about.
78. McGuire and Bayless quoted in "Claremore Bank Pioneers Internet Banking in Oklahoma," *Oklahoma Banker* (March 28, 1997), 4.
79. Hannah quoted in "Oklahoma Banks Begin to Offer True Internet Banking," 8.
80. Almon quoted in "Internet Banking High on Technology Wave," *Oklahoma Banker* (November 1998), 17.

81. "Despite Still Small Numbers Internet Banking Growing," *Oklahoma Banker* (April 1999), 19.

82. Fiechter quoted in "OCC Studies Banks with Online Services," *Oklahoma Banker* (September 2000), 5.

83. Garrett and Loy quoted in "'Gen-X' next Marketing Challenge for OK Banks," *Oklahoma Banker* (May 1999), 29.

84. Jackson and Hampton quoted in "Approach Y2K with Reason," *Oklahoman,* December 10, 1999.

85. "Bankers should be Educated on the Industry's Past," *Oklahoma Banker* (August 4, 1995), 4.

86. Ibid.

87. Ibid.

88. William Shakespeare, *Julius Caesar,* act 1, scene 2.

EPILOGUE

Epigraph: Tracy and Polly Kelly, interview by author, July 8, 2010, Bristow, Oklahoma, Hightower Oral History Collection. Tracy Kelly died before this book went to press.

1. Quiggin, *Zombie Economics,* 5–34.

2. Christopher Ketcham, "Stop Payment! A Homeowners' Revolt against the Banks," *Harper's* (January 2012): 28.

3. Levitt and Trott quoted in Frank Partnoy and Jesse Eisinger, "What's Inside America's Banks?," *Atlantic* (January–February 2013): 62–63.

4. Ibid., 65.

5. Ibid., 69.

6. Ibid., 71.

7. Haldane quoted in ibid., 70.

8. Warren quoted in Jason Stanford, "Shakespeare in the Senate," *Progressive Populist* (March 15, 2013), 11.

9. Brown quoted in William Greider, "Bank-Buster Brown," *Nation* (April 1, 2013), 8.

10. Brown quoted in Amy Dean, "The Left and Right Agree: Time to Break Up Banks," *Progressive Populist* (May 15, 2013), 6.

11. "Ten Banks to Pay $8.5B for Foreclosure Abuse," *Charlottesville (Va.) Daily Progress,* January 8, 2013.

12. Mears quoted in "Bank of America Whistle-Blower: We Were Told to Lie," *Progressive Populist* (August 1, 2013), 8.

13. Holder quoted in "JPMorgan, Government Finalize $13B Settlement," *Charlottesville (Va.) Daily Progress,* November 20, 2013.

14. "U.S. Approves Ban on High-Risk Bank Trades on Wall Street," *Charlottesville (Va.) Daily Progress,* December 11, 2013.

15. Leonard interview.

16. Shipp interview.

17. G. P. Johnson Hightower interview.

18. Clark interview.

19. Paul Freeman, interview by author, August 19, 2011, Texhoma, Oklahoma, Hightower Oral History Collection.

20. Tim Barnes, interview by author, August 18, 2011, Boise City, Oklahoma, Hightower Oral History Collection.

21. Lee Stidham, Mike Stidham, and Robert Jennings, interview by author, November 16, 2010, Checotah, Oklahoma, Hightower Oral History Collection.

22. Lindel Pettigrew, interview by author, August 15, 2011, Chickasha, Oklahoma, Hightower Oral History Collection.

23. John Massey, interview by author, October 25, 2011, Durant, Oklahoma, Hightower Oral History Collection.

24. Thompson interview.

25. Beverage interview.

26. Ben Walkingstick, interview by author, November 22, 2010, Chandler, Oklahoma, Hightower Oral History Collection.

27. David Rainbolt interview.

28. The Unassigned Lands, also known as the Oklahoma District, were later divided into six counties of what became central Oklahoma.

29. See chapter four, "The Dawn of Conservative Banking." For the complete story of the historic merger, see Hightower, "Brother Bankers," 388–415.

30. F. P. Johnson to the president of the American National Bank in 2013, April 22, 1913, Century Chest Collection, Research Division, Oklahoma Historical Society, Oklahoma City.

31. Jimmy Eppler, David Young, and Scott Estes, interview by author, July 19, 2010, Ada, Oklahoma, Hightower Oral History Collection.

32. Baggerly interview.

33. Pittman interview.

34. Bill and Guy Berry interview.

35. Ken Fergeson, interview by author, April 26, 2010, Oklahoma City, Hightower Oral History Collection.

36. V. Pauline Hodges, interview by author, August 19, 2011, Beaver, Oklahoma, Hightower Oral History Collection.

37. Tracy and Polly Kelly interview.

38. Quiggin, *Zombie Economics,* 72.

39. R. Bruce Hall, interview by author, January 30, 2012, McAlester, Oklahoma, Hightower Oral History Collection.

40. McCall interview.

41. Leonard interview.

42. McCormack interview.

43. Myers and Elliott interview.

44. Leonard interview.

45. Benbrook interview.

46. White interview.

47. *BancFirst Corporation Annual Report 2013,* inside front cover, p. 1, BancFirst Corporate Files, Oklahoma City.

48. Gene Rainbolt interview.

Bibliography

ARCHIVAL, CORPORATE, PERSONAL, AND VERTICAL FILE COLLECTIONS

BancFirst Corporate Files. BancFirst support center, Oklahoma City.
Banks and Banking Vertical Files. Research Division. Oklahoma Historical Society, Oklahoma City.
Frederick S. Barde Collection, 1890–1916. Research Division. Oklahoma Historical Society.
Century Chest Collection. Research Division. Oklahoma Historical Society.
Closed Bank Files. Oklahoma Department of Libraries, Oklahoma City.
Eisenhower National Historic Site Collection. Gettysburg, Pennsylvania.
First State Bank of Boise City Corporate Files. Boise City, Oklahoma.
Michael J. Hightower Oklahoma Bank and Commerce Oral History Collection. Research Division. Oklahoma Historical Society.
Indian-Pioneer Papers. Western History Collections. University of Oklahoma, Norman, Oklahoma.
Johnson-Hightower Family Archives. Private collection, Oklahoma City.
E. H. Kelley Collection. Research Division. Oklahoma Historical Society.
Oklahoma City Chamber of Commerce Collection. Research Division. Oklahoma Historical Society.
Oklahoma Oral History Collection. Research Division. Oklahoma Historical Society.
Oklahoma State Banking Department Collection. Oklahoma State Banking Commission, Oklahoma City.
Fred L. Wenner Collection. Western History Collections. University of Oklahoma.
Phillip L. Zweig Penn Square Bank Collection. Research Division. Oklahoma Historical Society.

NEWSPAPERS AND MAGAZINES

Ada Star-Democrat
American Banker

Atlantic
Beaver Herald
Blackwell Morning Tribune
Blackwell Sunday Tribune
Blackwell Times-Record
Cimarron News, Boise City
Boise City News
Chandler Tribune
Charlottesville (Va.) Daily Progress
Daily Oklahoman (later *Oklahoman*)
Indian Journal, Eufaula
Guthrie Daily Leader
Guymon Panhandle Herald
Harlow's Weekly
Harper's
Investor
Mangum Weekly Star
Marshall County News-Democrat
McMasters' Weekly
New York Times
Oklahoma Banker
Oklahoma City Black Dispatch
Oklahoma City Times
Oklahoma News
Oklahoma State Capital
Progressive Populist
Saturday Oklahoman and Times
Shawnee Daily Herald
Shawnee News-Star
Sunday Oklahoman
Tulsa Tribune
Tulsa World

BOOKS

Ahamed, Liaquat. *Lords of Finance: The Bankers Who Broke the World.* New York: Penguin, 2009.

Ameringer, Oscar. *If You Don't Weaken.* Foreword by Carl Sandburg. New York: Henry Holt, 1940.

Appleby, Joyce. *The Relentless Revolution: A History of Capitalism.* New York: W. W. Norton, 2010.

Brands, H. W. *American Colossus: The Triumph of Capitalism, 1865–1900.* New York: Anchor Books, 2010.

Brokaw, Tom. *The Greatest Generation.* New York: Dell Publishing, 1998.

Bruner, Robert F., and Sean D. Carr. *The Panic of 1907: Lessons Learned from the Market's Perfect Storm.* Hoboken, N.J.: Wiley, 2007.

Burbank, Garin. *When Farmers Voted Red: The Gospel of Socialism in the Oklahoma Countryside, 1910–1924.* Westport, Conn.: Greenwood Press, 1976.

Calomiris, Charles W. *U.S. Bank Deregulation in Historical Perspective.* Cambridge: Cambridge University Press, 2000.

Chernow, Ron. *The Death of the Banker: The Decline and Fall of the Great Financial Dynasties and the Triumph of the Small Investor.* New York: Vintage Books, 1997.

Colcord, Charles Francis. *The Autobiography of Charles Francis Colcord, 1859–1934.* Tulsa: privately printed, 1970.

Conn, Jack T. *One Man in His Time.* Edited by Odie B. Faulk. Oklahoma City: Western Heritage Books, 1979.

Cronon, William, George Miles, and Jay Gitlin, eds. *Under an Open Sky: Rethinking America's Western Past.* New York: W. W. Norton, 1992.

Debo, Angie. *Tulsa: From Creek Town to Oil Capital.* Norman: University of Oklahoma Press, 1943.

Delamaide, Darrell. *Debt Shock: The Full Story of the World Credit Crisis.* New York: Doubleday, 1984.

Dornblaser, Susan. *Liberty and Tulsa: Making History Together for 100 Years, 1895–1995.* Tulsa: Liberty Bank and Trust Company, N.A., 1995.

Doti, Lynne Pierson, and Larry Schweikart. *Banking in the American West: From the Gold Rush to Deregulation.* Norman: University of Oklahoma Press, 1991.

Eichler, Ned. *The Merchant Builders.* Cambridge, Mass.: MIT Press, 1982.

———. *The Thrift Debacle.* Berkeley: University of California Press, 1989.

Ferguson, Niall. *The Ascent of Money: A Financial History of the World.* New York: Penguin, 2008.

———. *Civilization: The West and the Rest.* New York: Penguin, 2011.

Friedman, Milton, and Anna Jacobson Schwartz. *A Monetary History of the United States, 1867–1960.* Princeton: Princeton University Press, 1971.

Glasscock, C. B. *Then Came Oil: The Story of the Last Frontier.* Westport, Conn.: Hyperion Press, 1976.

Gorton, George. *A "Big-Ass Boy" in the Oil Fields: My Adventures, 1918–28.* New Berlin, Wis.: Napco Graphic Arts, 1975.

Green, James R. *Grass-Roots Socialism: Radical Movements in the Southwest, 1895–1943.* Baton Rouge: Louisiana State University Press, 1978.

Haller, Ben, Jr. *A History of Banking in Nebraska, 1854–1990.* Lincoln: Nebraska Bankers Association, 1990.

Heilbroner, Robert L. *The Economic Transformation of America.* In collaboration with Aaron Singer. New York: Harcourt Brace Jovanovich, 1977.

Hendrickson, Jill M. *Regulation and Instability in U.S. Commercial Banking: A History of Crises.* New York: Palgrave MacMillan, 2011.

Hightower, Michael J. *Banking in Oklahoma before Statehood.* Norman: University of Oklahoma Press, 2013.

———. *Frontier Families: The Records and Johnstons in American History.* Oklahoma City: Cottonwood Press, 2010.

Holland, David S. *When Regulation Was Too Successful—The Sixth Decade of Deposit Insurance: A History of the Troubles of the U.S. Banking Industry in the 1980s and Early 1990s.* Westport, Conn.: Praeger, 1998.

Hurst, Irvin. *The 46th Star: A History of Oklahoma's Constitutional Convention and Early Statehood.* Oklahoma City: Western Heritage Books, 1980.

Kazin, Michael. *American Dreamers: How the Left Changed a Nation.* New York: Vintage Books, 2012.

Kindleberger, Charles P., and Robert Z. Aliber. *Manias, Panics, and Crashes: A History of Financial Crises.* Basingstoke, UK: Palgrave MacMillan, 2005.

Lenthall, Bruce. *Radio's America: The Great Depression and the Rise of Modern Mass Culture.* Chicago: University of Chicago Press, 2007.

Lippmann, Walter. *Drift and Mastery: An Attempt to Diagnose the Current Unrest.* Madison: University of Wisconsin Press, 1985.

Mayer, Martin. *The Bankers: The Next Generation.* New York: Truman Talley Books, 1997.

———. *The Greatest-Ever Bank Robbery: The Collapse of the Savings and Loan Industry.* New York: Scribner's, 1990.

———. *The Money Bazaars: Understanding the Banking Revolution around Us.* New York: E. P. Dutton, 1984.

McCollom, James P. *The Continental Affair: The Rise and Fall of the Continental Illinois Bank.* New York: Dodd, Mead, 1987.

McReynolds, Edwin C. *Oklahoma: A History of the Sooner State.* Norman: University of Oklahoma Press, 1954.

McRill, Albert. *And Satan Came Also: An Inside Story of a City's Social and Political History.* Oklahoma City: Britton Publishing, 1955.

Meacham, Jon. *American Lion: Andrew Jackson in the White House.* New York: Random House, 2008.

Money, Jack, and Steve Lackmeyer. *Skirvin.* Oklahoma City: Full Circle, 2009.

Nichols, Max J. *John and Eleanor: A Sense of Community.* Tulsa: Council Oak Books, 1995.

Nichols, Max J., and David R. "Dusty" Martin. *Continuing an Oklahoma Banking Tradition.* Oklahoma City: First Interstate Bank of Oklahoma, N.A., 1989.

Quiggin, John. *Zombie Economics: How Dead Ideas Still Walk among Us.* Princeton, N.J.: Princeton University Press, 2010.

Robb, Thomas Bruce. *The Guaranty of Bank Deposits.* Boston: Houghton Mifflin, 1921.

Samuelson, Robert J. *The Great Inflation and Its Aftermath: The Past and Future of American Affluence.* New York: Random House, 2010.

Santayana, George. *The Life of Reason, or the Phases of Human Progress: Reason in Common Sense.* London: Constable, 1906.

Scales, James R., and Danney Goble. *Oklahoma Politics: A History.* Norman: University of Oklahoma Press, 1982.

Schlesinger, Arthur M., Jr., gen. ed. *The Almanac of American History.* New York: Putnam, 1983.

Schneider, Steven A. *The Oil Price Revolution.* Baltimore: Johns Hopkins University Press, 1983.

Schweikart, Larry, ed. *Banking in the West.* Manhattan, Kans.: Sunflower University Press, 1984.

Scott, Angelo C. *The Story of Oklahoma City.* Oklahoma City: Times-Journal Publishing, 1939.

Singer, Mark. *Funny Money.* New York: Knopf, 1985.

Smallwood, James M. *An Oklahoma Adventure of Banks and Bankers.* Norman: University of Oklahoma Press, 1979.

Stein, Judith. *Pivotal Decade: How the United States Traded Factories for Financing in the Seventies.* New Haven, Conn.: Yale University Press, 2010.

Stewart, Roy P. *Born Grown: An Oklahoma City History.* Oklahoma City: Fidelity Bank, N.A., 1974.

Studenski, Paul, and Herman E. Krooss. *Financial History of the United States.* New York: McGraw-Hill, 1963.

Thompson, John. *Closing the Frontier: Radical Response in Oklahoma, 1889–1923.* Norman: University of Oklahoma Press, 1986.

Todd, Tim. *Confidence Restored: The History of the Tenth District's Federal Reserve Bank.* Kansas City, Mo.: Public Affairs Department, Federal Reserve Bank of Kansas City, 2008.
Trescott, Paul B. *Financing American Enterprise: The Story of Commercial Banking.* New York: Harper and Row, 1963.
Wallis, Michael. *Pretty Boy: The Life and Times of Charles Arthur Floyd.* New York: St. Martin's Press, 1992.
Wapshott, Nicholas. *Keynes Hayek: The Clash that Defined Modern Economics.* New York: W. W. Norton, 2012.
White, Lawrence H., ed. *The Crisis in American Banking.* New York: New York University Press, 1993.
Zimmerman, William, ed. *Banking's Past, Financial Services' Future.* New York: American Banker, 1986.
Zinn, Howard. *The Twentieth Century: A People's History.* New York: HarperPerennial, 2003.
Zweig, Phillip L. *Belly Up: The Collapse of the Penn Square Bank.* New York: Crown, 1985.

ARTICLES, SPEECHES, AND BOOK CHAPTERS

Andrew, A. Piatt. "The Crux of the Currency Question." *Yale Review*, n.s., 2 (July 1913): 595–620.
———. "Hoarding in the Panic of 1907." *Quarterly Journal of Economics* 22, no. 2 (1908): 290–99.
———. "Substitutes for Cash in the Panic of 1907." *Quarterly Journal of Economics* 22, no. 4 (1908): 497–516.
Badger, Tony. "FDR: A Model for Obama?" *Nation* (January 26, 2009): 20–22.
Bass, Henry B. "Herbert Hiram Champlin." *Chronicles of Oklahoma* 33, no. 1 (Spring 1955): 43–48.
Bernanke, Ben S. "The Crisis as a Classic Financial Panic." Speech delivered at Fourteenth Jacques Polak Annual Research Conference, Washington, D.C., November 8, 2013. http://www.federalreserve.gov/newsevents/speech/bernanke20131108a.htm.
Chandler, Alfred D. "The Beginnings of 'Big Business' in American Industry." *Business History Review* 33, no. 1 (Spring 1959): 1–31.
Dayen, David. "Bank of America Whistle-Blower: We Were Told to Lie." *Progressive Populist* (August 1, 2013): 1, 8.
Dean, Amy. "The Left and Right Agree: Time to Break Up Banks." *Progressive Populist* (May 15, 2013): 6.
"The Economy: 'We Are All Keynesians Now.'" *Time* (December 31, 1965): 64–67.
Ellinger, Charles Wayne. "Congressional Viewpoint toward the Admission of Oklahoma as a State: 1902–1906." *Chronicles of Oklahoma* 58, no. 3 (Fall 1980): 282–95.
———. "The Drive for Statehood in Oklahoma, 1889–1906." *Chronicles of Oklahoma* 41, no. 1 (Spring 1963): 15–37.
Fabian, Ann. "History for the Masses: Commercializing the Western Past." In *Under an Open Sky: Rethinking America's Western Past,* edited by William Cronon, George Miles, and Jay Gitlin, 223–38. New York: W. W. Norton, 1992.
Garsson, Robert M. "'The Ballyhoo Years' End in a Crash and a Hangover." In *Banking's Past, Financial Services' Future,* edited by William Zimmerman, 33–46. New York: American Banker, 1986.
Gatch, Loren C. "'An' the west jes' smiled': Oklahoma Banking and the Panic of 1907." *Chronicles of Oklahoma* 87, no. 1 (Spring 2009): 4–33.

Greider, William. "Bank-Buster Brown." *Nation* (April 1, 2013): 8–9.
Hightower, Michael J. "Brother Bankers: Frank P. and Hugh M. Johnson, Founders of the First National Bank and Trust Company of Oklahoma City." *Chronicles of Oklahoma* 88, no. 4 (Winter 2010–11): 388–415.
———. "The Businessman's Frontier: C. C. Hightower, Commerce, and Old Greer County, 1891–1903." *Chronicles of Oklahoma* 86, no. 1 (Spring 2008): 4–31.
———. "Penn Square: The Shopping Center Bank that Shook the World, Part 1—Boom." *Chronicles of Oklahoma* 90, no. 1 (Spring 2012): 68–99.
———. "Penn Square: The Shopping Center Bank that Shook the World, Part 2—Bust." *Chronicles of Oklahoma* 90, no. 2 (Summer 2012): 204–36.
Ketcham, Christopher. "Stop Payment! A Homeowners' Revolt against the Banks." *Harper's* (January 2012): 28–36.
Lewallen, Robert D. "'Let the People Rule': William Jennings Bryan and the Oklahoma Constitution." *Chronicles of Oklahoma* 73, no. 3 (Fall 1995): 278–307.
Mahnken, Norbert R. "No Oklahoman Lost a Penny: Oklahoma's State Bank Guarantee Law, 1907–1923." *Chronicles of Oklahoma* 71, no. 1 (Spring 1993): 42–63.
———. "William Jennings Bryan in Oklahoma." *Nebraska History* 31, no. 4 (December 1950): 247–74.
Marshall, Jeffrey. "Twixt Booms and Panics: Banking in the Gilded Age." In *Banking's Past, Financial Services' Future*, edited by William Zimmerman, 25–32. New York: American Banker, 1986.
Meredith, H. L. "Oscar Ameringer and the Concept of Agrarian Socialism." *Chronicles of Oklahoma* 45, no. 1 (Spring 1967): 77–83.
Meredith, Howard L., and George H. Shirk. "Oklahoma City: Growth and Reconstruction, 1889–1939." *Chronicles of Oklahoma* 55, no. 3 (Fall 1977): 293–308.
Moore, Bill. "Race to the Top: The Great Skyscraper Race of 1931." *Oklahoma Gazette* 19 (November 6, 1997): 17–20.
Mullins, William H. "In the Midst of Adversity: The City, the Governor, and the FERA, Part I." *Chronicles of Oklahoma* 76, no. 4 (Winter 1998–99): 374–91.
———. "In the Midst of Adversity: The City, the Governor, and the FERA, Part II." *Chronicles of Oklahoma* 77, no. 1 (Spring 1999): 54–73.
Naylor, Bartlett. "Bankers Spilled Blood in Nation's Early Years." In *Banking's Past, Financial Services' Future*, edited by William Zimmerman, 18–24. New York: American Banker, 1986.
Noyes, Alexander D. "A Year after the Panic of 1907." *Quarterly Journal of Economics* 23 (February 1909): 185–212.
Partnoy, Frank, and Jesse Eisinger. "What's Inside America's Banks?" *Atlantic* (January/February 2013): 60–71.
Perlstein, Rick. "That Seventies Show." *Nation* (November 8, 2010): 32.
Rockoff, Hugh. "Banking and Finance, 1789–1914." In *The Long Nineteenth Century*. Vol. 2 of *The Cambridge Economic History of the United States*, edited by Stanley L. Engerman and Robert E. Gallman, 643–84. Cambridge: Cambridge University Press, 2000.
Rogers, William Warren. "'I Want You All to Come': John C. Walton and America's Greatest Barbecue." *Chronicles of Oklahoma* 75, no. 1 (Spring 1997): 20–31.
Salsman, Richard M. "Bankers as Scapegoats for Government-Created Banking Crises in U.S. History." In *The Crisis in American Banking*, edited by Lawrence H. White, 81–118. New York: New York University Press, 1993.
Smallwood, James M. "Partners in Progress: Banking and Agribusiness in Oklahoma." In

Banking in the West, edited by Larry Schweikart. Manhattan, Kans.: Sunflower University Press, 1984.
Sprague, O. M. W. "The American Crisis of 1907." Economic Journal 18 (September 1908): 353–72.
Stanford, Jason. "Shakespeare in the Senate." Progressive Populist (March 15, 2013): 11.
Tolman, Keith. "Will Rogers Field: The Life and Death of a World War II Airbase." Chronicles of Oklahoma 79, no. 1 (Spring 2001): 4–17.
Vanderlip, Frank A. "The Aldrich Plan for Banking Legislation: An Address by the Honorable Frank A. Vanderlip, President of the National City Bank, New York, before The Commercial Club of Chicago." Madison: Wisconsin Library Services, n.d., ca. 1911.
Williams, Robert L. "James Dwight Lankford." Chronicles of Oklahoma 3, no. 1 (April 1925): 86–89.
Wright, Muriel H. "The Wedding of Oklahoma and Miss Indian Territory." Chronicles of Oklahoma 35, no. 3 (Fall 1957): 255–63.

INTERVIEWS

Steve Baggerly, August 18, 2011. Guymon, Oklahoma.
Tim Barnes, August 18, 2011. Boise City, Oklahoma.
Bruce Benbrook, August 24, 2010. Woodward, Oklahoma.
Bill and Guy Berry, April 18, 2012. Sapulpa, Oklahoma.
Nick Berry, September 5 and 6, 2013. Oklahoma City.
Roger Beverage, June 21, 2011. Oklahoma City.
Margery Bird (formerly Mayo), July 16, 2010. Tulsa, Oklahoma.
Jim Bowles, April 10, 2012. Shawnee, Oklahoma.
Craig Buford, August 10, 2011. Oklahoma City.
Charlie and Charlotte Butler, August 19, 2011. Hooker, Oklahoma.
Joel Champlin, April 27, 2011. Enid, Oklahoma.
Don and Kitty Clark, January 23, 2012. Anadarko, Oklahoma.
Kent Crain and Felix Hensley, March 16, 2011. Ponca City, Oklahoma.
Jimmy Eppler, David Young, and Scott Estes, July 19, 2010. Ada, Oklahoma.
Ken Fergeson, April 26, 2010. Oklahoma City.
Paul Freeman, August 19, 2011. Texhoma, Oklahoma.
Gordon Greer, November 13, 2012. Tulsa, Oklahoma.
R. Bruce Hall, January 30, 2012. McAlester, Oklahoma.
Jim Hamby and Denver Davison, July 19, 2010. Ada, Oklahoma.
Dannie Bea Hightower, June 28 and 29, 2008, Harbor Springs, Mich.; February 16, 2009, Oklahoma City.
G. P. Johnson Hightower, October 17 and 22, 2013. Oklahoma City.
V. Pauline Hodges, August 19, 2011. Beaver, Oklahoma.
Matt Jackson and Linda Christensen, August 17, 2011. Thomas, Oklahoma.
George W. James, August 14, 2013. Harbor Springs, Michigan.
Bill Jordan, Kelly Jordan, Laura Miller, and Jerry Fowler, October 24, 2011. Quinton, Oklahoma.
George Kaiser and Stan Lybarger, August 2, 2012. Tulsa, Oklahoma.
Tracy and Polly Kelly, July 8, 2010. Bristow, Oklahoma.
Mike Leonard, April 17, 2012. Muskogee, Oklahoma.
Tom Loy, November 5, 2012. Oklahoma City.

Carlisle and John Mabrey, October 11, 2011. Bixby, Oklahoma.
Gerald R. Marshall, March 11, 2011. Oklahoma City.
John Massey, October 25, 2011. Durant, Oklahoma.
Charles McCall, October 25, 2011. Atoka, Oklahoma.
Bob McCormack, June 22, 2011. Duncan, Oklahoma.
Marilyn Myers and Clint Elliott, November 17, 2010. Alva, Oklahoma.
Lindel Pettigrew, August 15, 2011. Chickasha, Oklahoma.
Jim and Kirk Pittman, June 23, 2011. Seiling, Oklahoma.
Steve Plunk, August 3, 2012. Oklahoma City.
Roma Lee Porter, Paul Ellwanger, and Teresa Heater, August 23, 2010. Lawton, Oklahoma.
David Rainbolt, June 21, 2011. Oklahoma City.
H. E. "Gene" Rainbolt, October 18, 2011. Oklahoma City.
George and Nancy Records, June 4, 2009. Oklahoma City.
Betty Rodgers-Johnson, February 13, 2009. Oklahoma City.
Michael Rogers, October 18, 2011. Oklahoma City.
Meg Salyer, April 23, 2012. Oklahoma City.
Gayla Sherry, March 9, 2011. Oklahoma City.
Brian Shipp, October 26, 2011. Idabel, Oklahoma.
Gary Simpson, November 9, 2012. Stillwater, Oklahoma.
Lee Stidham, Mike Stidham, and Robert Jennings, November 16, 2010. Checotah, Oklahoma.
Mick Thompson, February 6, 2012. Oklahoma City.
Ben Walkingstick, November 22, 2010. Chandler, Oklahoma.
Mark White, March 17, 2011. Pawhuska, Oklahoma.

Index

Abedi, Agha Hasan, 184
Ackerman, Ray, 368
Ada Chamber of Commerce, 167
Adair, John J., 323
Adair County Savings and Loan, 188
Adams, Frederick Upham, 5
Adams, John and Mary Ann, 376
Adams, J. W., 56
Adams, K. S., 164–66
Agriculture: bankers' commitment to, 21, 60–62, 79, 94, 98, 131, 134–35, 162–64, 172, 245; Indian Territory, crisis in (early 1900s), 45–46; Oklahoma, crisis in (1980s), 289–90, 293–96; Oklahoma, crisis in (1990s), 369–71
Air Base Oklahoma City, 151
Aldrich, Nelson W., U.S. senator, 13, 38–40
Aldrich-Vreeland Act (1908), 37
Alexander, Bob, and Alexander Energy Corporation, 349
Alexander, W. L., 29
Alfred P. Murrah Federal Building (Oklahoma City), 363. *See also under* Oklahoma City; McVeigh, Timothy
Allen, J. D., 207
Allen, J. P., 145
Almon, Terry, 382–83

Alva State Bank and Trust Co., 300, 330
Amalgamated Copper Co., 7
American AgCredit, 294–95
American Bank and Trust Co. of Edmond, 314
American Banker, 192, 225–27, 230, 233–35, 240, 272–73, 358
American Bankers Association (ABA), 39, 106, 109, 112, 159, 162, 167, 294, 301–302, 330, 334–36, 342, 360, 363, 371–72, 378; Communications Council, 357; Human Resources Division, 288; Protective Department, 124; State Bank Division, 124
American Diversified Savings and Loan (Calif.), 320
American Express, 302
American Heritage Bank: of El Reno, 335, 360, 371; of Sapulpa (formerly, American National Bank), 278, 401
American Home Savings and Loan Association of Edmond, 325
American National Bank: of Bartlesville, 26; of Bristow (later, Spirit Bank), 298, 338–39; of Duncan, 341; of Lawton, 300, 314; of Oklahoma City, 8, 12, 23–24, 29, 41, 49–50, 84–86, 102, 150, 154–55, 287,

American National Bank (*continued*)
399–400; of Sapulpa (later, American Heritage Bank), 115, 155
American Red Cross, 249, 386
American Smelting and Refining Co., 7
American Society of Farm Managers and Rural Appraisers (ASFMRA), 296
Americans with Disabilities Act (1990), 347
Ameringer, Oscar, 44–47, 414n21
Ameristate Bank (formerly, Atoka State Bank), 403
Ames, C. B, 141
Amis, R. S. "Bob," 308
Anadarko Basin, 165, 192–98, 201–202, 207, 210–15, 217, 225, 234, 244, 250, 276, 345
Anadarko Indian Agency, 248
Andersen, Carl Jr., 228
Anderson, Brian, 380, 385
Anderson, Roger, 198–200, 207, 229
Andrew, A. Piatt, 11–12, 16–17, 38
And Satan Came Also (McRill), 160
Anthony, W. B., 28–29
Apache Tribe of Oklahoma, 375
Appeal to Reason, 45
Appleby, Buddy, 212
Applegate, Michael, 329
Arab Oil embargo (1973), 193
Ardmore National Bank, 30
Arthur Andersen and Co., 302–303, 332
Arthur Young and Co., 242
Arvest Bank, 220, 300, 325
Association of Oilwell Servicing Contactors, 244
Atoka State Bank (later, Ameristate Bank), 285, 403
Automated clearing house (ACH), 297, 301
Automated teller machines (ATMs), 289–90, 297–99, 301
Automatic transfer system (ATS), 267

Baggerly, Steve, 246, 400
Bailey, W. J., Federal Reserve Board governor, 99
Baker, Howard H., U.S. senator, 263
Baker, James (financial analyst), 264
Baker, James (securities firm founder), 303
BancFirst Corporation, 185–86, 236, 240, 246, 308, 336–37, 360, 380, 383, 399, 405–406. *See also under* Thunderbird Financial Corporation; Tradesmen's National Bank/Building (Oklahoma City); United Community Corporation
BancOklahoma Corporation of Tulsa, 313–14
BancOne Corporation of Columbus, Ohio, 299
Bandura, Joseph W., 322
Bank: of America, 199, 284, 290–91, 308, 394; of Amorita, 149; of Buffalo, 417n16; of Canton (later, Community State Bank of Canton), 71, 74, 101, 105–108, 148, 279; of Carney, 55; of Credit and Commerce International (BCCI), 184–87; of Cushing, 356; of England, 393; of Healdton, 202, 352; of Indian Territory, 72; of Kremlin, 376; of Locust Grove, 330, 363; of Millerton, 53; The, N.A. (formerly, National Bank of McAlester), 297, 316; of Ocheleta, 52; of Oklahoma (BOK), 284, 315–16, 373, 380; of Oklahoma (BOK) Oklahoma City (formerly, Fidelity National Bank and Trust Co.), 284, 315–16; of the Panhandle (Guymon), 246, 400; of Pawnee, 57; of Pontotoc, 53; of Red Oak, 173; of Southern Oklahoma, N.A. (Madill), 339; of Tulsa, 326; of Union, 330; of the West (Thomas), 288, 300; of the Wichitas (Snyder), 369; of Woodward, 403
Bank Administration Institute, 338
Bankers Trust Co. of New York, 38
Bank IV, 299–300, 352
Bank Holding Co. Act (1956), 168
Banking Act: of 1935, 305–306; of 1937, in Oklahoma, 147–48. *See also* Glass-Steagall Banking Act (1933)
Banking codes: Oklahoma, 17, 166; revision of, in Oklahoma (1965), 167–68

INDEX   463

Bank Insurance Fund, 360
Bank Marketing Association, 304
Bank Merger Act (1960), 168
Bank of Commerce: Chouteau, 330, 363; McLoud, 330, 363; Norman, 280; Tulsa, 307
Bank Protection Act (1968), 173–74
Bankruptcy Court, Western District of Oklahoma, 244
Banks of Mid-America, 313–14. *See also under* Liberty National Bank and Trust Co.; First National Bank
Barde, Frederick S., 23, 57, 60–62
Baresel, Larry, 376
Barkema, Alan, 327
Barnard, H. G., 315
Barnes, Tim, 397
Barnes, Wayne, 332–33
Barnett, W. J., 94, 113, 122
Barnsdall State Bank, 301
Barr, George, 312
Barrow, Clyde, 124
Bartlesville Clearing House Association, 54
Bartlett, Dewey, 181–83
Bass, Clark, 402–403
Bates, Albert L., 139
Bates, Jeff, 382
Bauer Financial Reports, 324
Baum, James E., 106–107, 124
Bauman, Marion C., 233, 341, 355
Bayless, Tom, 383
Beacon Club (Oklahoma City), 287
Bear Creek Wildlife, Inc., 377
Beitman (later, Heaney), Alice, 27–28, 411n108
Bell, Edgar T., 117
Beller, Eldon, 219–20, 227, 235, 242, 247–48
Bellmon, Henry, 183, 281, 291–92
Bellmon, Shirley, 298
Belly Up: The Collapse of the Penn Square Bank (Zweig), 192–93, 225–35, 240, 251. *See also* Penn Square National Bank of Oklahoma City

Benbrook, A. M., 328
Benbrook, Bruce, 290, 328, 334, 404–405
Benbrook, Temple, 328
Benjamin, Gary, 289
Bennett, Robert A., 273
Bergman, Roy, 161
Berle, Adolph A., 121–22
Bernanke, Ben, 13
Bernstein, Carl, 233
Berry, Bill, 115, 278, 401
Berry, Chris, 401
Berry, Guy III, 115, 278, 401
Berry, Nick, 221–25
Beverage, Roger, 325–26, 333–35, 350–52, 365–66, 372, 398
Bierer, A. G. C., 72
Biltmore Hotel (Oklahoma City), 94, 144
Bimson, Walter, 119
Bird (née Mayo), Margery, 137–39, 424n20
Birdwell, George, 108
Bitseedy, Martin, 375
Blaise, E. F., 26
Blinco, Ken, 356
Block, Dennis, 258
Bluestone, Barry, 277
Boatmen's National Bank of Oklahoma (formerly, First Interstate Bank of Oklahoma City), 340, 365, 380
Bolen, Hubert, 145
Bolshevik Revolution (1917), 48
Bonaparte, Charles J., 21, 70
Bond, Catherine L., 299
Bond, Cheryl, 299–300
Boren, David L., 257, 264–65, 281, 293
Boskin, Michael J., 271–72
Bowers Financial Services, 282
Bowles, Jim, 184
Bowman, Will, 275–77
Boyd, John R., 200, 204, 208, 215
Brackin, Mark, 338
Brady, Nicholas F., 323
Bragg, George, 325

464   INDEX

Branch banking, 18, 79–80, 91–93, 109, 123, 166–68, 184–88, 201, 251, 260, 278, 290, 297–99, 305–18, 324, 331–39, 350, 361, 365–69, 382, 395, 403–04. *See also* Federal Reserve System; Unit banking
Branstetter, Otto, 43–44
Briggs, Larry, 336–38
Broadhurst Financial Group (Tulsa), 338
Brock, Sidney L., 29–30
Brokaw, Tom, 129, 261
Brooks Theatre (Guthrie), 17
Brown, C. W., 135
Brown, Sherrod, 394
Brown, Wesley E., 183
Browning, Bill, 302–303
Bryan, William Jennings, 14, 17, 201, 307
Bryant, John, 356
Buford, Craig, 308–309
Building and loan associations, 89–90, 122
Bulling, Scott, 371
Burns, Ken, 402
Burrage, Steve, 362–63, 370
Busby, Miles, 379
Bush, George H. W., 323, 326
Bush, Neil, 323–24
Buss, Dennis, 296–97
Butler, Charlie, 246
Byars State Bank, 53

Cache Road National Bank (Lawton), 341
Cairns, James G., Jr., 285–87
Calhoun First National Bank of Georgia, 184
California gold rush (1849), 191, 392
Calmez Hotel (Clinton), 250
Cameron, Edgar Spier, 103
Campbell, Colin, 41–43
Cane, T. P., 20–21
Canton, Frank M., 72
Capitalism, 23, 35–36, 40–41, 61, 64, 89, 105, 110, 126, 156–57, 172, 190, 260, 274, 287, 326, 406
Capitol National Bank of Guthrie, 192
Capone, Al, 116

Carlile, Homer, 164
Carney State Bank, 53
Carroll, Sid, 236, 355, 361
Carson, Jack, 370
Carter, Jimmy, 181, 184, 195–98, 204, 260, 354
Cartwright, David, 213
Cash, Allen J., 49–50
Cash reserve association, Oklahoma City, 118
Cates, David, 271
Cellar Restaurant (Oklahoma City), 188
Central National Bank: of Alva, 330, 344, 403; of Poteau, 292, 309, 355
Central National Bank and Trust Co. of Enid, 314, 340
Central State Bank of Keifer, 53
Century Chest (Oklahoma City), 400
Chambers, Bill, 206
Champion, George, 270–71
Champlin, Herbert H., and Champlin Refining Co. (Enid), 114–15
Champlin, Joel, 114–15, 205, 219
Chaplin, Charlie, 138
Chapman, Clark, 163
Chapman, J. A., 315
Charles Dunning and Co., 152
Chase Manhattan Bank of New York, 198–200, 209–11, 221, 231–33, 258, 270
Check cashing shops, 289
Check imaging, 300
Chemical Bank of New York, 261
Cherokee Nation, 88, 97
Cherokee Outlet, 68
Cherokee Strip, 43–44
Cheyenne State Bank, 69
Cheyenne Tribe of Oklahoma, 376
Chickasha Bank and Trust Co., 397
Childers, C. C., 73
Choctaw State Bank, 301
Choney, Chuck, 380
Christensen, Linda, 288, 300
Christiansen, Bill, and Aviation Co., 374
Churchill, Winston, 162

INDEX 465

Cimarron (Ferber), 131
Cimarron Field (Oklahoma City), 152
Citibank, 199
Citicorp, 274
Citizens Bank: of Ada, 400; of Lawton (later, Local Oklahoma Bank), 375; of Wardville, 53
Citizens Security Bank of Bixby, 220, 252
City National Bank: of Lawton, 344–45; of Oklahoma City, 12, 132; of Tulsa, 136
City National Bank and Trust Co. of Guymon, 380
Civil Rights Act (1964), 169, 345–47
Clark, Don and Kitty, 252, 396
Clearing House Association of Oklahoma City, 11, 23, 49, 141, 144
Clearinghouses, 10–11, 14, 118
Cline, William R., 263, 274
Cockrell, E. B., 71, 418n29
Colcord, Charles F., 30–32, 57, 65–67, 94, 141
Colley, B. F., 135
Columbia Bank and Trust Co. of Oklahoma City, 21–26, 31, 49, 71–72
Commercial Bank of El Reno, 69
Commercial clubs, 50–51, 60, 122; of Chicago, 40. *See also under* Oklahoma City; Tulsa
Commercial National Bank of Chicago, 71
Commerce and Exchange Building (Oklahoma City), 94
Committee for Relief of Unemployed Women, 106
Commodity Futures Trading Commission (CFTC), 395
Communism, 123, 389
Community Bank: of Oklahoma City, 283; of Seiling, 281
Community Bankers Association of Oklahoma (CBAO; formerly Independent Bankers of Oklahoma), 291, 308–309, 334
Community Reinvestment Act (CRA; 1977), 267–68, 332–34, 363

Community State Bank: of Canton (formerly, Bank of Canton), 279; of Hennessey, 368
Compensating balances, 185–88
Condon, Brian, 375–76
Conference of State Bank Supervisors, 360
Conn, Chris, 340
Conn, Jack T., 167–71, 202, 268, 357–59, 428n35; Oklahoma banking statutes, revision of, 167–68
Conn, Mayhue, Kerr, and Harris Law Firm, 167
Conn Graduate School of Community Banking, Oklahoma City University, 385–87
Conner, L. A., 20
Conover, Todd, 238, 348
Consumer Credit Protection Act (1968), 169. *See also* Truth-in-Lending Act
Consumer Federation of America (CFA), 372
Consumer Finance Protection Agency, 397
Continental Building (Oklahoma City), 82, 86
Continental Federal Savings and Loan, 324–25
Continental Illinois Corporation (parent company of Continental Illinois National Bank of Chicago), 229, 263, 271
Continental National Bank of Chicago, 198–200, 205–11, 221, 227–35, 248, 258–64, 269–73, 278, 322, 393
Cooksey, Terrence, 341–42
Coolidge, Calvin, 133
Cordell National Bank, 280
Corn, Roy L., 373
Cortright, Steve, 386
Cotteral, John H., 72
Council of Economic Advisors (Johnson administration), 180
Cowboys Bar (Oklahoma City), 219–20
Crain, Kent, 295
Crawford, Bill, 293–94

466   INDEX

Credit Union National Association (CUNA), 372
Credit unions, 234, 247–48, 259, 327, 359–61, 366, 372
Crime Control Act (1990), 331
Cronkite, Walter, 197–98
Cross Roads Savings and Loan of Checotah, 325
Cruce, A. C., 72
Cruce, Lee, 30, 33, 53, 70
C-Teq (Oklahoma City), 300
Cudahy Oil Co., 88
Culbertson, J. J., 30
Curry, Paul, 56
Cut the Red Tape campaign, 334, 361

Dann, Tom, 248
Data processing, 286, 300–301, 341
Dauffenbach, Robert C., 327–29
Davis, Abner, 26–27
Davis, Bert, 234
Davis, Bud, 76
Davis, Jon, 351
Davison, Denver, 167
Davison, Henry, 38
Dawes, Henry M., 92
Dean, John, 287
Dean, Walter C., 145, 425n45
Dean Witter, 302
Debs, Eugene, 45
Deets, Larry, 301
De Gaulle, Charles, 162
Democracy: 5, 36, 40–41, 66, 105, 172, 190, 215, 273–74, 326, 406; frontier, 91; industrial, 44
Democratic National Committee, 145
Democratic National Convention: in Chicago (1968), 182; in Denver (1908), 20
Democratic Party of Oklahoma, 4–5, 8–9, 17, 45, 144, 241, 309
Denton, Lola Faye, 377
Deposit Insurance National Bank (DINB), 257

Depository Institutions Deregulation and Monetary Control Act (DIDMCA; 1980), 266–67
Depository Institutions Deregulation Committee, 266
Derebery, Murlin, 291
Dewald, Scott, 370
Dewey Bank, 314
DeWitt, Larry, 370–72
Diefenbach, John, 304
Dikeman, Neil J., Jr., 196
Dillinger, John, 124
Dirksen, Everett, 392
Divisibility theory of banking, 299
Dodd, Chris, 393. *See also* Wall Street Reform and Consumer Protection Act (2010)
Dodd-Frank Law (2010), 393–99
Dodson, W. H., 5
Domnick, Kenneth N., 163–64
Doolin, Bill, 57
Downriver Community Federal Credit Union (Ecorse, Mich.), 234, 248
Drabenstott, Mark, 294
Dressen, Vada, 373
Dresser Industries, 244
Drexel Burnham Lambert, Inc., 230, 321
Drovers National Bank of Kansas City, 80–81
Drysdale Government Securities, Inc., 211
Dukakis, Michael, 326
Dun and Bradstreet, 275
Duncan, Betty, 344
Duncan Savings and Loan Association, 325
Dunjee, Roscoe, and the *Black Dispatch*, 146–47
Dunkelberg, William C., 275
Dunlap, Elijah Thomas, Jr./Sr., and Dunlap Funeral Services, 377–78
Dun's Review, 199, 207–208, 260
Dust Bowl, The (Ken Burns), 402

Economic Club of Chicago, 261
Economic Development Administration (EDA), 168

INDEX   467

Economist, 230–31
Ederington, Louis, 342–43
Edwards, Mickey, 264
Edwards, Ronald P., 319, 326–27
Eisenhower, Dwight D., 162, 427–28n20
Eisinger, Jesse, 391–93
Electronic Funds Transfer (EFT), 176–77, 297, 340
Elliott, Clint, 403–404
Elliott and Gann Architects (Oklahoma City), 312
Ellis, Ed, 76
Ellis County Bank of Arnett, 69
Ellison, Clark, 212–13
Emergency Banking Relief Act (1933), 119, 423n67
Empie, Robert, 202–203, 279, 291–92, 311, 351
Enabling Act (1906), 4, 27
Enlai, Zhou, 389
Equal Credit Opportunity Act (Regulation B, 1974), 333
Equal Employment Opportunity Commission (EEOC), 288, 346
Erwin, William A., 110–12
Estes, Lewis, 56
Estes, Scott, 400
Everest, Pete, 285
Ewing, Sam, 181
Exchange National Bank and Trust Co. of Ardmore, 341, 374–75; of Perry, 297–98, 381–82
Exchange National Bank of Tulsa, 22, 98, 314–15
Expressway Bank of Oklahoma City, 281–83
Extension Service, USDA, 295–96

Fain, Leslie, 154, 426–27n74
Fair Housing Act (Title VIII of the Civil Rights Act, 1968), 169, 333
Fairlawn Cemetery (Oklahoma City), 144, 154
Fair value, 392

Fairview State Bank, 314
F&M Bank of Tulsa, 328, 340, 345–47
Fannie Mae, 394
Farmers Alliance, 44
Farmers and Merchants National Bank of Fairview, 330
Farmers Exchange Bank of Cherokee, 370
Farmers Home Administration (FHA), 160, 297
Farmers National Bank: of Kaw City, 54; of Tulsa, 26; of Tupelo, 53
Farmers State Bank: of Afton, 279; of Allen, 374; of Alva, 68–69; of Glencoe, 53; of Quinton, 245–46
FDIC Improvement Act (FDICIA, 1991), 335, 349
Federal Deposit Insurance Corporation (FDIC), 121, 124, 148, 173–75, 218, 226, 232–33, 236–42, 247–48, 251–52, 257–65, 270–74, 277–82, 285, 292, 307, 315, 320–22, 330–31, 334–35, 348–50, 355–70, 395
Federal Emergency Relief Administration (FERA), 140
Federal Equal Pay Act (1963), 345
Federal Home Loan Bank, 371; of San Francisco, 320
Federal Home Loan Bank Board, 173, 259, 322, 333
Federal National Bank and Trust Co. of Shawnee, 162–63, 181–83, 236
Federal Reserve Bank, 40, 83–87, 232–34, 237, 257–58, 261–62, 271, 294, 355, 394, 419n63; of Atlanta, 39, 85; of Boston, 39; of Chicago, 39, 261, 289; of Cleveland, 39; of Dallas, 39, 82–84; of Kansas City, 39, 82–87, 99, 176–78, 181, 237, 281, 294, 327, 341, 362; of Minneapolis, 39; of New York, 38–39; of Oklahoma City, Tenth District branch, 82–89, 99, 131, 152, 281, 341, 346, 351, 419n62; of Philadelphia, 39; of Richmond, 39; of Saint Louis, 39; of San Francisco, 39, 85

468   INDEX

Federal Reserve Board of Governors, 39–41, 43, 83–85, 91–92, 99, 168, 173–75, 178, 181, 236, 261, 306, 312–13, 317, 395
Federal Reserve Reform Act (1977), 178
Federal Reserve System, 8, 39–41, 74–75, 82–88, 109–12, 119–23, 161, 174, 178, 232–34, 268, 330. *See also* Owen-Glass Federal Reserve Act (1913)
Federal Savings and Loan Insurance Corporation (FSLIC), 322, 325
Ferber, Edna, 131
Fergeson, Ken, 330, 335, 356, 401
Ferris, Scott, 145
Fidelity National Bank and Trust Co. of Oklahoma City (later, BOK Oklahoma City), 170, 202, 229, 243, 268, 284, 313–15, 357–59, 380
Fiechter, Jonathan, 384
Filson, Charles H., 5, 9–10
Financial Corporation of America, 269
Financial Institutions Act (1976), 178
Financial Institutions Marketing Association (FIMA), 305
Financial Institutions Reform, Recovery, and Enforcement Act (FIRREA; 1989), 322–23, 332–34, 349, 446n50
Fireside chats, 119, 123. *See also under* Great Depression (1930s)
First American Bank and Trust Co. of Purcell, 181
First American Bank of Stonewall, 374
First Americans Bank of Anadarko, 375
Firstar Bank (formerly, First National Bank and Trust Co. of Muskogee), 395, 404
First Bank and Trust Co.: of Duncan, 330; of Fort Gibson, 330
First Bank: of Apache, 330; of Cleveland, 368
First City Bank of Atoka, 281
First Continental Bank and Trust Co. of Del City (later, United Del City Bank), 229, 264, 278–79
First Data Management Co. (Oklahoma City), 301

First Federal Savings and Loan Association of Seminole, 325
First Fidelity Bank of Oklahoma City, 380
First Heritage National Bank of Davis, 339
First Interstate Bank: of Los Angeles, 285–87; of Oklahoma City (formerly, First National Bank and Trust Co.), 285–87, 317–18
First Mustang State Bank, 308, 338
First National Bank and Trust Co.: of Chickasha, 368; of Heavener, 382; of McAlester, 368, 402–403; of Muskogee (later, Firstar Bank), 134, 297, 310, 395, 404; of Oklahoma City (later, First Interstate Bank of Oklahoma City), 12, 50, 79, 99–105, 113, 117–18, 126, 130–31, 140–47, 150, 153–55, 159, 170, 182, 203, 220–21, 229, 283–87, 307, 317–18, 343, 349, 353, 399, 440n108; of Tulsa (formerly, Tulsa Banking Co., a.k.a. Oilman's Bank), 99, 135–40, 159, 166, 281, 297, 313–14, 343, 346–48, 425n31; of Vinita, 339
First National Bank: of Altus, 368–69; of Amarillo, Tex., 203; of Antlers, 362; of Bartlesville, 314; of Buffalo, 69; of Chandler, 55–56, 61, 102; of Dallas, Tex. (later, Bank of America), 284; of Enid, 114, 314; of Frederick, 293; of Geary, 301, 344; of Georgia, 184; of Gracemont, 252; of Guymon, 62; of Holdenville, 336; of Hooker, 246; of Konawa, 330; of Lindsay, 330; of Maud, 173; of McLoud, 71; of Miami, 376; of Midwest City, 308; of Nash, 173; of Nowata, 368; of Okeene, 108, 330; of Owasso, 53; of Pauls Valley, 173; of Pawhuska, 76; of Pryor, 382; of Rush Springs, 281; of Sapulpa, 281; of Seiling, 282, 400; of Skiatook, 281; of Stigler, 164; of Terlton, 53; of Texhoma, 396
First National Building Corporation (Oklahoma City), 103, 154

First Penn Corporation (Oklahoma City), 204
First Pennsylvania Bank (First Penny), 387
First Security Bank of Beaver, 401
First State Bank and Trust Co.: of Oklahoma City, 173; of Shawnee, 301
First State Bank: of Anadarko, 252, 396; of Avery, 76; of Boise City, 397; of Gould, 330; of Harrah, 173, 330; of Mead, 52; of Stonewall, 108, 149; of Talihina, 163
First Trust and Savings Bank of Tulsa, 136
First Tulsa Bancorp., 313
First United Bank of Durant, 398
Fisher, John F., 299
Fite, Theo, 340
Flint, J. Don and J. N., 374
Floyd, Charles Arthur "Pretty Boy," 77–78, 108–109, 139
Flynn, Dennis T., 141
Fogg, Capt. R. S., 150
Ford, Gerald, 179
Forsythe, Jay, 135
Fort Sill National Bank, 368
Founders Bank and Trust Co. of Oklahoma City, 283
4-H movement, 134, 153, 162
Fourth National Bank of Tulsa, 348
Fowler, Jerry, 246
Frank, Barney, 393. *See also* Wall Street Reform and Consumer Protection Act (2010)
Frantz, Frank, 5, 9
Freeman, Paul, 396–97
French Revolution (1789), 389
Fuller, Lawrence, 230
Funny Money (Singer), 192, 197, 214–15, 231, 251. *See also* Penn Square National Bank of Oklahoma City
Future Farmers of America (FFA), 162

Gallatin, Albert, 141
Garber State Bank, 54
Garnett, R. L., 72
Garn–St. Germain Act (1982), 320

Garrett, Jan, 385
Gary, Raymond, 183
Generation X, 385, 388
George, E. L., 87
Getty, J. Paul, 136
GHK Co., 194–96, 232–33, 243–44
Gibson, Fred, 374
Gilcrease Bank of Tulsa, 307
Glascoe Usury Bill, 58
Glass, Carter, 39, 120, 268. *See also* Owen-Glass Federal Reserve Act (1913); Glass-Steagall Banking Act (1933)
Glass-Steagall Banking Act (1933), 120–22, 268, 305–306, 393, 438n44
Glenn, Ida, and Glenn Pool, 94, 135
Glomski, Robert, 250
Glover, Laurence, 194
Gloyd, Samuel, L., 143
Good roads associations, 34–35
Gore, Thomas P., 15
Gorton, George, 34, 97
Graham, Clint, 15
Graham, Mark, 300
Grant, Whit, 32
Grapes of Wrath, The (Steinbeck), 77–78
Gray, Edwin J., 322
Gray, Jonathan, 320
Great Depression (1930s), 99–100, 129, 135, 139, 156, 192, 239, 265–66, 268–69, 272, 287, 294, 305–306, 315, 319, 391
Great Moderation theory, 390
Great Plains Savings Association of Weatherford, 325
Great Recession (a.k.a. subprime mortgage crisis, 2008), 13–14, 191, 324, 333, 390–95, 402
Great Skyscraper Race (Oklahoma City, 1931), 99–100, 102–104, 421n12
Grecian, O. E., 71
Green, D. B., 340
Green Corn Rebellion (1917), 48–49, 123
Greenspan, Alan, 329
Greer, Gordon, 186–87, 266, 352
Grissom, John W., 298

Grubb, Ronald, 307
Grubner, James, 346
Guaranty Bank and Trust Co. of Oklahoma City, 314, 385
Guard, Mary Beth, 331–34, 347–49
Guffey, Roger, 176–79
Gum, Eugene P., 77
Gunter, Charles W., 103, 145–47
Guthrie National Bank of Commerce, 20

Hackbert, Peter H., 300–301
Haggard, Merle, 193, 204
Haggin, John, 244
Haldane, Andrew, 393
Hales, W. T. "Papa," 126, 130–31, 145
Hall, Bruce, 402–403
Hall, Chuck, 381
Hall, David, 183
Hall, F. C., 145, 426–27n74
Hall, J. M., 135
Halliburton, 244
Halsell, William H., 136
Hamilton, Alexander, 23, 38–40
Hamilton, Edward L., 4
Hammons, Sam, 244
Hampton, Debbie, 386
Hannah, Jay, 383
Hannah, John T., 291
Harding, W. P. G., 86
Harkess, John, 347
Harlow, Rex F., and *Harlow's Weekly*, 35, 46, 49, 65, 73–75, 85–86, 90, 93, 97–98
Harn, W. F., 30
Harper, Denton A., 375
Harris, Robert E. "Bob," 291, 348–52
Harris, Ronald M., 373
Harrison, W. B., 83
Haskell, Charles N., 5, 9, 14–15, 19–30, 33, 70, 261–62, 272, 307, 321
Hayes, Kent, 147
Hayes, S. W., 151
Haynes, Tim, and wrecker service, 249
Head, Ben T., 173

Heaney, A. S., and Mrs. A. S. (née Beitman), 27–28, 411n108
Heaton, Joe, 376
Hecht, R. S., 109–10
Hefner, Robert A., 148–49
Hefner, Robert A., III, 194–98, 201, 204, 207, 211–14, 228, 242–43
Hefter, Tom J., 304–305
Heinze, Fritz Augustus, Otto, and Arthur, and Otto C. Heinze and Co., 7–8, 13
Helena National Bank, 344
Helmerich, Hans, and Helmerich and Payne Co. (Tulsa), 243, 276
Helmerich, Walter III, 314
Hendricks, H. G., 101
Hensley, Felix, 295
Hibernia Bank and Trust Co. of New Orleans, 109, 211, 259
Higgins, Thomas, 259
High, S. J., 124
Hightower, C. C., 150
Hightower, Dannie Bea (Mrs. Frank J., née James), 153, 424n91, 426n70
Hightower, Ethlyn (Mrs. W. E., née Johnson), 41–43, 126, 141, 150, 413–14n16, 426n62
Hightower, Frank J., 150, 153–55, 188, 413–14n16, 424n91
Hightower, G. P. Johnson, 220, 284–85, 300, 315–16, 325, 353, 368, 396, 426n62, 433n13
Hightower, Michael J. (author), 246, 401, 426n62
Hightower, Phyllis (later, Mrs. Roby Penn), 150, 413–14n16, 427n75
Hightower, Wilbur E. "Billy," 147, 150–51, 153–55, 284–86, 413–14n16, 426n62n63, 427n75
Hightower Building (Oklahoma City), 144, 188
Himelic, L. L., 249
Hinson, H. C., 76
Hirshfield, Jim, 174
Hitchcock, Frank H., 62

Hobbs, Gary B., 325
Hodges, Jim, 373
Hodges, V. Pauline, 401–402
Hoefer, John, 54
Hogan, D. W., 12, 132
Holder, Eric, 394–95
Holder, Todd, 300
Holland, Rebecca, 343
Holmes, Sven Erik, 373
Home Mortgage Disclosure Act (Regulation C; 1975), 333–34
Homestead Act (1862), 44–45
Hoover, Herbert, 104, 114, 131–32
Hope, Bob, 138
Hopeton State Bank, 330
Hopkins, Harry, 140
Hoysler, Layton C., 296
Huckabay, Gary, 308, 338
Huckabay, Todd, 369–70
Hudson, Hubert, 117
Hudson, John, 376
Hughes Tool Co., 242–44, 275
Humphrey, Ryan, 378
Hundred Days, 117. *See also* Great Depression (1930s)
Hunt, Roy O., 154
Hurst, Irvin, 5–6, 29–31
Huston, U.S. district judge, 20
Hutto, R. W., 91–92

Iacocca, Lee, 261–63
Idabel National Bank, 245, 252, 316, 395–96
If You Don't Weaken (Ameringer), 44–47, 414n21
Independent Community Bankers of America (ICBA), 309
Independent Gas Producers Committee, 194–95
Indian Territory, 4–6, 10–11, 39, 44–45, 55, 97, 126, 142, 193, 215
Indian Territory Illuminating Oil Co. (ITIO), 95
Industries Foundation of Oklahoma, Inc., 151

Inflation: from 1907 to 1944, 30; from 1945 to 1975, 156, 159, 178–81, 190; from 1976 to 2000, 196, 211–12, 229, 265–67, 272, 289, 295, 326, 329–30, 354
Inhofe, James, U.S. representative, 281
Intensive Financial Management and Planning Support (IFMAPS) program, 295–96
International Association of Drilling Contractors, 214
International Association of Financial Crime Investigators, 378
International Banking Act (1978), 178
International Bank of Coalgate, 19
International Petroleum Exposition (IPE), 136–37
Iran hostage crisis (1979), 197–98, 205
Isaac, William M., 232, 237, 262–63, 270, 274, 277–78

Jackson, Andrew, 33, 65–66, 91, 110, 320
Jackson, Eddie, 283
Jackson, Gary, 386
Jackson, Lewis B., 115, 155
Jackson, Roy E., 242
Jackson, R. R., 134
James, Dannie Bea (later, Mrs. Frank J. Hightower), 153, 424n91, 426n70
James, Dan W., 152–53, 426n70
James, George W., 153, 426n70
James, Jesse, 55–56
James, T. L., and T. L. James Construction Co. (later, James Construction Group, LLC), 152, 426n70
Jarrett, Walter, 139
Jefferson, Thomas, 23, 38, 44, 110, 141, 201
Jennings, Peter, 261
Jennings, Robert, 397
Jennings, William P. "Beep," 191, 202–204, 208–10, 214, 218–20, 226–29, 233, 240–42, 245–47, 252, 351–52
Jerome, Norma, 297–98
Johnson, Aida Allen (Mrs. Frank P.), 41–42, 126, 142–44, 153–55, 413–14n16

472   INDEX

Johnson, Edith C., 42
Johnson, Ethlyn. *See* Hightower, Ethlyn
Johnson, Frank P., 8, 11–12, 23–25, 29–30, 34, 41–43, 50, 84–86, 92–93, 102–103, 113–15, 126, 130–31, 141–47, 150, 153–55, 284–87, 399–400, 408n25, 413–14n16, 424n88, 424n91, 425n48
Johnson, Gary, 379
Johnson, Hugh, 268
Johnson, Hugh M., 34–35, 43, 58, 61, 102–103, 141–43, 147, 150, 153–54, 284–87, 399, 413n137
Johnson, Lyndon B., 180–81, 326
Johnson, Mary (Mrs. Hugh M.), 43, 155
Johnson, T. T., 130–31
Johnston, W. R. "Ross," 188
Johnstone, Anne, 300
Jones, Charles G. "Gristmill," 5, 94
Jones, Stephen, 378
Jordan, Bill, 245
Jordan and Associates (Oklahoma City), 221–22
Joullian, Edward C., III, 284, 287
JPMorgan Chase and Co., 394–95. *See also* Morgan, J. P., and Co. of New York
Junior League of Oklahoma City, 106
Junior's Restaurant (Oklahoma City), 231
Junk bonds, 273, 321

Kaiser, George, 315–16
Kansas, deposit guaranty in, 18, 73–74
Kattigan, William P., 143
Kaufman, Henry, 273–74
Keating, Frank, Okla. governor, 359
Keeler, George B., 88
Keeton, William, 362
Keller, Ed, 348
Kelley, E. H., 68
Kelly, Albert, 164
Kelly, George "Machine Gun," 124, 139
Kelly, Tracy, 298, 338–39, 389, 402, 451
Kennedy, David O'D., 194
Kennedy, John F., 138, 179–80, 326
Kernodle, Stratton D., 144

Kerr, Robert S., 158
Kerr-McGee Co., 167
Ketcha, Nicholas J., 369
Keynes, John Maynard, and Keynesianism, 156–58, 180, 423n60, 427n3
Keystone State Bank, 53
Khomeini, Ayatollah, 197
Khrushchev, Nikita, 162
Kilpatrick, E. D., 82
Kimberling, C. F., 247
King, Martin Luther, 169
Kirby, Doyle and Bobbie, 278–79
Kirkpatrick, John E. and Eleanor B., 314–15
Kleindienst, Richard, 183
Kliewer, Frank G., Jr., 171
Knickerbocker Trust Co. of New York, 8
Knox, Steve, 226
Kotarski, Bob, 209
Ku Klux Klan, 146

Lage, Gerald, 362–63
Laissez-faire economics, 132, 158, 172, 260, 269
Lake Overholser, 150
Lakeside Bank of Salina, 363
Lance, Bert, 184–87
Landmark Bank of Ada, 370
Land run (1889), 41–42, 103, 142, 148, 399, 452n28
Lane, Jimmy, 250
Lankford, J. D., 31–32, 63, 74, 412n121, 416–17n103
Larson, Gloria, 250
Lawrence, Bob, 345
Lawson, Kenneth, Jr., 283
Lee, Nita, 250–51
Lee, Roger, 250
Lee, Stanley, 202
Lee Huckins Hotel, Oklahoma City, 28–29, 287
Lehman Brothers, 373, 397
Lehr, John, 213
Leonard, H. E. "Harry," 156, 175–76, 297, 310–11, 403

INDEX   473

Leonard, Mike, 310–11, 395, 404
Levitt, Arthur, 391
Lewis, Carl, 305
Lewis, Clarence, 250
Lewis, George Chase, 78–79
Liberty Bancorp., Inc., 350
Liberty Bank of Midwest City, 316
Liberty Loan Campaigns: World War I, 59–60, 123, 153; World War II, 153
Liberty National Bank and Trust Co.: of Oklahoma City, 159, 167, 182, 206, 221, 229, 238, 266, 281, 313–14, 338, 345–48, 352; of Tulsa, 316, 351, 374
Liberty National Bank of Pawhuska, 76
Liberty National Corporation, 313
Lincoln Bank and Trust Co. of Ardmore, 298
Lincoln National Bank, 283
Lindbergh, Charles, 138–39
Lippmann, Walter, 110
Livshee, Steve, 244
Local Oklahoma Bank of Lawton (formerly, Citizens Bank), 375
Longhorn Oil and Gas Co., 207
Loy, Tom, 185–87, 265–66, 321–22, 354, 385–88
Lucas, Vane, 316
Lybarger, Stan, 315–16
Lytle, John R., 207–208, 259–60

Mabrey, Carlisle, III, 252–53
Mabrey, John, 220–21, 225, 253
Madill National Bank, 47
Mahan, Frank, 231
Mahan and Rowsey, Inc., 231
Manufacturers Hanover Trust Co. of New York, 219
Markham, B. H., 66
Marshall, Gerald R., 284
Martin, John F., 145, 425n45
Marxism, 44, 47–48, 180
Massey, C. H., 167
Massey, John, 398
May, Keith, 243, 435n82
May Avenue Bank of Oklahoma City, 173

Mayer, Martin, 280
Mayo (later, Bird), Margery, 137–39, 424n20
Mayo, Burch, 138
Mayo, Cass A., 137
Mayo, John D., 137–38
Mayo Building (a.k.a. Petroleum Building; Tulsa), 138
Mayo Hotel (Tulsa), 99, 137–38
McAfee and Taft, P.C. (Oklahoma City), 233, 341, 354–55
McCall, C. A. "Barney," 285–86, 403
McCall, Charles, 285–86, 403
McCaskill, James Dan, 374–75
McClellan, John L., 158
McClelland, J. C., 32
McClellan-Kerr Arkansas River Navigation System, 158–59
McClintock, R. Otis, 136–39
McClure, M. L., 99–101
McCollom, James P., 260–61
McCormack, Bob, and Association (Duncan), 214, 240, 403
McCormick, Robert, Jr., 324–25, 336
McCurtain County National Bank of Broken Bow, 368
McEuen, Joe, 245
McFadden Act (1927), 91, 168, 305–306
McGraw, James J., 98–99
McGuire, Bird, 4
McGuire, Ted, 382–83
McKee, P. N., 107
McKeown, James P., 291
McKinsey and Co., 199–200, 210
McLean, George, 39
McLean, J. W. (Banks of Mid-America chairman), 313
McNeal, J. W. (Guthrie National Bank of Commerce president), 20
McPheters, W. H., 133
McRill, Albert, 160
McVeigh, Timothy, 363
Meadows, Virginia, 343
Mears, Peggy, 394
Mee, William, 83

474 INDEX

Meltzer, Alan, 274–75
Menefee, James A., 20–21
Meno Guaranty Bank, 330
Mercantile National Bank of New York, 7
Merrill Lynch, 263, 302
Metafund (Oklahoma City), 185, 265
Metrobank, N.A., of Oklahoma City, 368
Metropolitan Area Projects (MAPS), 367–68
Michigan National Bank, 271
Michigan National Corporation, 211, 258–59
MidFirst Bank, 189
Midland Mortgage Co. of Oklahoma City, 188–89
Midwest Air Depot (Oklahoma City), 152
Midwest National Bank of Midwest City, 346
Milken, Michael, 321
Miller, Laura, 245–46
Miller, Terry, 376–77
Millers' Association, 134
Mingo, John, 306
Mississippi, deposit guaranty in, 18, 73–74
Mississippi A&M College, 126, 146
Mississippi Bank of Jackson, 278
Miss Jackson's Shop (Tulsa), 138
Mitchell, Dale, 307
Mitchell, John, 183
Mixed economy, 157–59, 172
Model Banking Code, ABA, 167
Money Any Time (MAT), 297
Moody's, 262
Moore, Bob, 53–54
Morgan, J. P., and Co. of New York, 8, 11–13, 38–40, 75–76. *See also* JPMorgan Chase and Co.
Morgan Guaranty Trust Co. of New York, 230
Morris, Charles, 327
Morris, Dave, 332
Morris, Jeff, 370
Morrow, Diana, 346–47
Morrow, Preston, 227

Mortgage-backed securities, 157, 188, 394. *See also* Great Recession (a.k.a. subprime mortgage crisis, 2008)
Mortgages, 13, 57, 89, 157, 169, 189, 205, 265, 322–25, 333–34, 383, 390–95, 402; reverse, 404
Motley, Merleta, 380
Multibank holding companies, 187, 201, 297, 306–13, 318, 336, 350
Murphy, Dennis, 380
Murphy, Frank, 204, 209, 219
Murphy, John, 76
Murray, William H. "Alfalfa Bill," 17, 27–28, 113–14, 118, 140
Myers, Marilyn, 344, 403
Myers, W. D., Sr., 344

Nance, Teri, 305
Nassau Savings and Loan of Princeton, N.J., 322
National Conference of State Bank Supervisors, 131, 360
National Bank: of Carmel, Calif., 278; of Frederick, 281; of McAlester (later, The Bank, N.A.), 297; of Tulsa (NBT, later, Bank of Oklahoma), 159, 163, 315
National Banking Acts (1863, 1864), 111, 167, 302
National Bank of Commerce (NBC): of Altus, 330, 401; of Guthrie, 20
National City Bank of New York, 38
National Monetary Commission, 37–39
National Retail Credit Association, 80–81
NationsBank, 365
Natural gas industry, 164, 192–97, 204, 211–13, 226, 240, 243, 275, 348–49. *See also* Anadarko Basin; Natural Gas Policy Act (NGPA, 1978); Oil industry; Penn Square National Bank of Oklahoma City
Natural Gas Policy Act (NGPA, 1978), 197, 204, 211, 348
Naylor, Frank W., 293
Neal, Linwood O., 149

INDEX   475

Neary, William D., 244–45
Nebraska, deposit guaranty in, 17–18, 73
Nebraska Bankers Association, 359
Negotiable order of withdrawal (NOW) accounts, 267, 290. *See also* Super NOW accounts
Nelson, Chuck, 338, 350
New Deal, 116–17, 126, 157–58, 268. *See also* Great Depression (1930s)
Newton, Wayne, 207
New York State Safety Fund System, 17, 262
New York Stock Exchange, 7
New York University, 271–73
Nichols Hills, 225
Nichols Hills Bank and Trust Co. of Oklahoma City, 283, 314
Nigh, George, 279, 311, 316
Night and Day Bank of Oklahoma City, 26–27, 30–31
Nixon, Richard M., 158, 181–82, 354
Noble State Bank, 20
Nonbank banks, 168, 266, 290, 297, 302–305, 316–17, 336–38, 372
Noonan, John, 272
Norick, Ron, 368
North Dakota, deposit guaranty in, 18, 73–74
Northern Trust Bank, 211
Northwest Bank of Oklahoma City, 363
Norton, W. L., 21, 25–26
Noyes, Alexander D., 11–13, 112
Nunn, Wesley I., 97–98

Ocean Accident and Guaranty Corporation, 53
Office of the Comptroller of the Currency (OCC), 15–16, 23, 26, 58, 92, 119, 168, 173–75, 179, 259, 265, 271–72, 302, 339, 384, 394–95; and First National Bank and Trust Co. of Oklahoma City, 285; and Penn Square National Bank, 202, 206–207, 217–18, 227, 232–38, 348
Office of Thrift Supervision, 324, 333

Ogden, H. H., 134
Ogilvie, Donald G., 335
Oil and Gas Men for Carter, 195
"Oil Capital of the World" (Tulsa), 22, 135–38, 315
Oil industry, 35, 43, 49, 87–88, 97–99, 114–15, 122, 144, 164–66, 192–202, 212–16, 226–30, 242–53, 270, 275–77, 283–87, 345, 348, 352–54, 403; and Columbia Bank and Trust Co., 21–23; and Penn Square National Bank, 203–207, 210, 214–15, 221, 226–31, 235–37, 240–42, 247, 352. *See also* Anadarko Basin; Arab Oil Embargo (1973); Natural gas industry; Organization of Petroleum Exporting Countries (OPEC)
Okemah National Bank, 330
Oklahoma: Appropriations and Budget Committee, 309; Bank Guaranty Law (1908) and guaranty fund, 16–23, 30–34, 43, 69–75, 261–62; Beginning Farmer Loan Program, 296–97; Business Development Corporation, 169; Cattlemen's Association, 370; Constitutional Convention, 5; Cooperative Extension Services, 295–96; county commissioner scandal, 230–31; Dept. of Agriculture, 296, 370; Dept. of Commerce, Bureau of Economic Analysis, 213; Dept. of Health, 347; Development Finance Authority, 296, 355; Employment Securities Commission, 250, 275; Farm Bureau, 371; Finance Authority, 162; Highway Commission, 145, 184; Historical Society, 68, 192, 264; House Bill 11A, 15; House Bill 1123, 311–13; House Committee on Banking and Currency, 168, 355; legislature, 15–18, 30, 33–34, 45, 52–54, 69–71, 146–47, 158, 166, 169, 241, 272, 302, 309, 317, 350–51, 355; National Guard, 66, 72, 114–15, 386; Natural Gas Co., 143; Natural Gas Policy Commission, 349; Plan, 314;

476   INDEX

Oklahoma (*continued*)
  Railway Co., 59; Savings and Loan Association, 144; Senate Bill 502, 317; Senate Bill 553, 317; Senate Committee on Banking and Currency, 168; State Auctioneers Association, 249; State Banking Board, 16, 19–20, 25, 32–33, 70–72, 148, 291, 339; State Banking Department, 14, 354–56, 359; State Data Center, 346; State Econometric Model, 329; State Federation of Commercial Clubs, 37, 50; statehood, 3–10, 14, 140–41; State Regents for Higher Education, 378, 398; Territory (later, western Oklahoma), 4–10, 57, 102, 146–47, 154; Tower (Oklahoma City), 287; University Club, 144
Oklahoma Bank and Trust Co. of Clinton, 305, 368
Oklahoma Banker, 50, 53, 59–61, 74–81, 89, 98, 108–109, 112, 131, 140, 143–44, 164, 241, 293, 299–303, 317, 327, 356, 366, 379–83, 387
Oklahoma Bankers Association (OBA), 15, 53, 58–59, 60, 72, 82–83, 86, 92, 101–102, 109, 122, 130, 163, 167, 241, 301, 308, 353, 378; Agricultural Committee of, 61, 79; New Regulations Workshop, 175; vigilance committees, 75–77, 124
Oklahoma City: airport, 151; bombing (1995), 363; Building and Loan Association, 89; Building and Loan Co., 144; Chamber of Commerce, 59–60, 87–89, 139, 144, 149–52, 368; Clearing House Association, 11, 23, 49, 141, 144; Commercial Club, 4; oil field, 94–97; University, 277, 385–87
Oklahoma Economic Outlook, 362–66
Oklahoma National Bank of Tulsa, 136
Oklahoma State Bank of Ada, 167–70
Oklahoma State University (formerly, Oklahoma A&M College/University), 133, 185, 307, 376; College of Business Administration, 362; Department of Economics, 295–96; Office of Business and Economic Research, 275, 327
Okun, Arthur, 180
Omnibus Credit Solution Act, 323
One Man in His Time (Conn), 167
Online banking, 282–83, 290, 340, 380–85, 392, 450n75
Organic Act (1890), 4
Organization of Petroleum Exporting Countries (OPEC), 193, 198, 226, 354
Orr, Thomas S., 247
Osage Federal Bank of Pawhuska, 319, 405
Osage State Bank, 53
Osborn, Wayne, 292, 336, 342, 349, 354–55
Overholser, Henry, 29
Overholser Theater, 42
Owen, Robert L., 15–16, 39, 70, 83
Owen-Glass Federal Reserve Act (1913), 39–41, 43, 60, 63, 82, 287. *See also* Federal Reserve System
Ozan, George, 343

Pabst, Mark, 288–89
Pahlavi, Shah Mohammad Reza, 197
Panics, financial: of 1837, 11, 17; of 1857, 11; of 1873, 11; of 1893, 11, 13, 112, 192, 287; of 1907, 6–14, 19, 37, 43, 46, 68, 112–14, 117, 287, 391
Partnoy, Frank, 391–93
Patronage payments, 295
Patterson, Ray, and Associates of Frederick, 249
Patterson, Robert U., 152
Patterson, William George "Bill," 203–208, 214, 218–21, 231–35, 239–42, 247–48
Patterson Steel Co., 152
Paul, Homer, 314
Pay Any Time (PAT), 297
Pay Equity Technical Assistance Act, 346
Payne, David L., 27
Peat, Marwick, Mitchell and Co., 242, 271
Penn Square National Bank of Oklahoma City, 191–93, 202–11, 214, 217–37, 240–42, 245–46, 250–53, 283, 288, 303,

INDEX   477

310, 319, 322, 331, 336, 380, 387; FDIC closure of, 238–40; lawsuits stemming from closure of, 246–48; nationwide consequences stemming from closure of, 257–65, 270–74, 277–78; reflections on (1992), 348–55. *See also* Singer, Mark; Zweig, Phillip L.
Penn Square Shopping Center (Oklahoma City), 230, 240, 283
Pentecost, Col. H. W., 59
People's National Bank: of Checotah, 397; of Seattle, 285
People's State Bank and Trust Co. of Holdenville, 281
Permenter, Morris, 283
Persian Gulf War (Operation Desert Storm, 1991), 329
Peters, A. J., 155
Petrodollars, 198
Petroleum Information Corporation (Denver), 213
Pettigrew, Lindel, 397–98
Phillips, Waite, 131, 137
Phillips Petroleum Co., 164
Pickel, James A., 312
Pickens, T. Boone, 314
Pickwick Club (Oklahoma City), 41
Pittman, James D. "Jim" and Kirk, 282–83, 400–401
Pitzer, Greg, 332
Planters and Mechanics Bank of Oklahoma City, 30–31
Platt, John D., 243
Plunk, Steve, 217, 233–38, 248, 271, 322, 348, 351, 434n63
PNB Financial Corporation (Kingfisher), 300
Poole, Clifton, 217–18, 232–35, 242
Populism, 14–15, 45, 201, 306–307
Porter, Frank, 155
Porter, Roma Lee, 344–45
Port of Catoosa, 158
Ports of Call Oil Co. (Oklahoma City), 212–13
Post, Wiley, 108, 426–27n74

Postal savings banks, 62–63
Prager, Jonas, 273
Preston, John R., 247
Preston State Bank, 53
Price, Jimmie, 301
Price, William S., 247
Priest, Linda Carol, 374
Pringle, Laura N., 312, 317
Production Credit Associations, 160, 163
Professional Asset Management of Los Angeles, 259
Professional Bank Systems, 332
Prosperity League, 13
Prue State Bank, 53
Pujo, Arsène P., 38–39
Pulley, P. E., 117–18
Putnam, I. M., 26–27, 30–31
Pyron, R. L., 249–50

Quiggin, John, 402
Quinn, R. B., 62–63

Rackley, Jack Butler, 376
Rainbolt, David, 236, 240, 308, 311, 350, 360–61, 399, 405
Rainbolt, H. E. "Gene," 162–63, 171, 181–87, 236, 245, 307, 313, 336–38, 405–406
Raines, Bruce, 328
Ramsey, Arthur and W. R., 99
Ramsey Tower, 99–102, 421nn11–12
Rather, Dan, 261
RCB Bank (formerly, Rogers County Bank), 382–83
Reagan, Ronald, 196–97, 260, 266–68, 278, 297, 320, 326, 354
Reasoner, Harry, 196
Reconstruction Finance Corporation, 260
Records, George J., 187–89, 307, 430n86
Regulation Q, 266–67, 354, 438n44
Reno, Janet, 361–63
Republican Party of Oklahoma, 5, 9, 65, 183, 264, 326
Republic Bank: of Dallas, 236, 308; of Norman, 330

Resolution Trust Corporation (RTC), 323, 333
Reverse mortgage, 404
Richardson, Mrs. D. A., 144
Richardson, T. M., 287
Ridgely, William Barret, 16
Riegle Community Development and Regulatory Improvement Act (1994), 361
Riegle-Neal Interstate Banking and Branching Efficiency Act (1994), 361
Rivers and Harbors Act (1946), 158
Robb, Thomas Bruce, 16–19, 22, 25–27, 32, 35, 63–64
Roberts, George E., 71
Robertson, Guy, 83
Robertson, J. B. A., 145
Roddie, Reuben M., 15
Roddie-Williams bill, 15
Rodgers-Johnson, Betty, 189
Rogers, John, 300
Rogers, Michael, 243, 246
Rogers, Will, 81, 104–105, 116–17, 292–93
Rooney, Larry, 202
Roosevelt, Franklin D., 113–23, 132–33, 150–52
Roosevelt, Theodore, 3–5, 9–10, 13
Rose Anti-Wildcat Banking Bill (1897), 192
Ross, Blanche, 305
Rowsey, William E. "Billy," 231
Roy, Sydney J., 37, 50
Ruddy, George, 154
Rukeyser, Louis, 264
Ruth, Babe, 138

Safenet Home Banking Services, 383
Salem, George M., 274
Salomon Brothers, 273–74, 277
Salyer (née Sipperly), Meg, 209–11, 231, 432n57
Samson Properties (Tulsa), 213
Sand Springs State Bank, 330
San Francisco earthquake (1906), 7, 13
Santayana, George, 193, 430n3

Savings and loans, 188–89, 247, 259, 272, 297, 303–304, 307, 312–13, 359; crisis (1980s), 319–26, 331–34, 338–39, 349, 387
Scoggins, Ken, 329
Scott, Angelo C., 29, 35, 102, 142–43
Seagraves, Ronald A., 322
Sears, Roebuck and Co., 302
Seattle First National Bank (a.k.a. Seafirst), 174, 200, 204, 208–11, 232–33, 258, 290–91
Seay, Frank, 377
Sebring, Carl, 181
Second Bank of the United States, 63, 91, 320
Security Bank and Trust Co. of Miami (Okla.), 279
Security Bank of Oklahoma City, 83
Security Corporation of Duncan, 341
Security National Bank and Trust Co.: of Duncan, 240, 341; of Norman, 91, 281, 382
Security Savings and Loan Association (N.J.), 322
Seeing Oklahoma City, 41–43
Seidler, Lee, 271
Service Bank of Tonkawa, 296–97
Shakeout theory of banking, 299
Shawnee Chamber of Commerce, 37, 50
Shearson American Express, 302
Shearson Lehman Brothers, Inc., 373
Shearson Loeb Rhoades, 302
Shelton, Dan, 345
Sheridan Bank and Trust Co. of Lawton, 314
Sherry, Gayla, 206–207, 215, 238–41, 280–82
Sheshunoff Information Services (a.k.a. Alex Sheshunoff and Co.; Sheshunoff Rating Services, Inc.), 225, 280, 360
Shewey, Bill, 340
Shipp, Brian, 245, 252, 395–96
Sigma Alpha Epsilon Fraternity, 144–45
Sigma Chi Fraternity, 203–204, 208, 218–19

Silverado Banking, Savings and Loan Association of Denver, 323–24
Simonson, Donald G., 292, 299
Simpson, Gary, 185–87, 279–80, 307–308, 324, 330–32, 342, 349–53, 362–69
Sims, R. N., 131
Sinclair, Harry F., 136, 315
Singer, Mark, 192, 197, 214–15, 231, 251. *See also* Penn Square National Bank of Oklahoma City
Singletary, R. A., 151
Skeen, C. A., 15
Skelly, W. G., 136
Skipper, Michelle, 343–44
Skirvin Hotel (Oklahoma City), 65, 152–53, 426n69
Smith, Adam, 265, 268
Smith, Ben, 182–83
Smith, James, 179
Smith, Randy, 249
Smith International, 244
Smock, Herbert H., 9, 11, 19–21, 69, 408n30
Snyder, D. K., 80–82
Socialism/Socialist Party of Oklahoma, 43–49, 61, 75, 79, 123, 157, 287
Social issues (gender equality, sexual discrimination, child care, AIDS, substance abuse, 1980s–1990s), 343–48
Sohlberg, George, 141
Sooner Federal Savings Association of Tulsa, 325
South Dakota, deposit guaranty in, 18, 73–74
South Sea Bubble, 191
Southwestern Cotton Oil Co. (Oklahoma City), 154
Sparks, Ronald G., 375–76
Speakman, Streeter, 56
Spears, Kate, 325
Spirit Bank: (formerly, American National Bank) of Bristow, 389, 402; of Sapulpa, 374
Sprague, O. M. W., 7, 13

St. Germain, Fernand, 263. *See also* Garn–St. Germain Act (1982)
Standard and Poor's, 261–62, 277
Starr, Belle and Sam, 55
Starr, Henry, 55–58, 75, 78, 87
State National Bank: of Depew, 173; of Marlow, 340; of Oklahoma City, 49–50, 287
Steagall, Henry B., 120, 268. *See also* Glass-Steagall Act (1933)
Steinbeck, John, 77–78
Stephens, Walter B., 129–31, 155
Stephenson, Owen K., 375–76
Sterkel, Mike, 340
Stidham, Lee and Mike, 397
Stidham, Steve, 377
Stillwater National Bank and Trust Co. (later, Bank SNB), 324–25, 336, 377–78, 382–83
Stipe, Gene, 183–84
Stock Exchange Bank of Woodward, 290, 328, 404
Stockman, David, 196–97
Stone, Wayne, 283
Story of Oklahoma City, The (Scott), 29, 35, 102, 142–43
Strohm, Thomas G., 357–58
Strong, Benjamin, 38–39
Stroud National Bank, 55–56, 298
Sudik, Vincent and Mary, and Mary Sudik No. 1, 95–97
Sue Bland No. 1, 135
Super NOW accounts, 267, 303. *See also* Negotiable Order of Withdrawal (NOW) accounts
Swan, Carl, 207, 228, 247
Swearingen, Wayne, and Management Association, 243, 275
Swords, M. J., 181
Sykes, Cherie, 346

Taft, William, 11, 16
Talley, William, 275
Taylor, David G., 263

480 INDEX

Taylor, Tony, 374
Tenancy, land, 45–47, 135
Texas, deposit guaranty in, 18, 73–74
Texas Bankers Association, 348
Thatcher, Margaret, 266
The Bank, N.A. (formerly, National Bank of McAlester), 297, 316
Thomas, Heck, 57
Thompson, Ben, 75
Thompson, Mick, 241, 292, 309–10, 313, 339, 355–56, 359–61, 398
Thunderbird Financial Corporation, 236, 243, 246. *See also* BancFirst Corporation; United Community Corporation
Thurmond, E. K., 83
Thurow, Lester C., 269–70
Tibbs, P. W., and Tibbs-Dorsey Manufacturing Co., 86
Tinker, Clarence L., 152
Tinker Field (formerly, Midwest Air Depot, Oklahoma City), 152–53, 426n70
Tippens, Doug, 371
Tippetts, Charles S., 69
Tipton Bank, 376
Titchywy, Bill, 248–49
Tomcat No. 1, 212–13
Townsend, Kenneth W., 284, 368
Tradesmen's National Bank/Building (Oklahoma City), 132, 145, 336–37, 405
Trading with the Enemy Act (1917), 117–19
Trott, Ed, 391
Truman, Harry, 190
Truth-in-Lending Act (Title I, Consumer Credit Protection Act, 1968), 169
Tucker, Morrison G., 185–87, 265, 291, 307
Tulipomania, 191
Tulsa Bomber Plant, 152–53
Tulsa Commercial Club, 50–52
Tulsa National Bank, 137
Turpen, Mike, 312
Twin Territories (Okla. and Indian Terr.), 3–5, 8–9, 35, 201
Tyler, Don, 163–64

UMB, Bank of Oklahoma City and Financial Corporation, 382
Union Bank and Trust Co. of Oklahoma City, 282, 351
Union National Bank: of Bartlesville 163–64, 314; of Chandler (later, BancFirst), 398; of Tulsa, 136
Unit banking, 18, 91, 109–11, 171, 188, 201, 251, 290–91, 307–12, 339, 350
United Community Corporation, 246. *See also* BancFirst Corporation; Thunderbird Financial Corporation
United Copper Co., 7
United Del City Bank (formerly, First Continental Bank and Trust Co. of Del City), 278–79
United Oklahoma Bank, 291–92
United Oklahoma Bankshares, 313–14
United States: Bureau of Printing and Engraving, 119; Bureau of the Census, 164; Chamber of Commerce Foundation (formerly, National Chamber Foundation), 323; Congress, 3–4, 37–39, 62, 91, 116–21, 152, 158, 168–69, 173–75, 178, 193–96, 229, 242, 265–69, 272–73, 281, 289, 294, 305, 316–17, 321–25, 331–35, 343, 348–49, 361, 365–66, 372, 393–98; Dept. of Agriculture, 293; Dept. of Commerce, 381; Dept. of the Treasury, 20; District Court, Oklahoma City, 183; Equal Employment Opportunity Commission (EEOC), 288; House Banking, Finance, and Urban Affairs Committee, 242, 263; House Bill 12707, 4; House Committee on Banking and Currency, 39, 268; House Committee on Interstate and Foreign Commerce, 195; House Resolution 3474, 335; Office of the Comptroller of the Currency (OCC), 339, 384; Securities and Exchange Commission (SEC), 120, 174, 395; Senate Committee on Banking and Currency, 39, 268; Senate

INDEX 481

Committee on Banking, Housing, and Urban Affairs, 242; Senate Committee on Energy and Natural Resources, 211; Senate Committee on Interstate and Foreign Commerce, 194–95; Small Business Administration (SBA), 162; Tenth Circuit Court, Denver, 259
University of Oklahoma, 194, 203, 292, 342; Center for Economic and Management Research, 196
Upstreaming of interest, 221, 242, 248
Urschel, Charles F., 139
Utt, Ronald, 323

Valley National Bank of Phoenix, 119
Valparaiso, Chile, earthquake (1906), 13
Vanderlip, Frank A., 38–40
Vandever, Charley, 57
Variable-interest entities (VIEs), 392
Vera State Bank, 54
Vernon, Dennis, 369–70
Vietnam War, 181
Vigilance committees, 76–77
Vint, Shirley, 233–36
Vision Bank of Ada, 167
Vitter, David, 394
Volcker, Paul, 235–38, 262, 266–67, 274, 354, 390
Volcker Rule, 395
Vose, C. A. "Chuck," Jr., 284–86, 307, 427n75
Vose, C. A. "Chuck," Sr., 147, 220, 284–86, 307, 419n54, 427n75
Vose, R. A., 103, 141, 147, 154–55, 427n75

Wade, Jess, 324
Walker, E. A., 132–33, 145
Walker, Gene, 316
Walkingstick, Ben, 398–99
Wall Street, 8, 37, 75, 99, 106, 120, 263, 402
Wall Street Reform and Consumer Protection Act (2010), 393–99
Wal-Mart, 316, 378, 400, 403
Walters, David, 355, 359

Walton, John Calloway "Jack," as Oklahoma City mayor, 65–67, 72, 146, 417n1, 417n5
Warburg, Paul, 38
Ward, Glenn P. "Red," 331
Warren, Elizabeth, 393
Warren, W. K., 136
War Stamp Savings Bank of Oklahoma City, 59–60
Washington, Albert, 143–44
Washington Gas Light Co., 213
Washington State, deposit guaranty in, 18, 73–74
Washita State Bank of Burns Flat, 343, 377
Watergate Hotel (Washington, D.C.) and scandal (1970s), 182, 233
Wealth of Nations, The (Smith), 265, 268
Weaver, Claude, 39
Weber, Max, 126
Weiss, Martin, and Weiss Ratings, Inc., 368
Welge, William D., 264–65
Wells Fargo Bank, 391–94, 397
Wenner, Fred L., 8, 27
Wentz, Lew, 131
Wertzberger, Ed, 302–303
West, Mae, 138
WestStar Bank of Bartlesville, 305
Wheat Improvement Association, 134
Wheeler, Burton K., 116
Wheeler, Glen E. and Kim, 298
White, Mark, 319–20
White House Office of Management and Budget, 184, 323
Whitney, Alan, 280
Whittaker, David, 380
Will Rogers Field (Oklahoma City), 151–53
Williams, Carl, 46
Williams, Joe, 335, 360
Williams, J. Roy, 15
Williams, J. S., 58
Williams, Penny, 373
Willis, Bert, 68, 71, 74, 101, 105–108, 115–17, 121, 124–25, 130, 148–50, 156, 279

Willis, Clay, 115
Willis, H. Parker, 116
Willis, Oliver, 107–108, 115
Willis, Ruth, 107
Williston, Sheila A., 376
Wilson, Edwin, and Edwin Bird Wilson, Inc., of New York and Chicago, 80
Wilson, Woodrow, 39, 48, 91, 126, 133
Winans District (later, Heritage Hills, Oklahoma City), 126
Windsor, Brad, 346
Winkler, George, 137
Winters, Leo, 181–84
Wood, Jerry N., 373
Woodall, Lora, 344
Wooden, James, 263
Woodward, Bob, 233
World Banking Credit Committee, 200
World War I, 49, 59, 67–68, 74, 80, 97, 123, 126, 133, 138, 150, 153, 287, 391
World War II, 156–57, 172, 191, 352, 370
WPPSS bonds, 387
Wright, Paul S., 144
Wriston, Walter B., 274

Y2K, 386–87
Yarbrough, Brent, 378–79
Yegg, John, and yeggmen/yeggs, 77, 108, 419n49
Younes, Leigh, 174
Young, A. M., 23–25, 411n90
Young, Brigam (policeman), 52
Young Ladies' Seminary (Oklahoma City), 27, 411n108
Younger brothers, 55

Zimmerman, Hugh, 108–109
Zweig, Phillip L., 192–93, 225–35, 240, 251. *See also* Penn Square National Bank of Oklahoma City

www.ingramcontent.com/pod-product-compliance
Lightning Source LLC
Chambersburg PA
CBHW031424160426
43195CB00010BB/608